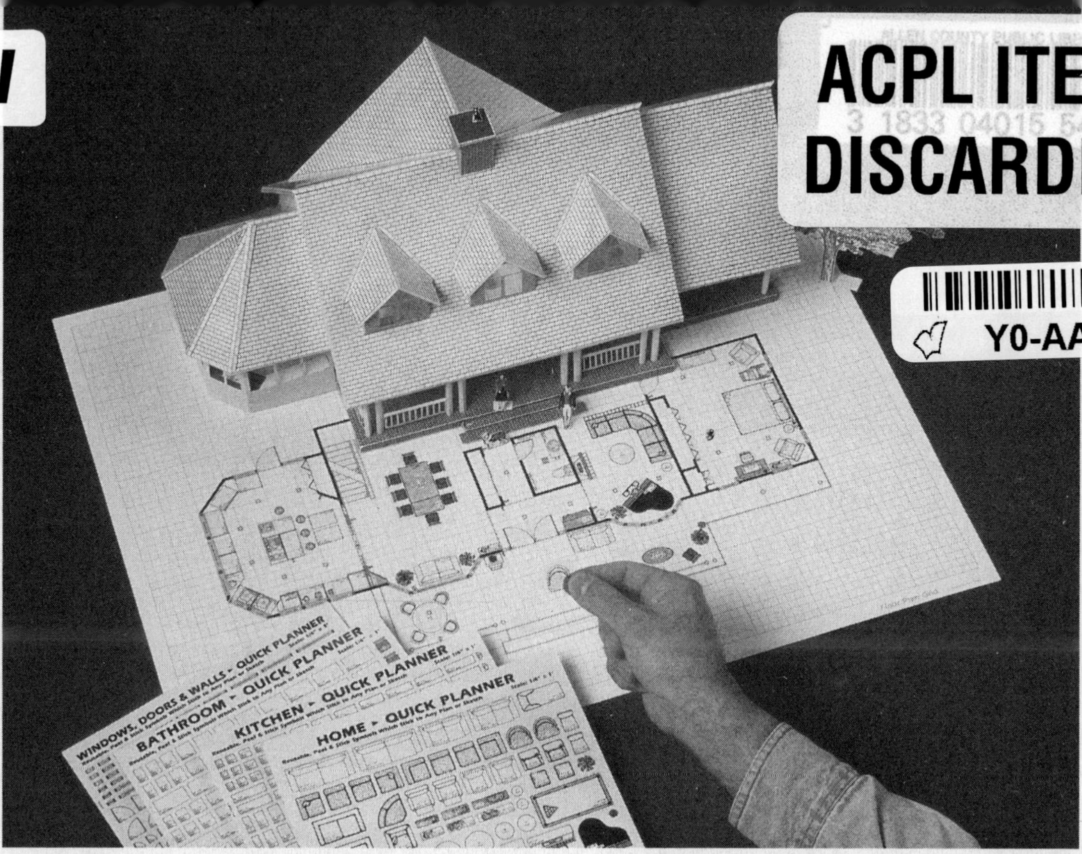
WINDOWS, DOORS & WALLS - QUICK PLANNER
BATHROOM - QUICK PLANNER
KITCHEN - QUICK PLANNER
HOME - QUICK PLANNER

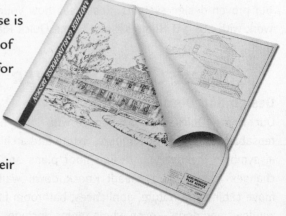

NEW HOME DESIGNS for 2003
A SABOT PUBLICATION

Contents

ISBN: 1-893536-03-3
Library of Congress No: 00-136082

Cover Design
Melani Gonzalez

Submit all Canadian plan orders to: Garlinghouse Company, 102 Ellis Street, Penticton, BC V2A 4L5

Hot New Designs

We are pleased to bring you this exciting feature, a special section presenting the newest home designs from our talented network of designers. These innovative floor plans are on the cutting edge of today's market, offering the ultimate in convenience, style and luxurious detailing.

Design 64156

See Order Pages and Index for Info

Units	Single
Price Code	H
Total Finished	2,755 sq. ft.
First Finished	2,073 sq. ft.
Second Finished	682 sq. ft.
Garage Unfinished	528 sq. ft.
Porch Unfinished	120 sq. ft.
Dimensions	64'x76'2"
Foundation	Crawlspace
Bedrooms	3
Full Baths	2
Half Baths	1
Max Ridge Height	28'
Exterior Walls	2x6

* Alternate foundation options available at an additional charge
Please call 1-800-235-5700 for more information.

Hot New Design

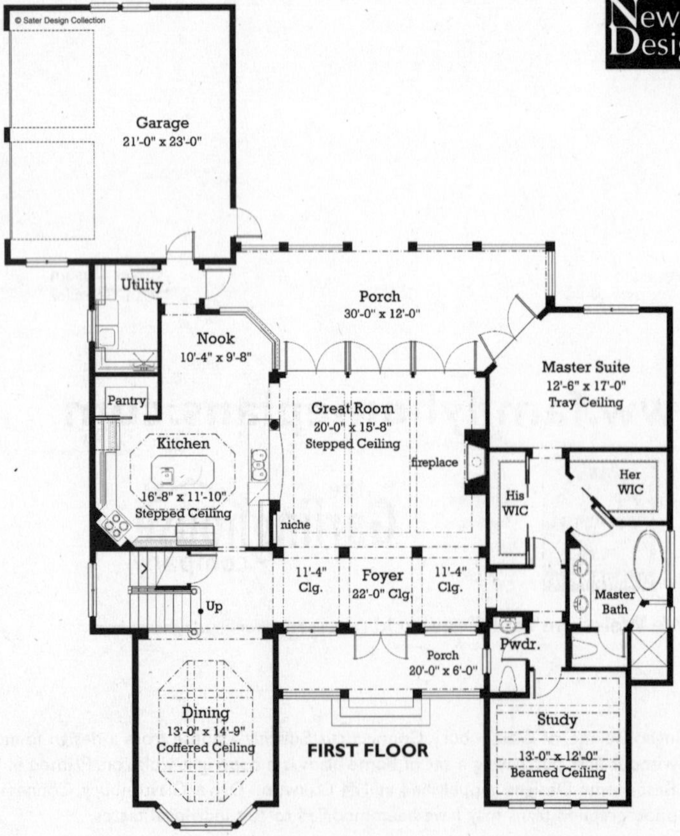
© Sater Design Collection
Garage
21'-0" x 23'-0"
Utility
Porch
30'-0" x 12'-0"
Nook
10'-4" x 9'-8"
Master Suite
12'-6" x 17'-0"
Tray Ceiling
Pantry
Great Room
20'-0" x 15'-8"
Stepped Ceiling
Kitchen
16'-8" x 11'-10"
Stepped Ceiling
fireplace
His WIC
Her WIC
niche
11'-4" Clg.
Foyer
22'-0" Clg
11'-4" Clg.
Master Bath
Up
Pwdr.
Porch
20'-0" x 6'-0"
Dining
13'-0" x 14'-9"
Coffered Ceiling
Study
13'-0" x 12'-0"
Beamed Ceiling

FIRST FLOOR

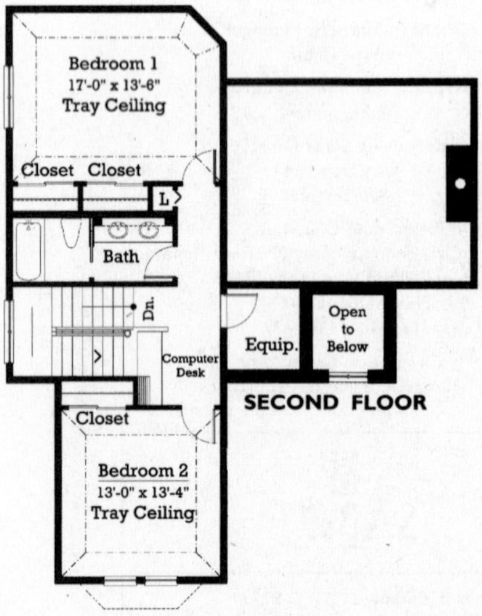
Bedroom 1
17'-0" x 13'-6"
Tray Ceiling
Closet
Closet
L
Bath
Dn.
Computer Desk
Equip.
Open to Below
Closet
Bedroom 2
13'-0" x 13'-4"
Tray Ceiling

SECOND FLOOR

Design 64200

See Order Pages and Index for Info

Units	Single
Price Code	K
Total Finished	2,925 sq. ft.
First Finished	1,373 sq. ft.
Second Finished	1,552 sq. ft.
Dimensions	64'6"x52'
Foundation	Crawlspace
Bedrooms	4
Full Baths	2
Half Baths	1
Exterior Walls	2x6

* Alternate foundation options available at an additional charge. Please call 1-800-235-5700 for more information.

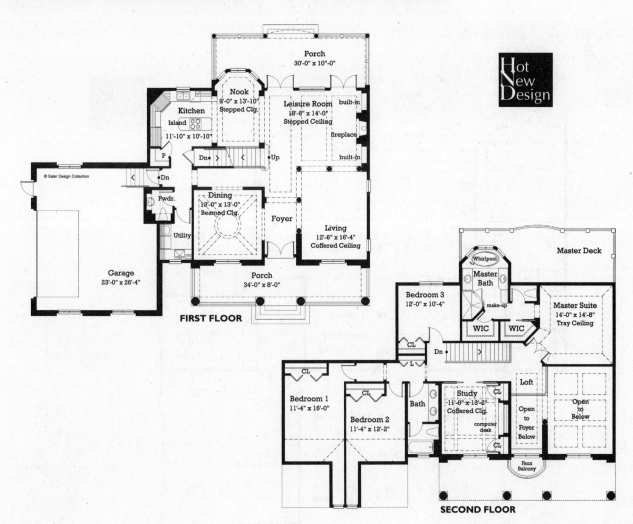

Hot New Design

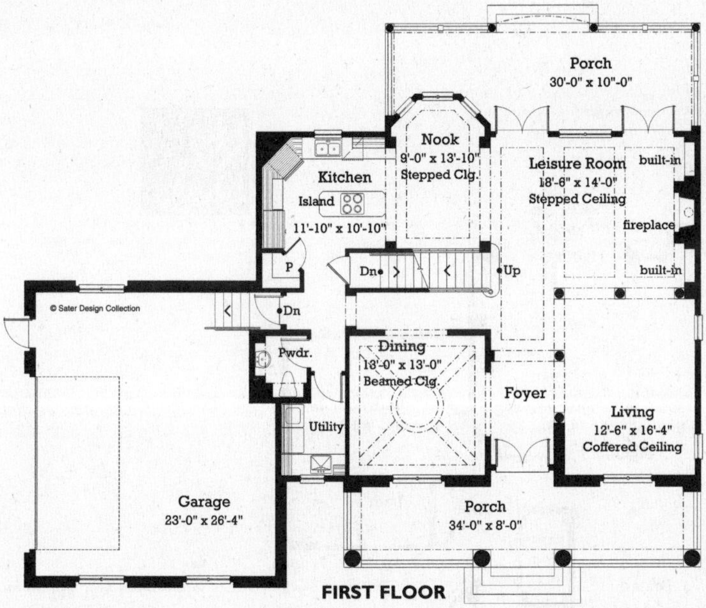
Porch
30'-0" x 10"-0"
Nook
9'-0" x 13'-10"
Stepped Clg.
Kitchen
Island
11'-10" x 10'-10"
Leisure Room
18'-6" x 14'-0"
Stepped Ceiling
built-in
fireplace
built-in
P
Dn
Up
Dn
© Sater Design Collection
Pwdr.
Dining
13'-0" x 13'-0"
Beamed Clg.
Foyer
Living
12'-6" x 16'-4"
Coffered Ceiling
Utility
Garage
23'-0" x 26'-4"
Porch
34'-0" x 8'-0"

FIRST FLOOR

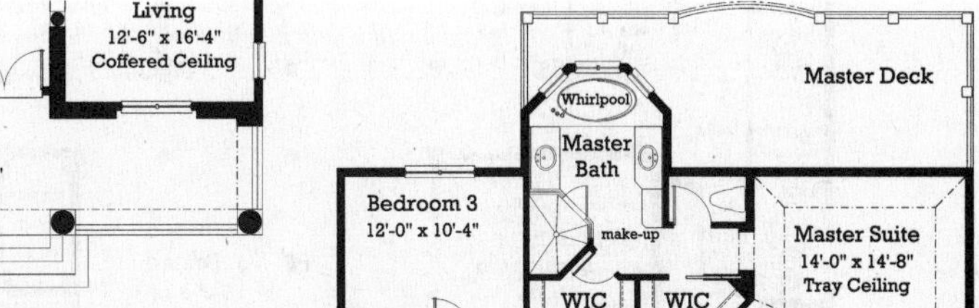
Master Deck
Whirlpool
Master
Bath
Bedroom 3
12'-0" x 10'-4"
make-up
Master Suite
14'-0" x 14'-8"
Tray Ceiling
WIC
WIC
CL
Dn
L
CL
Loft
Bedroom 1
11'-4" x 16'-0"
CL
Bath
Study
11'-0" x 13'-2"
Coffered Clg.
CL
Bedroom 2
11'-4" x 12'-2"
computer
desk
CL
Open
to
Foyer
Below
Open
to
Below
Faux
Balcony

SECOND FLOOR

Design 64178

See Order Pages and Index for Info

Units	Single
Price Code	H
Total Finished	2,555 sq. ft.
Main Finished	2,555 sq. ft.
Garage Unfinished	640 sq. ft.
Porch Unfinished	315 sq. ft.
Dimensions	70'x76'6"
Foundation	Crawlspace
Bedrooms	3
Full Baths	2
Half Baths	1
Max Ridge Height	28'4"
Exterior Walls	2x6

* Alternate foundation options available at an additional charge. Please call 1-800-235-5700 for more information.

Hot New Design

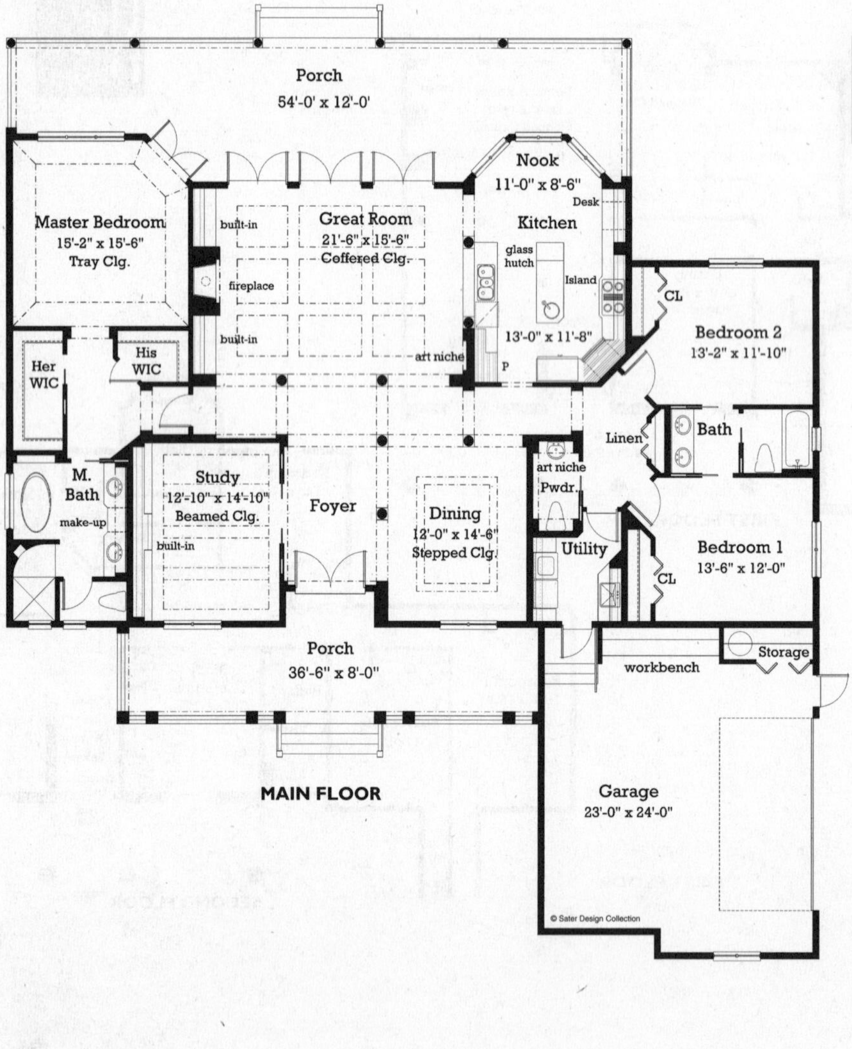
Porch
54'-0' x 12'-0'
Nook
11'-0" x 8'-6"
Desk
Kitchen
glass hutch
Island
13'-0" x 11'-8"
Master Bedroom
15'-2" x 15'-6"
Tray Clg.
built-in
Great Room
21'-6" x 15'-6"
Coffered Clg.
fireplace
built-in
art niche
Her WIC
His WIC
CL
Bedroom 2
13'-2" x 11'-10"
Linen
Bath
M. Bath
make-up
Study
12'-10" x 14'-10"
Beamed Clg.
built-in
Foyer
Dining
12'-0" x 14'-6"
Stepped Clg.
art niche
Pwdr.
Utility
Bedroom 1
13'-6" x 12'-0"
CL
Porch
36'-6" x 8'-0"
workbench
Storage
Garage
23'-0" x 24'-0"
© Sater Design Collection

MAIN FLOOR

Design 64146

See Order Pages and Index for Info

Units	Single
Price Code	1
Total Finished	2,847 sq. ft.
First Finished	1,642 sq. ft.
Second Finished	1,205 sq. ft.
Bonus Unfinished	340 sq. ft.
Garage Unfinished	541 sq. ft.
Porch Unfinished	300 sq. ft.
Dimensions	53'7"x72'6"
Foundation	Crawlspace
Bedrooms	3
Full Baths	3
Half Baths	1
Max Ridge Height	33'6"
Exterior Walls	2x6

* Alternate foundation options available at an additional charge. Please call 1-800-235-5700 for more information.

Hot New Design

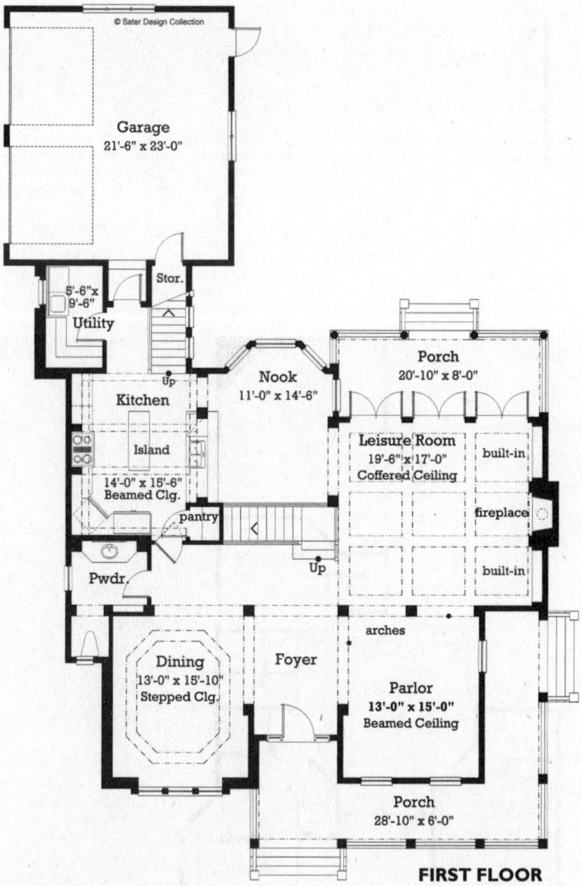
© Sater Design Collection
Garage
21'-6" x 23'-0"
Stor.
5'-6"x
9'-6"
Utility
Up
Kitchen
Island
14'-0" x 15'-6"
Beamed Clg.
pantry
Nook
11'-0" x 14'-6"
Porch
20'-10" x 8'-0"
Leisure Room
19'-6" x 17'-0"
Coffered Ceiling
built-in
fireplace
built-in
Up
Pwdr.
arches
Dining
13'-0" x 15'-10"
Stepped Clg.
Foyer
Parlor
13'-0" x 15'-0"
Beamed Ceiling
Porch
28'-10" x 6'-0"

FIRST FLOOR

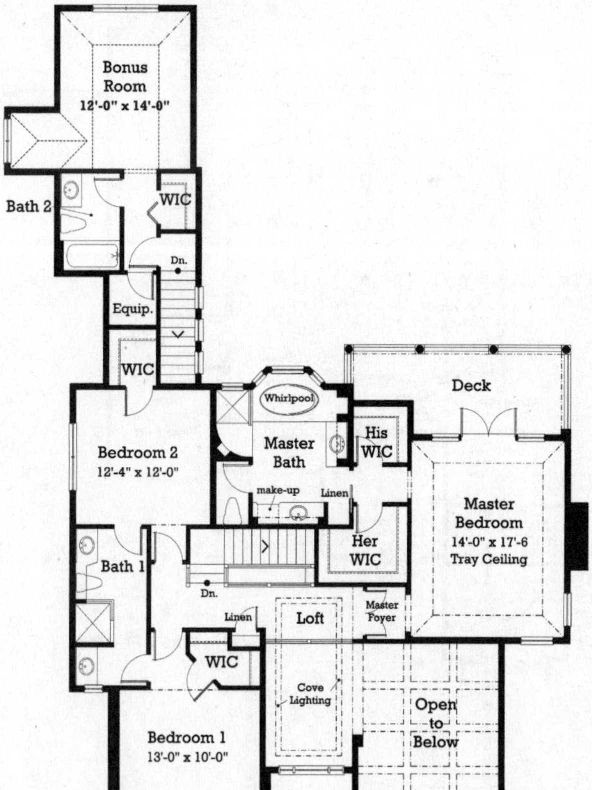
Bonus
Room
12'-0" x 14'-0"
Bath 2
WIC
Dn.
Equip.
WIC
Whirlpool
Master
Bath
His
WIC
Deck
make-up
Linen
Bedroom 2
12'-4" x 12'-0"
Her
WIC
Master
Bedroom
14'-0" x 17'-6
Tray Ceiling
Bath 1
Dn.
Linen
Loft
Master
Foyer
WIC
Cove
Lighting
Open
to
Below
Bedroom 1
13'-0" x 10'-0"

SECOND FLOOR

Design 64184

See Order Pages and Index for Info

Units	Single
Price Code	K
Total Finished	3,096 sq. ft.
First Finished	2,083 sq. ft.
Second Finished	1,013 sq. ft.
Garage Unfinished	497 sq. ft.
Porch Unfinished	369 sq. ft.
Dimensions	74'x88'
Foundation	Crawlspace
Bedrooms	3
Full Baths	3
Half Baths	1
Max Ridge Height	33'
Exterior Walls	2x6

* Alternate foundation options available at an additional charge. Please call 1-800-235-5700 for more information.

Hot New Design

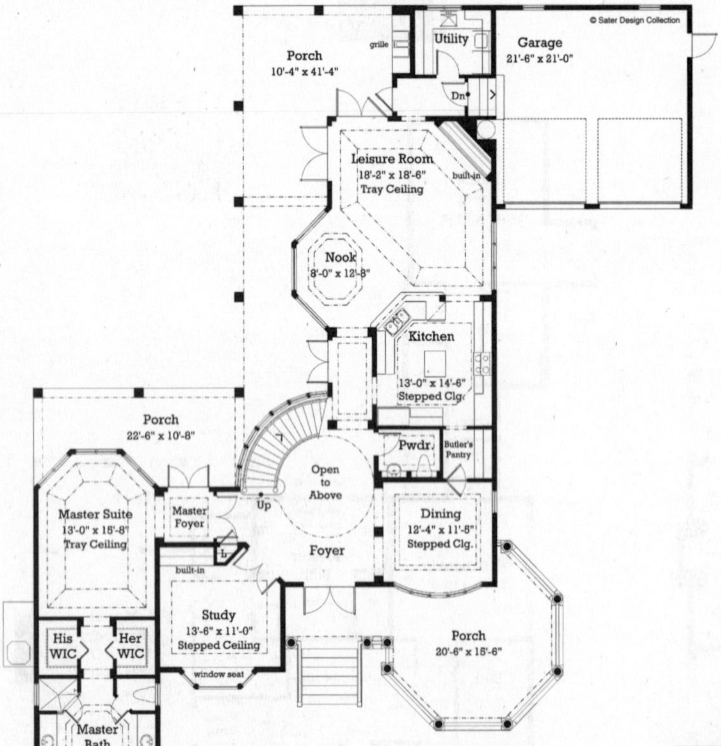
© Sater Design Collection
Porch
10'-4" x 41'-4"
grille
Utility
Garage
21'-6" x 21'-0"
Dn
Leisure Room
18'-2" x 18'-6"
Tray Ceiling
built-in
Nook
8'-0" x 12'-8"
Kitchen
13'-0" x 14'-6"
Stepped Clg.
Porch
22'-6" x 10'-8"
Pwdr.
Butler's Pantry
Open to Above
Up
Master Suite
13'-0" x 15'-8"
Tray Ceiling
Master Foyer
Dining
12'-4" x 11'-8"
Stepped Clg.
Foyer
built-in
Study
13'-6" x 11'-0"
Stepped Ceiling
window seat
Porch
20'-6" x 15'-6"
His WIC
Her WIC
Master Bath
Whirlpool

FIRST FLOOR

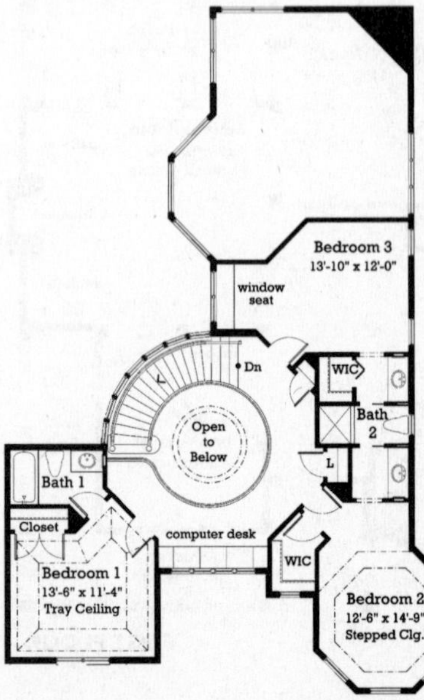
Bedroom 3
13'-10" x 12'-0"
window seat
Dn
WIC
Bath 2
Open to Below
L
Bath 1
Closet
computer desk
WIC
Bedroom 1
13'-6" x 11'-4"
Tray Ceiling
Bedroom 2
12'-6" x 14'-9"
Stepped Clg.

SECOND FLOOR

Design 65369

See Order Pages and Index for Info

Units	Single
Price Code	G
Total Finished	2,867 sq. ft.
First Finished	1,905 sq. ft.
Second Finished	962 sq. ft.
Basement Unfinished	1,905 sq. ft.
Garage Unfinished	608 sq. ft.
Porch Unfinished	181 sq. ft.
Dimensions	70'x53'
Foundation	Basement
Bedrooms	4
Full Baths	3
Half Baths	1
First Ceiling	9'
Second Ceiling	8'
Max Ridge Height	32'
Roof Framing	Truss
Exterior Walls	2x6

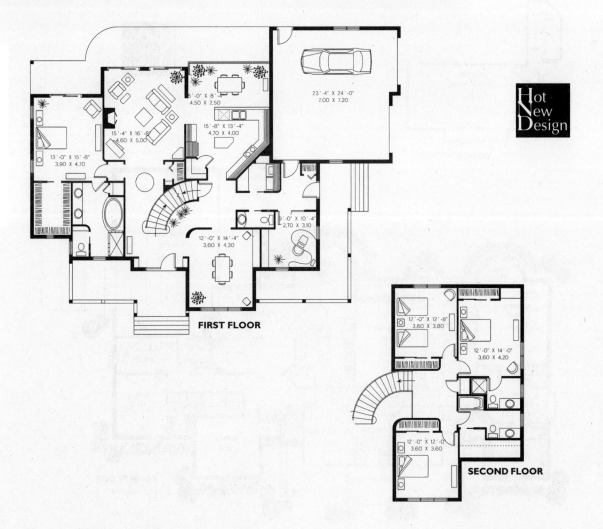

Hot New Design

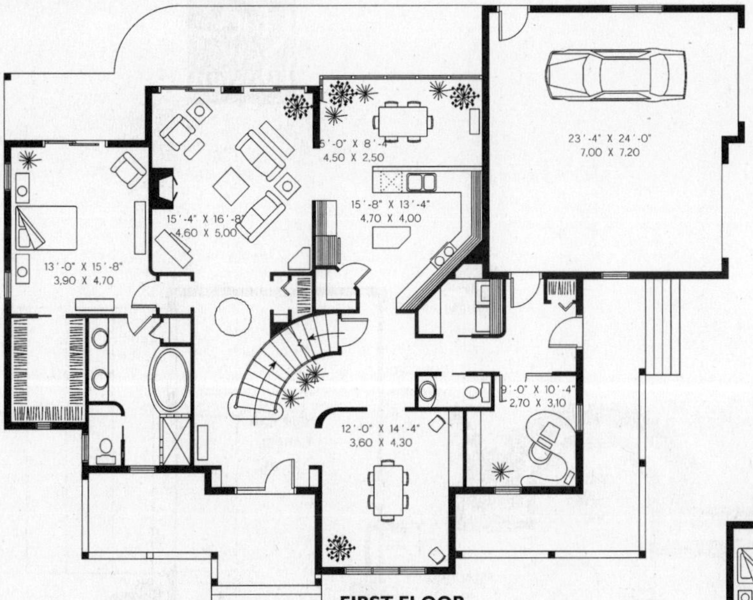
23'-4" X 24'-0"
7,00 X 7,20
5'-0" X 8'-4"
4,50 X 2,50
15'-8" X 13'-4"
4,70 X 4,00
15'-4" X 16'-8"
4,60 X 5,00
13'-0" X 15'-8"
3,90 X 4,70
9'-0" X 10'-4"
2,70 X 3,10
12'-0" X 14'-4"
3,60 X 4,30

FIRST FLOOR

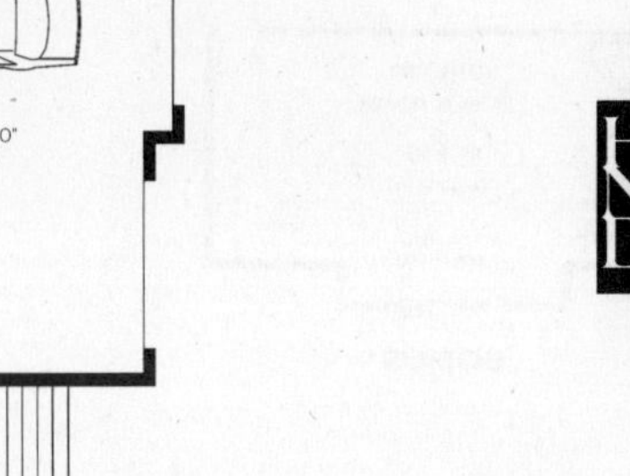
12'-0" X 12'-8"
3,60 X 3,80
12'-0" X 14'-0"
3,60 X 4,20
12'-0" X 12'-0"
3,60 X 3,60

SECOND FLOOR

Design 66010

See Order Pages and Index for Info

Units	Single
Price Code	J
Total Finished	3,578 sq. ft.
Main Finished	3,578 sq. ft.
Bonus Unfinished	460 sq. ft.
Garage Unfinished	864 sq. ft.
Porch Unfinished	292 sq. ft.
Dimensions	100'x72'8"
Foundation	Basement Crawlspace Slab
Bedrooms	4
Full Baths	3
Half Baths	1
Main Ceiling	9'-12'
Max Ridge Height	30'
Roof Framing	Stick
Exterior Walls	2x4

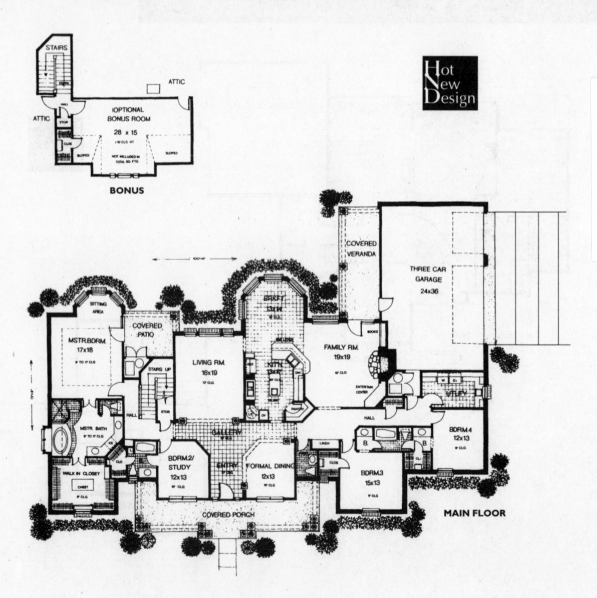

Hot New Design

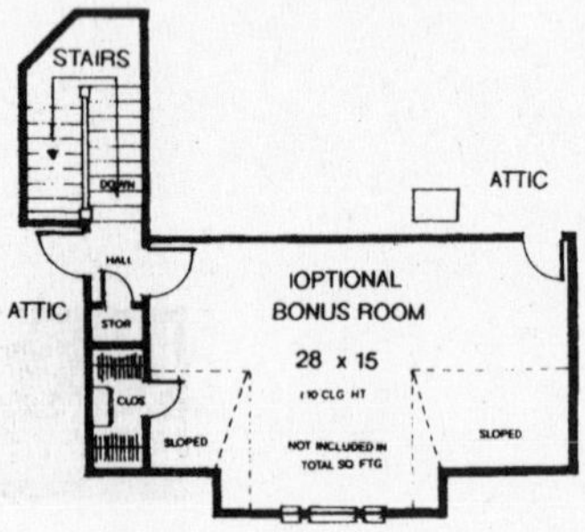
STAIRS
ATTIC
ATTIC
OPTIONAL
BONUS ROOM
28 x 15
NOT INCLUDED IN TOTAL SQ FTG
SLOPED
SLOPED

BONUS

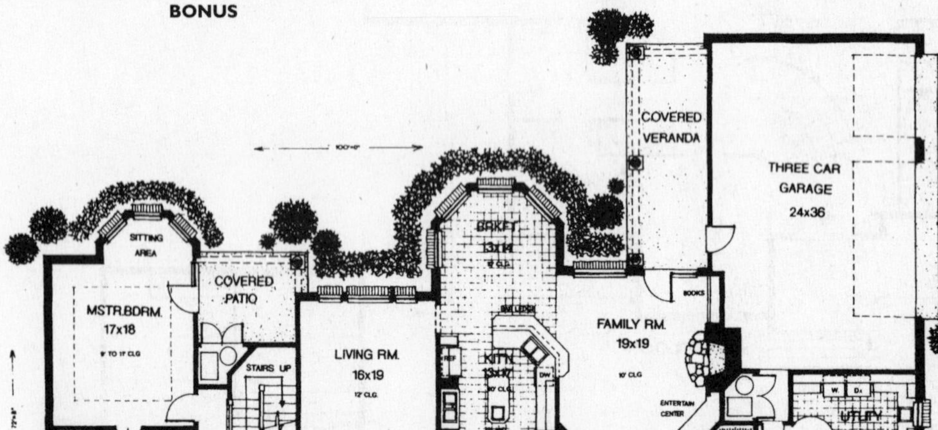
COVERED VERANDA
THREE CAR GARAGE
24x36
SITTING AREA
COVERED PATIO
MSTR.BDRM.
17x18
BRKFT
13x14
FAMILY RM.
19x19
LIVING RM.
16x19
KIT'N
STAIRS UP
ENTERTAIN CENTER
UTILITY
MSTR. BATH
HALL
GALLERY
HALL
BDRM.4
12x13
WALK IN CLOSET
BDRM.2/ STUDY
12x13
ENTRY
FORMAL DINING
12x13
BDRM.3
15x13
COVERED PORCH

MAIN FLOOR

Design 66014

See Order Pages and Index for Info

Units	Single
Price Code	J
Total Finished	3,510 sq. ft.
First Finished	2,498 sq. ft.
Second Finished	1,012 sq. ft.
Bonus Unfinished	340 sq. ft.
Garage Unfinished	810 sq. ft.
Porch Unfinished	60 sq. ft.
Dimensions	72'x62'
Foundation	Crawlspace Slab
Bedrooms	4
Full Baths	3
Half Baths	1
First Ceiling	10'
Second Ceiling	8'
Max Ridge Height	34'
Roof Framing	Stick
Exterior Walls	2x4

Hot New Design

FIRST FLOOR

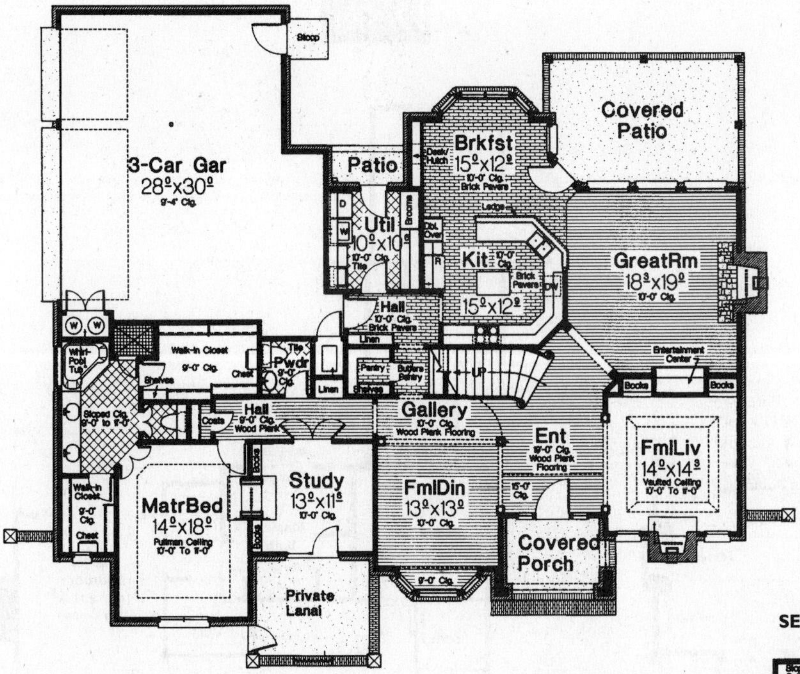
Stoop
3-Car Gar
28⁰x30⁰
Patio
Util
10⁰x10
Brkfst
15⁰x12⁰
Covered Patio
Kit
15⁰x12⁰
GreatRm
18³x19⁰
Hall
Walk-In Closet
Pwdr
Gallery
Ent
FmlLiv
14⁰x14³
Vaulted Ceiling
Hall
MatrBed
14⁰x18⁰
Study
13⁰x11⁵
FmlDin
13⁰x13⁰
Covered Porch
Private Lanai

SECOND FLOOR

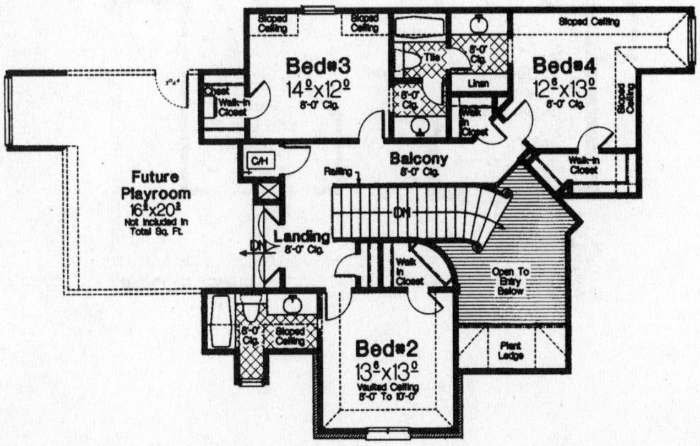
Bed#3
14⁰x12⁰
Bed#4
12⁶x13⁰
Balcony
Future Playroom
16⁴x20⁸
Not Included In Total Sq. Ft.
Landing
Open To Entry Below
Bed#2
13⁶x13⁰
Vaulted Ceiling

Design 64147

See Order Pages and Index for Info

Units	Single
Price Code	I
Total Finished	2,847 sq. ft.
First Finished	1,642 sq. ft.
Second Finished	1,205 sq. ft.
Bonus Unfinished	340 sq. ft.
Dimensions	53'7"x72'6"
Foundation	Crawlspace
Bedrooms	3
Full Baths	3
Half Baths	1
Exterior Walls	2x6

* Alternate foundation options available at an additional charg
Please call 1-800-235-5700 for more information.

Hot New Design

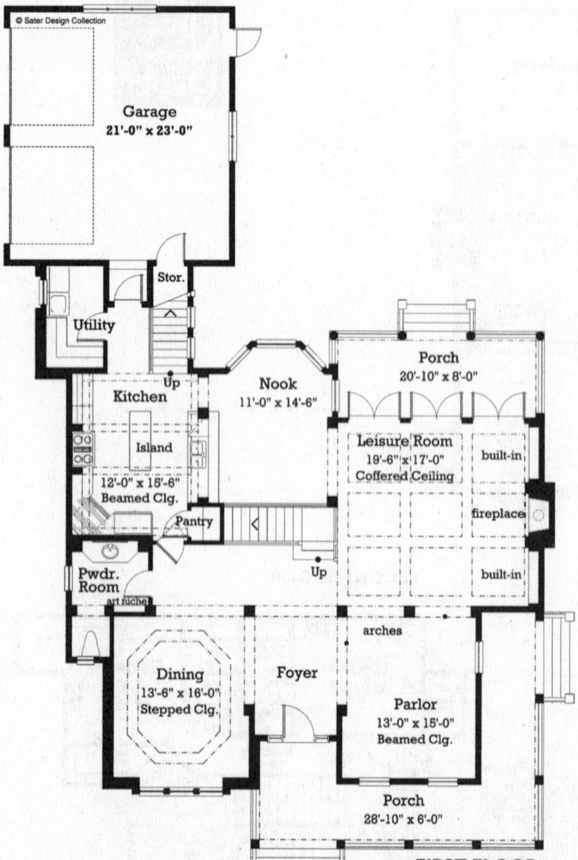
© Sater Design Collection
Garage
21'-0" x 23'-0"
Stor.
Utility
Up
Kitchen
Island
12'-0" x 15'-6"
Beamed Clg.
Nook
11'-0" x 14'-6"
Porch
20'-10" x 8'-0"
Leisure Room
19'-6" x 17'-0"
Coffered Ceiling
built-in
fireplace
built-in
Pantry
Up
Pwdr. Room
art niche
Dining
13'-6" x 16'-0"
Stepped Clg.
Foyer
arches
Parlor
13'-0" x 15'-0"
Beamed Clg.
Porch
28'-10" x 6'-0"

FIRST FLOOR

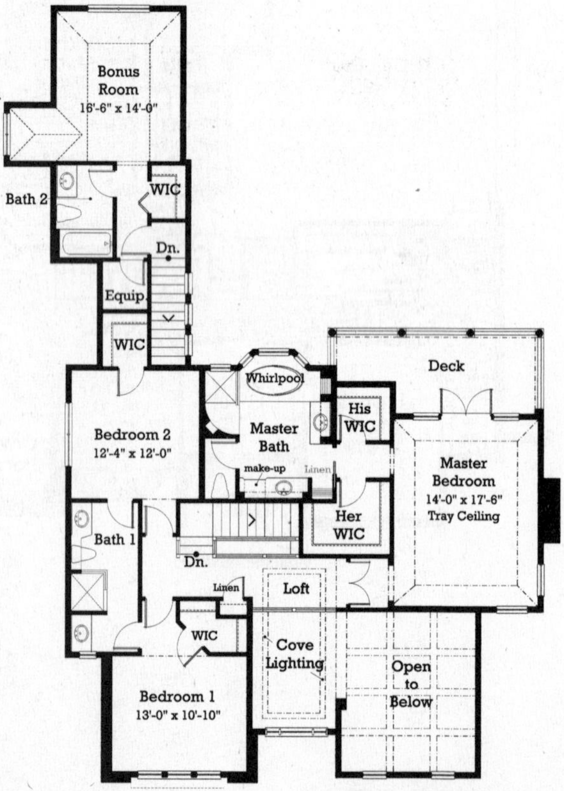
Bonus Room
16'-6" x 14'-0"
Bath 2
WIC
Dn.
Equip.
WIC
Bedroom 2
12'-4" x 12'-0"
Whirlpool
Master Bath
make-up
Linen
His WIC
Her WIC
Deck
Master Bedroom
14'-0" x 17'-6"
Tray Ceiling
Bath 1
Dn.
Linen
Loft
WIC
Cove Lighting
Open to Below
Bedroom 1
13'-0" x 10'-10"

SECOND FLOOR

Design 65240

See Order Pages and Index for Info

Units	Single
Price Code	L
Total Finished	4,204 sq. ft.
First Finished	2,482 sq. ft.
Second Finished	1,722 sq. ft.
Garage Unfinished	792 sq. ft.
Dimensions	95'x51'
Foundation	Basement
Bedrooms	5
Full Baths	3
Half Baths	1
First Ceiling	9'
Second Ceiling	8'
Max Ridge Height	37'8"
Roof Framing	Truss
Exterior Walls	2x6

Hot New Design

4,80 X 3,30
16'-0" X 11'-0"
4,30 X 4,30
14'-4" X 14'-4"
3,60 X 4,40
12'-0" X 14'-8"
4,20 X 3,20
14'-0" X 10'-8"

SECOND FLOOR

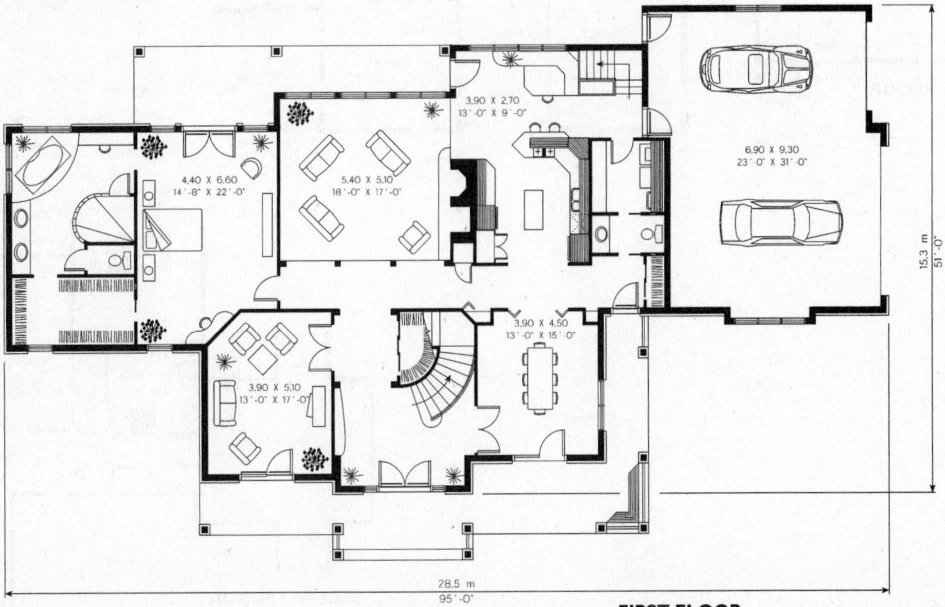
3,90 X 2,70
13'-0" X 9'-0"
6,90 X 9,30
23'-0" X 31'-0"
4,40 X 6,60
14'-8" X 22'-0"
5,40 X 5,10
18'-0" X 17'-0"
15,3 m
51'-0"
3,90 X 4,50
13'-0" X 15'-0"
3,90 X 5,10
13'-0" X 17'-0"
28,5 m
95'-0"

FIRST FLOOR

Design 64190

See Order Pages and Index for Info

Units	Single
Price Code	K
Total Finished	3,082 sq. ft.
First Finished	2,138 sq. ft.
Second Finished	944 sq. ft.
Bonus Unfinished	427 sq. ft.
Garage Unfinished	596 sq. ft.
Dimensions	76'8"x64'
Foundation	Crawlspace
Bedrooms	3
Full Baths	3
Half Baths	1
Max Ridge Height	32'
Exterior Walls	2x6

* Alternate foundation options available at an additional charge. Please call 1-800-235-5700 for more information.

Hot New Design

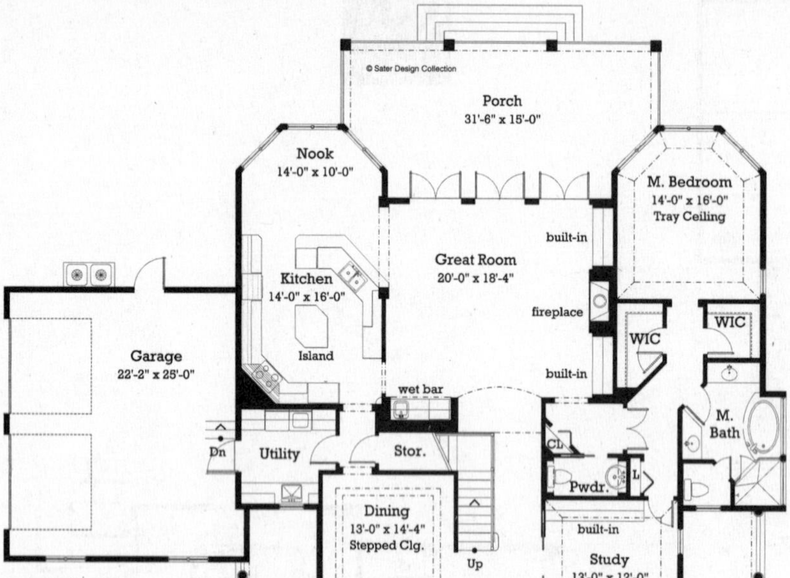
© Sater Design Collection
Porch
31'-6" x 15'-0"
Nook
14'-0" x 10'-0"
M. Bedroom
14'-0" x 16'-0"
Tray Ceiling
Great Room
20'-0" x 18'-4"
built-in
Kitchen
14'-0" x 16'-0"
fireplace
WIC
WIC
Garage
22'-2" x 25'-0"
Island
built-in
wet bar
M. Bath
Dn
Utility
Stor.
CL
L
Pwdr.
Dining
13'-0" x 14'-4"
Stepped Clg.
built-in
Study
13'-0" x 12'-0"
Tray Ceiling
Up
Foyer
Porch
52'-0" x 8'-0"

FIRST FLOOR

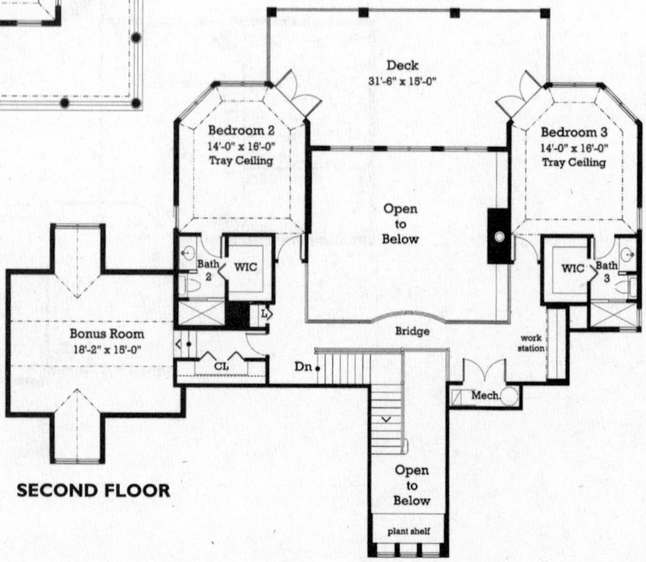
Deck
31'-6" x 15'-0"
Bedroom 2
14'-0" x 16'-0"
Tray Ceiling
Bedroom 3
14'-0" x 16'-0"
Tray Ceiling
Open
to
Below
Bath
2
WIC
WIC
Bath
3
Bonus Room
18'-2" x 15'-0"
L
Bridge
work
station
CL
Dn
Mech.
Open
to
Below
plant shelf

SECOND FLOOR

Design 64167

See Order Pages and Index for Info

Units	Single
Price Code	K
Total Finished	3,342 sq. ft.
First Finished	1,865 sq. ft.
Second Finished	1,477 sq. ft.
Bonus Unfinished	282 sq. ft.
Garage Unfinished	584 sq. ft.
Dimensions	79'x79'2"
Foundation	Crawlspace
Bedrooms	4
Full Baths	2
Half Baths	1
Max Ridge Height	37'
Exterior Walls	2x6

* Alternate foundation options available at an additional charge. Please call 1-800-235-5700 for more information.

Hot New Design

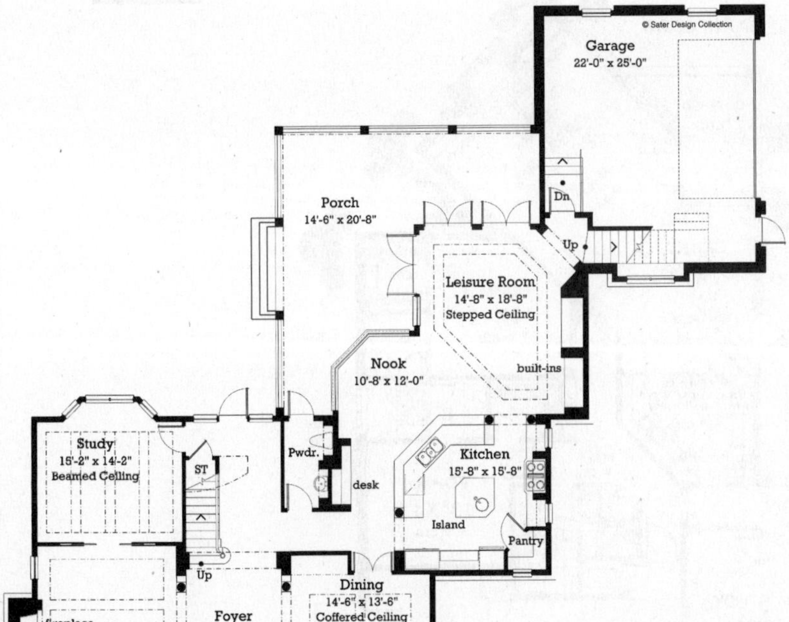
© Sater Design Collection
Garage
22'-0" x 25'-0"
Dn
Up
Porch
14'-6" x 20'-8"
Leisure Room
14'-8" x 18'-8"
Stepped Ceiling
Nook
10'-8' x 12'-0"
built-ins
Study
15'-2" x 14'-2"
Beamed Ceiling
ST
Pwdr.
desk
Kitchen
15'-8" x 15'-8"
Island
Pantry
Up
Dining
14'-6" x 13'-6"
Coffered Ceiling
fireplace
Foyer
Living
14'-6" x 16'-6"
Coffered Ceiling
Porch
42'-0" x 8'-0"

FIRST FLOOR

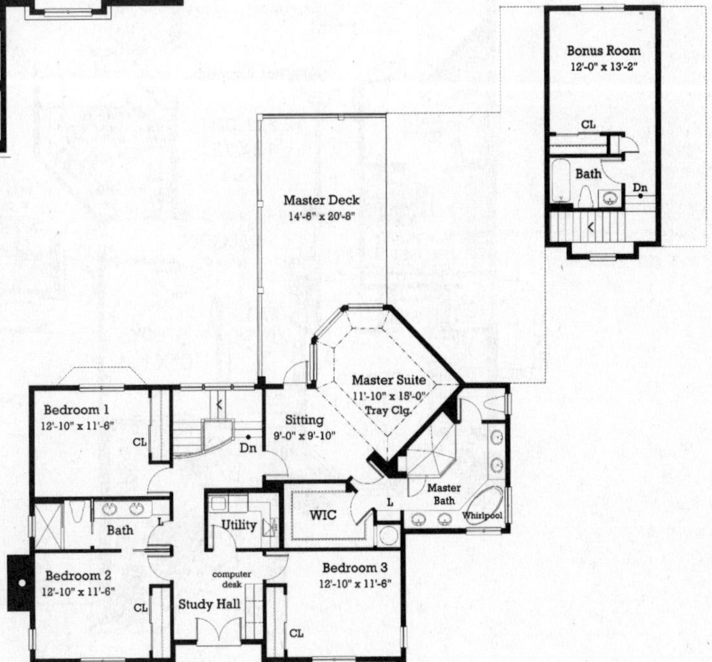
Bonus Room
12'-0" x 13'-2"
CL
Bath
Dn
Master Deck
14'-6" x 20'-8"
Master Suite
11'-10" x 18'-0"
Tray Clg.
Bedroom 1
12'-10" x 11'-6"
CL
Dn
Sitting
9'-0" x 9'-10"
WIC
L
Master Bath
Whirlpool
Bath
L
Utility
Bedroom 2
12'-10" x 11'-6"
CL
computer desk
Study Hall
Bedroom 3
12'-10" x 11'-6"
CL
Porch
42'-0" x 8'-0"

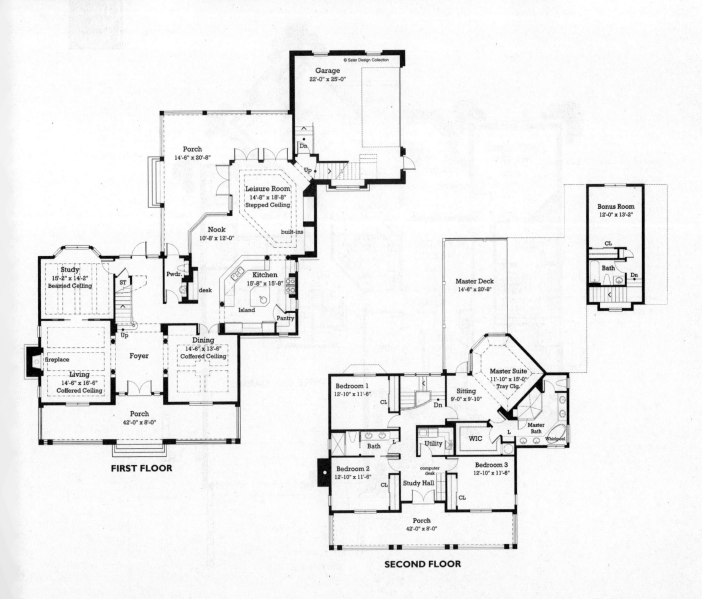

SECOND FLOOR

Design 66009

See Order Pages and Index for Info

Units	Single
Price Code	L
Total Finished	2,684 sq. ft.
Main Finished	2,684 sq. ft.
Garage Unfinished	638 sq. ft.
Porch Unfinished	32 sq. ft.
Dimensions	65'x76'6"
Foundation	Slab
Bedrooms	4
Full Baths	3
Half Baths	1
Max Ridge Height	32'
Roof Framing	Stick
Exterior Walls	2x4

Hot New Design

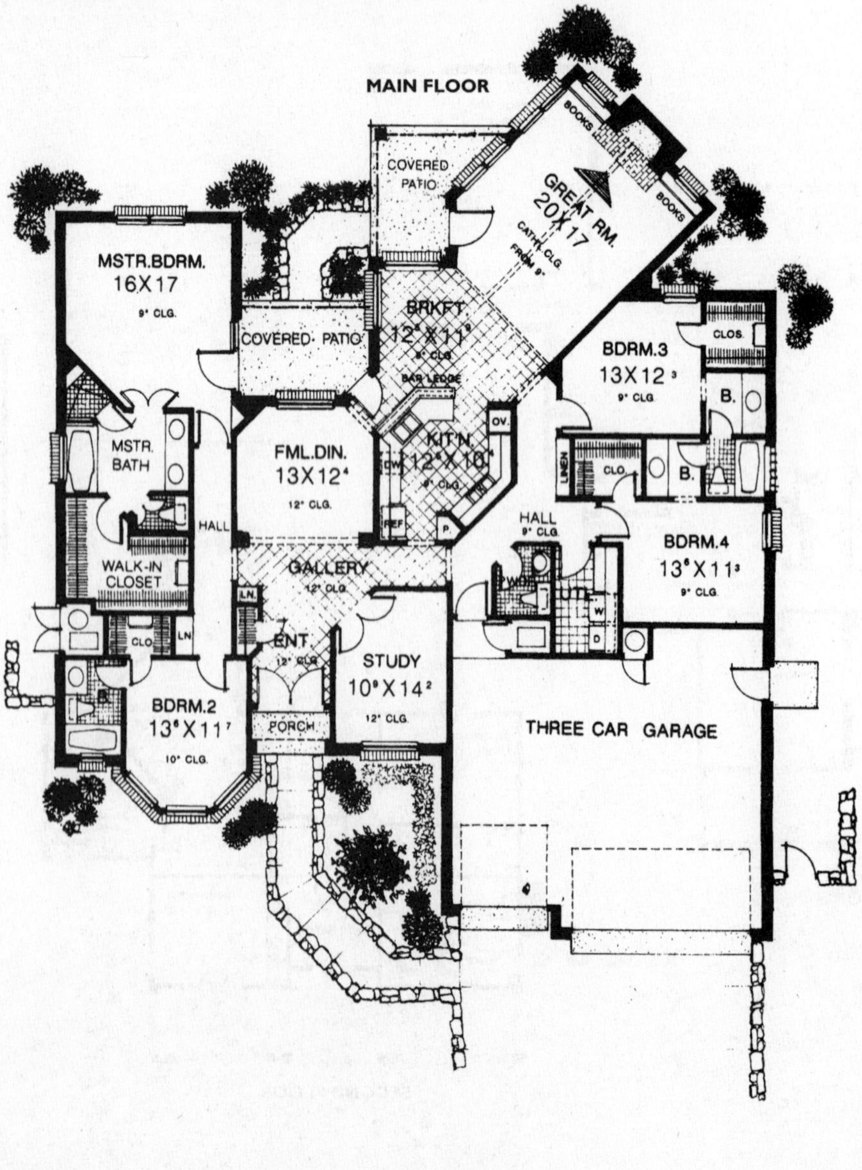
MAIN FLOOR
COVERED PATIO
BOOKS
GREAT RM. 20X17
CATH. CLG.
BOOKS
MSTR.BDRM. 16X17
9' CLG.
COVERED PATIO
BRKFT 12⁶X11⁶
BAR LEDGE
BDRM.3 13X12³
9' CLG.
CLOS.
B.
MSTR. BATH
FML.DIN. 13X12⁴
12' CLG.
KIT'N. 12⁶X10⁶
OV.
REF
P.
LINEN
CLO.
B.
HALL
HALL 9' CLG.
BDRM.4 13⁶X11³
9' CLG.
WALK-IN CLOSET
GALLERY 12' CLG.
W
D
CLO
LN
LN
ENT 12' CLG.
STUDY 10⁸X14²
12' CLG.
B
BDRM.2 13⁶X11⁷
10' CLG.
PORCH
THREE CAR GARAGE

Design 64149

See Order Pages and Index for Info

Units	Single
Price Code	K
Total Finished	3,136 sq. ft.
First Finished	1,673 sq. ft.
Second Finished	1,463 sq. ft.
Dimensions	60'10"x62'
Foundation	Crawlspace
Bedrooms	3
Full Baths	2
Half Baths	1
Max Ridge Height	34'4"
Exterior Walls	2x6

* Alternate foundation options available at an additional charge. Please call 1-800-235-5700 for more information.

Hot New Design

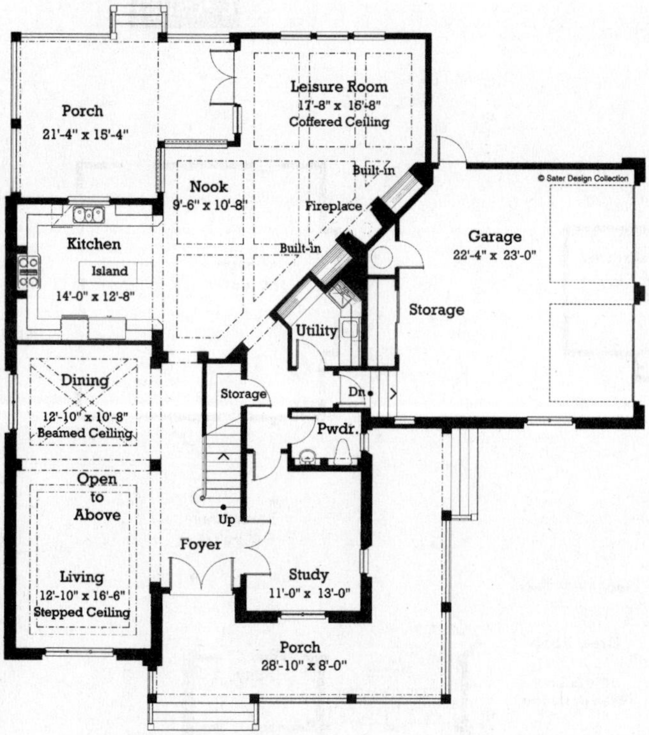
Porch
21'-4" x 15'-4"
Leisure Room
17'-8" x 16'-8"
Coffered Ceiling
Built-in
Nook
9'-6" x 10'-8"
Fireplace
Built-in
© Sater Design Collection
Garage
22'-4" x 23'-0"
Kitchen
Island
14'-0" x 12'-8"
Storage
Utility
Dining
12'-10" x 10'-8"
Beamed Ceiling
Storage
Dn
Pwdr.
Open
to
Above
Up
Foyer
Study
11'-0" x 13'-0"
Living
12'-10" x 16'-6"
Stepped Ceiling
Porch
28'-10" x 8'-0"

FIRST FLOOR

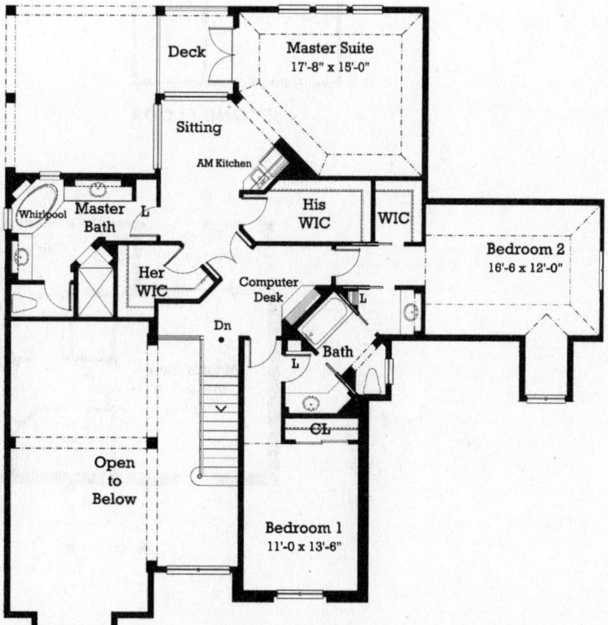
Deck
Master Suite
17'-8" x 15'-0"
Sitting
AM Kitchen
Master
Bath
Whirlpool
L
His
WIC
WIC
Bedroom 2
16'-6 x 12'-0"
Her
WIC
Computer
Desk
L
Dn
L
Bath
CL
Open
to
Below
Bedroom 1
11'-0 x 13'-6"

SECOND FLOOR

Design 64161

See Order Pages and Index for Info

Units	Single
Price Code	I
Total Finished	2,626 sq. ft.
First Finished	1,627 sq. ft.
Second Finished	999 sq. ft.
Garage Unfinished	499 sq. ft.
Porch Unfinished	438 sq. ft.
Dimensions	78'6"x80'6"
Foundation	Crawlspace
Bedrooms	3
Full Baths	3
Half Baths	1
Max Ridge Height	32'
Exterior Walls	2x6

* Alternate foundation options available at an additional charge. Please call 1-800-235-5700 for more information.

Hot New Design

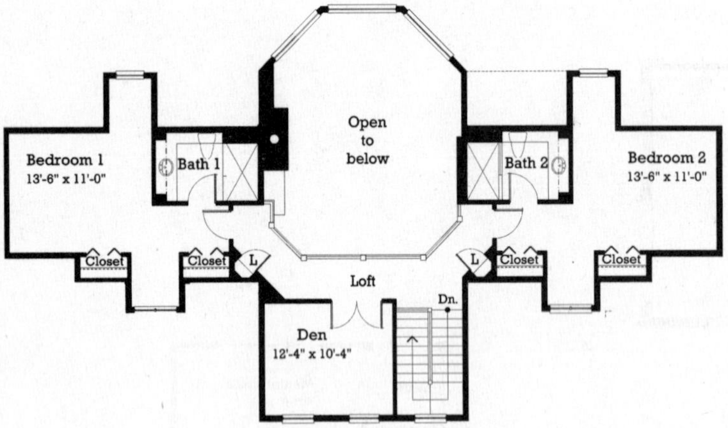
Open to below
Bedroom 1
13'-6" x 11'-0"
Bath 1
Bath 2
Bedroom 2
13'-6" x 11'-0"
Closet
Closet
L
L
Closet
Closet
Loft
Dn.
Den
12'-4" x 10'-4"

SECOND FLOOR

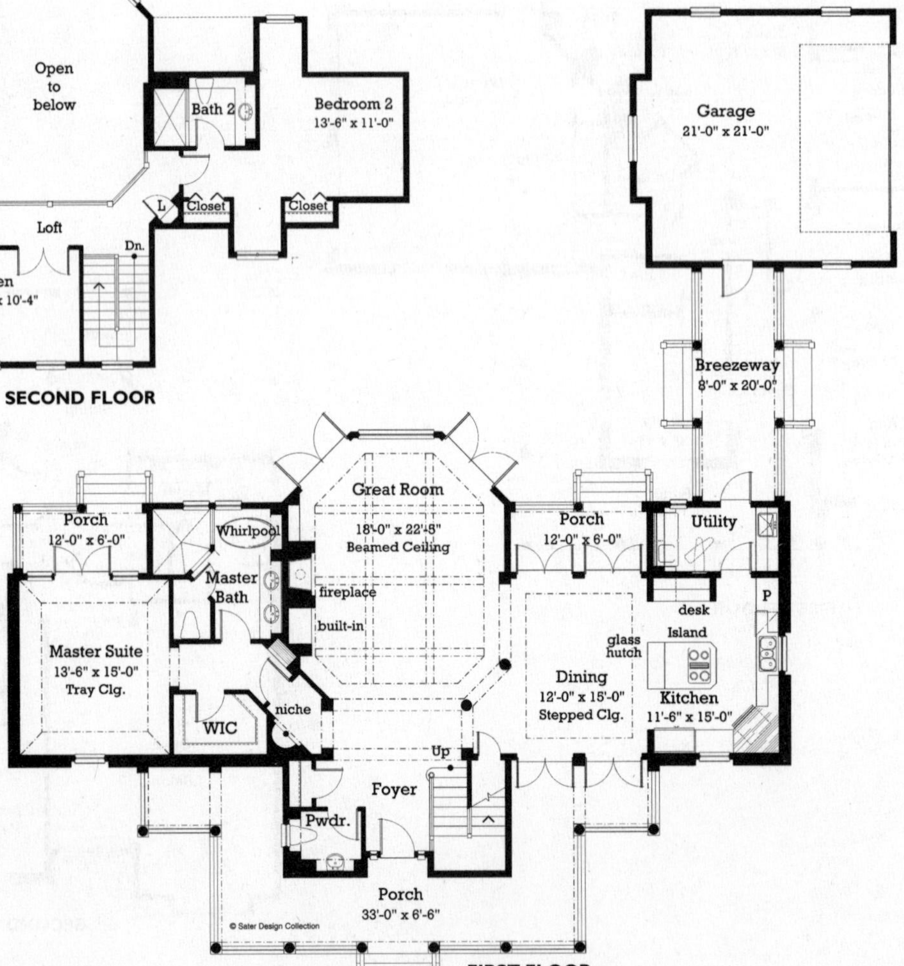
Garage
21'-0" x 21'-0"
Breezeway
8'-0" x 20'-0"
Great Room
18'-0" x 22'-8"
Beamed Ceiling
Porch
12'-0" x 6'-0"
Whirlpool
Master Bath
fireplace
built-in
Porch
12'-0" x 6'-0"
Utility
P
desk
Island
glass hutch
Master Suite
13'-6" x 15'-0"
Tray Clg.
Dining
12'-0" x 15'-0"
Stepped Clg.
Kitchen
11'-6" x 15'-0"
niche
WIC
Up
Foyer
Pwdr.
Porch
33'-0" x 6'-6"
© Sater Design Collection

FIRST FLOOR

Design 66011

See Order Pages and Index for Info

Units	Single
Price Code	H
Total Finished	3,012 sq. ft.
Main Finished	3,012 sq. ft.
Bonus Unfinished	392 sq. ft.
Garage Unfinished	851 sq. ft.
Dimensions	80'x72'
Foundation	Slab
Bedrooms	4
Full Baths	3
Half Baths	2
Main Ceiling	9'-11'
Max Ridge Height	30'6"
Roof Framing	Stick
Exterior Walls	2x4

Hot New Design

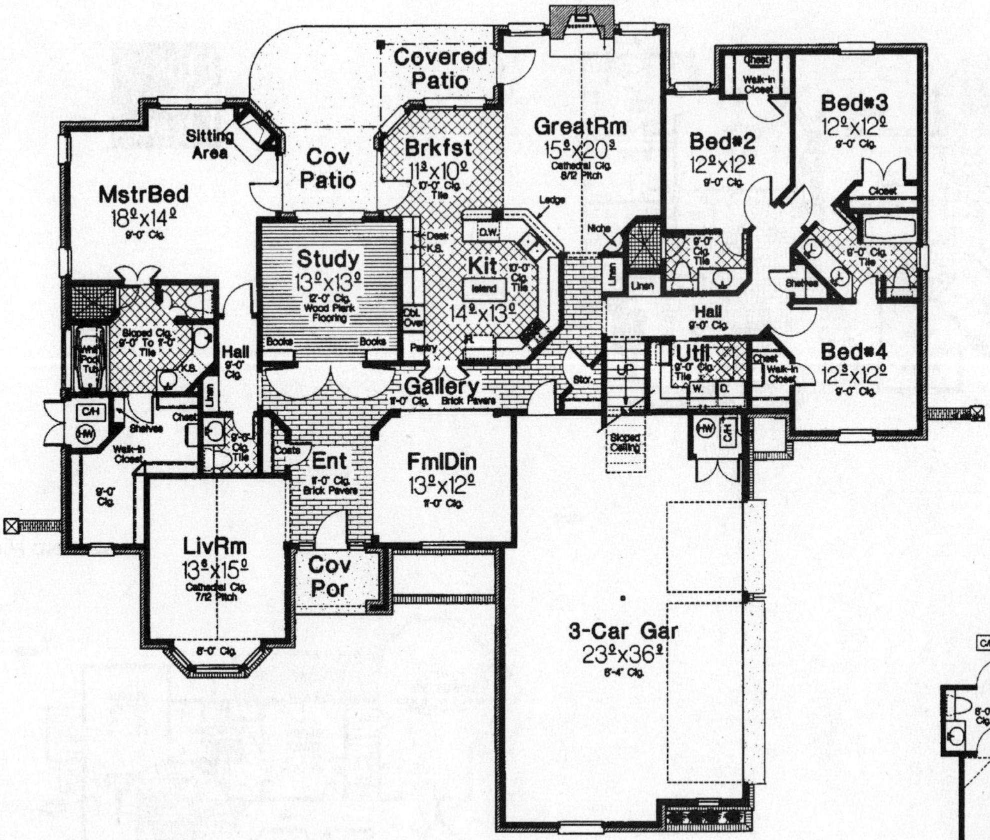
Covered Patio
GreatRm
Cathedral Clg.
8/12 Pitch
Bed#2
9'-0" Clg.
Bed#3
9'-0" Clg.
Sitting Area
Cov Patio
Brkfst
Tile
MstrBed
9'-0" Clg.
Study
Wood Plank Flooring
Kit
Island
Hall
9'-0" Clg.
Util
Bed#4
9'-0" Clg.
Gallery
Brick Pavers
Ent
Brick Pavers
FmlDin
LivRm
Cathedral Clg.
7/12 Pitch
Cov Por
3-Car Gar

MAIN FLOOR

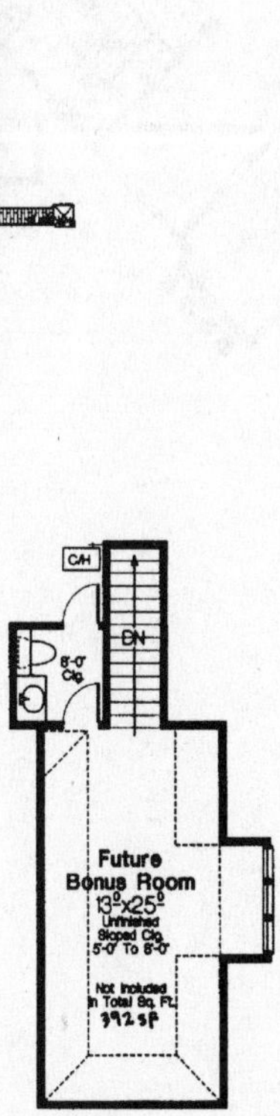
DN
Future
Bonus Room
Unfinished
Sloped Clg.
Not Included
In Total Sq. Ft.
392 sf

BONUS

Design 66015

See Order Pages and Index for Info

Units	Single
Price Code	L
Total Finished	5,354 sq. ft.
First Finished	3,920 sq. ft.
Second Finished	1,434 sq. ft.
Bonus Unfinished	427 sq. ft.
Garage Unfinished	740 sq. ft.
Porch Unfinished	220 sq. ft.
Dimensions	107'10"x92'8"
Foundation	Basement Slab
Bedrooms	5
Full Baths	4
Half Baths	1
First Ceiling	10'
Second Ceiling	9'
Max Ridge Height	34'6"
Roof Framing	Stick
Exterior Walls	2x4,2x6

FIRST FLOOR

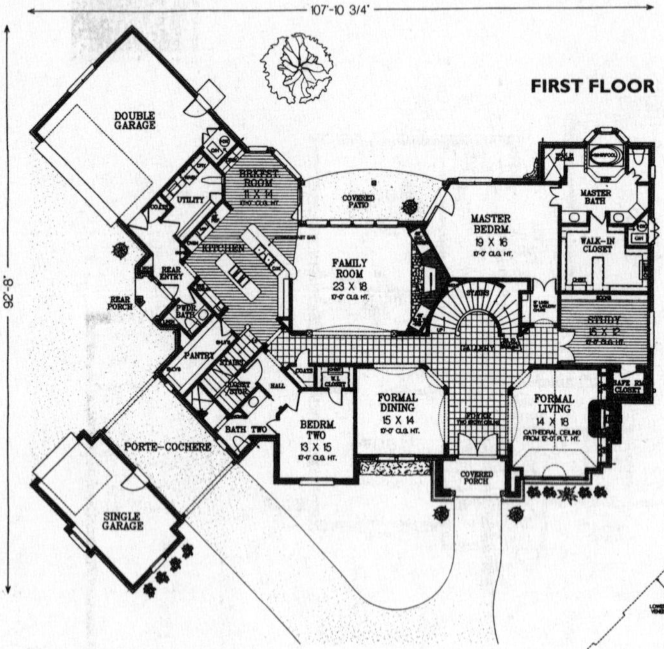
107'-10 3/4"
92'-8"
DOUBLE GARAGE
BRKFST. ROOM 11 X 14
UTILITY
COVERED PATIO
MASTER BEDRM. 19 X 16
MASTER BATH
WALK-IN CLOSET
KITCHEN
FAMILY ROOM 23 X 18
REAR ENTRY
REAR PORCH
STUDY 15 X 12
GALLERY
PANTRY
FORMAL DINING 15 X 14
FORMAL LIVING 14 X 18
FOYER
BEDRM. TWO 13 X 15
BATH TWO
PORTE-COCHERE
COVERED PORCH
SINGLE GARAGE

Hot New Design

SECOND FLOOR

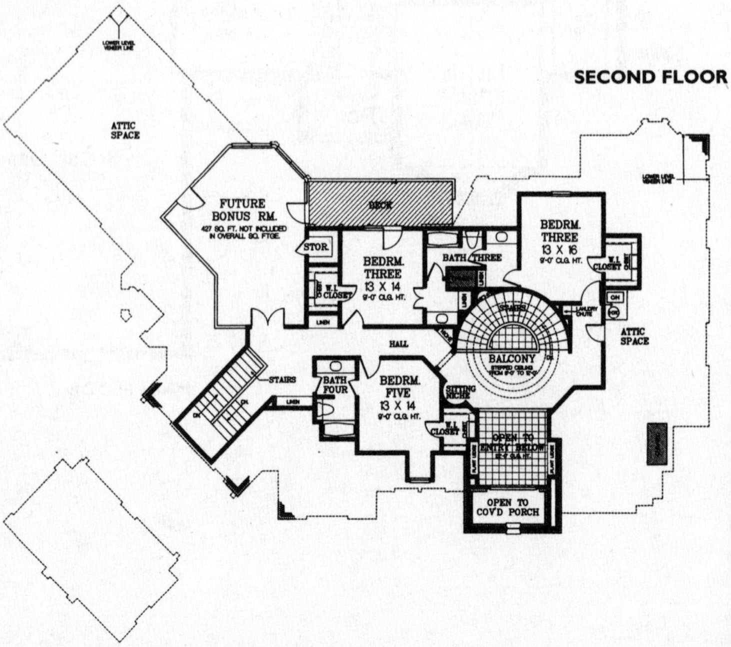
ATTIC SPACE
FUTURE BONUS RM.
427 SQ. FT. NOT INCLUDED IN OVERALL SQ. FTGE.
STOR.
BEDRM. THREE 13 X 14
BATH THREE
BEDRM. THREE 13 X 16
W.I. CLOSET
HALL
BALCONY
ATTIC SPACE
STAIRS
BATH FOUR
BEDRM. FIVE 13 X 14
SITTING NICHE
OPEN TO ENTRY BELOW
OPEN TO COV'D PORCH

Design 66012

See Order Pages and Index for Info

Units	Single
Price Code	G
Total Finished	2,569 sq. ft.
Main Finished	2,569 sq. ft.
Dimensions	90'6"x62'11"
Foundation	Crawlspace Slab
Bedrooms	3
Full Baths	2
Half Baths	1
Main Ceiling	10'
Max Ridge Height	28'
Roof Framing	Stick
Exterior Walls	2x4

Hot New Design

MAIN FLOOR

90 - 6 1/2

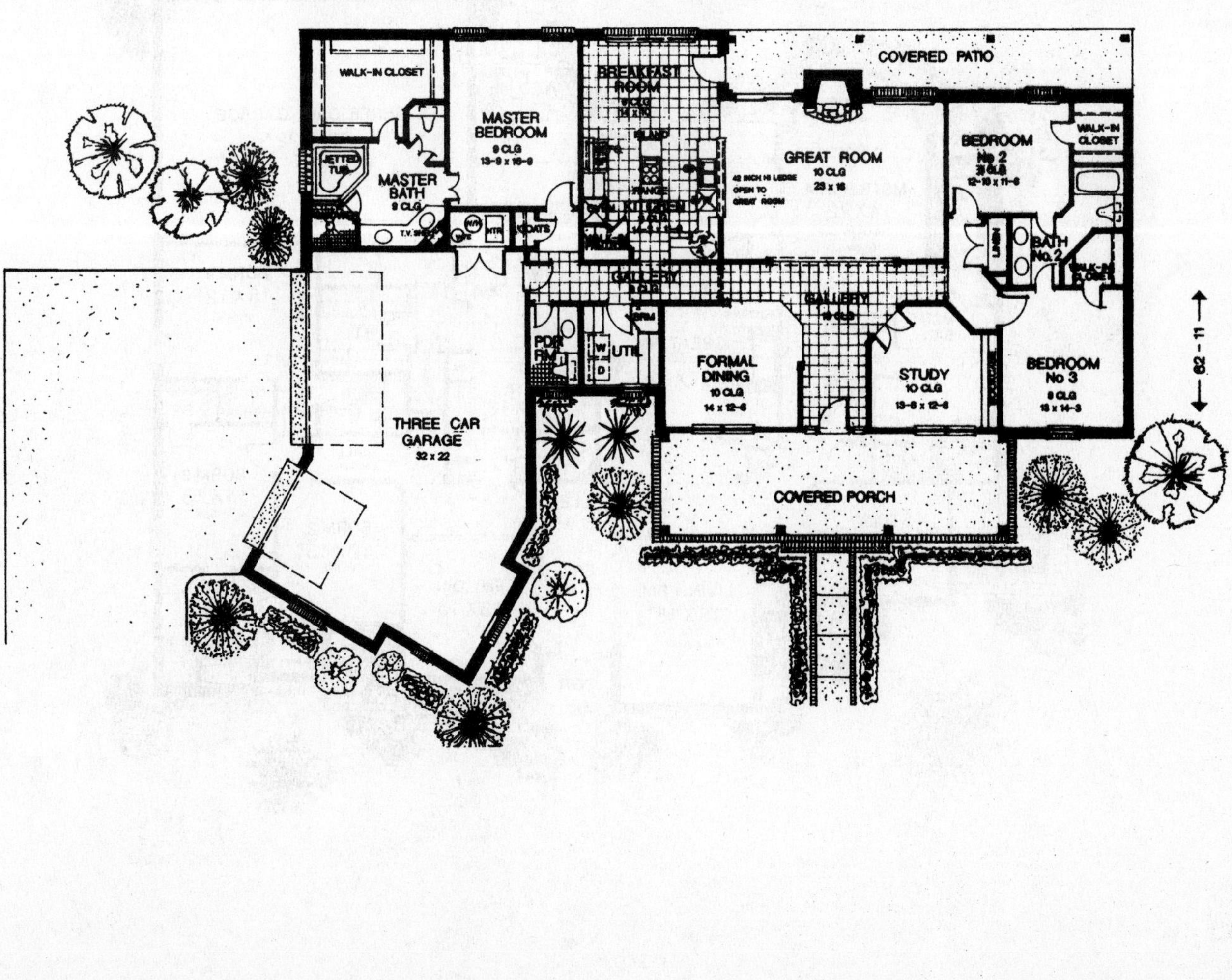
WALK-IN CLOSET
MASTER BEDROOM
9 CLG
JETTED TUB
MASTER BATH
9 CLG
BREAKFAST ROOM
COVERED PATIO
GREAT ROOM
10 CLG
23 x 16
BEDROOM No 2
WALK-IN CLOSET
BATH No 2
GALLERY
FORMAL DINING
10 CLG
14 x 12-6
STUDY
10 CLG
BEDROOM No 3
PDR RM
UTIL
THREE CAR GARAGE
32 x 22
COVERED PORCH
62 - 11

Design 66013

See Order Pages and Index for Info

Units	Single
Price Code	I
Total Finished	3,262 sq. ft.
Main Finished	3,262 sq. ft.
Garage Unfinished	662 sq. ft.
Porch Unfinished	285 sq. ft.
Dimensions	79'8"x65'4"
Foundation	Slab
Bedrooms	4
Full Baths	3
Half Baths	1
Main Ceiling	9'-10'
Max Ridge Height	31'6"
Roof Framing	Stick
Exterior Walls	2x4

Hot New Design

MAIN FLOOR

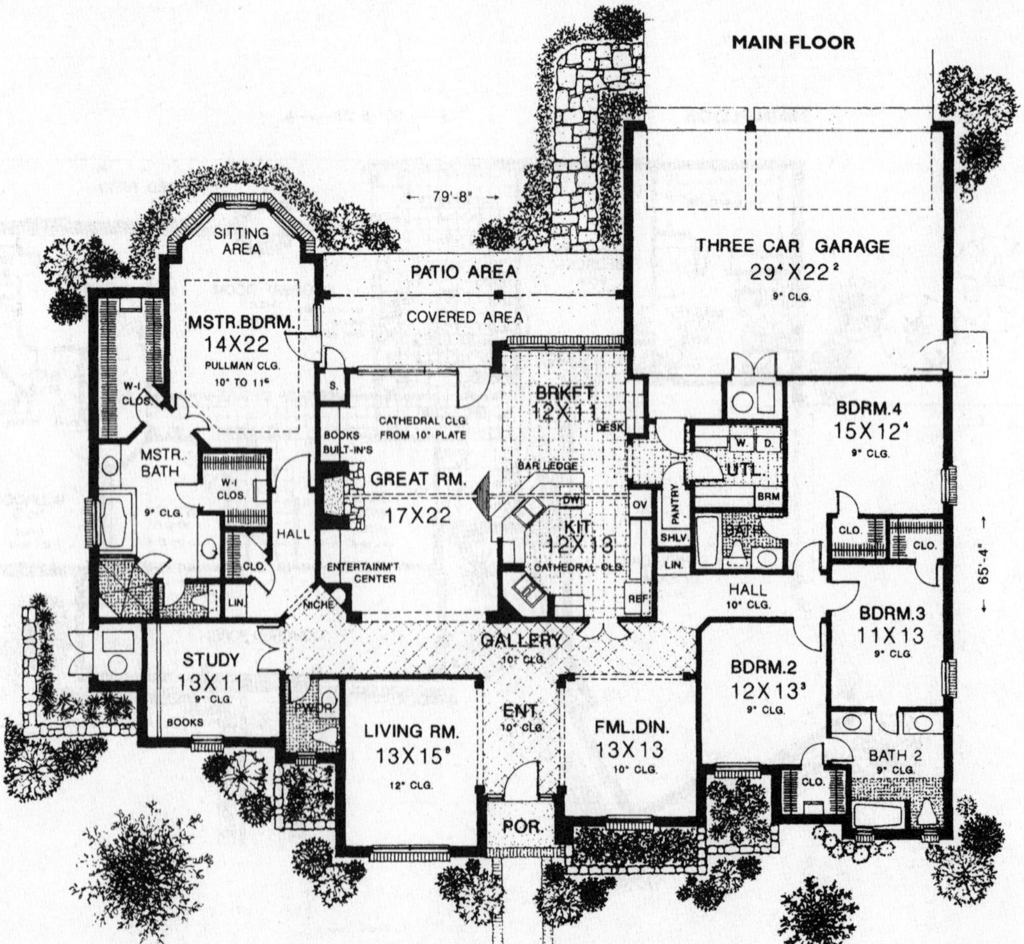
79'-8"
65'-4"
SITTING AREA
PATIO AREA
COVERED AREA
THREE CAR GARAGE
29⁴X22²
9" CLG.
MSTR.BDRM.
14X22
PULLMAN CLG.
10" TO 11⁶
W-I CLOS.
S.
BOOKS BUILT-IN'S
CATHEDRAL CLG. FROM 10" PLATE
BRKFT.
12X11
DESK
BDRM.4
15X12⁴
9" CLG.
MSTR. BATH
9" CLG.
W-I CLOS.
GREAT RM.
17X22
BAR LEDGE
DW
KIT.
12X13
CATHEDRAL CLG.
OV
PANTRY
SHLV.
LIN.
REF.
W.
D.
UTL.
BRM
BATH
CLO.
CLO.
HALL
CLO.
LIN.
ENTERTAINM'T CENTER
NICHE
HALL
10" CLG.
BDRM.3
11X13
9" CLG.
GALLERY
10" CLG.
STUDY
13X11
9" CLG.
BOOKS
PWDR
ENT.
10" CLG.
BDRM.2
12X13³
9" CLG.
LIVING RM.
13X15⁸
12" CLG.
FML.DIN.
13X13
10" CLG.
CLO.
BATH 2
9" CLG.
POR.

Design 64150

See Order Pages and Index for Info

Units	Single
Price Code	K
Total Finished	3,135 sq. ft.
First Finished	1,664 sq. ft.
Second Finished	1,471 sq. ft.
Garage Unfinished	611 sq. ft.
Porch Unfinished	288 sq. ft.
Dimensions	60'10"x62'
Foundation	Crawlspace
Bedrooms	3
Full Baths	2
Half Baths	1
Max Ridge Height	34'4"
Exterior Walls	2x6

* Alternate foundation options available at an additional charge. Please call 1-800-235-5700 for more information.

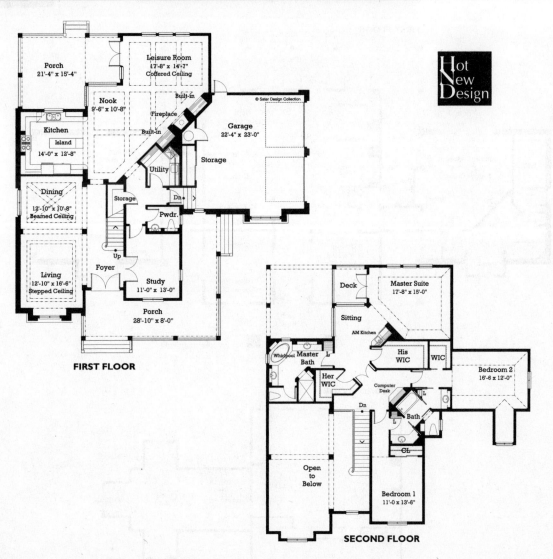

Hot New Design

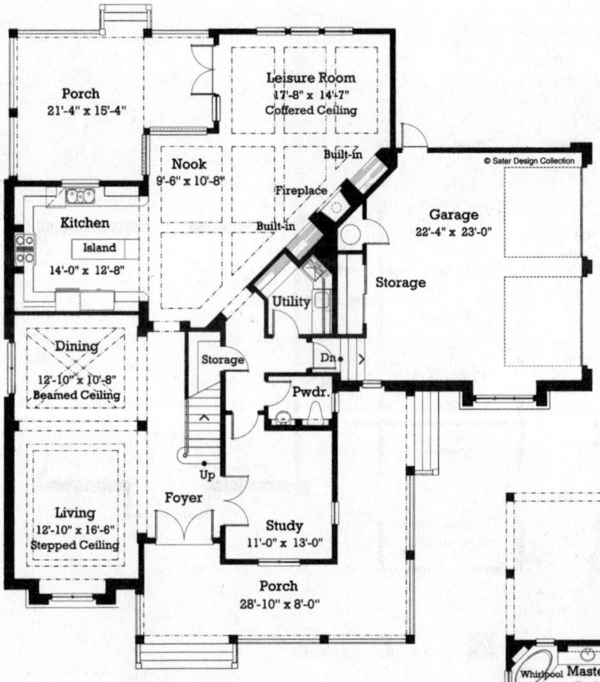
Porch
21'-4" x 15'-4"
Leisure Room
17'-8" x 14'-7"
Coffered Ceiling
Nook
9'-6" x 10'-8"
Built-in
Fireplace
Built-in
© Sater Design Collection
Garage
22'-4" x 23'-0"
Kitchen
Island
14'-0" x 12'-8"
Storage
Utility
Dining
12'-10" x 10'-8"
Beamed Ceiling
Storage
Dn
Pwdr.
Up
Living
12'-10" x 16'-6"
Stepped Ceiling
Foyer
Study
11'-0" x 13'-0"
Porch
28'-10" x 8'-0"

FIRST FLOOR

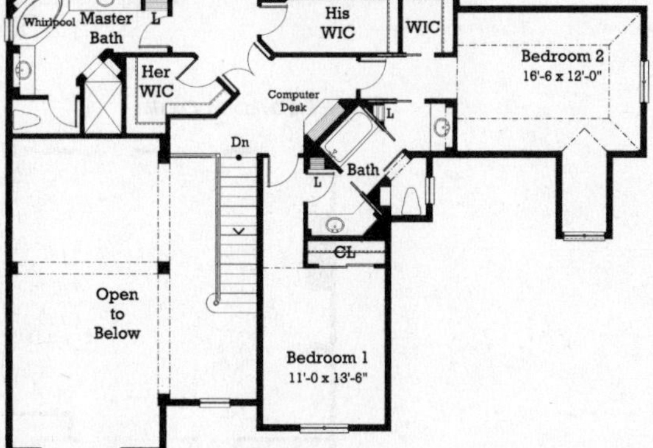
Deck
Master Suite
17'-8" x 15'-0"
Sitting
AM Kitchen
Whirlpool
Master Bath
His WIC
WIC
Bedroom 2
16'-6 x 12'-0"
Her WIC
Computer Desk
Dn
Bath
CL
Open to Below
Bedroom 1
11'-0 x 13'-6"

SECOND FLOOR

Design 64153

See Order Pages and Index for Info

Units	Single
Price Code	I
Total Finished	2,885 sq. ft.
First Finished	2,151 sq. ft.
Second Finished	734 sq. ft.
Bonus Unfinished	522 sq. ft.
Garage Unfinished	612 sq. ft.
Dimensions	99'x56'
Foundation	Crawlspace
Bedrooms	3
Full Baths	2
Half Baths	1
Max Ridge Height	33'
Exterior Walls	2x6

* Alternate foundation options available at an additional charge. Please call 1-800-235-5700 for more information.

Hot New Design

FIRST FLOOR

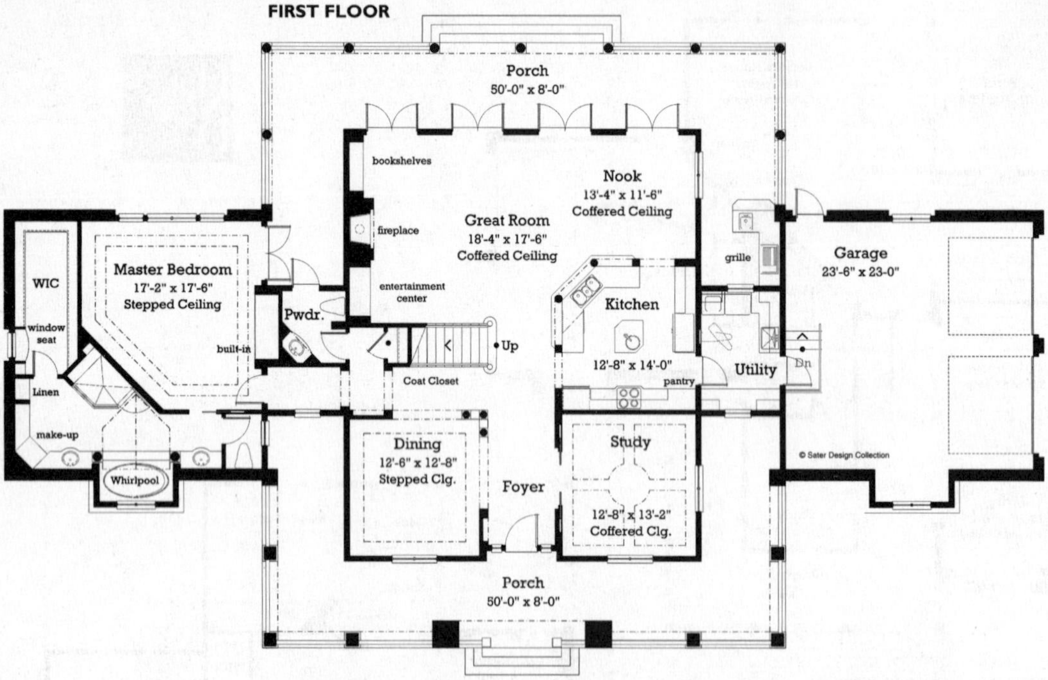
Porch
50'-0" x 8'-0"
bookshelves
fireplace
Great Room
18'-4" x 17'-6"
Coffered Ceiling
entertainment center
Nook
13'-4" x 11'-6"
Coffered Ceiling
Kitchen
12'-8" x 14'-0"
pantry
grille
Utility
Garage
23'-6" x 23-0"
Dn
WIC
window seat
Master Bedroom
17'-2" x 17'-6"
Stepped Ceiling
built-in
Linen
make-up
Whirlpool
Pwdr.
Up
Coat Closet
Dining
12'-6" x 12'-8"
Stepped Clg.
Foyer
Study
12'-8" x 13'-2"
Coffered Clg.
© Sater Design Collection
Porch
50'-0" x 8'-0"

SECOND FLOOR

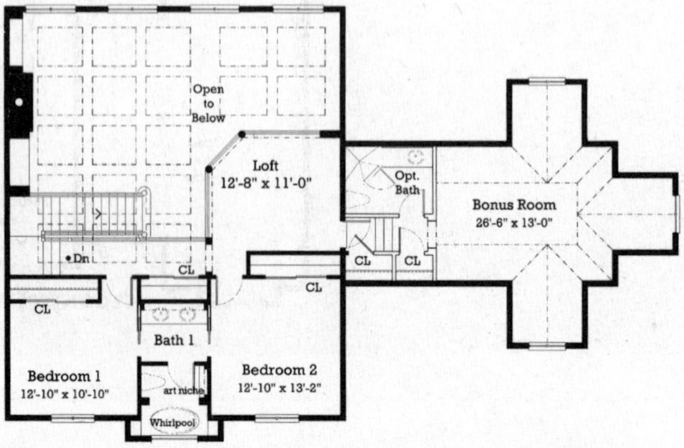
Open to Below
Loft
12'-8" x 11'-0"
Opt. Bath
Bonus Room
26'-6" x 13'-0"
CL
CL
Dn
CL
CL
CL
Bath 1
Bedroom 1
12'-10" x 10'-10"
art niche
Whirlpool
Bedroom 2
12'-10" x 13'-2"

Weather Shield™

Weather Shield Windows & Doors is a leading manufacturer of innovative window and door products. We offer countless styles, options, custom capabilities and our patented ThermoGold™ glazing.

IndyMac Bank

www.indymacbank.com 1-866-813-2787

IndyMac Bank is one of the largest and most experienced construction lenders in the country. Our Construction-to-Permanent Loan takes you all the way from construction through home ownership. One loan. One application. One set of closing costs. You can even apply online for fast approval.

IndyMac Bank. Home Construction Lending

We're experts in construction, not red tape.

Member FDIC NYSE:NDE

Heat-N-Glo HearthFire Fireplace

www.heatnglo.com 1-888-427-3973

Heat-N-Glo has created a gas fireplace that has the most authentic masonry-look available. The HearthFire model CFX-36T, allows you to finish the fireplace right up to the opening. With 60,000 BTUs/hour onput, the flames are more intense and the realistic split logs and burning embers have a spectacular radiance. Heat-n-Glo's model HearthFire is the best choice for a fireplace when you are in the market for a traditional masonry-look, but still want the convenience of clean burning gas.

HEAT-N-GLO
No one builds a better fire

Design 65078

See Order Pages and Index for Info

Units	Single
Price Code	A
Total Finished	1,059 sq. ft.
Main Finished	1,059 sq. ft.
Garage Unfinished	300 sq. ft.
Dimensions	38'x46'8"
Foundation	Basement
Bedrooms	2
Full Baths	1
Main Ceiling	8'
Max Ridge Height	17'1"
Roof Framing	Truss
Exterior Walls	2x6

Hot New Design

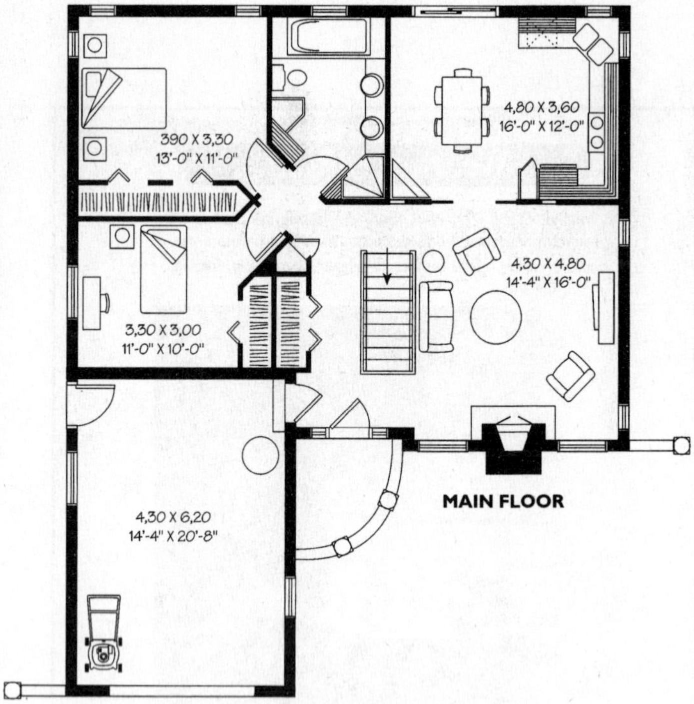
390 X 3,30
13'-0" X 11'-0"
4,80 X 3,60
16'-0" X 12'-0"
4,30 X 4,80
14'-4" X 16'-0"
3,30 X 3,00
11'-0" X 10'-0"
4,30 X 6,20
14'-4" X 20'-8"
MAIN FLOOR

Design 65636

See Order Pages and Index for Info

Units	Single
Price Code	A
Total Finished	1,420 sq. ft.
Main Finished	1,420 sq. ft.
Dimensions	52'x56'
Foundation	Crawlspace Slab
Bedrooms	3
Full Baths	2
Max Ridge Height	28'
Roof Framing	Stick
Exterior Walls	2x6

Hot New Design

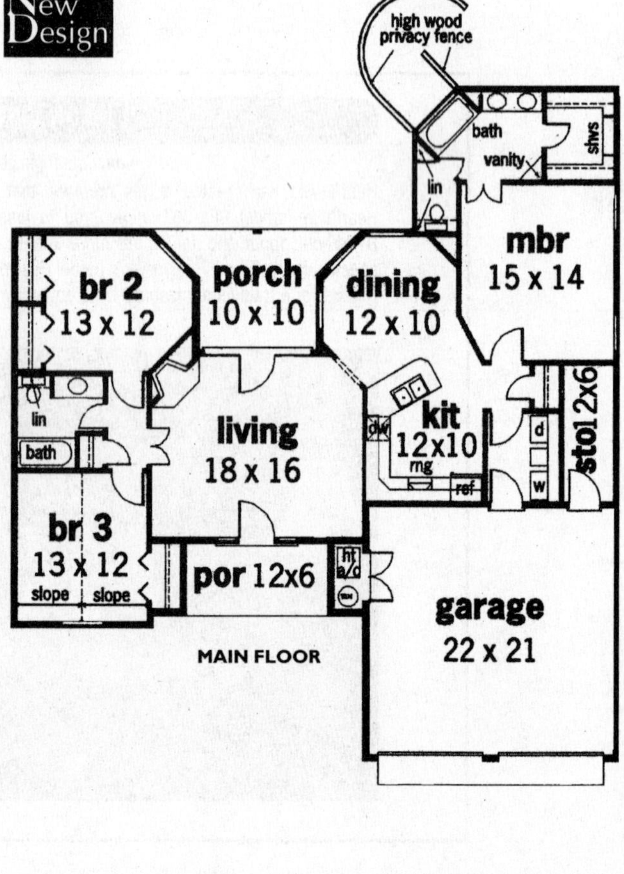
high wood privacy fence
bath
vanity
shws
lin
mbr
15 x 14
br 2
13 x 12
porch
10 x 10
dining
12 x 10
kit
12x10
dw
mg
ref
d
w
sto 12x6
lin
bath
living
18 x 16
br 3
13 x 12
slope
slope
por 12x6
ht a/c
garage
22 x 21
MAIN FLOOR

Design 65637

See Order Pages and Index for Info

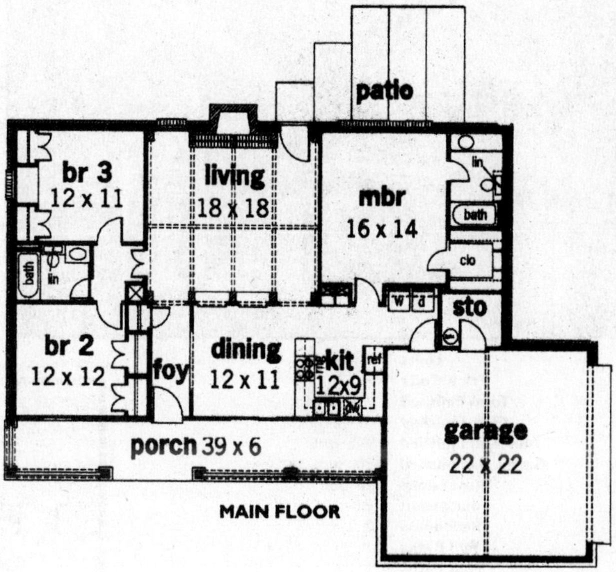
patio
br 3
12 x 11
living
18 x 18
mbr
16 x 14
lin
bath
clo
bath
lin
w
d
sto
br 2
12 x 12
foy
dining
12 x 11
kit
12x9
ref
porch 39 x 6
garage
22 x 22
MAIN FLOOR

Units	Single
Price Code	A
Total Finished	1,418 sq. ft.
Main Finished	1,418 sq. ft.
Dimensions	61'x44'
Foundation	Crawlspace Slab
Bedrooms	3
Full Baths	2
Max Ridge Height	25'
Roof Framing	Stick
Exterior Walls	2x4

Hot New Design

Design 65635

See Order Pages and Index for Info

Photography supplied by PBF Design Group

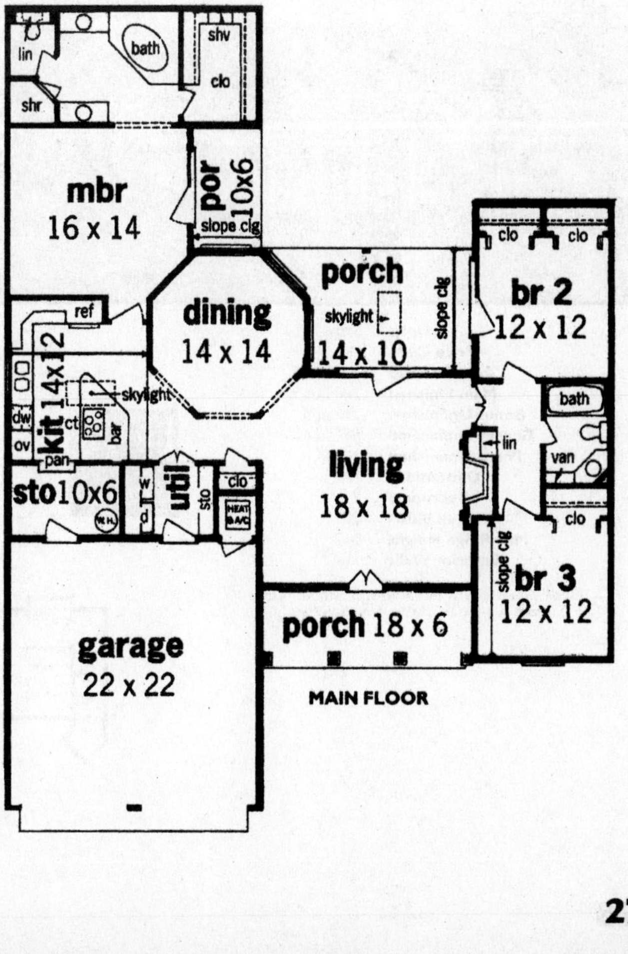
lin
bath
shv
clo
shr
mbr
16 x 14
por
10x6
slope clg
clo
clo
br 2
12 x 12
porch
skylight
14 x 10
slope clg
dining
14 x 14
ref
kit 14x12
skylight
dw
ov
ct
bar
pan
bath
lin
van
living
18 x 18
clo
sto 10x6
w
d
util
sto
clo
HEAT A/C
slope clg
br 3
12 x 12
porch 18 x 6
garage
22 x 22
MAIN FLOOR

Units	Single
Price Code	B
Total Finished	1,655 sq. ft.
Main Finished	1,655 sq. ft.
Dimensions	52'x66'
Foundation	Crawlspace Slab
Bedrooms	3
Full Baths	2
Max Ridge Height	26'
Roof Framing	Stick
Exterior Walls	2x6

Hot New Design

Design 65251

See Order Pages and Index for Info

Hot New Design

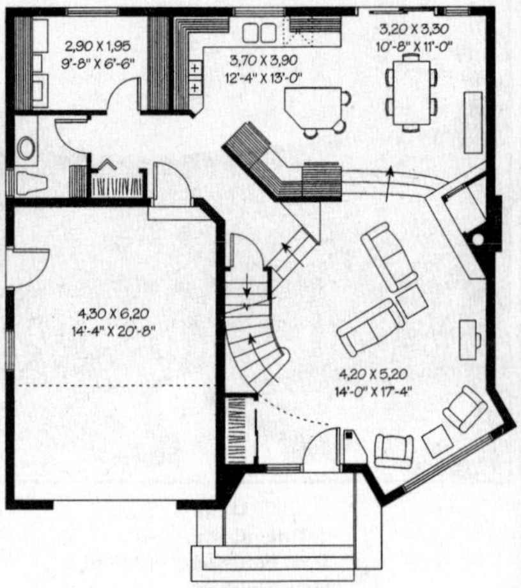
2,90 X 1,95
9'-8" X 6'-6"
3,70 X 3,90
12'-4" X 13'-0"
3,20 X 3,30
10'-8" X 11'-0"
4,30 X 6,20
14'-4" X 20'-8"
4,20 X 5,20
14'-0" X 17'-4"

FIRST FLOOR

Units	Single
Price Code	B
Total Finished	1,659 sq. ft.
First Finished	917 sq. ft.
Second Finished	742 sq. ft.
Garage Unfinished	300 sq. ft.
Dimensions	38'x36'
Foundation	Basement
Bedrooms	3
Full Baths	1
Half Baths	1
First Ceiling	8'
Second Ceiling	8'
Max Ridge Height	26'1"
Roof Framing	Truss
Exterior Walls	2x6

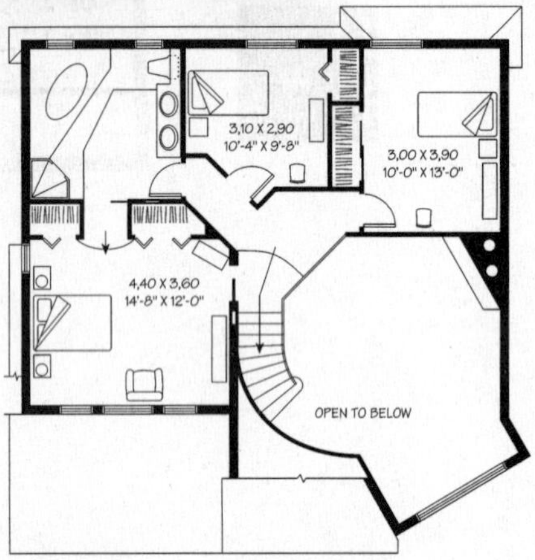
3,10 X 2,90
10'-4" X 9'-8"
3,00 X 3,90
10'-0" X 13'-0"
4,40 X 3,60
14'-8" X 12'-0"
OPEN TO BELOW

SECOND FLOOR

Design 64193

See Order Pages and Index for Info

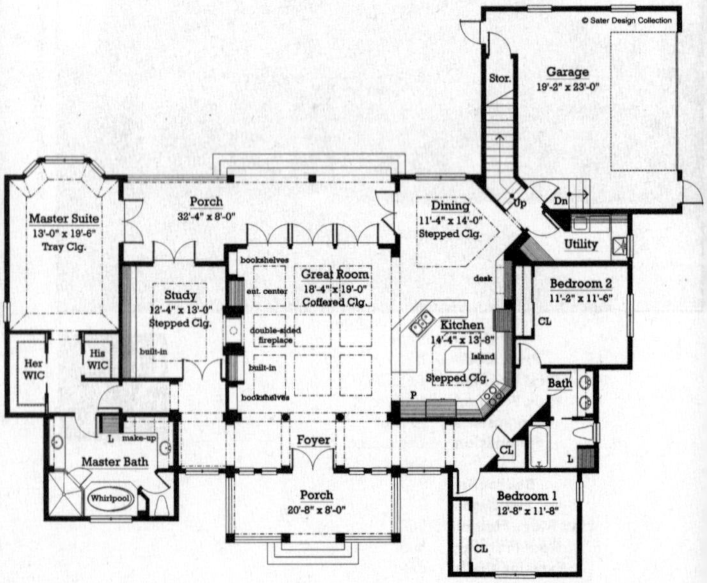
© Sater Design Collection
Stor.
Garage
19'-2" x 23'-0"
Master Suite
13'-0" x 19'-6"
Tray Clg.
Porch
32'-4" x 8'-0"
Dining
11'-4" x 14'-0"
Stepped Clg.
Up
Dn
Utility
bookshelves
Great Room
18'-4" x 19'-0"
Coffered Clg.
ent. center
double-sided fireplace
built-in
desk
Bedroom 2
11'-2" x 11'-6"
CL
Study
12'-4" x 13'-0"
Stepped Clg.
Kitchen
14'-4" x 13'-8"
Island
Stepped Clg.
Her WIC
His WIC
Bath
make-up
Master Bath
Whirlpool
Foyer
Porch
20'-8" x 8'-0"
Bedroom 1
12'-8" x 11'-8"

MAIN FLOOR

Units	Single
Price Code	H
Total Finished	2,454 sq. ft.
Main Finished	2,454 sq. ft.
Bonus Unfinished	256 sq. ft.
Garage Unfinished	547 sq. ft.
Porch Unfinished	165 sq. ft.
Dimensions	80'6"x66'
Bedrooms	3
Full Baths	2
Max Ridge Height	24'2"
Exterior Walls	2x6

Hot New Design

* Alternate foundation options available at an additional charge. Please call 1-800-235-5700 for more information.

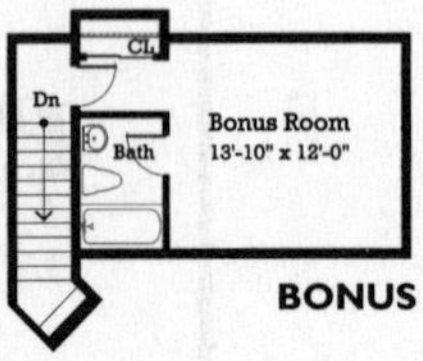
CL
Dn
Bath
Bonus Room
13'-10" x 12'-0"

BONUS

Design 64194

See Order Pages and Index for Info

Units	Single
Price Code	H
Total Finished	2,454 sq. ft.
Main Finished	2,454 sq. ft.
Bonus Unfinished	256 sq. ft.
Garage Unfinished	547 sq. ft.
Porch Unfinished	165 sq. ft.
Dimensions	80'6"x66'6"
Foundation	Crawlspace
Bedrooms	3
Full Baths	2
Max Ridge Height	24'2"
Exterior Walls	2x6

* Alternate foundation options available at an additional charge. Please call 1-800-235-5700 for more information.

Hot New Design

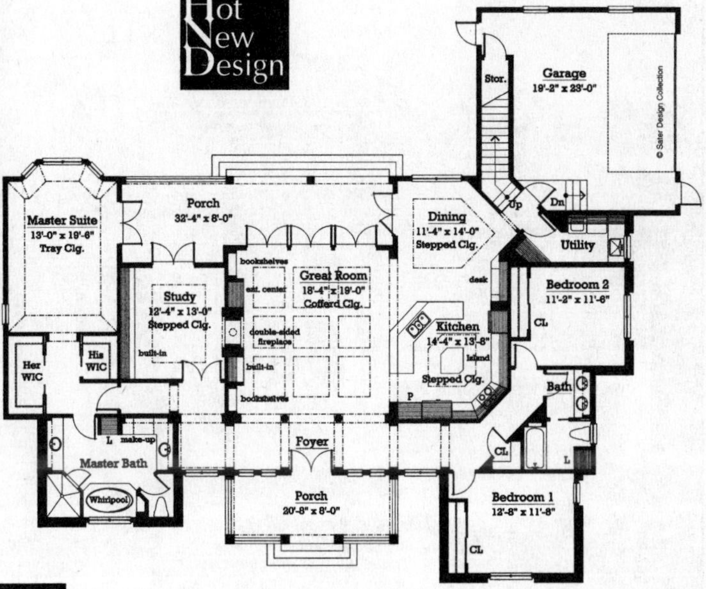
Garage
19'-2" x 23'-0"
Stor.
Master Suite
13'-0" x 19'-6"
Tray Clg.
Porch
32'-4" x 8'-0"
Dining
11'-4" x 14'-0"
Stepped Clg.
Utility
Study
12'-4" x 13'-0"
Stepped Clg.
Great Room
18'-4" x 19'-0"
Coffered Clg.
Kitchen
14'-4" x 13'-8"
Stepped Clg.
Bedroom 2
11'-2" x 11'-6"
Her WIC
His WIC
Master Bath
Whirlpool
Foyer
Porch
20'-8" x 8'-0"
Bedroom 1
12'-8" x 11'-8"
Bath
© Sater Design Collection

MAIN FLOOR

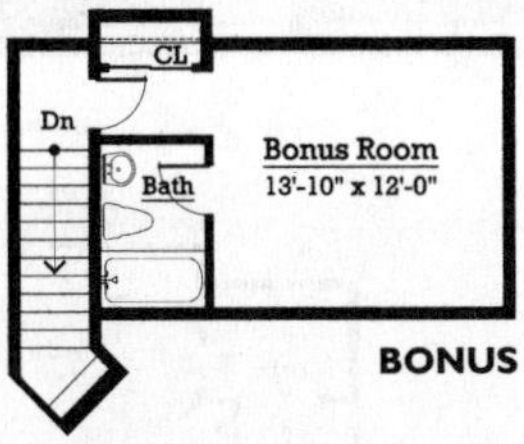
CL
Dn
Bath
Bonus Room
13'-10" x 12'-0"

BONUS

Design 64164

See Order Pages and Index for Info

Units	Single
Price Code	H
Total Finished	2,329 sq. ft.
First Finished	2,329 sq. ft.
Garage Unfinished	528 sq. ft.
Dimensions	72'x73'4"
Foundation	Crawlspace
Bedrooms	3
Full Baths	2
Half Baths	1
Max Ridge Height	27'
Exterior Walls	2x6

* Alternate foundation options available at an additional charge. Please call 1-800-235-5700 for more information.

Hot New Design

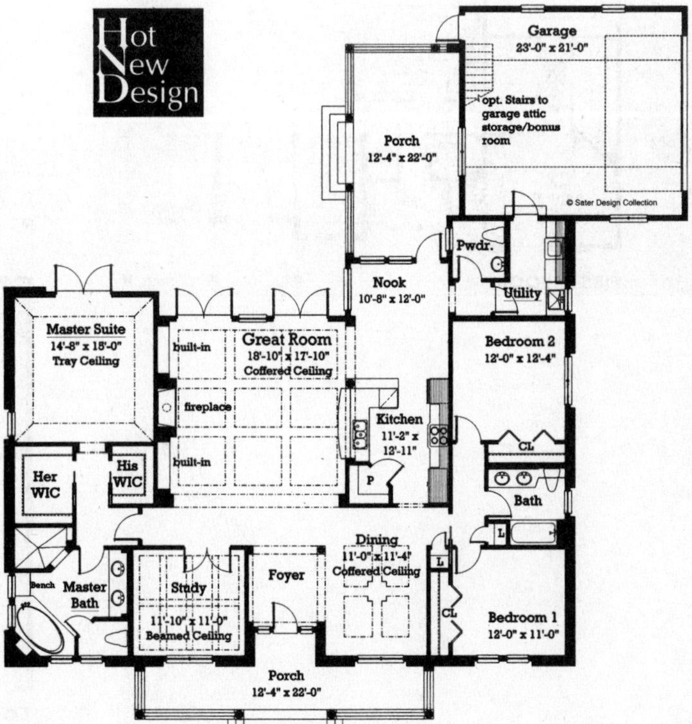
Garage
23'-0" x 21'-0"
opt. Stairs to garage attic storage/bonus room
Porch
12'-4" x 22'-0"
© Sater Design Collection
Pwdr.
Utility
Nook
10'-8" x 12'-0"
Master Suite
14'-8" x 15'-0"
Tray Ceiling
Great Room
18'-10" x 17'-10"
Coffered Ceiling
Bedroom 2
12'-0" x 12'-4"
fireplace
built-in
Kitchen
11'-2" x 12'-11"
Her WIC
His WIC
Bath
Master Bath
Study
11'-10" x 11'-0"
Beamed Ceiling
Foyer
Dining
11'-0" x 11'-4"
Coffered Ceiling
Bedroom 1
12'-0" x 11'-0"
Porch
12'-4" x 22'-0"

Design 94285

See Order Pages and Index for Info

Units	Single
Price Code	G
Total Finished	2,988 sq. ft.
First Finished	2,096 sq. ft.
Second Finished	892 sq. ft.
Lower Unfinished	1,948 sq. ft.
Dimensions	56'x54'
Foundation	Basement
Bedrooms	3
Full Baths	3
Half Baths	1
Max Ridge Height	36'
Exterior Walls	2x6

* Alternate foundation options available at an additional charge. Please call 1-800-235-5700 for more information.

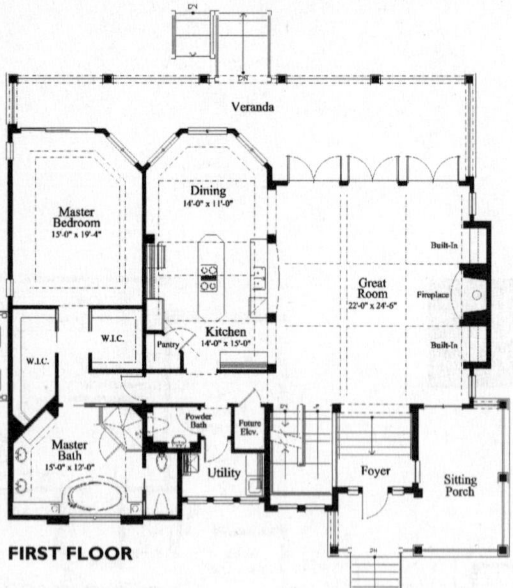

Veranda
Master Bedroom
15'-0" x 19'-4"
Dining
14'-0" x 11'-0"
Great Room
22'-0" x 24'-6"
Built-In
Fireplace
Built-In
Kitchen
14'-0" x 15'-0"
Pantry
W.I.C.
W.I.C.
Master Bath
15'-0" x 12'-0"
Powder Bath
Future Elev.
Utility
Foyer
Sitting Porch

FIRST FLOOR

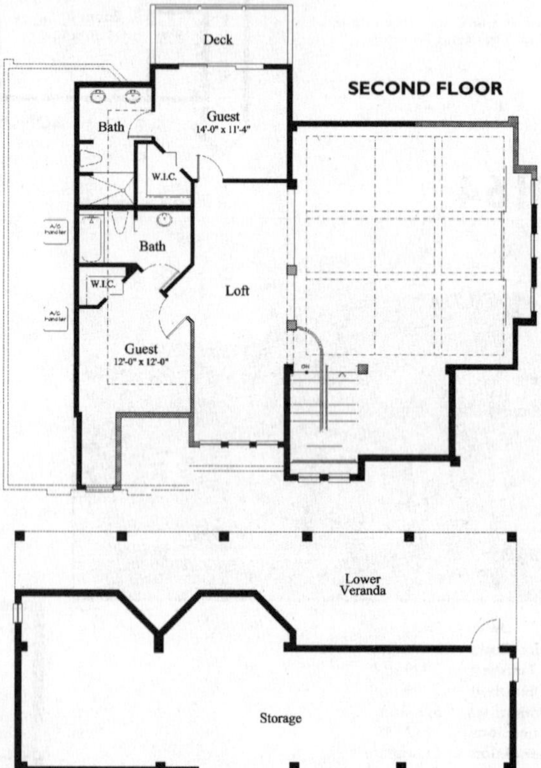

Deck
Bath
Guest
14'-0" x 11'-4"
W.I.C.
Bath
W.I.C.
Loft
Guest
12'-0" x 12'-0"

SECOND FLOOR

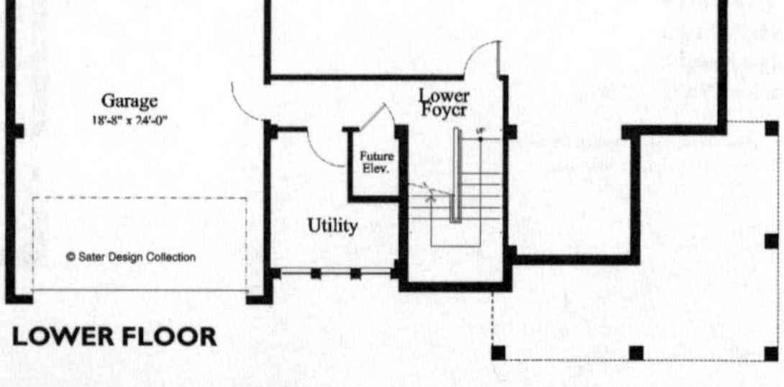

Lower Veranda
Storage
Garage
18'-8" x 24'-0"
Lower Foyer
Future Elev.
Utility
© Sater Design Collection

LOWER FLOOR

Design 24802

See Order Pages and Index for Info

Units	Single
Price Code	L
Total Finished	4,064 sq. ft.
Main Finished	2,466 sq. ft.
Lower Finished	1,598 sq. ft.
Basement Unfinished	876 sq. ft.
Garage Unfinished	665 sq. ft.
Dimensions	78'x52'4"
Foundation	Basement
Bedrooms	4
Full Baths	3
Main Ceiling	9'-11'
Max Ridge Height	32'
Roof Framing	Stick
Exterior Walls	2x6

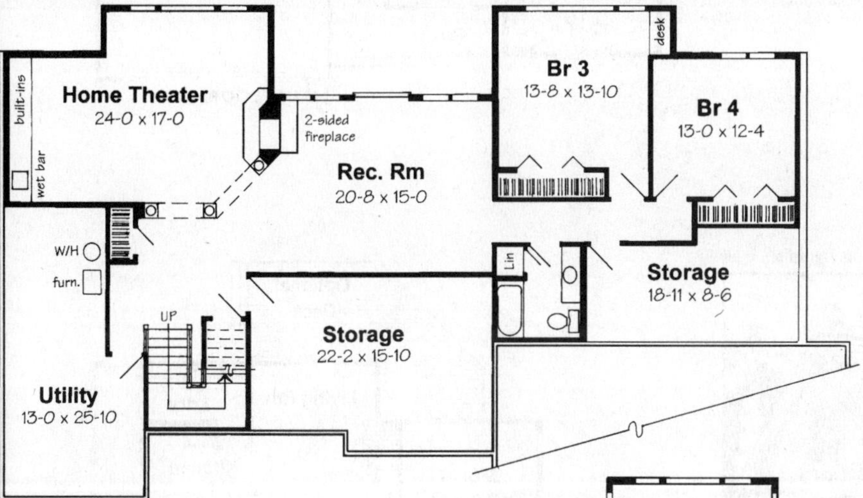
Home Theater
24-0 x 17-0
built-ins
wet bar
2-sided fireplace
Rec. Rm
20-8 x 15-0
Br 3
13-8 x 13-10
desk
Br 4
13-0 x 12-4
W/H
furn.
Lin
Storage
18-11 x 8-6
Storage
22-2 x 15-10
UP
Utility
13-0 x 25-10

LOWER FLOOR

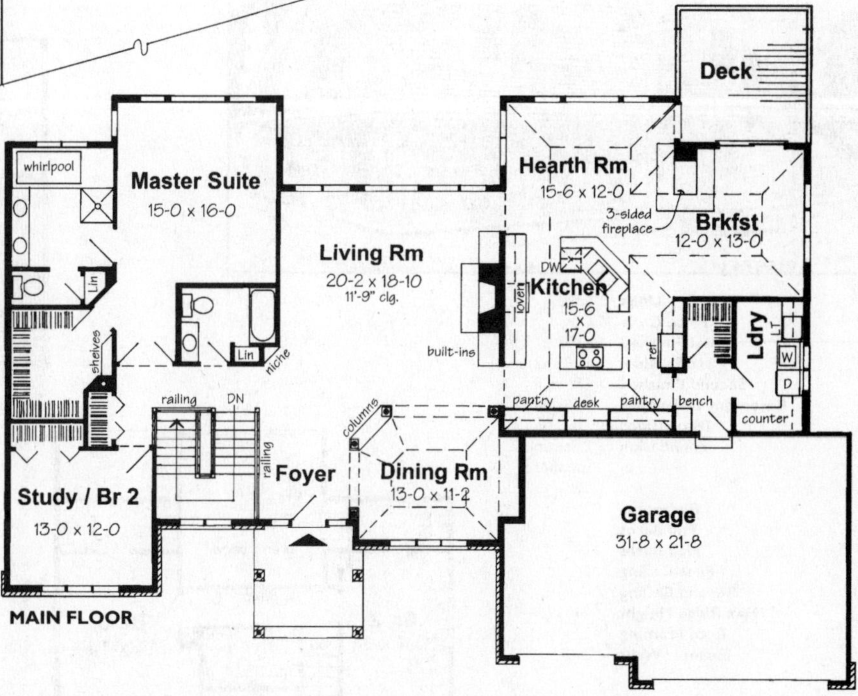
whirlpool
Master Suite
15-0 x 16-0
Lin
shelves
Lin
niche
Living Rm
20-2 x 18-10
11'-9" clg.
built-ins
Hearth Rm
15-6 x 12-0
3-sided fireplace
Deck
Brkfst
12-0 x 13-0
DW
Kitchen
15-6 x 17-0
oven
ref
Ldry
D
W
railing
DN
railing
columns
pantry
desk
pantry
bench
counter
Foyer
Dining Rm
13-0 x 11-2
Study / Br 2
13-0 x 12-0
Garage
31-8 x 21-8

MAIN FLOOR

Design 24700

See Order Pages and Index for Info

Units	Single
Price Code	A
Total Finished	1,312 sq. ft.
Main Finished	1,312 sq. ft.
Basement Unfinished	1,293 sq. ft.
Garage Unfinished	459 sq. ft.
Porch Unfinished	84 sq. ft.
Dimensions	50'x40'
Foundation	Basement Crawlspace Slab
Bedrooms	3
Full Baths	2
Main Ceiling	8'
Max Ridge Height	20'
Roof Framing	Stick
Exterior Walls	2x6

OPTIONAL CRAWLSPACE/SLAB

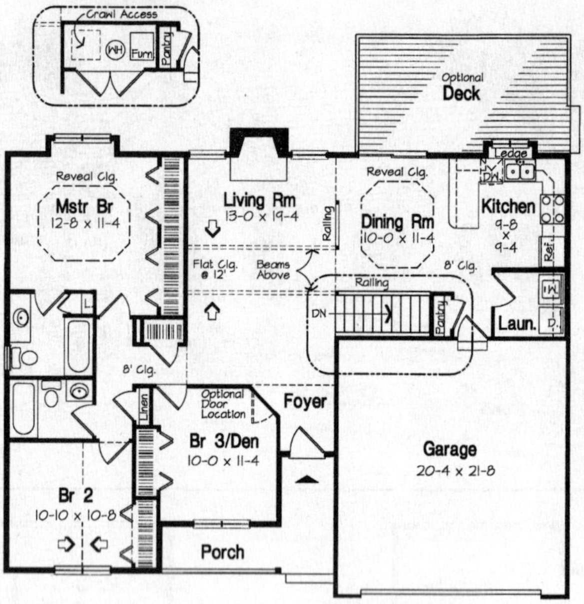
Crawl Access
WH
Furn.
Pantry
Optional Deck
Reveal Clg.
Mstr Br
12-8 x 11-4
Living Rm
13-0 x 19-4
Reveal Clg.
Dining Rm
10-0 x 11-4
Kitchen
9-8 x 9-4
Ledge
DW
Ref.
Railing
Flat Clg. @ 12'
Beams Above
8' Clg.
Railing
DN
Pantry
Laun.
8' Clg.
Linen
Optional Door Location
Foyer
Br 3/Den
10-0 x 11-4
Garage
20-4 x 21-8
Br 2
10-10 x 10-8
Porch

MAIN FLOOR

Design 10785

See Order Pages and Index for Info

Units	Single
Price Code	C
Total Finished	1,907 sq. ft.
First Finished	1,269 sq. ft.
Second Finished	638 sq. ft.
Basement Unfinished	1,269 sq. ft.
Dimensions	47'x39'
Foundation	Basement Crawlspace Slab
Bedrooms	3
Full Baths	2
Half Baths	1
First Ceiling	8'
Second Ceiling	8'
Max Ridge Height	24'
Roof Framing	Stick
Exterior Walls	2x6

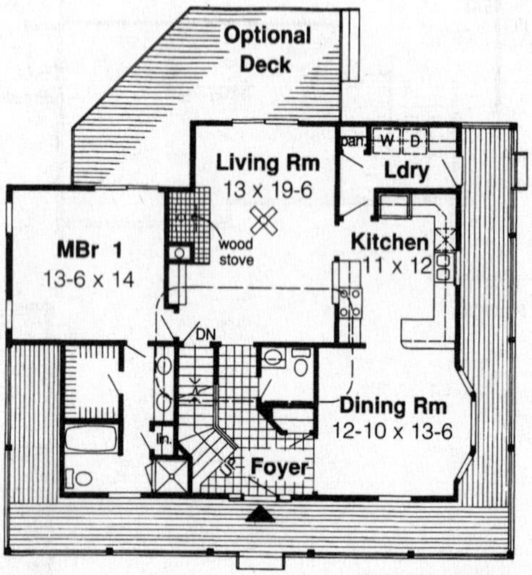
Optional Deck
Living Rm
13 x 19-6
pan
W D
Ldry
wood stove
MBr 1
13-6 x 14
Kitchen
11 x 12
DN
lin.
Dining Rm
12-10 x 13-6
Foyer

FIRST FLOOR

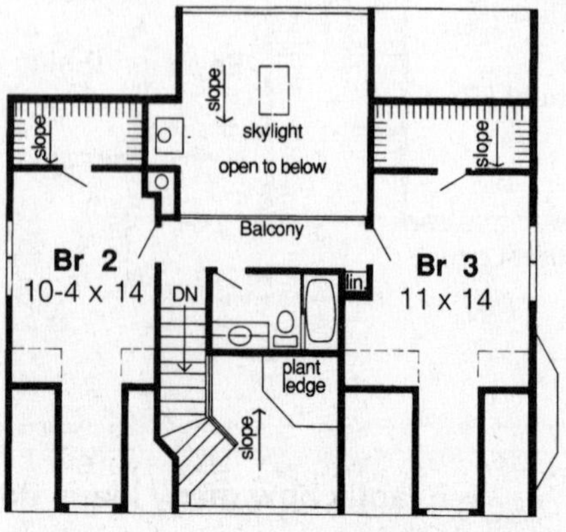
slope
skylight
open to below
slope
slope
Balcony
Br 2
10-4 x 14
Br 3
11 x 14
DN
lin
plant ledge
slope

SECOND FLOOR

Design 94297

See Order Pages and Index for Info

Units	Single
Price Code	E
Total Finished	2,349 sq. ft.
First Finished	1,537 sq. ft.
Second Finished	812 sq. ft.
Basement Unfinished	1,263 sq. ft.
Dimensions	45'4"x50'
Foundation	Basement
Bedrooms	3
Full Baths	2
Half Baths	1
Max Ridge Height	40'8"
Roof Framing	Truss
Exterior Walls	2x6

* Alternate foundation options available at an additional charge. Please call 1-800-235-5700 for more information.

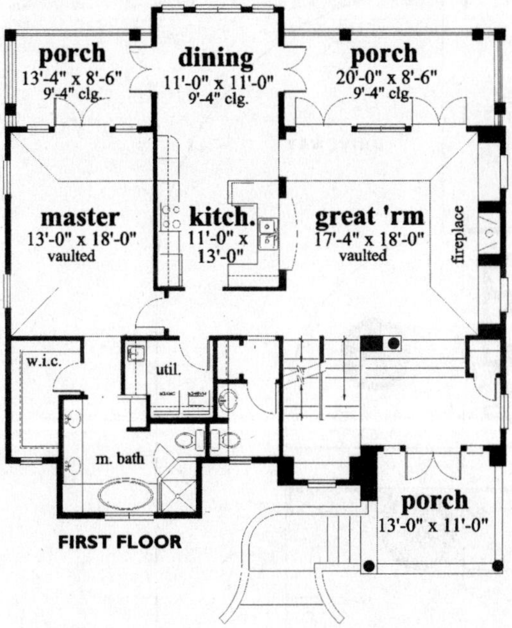
porch
13'-4" x 8'-6"
9'-4" clg.
dining
11'-0" x 11'-0"
9'-4" clg.
porch
20'-0" x 8'-6"
9'-4" clg.
master
13'-0" x 18'-0"
vaulted
kitch.
11'-0" x
13'-0"
great 'rm
17'-4" x 18'-0"
vaulted
fireplace
w.i.c.
util.
m. bath
porch
13'-0" x 11'-0"

FIRST FLOOR

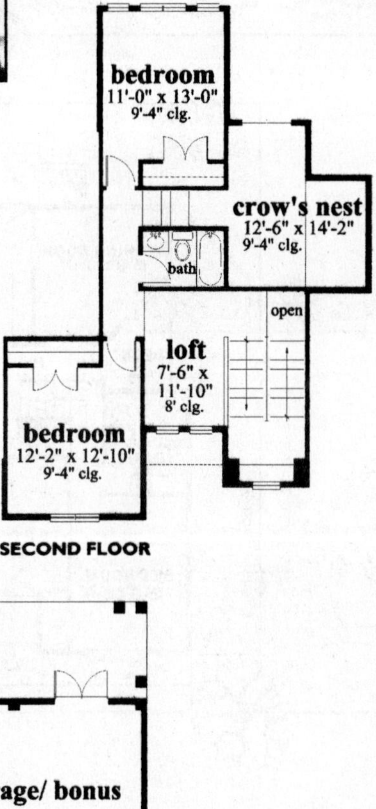
bedroom
11'-0" x 13'-0"
9'-4" clg.
crow's nest
12'-6" x 14'-2"
9'-4" clg.
bath
open
loft
7'-6" x
11'-10"
8' clg.
bedroom
12'-2" x 12'-10"
9'-4" clg.

SECOND FLOOR

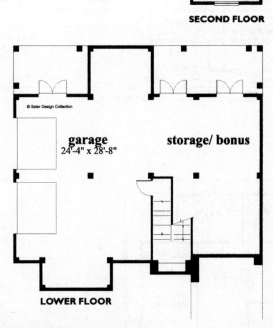

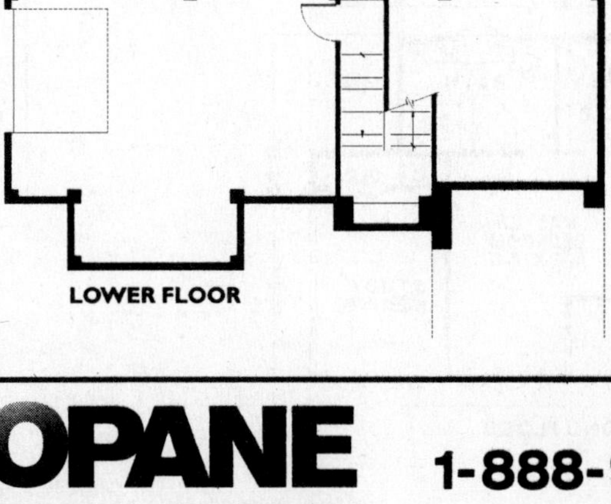
© Sater Design Collection
garage
24'-4" x 28'-8"
storage/ bonus

LOWER FLOOR

Design 10334

See Order Pages and Index for Info

Units	Single
Price Code	G
Total Finished	2,994 sq. ft.
First Finished	1,742 sq. ft.
Second Finished	809 sq. ft.
Lower Finished	443 sq. ft.
Basement Unfinished	1,270 sq. ft.
Garage Unfinished	558 sq. ft.
Dimensions	66'x54'
Foundation	Basement
Bedrooms	4
Full Baths	3
Half Baths	1
Max Ridge Height	24'
Roof Framing	Stick
Exterior Walls	2x6

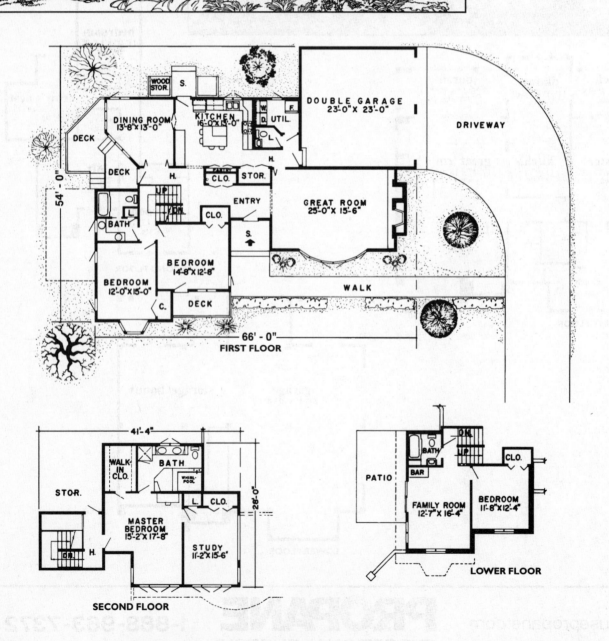

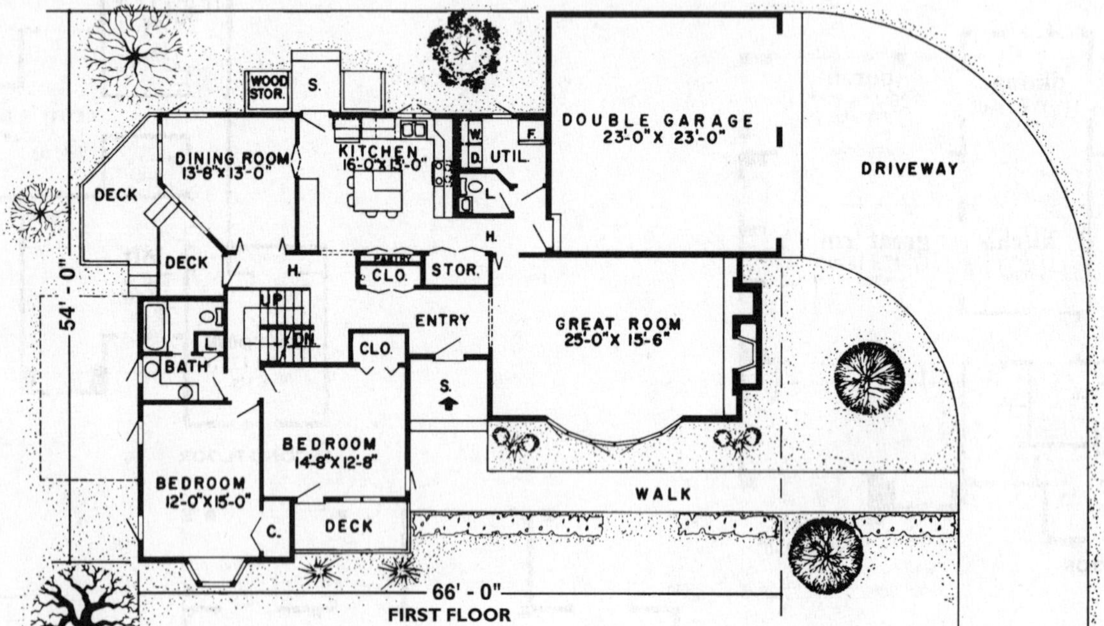
WOOD STOR.
S.
DINING ROOM 13'-8"x13'-0"
KITCHEN 16'-0"x13'-0"
W
D
F
UTIL.
L.
DOUBLE GARAGE 23'-0" X 23'-0"
DRIVEWAY
DECK
DECK
H.
H.
PANTRY
CLO.
STOR.
UP
DN.
BATH
L.
ENTRY
CLO.
S.
GREAT ROOM 25'-0" X 15'-6"
BEDROOM 14'-8"x12'-8"
BEDROOM 12'-0"x15'-0"
C.
DECK
WALK
54'-0"
66'-0"

FIRST FLOOR

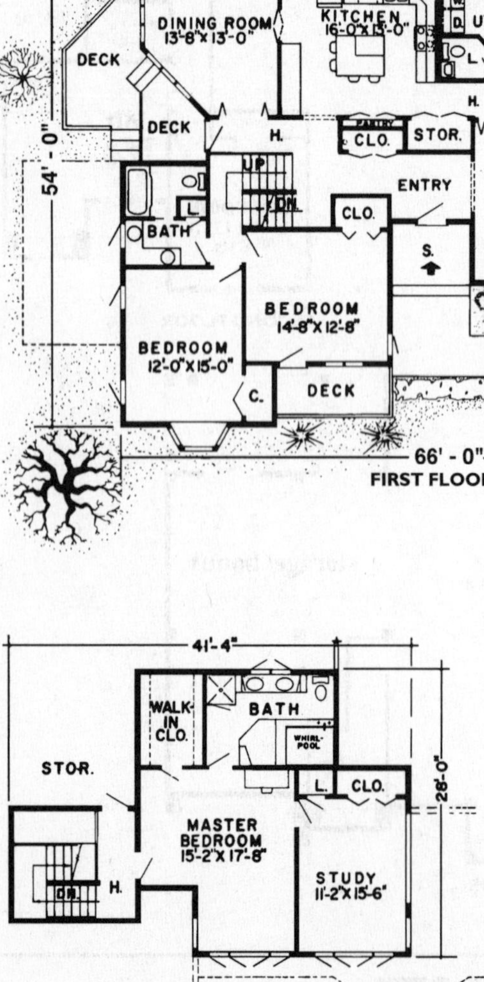
41'-4"
WALK-IN CLO.
BATH
WHIRL-POOL
STOR.
L.
CLO.
28'-0"
MASTER BEDROOM 15'-2"x17'-8"
STUDY 11'-2"x15'-6"
DN.
H.

SECOND FLOOR

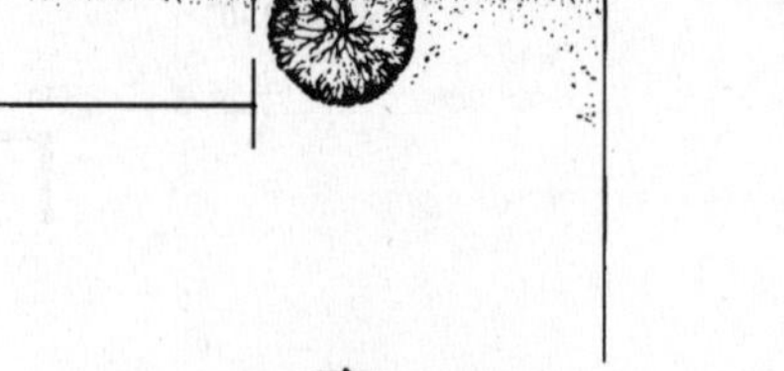
DN.
BATH
UP
CLO.
BAR
PATIO
FAMILY ROOM 12'-7" X 16'-4"
BEDROOM 11'-8"x12'-4"

LOWER FLOOR

Design 97219

See Order Pages and Index for Info

Units	Single
Price Code	D
Total Finished	2,128 sq. ft.
First Finished	1,257 sq. ft.
Second Finished	871 sq. ft.
Bonus Unfinished	444 sq. ft.
Basement Unfinished	1,275 sq. ft.
Garage Unfinished	462 sq. ft.
Dimensions	61'x40'6"
Foundation	Basement Crawlspace
Bedrooms	4
Full Baths	3
Half Baths	1
Max Ridge Height	32'
Roof Framing	Stick
Exterior Walls	2x4

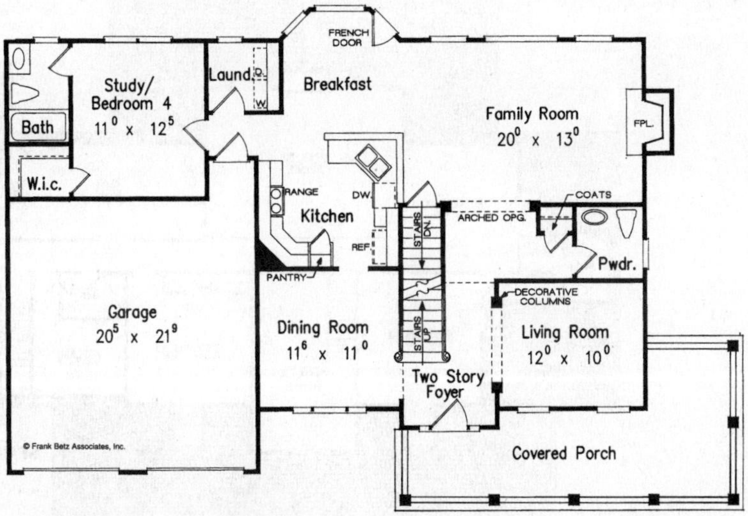

FRENCH DOOR
Bath
Study/ Bedroom 4
11^0 x 12^5
Laund.
Breakfast
Family Room
20^0 x 13^0
FPL.
W.i.c.
RANGE
DW.
Kitchen
REF
STAIRS DN.
ARCHED OPG.
COATS
Pwdr.
PANTRY
Garage
20^5 x 21^9
Dining Room
11^6 x 11^0
STAIRS UP
DECORATIVE COLUMNS
Living Room
12^0 x 10^0
Two Story Foyer
Covered Porch
© Frank Betz Associates, Inc.

FIRST FLOOR

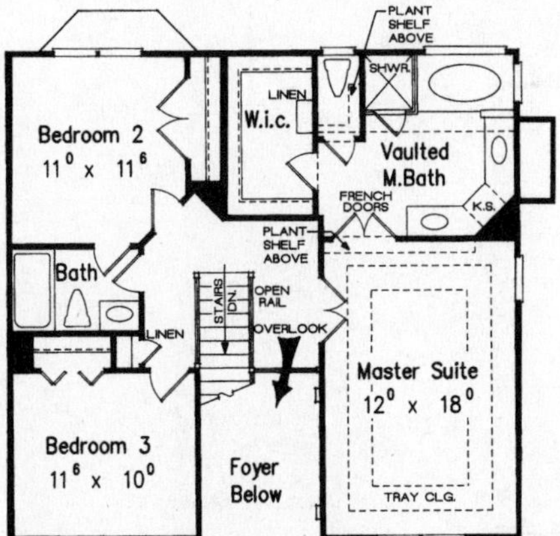

PLANT SHELF ABOVE
Bedroom 2
11^0 x 11^6
LINEN
W.i.c.
SHWR.
Vaulted M.Bath
FRENCH DOORS
K.S.
PLANT SHELF ABOVE
Bath
STAIRS DN.
OPEN RAIL
OVERLOOK
LINEN
Master Suite
12^0 x 18^0
Bedroom 3
11^6 x 10^0
Foyer Below
TRAY CLG.

SECOND FLOOR

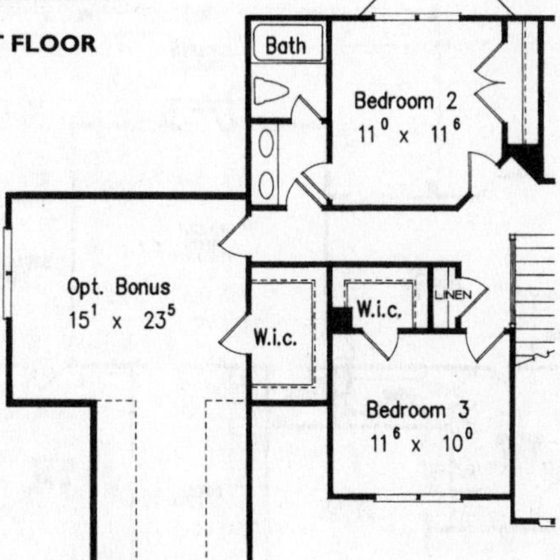

Bath
Bedroom 2
11^0 x 11^6
Opt. Bonus
15^1 x 23^5
W.i.c.
W.i.c.
LINEN
Bedroom 3
11^6 x 10^0

SECOND FLOOR W/OPTIONAL BONUS ROOM

Design 99096

See Order Pages and Index for Info

Units	Single
Price Code	L
Total Finished	4,929 sq. ft.
First Finished	2,600 sq. ft.
Second Finished	2,329 sq. ft.
Basement Unfinished	2,600 sq. ft.
Dimensions	96'x40'
Foundation	Basement
Bedrooms	4
Full Baths	2
3/4 Baths	1
Half Baths	1
First Ceiling	9'
Max Ridge Height	28'
Exterior Walls	2x6

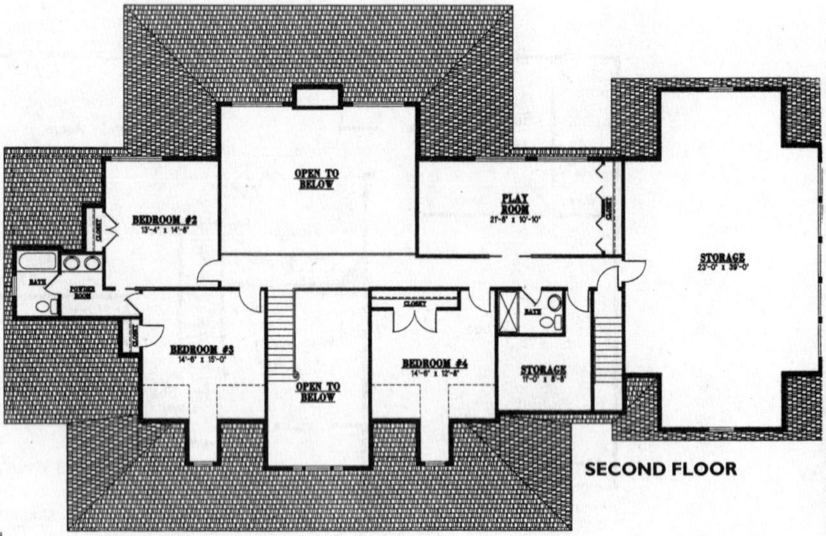

OPEN TO BELOW
PLAY ROOM
21'-8" x 10'-10"
CLOSET
BEDROOM #2
13'-4" x 14'-8"
CLOSET
BATH
POWDER ROOM
STORAGE
23'-0" x 39'-0"
CLOSET
BEDROOM #3
14'-6" x 15'-0"
OPEN TO BELOW
CLOSET
BEDROOM #4
14'-6" x 12'-8"
BATH
STORAGE
11'-0" x 8'-8"

SECOND FLOOR

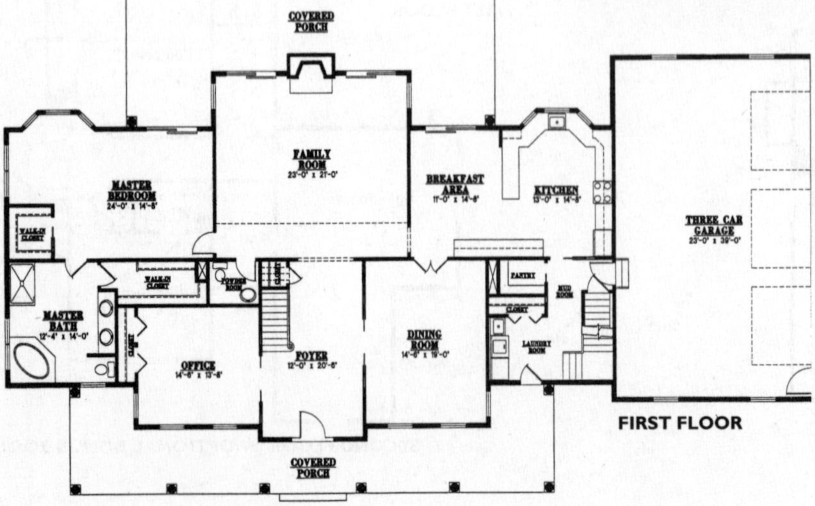

COVERED PORCH
FAMILY ROOM
23'-0" x 21'-0"
MASTER BEDROOM
24'-0" x 14'-8"
BREAKFAST AREA
11'-0" x 14'-8"
KITCHEN
13'-0" x 14'-8"
THREE CAR GARAGE
23'-0" x 39'-0"
WALK-IN CLOSET
WALK-IN CLOSET
POWDER ROOM
CLOSET
PANTRY
MUD ROOM
CLOSET
MASTER BATH
12'-4" x 14'-0"
CLOSET
DINING ROOM
14'-6" x 19'-0"
LAUNDRY ROOM
FOYER
12'-0" x 20'-6"
OFFICE
14'-6" x 13'-8"
COVERED PORCH

FIRST FLOOR

Design 10515

See Order Pages and Index for Info

Units	Single
Price Code	D
Total Finished	2,015 sq. ft.
First Finished	1,280 sq. ft.
Second Finished	735 sq. ft.
Porch Unfinished	80 sq. ft.
Dimensions	32'x40'
Foundation	Crawlspace
Bedrooms	3
Full Baths	2
Half Baths	1
First Ceiling	8'
Second Ceiling	8'
Max Ridge Height	32'
Roof Framing	Stick
Exterior Walls	2x6

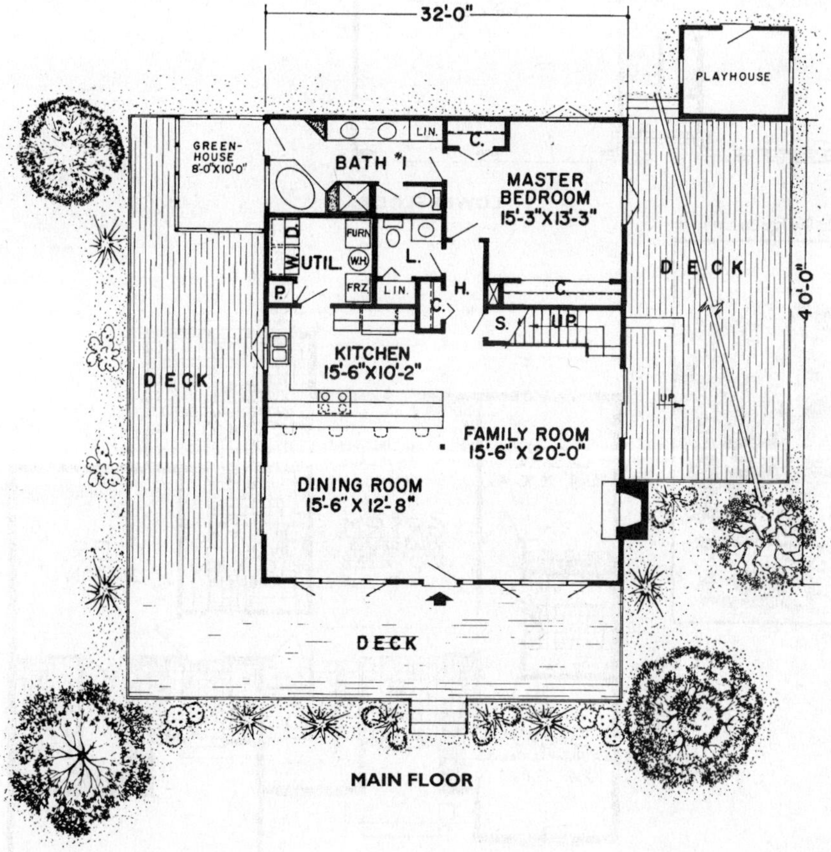
32'-0"
PLAYHOUSE
GREEN-HOUSE 8'-0"X10'-0"
LIN.
C.
BATH #1
MASTER BEDROOM 15'-3"X13'-3"
W.D.
UTIL.
FURN
W.H.
FRZ.
LIN.
L.
H.
C.
P.
S.
UP
DECK
40'-0"
KITCHEN 15'-6"X10'-2"
DECK
UP
FAMILY ROOM 15'-6" X 20'-0"
DINING ROOM 15'-6" X 12'-8"
DECK

MAIN FLOOR

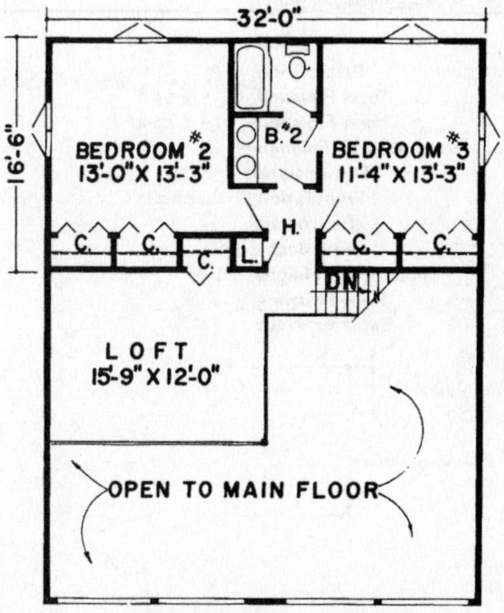
32'-0"
16'-6"
B.#2
BEDROOM #2 13'-0"X13'-3"
BEDROOM #3 11'-4"X13'-3"
H.
C.
C.
C.
L.
C.
C.
DN.
LOFT 15'-9"X12'-0"
OPEN TO MAIN FLOOR

ALTERNATE FOUNDATION

Design 98970

See Order Pages and Index for Info

Units	Single
Price Code	A
Total Finished	1,410 sq. ft.
Main Finished	1,396 sq. ft.
Lower Finished	14 sq. ft.
Garage Unfinished	646 sq. ft.
Dimensions	50'4"x31'
Foundation	Basement
Bedrooms	3
Full Baths	2
First Ceiling	8'
Max Ridge Height	26'
Roof Framing	Stick
Exterior Walls	2x4

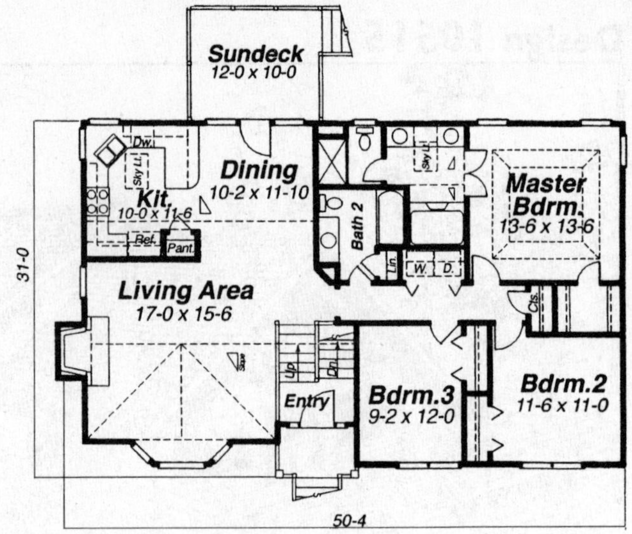
Sundeck
12-0 x 10-0
Dw.
Sky Lt.
Kit.
10-0 x 11-6
Ref.
Pant.
Dining
10-2 x 11-10
Bath 2
Master
Bdrm.
13-6 x 13-6
W.
D.
Lin.
Cls.
Living Area
17-0 x 15-6
Up
Dn.
Entry
Bdrm.3
9-2 x 12-0
Bdrm.2
11-6 x 11-0
31-0
50-4

MAIN FLOOR

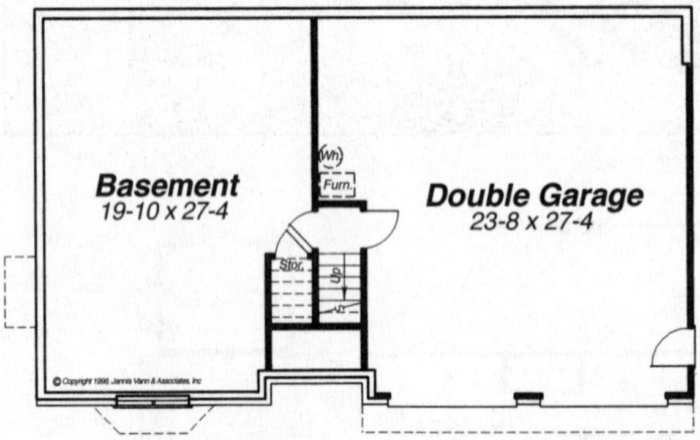
Basement
19-10 x 27-4
Wh
Furn.
Stor.
Double Garage
23-8 x 27-4

LOWER FLOOR

Design 97113

See Order Pages and Index for Info

Units	Single
Price Code	A
Total Finished	1,416 sq. ft.
Main Finished	1,416 sq. ft.
Basement Unfinished	1,416 sq. ft.
Dimensions	48'x55'4"
Foundation	Basement
Bedrooms	3
Full Baths	2
Max Ridge Height	21'8"
Roof Framing	Truss
Exterior Walls	2x6

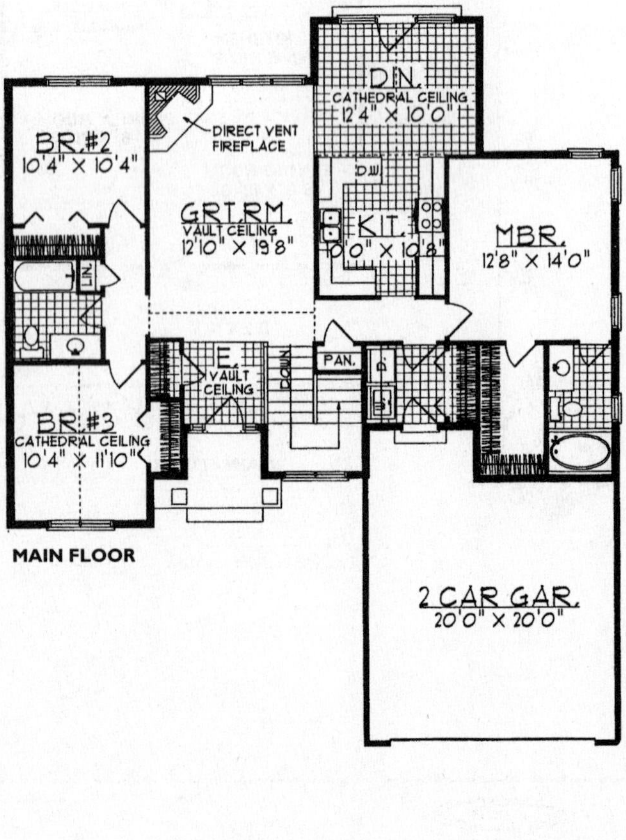
DIN.
CATHEDRAL CEILING
12'4" X 10'0"
BR.#2
10'4" X 10'4"
DIRECT VENT
FIREPLACE
DW
GRT.RM.
VAULT CEILING
12'10" X 19'8"
KIT.
10'0" X 10'8"
MBR.
12'8" X 14'0"
LIN.
E.
VAULT
CEILING
DOWN
PAN.
BR.#3
CATHEDRAL CEILING
10'4" X 11'10"
2 CAR GAR.
20'0" X 20'0"

MAIN FLOOR

Design 20198

See Order Pages and Index for Info

Units	Single
Price Code	C
Total Finished	1,792 sq. ft.
Main Finished	1,792 sq. ft.
Basement Unfinished	818 sq. ft.
Garage Unfinished	857 sq. ft.
Dimensions	56'x32'
Foundation	Basement
Bedrooms	3
Full Baths	2
Main Ceiling	8'
Max Ridge Height	25'
Roof Framing	Stick
Exterior Walls	2x4,2x6

Rear Elevation

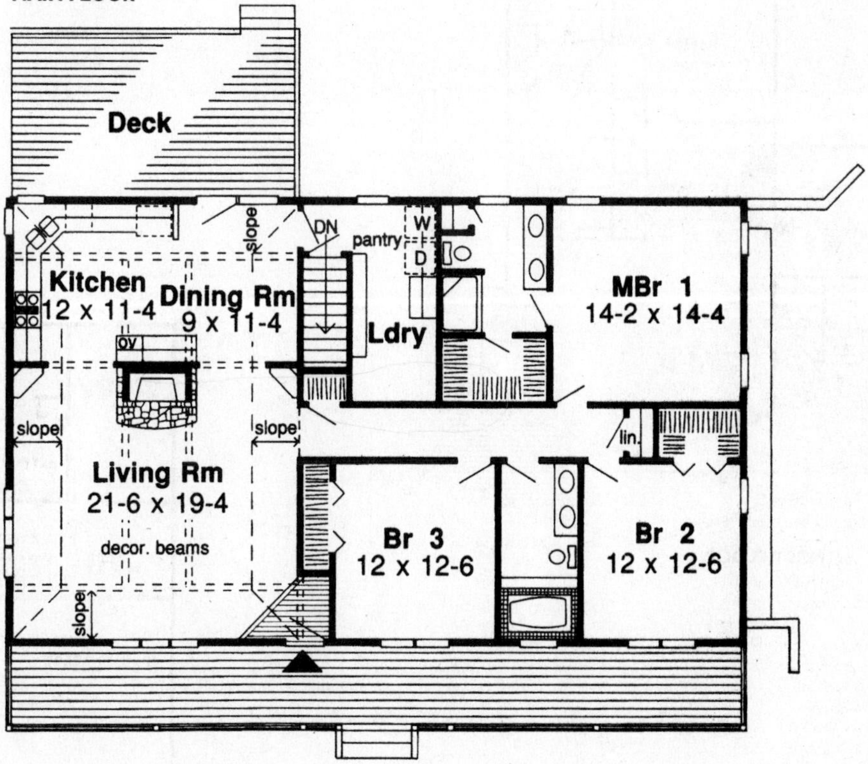
MAIN FLOOR
Deck
DN
pantry
W
D
slope
Kitchen
12 x 11-4
Dining Rm
9 x 11-4
OV
Ldry
MBr 1
14-2 x 14-4
lin.
slope
slope
Living Rm
21-6 x 19-4
decor. beams
Br 3
12 x 12-6
Br 2
12 x 12-6
slope

Design 61005

See Order Pages and Index for Info

Units	Single
Price Code	D
Total Finished	2,054 sq. ft.
First Finished	1,413 sq. ft.
Second Finished	641 sq. ft.
Dimensions	47'x63'
Foundation	Slab
Bedrooms	3
Full Baths	2
Half Baths	1

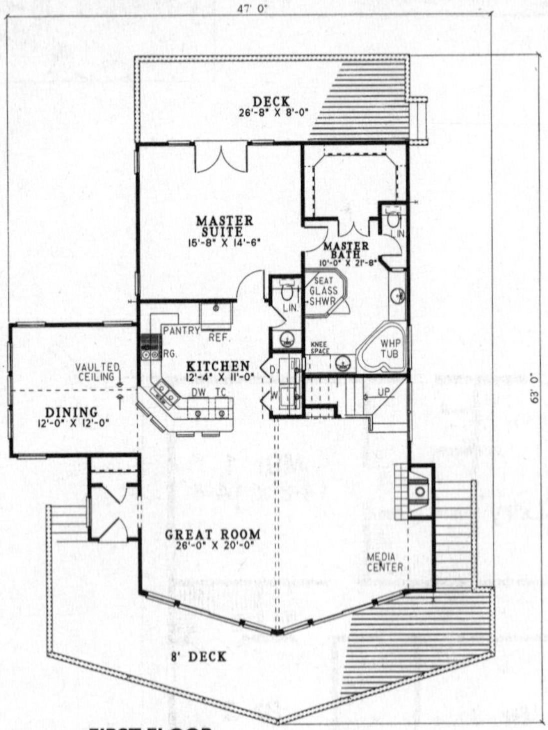
47' 0"
DECK
26'-8" X 8'-0"
MASTER SUITE
15'-8" X 14'-6"
MASTER BATH
10'-0" X 21'-8"
LIN
SEAT GLASS SHWR
LIN
KNEE SPACE
WHP TUB
PANTRY
REF.
RG.
KITCHEN
12'-4" X 11'-0"
DW TC
D
W
UP
VAULTED CEILING
DINING
12'-0" X 12'-0"
63' 0"
GREAT ROOM
26'-0" X 20'-0"
MEDIA CENTER
8' DECK

FIRST FLOOR

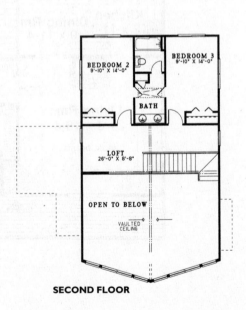

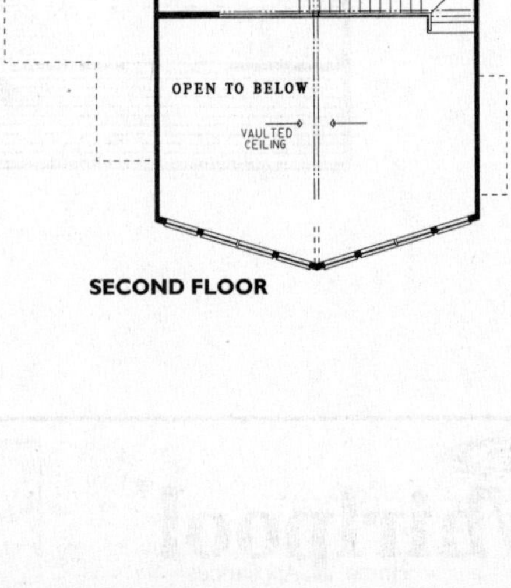
BEDROOM 2
9'-10" X 14'-0"
BEDROOM 3
9'-10" X 14'-0"
BATH
LOFT
26'-0" X 8'-8"
OPEN TO BELOW
VAULTED CEILING

SECOND FLOOR

Design 96509

See Order Pages and Index for Info

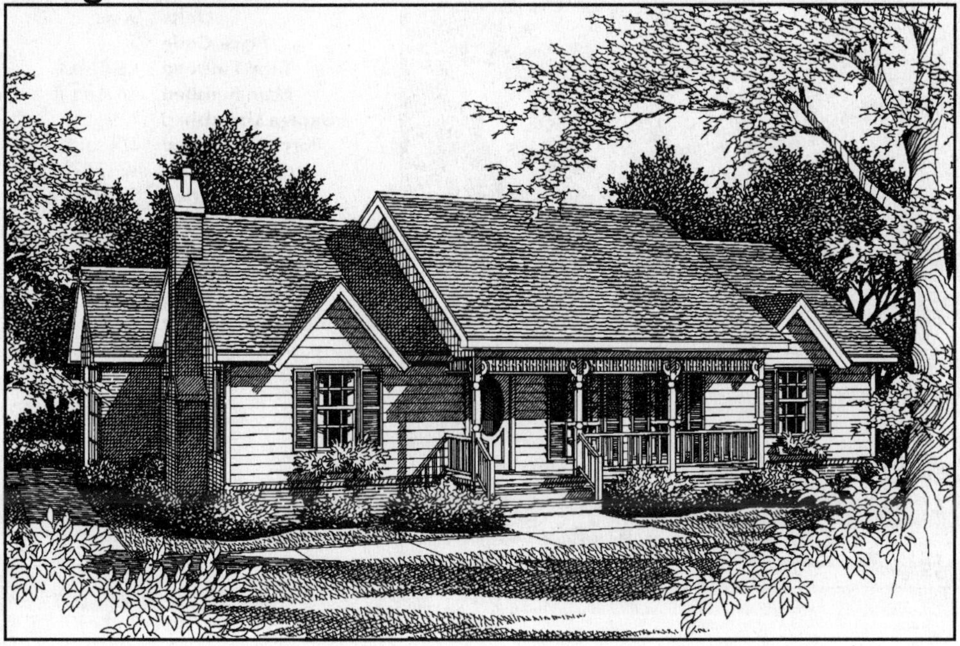

Units	Single
Price Code	A
Total Finished	1,438 sq. ft.
Main Finished	1,438 sq. ft.
Garage Unfinished	486 sq. ft.
Porch Unfinished	126 sq. ft.
Dimensions	54'x57'
Foundation	Crawlspace Slab
Bedrooms	3
Full Baths	2
Max Ridge Height	19'
Roof Framing	Stick
Exterior Walls	2x4

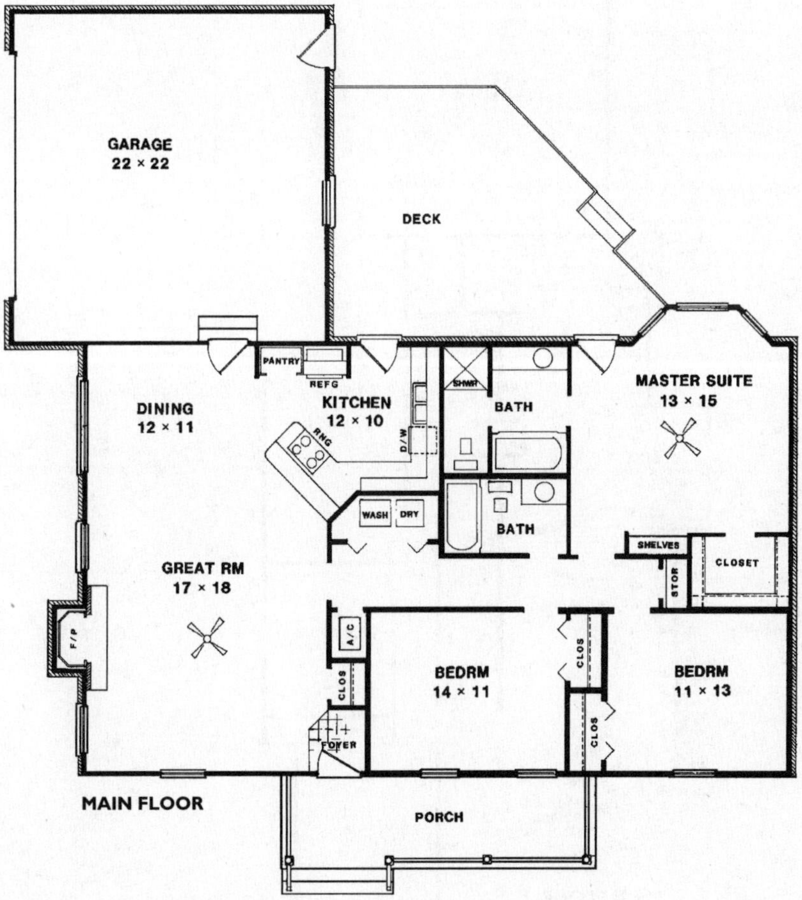
GARAGE
22 × 22
DECK
PANTRY
REFG
DINING
12 × 11
KITCHEN
12 × 10
RNG
D/W
SHWR
BATH
MASTER SUITE
13 × 15
WASH
DRY
BATH
SHELVES
CLOSET
STOR
GREAT RM
17 × 18
F/P
A/C
CLOS
FOYER
BEDRM
14 × 11
CLOS
CLOS
BEDRM
11 × 13
PORCH

MAIN FLOOR

Design 62058

See Order Pages and Index for Info

Units	Single
Price Code	C
Total Finished	1,601 sq. ft.
Main Finished	1,601 sq. ft.
Garage Unfinished	771 sq. ft.
Porch Unfinished	279 sq. ft.
Dimensions	39'x77'2"
Foundation	Crawlspace Slab
Bedrooms	3
Full Baths	2
Main Ceiling	9'
Max Ridge Height	22'
Roof Framing	Stick
Exterior Walls	2x4

39'-0"
© 2001 NELSON DESIGN GROUP, LLC.
GARAGE
21'-0" X 20'-0"
GRILLING PORCH
LAU.
STOR.
PATIO
KITCHEN
12'-4" X 10'-10"
WHP. TUB
M.BATH
7'-10" X 19'-8"
MASTER SUITE
12'-0" X 16'-8"
10' BOXED CEILING
DINING
17'-8" X 10'-0"
COMP CENTER
W.I.C.
77'-2"
8" COLUMNS
BATH
GREAT ROOM
14'-10" X 19'-9"
10' BOXED CEILING
BEDROOM 3
11'-0" X 12'-6"
FOYER
OPT. BOOK SHELVES
COVERED PORCH
20'-8" X 8'-0"
BEDROOM 2 / STUDY
12'-0" X 13'-8"

MAIN FLOOR

Design 92220

See Order Pages and Index for Info

Units	Single
Price Code	C
Total Finished	1,830 sq. ft.
Main Finished	1,830 sq. ft.
Garage Unfinished	759 sq. ft.
Porch Unfinished	390 sq. ft.
Dimensions	75'x52'3"
Foundation	Basement Crawlspace Slab
Bedrooms	3
Full Baths	2
Max Ridge Height	27'3"
Roof Framing	Stick
Exterior Walls	2x4

MAIN FLOOR

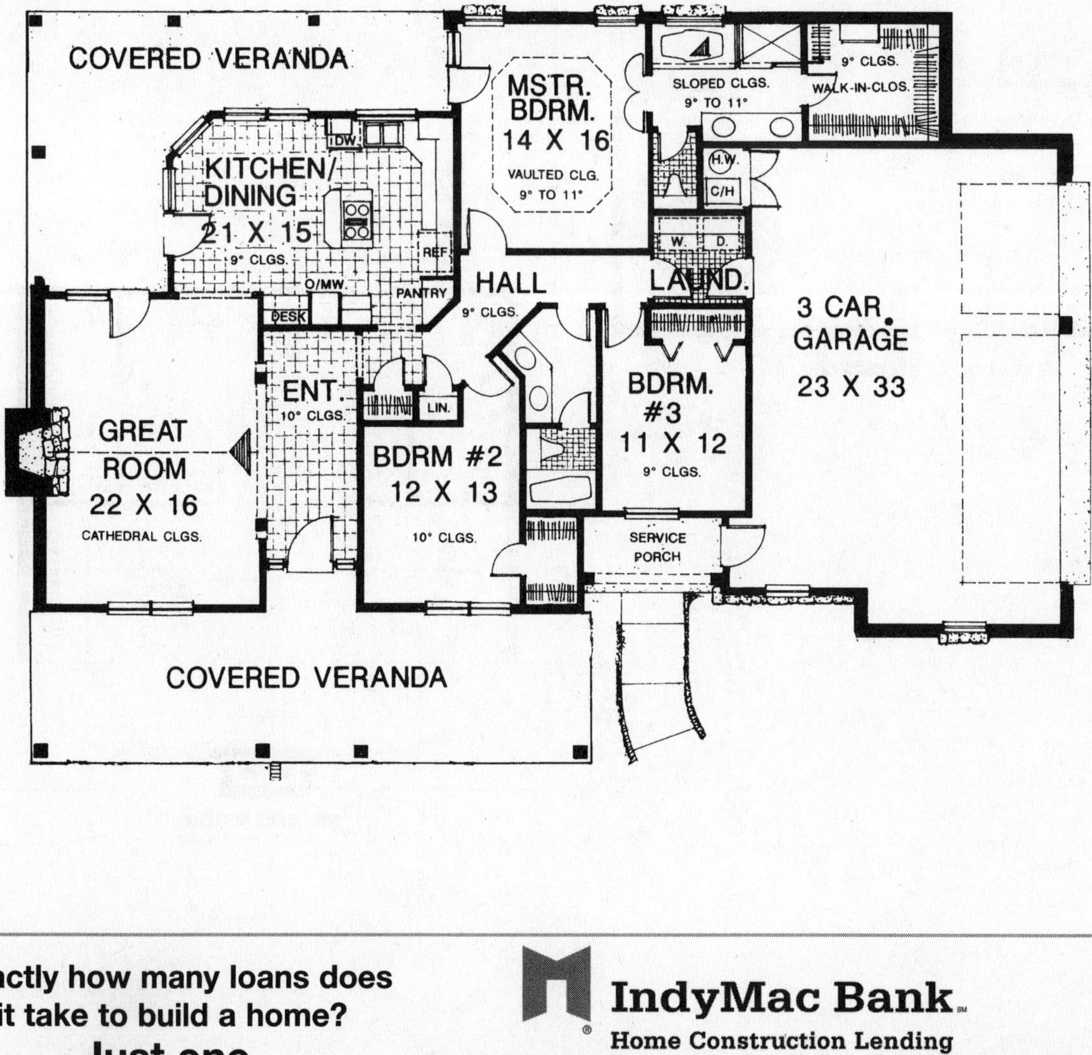
COVERED VERANDA
KITCHEN/ DINING 21 X 15
9° CLGS.
DW
REF.
O/MW.
PANTRY
DESK
MSTR. BDRM. 14 X 16
VAULTED CLG. 9° TO 11°
SLOPED CLGS. 9° TO 11°
9° CLGS.
WALK-IN-CLOS.
H.W.
C/H
W.
D.
LAUND.
HALL
9° CLGS.
3 CAR GARAGE 23 X 33
ENT.
10° CLGS.
LIN.
GREAT ROOM 22 X 16
CATHEDRAL CLGS.
BDRM #2 12 X 13
10° CLGS.
BDRM. #3 11 X 12
9° CLGS.
SERVICE PORCH
COVERED VERANDA

Design 65365

See Order Pages and Index for Info

Units	Single
Price Code	A
Total Finished	1,148 sq. ft.
First Finished	726 sq. ft.
Second Finished	420 sq. ft.
Bonus Unfinished	728 sq. ft.
Porch Unfinished	187 sq. ft.
Dimensions	28'x26'
Foundation	Basement
Bedrooms	1
Full Baths	1
Half Baths	1
First Ceiling	8'
Second Ceiling	8'
Max Ridge Height	29'8"
Exterior Walls	2x6

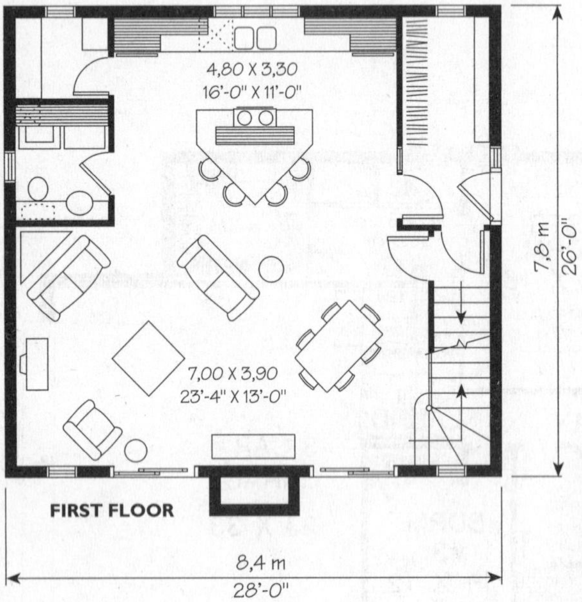
4,80 X 3,30
16'-0" X 11'-0"
7,00 X 3,90
23'-4" X 13'-0"
7,8 m
26'-0"
8,4 m
28'-0"
FIRST FLOOR

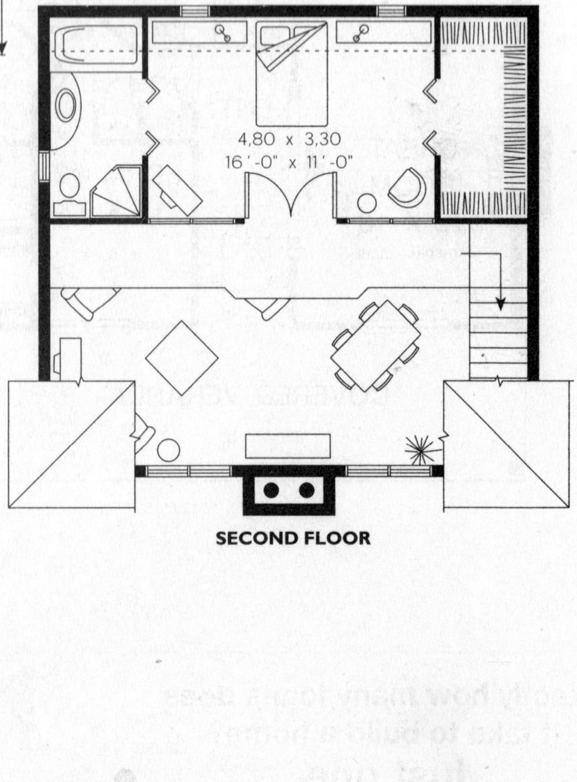
4,80 x 3,30
16'-0" x 11'-0"
SECOND FLOOR

Design 94614

See Order Pages and Index for Info

Units	Single
Price Code	F
Total Finished	2,533 sq. ft.
First Finished	1,916 sq. ft.
Second Finished	617 sq. ft.
Garage Unfinished	516 sq. ft.
Porch Unfinished	390 sq. ft.
Dimensions	66'x66'
Foundation	Crawlspace Slab
Bedrooms	4
Full Baths	3
Half Baths	1
First Ceiling	9'
Second Ceiling	8'
Roof Framing	Truss
Exterior Walls	2x4,2x6

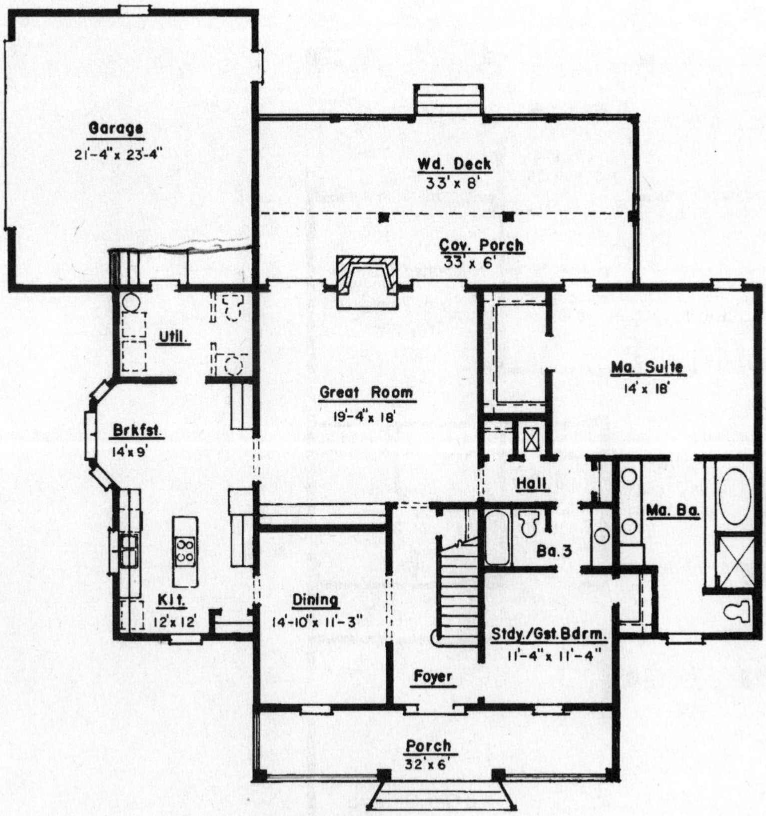
Garage
21'-4" x 23'-4"
Wd. Deck
33' x 8'
Cov. Porch
33' x 6'
Util.
Great Room
19'-4" x 18'
Ma. Suite
14' x 18'
Brkfst.
14'x 9'
Hall
Ma. Ba.
Ba. 3
Kit.
12'x 12'
Dining
14'-10" x 11'-3"
Stdy./Gst.Bdrm.
11'-4" x 11'-4"
Foyer
Porch
32' x 6'

FIRST FLOOR

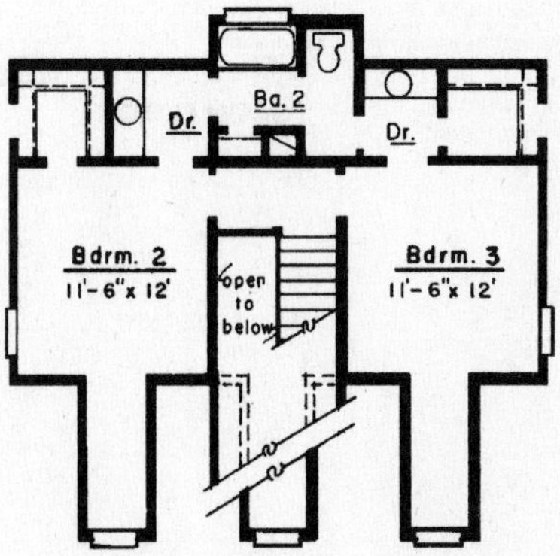
Ba. 2
Dr.
Dr.
Bdrm. 2
11'-6" x 12'
open
to
below
Bdrm. 3
11'-6" x 12'

SECOND FLOOR

Design 64132

See Order Pages and Index for Info

Units	Single
Price Code	G
Total Finished	1,822 sq. ft.
Main Finished	1,822 sq. ft.
Garage Unfinished	537 sq. ft.
Dimensions	58'x67'2"
Foundation	Basement
Bedrooms	3
Full Baths	2
Max Ridge Height	26'10"
Roof Framing	Stick
Exterior Walls	2x6

* Alternate foundation options available at an additional charge. Please call 1-800-235-5700 for more information.

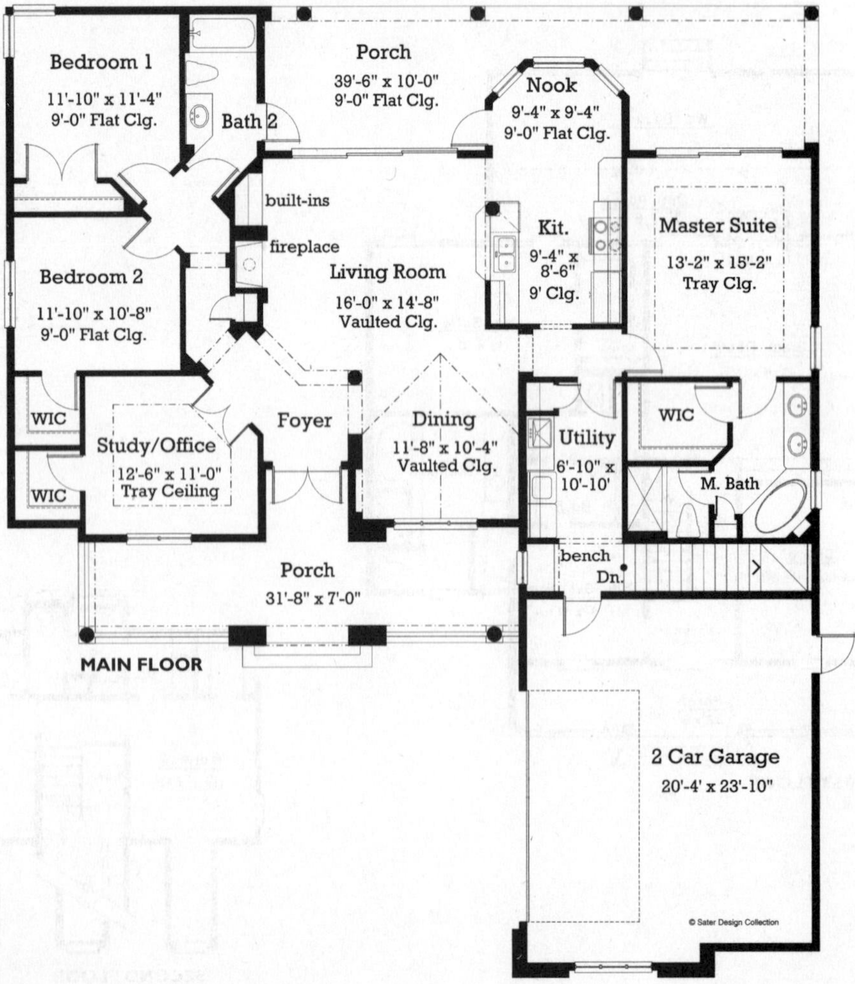
Bedroom 1
11'-10" x 11'-4"
9'-0" Flat Clg.
Bath 2
Porch
39'-6" x 10'-0"
9'-0" Flat Clg.
Nook
9'-4" x 9'-4"
9'-0" Flat Clg.
built-ins
fireplace
Kit.
9'-4" x 8'-6"
9' Clg.
Master Suite
13'-2" x 15'-2"
Tray Clg.
Bedroom 2
11'-10" x 10'-8"
9'-0" Flat Clg.
Living Room
16'-0" x 14'-8"
Vaulted Clg.
WIC
Study/Office
12'-6" x 11'-0"
Tray Ceiling
WIC
Foyer
Dining
11'-8" x 10'-4"
Vaulted Clg.
Utility
6'-10" x 10'-10'
WIC
M. Bath
bench
Dn.
Porch
31'-8" x 7'-0"
2 Car Garage
20'-4' x 23'-10"
© Sater Design Collection

MAIN FLOOR

Design 98532

See Order Pages and Index for Info

Units	Single
Price Code	H
Total Finished	3,112 sq. ft.
First Finished	2,263 sq. ft.
Second Finished	849 sq. ft.
Bonus Unfinished	430 sq. ft.
Garage Unfinished	630 sq. ft.
Porch Unfinished	37 sq. ft.
Dimensions	59'x66'6.5"
Foundation	Crawlspace Slab
Bedrooms	4
Full Baths	3
Half Baths	1
First Ceiling	9'-10'
Max Ridge Height	33'6"
Roof Framing	Stick
Exterior Walls	2x4

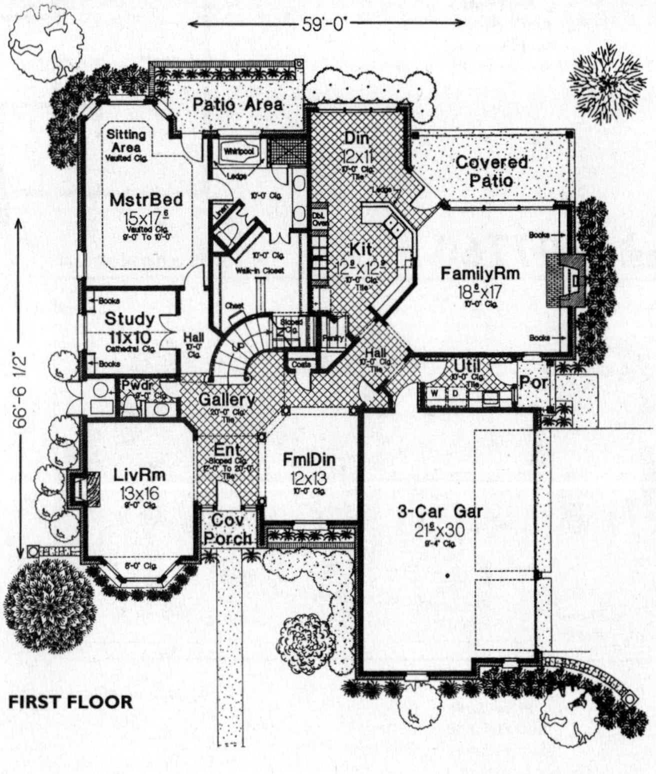
59'-0"
66'-6 1/2"
Patio Area
Sitting Area
MstrBed
15x17
Din
12x11
Covered Patio
Kit
FamilyRm
18x17
Study
11x10
Hall
Pwdr
Gallery
Util
Por
Ent
LivRm
13x16
FmlDin
12x13
3-Car Gar
Cov Porch

FIRST FLOOR

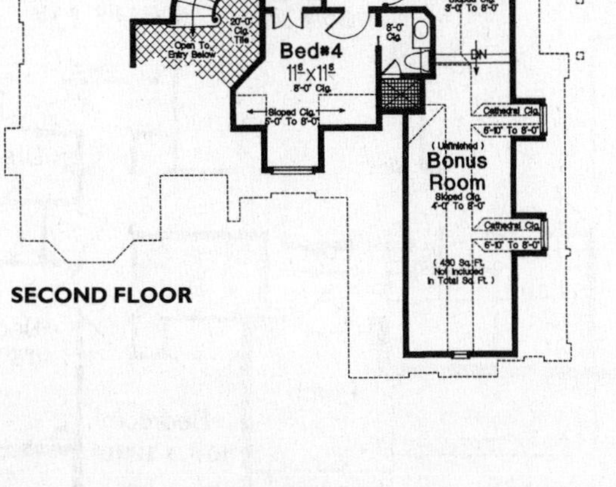
Bed#2
Bed#3
13x13
Balcony
Bed#4
Bonus Room

SECOND FLOOR

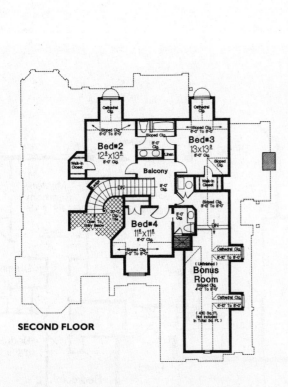

Design 97235

See Order Pages and Index for Info

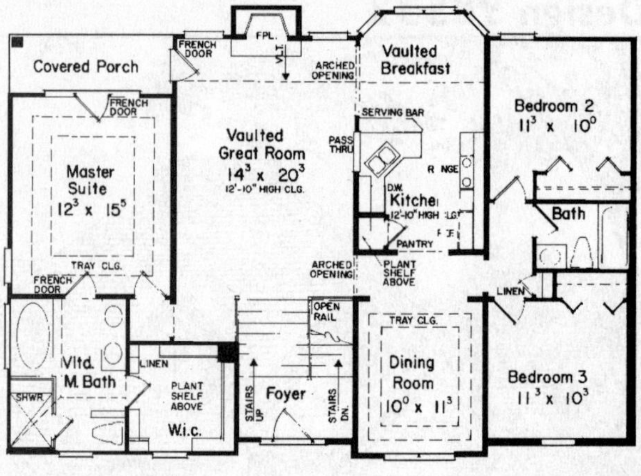
Covered Porch
FRENCH DOOR
FPL.
V.T.
ARCHED OPENING
Vaulted Breakfast
Master Suite
12^3 x 15^5
TRAY CLG.
FRENCH DOOR
Vaulted Great Room
14^3 x 20^3
12'-10" HIGH CLG.
SERVING BAR
PASS THRU
Kitchen
PANTRY
PLANT SHELF ABOVE
Bedroom 2
11^3 x 10^0
Bath
LINEN
ARCHED OPENING
OPEN RAIL
Vltd. M.Bath
SHWR
LINEN
PLANT SHELF ABOVE
W.i.c.
STAIRS UP
Foyer
STAIRS DN.
TRAY CLG.
Dining Room
10^0 x 11^3
Bedroom 3
11^3 x 10^3

MAIN FLOOR

Units	Single
Price Code	B
Total Finished	1,609 sq. ft.
Main Finished	1,509 sq. ft.
Lower Finished	100 sq. ft.
Basement Unfinished	954 sq. ft.
Garage Unfinished	484 sq. ft.
Dimensions	49'x34'4"
Foundation	Basement
Bedrooms	3
Full Baths	2
Max Ridge Height	28'
Roof Framing	Stick
Exterior Walls	2x4

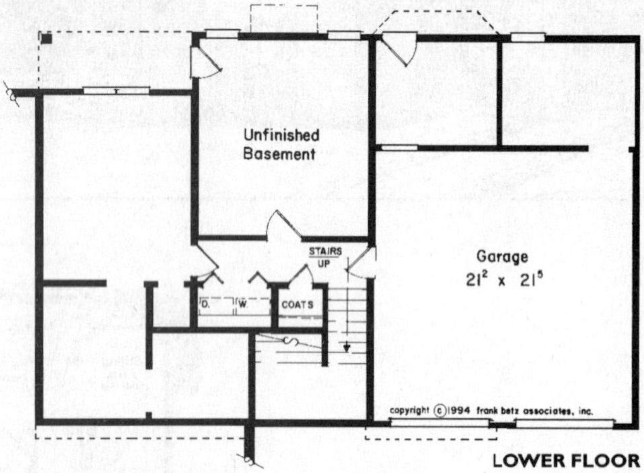
Unfinished Basement
STAIRS UP
COATS
Garage
21^2 x 21^5
copyright ©1994 frank betz associates, inc.

LOWER FLOOR

Design 97760

See Order Pages and Index for Info

Units	Single
Price Code	B
Total Finished	1,611 sq. ft.
Main Finished	1,611 sq. ft.
Garage Unfinished	430 sq. ft.
Porch Unfinished	163 sq. ft.
Dimensions	66'4"x43'10"
Foundation	Basement
Bedrooms	3
Full Baths	2
Main Ceiling	8'
Vaulted Ceiling	10'
Tray Ceiling	10'
Max Ridge Height	22'6"
Roof Framing	Truss
Exterior Walls	2x4

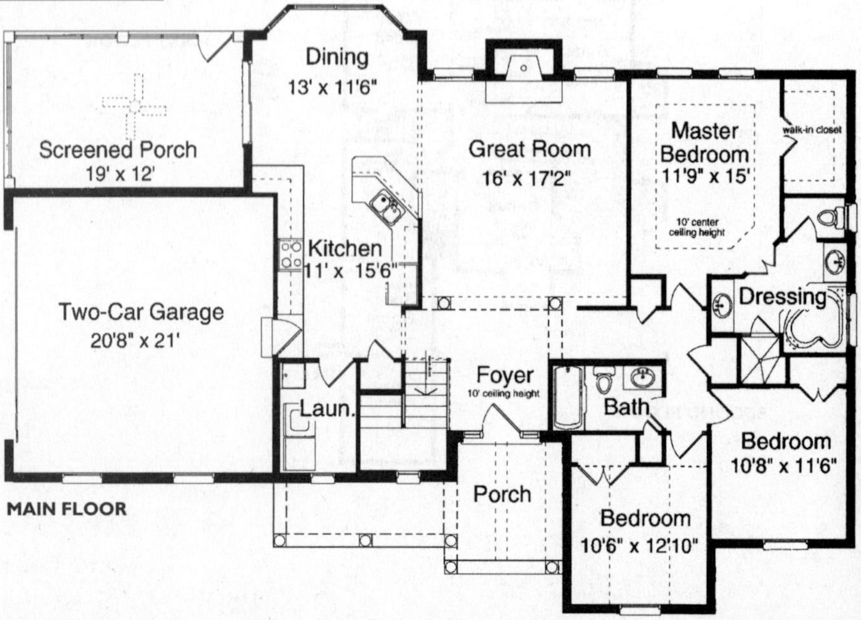
Dining
13' x 11'6"
Screened Porch
19' x 12'
Great Room
16' x 17'2"
Master Bedroom
11'9" x 15'
walk-in closet
10' center ceiling height
Kitchen
11' x 15'6"
Two-Car Garage
20'8" x 21'
Dressing
Foyer
10' ceiling height
Laun.
Bath
Bedroom
10'8" x 11'6"
Porch
Bedroom
10'6" x 12'10"

MAIN FLOOR

Design 34600

See Order Pages and Index for Info

Photography by Michelle Evans Christy

Units	Single
Price Code	A
Total Finished	1,328 sq. ft.
First Finished	1,013 sq. ft.
Second Finished	315 sq. ft.
Basement Unfinished	1,013 sq. ft.
Dimensions	36'x36'
Foundation	Basement Crawlspace Slab
Bedrooms	3
Full Baths	2
First Ceiling	8'
Second Ceiling	7'6"
Max Ridge Height	23'6"
Roof Framing	Stick
Exterior Walls	2x4,2x6

Rear Elevation

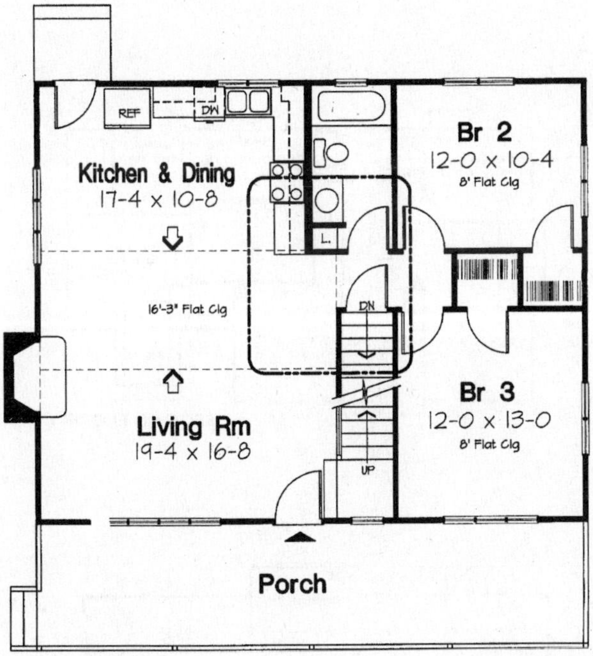
REF
DW
Kitchen & Dining
17-4 x 10-8
16'-3" Flat Clg
Living Rm
19-4 x 16-8
Br 2
12-0 x 10-4
8' Flat Clg
Br 3
12-0 x 13-0
8' Flat Clg
L.
DN
UP
Porch

FIRST FLOOR

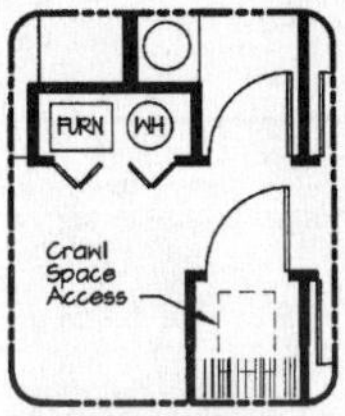
FURN
WH
Crawl Space Access

CRAWLSPACE OPTION

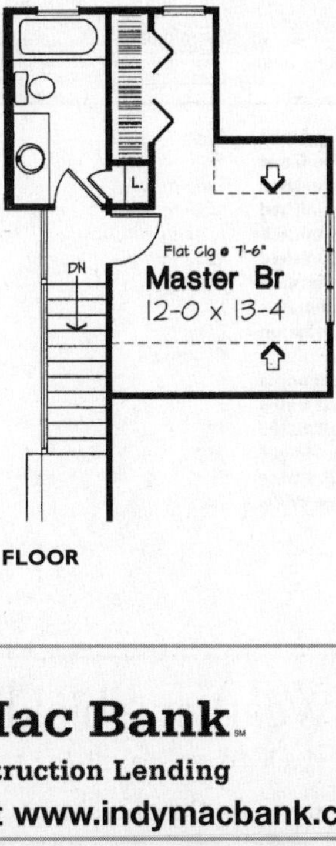
L.
Flat Clg @ 7'-6"
DN
Master Br
12-0 x 13-4

SECOND FLOOR

Design 97224

See Order Pages and Index for Info

Units	Single
Price Code	A
Total Finished	1,363 sq. ft.
Main Finished	1,363 sq. ft.
Basement Unfinished	715 sq. ft.
Garage Unfinished	677 sq. ft.
Dimensions	47'x35'4"
Foundation	Basement
Bedrooms	3
Full Baths	2
Main Ceiling	9'
Max Ridge Height	22'4"
Roof Framing	Stick
Exterior Walls	2x4

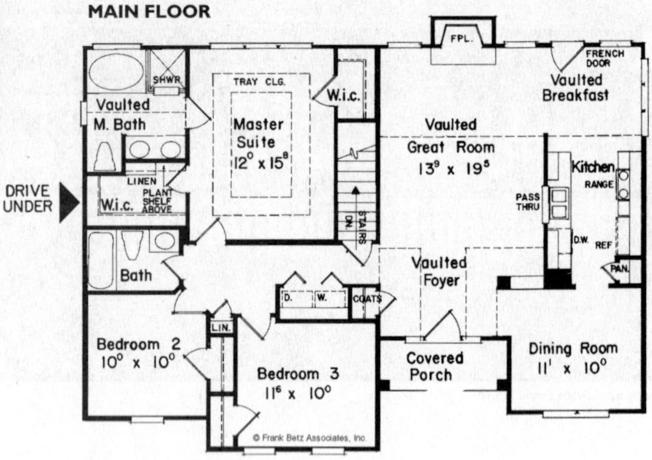
MAIN FLOOR
FPL.
FRENCH DOOR
Vaulted Breakfast
SHWR.
TRAY CLG.
Vaulted M. Bath
Master Suite 12⁰ x 15⁸
W.i.c.
Vaulted Great Room 13⁹ x 19⁵
Kitchen RANGE
PASS THRU
DRIVE UNDER
LINEN
W.i.c. PLANT SHELF ABOVE
DN. STAIRS
D.W. REF.
PAN.
Bath
Vaulted Foyer
D. W. COATS
LIN.
Bedroom 2 10⁰ x 10⁰
Bedroom 3 11⁶ x 10⁰
Covered Porch
Dining Room 11' x 10⁰
© Frank Betz Associates, Inc.

Design 97220

See Order Pages and Index for Info

Units	Single
Price Code	G
Total Finished	2,892 sq. ft.
First Finished	1,269 sq. ft.
Second Finished	1,623 sq. ft.
Basement Unfinished	1,269 sq. ft.
Garage Unfinished	672 sq. ft.
Dimensions	58'x41'6"
Foundation	Basement Crawlspace
Bedrooms	4
Full Baths	3
Half Baths	1
Max Ridge Height	33'
Roof Framing	Stick
Exterior Walls	2x4

Bedroom 2 13⁰ x 11⁰
W.i.c.
LINEN
Laundry
Master Suite 15⁰ x 17¹⁰
Vaulted Sitting Room 9⁸ x 10⁰
W.i.c.
PLANT SHELF ABOVE
Bath
OPEN RAIL
Vaulted Master Bath
SHWR.
W.i.c.
OVERLOOK
STAIRS DN.
Bath
LINEN
Bedroom 3 13⁰ x 11⁰
Foyer Below
Bedroom 4 13' x 12⁰
W.i.c.
SECOND FLOOR

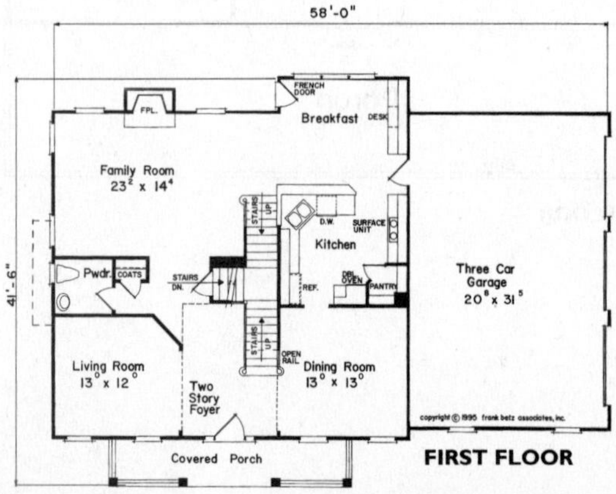
58'-0"
FRENCH DOOR
FPL.
Breakfast DESK
Family Room 23² x 14⁴
Kitchen
SURFACE UNIT
D.W.
41'-6"
Pwdr. COATS
STAIRS DN.
REF.
PANTRY
Three Car Garage 20⁶ x 31⁵
OPEN RAIL
Living Room 13⁰ x 12⁰
Two Story Foyer
Dining Room 13⁰ x 13⁰
copyright © 1995 frank betz associates, inc.
Covered Porch
FIRST FLOOR

Design 96513

See Order Pages and Index for Info

Units	Single
Price Code	B
Total Finished	1,648 sq. ft.
Main Finished	1,648 sq. ft.
Garage Unfinished	479 sq. ft.
Dimensions	68'x50'
Foundation	Crawlspace Slab
Bedrooms	3
Full Baths	2
Half Baths	1
Main Ceiling	9'
Max Ridge Height	20'
Roof Framing	Stick
Exterior Walls	2x4

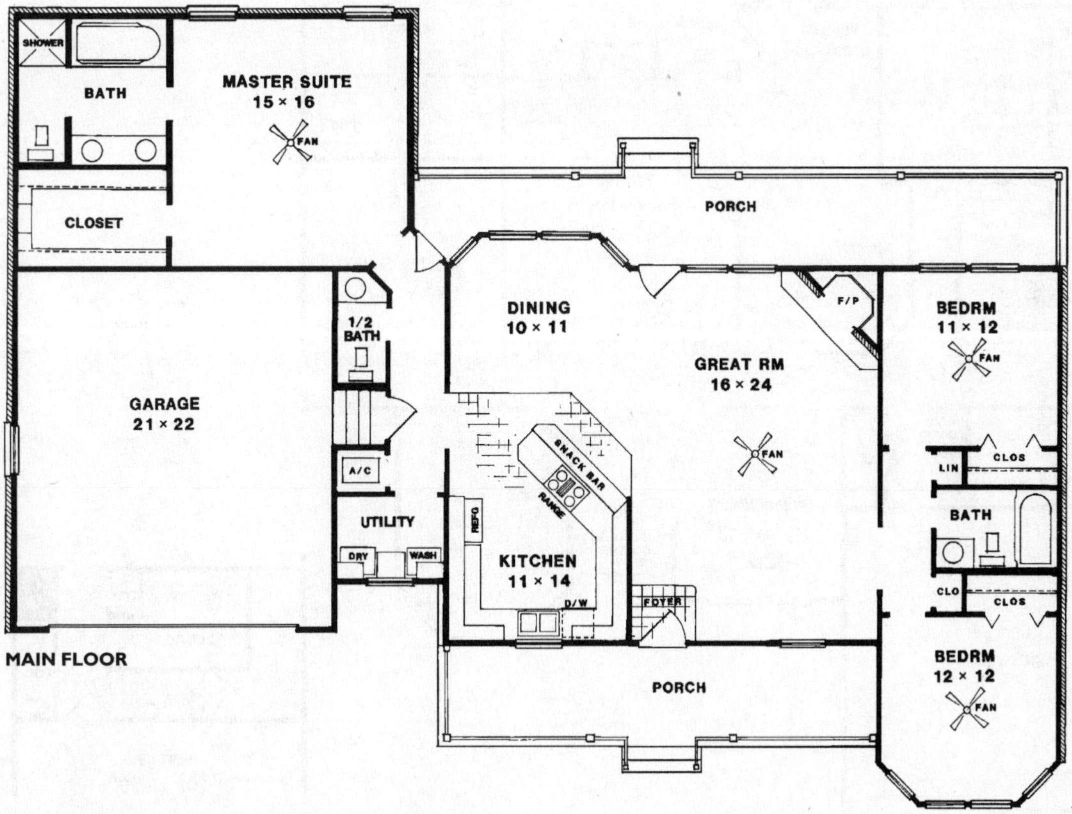
SHOWER
BATH
MASTER SUITE
15 × 16
FAN
CLOSET
PORCH
DINING
10 × 11
F/P
BEDRM
11 × 12
FAN
1/2
BATH
GREAT RM
16 × 24
GARAGE
21 × 22
SNACK BAR
RANGE
FAN
A/C
CLOS
LIN
REFG
UTILITY
BATH
DRY
WASH
KITCHEN
11 × 14
CLO
CLOS
D/W
FOYER
BEDRM
12 × 12
FAN
PORCH

MAIN FLOOR

Design 97228

See Order Pages and Index for Info

Units	Single
Price Code	D
Total Finished	2,201 sq. ft.
Main Finished	2,201 sq. ft.
Basement Unfinished	2,201 sq. ft.
Garage Unfinished	452 sq. ft.
Dimensions	59'6"x62'
Foundation	Basement Crawlspace
Bedrooms	3
Full Baths	2
Half Baths	1
Max Ridge Height	25'
Roof Framing	Stick
Exterior Walls	2x4

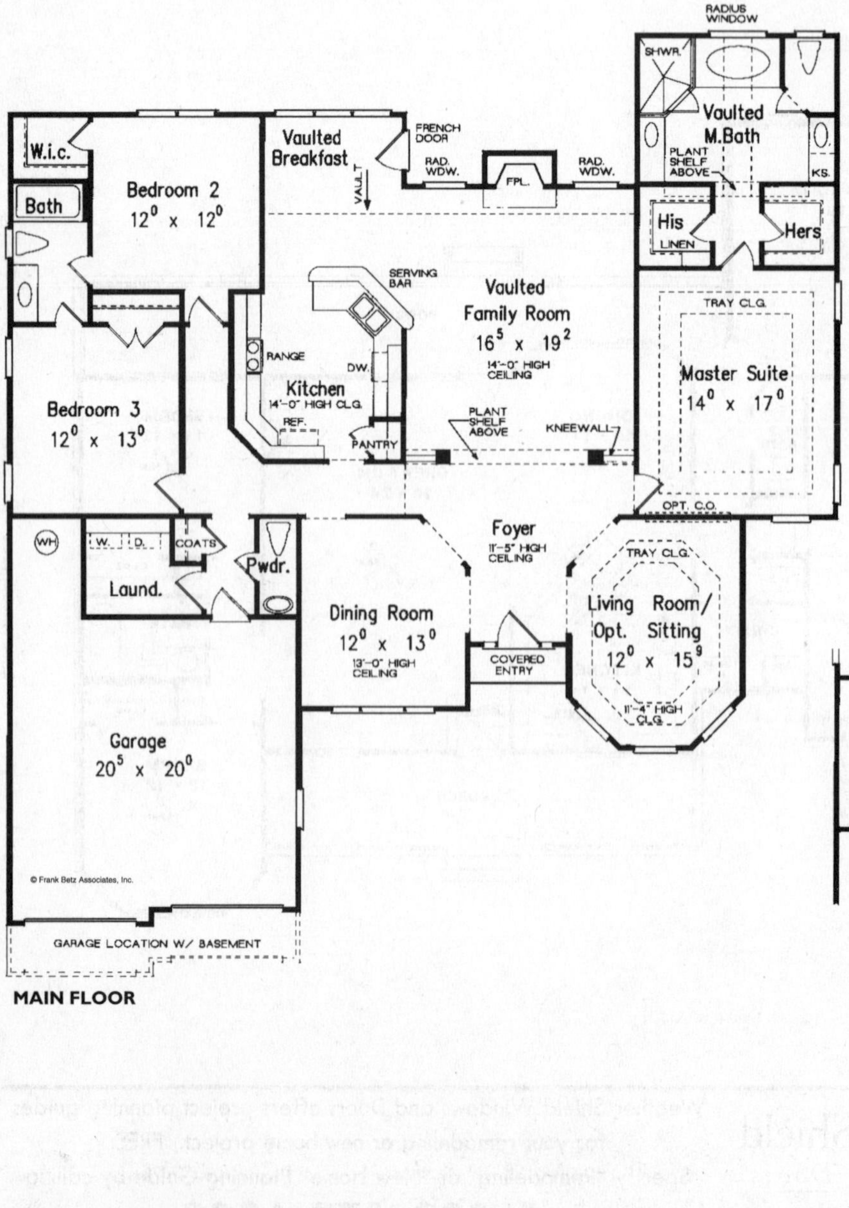
RADIUS WINDOW
SHWR.
Vaulted M.Bath
PLANT SHELF ABOVE
KS.
His
LINEN
Hers
W.i.c.
Bath
Bedroom 2
12^{0} x 12^{0}
Vaulted Breakfast
VAULT
FRENCH DOOR
RAD. WDW.
FPL.
RAD. WDW.
SERVING BAR
Vaulted Family Room
16^{5} x 19^{2}
14'-0" HIGH CEILING
TRAY CLG.
Master Suite
14^{0} x 17^{0}
RANGE
DW.
Kitchen
14'-0" HIGH CLG.
REF.
PANTRY
PLANT SHELF ABOVE
KNEEWALL
Bedroom 3
12^{0} x 13^{0}
OPT. C.O.
WH
W. D.
COATS
Pwdr.
Laund.
Foyer
11'-5" HIGH CEILING
TRAY CLG.
Dining Room
12^{0} x 13^{0}
13'-0" HIGH CEILING
COVERED ENTRY
Living Room/ Opt. Sitting
12^{0} x 15^{9}
11'-4" HIGH CLG.
Garage
20^{5} x 20^{0}
© Frank Betz Associates, Inc.
GARAGE LOCATION W/ BASEMENT

MAIN FLOOR

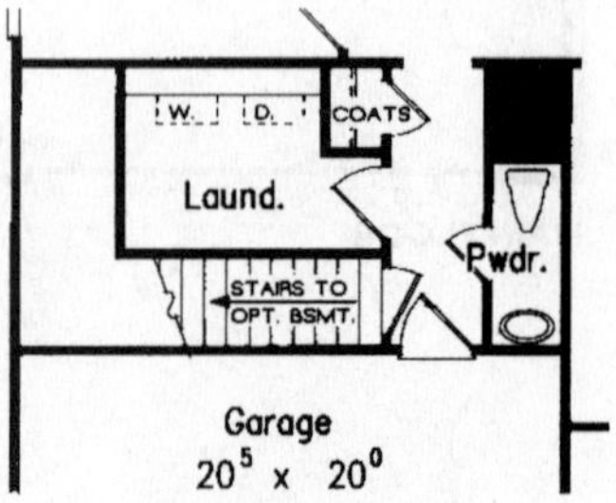
W. D.
COATS
Laund.
Pwdr.
STAIRS TO OPT. BSMT.
Garage
20^{5} x 20^{0}

BASEMENT OPTION

Design 98431

See Order Pages and Index for Info

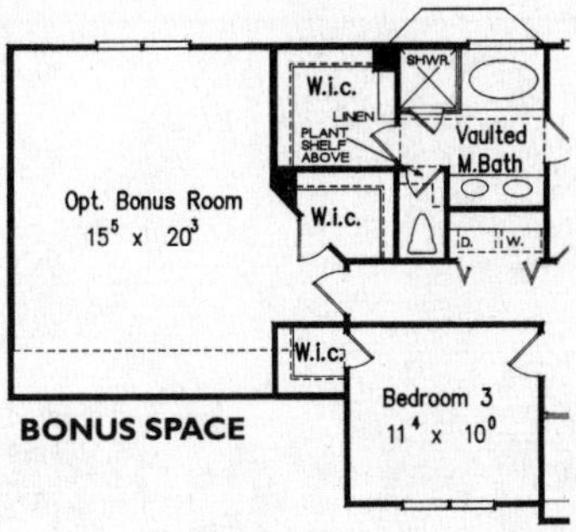

Opt. Bonus Room
15^5 x 20^3
W.i.c.
SHWR.
LINEN
PLANT SHELF ABOVE
Vaulted M.Bath
W.i.c.
D. W.
W.i.c.
Bedroom 3
11^4 x 10^0

BONUS SPACE

Units	Single
Price Code	B
Total Finished	1,675 sq. ft.
First Finished	882 sq. ft.
Second Finished	793 sq. ft.
Bonus Unfinished	416 sq. ft.
Basement Unfinished	882 sq. ft.
Garage Unfinished	510 sq. ft.
Dimensions	49'6"x35'4"
Foundation	Basement Crawlspace Slab
Bedrooms	3
Full Baths	2
Half Baths	1
First Ceiling	8'
Second Ceiling	8'
Max Ridge Height	29'6"
Roof Framing	Stick
Exterior Walls	2x4

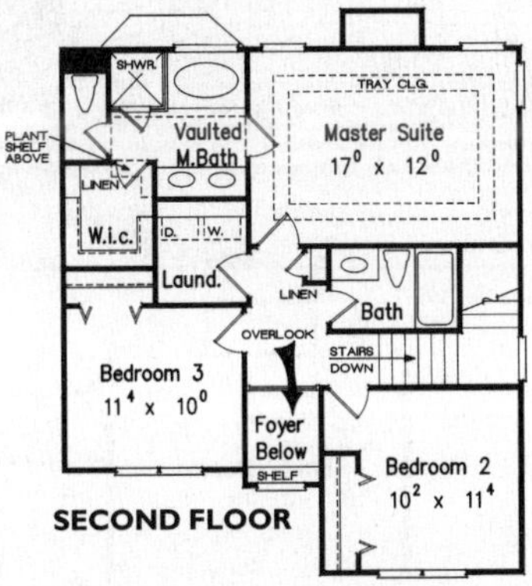

SHWR.
PLANT SHELF ABOVE
Vaulted M.Bath
TRAY CLG.
Master Suite
17^0 x 12^0
LINEN
W.i.c.
D. W.
Laund.
LINEN
Bath
OVERLOOK
STAIRS DOWN
Bedroom 3
11^4 x 10^0
Foyer Below
SHELF
Bedroom 2
10^2 x 11^4

SECOND FLOOR

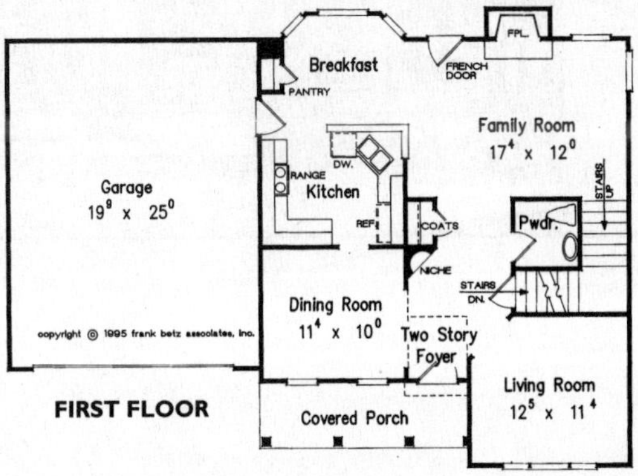

Breakfast
PANTRY
FRENCH DOOR
FPL.
Family Room
17^4 x 12^0
STAIRS UP
Garage
19^9 x 25^0
RANGE
DW.
Kitchen
REF.
COATS
Pwdr.
NICHE
STAIRS DN.
Dining Room
11^4 x 10^0
Two Story Foyer
Living Room
12^5 x 11^4
Covered Porch
copyright © 1995 frank betz associates, inc.

FIRST FLOOR

Design 99327

See Order Pages and Index for Info

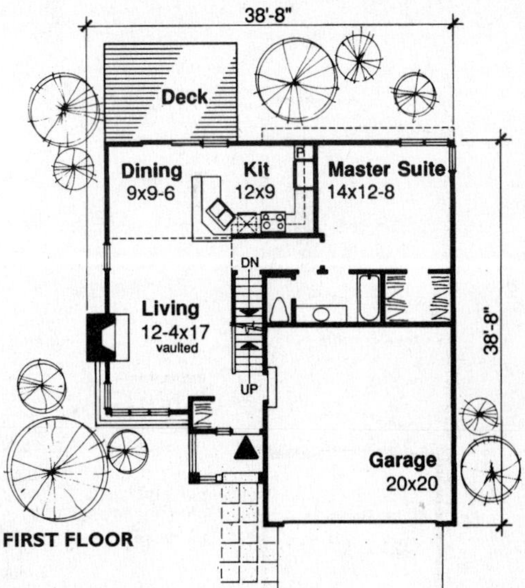

38'-8"
Deck
Dining
9x9-6
Kit
12x9
R
Master Suite
14x12-8
DN
Living
12-4x17
vaulted
UP
38'-8"
Garage
20x20

FIRST FLOOR

Units	Single
Price Code	A
Total Finished	1,289 sq. ft.
First Finished	858 sq. ft.
Second Finished	431 sq. ft.
Basement Unfinished	858 sq. ft.
Garage Unfinished	400 sq. ft.
Dimensions	38'8"x38'8"
Foundation	Basement
Bedrooms	3
Full Baths	2
Max Ridge Height	23'
Roof Framing	Stick/Truss
Exterior Walls	2x4

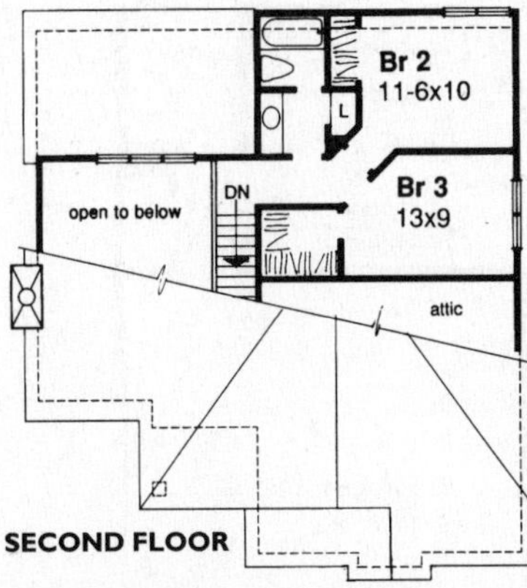

Br 2
11-6x10
L
Br 3
13x9
DN
open to below
attic

SECOND FLOOR

Design 97217

See Order Pages and Index for Info

Units	Single
Price Code	E
Total Finished	2,430 sq. ft.
First Finished	1,415 sq. ft.
Second Finished	1,015 sq. ft.
Bonus Unfinished	169 sq. ft.
Basement Unfinished	1,415 sq. ft.
Garage Unfinished	471 sq. ft.
Dimensions	54'x43'4"
Foundation	Basement Crawlspace
Bedrooms	4
Full Baths	3
Half Baths	1
Max Ridge Height	30'
Roof Framing	Stick
Exterior Walls	2x4

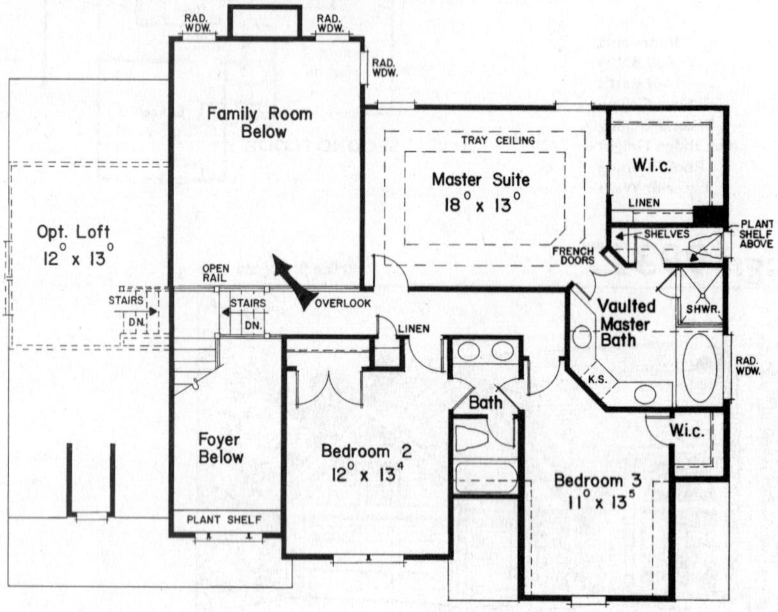
RAD. WDW.
RAD. WDW.
RAD. WDW.
Family Room Below
TRAY CEILING
Master Suite
18⁰ x 13⁰
W.i.c.
LINEN
PLANT SHELF ABOVE
SHELVES
FRENCH DOORS
Opt. Loft
12⁰ x 13⁰
OPEN RAIL
STAIRS DN.
STAIRS DN.
OVERLOOK
LINEN
Vaulted Master Bath
SHWR.
K.S.
RAD. WDW.
Bath
W.i.c.
Foyer Below
Bedroom 2
12⁰ x 13⁴
Bedroom 3
11⁰ x 13⁵
PLANT SHELF

SECOND FLOOR

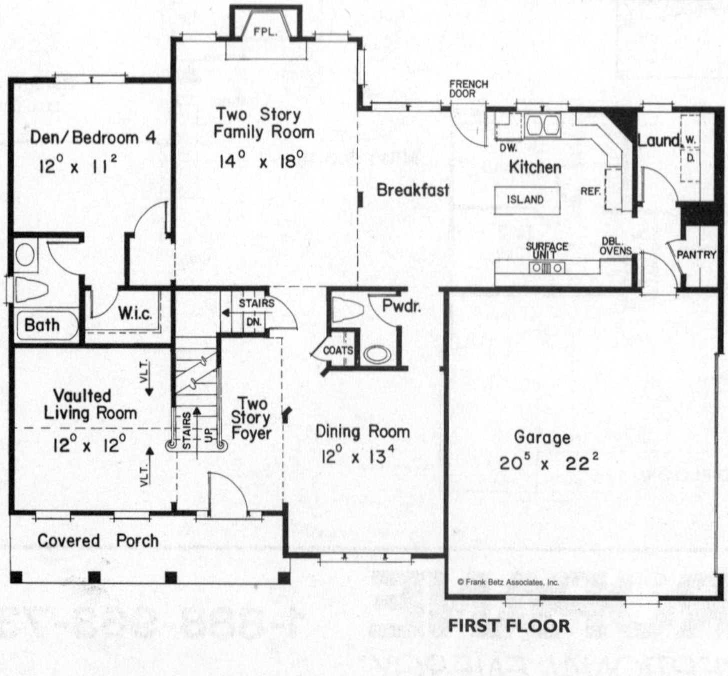
FPL.
Den/Bedroom 4
12⁰ x 11²
Two Story Family Room
14⁰ x 18⁰
FRENCH DOOR
DW.
Kitchen
Laund.
W.
D.
Breakfast
ISLAND
REF.
SURFACE UNIT
DBL. OVENS
PANTRY
Bath
W.i.c.
STAIRS DN.
Pwdr.
COATS
VLT.
Vaulted Living Room
12⁰ x 12⁰
STAIRS UP
Two Story Foyer
Dining Room
12⁰ x 13⁴
Garage
20⁵ x 22²
VLT.
Covered Porch
© Frank Betz Associates, Inc.

FIRST FLOOR

Design 24701

See Order Pages and Index for Info

Units	Single
Price Code	B
Total Finished	1,625 sq. ft.
Main Finished	1,625 sq. ft.
Basement Unfinished	1,625 sq. ft.
Garage Unfinished	455 sq. ft.
Dimensions	54'x48'4"
Foundation	Basement Crawlspace Slab
Bedrooms	3
Full Baths	2
Main Ceiling	8'- 9'
Max Ridge Height	22'
Roof Framing	Stick
Exterior Walls	2x4,2x6

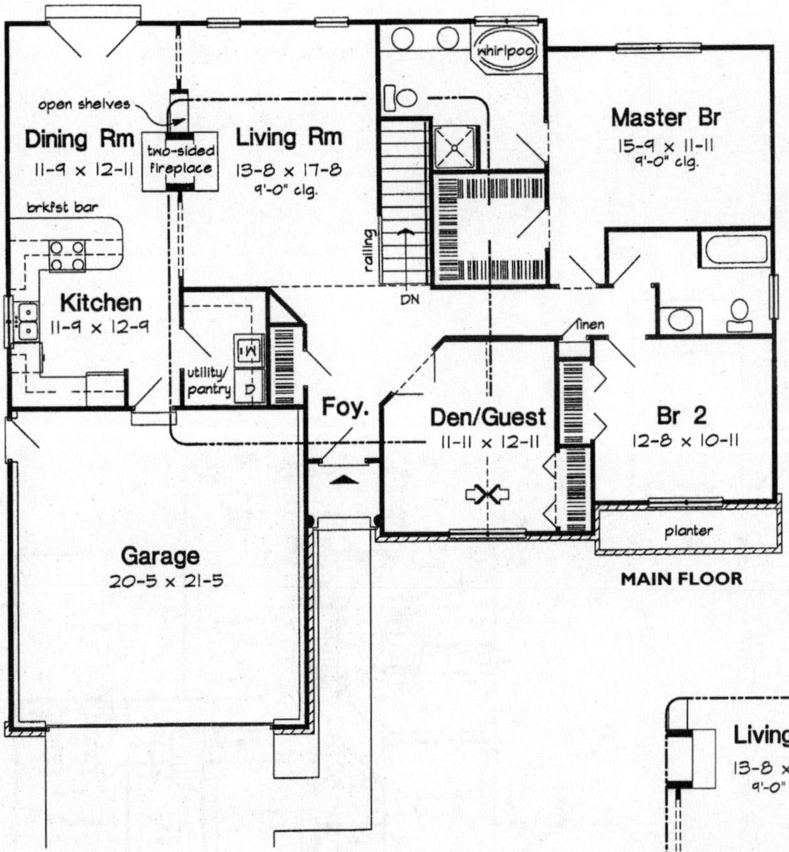
open shelves
Dining Rm
11-9 x 12-11
two-sided fireplace
Living Rm
13-8 x 17-8
9'-0" clg.
whirlpool
Master Br
15-9 x 11-11
9'-0" clg.
brkfst bar
Kitchen
11-9 x 12-9
railing
DN
linen
utility/ pantry
W
D
Foy.
Den/Guest
11-11 x 12-11
Br 2
12-8 x 10-11
planter
Garage
20-5 x 21-5

MAIN FLOOR

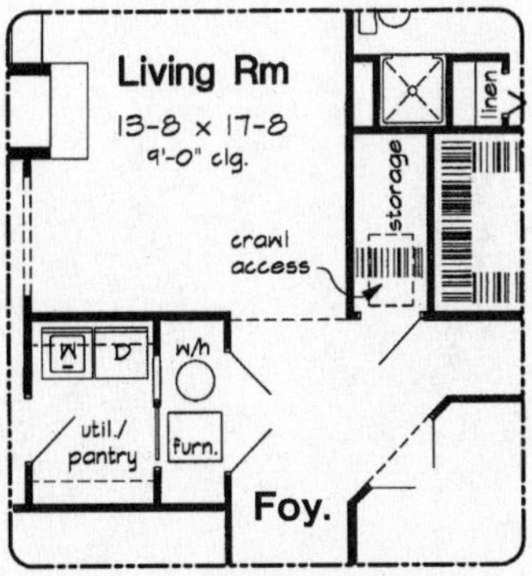
Living Rm
13-8 x 17-8
9'-0" clg.
linen
storage
crawl access
W
D
w/h
util./ pantry
furn.
Foy.

ALTERNATE FOUNDATION

Design 60137

See Order Pages and Index for Info

Units	Single
Price Code	L
Total Finished	4,464 sq. ft.
First Finished	2,092 sq. ft.
Second Finished	2,372 sq. ft.
Basement Unfinished	2,092 sq. ft.
Garage Unfinished	674 sq. ft.
Dimensions	75'5"x64'
Foundation	Basement Crawlspace
Bedrooms	5
Full Baths	4
Half Baths	1
First Ceiling	9'
Second Ceiling	8'
Max Ridge Height	34'
Roof Framing	Stick
Exterior Walls	2x4

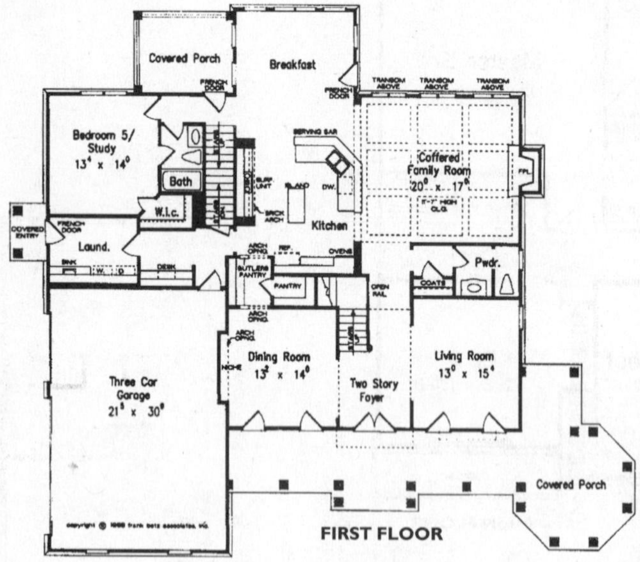
Covered Porch
Breakfast
French Door
Bedroom 5/ Study
Bath
W.I.c.
Covered Entry
Laund.
Kitchen
Coffered Family Room
Pwdr.
Three Car Garage
Dining Room
Two Story Foyer
Living Room
Covered Porch

FIRST FLOOR

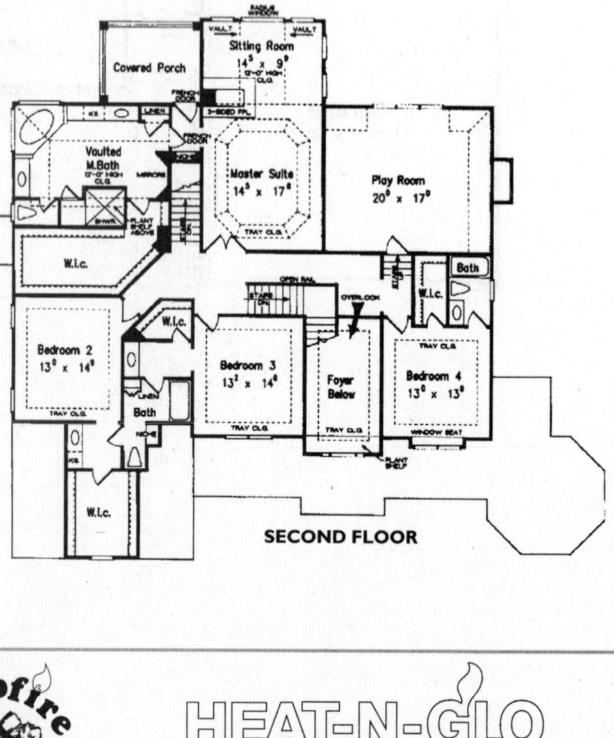
Covered Porch
Sitting Room
Vaulted M.Bath
Master Suite
Play Room
W.I.c.
Bath
Bedroom 2
Bedroom 3
Foyer Below
Bedroom 4
Bath
W.I.c.

SECOND FLOOR

Design 19422

See Order Pages and Index for Info

Photography supplied by the Meredith Corporation

Units	Single
Price Code	B
Total Finished	1,695 sq. ft.
Main Finished	1,290 sq. ft.
Second Finished	405 sq. ft.
Garage Unfinished	513 sq. ft.
Dimensions	50'8"x61'8"
Foundation	Basement Crawlspace
Bedrooms	2
Full Baths	2
Main Ceiling	9'
Second Ceiling	8'
Max Ridge Height	29'
Roof Framing	Stick/Truss
Exterior Walls	2x4

SECOND FLOOR

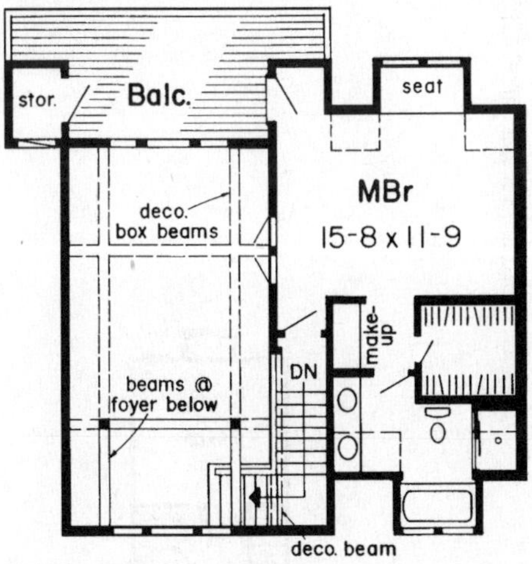
stor.
Balc.
seat
MBr
15-8 x 11-9
deco. box beams
make-up
DN
beams @ foyer below
deco. beam

FIRST FLOOR

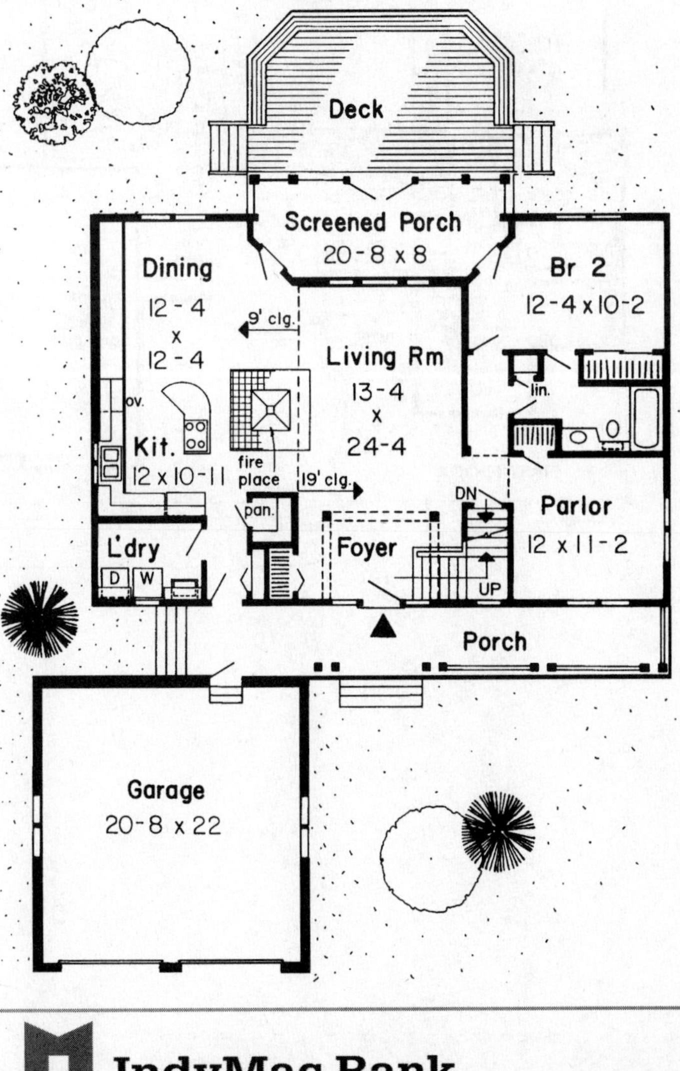
Deck
Screened Porch
20-8 x 8
Dining
12-4
x
12-4
9' clg.
Living Rm
13-4
x
24-4
Br 2
12-4 x 10-2
lin.
ov.
Kit.
12 x 10-11
fire place
19' clg.
pan.
DN
Parlor
12 x 11-2
L'dry
D
W
Foyer
UP
Porch
Garage
20-8 x 22

Design 94995

See Order Pages and Index for Info

Units	Single
Price Code	H
Total Finished	3,172 sq. ft.
First Finished	2,252 sq. ft.
Second Finished	920 sq. ft.
Basement Unfinished	2,252 sq. ft.
Garage Unfinished	646 sq. ft.
Dimensions	73'4"x57'4"
Foundation	Basement
Bedrooms	4
Full Baths	2
Half Baths	1
3/4 Baths	1
Max Ridge Height	28'
Roof Framing	Stick
Exterior Walls	2x4

* Alternate foundation options available at an additional charge. Please call 1-800-235-5700 for more information.

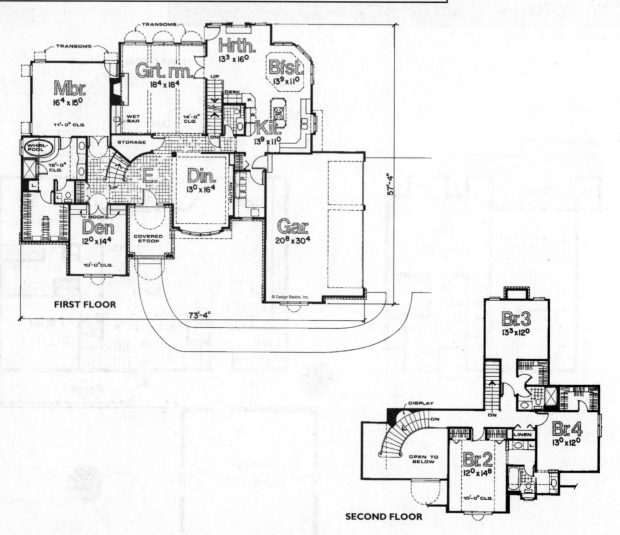

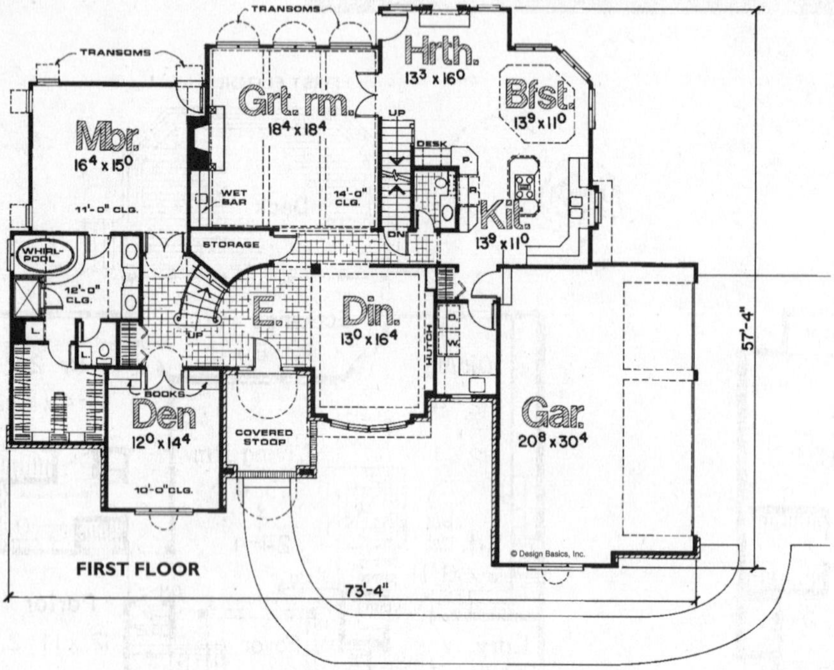
TRANSOMS
TRANSOMS
Hrth.
13³ x 16⁰
Bfst.
13⁹ x 11⁰
Grt. rm.
18⁴ x 18⁴
Mbr.
16⁴ x 15⁰
WET BAR
14'-0" CLG.
11'-0" CLG.
UP
DESK
DN
Kit.
13⁹ x 11⁰
WHIRLPOOL
STORAGE
12'-0" CLG.
E.
Din.
13⁰ x 16⁴
HUTCH
UP
BOOKS
Den
12⁰ x 14⁴
COVERED STOOP
10'-0" CLG.
Gar.
20⁸ x 30⁴
57'-4"
73'-4"
© Design Basics, Inc.

FIRST FLOOR

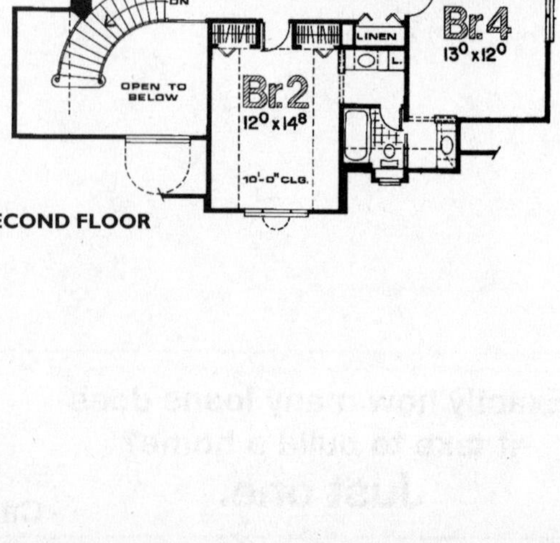
Br. 3
13³ x 12⁰
DISPLAY
DN
DN
LINEN
Br. 4
13⁰ x 12⁰
OPEN TO BELOW
Br. 2
12⁰ x 14⁸
10'-0" CLG.

SECOND FLOOR

Design 62006

See Order Pages and Index for Info

Units	Single
Price Code	F
Total Finished	2,701 sq. ft.
First Finished	2,352 sq. ft.
Second Finished	349 sq. ft.
Garage Unfinished	697 sq. ft.
Porch Unfinished	724 sq. ft.
Dimensions	69'x69'10"
Foundation	Basement Crawlspace Slab
Bedrooms	3
Full Baths	4
Half Baths	1
First Ceiling	9'
Second Ceiling	8'
Roof Framing	Stick
Exterior Walls	2x4

FIRST FLOOR

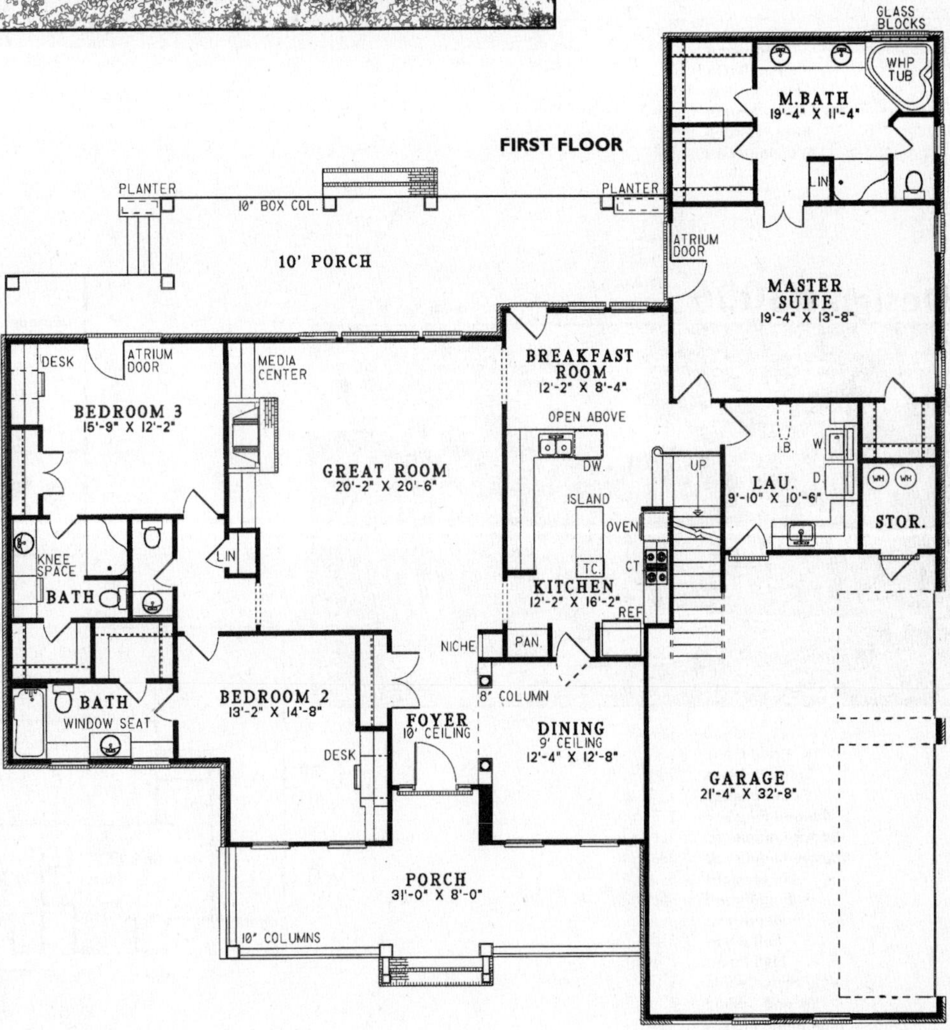
GLASS BLOCKS
WHP TUB
M.BATH
19'-4" X 11'-4"
LIN
PLANTER
10' BOX COL.
PLANTER
10' PORCH
ATRIUM DOOR
MASTER SUITE
19'-4" X 13'-8"
DESK
ATRIUM DOOR
MEDIA CENTER
BEDROOM 3
15'-9" X 12'-2"
BREAKFAST ROOM
12'-2" X 8'-4"
OPEN ABOVE
GREAT ROOM
20'-2" X 20'-6"
DW.
ISLAND
OVEN
UP
I.B.
W
D
WH
WH
LAU.
9'-10" X 10'-6"
STOR.
KNEE SPACE
BATH
LIN
TC.
CT
KITCHEN
12'-2" X 16'-2"
REF.
NICHE
PAN.
BATH
WINDOW SEAT
BEDROOM 2
13'-2" X 14'-8"
8' COLUMN
FOYER
10' CEILING
DINING
9' CEILING
12'-4" X 12'-8"
DESK
GARAGE
21'-4" X 32'-8"
PORCH
31'-0" X 8'-0"
10' COLUMNS

SECOND FLOOR

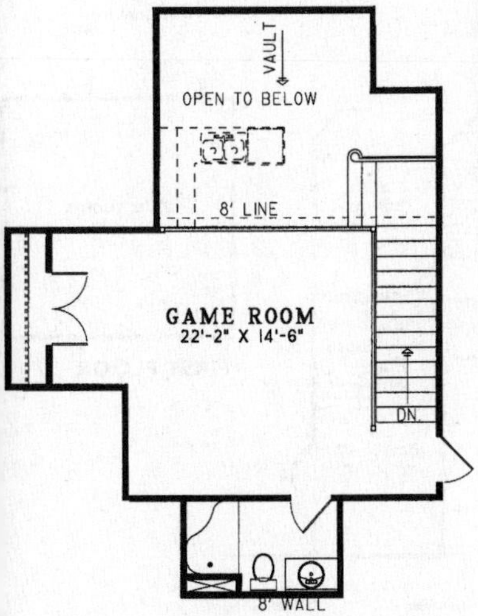
VAULT
OPEN TO BELOW
8' LINE
GAME ROOM
22'-2" X 14'-6"
DN
8' WALL

Design 98456

See Order Pages and Index for Info

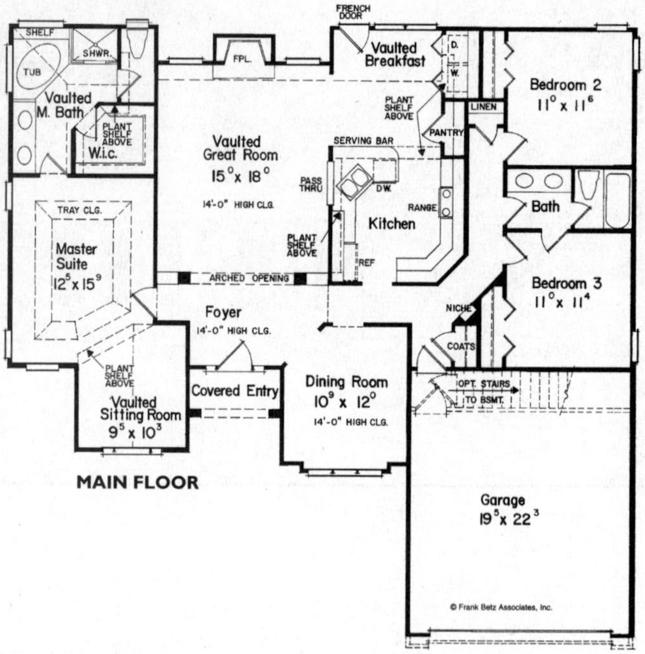
SHELF
TUB
SHWR.
Vaulted M. Bath
PLANT SHELF ABOVE
W.i.c.
FPL.
FRENCH DOOR
Vaulted Breakfast
D.
W.
Bedroom 2
11° x 11⁶
LINEN
PLANT SHELF ABOVE
PANTRY
Vaulted Great Room
15° x 18°
14'-0" HIGH CLG.
SERVING BAR
PASS THRU
DW.
RANGE
Kitchen
Bath
TRAY CLG.
Master Suite
12⁵ x 15⁹
PLANT SHELF ABOVE
REF
ARCHED OPENING
Bedroom 3
11° x 11⁴
NICHE
Foyer
14'-0" HIGH CLG.
COATS
PLANT SHELF ABOVE
Vaulted Sitting Room
9⁵ x 10³
Covered Entry
Dining Room
10⁹ x 12°
14'-0" HIGH CLG.
OPT. STAIRS TO BSMT.
MAIN FLOOR
Garage
19⁵ x 22³
© Frank Betz Associates, Inc.

Units	Single
Price Code	B
Total Finished	1,715 sq. ft.
Main Finished	1,715 sq. ft.
Basement Unfinished	1,715 sq. ft.
Garage Unfinished	450 sq. ft.
Dimensions	55'x51'6"
Foundation	Basement Crawlspace Slab
Bedrooms	3
Full Baths	2
Main Ceiling	9'1"
Max Ridge Height	25'
Roof Framing	Stick
Exterior Walls	2x4

Design 63006

See Order Pages and Index for Info

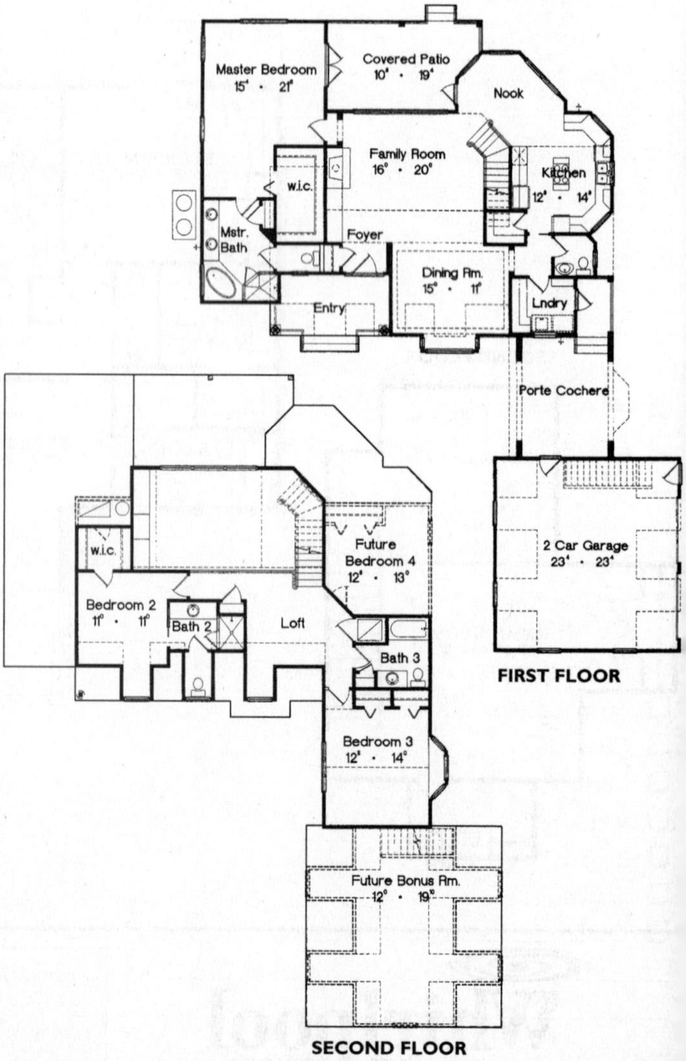
Master Bedroom
15' · 21'
Covered Patio
10' · 19'
Nook
Family Room
16' · 20'
Kitchen
12' · 14'
w.i.c.
Mstr. Bath
Foyer
Dining Rm.
15' · 11'
Entry
Lndry
Porte Cochere
2 Car Garage
23' · 23'
FIRST FLOOR
w.i.c.
Future Bedroom 4
12' · 13'
Bedroom 2
11' · 11'
Bath 2
Loft
Bath 3
Bedroom 3
12' · 14'
Future Bonus Rm.
12' · 19'
SECOND FLOOR

Units	Single
Price Code	E
Total Finished	2,307 sq. ft.
First Finished	1,530 sq. ft.
Second Finished	777 sq. ft.
Bonus Unfinished	361 sq. ft.
Garage Unfinished	576 sq. ft.
Dimensions	61'4"x78'
Foundation	Slab
Bedrooms	3
Full Baths	3
Half Baths	1
First Ceiling	9'
Second Ceiling	8'
Max Ridge Height	24'9"
Roof Framing	Truss
Exterior Walls	2x4

FREE! Traditional Family Home Plans

Thanks for buying this Garlinghouse magazine and giving us a chance to better understand your needs and desires. To receive your FREE copy of Traditional Family Home Plans book, please:

PREMIER EDITION
TRADITIONAL
Family
HOME PLANS
FEATURING OUR PLATINUM AND GOLD DESIGN NETWORK

1. Fill out the questionnaire.
2. Cut out the bar code on the front of this magazine and affix it to the questionnaire.
3. Enclose a check for $3.50 to cover postage and handling. Your book will be shipped book rate and will arrive in about 1-3 weeks.
4. Mail your questionnaire, bar code and check for postage to:
   Publisher
   Garlinghouse Inc.
   174 Oakwood Drive
   Glastonbury, CT 06033

FREE! FREE! FREE!

Name: ______________________________

Address: ______________________________

City: ______________ **State:** ________ **Zip:** ________

Daytime telephone number: (   ) ______________

FREE Traditional Family Home Plans | Affix Bar Code Here

Where did you buy this magazine?

- ❑ Newsstand
- ❑ Grocery store
- ❑ Pharmacy/Conv. Store
- ❑ Lumberyard
- ❑ Bookstore
- ❑ Other

When are you planning to build?

- ❑ Within 6 months
- ❑ 6 months to 12 months
- ❑ 1 to 2 years
- ❑ More than 2 years
- ❑ Undecided

What style are you most interested in?

- ❑ Farmhouse or Country Style
- ❑ Colonial
- ❑ Rustic Cottage or Cabin
- ❑ Victorian
- ❑ Eurostyle
- ❑ Traditional
- ❑ Other ______________________________

What is the approximate size of the home?

- ❑ Under 1,000 square feet
- ❑ 1,000 to 2,000
- ❑ 2,000 to 3,000
- ❑ 3,000 to 4,000
- ❑ Over 4,000

What type of home?

- ❑ One level
- ❑ Two story with all bedrooms on second floor
- ❑ Two story with one or two bedrooms on first floor
- ❑ Other ______________________________

Please provide any other comments.

Please tell us anything else about the dream house you'd like to build. Let us know if you have special floor plan requirements (i.e. you want a great room but no living room) or specific property features (i.e. you have a sloped or narrow lot).

Design 94298

See Order Pages and Index for Info

Units	Single
Price Code	E
Total Finished	2,349 sq. ft.
First Finished	1,537 sq. ft.
Second Finished	812 sq. ft.
Lower Unfinished	1,263 sq. ft.
Dimensions	45'4"x50'
Foundation	Basement
Bedrooms	3
Full Baths	2
Half Baths	1
Max Ridge Height	40'8"
Roof Framing	Truss
Exterior Walls	2x6

* Alternate foundation options available at an additional charge. Please call 1-800-235-5700 for more information.

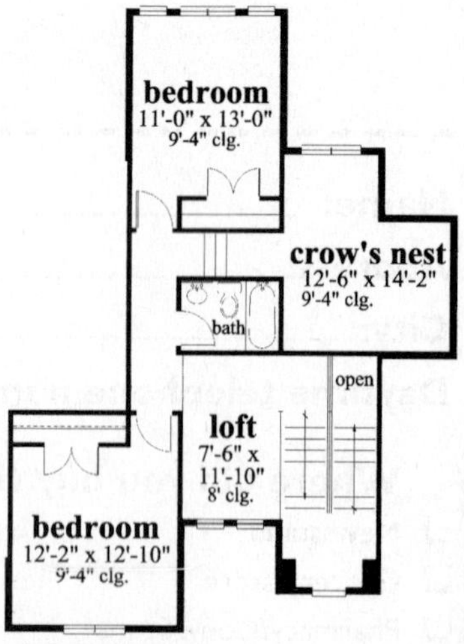
bedroom
11'-0" x 13'-0"
9'-4" clg.
crow's nest
12'-6" x 14'-2"
9'-4" clg.
bath
open
loft
7'-6" x
11'-10"
8' clg.
bedroom
12'-2" x 12'-10"
9'-4" clg.

SECOND FLOOR

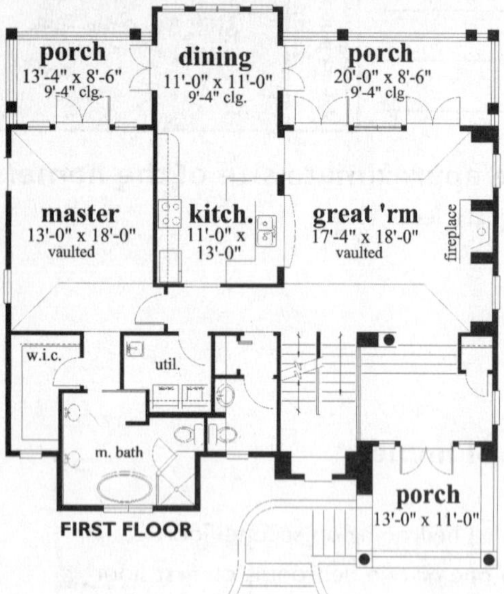
porch
13'-4" x 8'-6"
9'-4" clg.
dining
11'-0" x 11'-0"
9'-4" clg.
porch
20'-0" x 8'-6"
9'-4" clg.
master
13'-0" x 18'-0"
vaulted
kitch.
11'-0" x
13'-0"
great 'rm
17'-4" x 18'-0"
vaulted
fireplace
w.i.c.
util.
m. bath
porch
13'-0" x 11'-0"

FIRST FLOOR

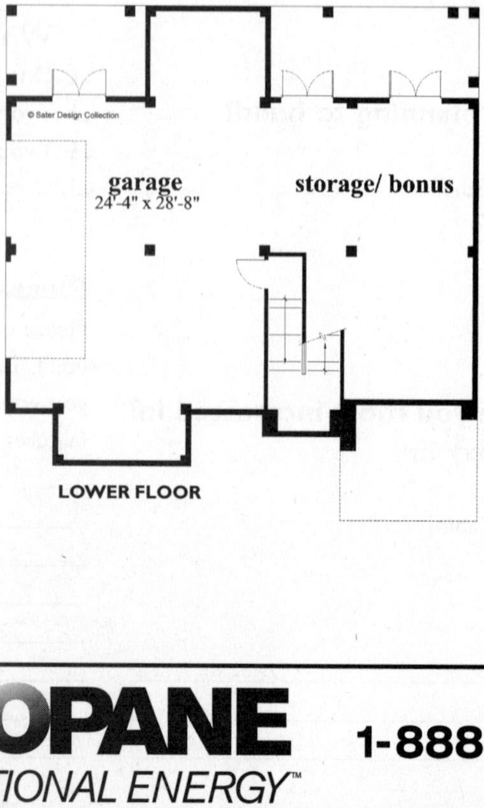
© Sater Design Collection
garage
24'-4" x 28'-8"
storage/ bonus

LOWER FLOOR

Design 62003

See Order Pages and Index for Info

Units	Single
Price Code	F
Total Finished	2,582 sq. ft.
Main Finished	2,582 sq. ft.
Garage Unfinished	552 sq. ft.
Porch Unfinished	365 sq. ft.
Dimensions	77'x57'8"
Foundation	Basement Crawlspace Slab
Bedrooms	4
Full Baths	2
Half Baths	1
Main Ceiling	9'
Roof Framing	Stick
Exterior Walls	2x4

MAIN FLOOR

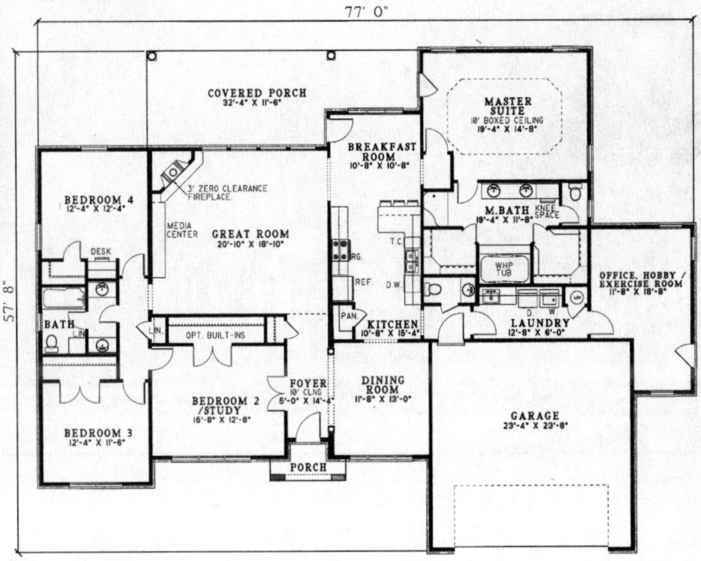
77' 0"
57' 8"
COVERED PORCH
32'-4" X 11'-6"
MASTER SUITE
10' BOXED CEILING
19'-4" X 14'-8"
BREAKFAST ROOM
10'-8" X 10'-8"
BEDROOM 4
12'-4" X 12'-4"
3' ZERO CLEARANCE FIREPLACE
MEDIA CENTER
GREAT ROOM
20'-10" X 18'-10"
M.BATH
19'-4" X 11'-8"
KNEE SPACE
DESK
WHP TUB
OFFICE, HOBBY / EXERCISE ROOM
11'-8" X 18'-8"
BATH
OPT. BUILT-INS
KITCHEN
10'-8" X 15'-4"
LAUNDRY
12'-8" X 6'-0"
FOYER
10' CLNG
5'-0" X 14'-4"
DINING ROOM
11'-8" X 13'-0"
BEDROOM 2 /STUDY
15'-8" X 12'-8"
BEDROOM 3
12'-4" X 11'-6"
GARAGE
23'-4" X 23'-8"
PORCH

Design 98402

See Order Pages and Index for Info

Units	Single
Price Code	H
Total Finished	3,027 sq. ft.
First Finished	2,130 sq. ft.
Second Finished	897 sq. ft.
Basement Unfinished	2,130 sq. ft.
Garage Unfinished	494 sq. ft.
Dimensions	62'4"x54'6"
Foundation	Basement Crawlspace Slab
Bedrooms	4
Full Baths	3
Half Baths	1
First Ceiling	9'
Second Ceiling	8'
Max Ridge Height	29'
Roof Framing	Stick
Exterior Walls	2x4

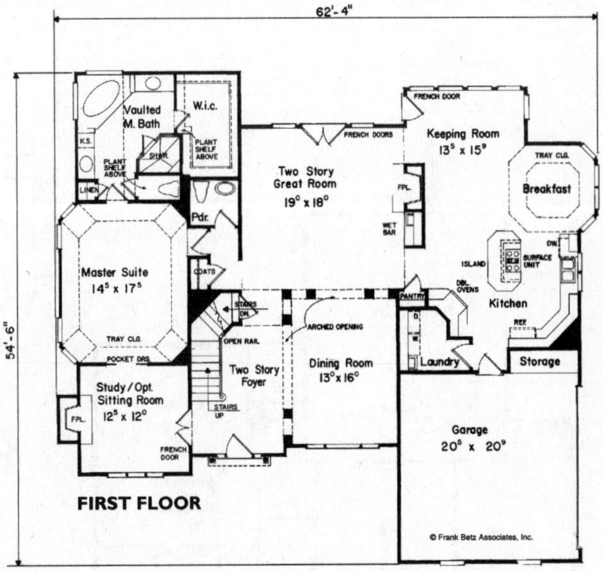
62'-4"
54'-6"
Vaulted M. Bath
W.i.c.
Two Story Great Room
19⁰ x 18⁰
Keeping Room
13⁵ x 15⁹
Breakfast
Master Suite
14⁵ x 17⁵
Kitchen
Two Story Foyer
Dining Room
13⁰ x 16⁰
Study / Opt. Sitting Room
12⁵ x 12⁰
Laundry
Storage
Garage
20⁵ x 20⁹
FIRST FLOOR
© Frank Betz Associates, Inc.

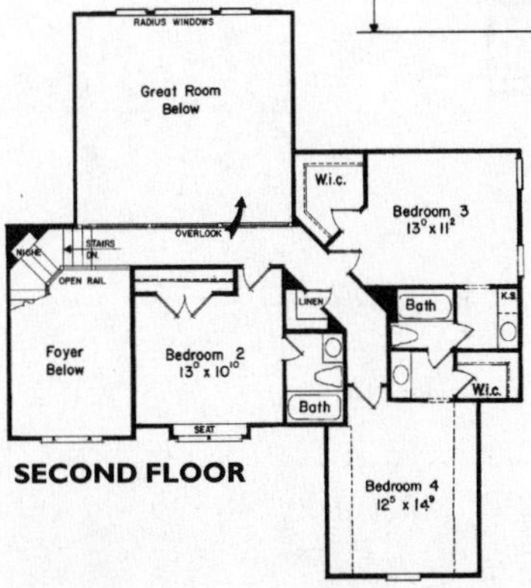
RADIUS WINDOWS
Great Room Below
W.i.c.
Bedroom 3
13⁰ x 11²
OVERLOOK
Foyer Below
Bedroom 2
13⁰ x 10¹⁰
Bath
Bath
W.i.c.
Bedroom 4
12⁵ x 14⁹

SECOND FLOOR

Design 98452

See Order Pages and Index for Info

Units	Single
Price Code	H
Total Finished	3,083 sq. ft.
First Finished	2,429 sq. ft.
Second Finished	654 sq. ft.
Bonus Unfinished	420 sq. ft.
Basement Unfinished	2,429 sq. ft.
Garage Unfinished	641 sq. ft.
Dimensions	63'6"x71'4"
Foundation	Basement Crawlspace
Bedrooms	3
Full Baths	3
Half Baths	1
Max Ridge Height	34'9"
Roof Framing	Stick
Exterior Walls	2x4

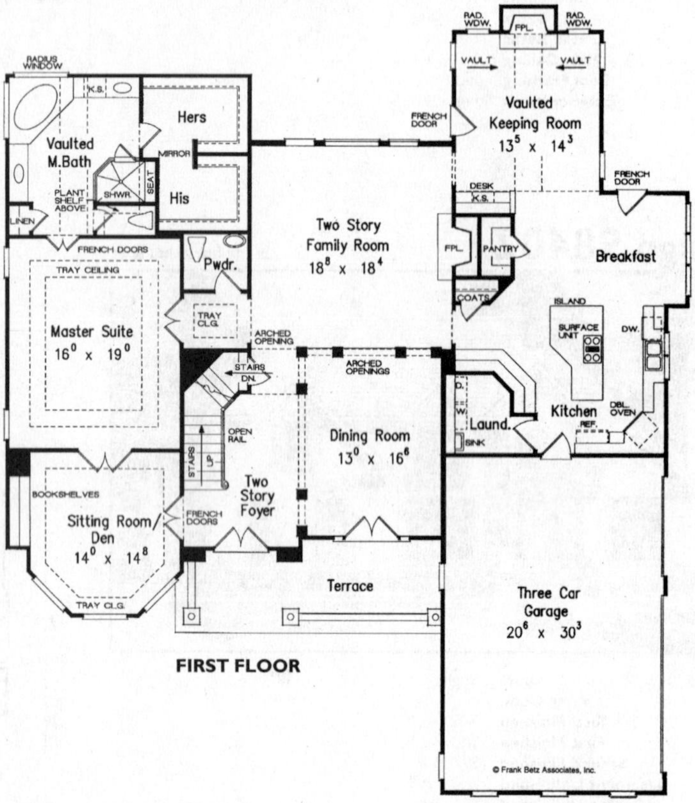
RAD. WDW.
FPL.
RAD. WDW.
VAULT
VAULT
FRENCH DOOR
Vaulted Keeping Room
13⁵ x 14³
FRENCH DOOR
DESK
K.S.
RADIUS WINDOW
K.S.
Hers
Vaulted M.Bath
MIRROR
PLANT SHELF ABOVE
SHWR
SEAT
His
LINEN
Two Story Family Room
18⁸ x 18⁴
FPL.
PANTRY
Breakfast
FRENCH DOORS
TRAY CEILING
Pwdr.
COATS
TRAY CLG.
ISLAND
SURFACE UNIT
DW.
Master Suite
16⁰ x 19⁰
ARCHED OPENING
ARCHED OPENINGS
STAIRS DN.
Kitchen
DBL. OVEN
Laund.
REF.
SINK
OPEN RAIL
Dining Room
13⁰ x 16⁶
STAIRS
UP
Two Story Foyer
BOOKSHELVES
Sitting Room/ Den
14⁰ x 14⁸
FRENCH DOORS
TRAY CLG.
Terrace
Three Car Garage
20⁶ x 30³
© Frank Betz Associates, Inc.

FIRST FLOOR

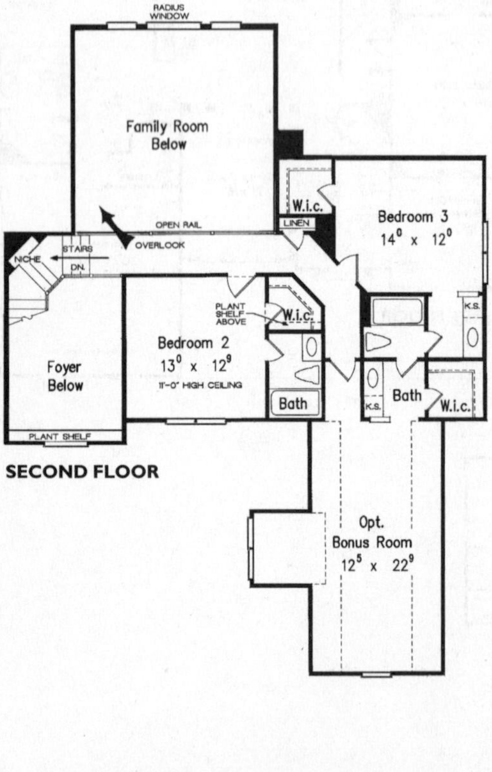
RADIUS WINDOW
Family Room Below
W.i.c.
LINEN
Bedroom 3
14⁰ x 12⁰
OPEN RAIL
OVERLOOK
STAIRS
NICHE
DN.
PLANT SHELF ABOVE
W.i.c.
K.S.
Bedroom 2
13⁰ x 12⁹
11'-0" HIGH CEILING
Foyer Below
Bath
K.S.
Bath
W.i.c.
PLANT SHELF
Opt. Bonus Room
12⁵ x 22⁹

SECOND FLOOR

Design 92052

See Order Pages and Index for Info

Units	Single
Price Code	A
Total Finished	1,189 sq. ft.
First Finished	615 sq. ft.
Second Finished	574 sq. ft.
Dimensions	36'x35'8"
Foundation	Basement
Bedrooms	3
Full Baths	2
Half Baths	1
Max Ridge Height	27'
Roof Framing	Truss
Exterior Walls	2x4

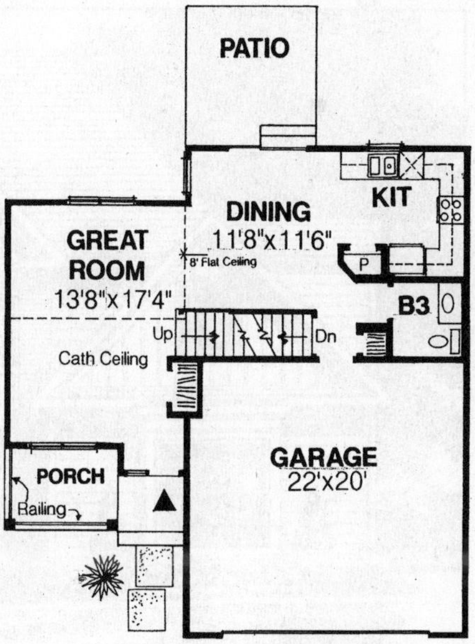
PATIO
DINING
11'8"x11'6"
KIT
GREAT ROOM
13'8"x17'4"
8' Flat Ceiling
B3
Up
Dn
Cath Ceiling
PORCH
Railing
GARAGE
22'x20'

FIRST FLOOR

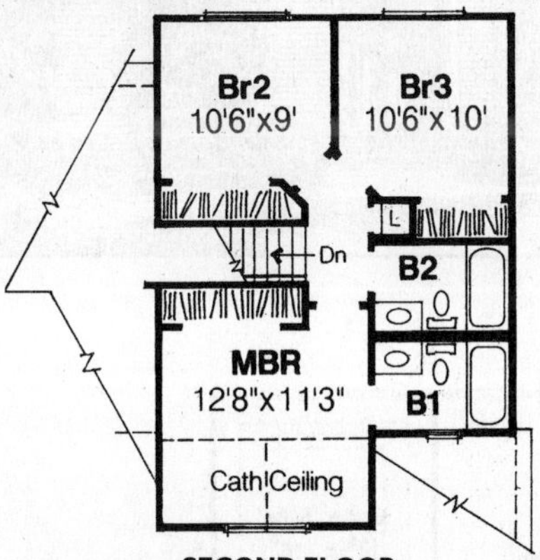
Br2
10'6"x9'
Br3
10'6"x10'
L
Dn
B2
MBR
12'8"x11'3"
B1
Cath Ceiling

SECOND FLOOR

Design 94109

See Order Pages and Index for Info

Units	Single
Price Code	D
Total Finished	2,013 sq. ft.
First Finished	1,025 sq. ft.
Second Finished	988 sq. ft.
Dimensions	56'x34'
Foundation	Basement
Bedrooms	4
Full Baths	2
Half Baths	1
Max Ridge Height	29'
Roof Framing	Stick/Truss
Exterior Walls	2x6

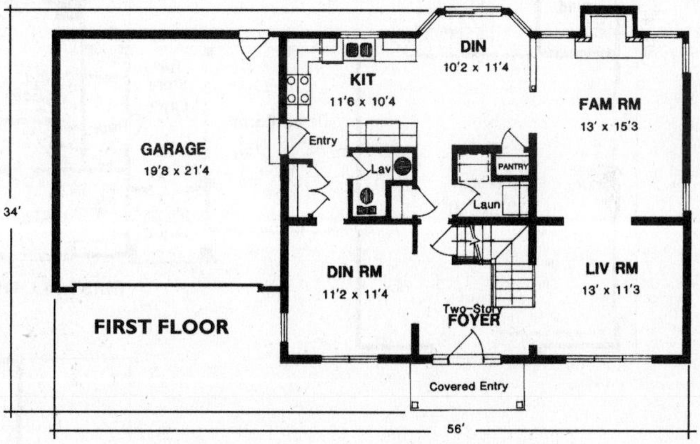
DIN
10'2 x 11'4
KIT
11'6 x 10'4
FAM RM
13' x 15'3
GARAGE
19'8 x 21'4
Entry
Lav
PANTRY
Laun
34'
DIN RM
11'2 x 11'4
LIV RM
13' x 11'3
Two-Story
FOYER
FIRST FLOOR
Covered Entry
56'

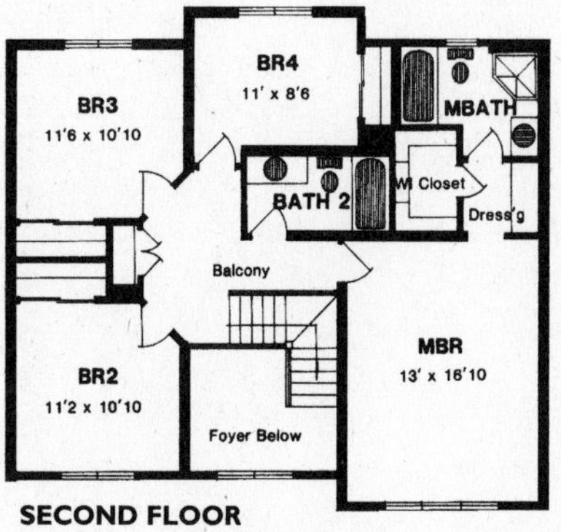
BR4
11' x 8'6
BR3
11'6 x 10'10
MBATH
BATH 2
W. Closet
Dress'g
Balcony
MBR
13' x 16'10
BR2
11'2 x 10'10
Foyer Below

SECOND FLOOR

Design 60105

See Order Pages and Index for Info

Units	Single
Price Code	D
Total Finished	2,044 sq. ft.
First Finished	1,544 sq. ft.
Second Finished	500 sq. ft.
Bonus Unfinished	242 sq. ft.
Basement Unfinished	1,544 sq. ft.
Garage Unfinished	471 sq. ft.
Dimensions	53'x46'4"
Foundation	Basement Crawlspace
Bedrooms	4
Full Baths	2
Half Baths	1
First Ceiling	9'
Second Ceiling	8'
Max Ridge Height	31'
Roof Framing	Stick
Exterior Walls	2x4

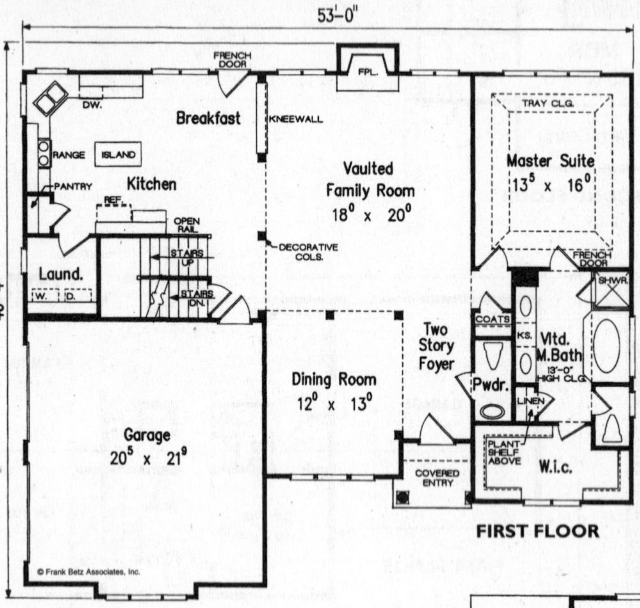
53'-0"
46'-4"
FRENCH DOOR
FPL.
DW.
Breakfast
KNEEWALL
RANGE
ISLAND
Kitchen
PANTRY
REF.
OPEN RAIL
Vaulted Family Room
18^{0} x 20^{0}
TRAY CLG.
Master Suite
13^{5} x 16^{0}
DECORATIVE COLS.
STAIRS UP
STAIRS DN.
Laund.
W. D.
FRENCH DOOR
SHWR.
COATS
KS.
Vltd. M.Bath
13'-0" HIGH CLG.
Two Story Foyer
Dining Room
12^{0} x 13^{0}
Pwdr.
LINEN
Garage
20^{5} x 21^{9}
PLANT SHELF ABOVE
W.i.c.
COVERED ENTRY
© Frank Betz Associates, Inc.

FIRST FLOOR

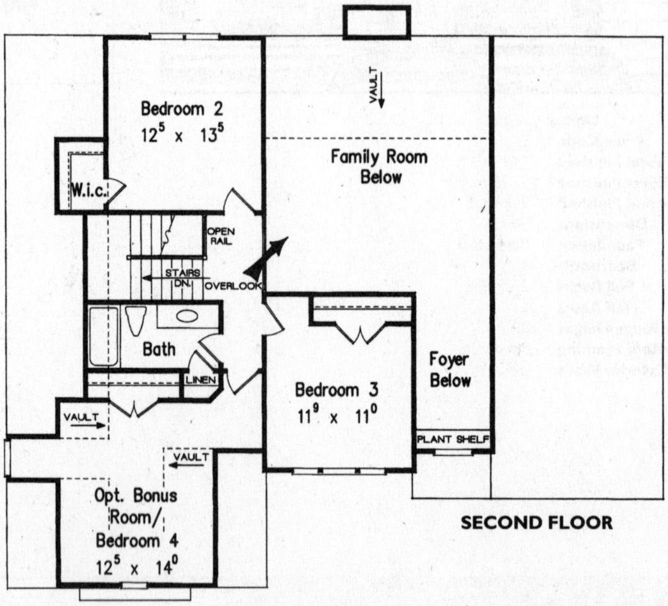
Bedroom 2
12^{5} x 13^{5}
VAULT
Family Room Below
W.i.c.
OPEN RAIL
STAIRS DN.
OVERLOOK
Bath
LINEN
Bedroom 3
11^{9} x 11^{0}
Foyer Below
PLANT SHELF
VAULT
VAULT
Opt. Bonus Room/ Bedroom 4
12^{5} x 14^{0}

SECOND FLOOR

Design 97456

See Order Pages and Index for Info

Units	Single
Price Code	C
Total Finished	1,758 sq. ft.
Main Finished	1,758 sq. ft.
Garage Unfinished	494 sq. ft.
Dimensions	55'4"x49'8"
Foundation	Basement
Bedrooms	3
Full Baths	2
Main Ceiling	9'
Max Ridge Height	26'
Roof Framing	Stick
Exterior Walls	2x4

* Alternate foundation options available at an additional charge. Please call 1-800-235-5700 for more information.

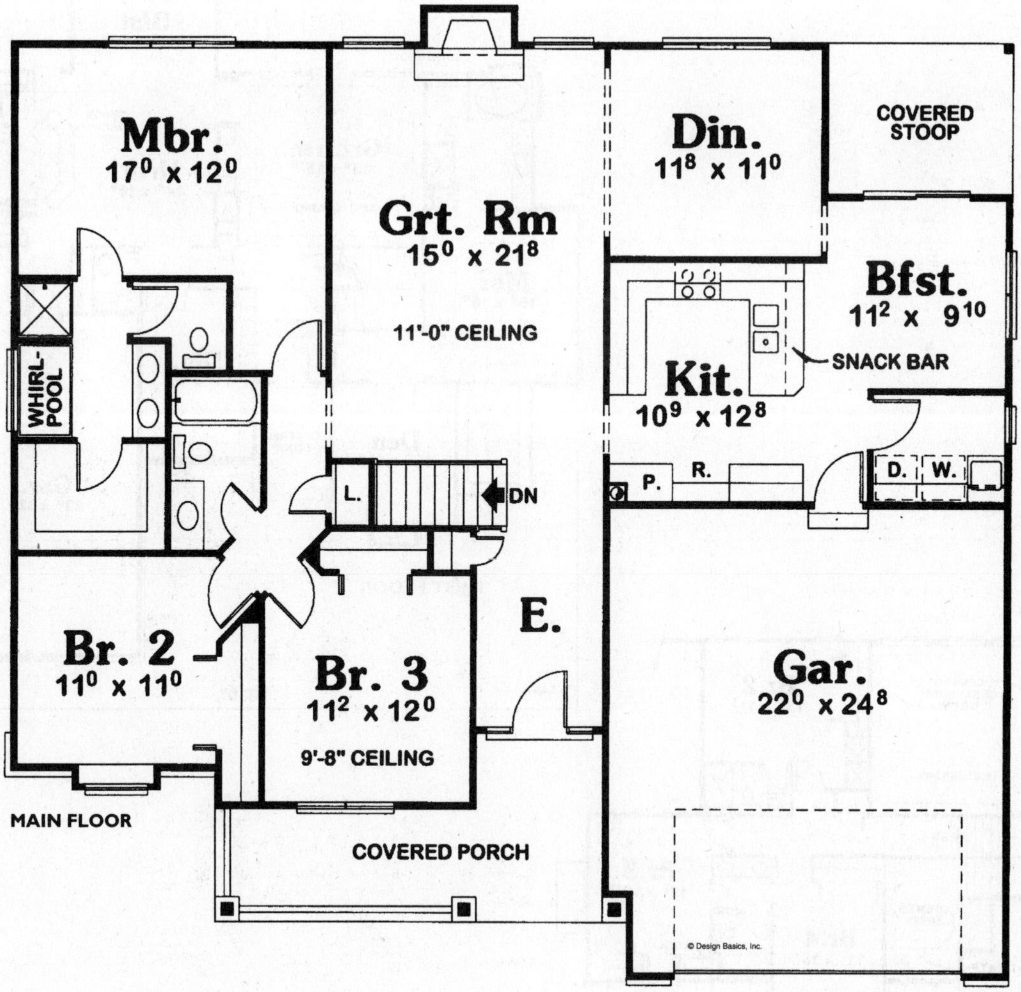

Mbr.
$17^0 \times 12^0$
Grt. Rm
$15^0 \times 21^8$
11'-0" CEILING
Din.
$11^8 \times 11^0$
COVERED STOOP
Bfst.
$11^2 \times 9^{10}$
SNACK BAR
Kit.
$10^9 \times 12^8$
WHIRL-POOL
L.
DN
P.
R.
D.
W.
E.
Br. 2
$11^0 \times 11^0$
Br. 3
$11^2 \times 12^0$
9'-8" CEILING
Gar.
$22^0 \times 24^8$
COVERED PORCH
© Design Basics, Inc.

MAIN FLOOR

Design 99470

See Order Pages and Index for Info

Units	Single
Price Code	H
Total Finished	3,040 sq. ft.
First Finished	2,215 sq. ft.
Second Finished	825 sq. ft.
Bonus Unfinished	186 sq. ft.
Garage Unfinished	728 sq. ft.
Dimensions	66'x66'
Foundation	Basement
Bedrooms	4
Full Baths	2
Half Baths	1
3/4 Baths	1
First Ceiling	9'
Max Ridge Height	28'9"
Roof Framing	Stick
Exterior Walls	2x4

* Alternate foundation options available at an additional cha
Please call 1-800-235-5700 for more information.

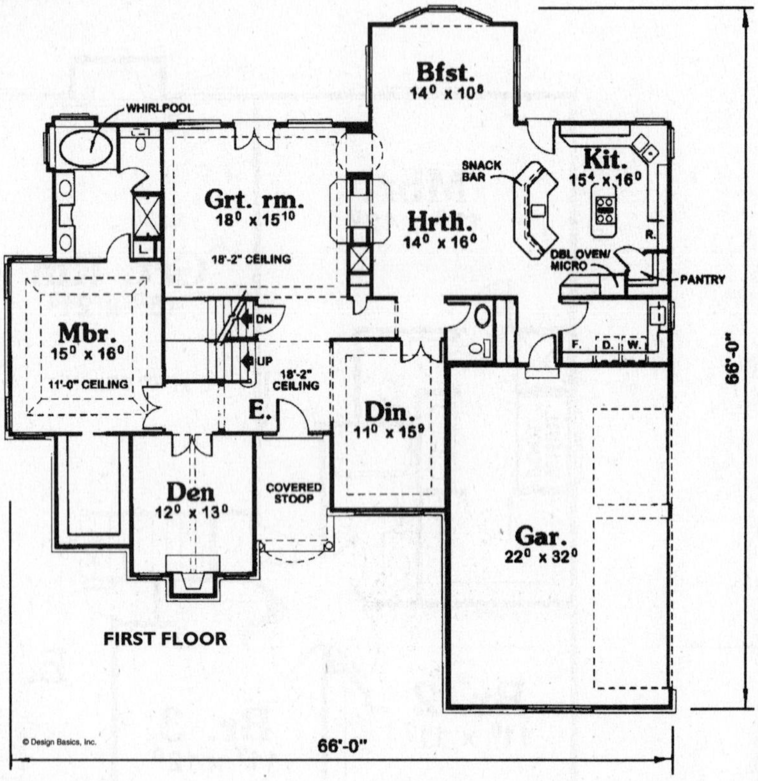
Bfst.
14⁰ x 10⁸
WHIRLPOOL
SNACK BAR
Kit.
15⁴ x 16⁰
Grt. rm.
18⁰ x 15¹⁰
18'-2" CEILING
Hrth.
14⁰ x 16⁰
DBL OVEN/ MICRO
PANTRY
R.
L
DN
UP
18'-2" CEILING
Mbr.
15⁰ x 16⁰
11'-0" CEILING
E.
Din.
11⁰ x 15⁹
F.
D.
W.
Den
12⁰ x 13⁰
COVERED STOOP
Gar.
22⁰ x 32⁰
66'-0"
66'-0"
© Design Basics, Inc.

FIRST FLOOR

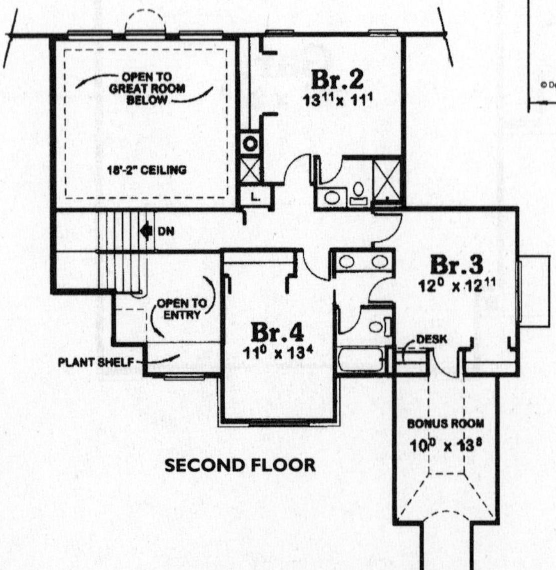
OPEN TO GREAT ROOM BELOW
18'-2" CEILING
Br.2
13¹¹ x 11¹
L
DN
OPEN TO ENTRY
PLANT SHELF
Br.4
11⁰ x 13⁴
Br.3
12⁰ x 12¹¹
DESK
BONUS ROOM
10⁰ x 13⁸

SECOND FLOOR

Design 99498

See Order Pages and Index for Info

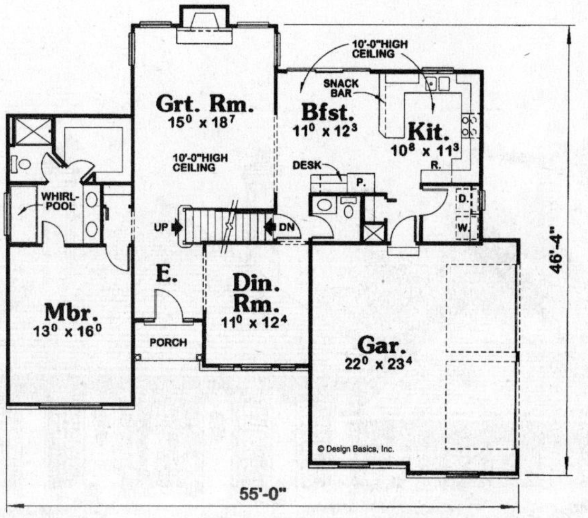
Grt. Rm.
15⁰ x 18⁷
10'-0"HIGH CEILING
10'-0"HIGH CEILING
SNACK BAR
Bfst.
11⁰ x 12³
Kit.
10⁸ x 11³
DESK
WHIRL-POOL
UP
DN
E.
Din. Rm.
11⁰ x 12⁴
Mbr.
13⁰ x 16⁰
PORCH
Gar.
22⁰ x 23⁴
© Design Basics, Inc.
55'-0"
46'-4"

FIRST FLOOR

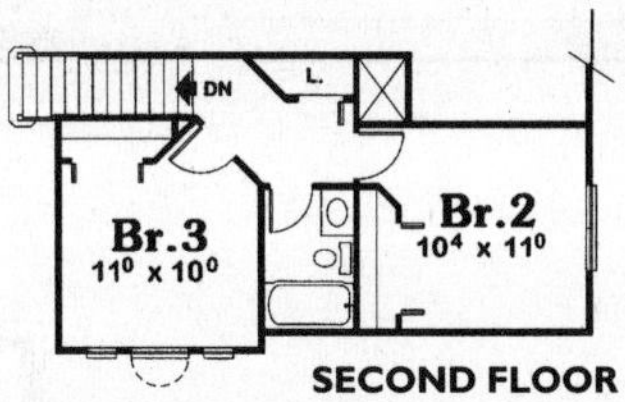
DN
Br.3
11⁰ x 10⁰
Br.2
10⁴ x 11⁰

SECOND FLOOR

Units	Single
Price Code	C
Total Finished	1,762 sq. ft.
First Finished	1,363 sq. ft.
Second Finished	399 sq. ft.
Garage Unfinished	524 sq. ft.
Dimensions	55'x46'4"
Foundation	Basement
Bedrooms	3
Full Baths	2
Half Baths	1
First Ceiling	9'
Max Ridge Height	27'
Roof Framing	Stick
Exterior Walls	2x4

* Alternate foundation options available at an additional charge. Please call 1-800-235-5700 for more information.

Design 24706

See Order Pages and Index for Info

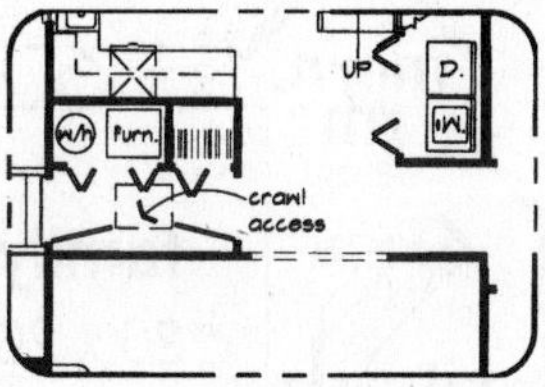
UP
D.
W
Furn.
crawl access

OPTIONAL CRAWLSPACE/SLAB

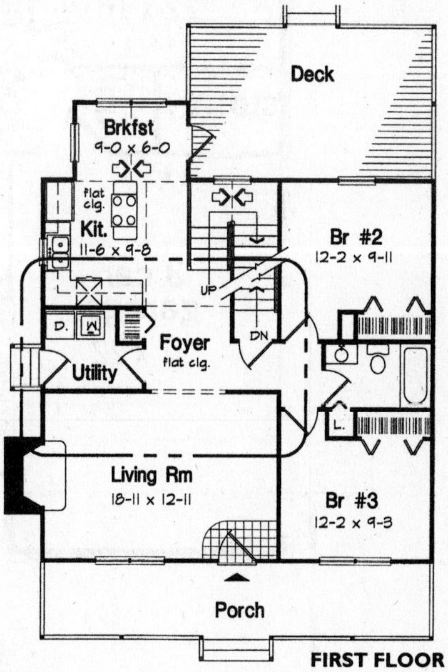
Deck
Brkfst
9-0 x 6-0
flat clg.
Kit.
11-6 x 9-8
Br #2
12-2 x 9-11
UP
DN
Foyer
flat clg.
Utility
Living Rm
18-11 x 12-11
Br #3
12-2 x 9-3
Porch

FIRST FLOOR

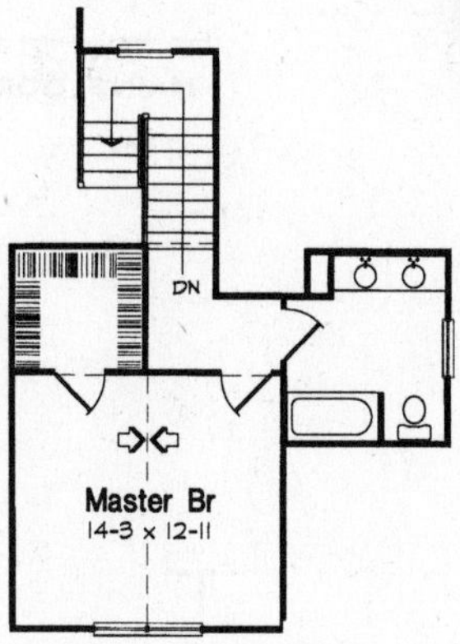
DN
Master Br
14-3 x 12-11

SECOND FLOOR

Units	Single
Price Code	A
Total Finished	1,470 sq. ft.
First Finished	1,035 sq. ft.
Second Finished	435 sq. ft.
Basement Unfinished	1,018 sq. ft.
Porch Unfinished	192 sq. ft.
Dimensions	35'x42'
Foundation	Basement Crawlspace Slab
Bedrooms	3
Full Baths	2
First Ceiling	8'
Second Ceiling	8'
Max Ridge Height	27'
Roof Framing	Stick
Exterior Walls	2x4,2x6

Design 65627

See Order Pages and Index for Info

Units	Single
Price Code	G
Total Finished	2,791 sq. ft.
Main Finished	2,791 sq. ft.
Dimensions	84'x54'
Foundation	Crawlspace Slab
Bedrooms	3
Full Baths	2
Main Ceiling	8'-12'
Max Ridge Height	29'
Exterior Walls	2x4

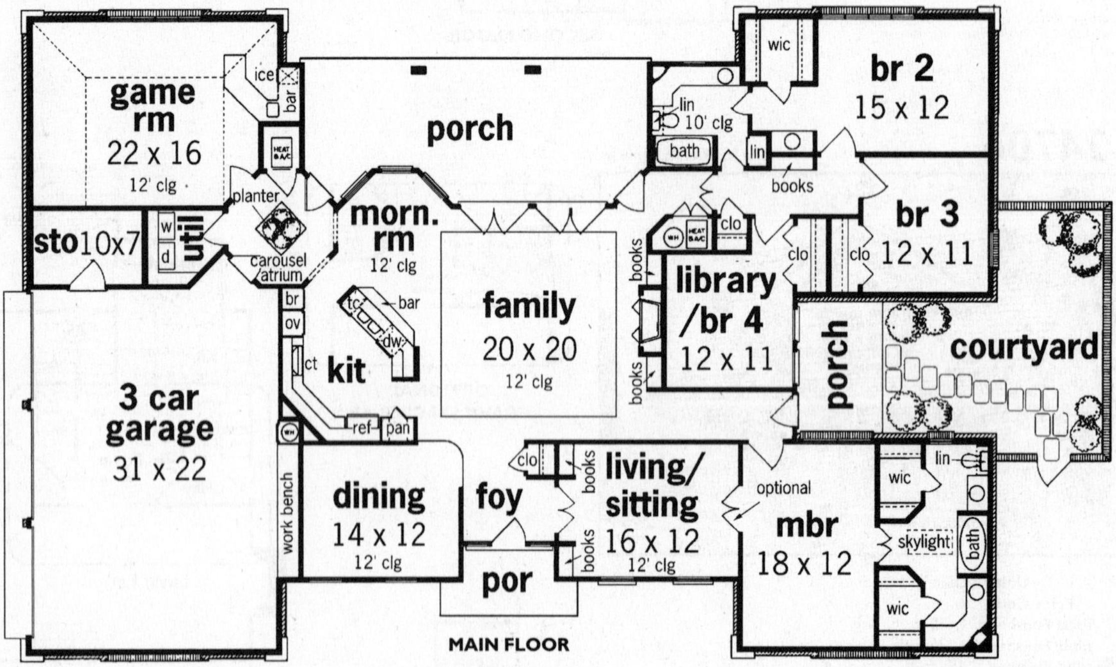
game rm
22 x 16
12' clg
ice
bar
porch
wic
br 2
15 x 12
lin
10' clg
bath
lin
books
br 3
12 x 11
clo
clo
clo
planter
carousel atrium
sto 10x7
w
d
util
morn. rm
12' clg
bar
family
20 x 20
12' clg
books
library /br 4
12 x 11
books
porch
courtyard
br
ov
ct
kit
dw
ref
pan
3 car garage
31 x 22
work bench
dining
14 x 12
12' clg
foy
clo
books
living/ sitting
16 x 12
12' clg
books
por
optional
mbr
18 x 12
wic
lin
skylight
bath
wic

MAIN FLOOR

Design 65631

See Order Pages and Index for Info

Units	Single
Price Code	G
Total Finished	1,485 sq. ft.
First Finished	924 sq. ft.
Second Finished	561 sq. ft.
Porch Unfinished	504 sq. ft.
Foundation	Basement Crawlspace Slab
Bedrooms	3
Full Baths	2
First Ceiling	8'
Second Ceiling	8'
Max Ridge Height	30'
Exterior Walls	2x6

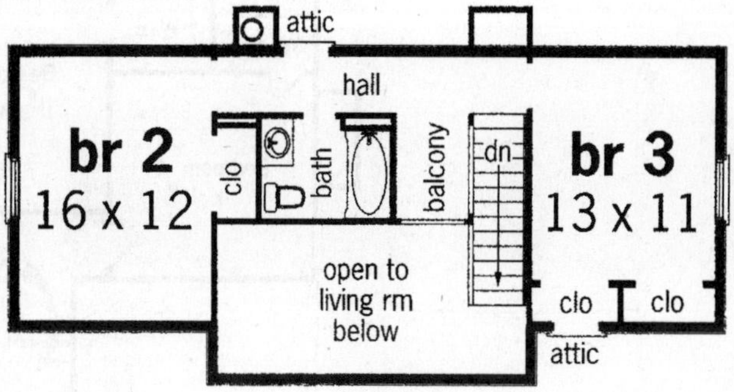
attic
hall
br 2
16 x 12
clo
bath
balcony
dn
br 3
13 x 11
open to
living rm
below
clo
clo
attic

SECOND FLOOR

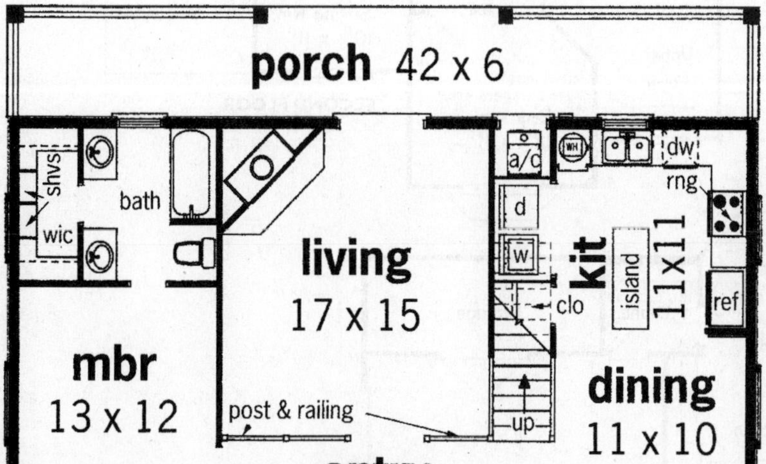
porch 42 x 6
shvs
bath
wic
a/c
WH
dw
rng
d
w
kit
island
11x11
living
17 x 15
clo
ref
mbr
13 x 12
post & railing
dining
11 x 10
up
entry
porch 42 x 6

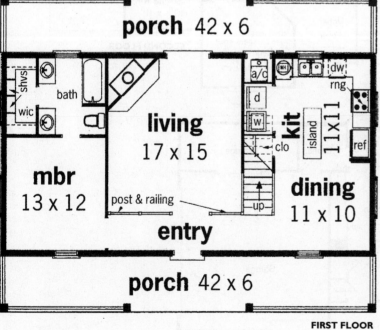

FIRST FLOOR

Design 97209

See Order Pages and Index for Info

Units	Single
Price Code	E
Total Finished	2,340 sq. ft.
First Finished	1,132 sq. ft.
Second Finished	1,208 sq. ft.
Basement Unfinished	1,132 sq. ft.
Garage Unfinished	514 sq. ft.
Dimensions	56'4"x39'6"
Foundation	Basement Crawlspace Slab
Bedrooms	4
Full Baths	2
Half Baths	1
First Ceiling	9'
Second Ceiling	8'
Max Ridge Height	33'
Roof Framing	Stick
Exterior Walls	2x4

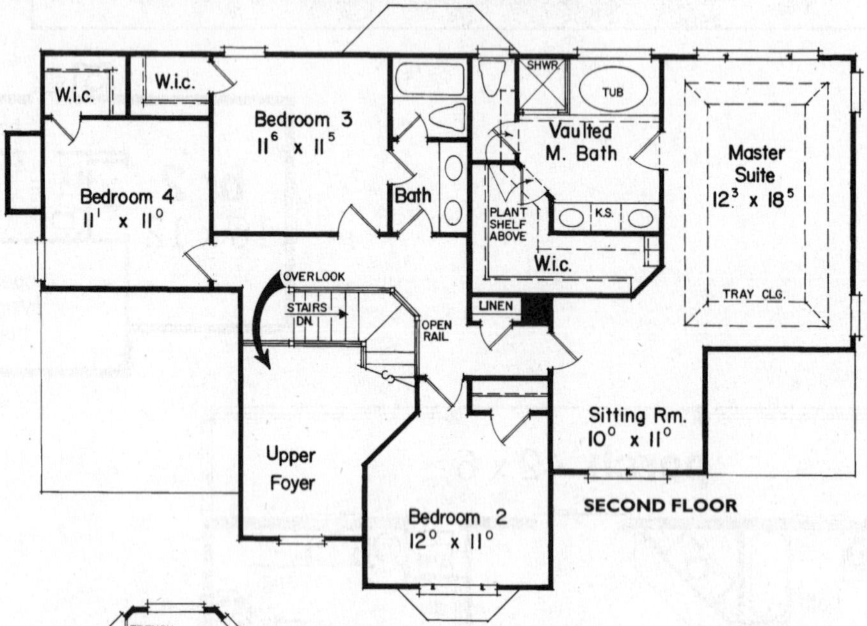
W.i.c.
W.i.c.
Bedroom 3
11^6 x 11^5
Bedroom 4
11^1 x 11^0
Bath
SHWR
TUB
Vaulted
M. Bath
PLANT
SHELF
ABOVE
K.S.
W.i.c.
Master
Suite
12^3 x 18^5
TRAY CLG.
LINEN
OVERLOOK
STAIRS
DN.
OPEN
RAIL
Upper
Foyer
Sitting Rm.
10^0 x 11^0
Bedroom 2
12^0 x 11^0

SECOND FLOOR

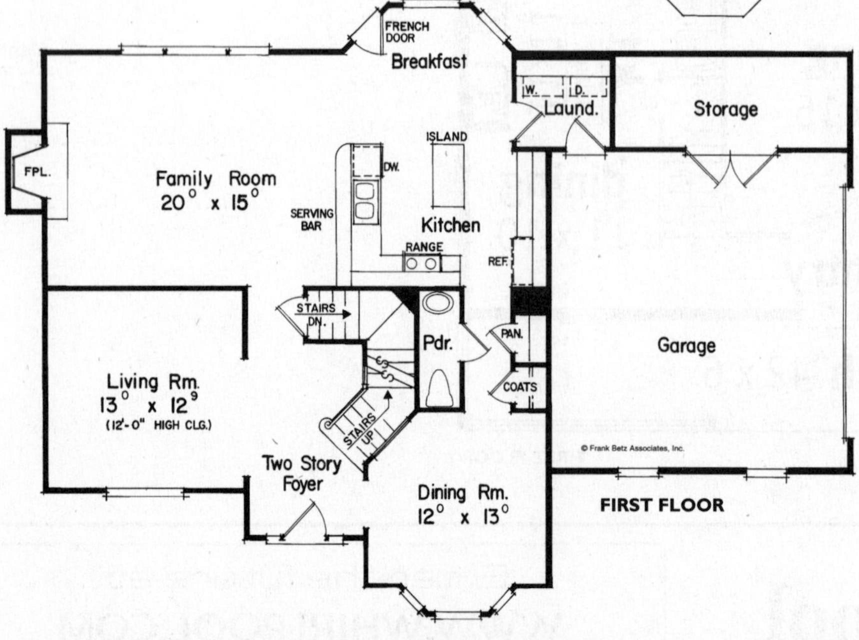
FRENCH
DOOR
Breakfast
W.
D.
Laund.
Storage
FPL.
Family Room
20^0 x 15^0
ISLAND
DW.
SERVING
BAR
Kitchen
RANGE
REF.
STAIRS
DN.
Pdr.
PAN.
COATS
Garage
Living Rm.
13^0 x 12^9
(12'-0" HIGH CLG.)
STAIRS
UP
Two Story
Foyer
Dining Rm.
12^0 x 13^0
© Frank Betz Associates, Inc.

FIRST FLOOR

Design 94938

See Order Pages and Index for Info

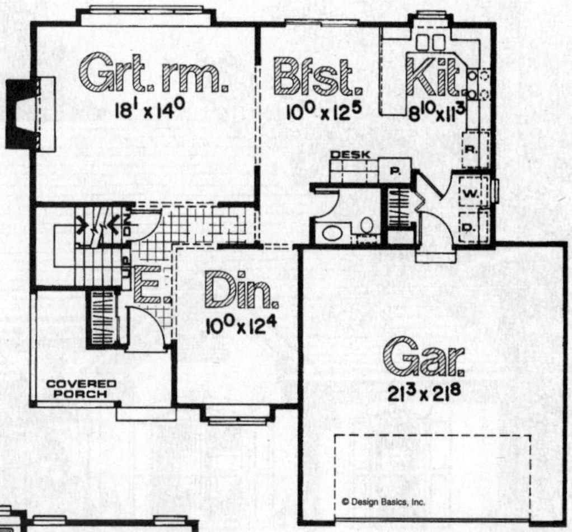
Grt. rm.
18¹ x 14⁰
Bfst.
10⁰ x 12⁵
Kit.
8¹⁰ x 11³
DESK
Din.
10⁰ x 12⁴
E.
COVERED PORCH
Gar.
21³ x 21⁸
© Design Basics, Inc.

FIRST FLOOR

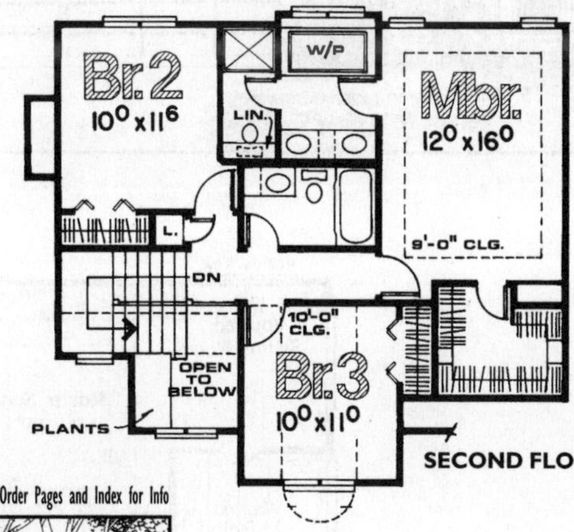
Br. 2
10⁰ x 11⁶
W/P
LIN.
Mbr.
12⁰ x 16⁰
9'-0" CLG.
L.
DN
10'-0" CLG.
Br. 3
10⁰ x 11⁰
OPEN TO BELOW
PLANTS

SECOND FLOOR

Units	Single
Price Code	B
Total Finished	1,650 sq. ft.
First Finished	891 sq. ft.
Second Finished	759 sq. ft.
Basement Unfinished	891 sq. ft.
Garage Unfinished	484 sq. ft.
Dimensions	44'x40'
Foundation	Basement
Bedrooms	3
Full Baths	2
Half Baths	1
Max Ridge Height	25'6"
Roof Framing	Stick
Exterior Walls	2x4

* Alternate foundation options available at an additonal charge. Please call 1-800-235-5700 for more information.

Design 93219

See Order Pages and Index for Info

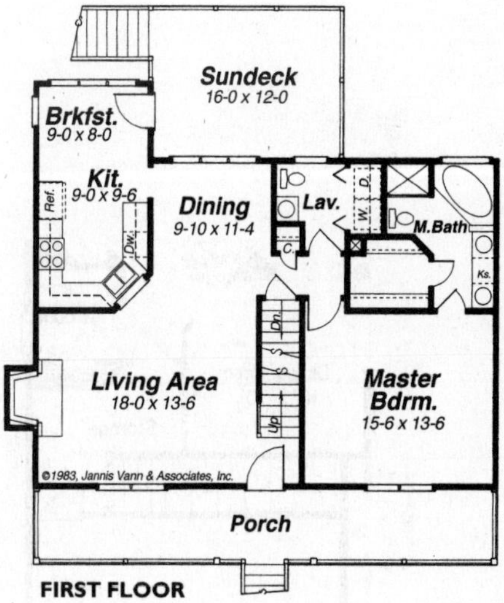
Sundeck
16-0 x 12-0
Brkfst.
9-0 x 8-0
Kit.
9-0 x 9-6
Dining
9-10 x 11-4
Lav.
M.Bath
Living Area
18-0 x 13-6
Master Bdrm.
15-6 x 13-6
©1983, Jannis Vann & Associates, Inc.
Porch

FIRST FLOOR

Units	Single
Price Code	B
Total Finished	1,668 sq. ft.
First Finished	1,057 sq. ft.
Second Finished	611 sq. ft.
Basement Unfinished	511 sq. ft.
Garage Unfinished	546 sq. ft.
Dimensions	40'4"x38'
Foundation	Basement
Bedrooms	3
Full Baths	2
Half Baths	1
First Ceiling	8'
Second Ceiling	8'
Max Ridge Height	23'
Roof Framing	Stick
Exterior Walls	2x4

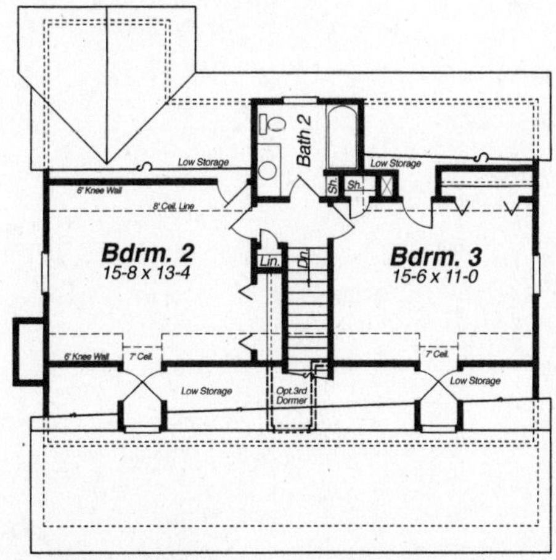
Low Storage
Bath 2
Low Storage
Bdrm. 2
15-8 x 13-4
Bdrm. 3
15-6 x 11-0
Low Storage
Opt.3rd Dormer
Low Storage

SECOND FLOOR

Design 98414

See Order Pages and Index for Info

Units	Single
Price Code	B
Total Finished	1,575 sq. ft.
Main Finished	1,575 sq. ft.
Basement Unfinished	1,658 sq. ft.
Garage Unfinished	459 sq. ft.
Dimensions	50'x52'6"
Foundation	Basement Crawlspace
Bedrooms	3
Full Baths	2
Main Ceiling	9'
Max Ridge Height	23'6"
Roof Framing	Stick
Exterior Walls	2x4

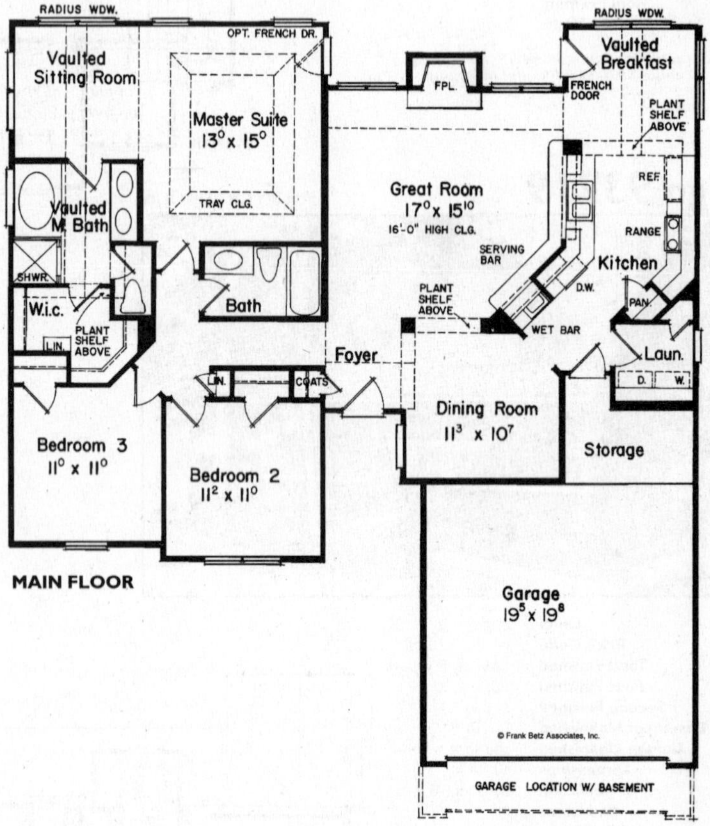
RADIUS WDW.
OPT. FRENCH DR.
Vaulted Sitting Room
Master Suite 13⁰ x 15⁰
TRAY CLG.
Vaulted M. Bath
SHWR.
W.i.c.
LIN.
PLANT SHELF ABOVE
Bath
FPL.
RADIUS WDW.
Vaulted Breakfast
FRENCH DOOR
PLANT SHELF ABOVE
Great Room 17⁰ x 15¹⁰
16'-0" HIGH CLG.
SERVING BAR
REF.
RANGE
Kitchen
D.W.
PAN.
PLANT SHELF ABOVE
WET BAR
Laun.
D. W.
Foyer
LIN.
COATS
Bedroom 3 11⁰ x 11⁰
Bedroom 2 11² x 11⁰
Dining Room 11³ x 10⁷
Storage
Garage 19⁵ x 19⁸
© Frank Betz Associates, Inc.
GARAGE LOCATION W/ BASEMENT

MAIN FLOOR

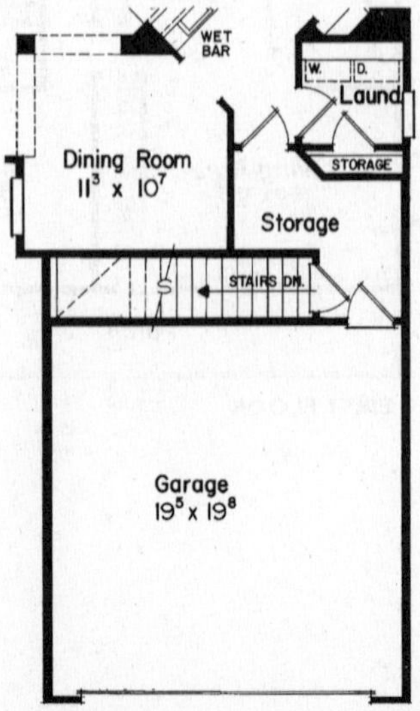
WET BAR
W. D.
Laund
STORAGE
Dining Room 11³ x 10⁷
Storage
STAIRS DN.
Garage 19⁵ x 19⁸

OPT. BASEMENT STAIR LOCATION

Design 97622

See Order Pages and Index for Info

Units	Single
Price Code	D
Total Finished	2,056 sq. ft.
Main Finished	2,056 sq. ft.
Bonus Unfinished	208 sq. ft.
Basement Unfinished	2,056 sq. ft.
Garage Unfinished	454 sq. ft.
Dimensions	60'6"x56'
Foundation	Basement Crawlspace
Bedrooms	4
Full Baths	2
Main Ceiling	9'
Second Ceiling	8'
Max Ridge Height	22'8"
Roof Framing	Stick
Exterior Walls	2x4

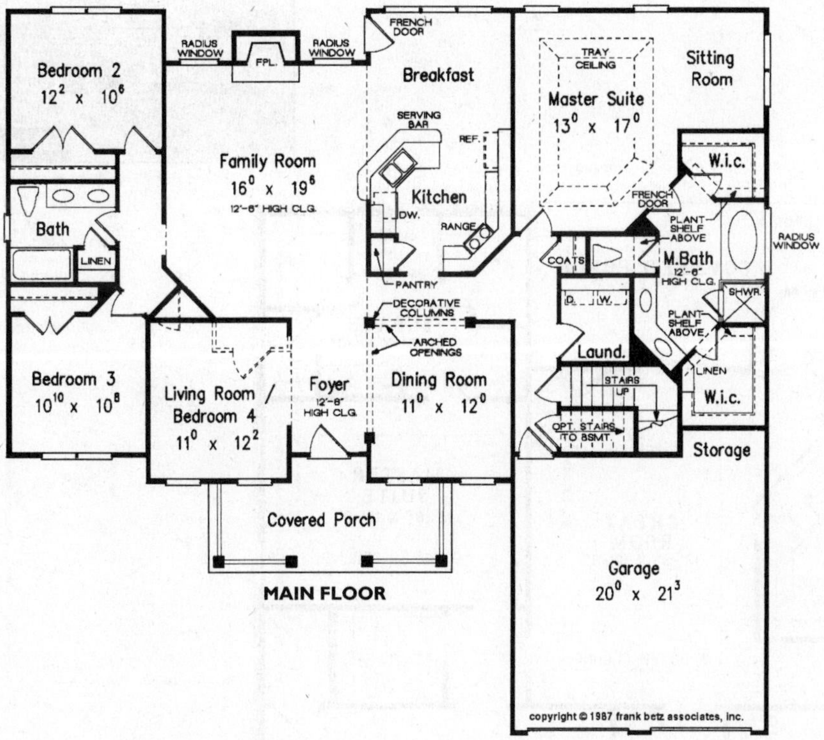
Bedroom 2
12^2 x 10^6
RADIUS WINDOW
FPL.
RADIUS WINDOW
FRENCH DOOR
Breakfast
TRAY CEILING
Master Suite
13^0 x 17^0
Sitting Room
Family Room
16^0 x 19^6
12'-6" HIGH CLG.
SERVING BAR
REF.
Kitchen
DW.
RANGE
W.i.c.
FRENCH DOOR
PLANT SHELF ABOVE
RADIUS WINDOW
Bath
LINEN
COATS
M.Bath
12'-6" HIGH CLG.
PANTRY
D
W
SHWR.
DECORATIVE COLUMNS
PLANT SHELF ABOVE
ARCHED OPENINGS
Laund.
LINEN
Bedroom 3
10^{10} x 10^8
Living Room / Bedroom 4
11^0 x 12^2
Foyer
12'-6" HIGH CLG.
Dining Room
11^0 x 12^0
STAIRS UP
W.i.c.
OPT. STAIRS TO BSMT.
Storage
Covered Porch
Garage
20^0 x 21^3
copyright © 1987 frank betz associates, inc.

MAIN FLOOR

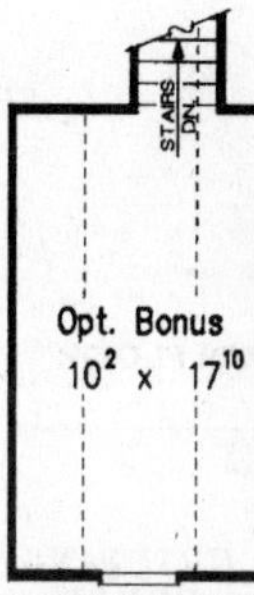
STAIRS DN.
Opt. Bonus
10^2 x 17^{10}

OPT. BONUS SPACE

Design 82026

See Order Pages and Index for Info

Units	Single
Price Code	A
Total Finished	1,485 sq. ft.
First Finished	1,485 sq. ft.
Garage Unfinished	415 sq. ft.
Porch Unfinished	180 sq. ft.
Dimensions	51'6"x49'10"
Foundation	Crawlspace Slab
Bedrooms	3
Full Baths	2
First Ceiling	9'
Roof Framing	Stick
Exterior Walls	2x4

Rear Elevation

MAIN FLOOR

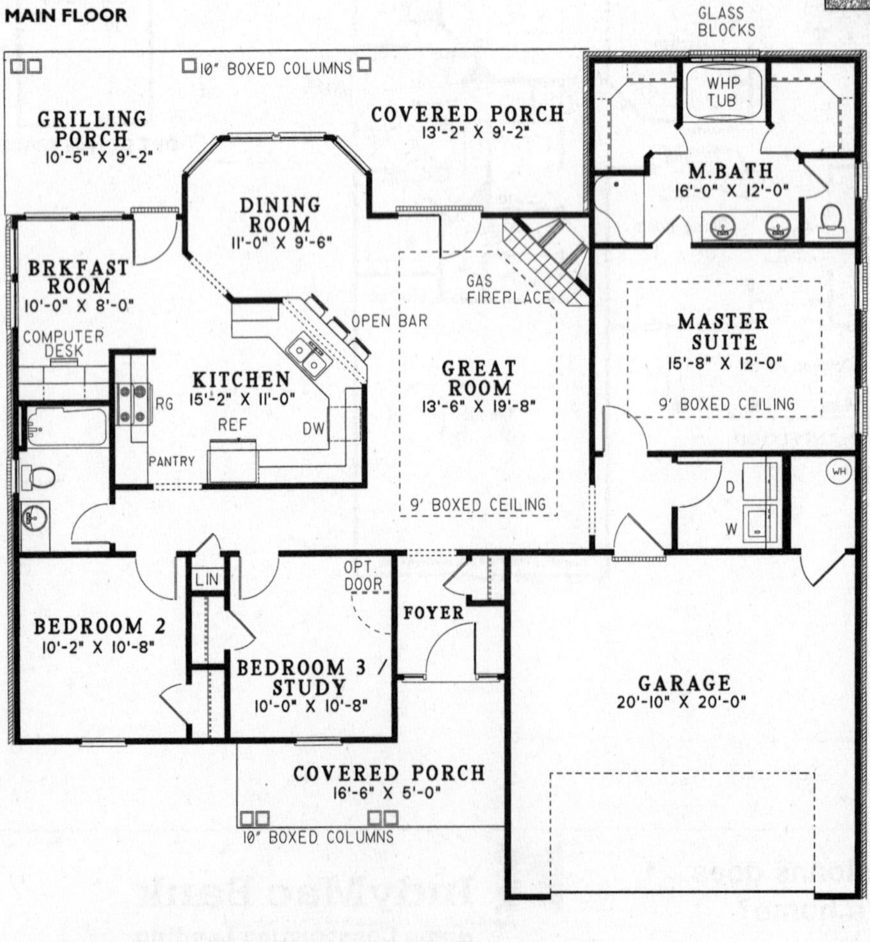
GLASS BLOCKS
10" BOXED COLUMNS
GRILLING PORCH
10'-5" X 9'-2"
COVERED PORCH
13'-2" X 9'-2"
WHP TUB
M.BATH
16'-0" X 12'-0"
DINING ROOM
11'-0" X 9'-6"
BRKFAST ROOM
10'-0" X 8'-0"
GAS FIREPLACE
OPEN BAR
MASTER SUITE
15'-8" X 12'-0"
9' BOXED CEILING
COMPUTER DESK
KITCHEN
15'-2" X 11'-0"
RG
REF
DW
PANTRY
GREAT ROOM
13'-6" X 19'-8"
9' BOXED CEILING
D
W
WH
LIN
OPT. DOOR
FOYER
BEDROOM 2
10'-2" X 10'-8"
BEDROOM 3 / STUDY
10'-0" X 10'-8"
GARAGE
20'-10" X 20'-0"
COVERED PORCH
16'-6" X 5'-0"
10" BOXED COLUMNS

Design 96819

See Order Pages and Index for Info

Units	Single
Price Code	C
Total Finished	1,840 sq. ft.
First Finished	1,014 sq. ft.
Second Finished	826 sq. ft.
Garage Unfinished	690 sq. ft.
Dimensions	62'7"x45'
Foundation	Basement Crawlspace Slab
Bedrooms	3
Full Baths	2
Half Baths	1
First Ceiling	9'
Roof Framing	Stick
Exterior Walls	2x4

SECOND FLOOR

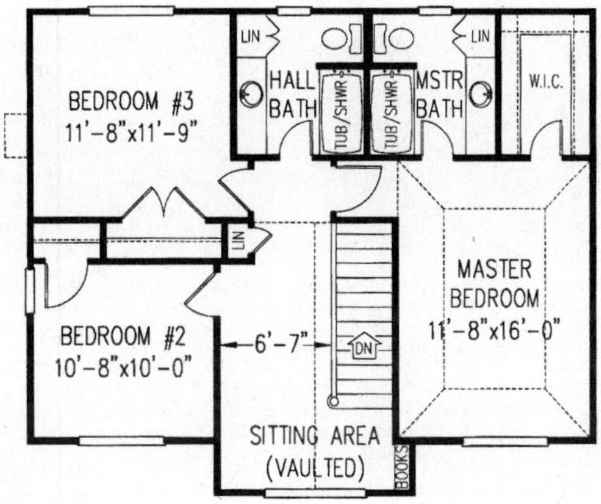
LIN
HALL BATH
TUB/SHWR
TUB/SHWR
MSTR BATH
LIN
W.I.C.
BEDROOM #3
11'-8"x11'-9"
LIN
BEDROOM #2
10'-8"x10'-0"
6'-7"
DN
MASTER BEDROOM
11'-8"x16'-0"
SITTING AREA
(VAULTED)
BOOKS

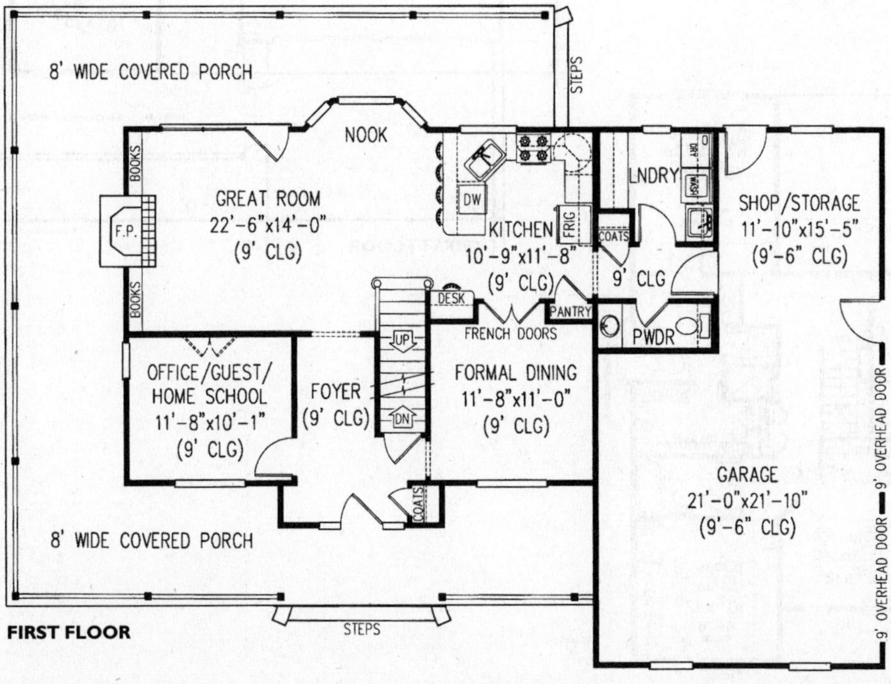
8' WIDE COVERED PORCH
STEPS
NOOK
BOOKS
F.P.
BOOKS
GREAT ROOM
22'-6"x14'-0"
(9' CLG)
DW
KITCHEN
10'-9"x11'-8"
(9' CLG)
FRIG
LNDRY
DRY
WASH
COATS
9' CLG
SHOP/STORAGE
11'-10"x15'-5"
(9'-6" CLG)
DESK
PANTRY
FRENCH DOORS
PWDR
UP
OFFICE/GUEST/
HOME SCHOOL
11'-8"x10'-1"
(9' CLG)
FOYER
(9' CLG)
DN
FORMAL DINING
11'-8"x11'-0"
(9' CLG)
COATS
GARAGE
21'-0"x21'-10"
(9'-6" CLG)
9' OVERHEAD DOOR
9' OVERHEAD DOOR
8' WIDE COVERED PORCH
STEPS

FIRST FLOOR

Design 99483

See Order Pages and Index for Info

G. McDONALD

Units	Single
Price Code	E
Total Finished	2,475 sq. ft.
First Finished	1,327 sq. ft.
Second Finished	1,148 sq. ft.
Dimensions	46'x49'4"
Foundation	Basement
Bedrooms	4
Full Baths	2
Half Baths	1
Max Ridge Height	29'8"

* Alternate foundation options available at an additional charge. Please call 1-800-235-5700 for more information.

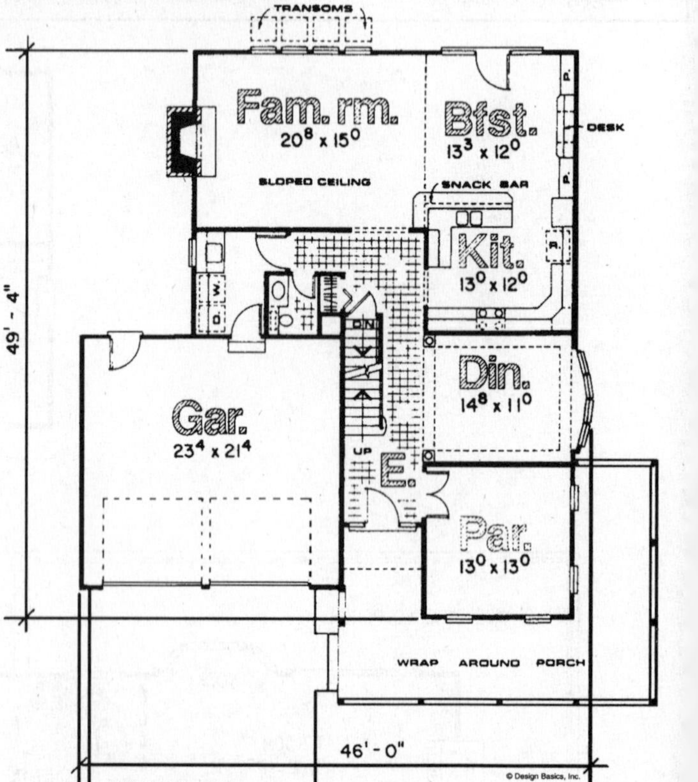
TRANSOMS
Fam. rm.
20⁸ x 15⁰
SLOPED CEILING
Bfst.
13³ x 12⁰
DESK
SNACK BAR
Kit.
13⁰ x 12⁰
Din.
14⁸ x 11⁰
Gar.
23⁴ x 21⁴
UP
DN
E.
Par.
13⁰ x 13⁰
WRAP AROUND PORCH
49' - 4"
46' - 0"
© Design Basics, Inc.

FIRST FLOOR

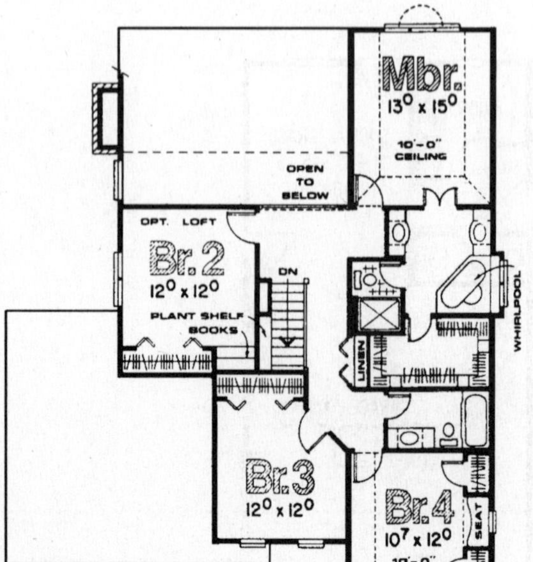
Mbr.
13⁰ x 15⁰
10'-0" CEILING
OPEN TO BELOW
OPT. LOFT
Br. 2
12⁰ x 12⁰
PLANT SHELF
BOOKS
DN
WHIRLPOOL
LINEN
Br. 3
12⁰ x 12⁰
Br. 4
10⁷ x 12⁰
10'-0" CLG.
SEAT

SECOND FLOOR

Design 94290

See Order Pages and Index for Info

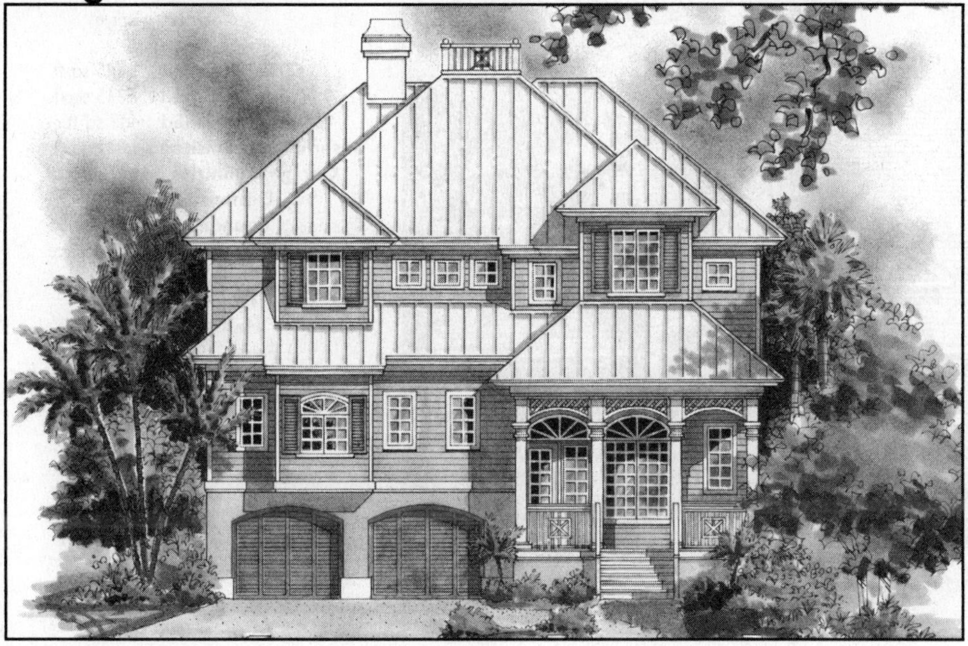

Units	Single
Price Code	E
Total Finished	2,374 sq. ft.
First Finished	1,510 sq. ft.
Second Finished	864 sq. ft.
Lower Unfinished	1,290 sq. ft.
Porch Unfinished	275 sq. ft.
Dimensions	44'x49'
Foundation	Basement
Bedrooms	3
Full Baths	3
Half Baths	1
Max Ridge Height	42'
Roof Framing	Truss
Exterior Walls	2x6

* Alternate foundation options available at an additional charge. Please call 1-800-235-5700 for more information.

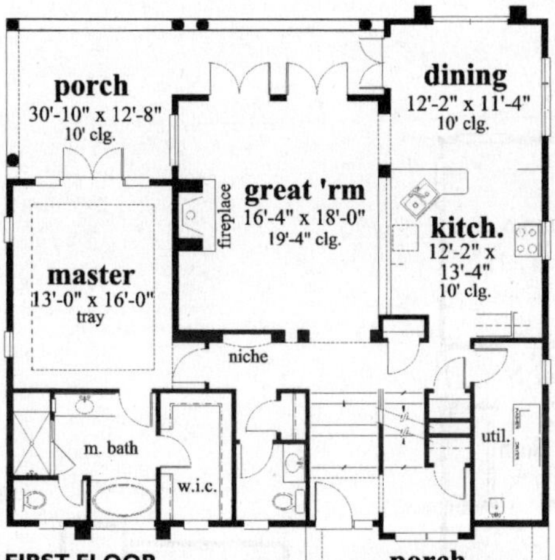
porch
30'-10" x 12'-8"
10' clg.
dining
12'-2" x 11'-4"
10' clg.
great 'rm
16'-4" x 18'-0"
19'-4" clg.
fireplace
kitch.
12'-2" x
13'-4"
10' clg.
master
13'-0" x 16'-0"
tray
niche
m. bath
w.i.c.
util.
porch
19'-8" x 8'-0"

FIRST FLOOR

open deck
30'-10" x 12'-8"
porch
8' clg.
porch
8' clg.
bedroom
12'-2" x 14'-0"
tray
open
bedroom
13'-2" x 12'-0"
tray
bath
w.i.c.
bath
loft
10'-4" x 11'-4"
8' clg.
open

SECOND FLOOR

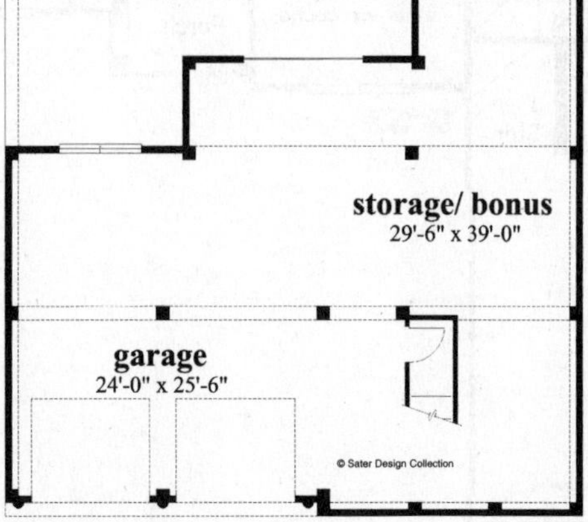
storage/ bonus
29'-6" x 39'-0"
garage
24'-0" x 25'-6"
© Sater Design Collection

LOWER FLOOR

Design 98425

See Order Pages and Index for Info

Units	Single
Price Code	C
Total Finished	1,845 sq. ft.
First Finished	1,845 sq. ft.
Bonus Unfinished	409 sq. ft.
Basement Unfinished	1,845 sq. ft.
Garage Unfinished	529 sq. ft.
Dimensions	56'x60'
Foundation	Basement Crawlspace
Bedrooms	3
Full Baths	2
Half Baths	1
First Ceiling	9'
Max Ridge Height	26'6"
Roof Framing	Stick
Exterior Walls	2x4

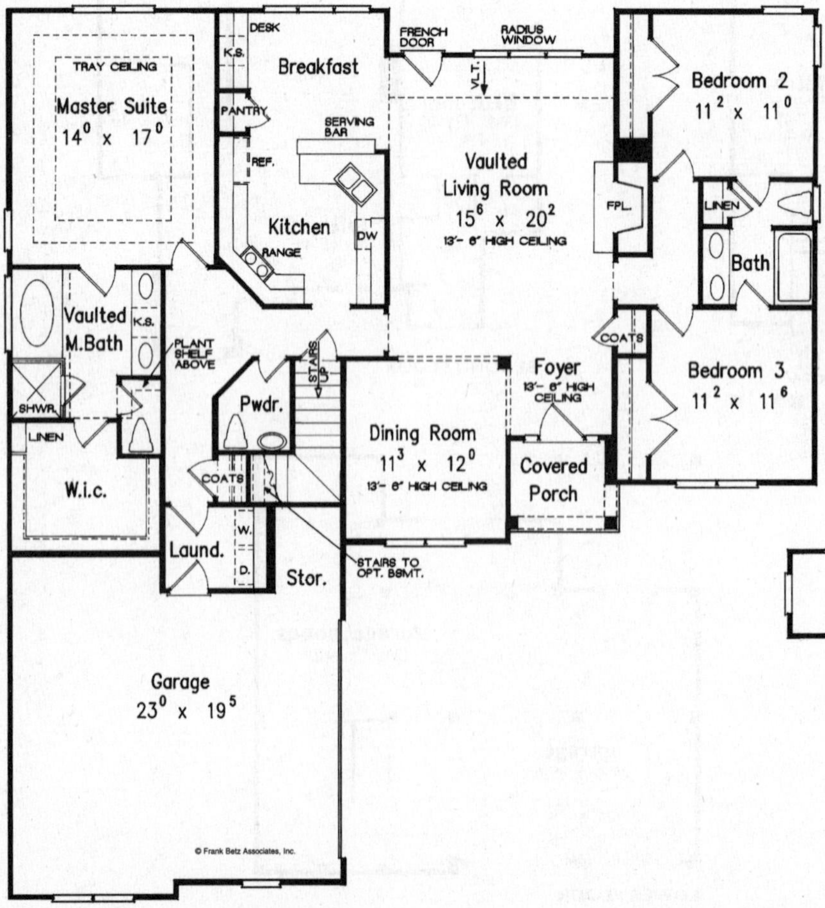
TRAY CEILING
Master Suite
14⁰ x 17⁰
K.S.
DESK
Breakfast
PANTRY
REF.
SERVING BAR
Kitchen
DW
RANGE
FRENCH DOOR
RADIUS WINDOW
V.T.
Vaulted Living Room
15⁶ x 20²
13'-6" HIGH CEILING
FPL.
Bedroom 2
11² x 11⁰
LINEN
Bath
COATS
Bedroom 3
11² x 11⁶
Vaulted M.Bath
K.S.
PLANT SHELF ABOVE
SHWR.
LINEN
W.i.c.
Pwdr.
STAIRS UP
COATS
Dining Room
11³ x 12⁰
13'-6" HIGH CEILING
Foyer
13'-6" HIGH CEILING
Covered Porch
Laund.
W.
D.
Stor.
STAIRS TO OPT. BSMT.
Garage
23⁰ x 19⁵
© Frank Betz Associates, Inc.

MAIN FLOOR

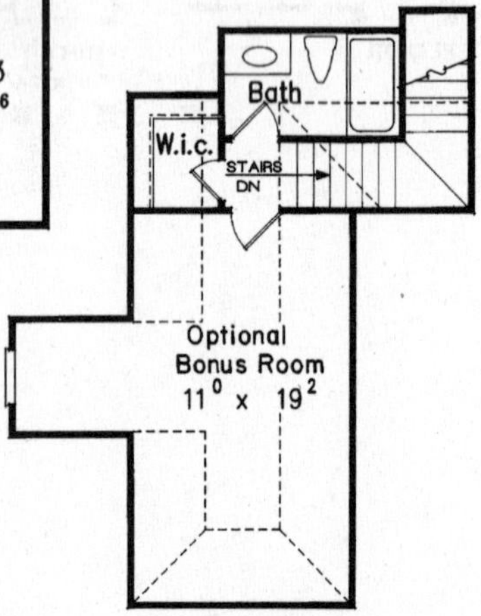
Bath
W.i.c.
STAIRS DN
Optional Bonus Room
11⁰ x 19²

BONUS SPACE

Design 90466

See Order Pages and Index for Info

Units	Single
Price Code	C
Total Finished	1,845 sq. ft.
Main Finished	1,845 sq. ft.
Garage Unfinished	512 sq. ft.
Porch Unfinished	38 sq. ft.
Dimensions	57'2"x54'10"
Foundation	Crawlspace Slab
Bedrooms	3
Full Baths	2
Half Baths	1
Main Ceiling	8'
Max Ridge Height	23'10"
Roof Framing	Stick
Exterior Walls	2x4

MAIN FLOOR

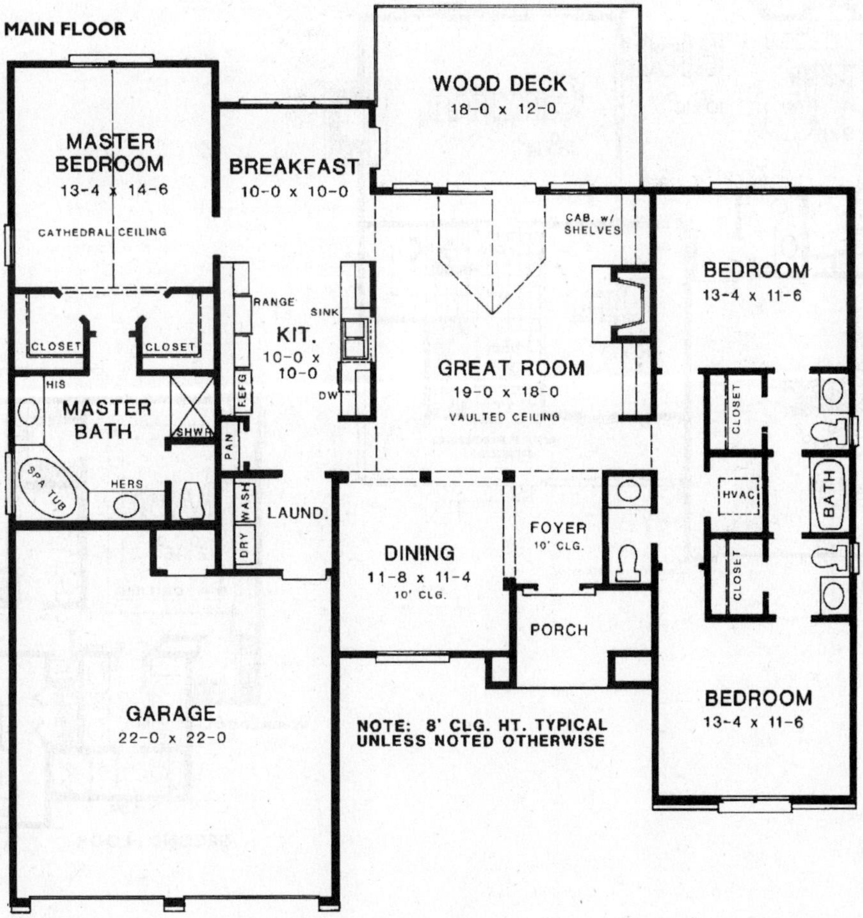
WOOD DECK
18-0 x 12-0
MASTER BEDROOM
13-4 x 14-6
CATHEDRAL CEILING
BREAKFAST
10-0 x 10-0
CAB. w/ SHELVES
BEDROOM
13-4 x 11-6
RANGE
SINK
KIT.
10-0 x 10-0
DW
REFG
CLOSET
CLOSET
HIS
MASTER BATH
SHWR
PAN
SPA TUB
HERS
WASH
DRY
LAUND.
GREAT ROOM
19-0 x 18-0
VAULTED CEILING
CLOSET
HVAC
BATH
CLOSET
DINING
11-8 x 11-4
10' CLG.
FOYER
10' CLG.
PORCH
GARAGE
22-0 x 22-0
NOTE: 8' CLG. HT. TYPICAL UNLESS NOTED OTHERWISE
BEDROOM
13-4 x 11-6

Design 99491

See Order Pages and Index for Info

Units	Single
Price Code	C
Total Finished	1,846 sq. ft.
First Finished	919 sq. ft.
Second Finished	927 sq. ft.
Garage Unfinished	414 sq. ft.
Dimensions	44'x40'
Foundation	Basement Slab
Bedrooms	4
Full Baths	2
Half Baths	1
Max Ridge Height	26'10"
Roof Framing	Stick
Exterior Walls	2x4

* Alternate foundation options available at an additional charge. Please call 1-800-235-5700 for more information.

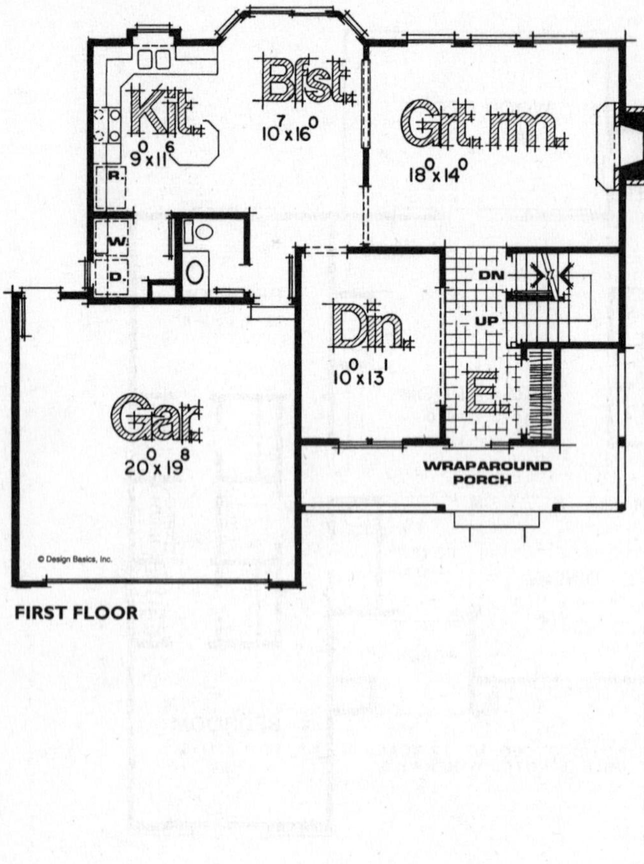
Kit.
9^0 x 11^6
Bfst.
10^7 x 16^0
Grt.rm.
18^0 x 14^0
R.
W.
D.
DN
UP
Din.
10^0 x 13^1
E.
Gar.
20^0 x 19^8
WRAPAROUND PORCH
© Design Basics, Inc.

FIRST FLOOR

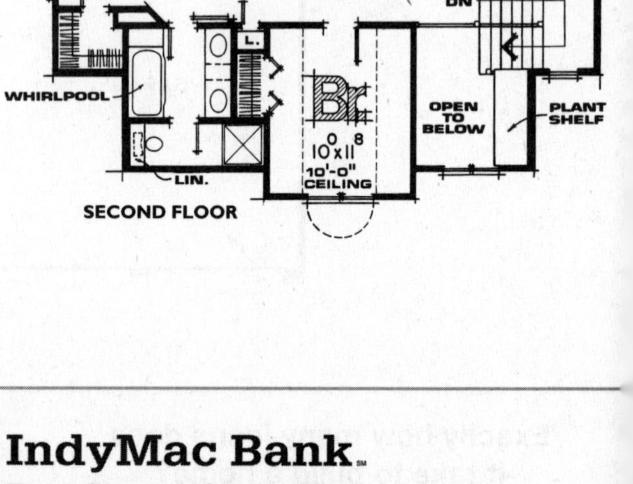
Mbr.
12^0 x 16^0
9'-4" CEILING
Br.
10^0 x 11^6
Br.
10^0 x 11^6
DN
L.
WHIRLPOOL
Br.
10^0 x 11^8
10'-0" CEILING
OPEN TO BELOW
PLANT SHELF
LIN.

SECOND FLOOR

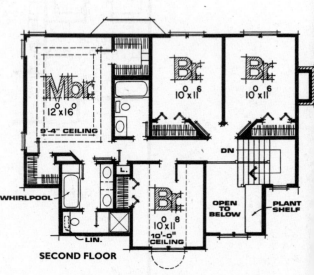

Design 94936

See Order Pages and Index for Info

Units	Single
Price Code	D
Total Finished	2,078 sq. ft.
First Finished	1,113 sq. ft.
Second Finished	965 sq. ft.
Basement Unfinished	1,113 sq. ft.
Garage Unfinished	486 sq. ft.
Dimensions	46'x41'5"
Foundation	Basement
Bedrooms	4
Full Baths	2
Half Baths	1
First Ceiling	8'
Second Ceiling	8'
Max Ridge Height	25'5"
Roof Framing	Stick
Exterior Walls	2x4

* Alternate foundation options available at an additional charge. Please call 1-800-235-5700 for more information.

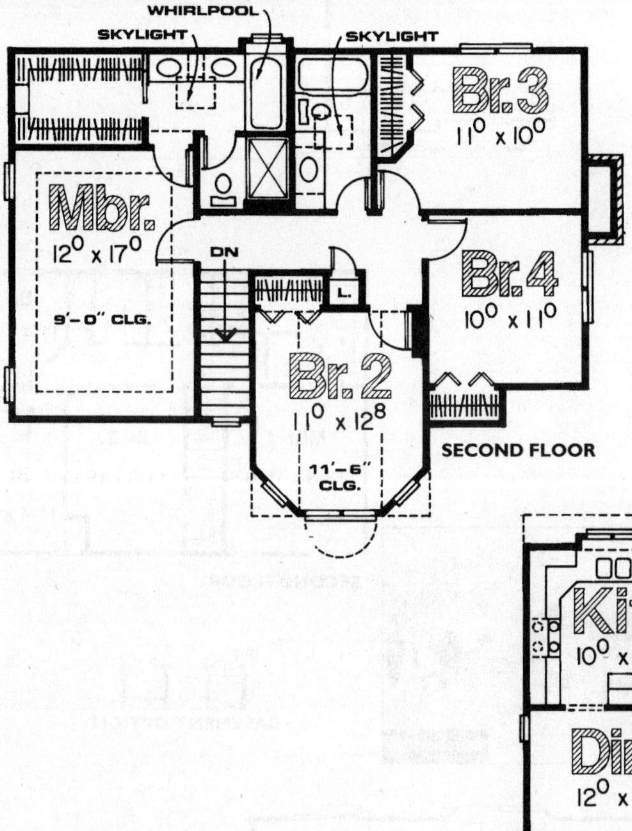
WHIRLPOOL
SKYLIGHT
SKYLIGHT
Br.3
11^0 x 10^0
Mbr.
12^0 x 17^0
9'-0" CLG.
DN
L.
Br.4
10^0 x 11^0
Br.2
11^0 x 12^8
11'-6" CLG.
SECOND FLOOR

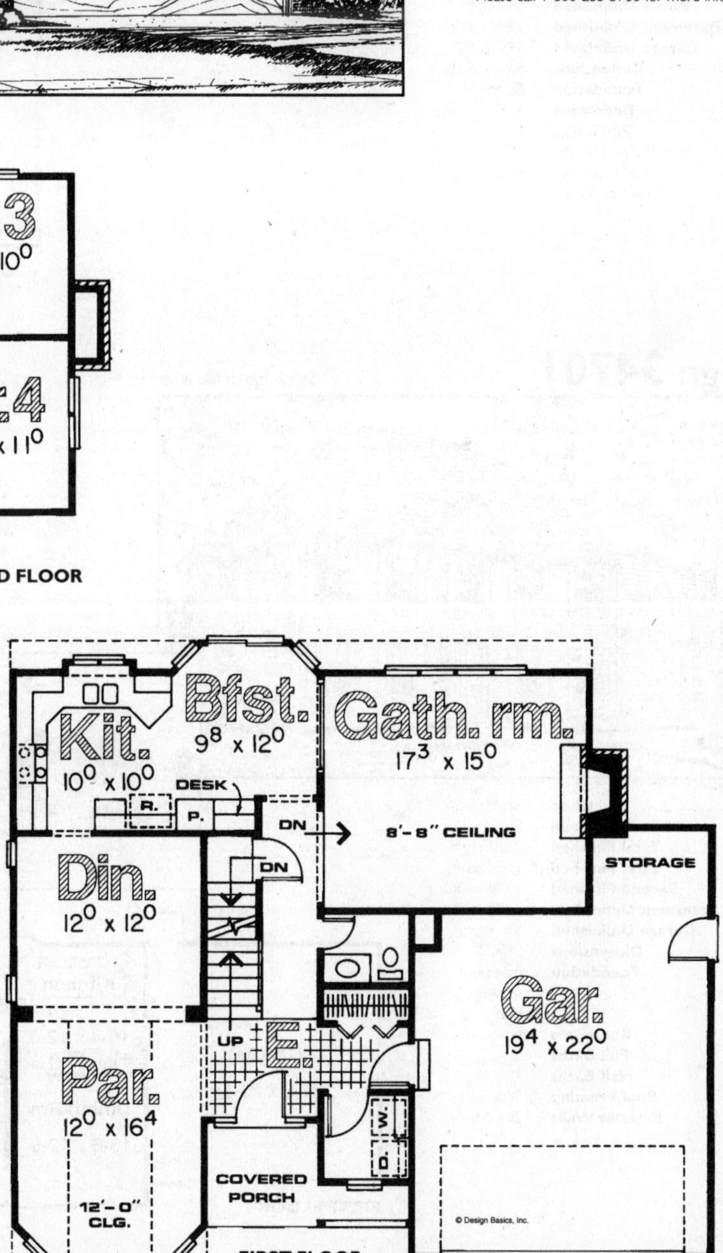
Kit.
10^0 x 10^0
Bfst.
9^8 x 12^0
Gath. rm.
17^3 x 15^0
DESK
R.
P.
DN
8'-8" CEILING
DN
STORAGE
Din.
12^0 x 12^0
Gar.
19^4 x 22^0
UP
E.
W.
D.
Par.
12^0 x 16^4
12'-0" CLG.
COVERED PORCH
© Design Basics, Inc.
FIRST FLOOR

Design 97615

See Order Pages and Index for Info

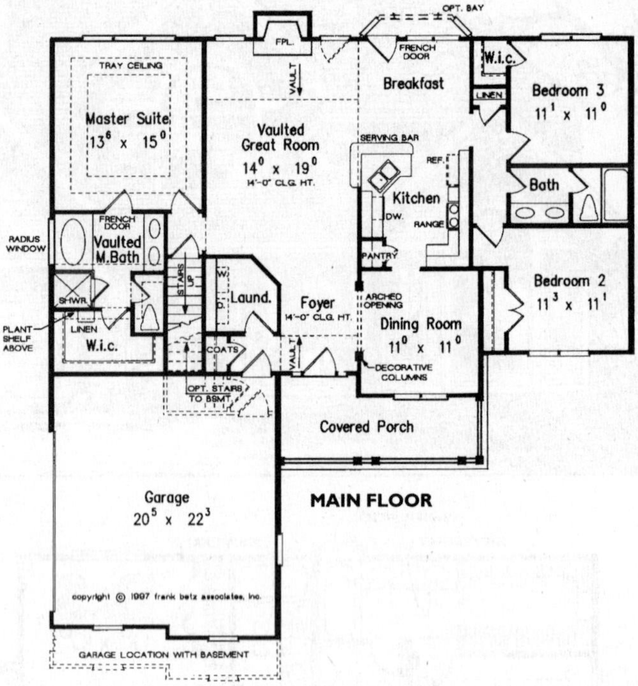

OPT. BAY
FPL.
FRENCH DOOR
TRAY CEILING
Master Suite 13⁶ x 15⁰
VAULT
Vaulted Great Room 14⁰ x 19⁰ 14'-0" CLG. HT.
Breakfast
W.i.c.
LINEN
Bedroom 3 11¹ x 11⁰
SERVING BAR
REF.
Kitchen
DW.
RANGE
Bath
RADIUS WINDOW
FRENCH DOOR
Vaulted M.Bath
PANTRY
Bedroom 2 11³ x 11¹
SHWR.
STAIRS UP
Laund.
Foyer 14'-0" CLG. HT.
ARCHED OPENING
Dining Room 11⁰ x 11⁰
PLANT SHELF ABOVE
LINEN
W.i.c.
COATS
DECORATIVE COLUMNS
OPT. STAIRS TO BSMT.
Covered Porch
Garage 20⁵ x 22³
copyright © 1997 frank betz associates, inc.
GARAGE LOCATION WITH BASEMENT

MAIN FLOOR

Units	Single
Price Code	B
Total Finished	1,571 sq. ft.
Main Finished	1,571 sq. ft.
Bonus Unfinished	334 sq. ft.
Basement Unfinished	1,642 sq. ft.
Garage Unfinished	483 sq. ft.
Dimensions	53'6"x55'10"
Foundation	Basement
Bedrooms	3
Full Baths	2
Max Ridge Height	23'6"
Roof Framing	Stick
Exterior Walls	2x4

Design 34701

See Order Pages and Index for Info

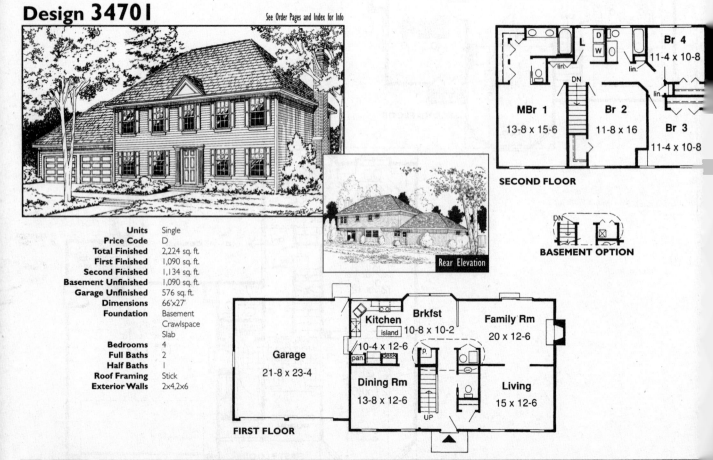

Rear Elevation

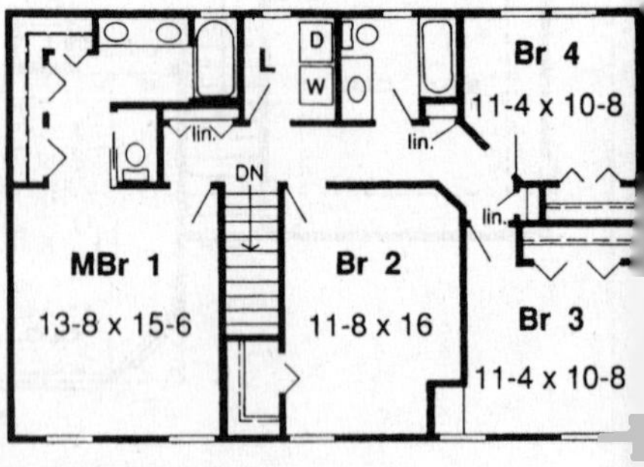

Br 4 11-4 x 10-8
lin.
DN
MBr 1 13-8 x 15-6
Br 2 11-8 x 16
Br 3 11-4 x 10-8

SECOND FLOOR

DN

BASEMENT OPTION

Units	Single
Price Code	D
Total Finished	2,224 sq. ft.
First Finished	1,090 sq. ft.
Second Finished	1,134 sq. ft.
Basement Unfinished	1,090 sq. ft.
Garage Unfinished	576 sq. ft.
Dimensions	66'x27'
Foundation	Basement Crawlspace Slab
Bedrooms	4
Full Baths	2
Half Baths	1
Roof Framing	Stick
Exterior Walls	2x4,2x6

Kitchen
island
10-4 x 12-6
pan.
desk
Brkfst 10-8 x 10-2
Family Rm 20 x 12-6
Garage 21-8 x 23-4
Dining Rm 13-8 x 12-6
UP
Living 15 x 12-6

FIRST FLOOR

Design 99193

See Order Pages and Index for Info

Units	Single
Price Code	H
Total Finished	3,040 sq. ft.
First Finished	2,190 sq. ft.
Second Finished	850 sq. ft.
Garage Unfinished	945 sq. ft.
Porch Unfinished	180 sq. ft.
Dimensions	66'8"x63'
Foundation	Basement
Bedrooms	4
Full Baths	2
Half Baths	1
3/4 Baths	1
First Ceiling	9'
Second Ceiling	8'
Max Ridge Height	35'
Roof Framing	Truss
Exterior Walls	2x6

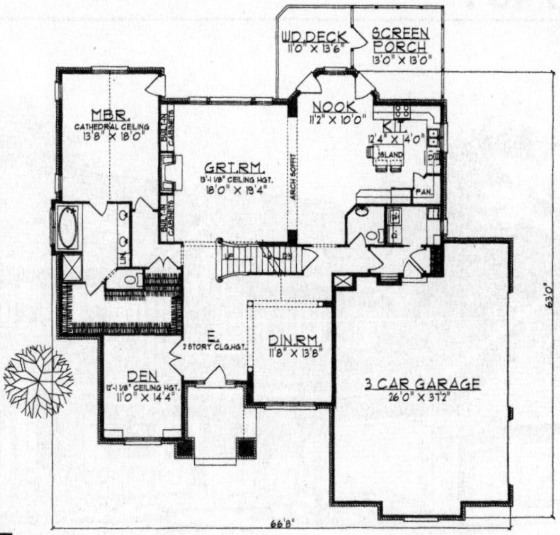
WD.DECK
11'0" X 13'6"
SCREEN PORCH
13'0" X 13'0"
MBR.
CATHEDRAL CEILING
13'8" X 18'0"
NOOK
11'2" X 10'0"
GRT.RM.
18'0" X 19'4"
ISLAND
DIN.RM.
11'8" X 13'8"
DEN
11'0" X 14'4"
3 CAR GARAGE
26'0" X 37'2"
66'8"
63'0"

FIRST FLOOR

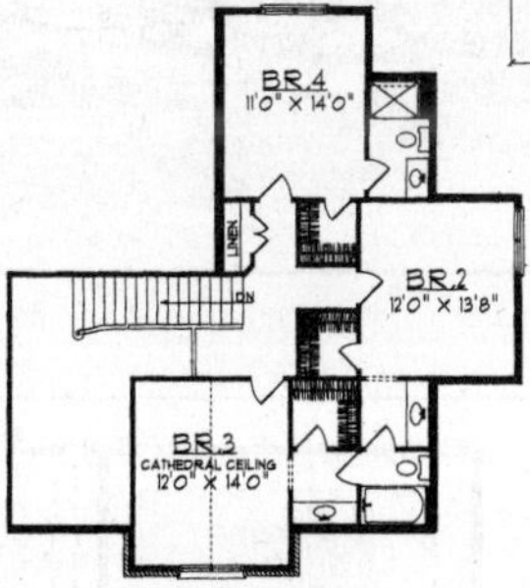
BR.4
11'0" X 14'0"
BR.2
12'0" X 13'8"
BR.3
CATHEDRAL CEILING
12'0" X 14'0"

SECOND FLOOR

Design 34043

See Order Pages and Index for Info

Rear Elevation

Units	Single
Price Code	B
Total Finished	1,583 sq. ft.
Main Finished	1,583 sq. ft.
Basement Unfinished	1,573 sq. ft.
Garage Unfinished	484 sq. ft.
Dimensions	70'x46'
Foundation	Basement Crawlspace Slab
Bedrooms	3
Full Baths	2
Main Ceiling	8'
Max Ridge Height	20'
Roof Framing	Stick
Exterior Walls	2x4,2x6

MAIN FLOOR

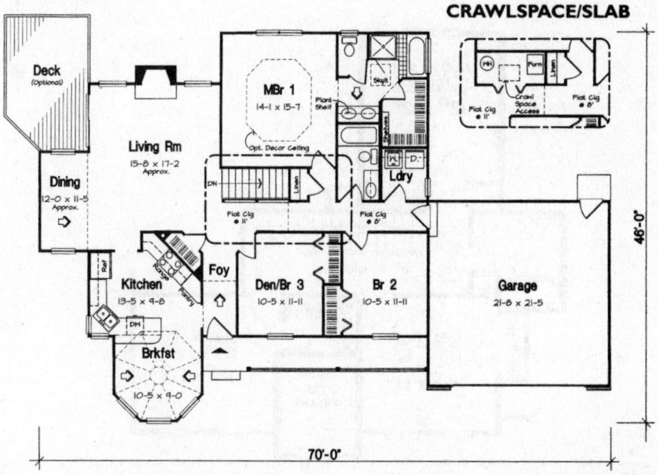
Deck
(Optional)
MBr 1
14-1 x 15-7
Living Rm
15-8 x 17-2
Approx.
Dining
12-0 x 11-5
Approx.
Ldry
Kitchen
13-5 x 9-8
Foy
Den/Br 3
10-5 x 11-11
Br 2
10-5 x 11-11
Garage
21-8 x 21-5
Brkfst
10-5 x 9-0
70'-0"
46'-0"

OPTIONAL CRAWLSPACE/SLAB

Design 99431

See Order Pages and Index for Info

Units	Single
Price Code	E
Total Finished	2,277 sq. ft.
First Finished	1,570 sq. ft.
Second Finished	707 sq. ft.
Basement Unfinished	1,570 sq. ft.
Garage Unfinished	504 sq. ft.
Dimensions	54'x52'
Foundation	Basement
Bedrooms	4
Full Baths	2
Half Baths	1
First Ceiling	8'
Second Ceiling	8'
Max Ridge Height	24'9"
Roof Framing	Stick
Exterior Walls	2x4

* Alternate foundation options available at an additional charge. Please call 1-800-235-5700 for more information.

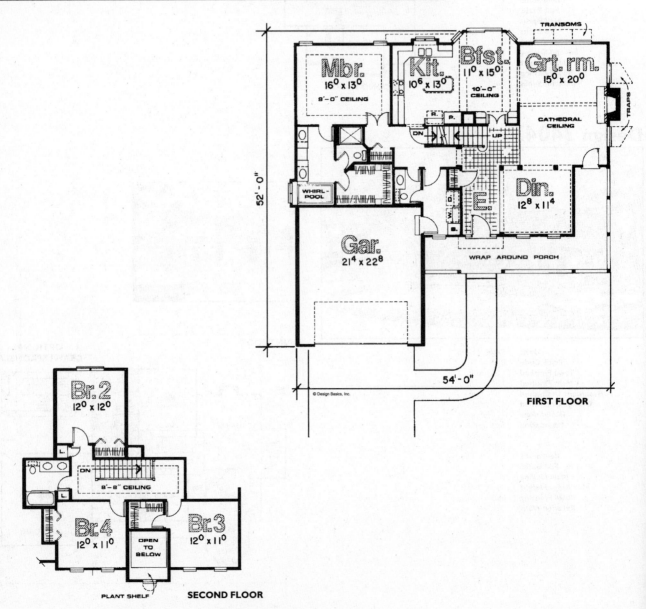

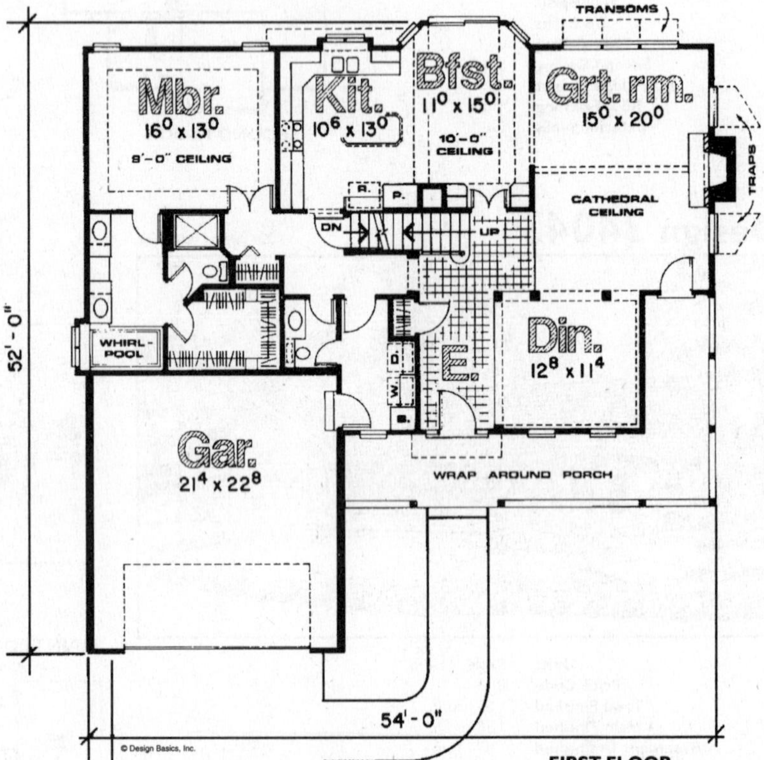
TRANSOMS
Mbr.
16⁰ x 13⁰
9'-0" CEILING
Kit.
10⁶ x 13⁰
Bfst.
11⁰ x 15⁰
10'-0" CEILING
Grt. rm.
15⁰ x 20⁰
TRAPS
CATHEDRAL CEILING
R.
P.
DN
UP
WHIRL-POOL
Din.
12⁸ x 11⁴
E.
D.
W.
B.
Gar.
21⁴ x 22⁸
WRAP AROUND PORCH
52'-0"
54'-0"
© Design Basics, Inc.

FIRST FLOOR

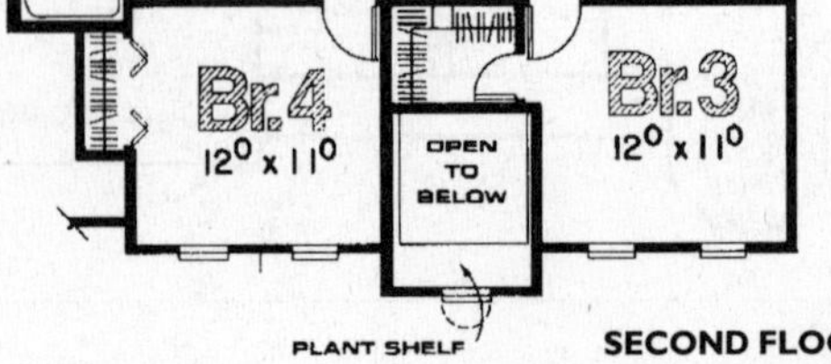
Br. 2
12⁰ x 12⁰
L.
DN
8'-8" CEILING
L.
Br. 4
12⁰ x 11⁰
OPEN TO BELOW
Br. 3
12⁰ x 11⁰
PLANT SHELF

SECOND FLOOR

Design 96945

See Order Pages and Index for Info

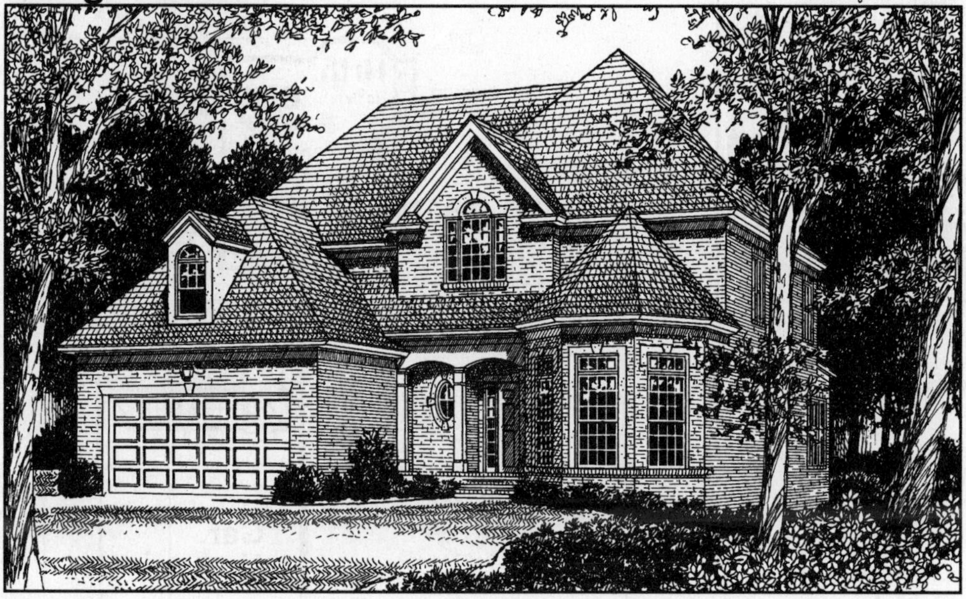

Units	Single
Price Code	H
Total Finished	3,042 sq. ft.
First Finished	1,725 sq. ft.
Second Finished	1,317 sq. ft.
Garage Unfinished	435 sq. ft.
Porch Unfinished	46 sq. ft.
Dimensions	45'10"x59'2"
Foundation	Crawlspace
Bedrooms	4
Full Baths	2
Half Baths	1
3/4 Baths	1
First Ceiling	9'
Second Ceiling	9'
Vaulted Ceiling	12'
Max Ridge Height	35'
Roof Framing	Stick
Exterior Walls	2x4

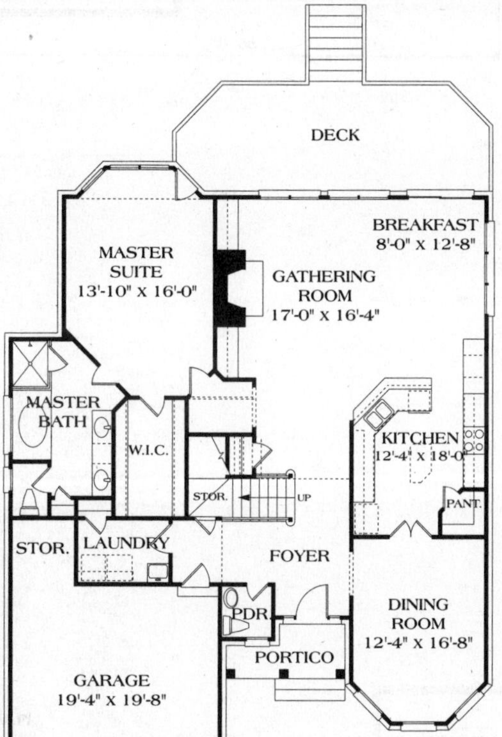
DECK
MASTER SUITE 13'-10" X 16'-0"
GATHERING ROOM 17'-0" X 16'-4"
BREAKFAST 8'-0" X 12'-8"
MASTER BATH
W.I.C.
KITCHEN 12'-4" X 18'-0"
STOR.
UP
PANT.
STOR.
LAUNDRY
FOYER
PDR
DINING ROOM 12'-4" X 16'-8"
PORTICO
GARAGE 19'-4" X 19'-8"

FIRST FLOOR

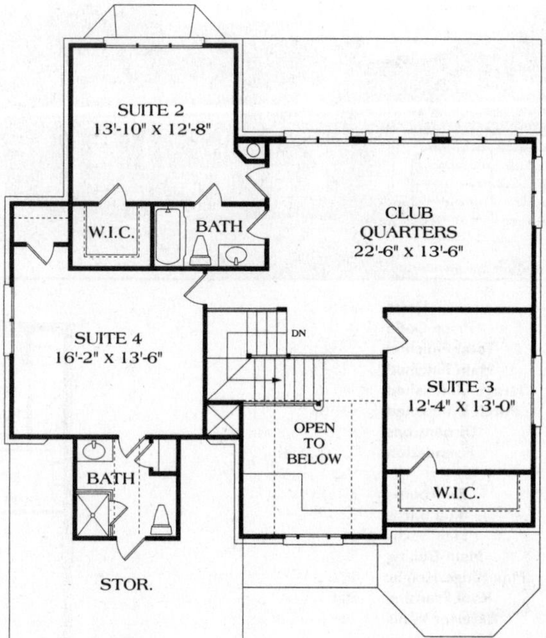
SUITE 2 13'-10" X 12'-8"
W.I.C.
BATH
CLUB QUARTERS 22'-6" X 13'-6"
SUITE 4 16'-2" X 13'-6"
DN
SUITE 3 12'-4" X 13'-0"
OPEN TO BELOW
BATH
W.I.C.
STOR.

SECOND FLOOR

Design 97912

See Order Pages and Index for Info

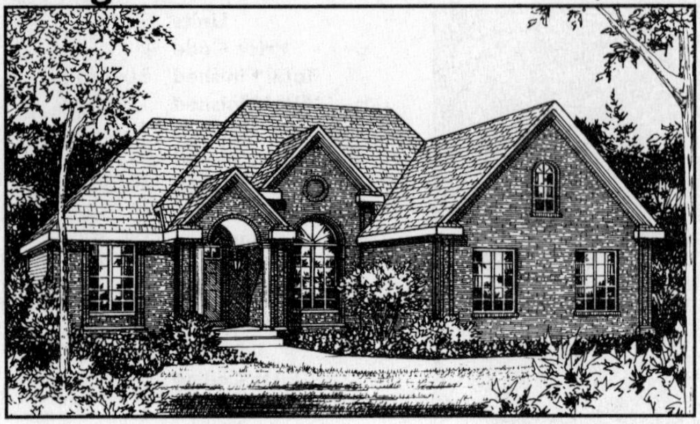

Units	Single
Price Code	C
Total Finished	1,995 sq. ft.
Main Finished	1,995 sq. ft.
Bonus Unfinished	308 sq. ft.
Basement Unfinished	1,995 sq. ft.
Dimensions	56'x62'
Foundation	Basement
Bedrooms	3
Full Baths	2
Main Ceiling	9'
Max Ridge Height	26'
Exterior Walls	2x4

* Alternate foundation options available at an additional charge. Please call 1-800-235-5700 for more information.

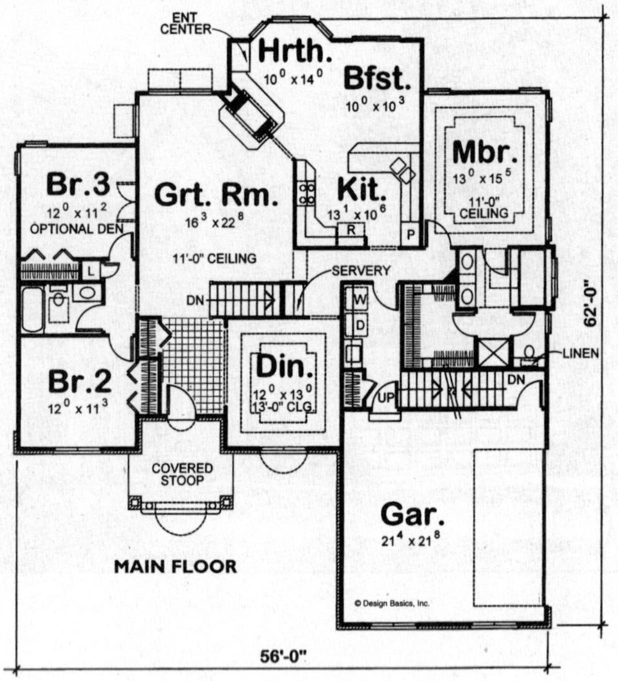
ENT CENTER
Hrth.
10⁰ x 14⁰
Bfst.
10⁰ x 10³
Mbr.
13⁰ x 15⁵
11'-0" CEILING
Br.3
12⁰ x 11²
OPTIONAL DEN
Grt. Rm.
16³ x 22⁸
11'-0" CEILING
Kit.
13¹ x 10⁶
SERVERY
DN
LINEN
Br.2
12⁰ x 11³
Din.
12⁰ x 13⁰
13'-0" CLG.
UP
DN
COVERED STOOP
Gar.
21⁴ x 21⁸
© Design Basics, Inc.
62'-0"
56'-0"

MAIN FLOOR

BONUS

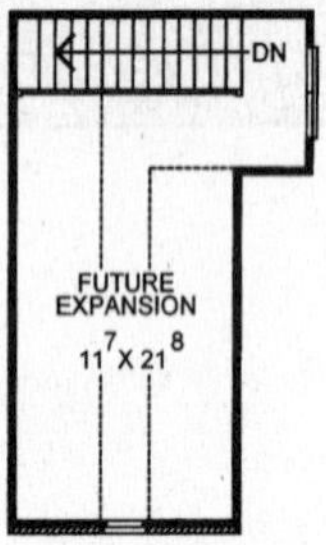
DN
FUTURE EXPANSION
11⁷ X 21⁸

Design 96506

See Order Pages and Index for Info

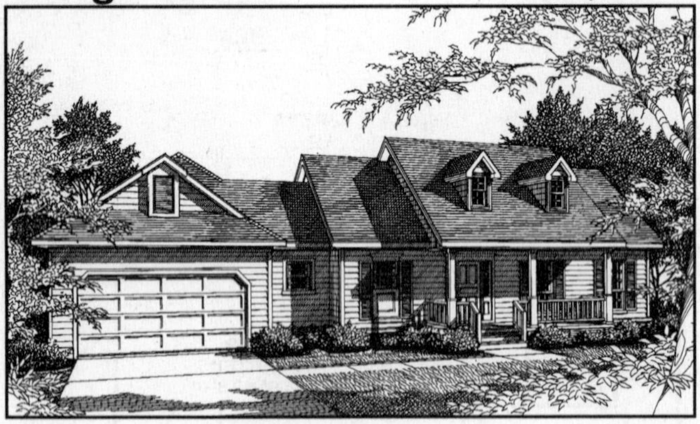

Units	Single
Price Code	B
Total Finished	1,654 sq. ft.
Main Finished	1,654 sq. ft.
Garage Unfinished	480 sq. ft.
Porch Unfinished	401 sq. ft.
Dimensions	68'x46'
Foundation	Crawlspace Slab
Bedrooms	3
Full Baths	2
Half Baths	1
Main Ceiling	9'
Max Ridge Height	21'
Roof Framing	Stick
Exterior Walls	2x4

MAIN FLOOR

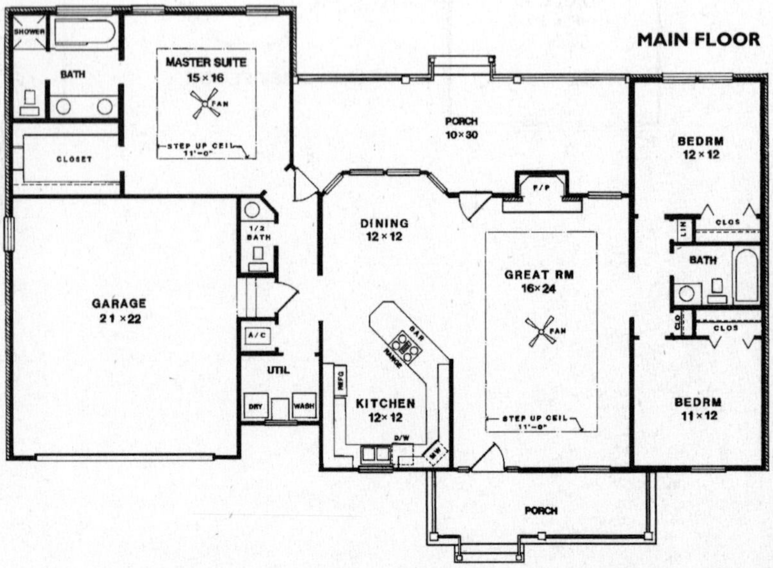
SHOWER
BATH
CLOSET
MASTER SUITE
15×16
FAN
STEP UP CEIL
11'-0"
PORCH
10×30
BEDRM
12×12
F/P
DINING
12×12
1/2 BATH
CLOS
LIN
BATH
GREAT RM
16×24
FAN
GARAGE
21×22
A/C
UTIL
BAR
RANGE
CLO
CLOS
DRY
WASH
REFG
KITCHEN
12×12
D/W
STEP UP CEIL
11'-0"
BEDRM
11×12
PORCH

Design 91838

See Order Pages and Index for Info

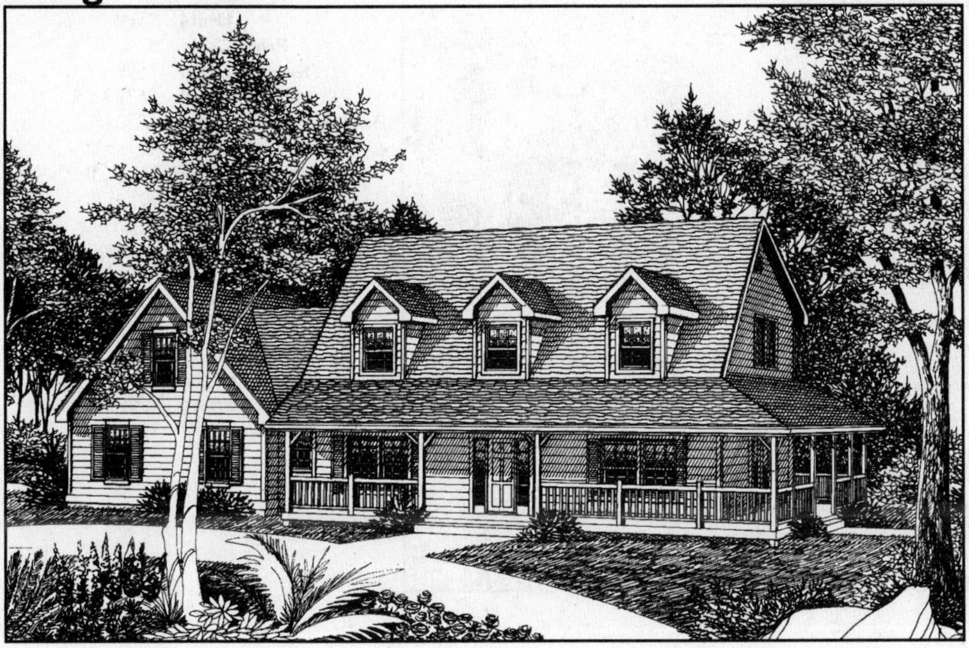

Units	Single
Price Code	E
Total Finished	2,487 sq. ft.
First Finished	1,624 sq. ft.
Second Finished	863 sq. ft.
Bonus Unfinished	407 sq. ft.
Basement Unfinished	1,624 sq. ft.
Garage Unfinished	573 sq. ft.
Porch Unfinished	228 sq. ft.
Dimensions	68'x50'
Foundation	Basement
Bedrooms	4
Full Baths	2
Half Baths	1
First Ceiling	8'
Second Ceiling	8'
Max Ridge Height	26'5'
Roof Framing	Stick
Exterior Walls	2x6

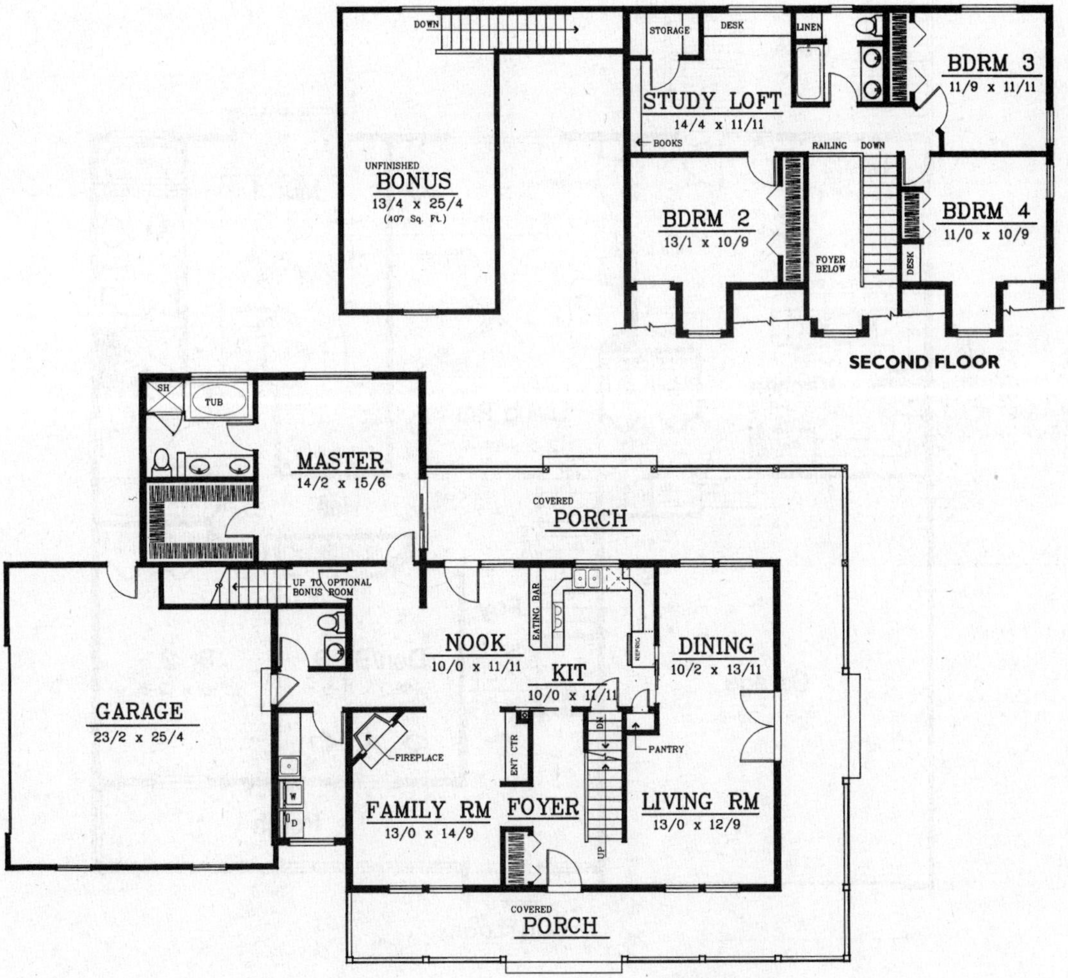
DOWN
STORAGE
DESK
LINEN
BDRM 3
11/9 x 11/11
STUDY LOFT
14/4 x 11/11
BOOKS
RAILING
DOWN
UNFINISHED
BONUS
13/4 x 25/4
(407 Sq. Ft.)
BDRM 2
13/1 x 10/9
FOYER BELOW
BDRM 4
11/0 x 10/9
DESK
SH
TUB
MASTER
14/2 x 15/6
COVERED
PORCH
UP TO OPTIONAL BONUS ROOM
EATING BAR
NOOK
10/0 x 11/11
KIT
10/0 x 11/11
DINING
10/2 x 13/11
GARAGE
23/2 x 25/4
FIREPLACE
ENT CTR
DN
PANTRY
W
D
FAMILY RM
13/0 x 14/9
FOYER
UP
LIVING RM
13/0 x 12/9
COVERED
PORCH

SECOND FLOOR

FIRST FLOOR

Design 24721

See Order Pages and Index for Info

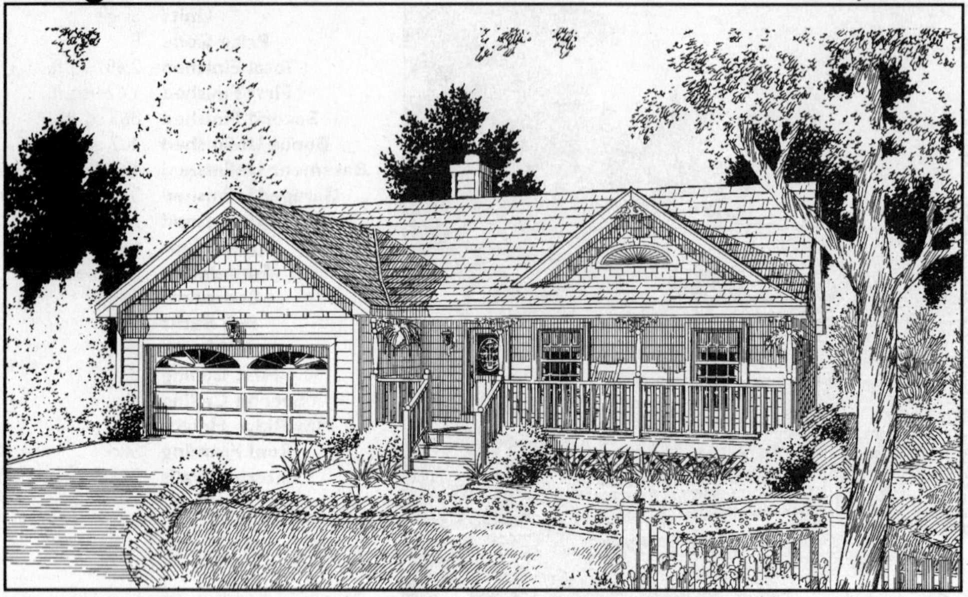

Units	Single
Price Code	B
Total Finished	1,539 sq. ft.
Main Finished	1,539 sq. ft.
Basement Unfinished	1,530 sq. ft.
Garage Unfinished	460 sq. ft.
Porch Unfinished	182 sq. ft.
Dimensions	50'x45'4"
Foundation	Basement Crawlspace Slab
Bedrooms	3
Full Baths	2
Main Ceiling	8'
Max Ridge Height	21'
Roof Framing	Stick
Exterior Walls	2x6

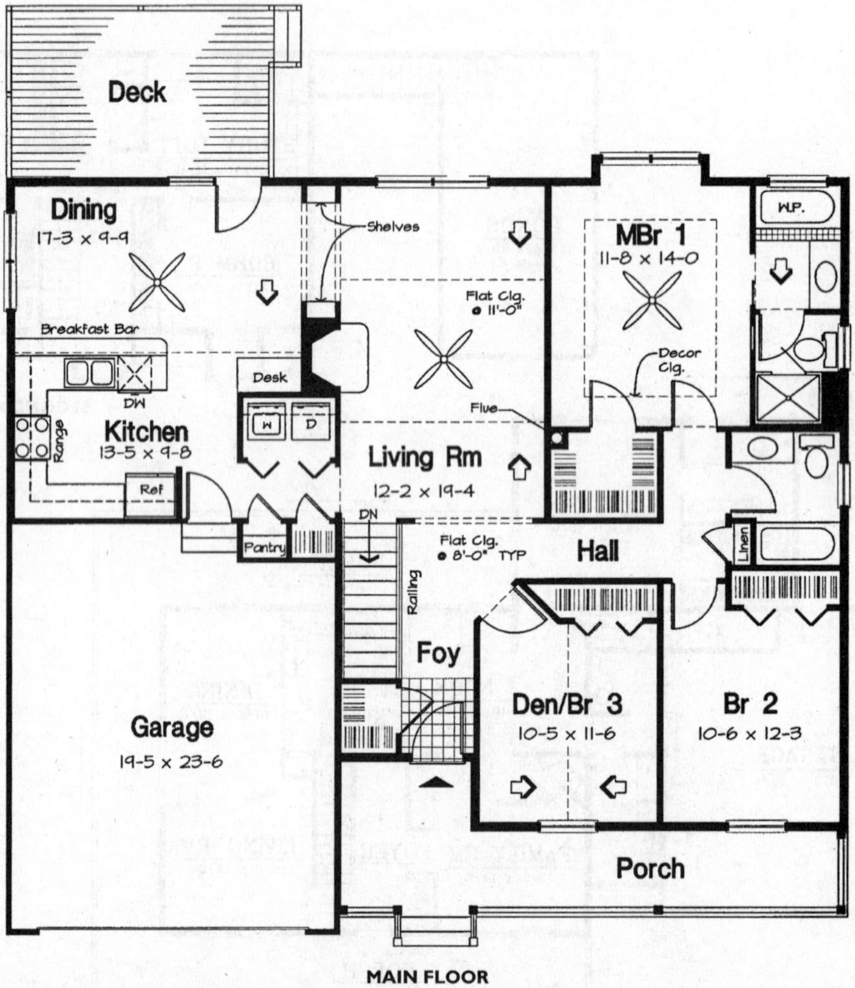
Deck
Dining
17-3 x 9-9
Shelves
Breakfast Bar
Desk
DW
Range
Kitchen
13-5 x 9-8
Ref
Pantry
Flat Clg. @ 11'-0"
Living Rm
12-2 x 19-4
Flue
DN
Flat Clg. @ 8'-0" TYP
MBr 1
11-8 x 14-0
Decor Clg.
W.P.
Linen
Hall
Railing
Foy
Den/Br 3
10-5 x 11-6
Br 2
10-6 x 12-3
Garage
19-5 x 23-6
Porch

MAIN FLOOR

Design 94274

See Order Pages and Index for Info

Units	Single
Price Code	H
Total Finished	3,138 sq. ft.
First Finished	2,341 sq. ft.
Second Finished	797 sq. ft.
Garage Unfinished	635 sq. ft.
Porch Unfinished	418 sq. ft.
Dimensions	65'x79'
Foundation	Slab
Bedrooms	3
Full Baths	4
Roof Framing	Truss

* Alternate foundation options available at an additional charge. Please call 1-800-235-5700 for more information.

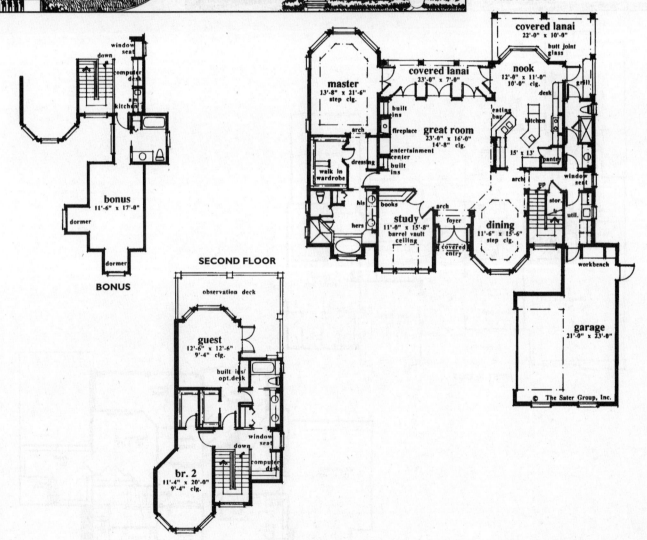

FIRST FLOOR

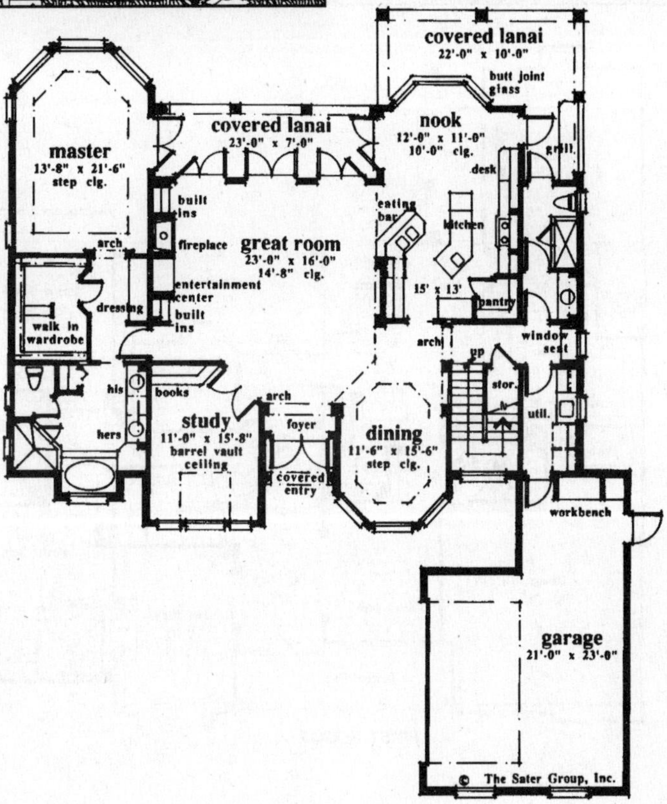
covered lanai
22'-0" x 10'-0"
butt joint glass
covered lanai
23'-0" x 7'-0"
master
13'-8" x 21'-6"
step clg.
nook
12'-0" x 11'-0"
10'-0" clg.
desk
grill
built ins
fireplace
great room
23'-0" x 16'-0"
14'-8" clg.
eating bar
kitchen
15' x 13'
pantry
entertainment center
built ins
arch
dressing
walk in wardrobe
window seat
arch
up
his
hers
books
study
11'-0" x 15'-8"
barrel vault ceiling
arch
foyer
covered entry
dining
11'-6" x 15'-6"
step clg.
stor.
util.
workbench
garage
21'-0" x 23'-0"
© The Sater Group, Inc.

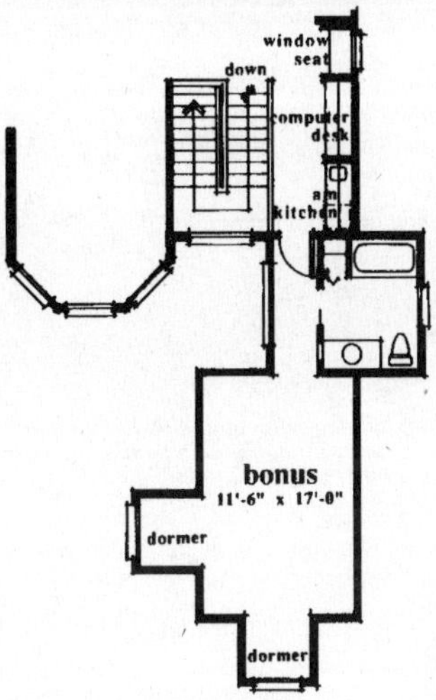
window seat
down
computer desk
am kitchen
bonus
11'-6" x 17'-0"
dormer
dormer

BONUS

SECOND FLOOR

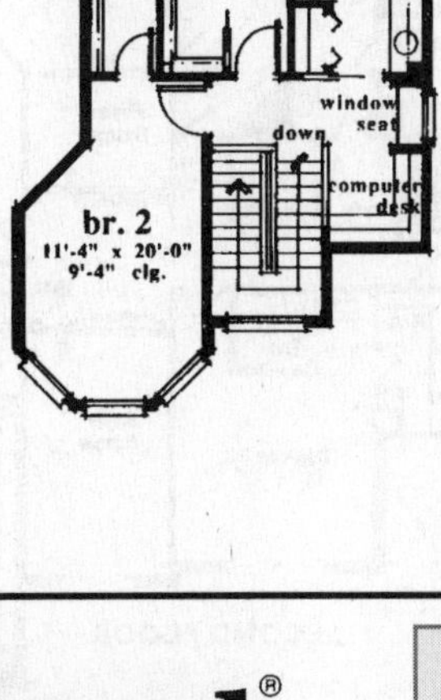
observation deck
guest
12'-6" x 12'-6"
9'-4" clg.
built ins/ opt.desk
window seat
down
computer desk
br. 2
11'-4" x 20'-0"
9'-4" clg.

Design 60136

See Order Pages and Index for Info

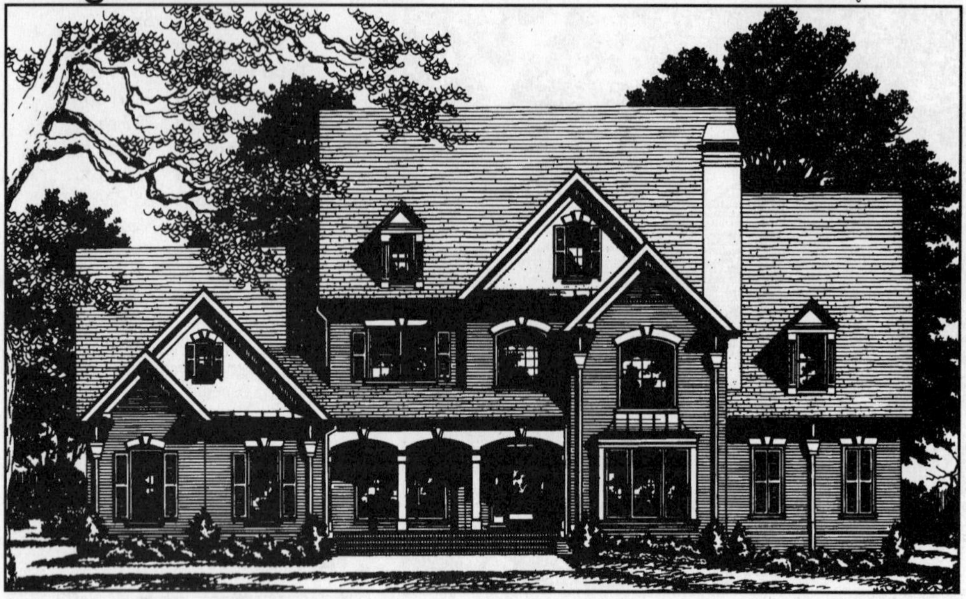

Units	Single
Price Code	L
Total Finished	4,418 sq. ft.
First Finished	3,197 sq. ft.
Second Finished	1,221 sq. ft.
Bonus Unfinished	656 sq. ft.
Basement Unfinished	3,197 sq. ft.
Garage Unfinished	537 sq. ft.
Dimensions	76'x73'10"
Foundation	Basement Crawlspace
Bedrooms	4
Full Baths	3
Half Baths	1
First Ceiling	10'4"
Second Ceiling	9'
Max Ridge Height	38'4"
Roof Framing	Stick
Exterior Walls	2x4

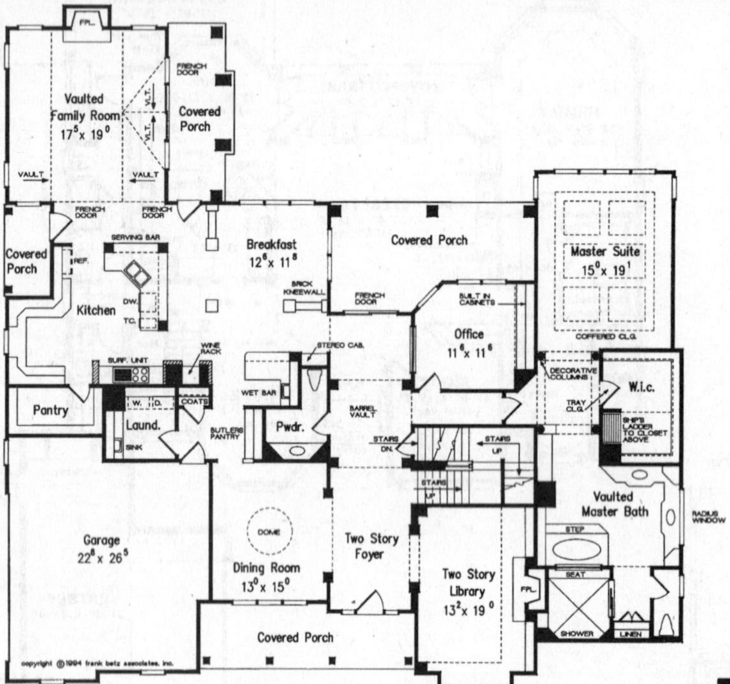
Vaulted Family Room 17⁵ x 19⁰
Covered Porch
Breakfast 12⁶ x 11⁸
Covered Porch
Master Suite 15⁰ x 19¹
Kitchen
Office 11⁶ x 11⁶
W.i.c.
Pantry
Laund.
Pwdr.
Vaulted Master Bath
Garage 22⁸ x 26⁵
Dining Room 13⁰ x 15⁰
Two Story Foyer
Two Story Library 13² x 19⁰
Covered Porch
copyright © 1994 frank betz associates, inc.

FIRST FLOOR

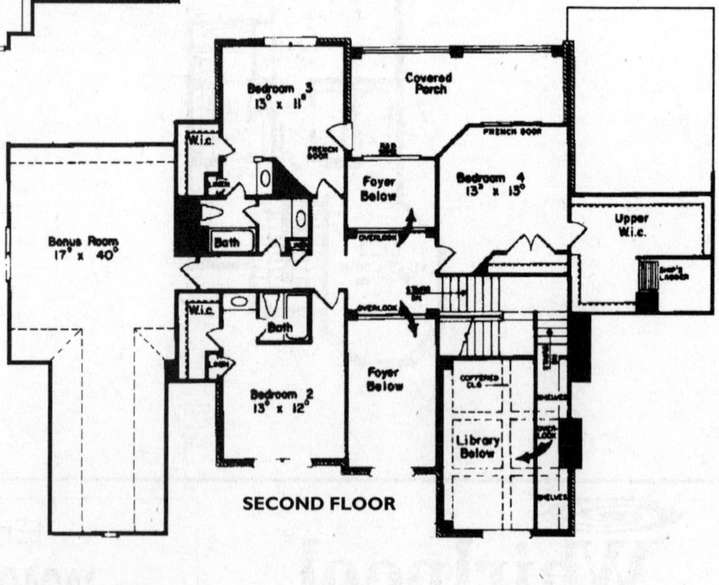
Bedroom 3 13⁰ x 11⁶
Covered Porch
Bedroom 4 13⁰ x 15⁰
Bonus Room 17⁹ x 40⁰
Foyer Below
Upper W.i.c.
Bath
Bath
Bedroom 2 13⁰ x 12⁰
Foyer Below
Library Below

SECOND FLOOR

Design 64129

See Order Pages and Index for Info

Units	Single
Price Code	H
Total Finished	2,324 sq. ft.
First Finished	1,710 sq. ft.
Second Finished	618 sq. ft.
Porch Unfinished	128 sq. ft.
Dimensions	47'x50'
Bedrooms	3
Full Baths	3
Max Ridge Height	30'2"
Exterior Walls	2x6

* Alternate foundation options available at an additional charge.
Please call 1-800-235-5700 for more information.

FIRST FLOOR

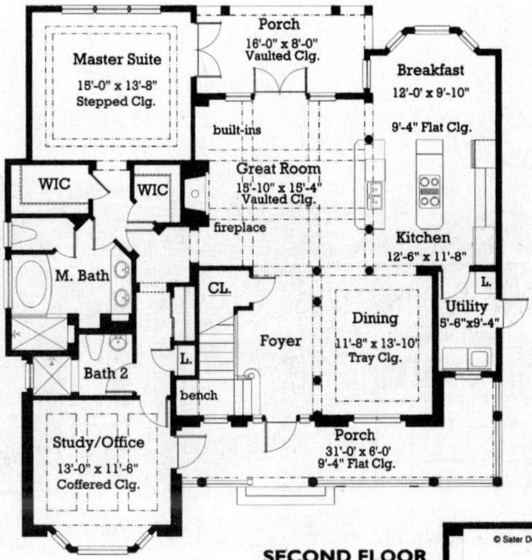

Porch
16'-0" x 8'-0"
Vaulted Clg.
Master Suite
15'-0" x 13'-8"
Stepped Clg.
Breakfast
12'-0' x 9'-10"
9'-4" Flat Clg.
built-ins
WIC
WIC
Great Room
15'-10" x 15'-4"
Vaulted Clg.
fireplace
Kitchen
12'-6" x 11'-8"
M. Bath
CL.
Foyer
Dining
11'-8" x 13'-10'
Tray Clg.
Utility
5'-6"x9'-4"
L.
L.
Bath 2
bench
Porch
31'-0' x 6'-0'
9'-4" Flat Clg.
Study/Office
13'-0" x 11'-8"
Coffered Clg.

SECOND FLOOR

© Sater Design Collection
open to below
WIC
Bedroom 1
11'-0" x 13'-0"
8'-0' Flat Clg.
Bath 3
desk
Dn.
Dn.
desk
WIC
L.
open to below
Bedroom 2
11'-0" x 13'-6"
8'-0' Flat Clg.
Equipment
plant shelf

Design 34150

See Order Pages and Index for Info

Rear Elevation

Units	Single
Price Code	A
Total Finished	1,492 sq. ft.
Main Finished	1,492 sq. ft.
Basement Unfinished	1,486 sq. ft.
Garage Unfinished	462 sq. ft.
Dimensions	56'x48'
Foundation	Basement Crawlspace Slab
Bedrooms	3
Full Baths	2
Main Ceiling	8'
Vaulted Ceiling	13'
Max Ridge Height	19'
Roof Framing	Stick
Exterior Walls	2x4,2x6

MAIN FLOOR

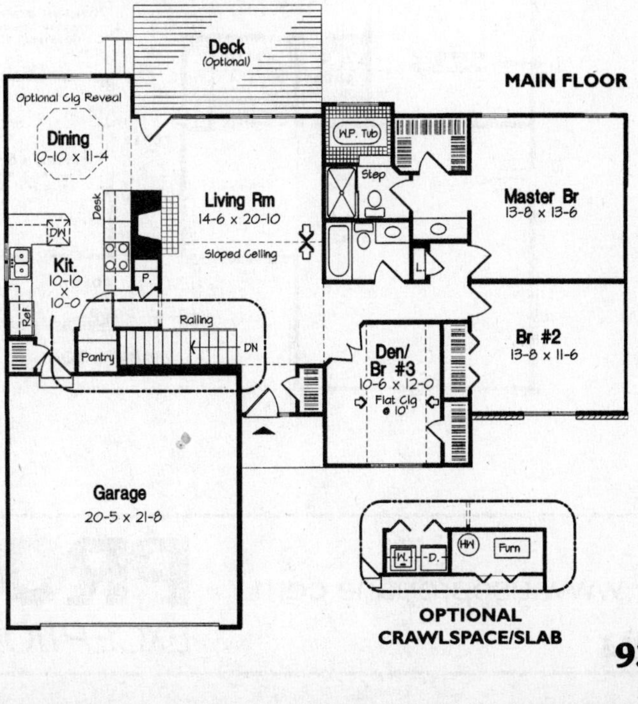

Deck
(Optional)
Optional Clg Reveal
Dining
10-10 x 11-4
Desk
Living Rm
14-6 x 20-10
Sloped Ceiling
W.P. Tub
Step
Master Br
13-8 x 13-6
DW
Kit.
10-10 x 10-0
P.
Ref
Pantry
Railing
DN
L
Br #2
13-8 x 11-6
Den/ Br #3
10-6 x 12-0
Flat Clg @ 10'
Garage
20-5 x 21-8
W
D.
HW
Furn

OPTIONAL CRAWLSPACE/SLAB

Design 24256

See Order Pages and Index for Info

Units	Single
Price Code	D
Total Finished	2,108 sq. ft.
Main Finished	2,108 sq. ft.
Dimensions	50'x66'
Foundation	Basement Crawlspace Slab
Bedrooms	3
Full Baths	2
Max Ridge Height	23'
Roof Framing	Stick
Exterior Walls	2x4

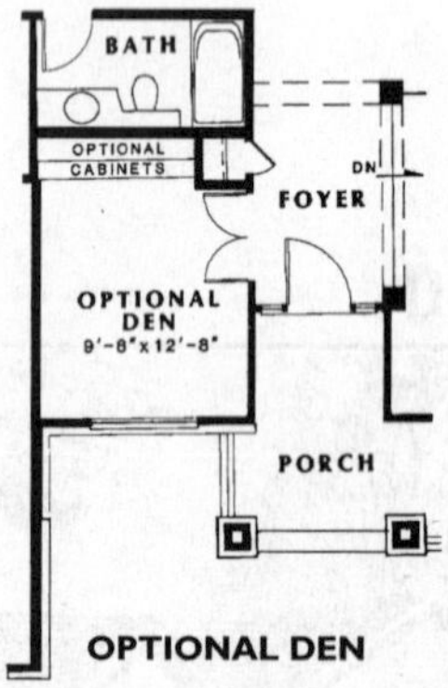
BATH
OPTIONAL CABINETS
FOYER
DN
OPTIONAL DEN 9'-8"x12'-8"
2-CAR GARAGE
PORCH

OPTIONAL DEN

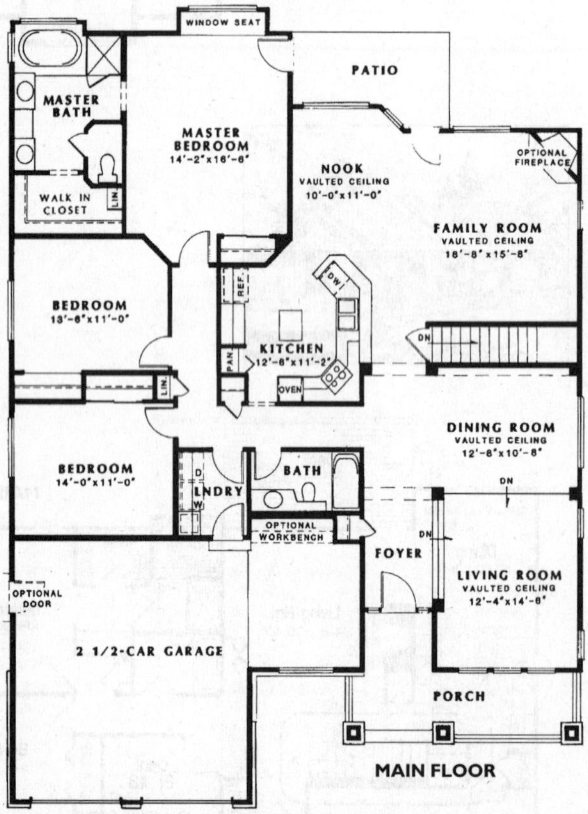
WINDOW SEAT
PATIO
MASTER BATH
MASTER BEDROOM 14'-2"x16'-6"
WALK IN CLOSET
LIN
NOOK VAULTED CEILING 10'-0"x11'-0"
OPTIONAL FIREPLACE
FAMILY ROOM VAULTED CEILING 18'-8"x15'-8"
BEDROOM 13'-6"x11'-0"
REF.
DW
KITCHEN 12'-8"x11'-2"
PAN
OVEN
DN
LIN
DINING ROOM VAULTED CEILING 12'-8"x10'-8"
BEDROOM 14'-0"x11'-0"
LNDRY
BATH
OPTIONAL WORKBENCH
FOYER
LIVING ROOM VAULTED CEILING 12'-4"x14'-8"
OPTIONAL DOOR
2 1/2-CAR GARAGE
PORCH

MAIN FLOOR

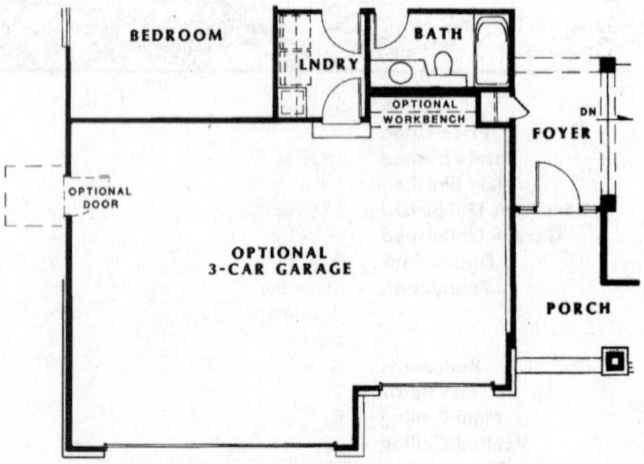
BEDROOM
LNDRY
BATH
OPTIONAL WORKBENCH
FOYER
DN
OPTIONAL DOOR
OPTIONAL 3-CAR GARAGE
PORCH

OPTIONAL 3-CAR GARAGE

Design 92538

See Order Pages and Index for Info

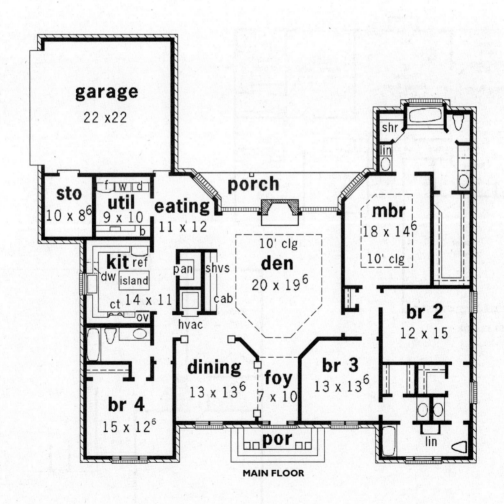

Units	Single
Price Code	F
Total Finished	2,733 sq. ft.
Main Finished	2,733 sq. ft.
Garage Unfinished	569 sq. ft.
Dimensions	70'10"x67'4"
Foundation	Crawlspace Slab
Bedrooms	4
Full Baths	3
Main Ceiling	9'
Max Ridge Height	28'
Roof Framing	Stick
Exterior Walls	2x4

garage
22 x22
sto
10 x 8⁶
f w d
util
9 x 10
b
eating
11 x 12
porch
shr
lin
mbr
18 x 14⁶
10' clg
10' clg
den
20 x 19⁶
kit
ref
dw
island
14 x 11
ct
ov
pan
shvs
cab
hvac
br 2
12 x 15
dining
13 x 13⁶
foy
7 x 10
br 3
13 x 13⁶
br 4
15 x 12⁶
por
lin

MAIN FLOOR

Design 60084

See Order Pages and Index for Info

ALLEN

Units	Single
Price Code	A
Total Finished	1,477 sq. ft.
First Finished	1,477 sq. ft.
Bonus Unfinished	283 sq. ft.
Basement Unfinished	1,477 sq. ft.
Garage Unfinished	420 sq. ft.
Dimensions	51'x51'4"
Foundation	Basement Crawlspace
Bedrooms	4
Full Baths	3
First Ceiling	8'
Second Ceiling	8'
Max Ridge Height	24'
Roof Framing	Stick
Exterior Walls	2x4

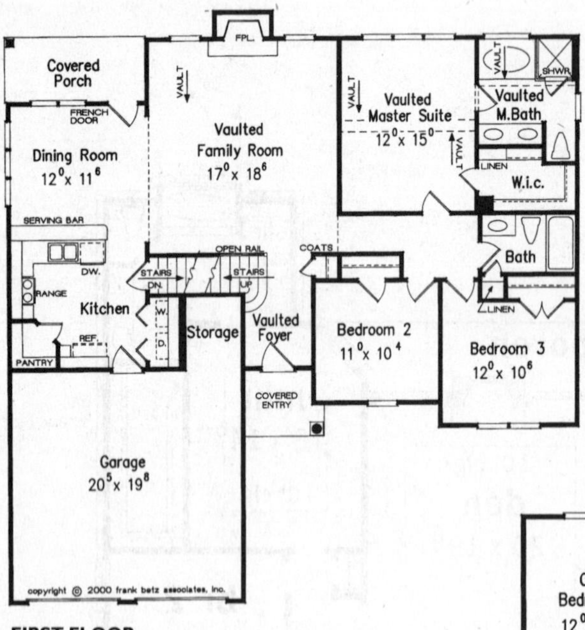
FPL.
Covered Porch
FRENCH DOOR
VAULT
Vaulted Family Room 17⁰x 18⁶
VAULT
Vaulted Master Suite 12⁰x 15⁰
VAULT
SHWR
Vaulted M.Bath
LINEN
W.i.c.
Dining Room 12⁰x 11⁶
SERVING BAR
DW.
RANGE
Kitchen
REF.
PANTRY
W.
D.
OPEN RAIL
STAIRS DN.
STAIRS UP
Storage
Vaulted Foyer
COATS
Bath
LINEN
Bedroom 2 11⁰x 10⁴
Bedroom 3 12⁰x 10⁶
COVERED ENTRY
Garage 20⁵x 19⁸
copyright © 2000 frank betz associates, inc.

FIRST FLOOR

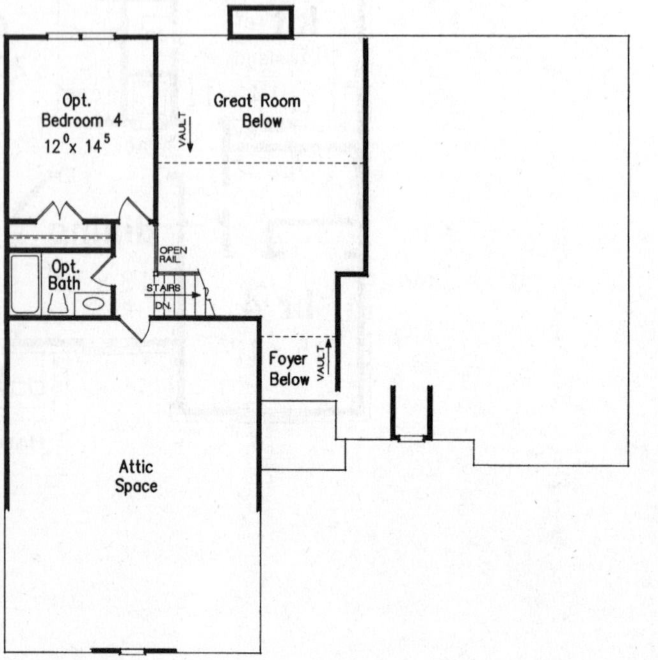
Opt. Bedroom 4 12⁰x 14⁵
VAULT
Great Room Below
OPEN RAIL
Opt. Bath
STAIRS DN.
Foyer Below
VAULT
Attic Space

SECOND FLOOR

Design 97100

See Order Pages and Index for Info

Units	Single
Price Code	D
Total Finished	2,120 sq. ft.
First Finished	995 sq. ft.
Second Finished	1,125 sq. ft.
Basement Unfinished	995 sq. ft.
Dimensions	56'4"x35'8"
Foundation	Basement
Bedrooms	4
Full Baths	2
Half Baths	1
Max Ridge Height	28'4"
Roof Framing	Truss
Exterior Walls	2x6

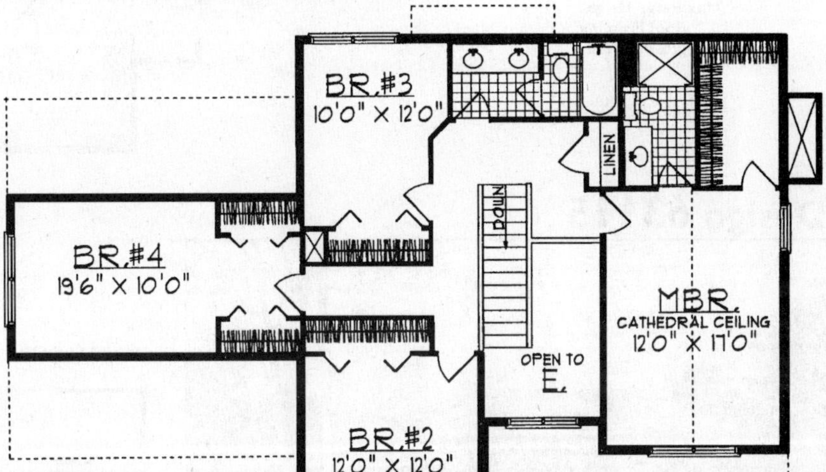
BR.#3
10'0" X 12'0"
LINEN
DOWN
BR.#4
19'6" X 10'0"
MBR.
CATHEDRAL CEILING
12'0" X 17'0"
OPEN TO
E.
BR.#2
12'0" X 12'0"

SECOND FLOOR

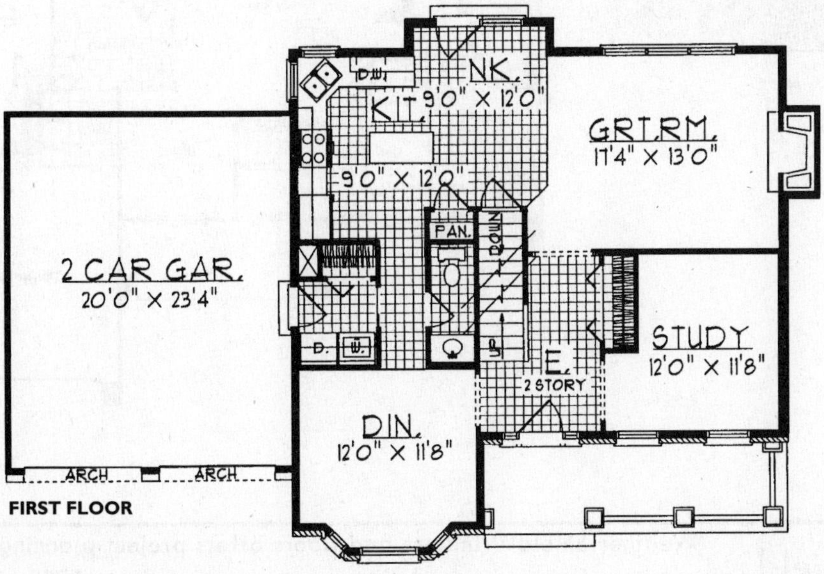
D.W.
NK.
9'0" X 12'0"
KIT.
9'0" X 12'0"
GRT.RM.
17'4" X 13'0"
PAN.
DOWN
2 CAR GAR.
20'0" X 23'4"
D.
W.
UP
E.
2 STORY
STUDY
12'0" X 11'8"
DIN.
12'0" X 11'8"
ARCH
ARCH

FIRST FLOOR

Design 65001

See Order Pages and Index for Info

Units	Single
Price Code	A
Total Finished	1,480 sq. ft.
First Finished	1,024 sq. ft.
Second Finished	456 sq. ft.
Basement Unfinished	1,024 sq. ft.
Dimensions	32'x40'
Foundation	Basement
Bedrooms	3
Full Baths	2
First Ceiling	8'
Second Ceiling	8'
Max Ridge Height	23'8"
Roof Framing	Truss
Exterior Walls	2x6

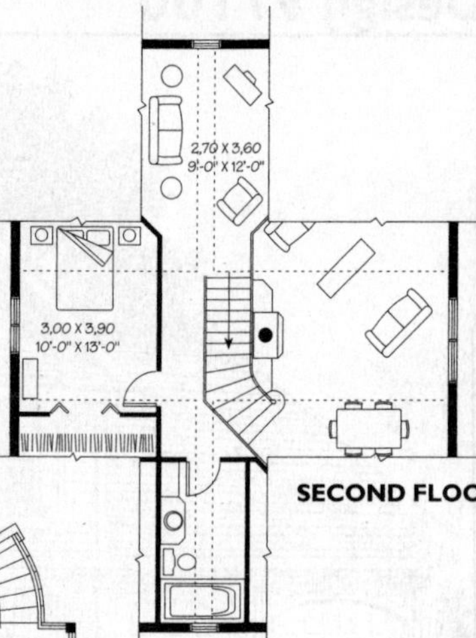
2,70 X 3,60
9'-0" X 12'-0"
3,00 X 3,90
10'-0" X 13'-0"

SECOND FLOOR

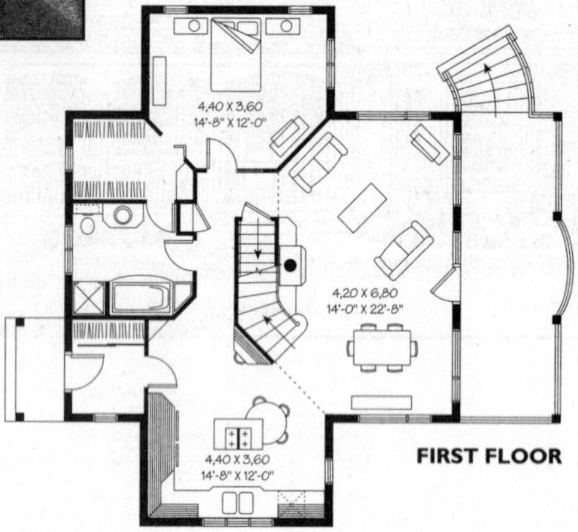
4,40 X 3,60
14'-8" X 12'-0"
4,20 X 6,80
14'-0" X 22'-8"
4,40 X 3,60
14'-8" X 12'-0"

FIRST FLOOR

Design 63115

See Order Pages and Index for Info

Units	Single
Price Code	C
Total Finished	1,869 sq. ft.
Main Finished	1,869 sq. ft.
Garage Unfinished	470 sq. ft.
Dimensions	61'8"x53'
Foundation	Slab
Bedrooms	4
Full Baths	2
Main Ceiling	10'
Max Ridge Height	20'
Roof Framing	Truss
Exterior Walls	2x4

MAIN FLOOR

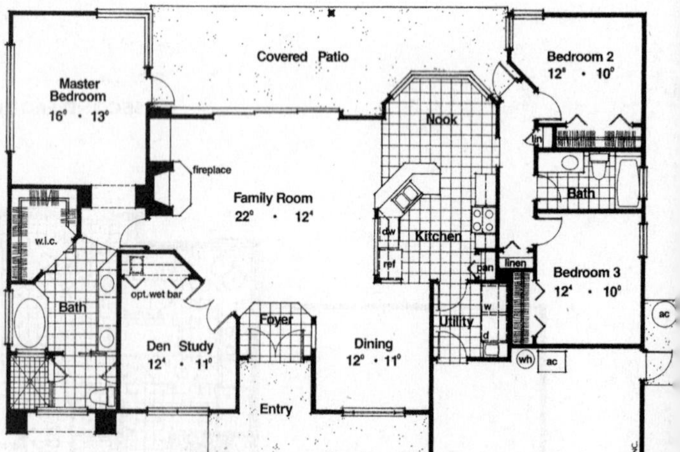
Covered Patio
Master Bedroom
16⁶ · 13⁰
Bedroom 2
12⁸ · 10⁰
Nook
fireplace
Family Room
22⁰ · 12⁴
Bath
w.i.c.
Kitchen
dw
ref
pan
linen
Bedroom 3
12⁴ · 10⁰
Bath
opt. wet bar
Foyer
Utility
Den Study
12⁴ · 11⁰
Dining
12⁰ · 11⁰
wh
ac
ac
Entry
Double Garage

Design 93152

See Order Pages and Index for Info

Units	Single
Price Code	E
Total Finished	2,493 sq. ft.
First Finished	1,185 sq. ft.
Second Finished	1,308 sq. ft.
Basement Unfinished	1,185 sq. ft.
Dimensions	58'4"x39'
Foundation	Basement
Bedrooms	4
Full Baths	2
Half Baths	1
Max Ridge Height	29'6"
Roof Framing	Stick
Exterior Walls	2x6

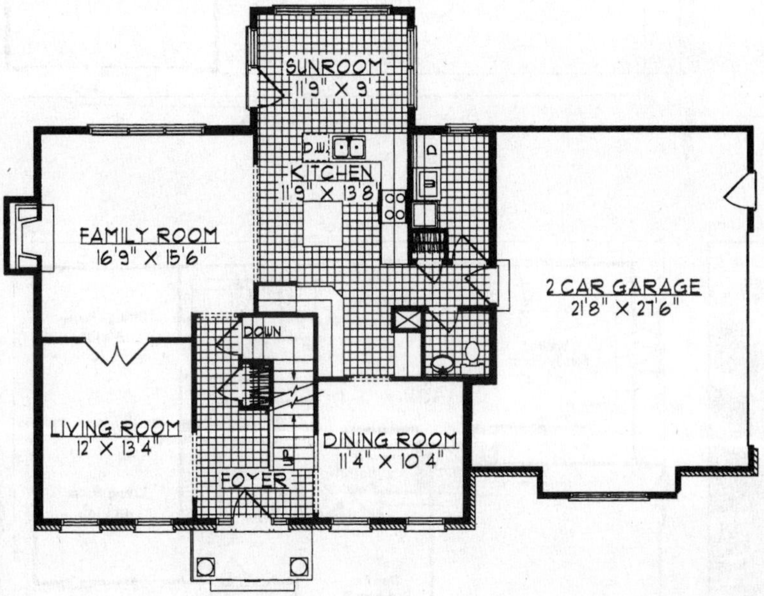
SUNROOM
11'9" X 9'
DW
KITCHEN
11'9" X 13'8"
FAMILY ROOM
16'9" X 15'6"
2 CAR GARAGE
21'8" X 27'6"
DOWN
LIVING ROOM
12' X 13'4"
DINING ROOM
11'4" X 10'4"
UP
FOYER

FIRST FLOOR

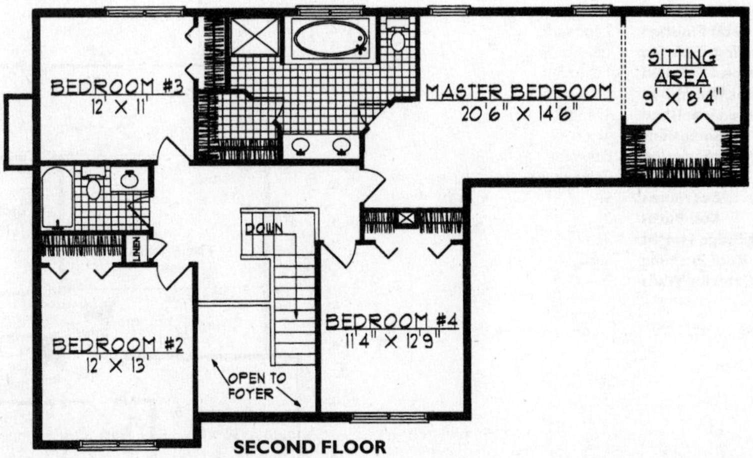
SITTING AREA
9' X 8'4"
BEDROOM #3
12' X 11'
MASTER BEDROOM
20'6" X 14'6"
DOWN
LINEN
BEDROOM #4
11'4" X 12'9"
BEDROOM #2
12' X 13'
OPEN TO FOYER

SECOND FLOOR

Design 94116

See Order Pages and Index for Info

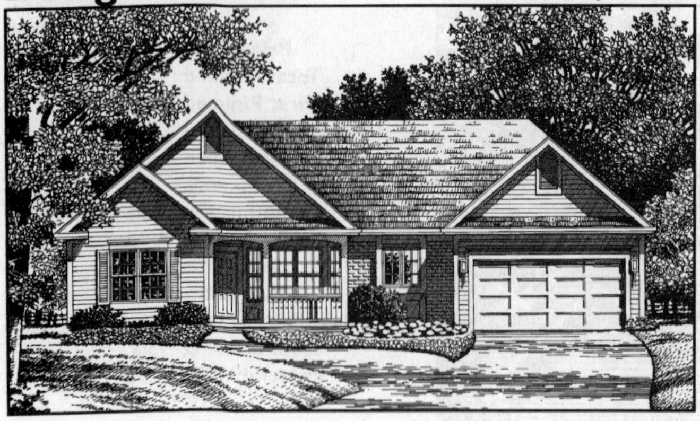

Units	Single
Price Code	B
Total Finished	1,546 sq. ft.
Main Finished	1,546 sq. ft.
Basement Unfinished	1,530 sq. ft.
Garage Unfinished	440 sq. ft.
Dimensions	60'x43'
Foundation	Basement
Bedrooms	3
Full Baths	1
3/4 Baths	1
Main Ceiling	9'2"
Max Ridge Height	23'
Roof Framing	Truss
Exterior Walls	2x4

MAIN FLOOR

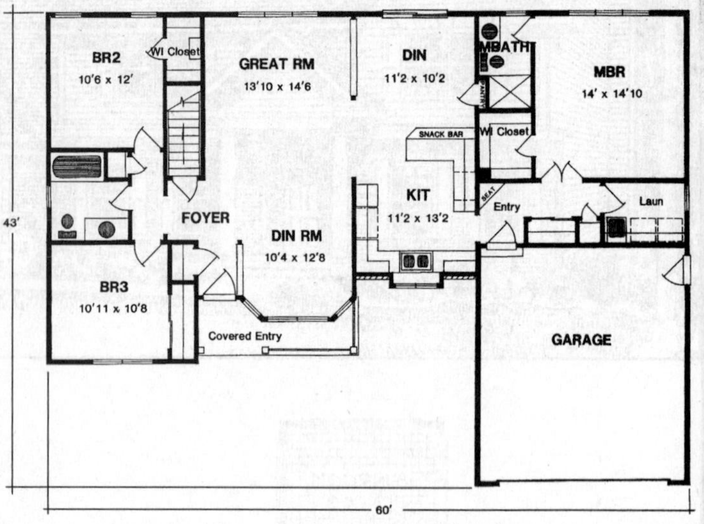
BR2
10'6 x 12'
WI Closet
GREAT RM
13'10 x 14'6
DIN
11'2 x 10'2
MBATH
MBR
14' x 14'10
SNACK BAR
WI Closet
KIT
11'2 x 13'2
Entry
Laun
FOYER
DIN RM
10'4 x 12'8
43'
BR3
10'11 x 10'8
Covered Entry
GARAGE
60'

Design 98418

See Order Pages and Index for Info

Units	Single
Price Code	F
Total Finished	2,680 sq. ft.
First Finished	1,424 sq. ft.
Second Finished	1,256 sq. ft.
Basement Unfinished	1,424 sq. ft.
Garage Unfinished	494 sq. ft.
Dimensions	57'x41'
Foundation	Basement Crawlspace
Bedrooms	5
Full Baths	3
Max Ridge Height	32'
Roof Framing	Stick
Exterior Walls	2x4

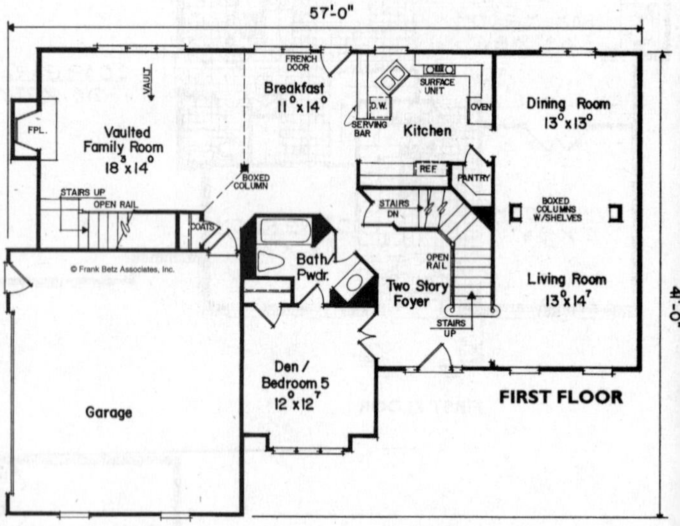
57'-0"
FRENCH DOOR
Breakfast
11⁰x14⁰
SURFACE UNIT
OVEN
D.W.
SERVING BAR
Kitchen
Dining Room
13⁰x13⁰
FPL.
Vaulted
Family Room
18⁵x14⁰
BOXED COLUMN
REF
PANTRY
STAIRS UP
OPEN RAIL
COATS
STAIRS DN
BOXED COLUMNS W/SHELVES
© Frank Betz Associates, Inc.
Bath/
Pwdr.
OPEN RAIL
Two Story
Foyer
Living Room
13⁰x14⁷
41'-0"
STAIRS UP
Garage
Den /
Bedroom 5
12⁰x12⁷
FIRST FLOOR

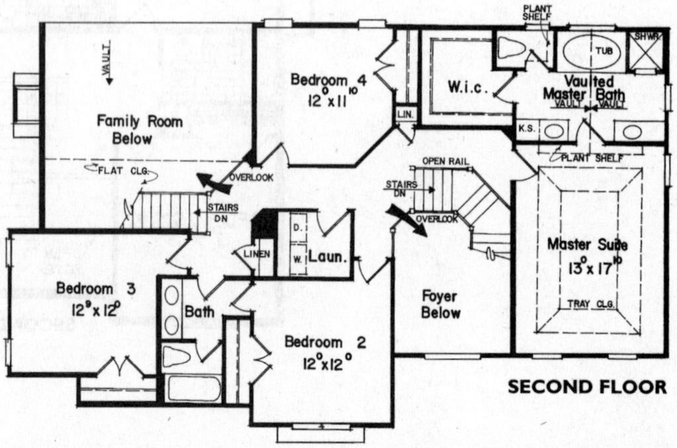
PLANT SHELF
TUB
SHWR
Bedroom 4
12⁰x11¹⁰
W.i.c.
Vaulted
Master Bath
LIN
K.S.
Family Room
Below
PLANT SHELF
OPEN RAIL
FLAT CLG.
OVERLOOK
STAIRS DN
OVERLOOK
STAIRS DN
LINEN
Laun.
Master Suite
13⁰x17¹⁰
Bedroom 3
12⁹x12⁰
Bath
Foyer
Below
TRAY CLG.
Bedroom 2
12⁰x12⁰
SECOND FLOOR

Design 98470

See Order Pages and Index for Info

Units	Single
Price Code	D
Total Finished	2,170 sq. ft.
Main Finished	2,170 sq. ft.
Basement Unfinished	2,184 sq. ft.
Garage Unfinished	484 sq. ft.
Dimensions	63'6"x61'
Foundation	Basement Crawlspace
Bedrooms	3
Full Baths	2
Half Baths	1
Main Ceiling	9'
Max Ridge Height	27'
Roof Framing	Stick
Exterior Walls	2x4

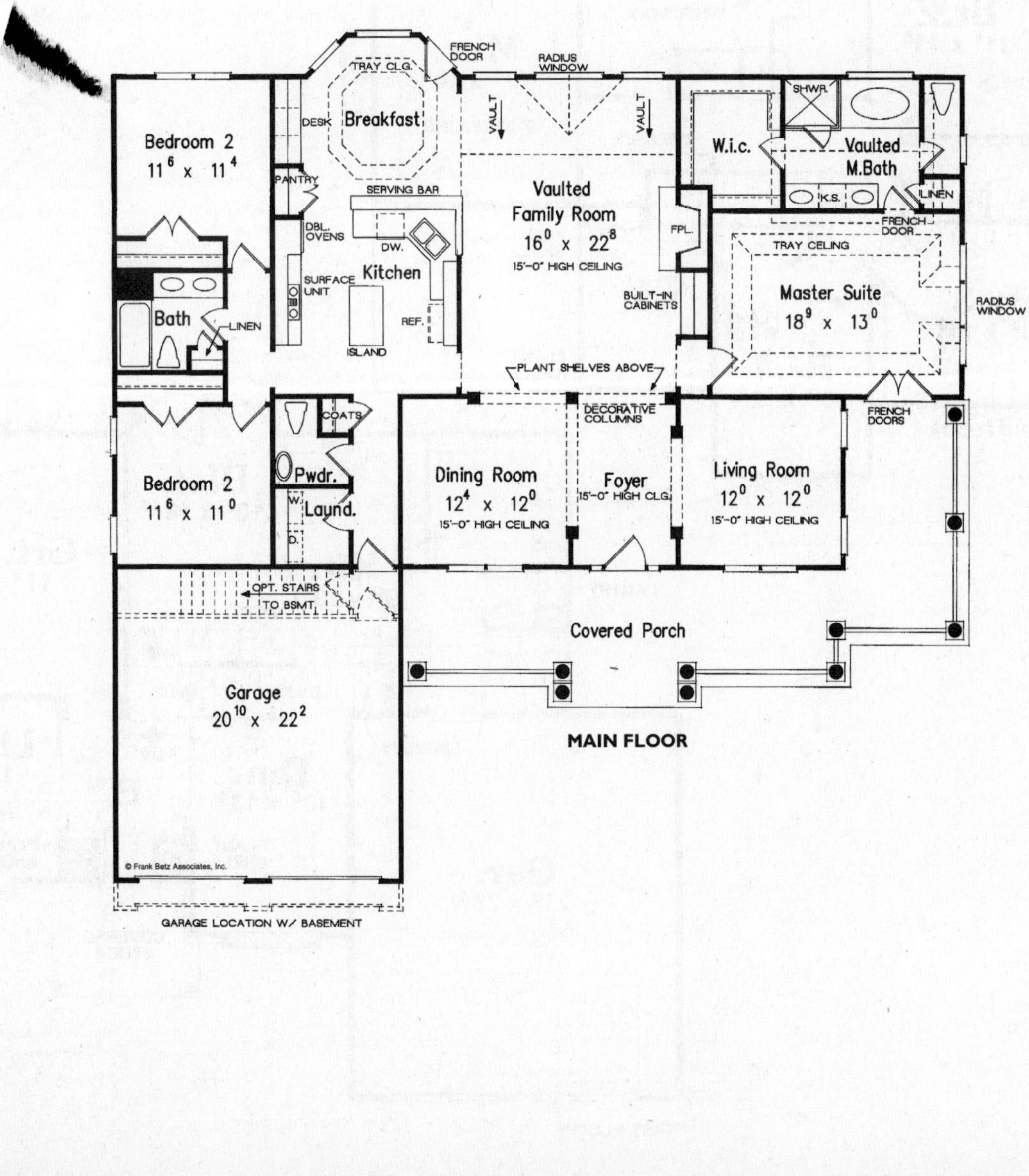
FRENCH DOOR
RADIUS WINDOW
TRAY CLG.
DESK
Breakfast
VAULT
VAULT
SHWR.
Bedroom 2
11⁶ x 11⁴
PANTRY
SERVING BAR
Vaulted Family Room
16⁰ x 22⁸
15'-0" HIGH CEILING
W.i.c.
Vaulted M.Bath
K.S.
LINEN
FRENCH DOOR
DBL. OVENS
DW.
Kitchen
SURFACE UNIT
REF.
ISLAND
FPL.
TRAY CEILING
Master Suite
18⁹ x 13⁰
RADIUS WINDOW
BUILT-IN CABINETS
Bath
LINEN
PLANT SHELVES ABOVE
DECORATIVE COLUMNS
COATS
FRENCH DOORS
Pwdr.
Bedroom 2
11⁶ x 11⁰
W.
Laund.
D.
Dining Room
12⁴ x 12⁰
15'-0" HIGH CEILING
Foyer
15'-0" HIGH CLG.
Living Room
12⁰ x 12⁰
15'-0" HIGH CEILING
OPT. STAIRS TO BSMT.
Covered Porch
Garage
20¹⁰ x 22²
© Frank Betz Associates, Inc.
GARAGE LOCATION W/ BASEMENT

MAIN FLOOR

Design 97427

See Order Pages and Index for Info

Units	Single
Price Code	E
Total Finished	2,332 sq. ft.
First Finished	1,214 sq. ft.
Second Finished	1,118 sq. ft.
Garage Unfinished	511 sq. ft.
Dimensions	54'x43'4"
Foundation	Basement
Bedrooms	4
Full Baths	2
Half Baths	1
Max Ridge Height	26'3"
Roof Framing	Stick
Exterior Walls	2x4

* Alternate foundation options available at an additional charge. Please call 1-800-235-5700 for more information.

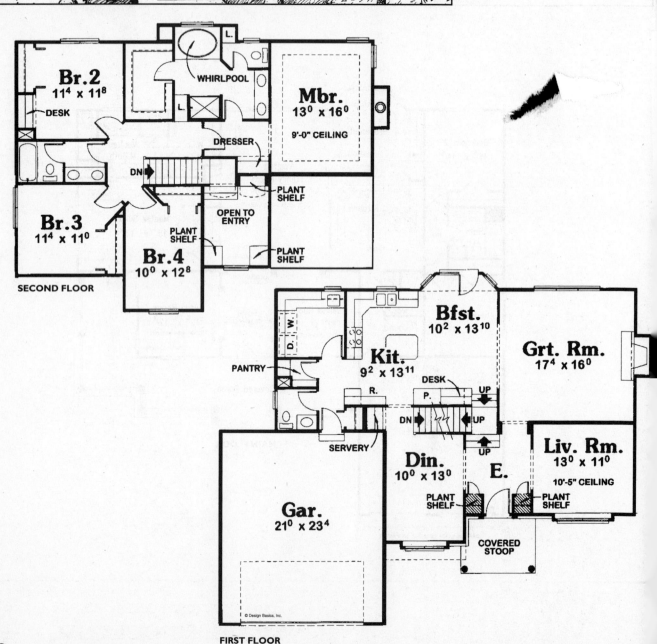

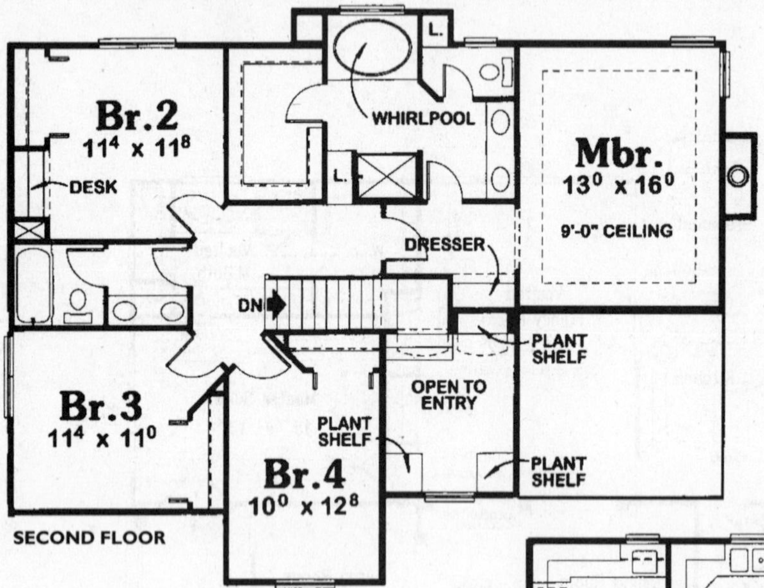
Br.2
11⁴ x 11⁸
DESK
WHIRLPOOL
L.
L.
Mbr.
13⁰ x 16⁰
9'-0" CEILING
DRESSER
DN
PLANT SHELF
OPEN TO ENTRY
Br.3
11⁴ x 11⁰
PLANT SHELF
Br.4
10⁰ x 12⁸
PLANT SHELF

SECOND FLOOR

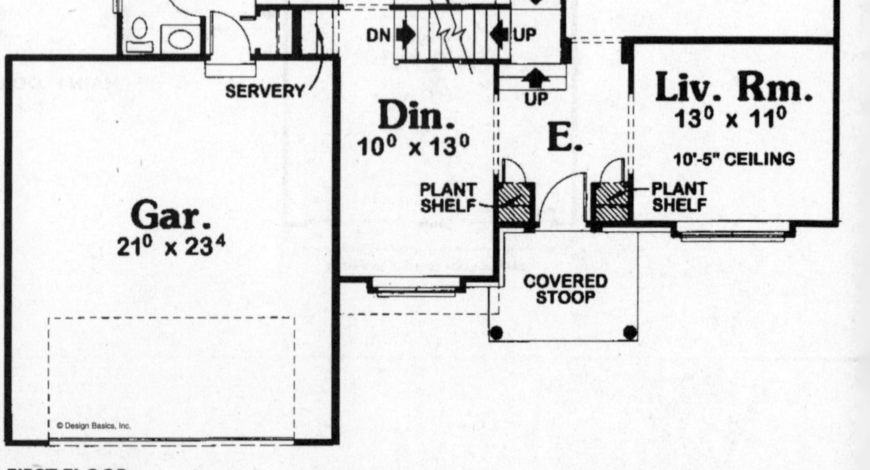
W.
D.
Bfst.
10² x 13¹⁰
Grt. Rm.
17⁴ x 16⁰
Kit.
9² x 13¹¹
PANTRY
DESK
R.
P.
UP
DN
UP
UP
SERVERY
Din.
10⁰ x 13⁰
E.
Liv. Rm.
13⁰ x 11⁰
10'-5" CEILING
PLANT SHELF
PLANT SHELF
Gar.
21⁰ x 23⁴
COVERED STOOP
© Design Basics, Inc.

FIRST FLOOR

Design 92546

See Order Pages and Index for Info

Units	Single
Price Code	E
Total Finished	2,387 sq. ft.
Main Finished	2,387 sq. ft.
Garage Unfinished	505 sq. ft.
Porch Unfinished	194 sq. ft.
Dimensions	64'10"x54'10"
Foundation	Crawlspace Slab
Bedrooms	4
Full Baths	2
Half Baths	1
Main Ceiling	9'
Max Ridge Height	28'
Roof Framing	Truss
Exterior Wall	2x4

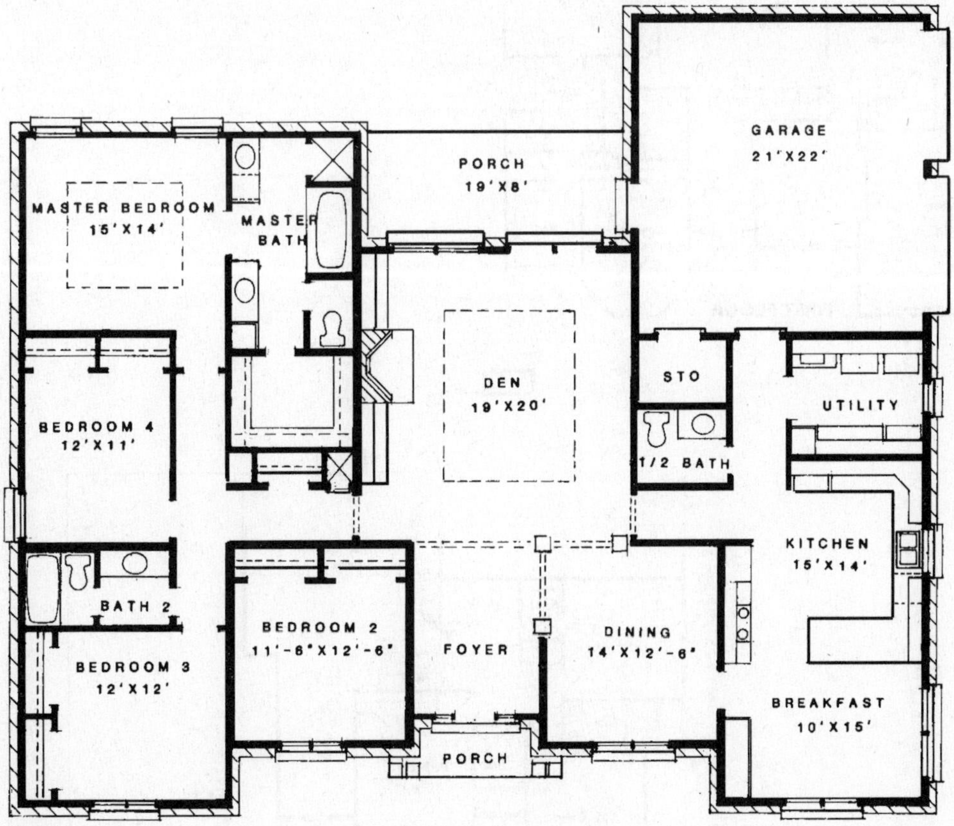
MASTER BEDROOM
15'X14'
MASTER BATH
PORCH
19'X8'
GARAGE
21'X22'
DEN
19'X20'
STO
UTILITY
1/2 BATH
BEDROOM 4
12'X11'
KITCHEN
15'X14'
BATH 2
BEDROOM 2
11'-6"X12'-6"
FOYER
DINING
14'X12'-6"
BEDROOM 3
12'X12'
BREAKFAST
10'X15'
PORCH

MAIN FLOOR

Design 60097

See Order Pages and Index for Info

Units	Single
Price Code	G
Total Finished	2,884 sq. ft.
First Finished	2,247 sq. ft.
Second Finished	637 sq. ft.
Bonus Unfinished	235 sq. ft.
Basement Unfinished	2,247 sq. ft.
Garage Unfinished	457 sq. ft.
Dimensions	64'x55'2"
Foundation	Basement Crawlspace
Bedrooms	4
Full Baths	4
First Ceiling	9'
Second Ceiling	8'
Max Ridge Height	29'4"
Roof Framing	Stick
Exterior Walls	2x4

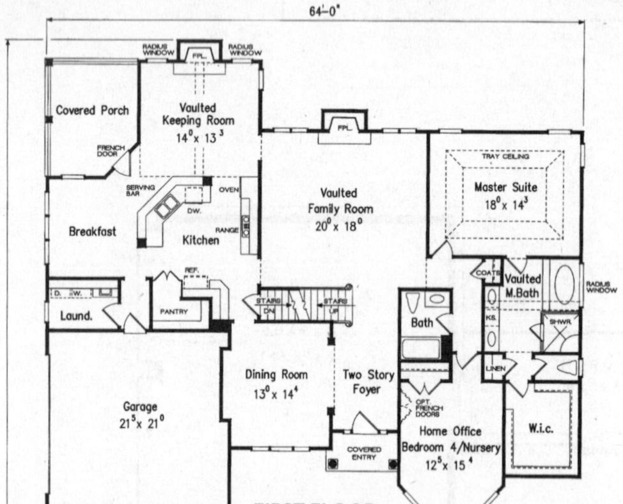
64'-0"
55'-2"
Covered Porch
Vaulted Keeping Room 14⁰ x 13³
Breakfast
Kitchen
Vaulted Family Room 20⁰ x 18⁰
Master Suite 18⁰ x 14³
Vaulted M.Bath
Laund.
Pantry
Bath
Dining Room 13⁰ x 14⁴
Two Story Foyer
Garage 21⁵ x 21⁰
Home Office Bedroom 4/Nursery 12⁵ x 15⁴
W.i.c.
Covered Entry
copyright © 2000 frank betz associates, inc.

FIRST FLOOR

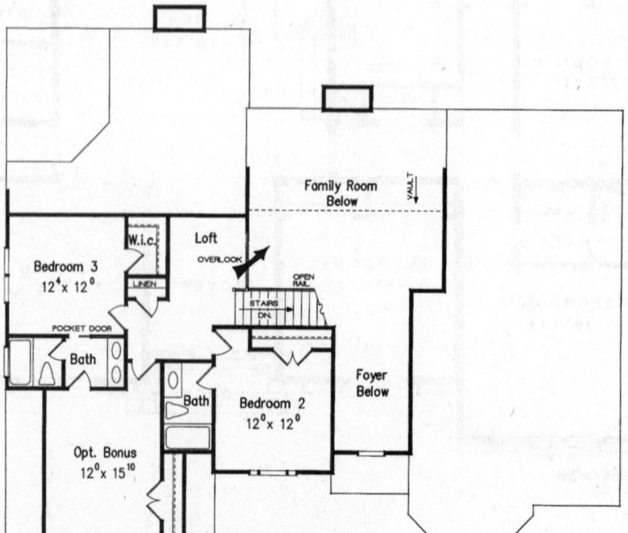
Family Room Below
Loft
Overlook
Bedroom 3 12⁴ x 12⁰
W.i.c.
Linen
Pocket Door
Bath
Bath
Bedroom 2 12⁰ x 12⁰
Foyer Below
Opt. Bonus 12⁰ x 15¹⁰

SECOND FLOOR

Design 92655

See Order Pages and Index for Info

Units	Single
Price Code	B
Total Finished	1,746 sq. ft.
Main Finished	1,746 sq. ft.
Basement Unfinished	1,697 sq. ft.
Garage Unfinished	480 sq. ft.
Porch Unfinished	111 sq. ft.
Dimensions	65'10"x56'
Foundation	Basement
Bedrooms	3
Full Baths	2
Max Ridge Height	21'6"
Roof Framing	Truss
Exterior Walls	2x4

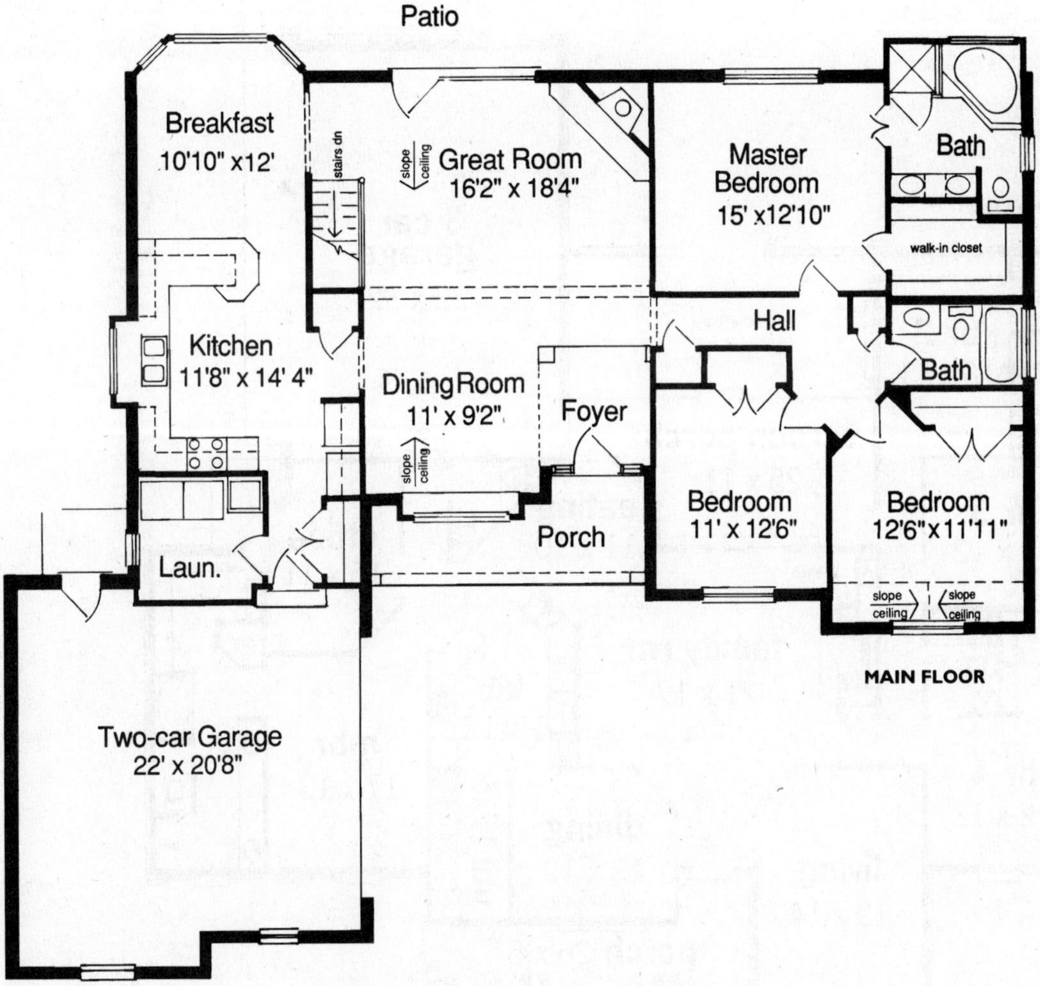
Patio
Breakfast
10'10" x12'
stairs dn
slope ceiling
Great Room
16'2" x 18'4"
Master Bedroom
15' x12'10"
Bath
walk-in closet
Hall
Kitchen
11'8" x 14' 4"
Dining Room
11' x 9'2"
Foyer
slope ceiling
Bath
Bedroom
11' x 12'6"
Bedroom
12'6"x11'11"
Porch
Laun.
slope ceiling
slope ceiling
Two-car Garage
22' x 20'8"

MAIN FLOOR

Design 65632

See Order Pages and Index for Info

Units	Single
Price Code	G
Total Finished	2,682 sq. ft.
Main Finished	2,682 sq. ft.
Dimensions	74'10"x75'
Foundation	Crawlspace Slab
Bedrooms	4
Full Baths	3
Half Baths	1
Main Ceiling	9'
Max Ridge Height	30'
Roof Framing	Stick
Exterior Walls	2x4

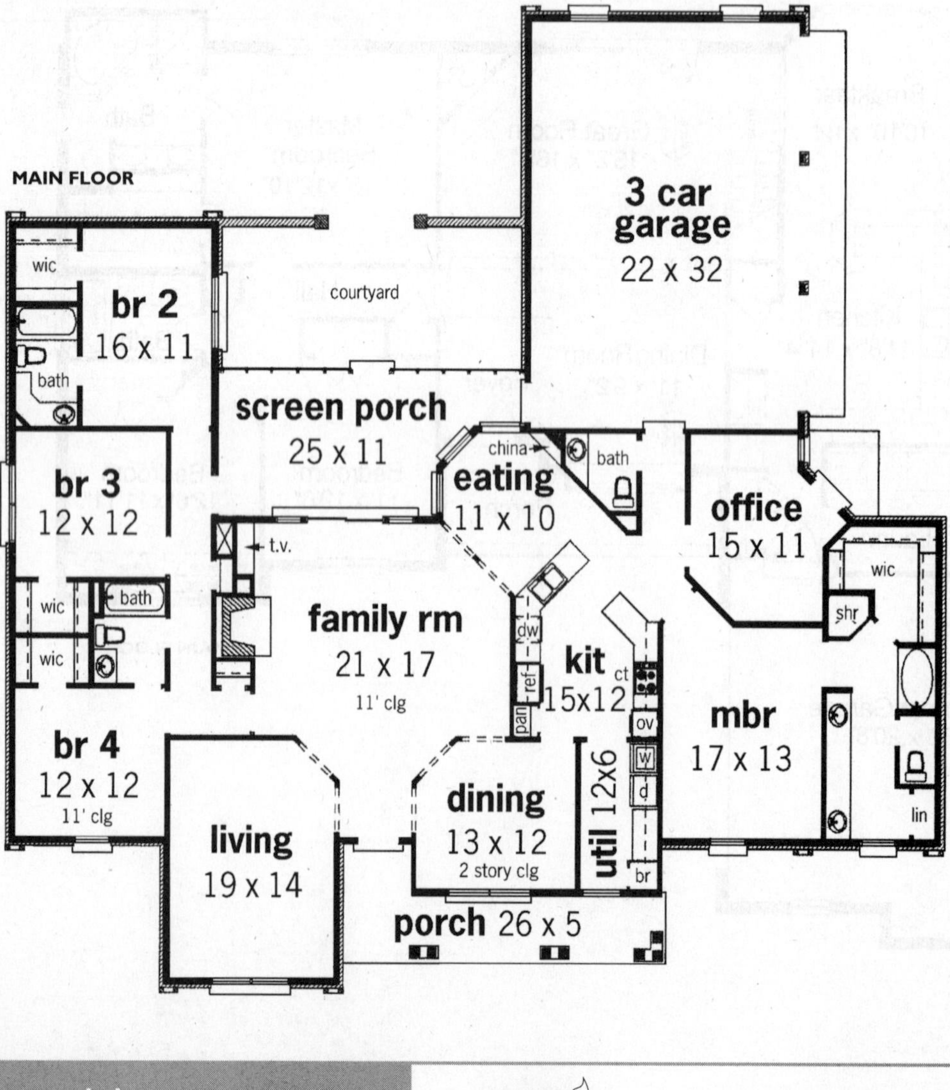
MAIN FLOOR
3 car garage
22 x 32
wic
br 2
16 x 11
bath
courtyard
screen porch
25 x 11
china
bath
eating
11 x 10
office
15 x 11
br 3
12 x 12
t.v.
wic
bath
wic
shr
family rm
21 x 17
11' clg
wic
dw
kit
ct
ref
15x12
pan
ov
w
d
mbr
17 x 13
br 4
12 x 12
11' clg
util 12x6
living
19 x 14
dining
13 x 12
2 story clg
br
lin
porch 26 x 5

Design 99492

See Order Pages and Index for Info

DESIGNERS' INK

Units	Single
Price Code	F
Total Finished	2,681 sq. ft.
First Finished	1,823 sq. ft.
Second Finished	858 sq. ft.
Garage Unfinished	515 sq. ft.
Dimensions	56'8"x50'8"
Foundation	Basement
Bedrooms	3
Full Baths	2
Half Baths	1
Max Ridge Height	28'6"
Roof Framing	Stick
Exterior Walls	2x4

* Alternate foundation options available at an additional charge. Please call 1-800-235-5700 for more information.

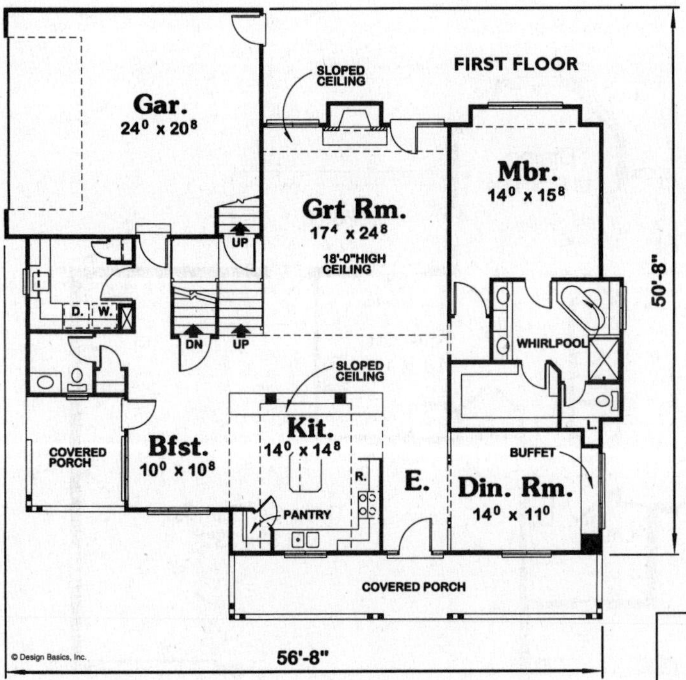
FIRST FLOOR
SLOPED CEILING
Gar.
24^{0} x 20^{8}
Grt Rm.
17^{4} x 24^{8}
18'-0"HIGH CEILING
Mbr.
14^{0} x 15^{8}
UP
D. W.
DN
UP
WHIRLPOOL
SLOPED CEILING
Kit.
14^{0} x 14^{8}
COVERED PORCH
Bfst.
10^{0} x 10^{8}
R.
E.
BUFFET
Din. Rm.
14^{0} x 11^{0}
L.
PANTRY
COVERED PORCH
50'-8"
56'-8"
© Design Basics, Inc.

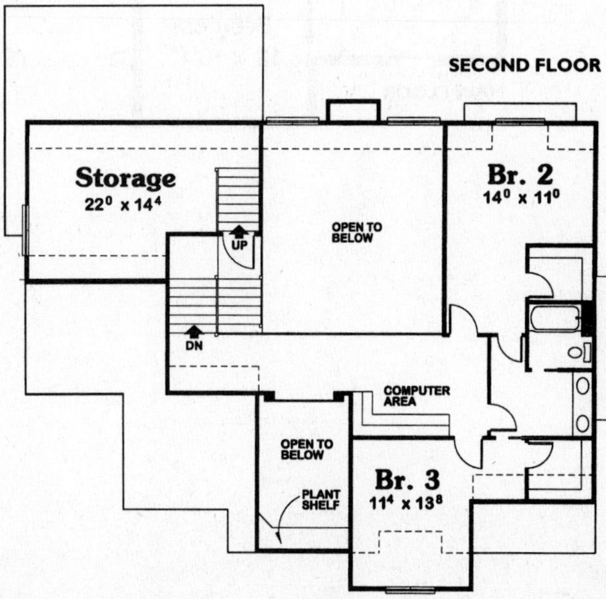
SECOND FLOOR
Storage
22^{0} x 14^{4}
Br. 2
14^{0} x 11^{0}
OPEN TO BELOW
UP
DN
COMPUTER AREA
OPEN TO BELOW
PLANT SHELF
Br. 3
11^{4} x 13^{8}

Design 97757

See Order Pages and Index for Info

Units	Single
Price Code	B
Total Finished	1,755 sq. ft.
Main Finished	1,755 sq. ft.
Basement Unfinished	1,725 sq. ft.
Garage Unfinished	796 sq. ft.
Porch Unfinished	138 sq. ft.
Dimensions	78'6"x47'7"
Foundation	Basement
Bedrooms	3
Full Baths	2
Main Ceiling	8'
Max Ridge Height	22'
Roof Framing	Truss
Exterior Walls	2x4

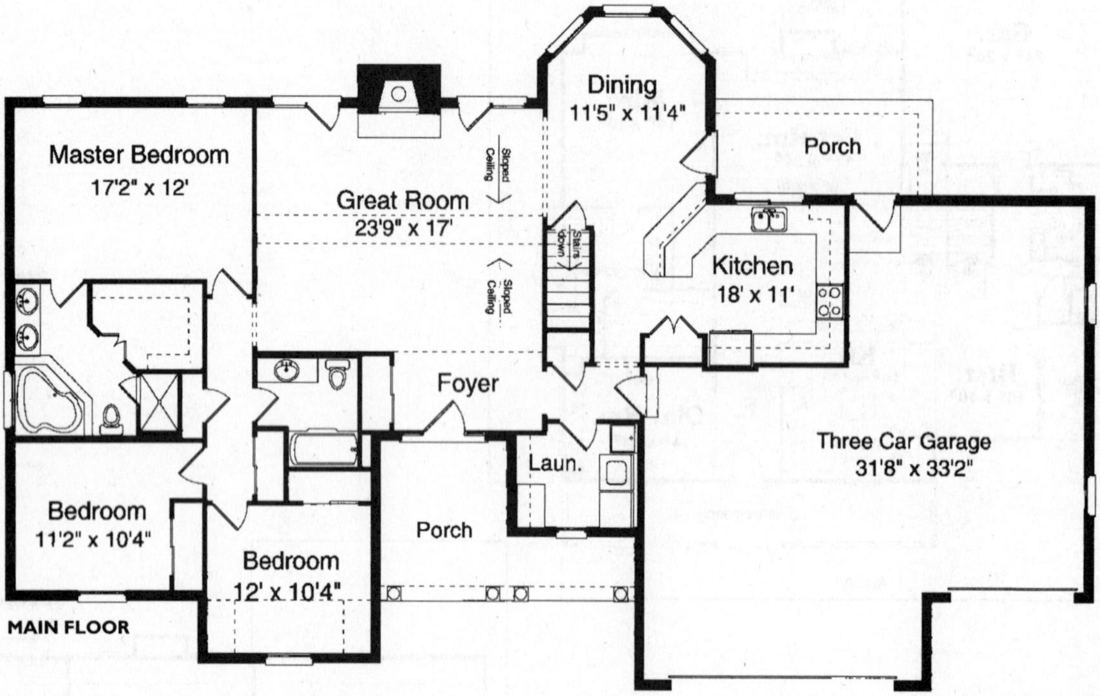
Dining
11'5" x 11'4"
Porch
Master Bedroom
17'2" x 12'
Sloped Ceiling
Great Room
23'9" x 17'
Stairs down
Kitchen
18' x 11'
Sloped Ceiling
Foyer
Laun.
Three Car Garage
31'8" x 33'2"
Bedroom
11'2" x 10'4"
Porch
Bedroom
12' x 10'4"

MAIN FLOOR

Design 99432

See Order Pages and Index for Info

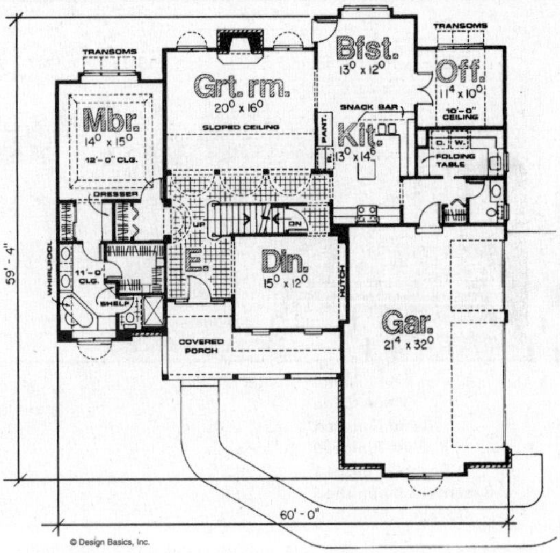

TRANSOMS
Mbr.
14⁰ x 15⁰
12'-0" CLG.
Grt. rm.
20⁰ x 16⁰
SLOPED CEILING
Bfst.
13⁰ x 12⁰
Off.
11⁴ x 10⁰
10'-0" CEILING
SNACK BAR
Kit.
13⁰ x 14⁶
FOLDING TABLE
DRESSER
WHIRLPOOL
UP
DN
E.
Din.
15⁰ x 12⁰
HUTCH
SHELF
COVERED PORCH
Gar.
21⁴ x 32⁰
59'-4"
60'-0"
© Design Basics, Inc.

FIRST FLOOR

Units	Single
Price Code	F
Total Finished	2,562 sq. ft.
First Finished	1,875 sq. ft.
Second Finished	687 sq. ft.
Basement Unfinished	1,875 sq. ft.
Dimensions	60'x59'4"
Foundation	Basement
Bedrooms	4
Full Baths	2
Half Baths	1
First Ceiling	8'
Second Ceiling	8'
Max Ridge Height	27'2"
Roof Framing	Stick
Exterior Walls	2x4

* Alternate foundation options available at an additional charge. Please call 1-800-235-5700 for more information.

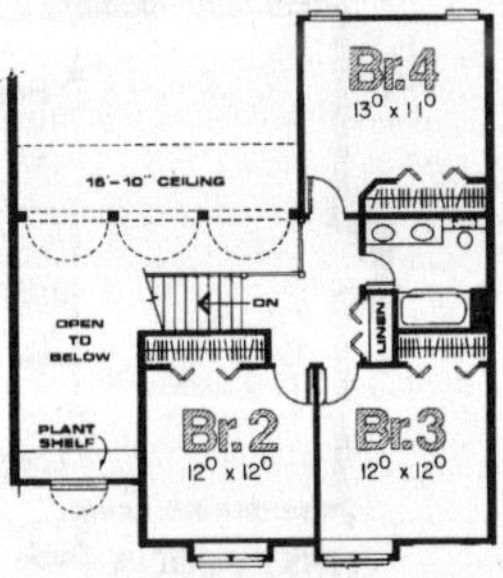

Br. 4
13⁰ x 11⁰
16'-10" CEILING
DN
OPEN TO BELOW
LINEN
PLANT SHELF
Br. 2
12⁰ x 12⁰
Br. 3
12⁰ x 12⁰

SECOND FLOOR

Design 99488

See Order Pages and Index for Info

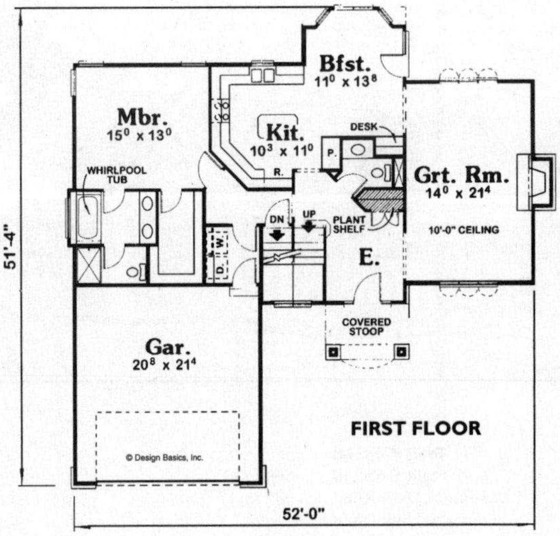

Bfst.
11⁰ x 13⁸
Mbr.
15⁰ x 13⁰
Kit.
10³ x 11⁰
DESK
WHIRLPOOL TUB
Grt. Rm.
14⁰ x 21⁴
10'-0" CEILING
DN
UP
PLANT SHELF
E.
COVERED STOOP
Gar.
20⁸ x 21⁴
© Design Basics, Inc.
51'-4"
52'-0"

FIRST FLOOR

Units	Single
Price Code	C
Total Finished	1,772 sq. ft.
First Finished	1,314 sq. ft.
Second Finished	458 sq. ft.
Garage Unfinished	454 sq. ft.
Dimensions	52'x51'4'
Foundation	Basement
Bedrooms	3
Full Baths	2
Half Baths	1
First Ceiling	8'
Second Ceiling	8'
Max Ridge Height	24'6"
Roof Framing	Stick/Truss
Exterior Walls	2x4

* Alternate foundation options available at an additional charge. Please call 1-800-235-5700 for more information.

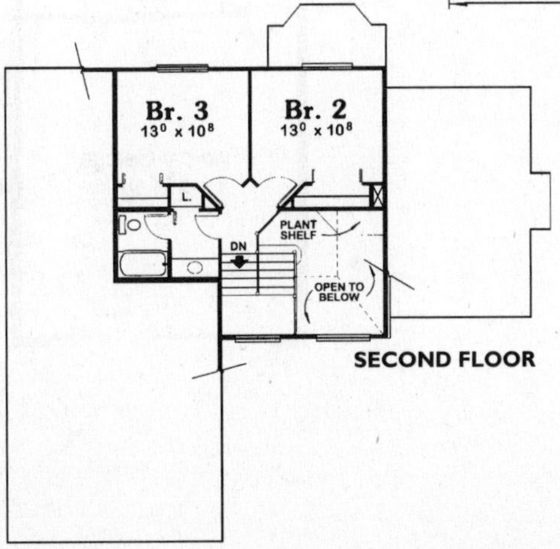

Br. 3
13⁰ x 10⁸
Br. 2
13⁰ x 10⁸
PLANT SHELF
DN
OPEN TO BELOW

SECOND FLOOR

Design 92622

See Order Pages and Index for Info

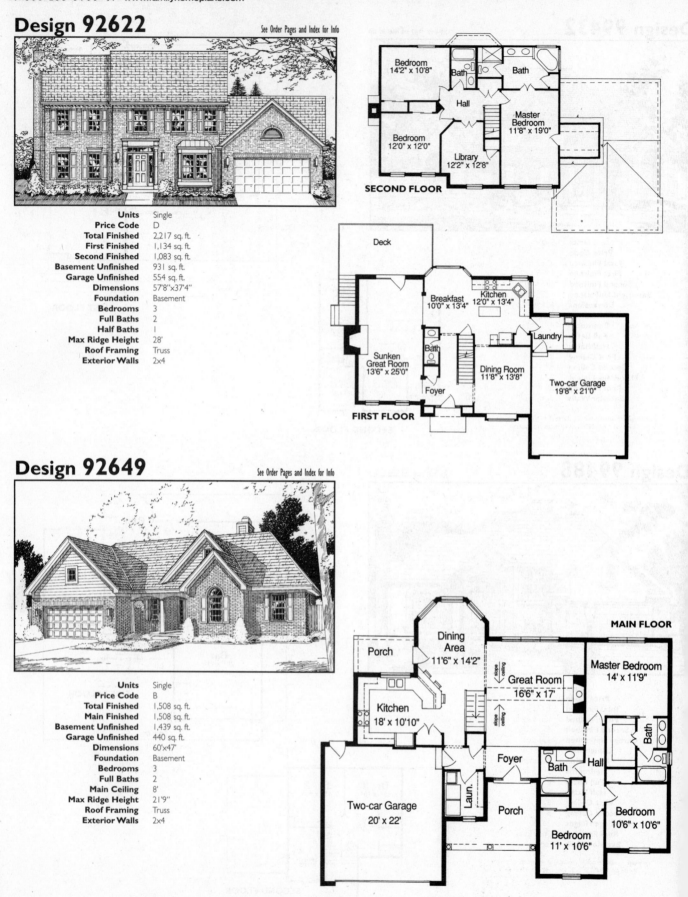

Units	Single
Price Code	D
Total Finished	2,217 sq. ft.
First Finished	1,134 sq. ft.
Second Finished	1,083 sq. ft.
Basement Unfinished	931 sq. ft.
Garage Unfinished	554 sq. ft.
Dimensions	57'8"x37'4"
Foundation	Basement
Bedrooms	3
Full Baths	2
Half Baths	1
Max Ridge Height	28'
Roof Framing	Truss
Exterior Walls	2x4

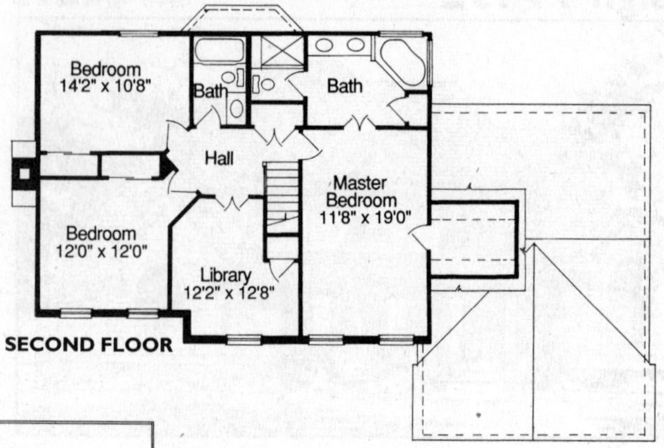
Bedroom
14'2" x 10'8"
Bath
Bath
Hall
Master
Bedroom
11'8" x 19'0"
Bedroom
12'0" x 12'0"
Library
12'2" x 12'8"

SECOND FLOOR

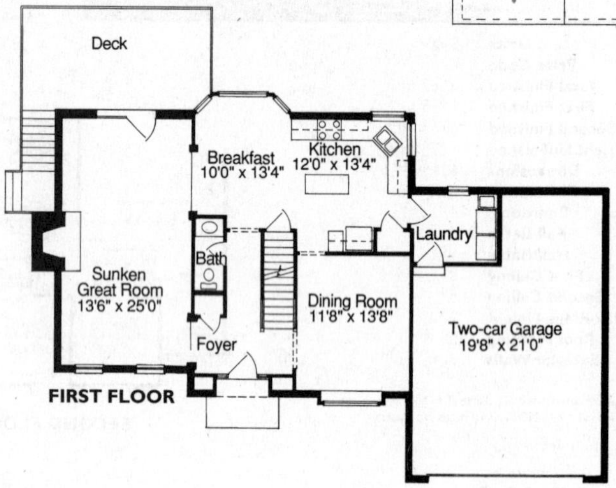
Deck
Breakfast
10'0" x 13'4"
Kitchen
12'0" x 13'4"
Laundry
Bath
Sunken
Great Room
13'6" x 25'0"
Dining Room
11'8" x 13'8"
Two-car Garage
19'8" x 21'0"
Foyer

FIRST FLOOR

Design 92649

See Order Pages and Index for Info

Units	Single
Price Code	B
Total Finished	1,508 sq. ft.
Main Finished	1,508 sq. ft.
Basement Unfinished	1,439 sq. ft.
Garage Unfinished	440 sq. ft.
Dimensions	60'x47'
Foundation	Basement
Bedrooms	3
Full Baths	2
Main Ceiling	8'
Max Ridge Height	21'9"
Roof Framing	Truss
Exterior Walls	2x4

MAIN FLOOR

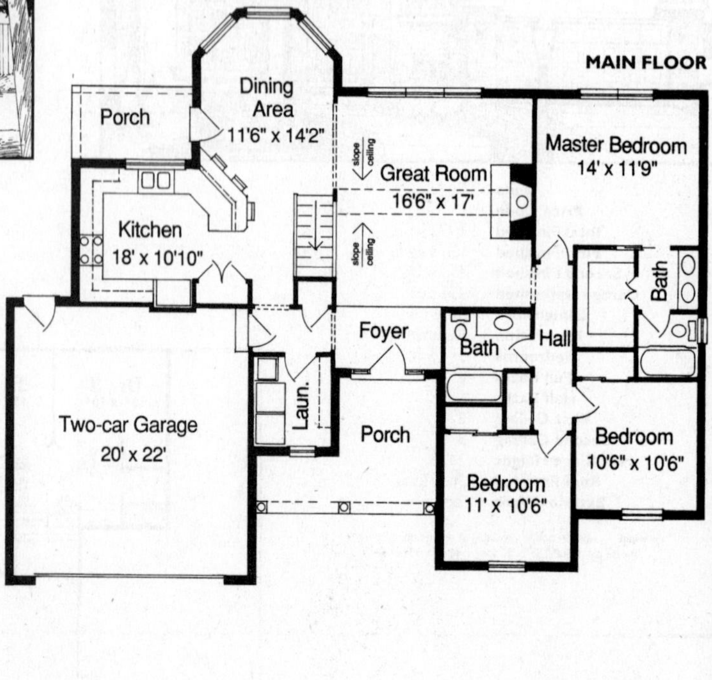
Dining
Area
11'6" x 14'2"
Porch
Master Bedroom
14' x 11'9"
slope
ceiling
Great Room
16'6" x 17'
slope
ceiling
Kitchen
18' x 10'10"
Bath
Foyer
Bath
Hall
Laun.
Two-car Garage
20' x 22'
Porch
Bedroom
10'6" x 10'6"
Bedroom
11' x 10'6"

Design 94223

See Order Pages and Index for Info

Units	Single
Price Code	G
Total Finished	3,896 sq. ft.
Main Finished	3,896 sq. ft.
Bonus Unfinished	356 sq. ft.
Garage Unfinished	846 sq. ft.
Porch Unfinished	930 sq. ft.
Dimensions	90'x128'8"
Foundation	Slab
Bedrooms	3
Full Baths	2
Half Baths	2
3/4 Baths	2
Main Ceiling	13'-4'
Max Ridge Height	36'6"
Roof Framing	Stick

* Alternate foundation options available at an additional charge. Please call 1-800-235-5700 for more information.

MAIN FLOOR

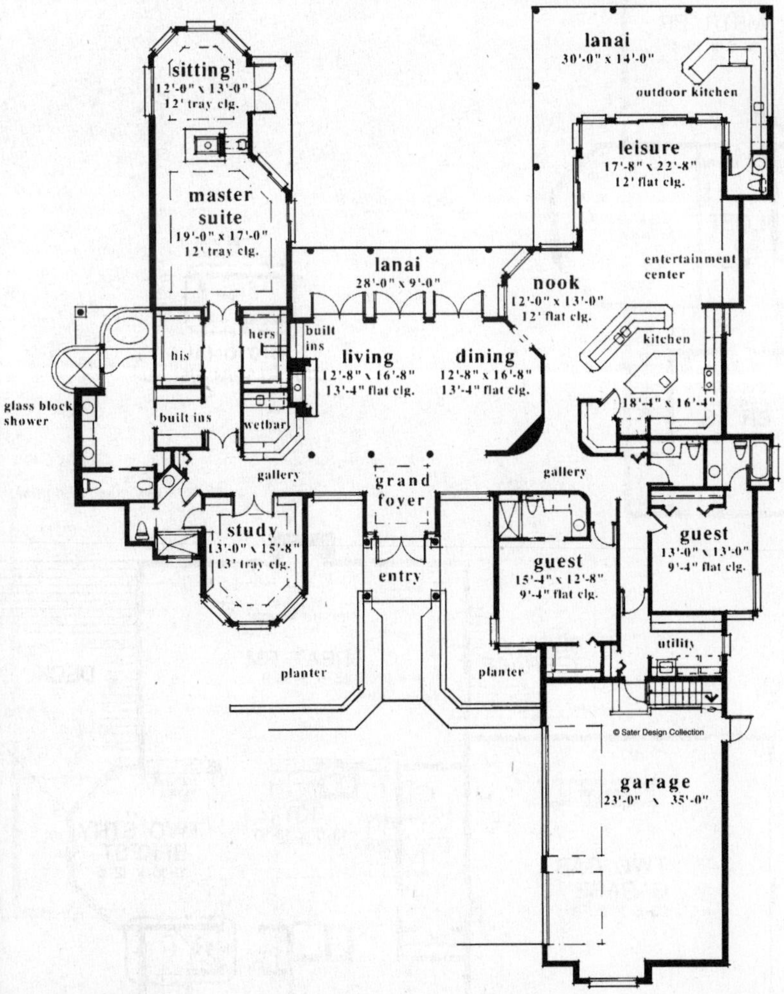
lanai
30'-0" x 14'-0"
outdoor kitchen
sitting
12'-0" x 13'-0"
12' tray clg.
leisure
17'-8" x 22'-8"
12' flat clg.
master
suite
19'-0" x 17'-0"
12' tray clg.
entertainment
center
lanai
28'-0" x 9'-0"
nook
12'-0" x 13'-0"
12' flat clg.
his
hers
built
ins
living
12'-8" x 16'-8"
13'-4" flat clg.
dining
12'-8" x 16'-8"
13'-4" flat clg.
kitchen
18'-4" x 16'-4"
glass block
shower
built ins
wetbar
gallery
grand
foyer
gallery
study
13'-0" x 15'-8"
13' tray clg.
entry
guest
15'-4" x 12'-8"
9'-4" flat clg.
guest
13'-0" x 13'-0"
9'-4" flat clg.
utility
planter
planter
© Sater Design Collection
garage
23'-0" x 35'-0"

BONUS

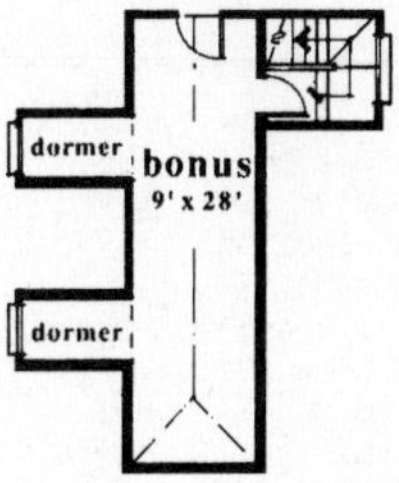
dormer
bonus
9' x 28'
dormer

Design 24964

See Order Pages and Index for Info

Units	Single
Price Code	D
Total Finished	2,240 sq. ft.
First Finished	1,195 sq. ft.
Second Finished	1,045 sq. ft.
Bonus Unfinished	338 sq. ft.
Basement Unfinished	1,195 sq. ft.
Garage Unfinished	635 sq. ft.
Porch Unfinished	130 sq. ft.
Dimensions	55'8"x46'
Foundation	Basement Crawlspace Slab
Bedrooms	3
Full Baths	2
Half Baths	1
First Ceiling	9'
Second Ceiling	8'
Max Ridge Height	34'
Roof Framing	Truss
Exterior Walls	2x4

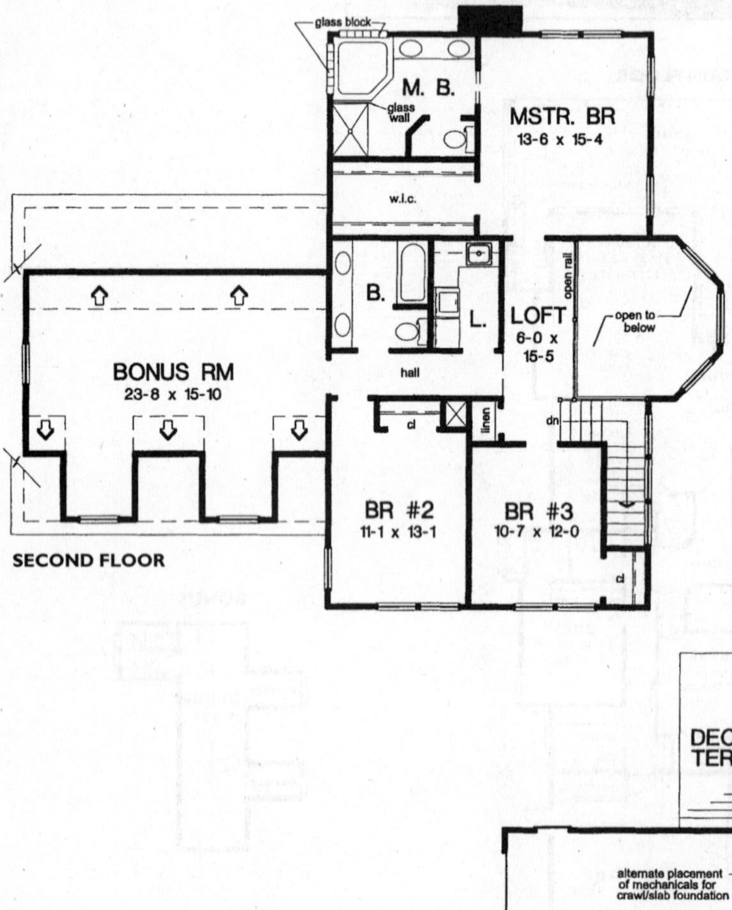

glass block
M. B.
glass wall
MSTR. BR
13-6 x 15-4
w.i.c.
B.
L.
LOFT
6-0 x
15-5
open rail
open to below
hall
BONUS RM
23-8 x 15-10
cl
linen
dn
BR #2
11-1 x 13-1
BR #3
10-7 x 12-0
cl

SECOND FLOOR

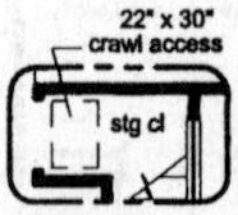

22" x 30"
crawl access
stg cl

OPTIONAL CRAWLSPACE/SLAB

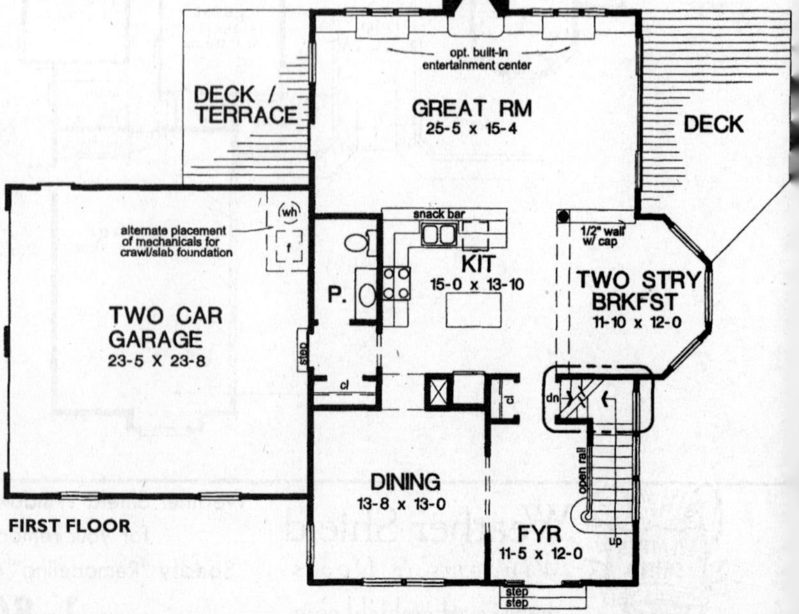

opt. built-in entertainment center
DECK / TERRACE
GREAT RM
25-5 x 15-4
DECK
wh
alternate placement of mechanicals for crawl/slab foundation
f
snack bar
KIT
15-0 x 13-10
1/2" wall w/ cap
TWO STRY BRKFST
11-10 x 12-0
P.
TWO CAR GARAGE
23-5 X 23-8
step
cl
cl
dn
open rail
DINING
13-8 x 13-0
FYR
11-5 x 12-0
up
step
step

FIRST FLOOR

Design 93453

See Order Pages and Index for Info

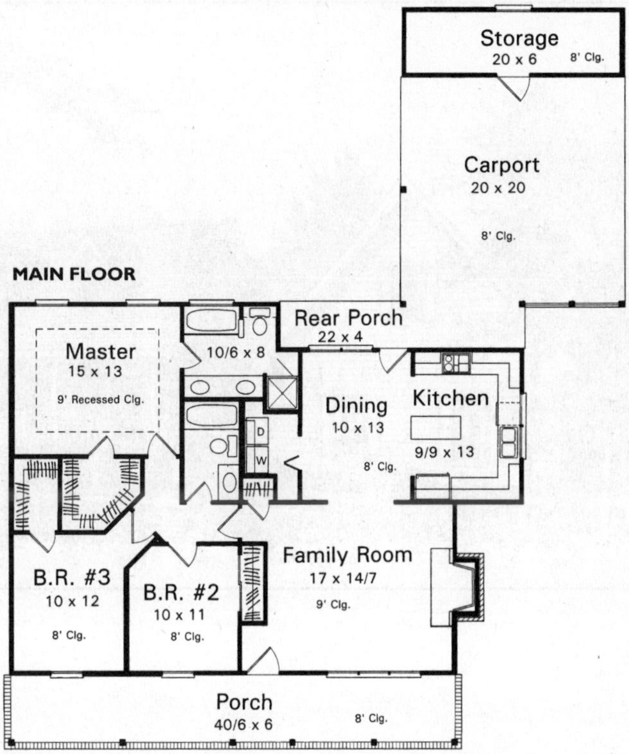
MAIN FLOOR
Storage
20 x 6
8' Clg.
Carport
20 x 20
8' Clg.
Rear Porch
22 x 4
Master
15 x 13
9' Recessed Clg.
10/6 x 8
Dining
10 x 13
8' Clg.
Kitchen
9/9 x 13
D
W
Family Room
17 x 14/7
9' Clg.
B.R. #3
10 x 12
8' Clg.
B.R. #2
10 x 11
8' Clg.
Porch
40/6 x 6
8' Clg.

Units	Single
Price Code	A
Total Finished	1,333 sq. ft.
Main Finished	1,333 sq. ft.
Garage Unfinished	520 sq. ft.
Dimensions	55'6"x64'3"
Foundation	Crawlspace Slab
Bedrooms	3
Full Baths	2
Main Ceiling	8'
Max Ridge Height	19'5"
Roof Framing	Stick
Exterior Walls	2x4

Design 94307

See Order Pages and Index for Info

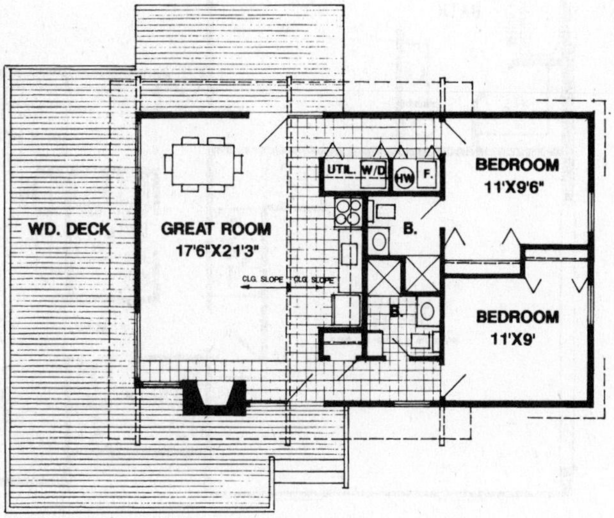
MAIN FLOOR
WD. DECK
GREAT ROOM
17'6"X21'3"
CLG. SLOPE
CLG. SLOPE
UTIL.
W/D
HW
F.
B.
B.
BEDROOM
11'X9'6"
BEDROOM
11'X9'

Units	Single
Price Code	A
Total Finished	786 sq. ft.
Main Finished	786 sq. ft.
Dimensions	46'x22'
Foundation	Crawlspace
Bedrooms	2
3/4 Baths	2
Main Ceiling	8'
Vaulted Ceiling	16'
Max Ridge Height	18'6"
Roof Framing	Truss
Exterior Walls	2x6

Design 96529

See Order Pages and Index for Info

Units	Single
Price Code	D
Total Finished	2,089 sq. ft.
Main Finished	2,089 sq. ft.
Bonus Unfinished	497 sq. ft.
Garage Unfinished	541 sq. ft.
Dimensions	79'x52'
Foundation	Crawlspace Slab
Bedrooms	3
Full Baths	2
Half Baths	1
Main Ceiling	9'
Max Ridge Height	22'
Roof Framing	Stick
Exterior Walls	2x4

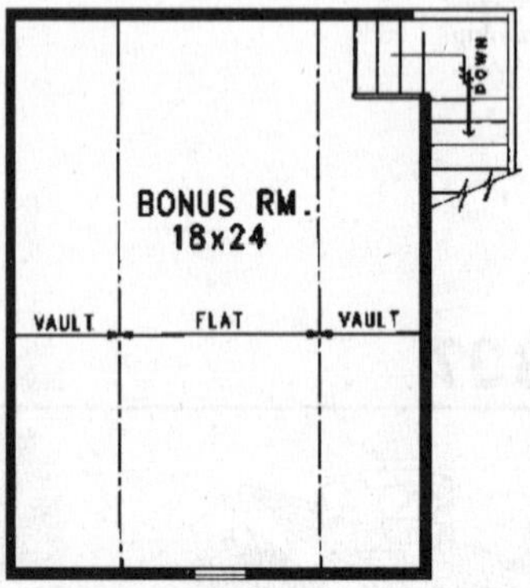
DOWN
BONUS RM.
18x24
VAULT
FLAT
VAULT

BONUS

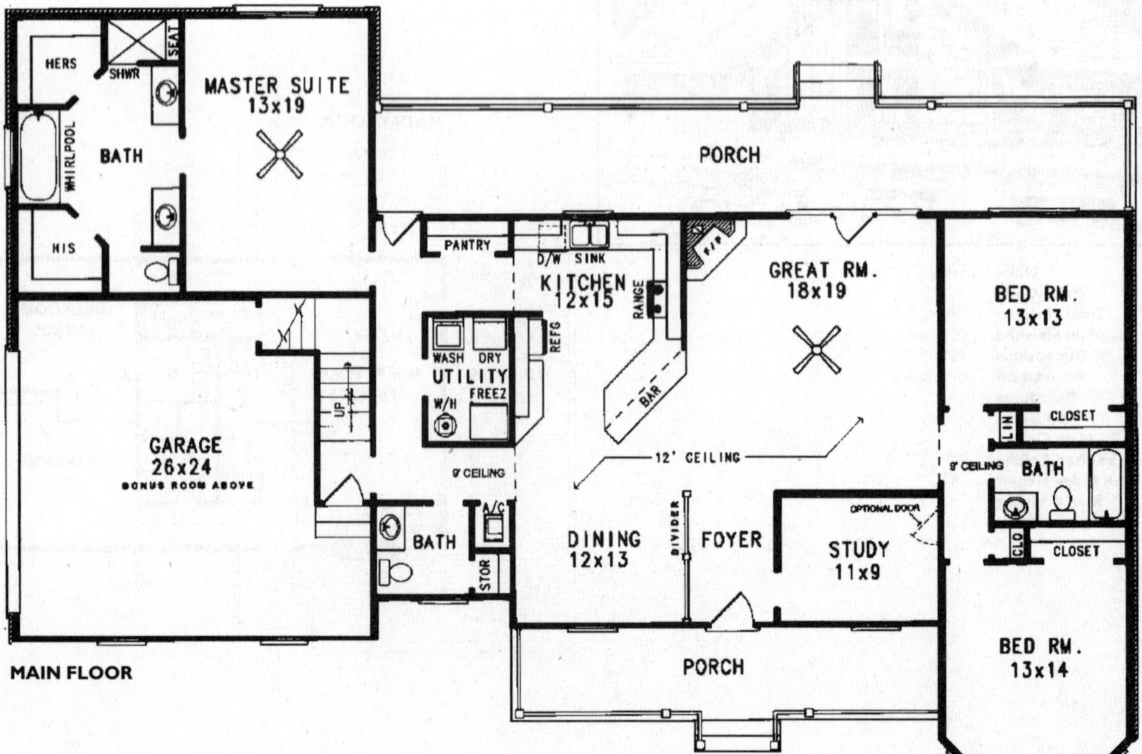
HERS
SHWR
SEAT
MASTER SUITE
13x19
WHIRLPOOL
BATH
HIS
PORCH
PANTRY
D/W SINK
KITCHEN
12x15
RANGE
GREAT RM.
18x19
BED RM.
13x13
WASH DRY
UTILITY
FREEZ
W/H
REFG
BAR
UP
GARAGE
26x24
BONUS ROOM ABOVE
12' CEILING
9' CEILING
CLOSET
LIN
BATH
A/C
BATH
STOR
DINING
12x13
DIVIDER
FOYER
OPTIONAL DOOR
STUDY
11x9
CLO
CLOSET
PORCH
BED RM.
13x14

MAIN FLOOR

Design 94640

See Order Pages and Index for Info

Units	Single
Price Code	F
Total Finished	2,558 sq. ft.
Main Finished	2,558 sq. ft.
Garage Unfinished	549 sq. ft.
Porch Unfinished	151 sq. ft.
Dimensions	63'6"x71'6"
Foundation	Crawlspace Slab
Bedrooms	4
Full Baths	3
Main Ceiling	9'
Max Ridge Height	21'6"
Roof Framing	Stick
Exterior Walls	2x4

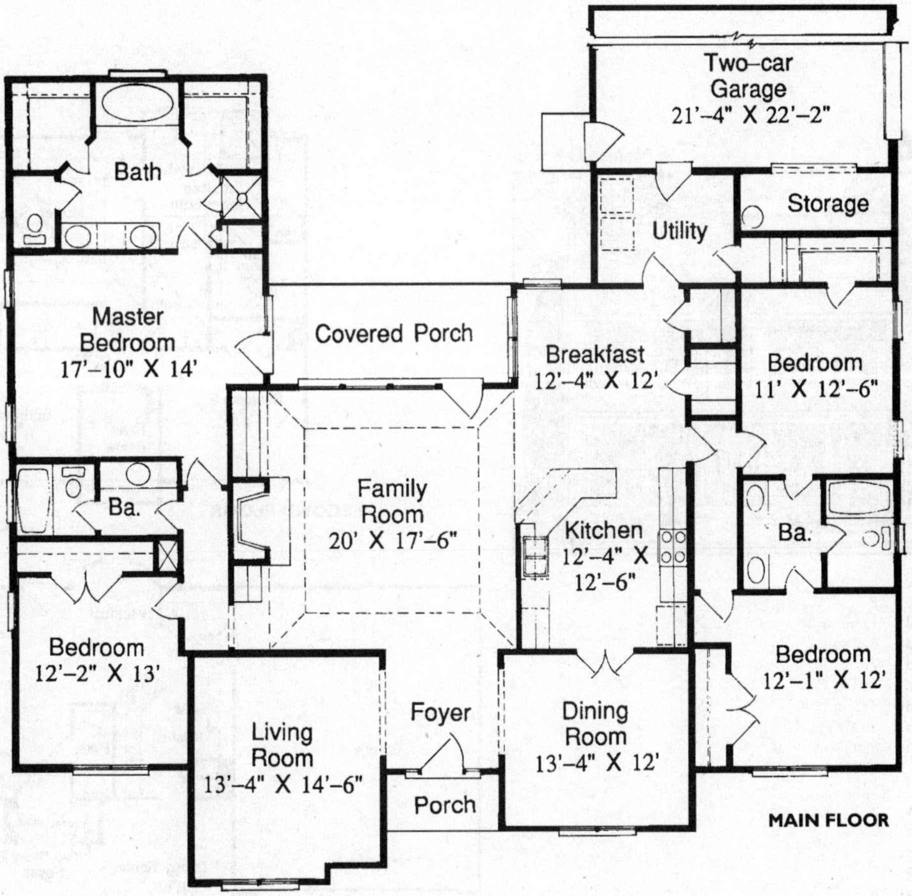
Two-car Garage 21'-4" X 22'-2"
Bath
Storage
Utility
Master Bedroom 17'-10" X 14'
Covered Porch
Breakfast 12'-4" X 12'
Bedroom 11' X 12'-6"
Family Room 20' X 17'-6"
Ba.
Kitchen 12'-4" X 12'-6"
Ba.
Bedroom 12'-2" X 13'
Bedroom 12'-1" X 12'
Foyer
Living Room 13'-4" X 14'-6"
Dining Room 13'-4" X 12'
Porch

MAIN FLOOR

Design 98441

See Order Pages and Index for Info

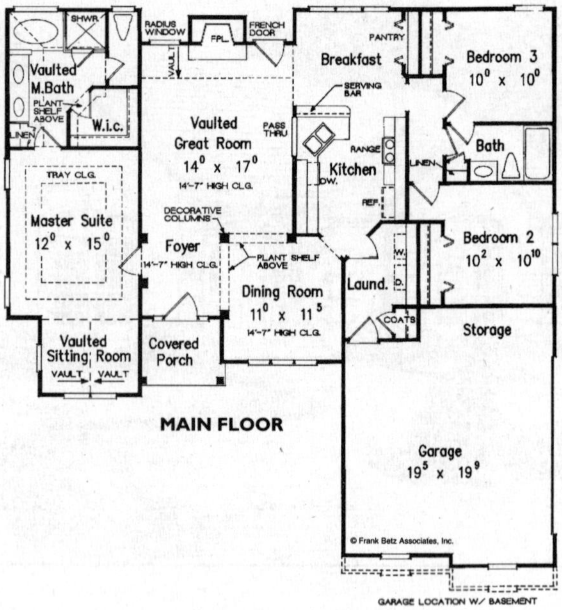

SHWR.
Vaulted M.Bath
PLANT SHELF ABOVE
LINEN
W.i.c.
RADIUS WINDOW
FPL.
FRENCH DOOR
VAULT
Vaulted Great Room
14^0 x 17^0
14'-7" HIGH CLG.
PASS THRU
Breakfast
PANTRY
SERVING BAR
RANGE
Kitchen
DW.
REF.
Bedroom 3
10^0 x 10^0
Bath
LINEN
TRAY CLG.
Master Suite
12^0 x 15^0
DECORATIVE COLUMNS
Foyer
14'-7" HIGH CLG.
PLANT SHELF ABOVE
Dining Room
11^0 x 11^5
14'-7" HIGH CLG.
Laund.
W.
D.
Bedroom 2
10^2 x 10^{10}
COATS
Storage
Vaulted Sitting Room
VAULT
VAULT
Covered Porch
Garage
19^5 x 19^9
© Frank Betz Associates, Inc.
GARAGE LOCATION W/ BASEMENT

MAIN FLOOR

Units	Single
Price Code	B
Total Finished	1,502 sq. ft.
Main Finished	1,502 sq. ft.
Basement Unfinished	1,555 sq. ft.
Garage Unfinished	448 sq. ft.
Dimensions	51'x50'6"
Foundation	Basement Crawlspace
Bedrooms	3
Full Baths	2
Max Ridge Height	24'9"
Roof Framing	Stick
Exterior Walls	2x4

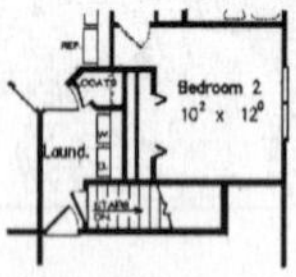

Bedroom 2
10^2 x 12^6
COATS
Laund.

BASEMENT OPTION

Design 98406

See Order Pages and Index for Info

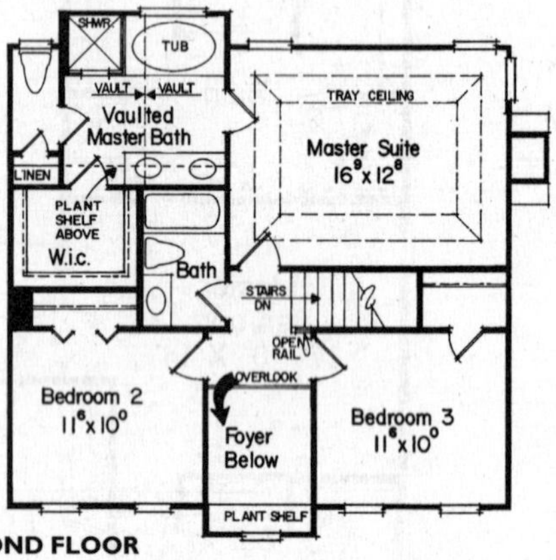

SHWR.
TUB
VAULT
VAULT
Vaulted Master Bath
LINEN
PLANT SHELF ABOVE
W.i.c.
TRAY CEILING
Master Suite
16^{9}x12^8
Bath
STAIRS DN
OPEN RAIL
OVERLOOK
Bedroom 2
11^{6}x10^0
Foyer Below
Bedroom 3
11^{6}x10^0
PLANT SHELF

SECOND FLOOR

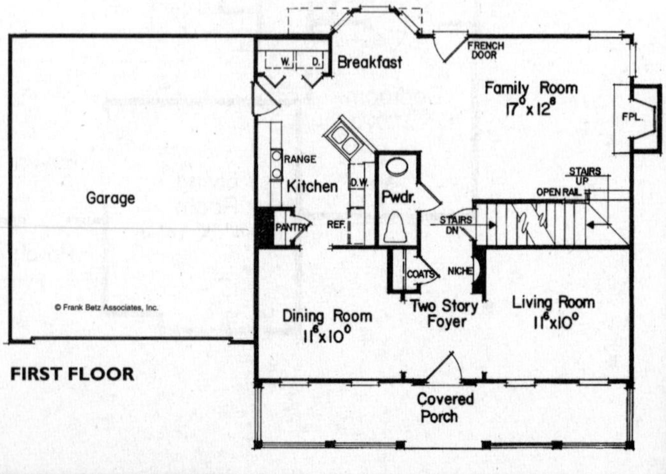

W.
D.
Breakfast
FRENCH DOOR
Family Room
17^{0}x12^8
FPL.
RANGE
Kitchen
D.W.
Pwdr.
STAIRS UP
OPEN RAIL
Garage
PANTRY
REF.
STAIRS DN
COATS
NICHE
© Frank Betz Associates, Inc.
Dining Room
11^{6}x10^0
Two Story Foyer
Living Room
11^{6}x10^0
Covered Porch

FIRST FLOOR

Units	Single
Price Code	B
Total Finished	1,600 sq. ft.
First Finished	828 sq. ft.
Second Finished	772 sq. ft.
Basement Unfinished	828 sq. ft.
Garage Unfinished	473 sq. ft.
Dimensions	52'4"x34'
Foundation	Basement Crawlspace Slab
Bedrooms	3
Full Baths	2
Half Baths	1
First Ceiling	9'
Second Ceiling	8'
Max Ridge Height	28'
Roof Framing	Stick
Exterior Walls	2x4

Design 99459

See Order Pages and Index for Info

Units	Single
Price Code	E
Total Finished	2,256 sq. ft.
First Finished	1,602 sq. ft.
Second Finished	654 sq. ft.
Dimensions	54'x50'
Foundation	Basement
Bedrooms	4
Full Baths	2
Half Baths	1
Max Ridge Height	26'
Roof Framing	Stick/Truss
Exterior Walls	2x4

* Alternate foundation options available at an additonal charge. Please call 1-800-235-5700 for more information.

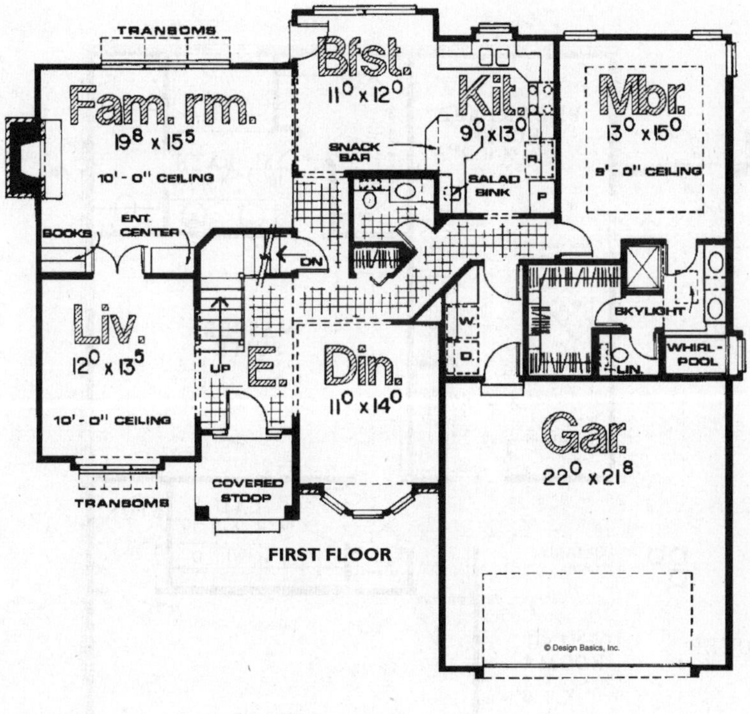
TRANSOMS
Bfst.
11⁰ x 12⁰
Fam. rm.
19⁸ x 15⁵
10' - 0" CEILING
Kit.
9⁰ x 13⁰
Mbr.
13⁰ x 15⁰
9' - 0" CEILING
SNACK BAR
SALAD SINK
R.
P
BOOKS
ENT. CENTER
DN
SKYLIGHT
Liv.
12⁰ x 13⁵
10' - 0" CEILING
UP
E.
Din.
11⁰ x 14⁰
W.
D.
LIN.
WHIRL-POOL
Gar.
22⁰ x 21⁸
COVERED STOOP
TRANSOMS
© Design Basics, Inc.

FIRST FLOOR

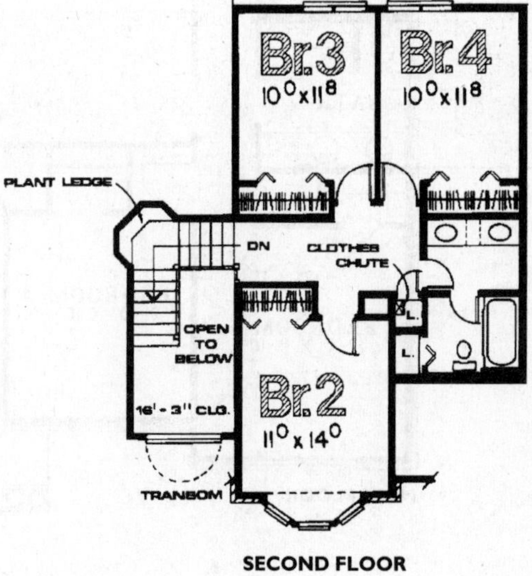
Br.3
10⁰ x 11⁸
Br.4
10⁰ x 11⁸
PLANT LEDGE
DN
CLOTHES CHUTE
L.
L.
OPEN TO BELOW
16' - 3" CLG.
Br.2
11⁰ x 14⁰
TRANSOM

SECOND FLOOR

Design 61096

See Order Pages and Index for Info

Units	Single
Price Code	D
Total Finished	2,148 sq. ft.
Main Finished	2,148 sq. ft.
Garage Unfinished	477 sq. ft.
Porch Unfinished	190 sq. ft.
Dimensions	63'x52'8"
Foundation	Crawlspace Slab
Bedrooms	4
Full Baths	2
Main Ceiling	9'
Roof Framing	Stick
Exterior Walls	2x4

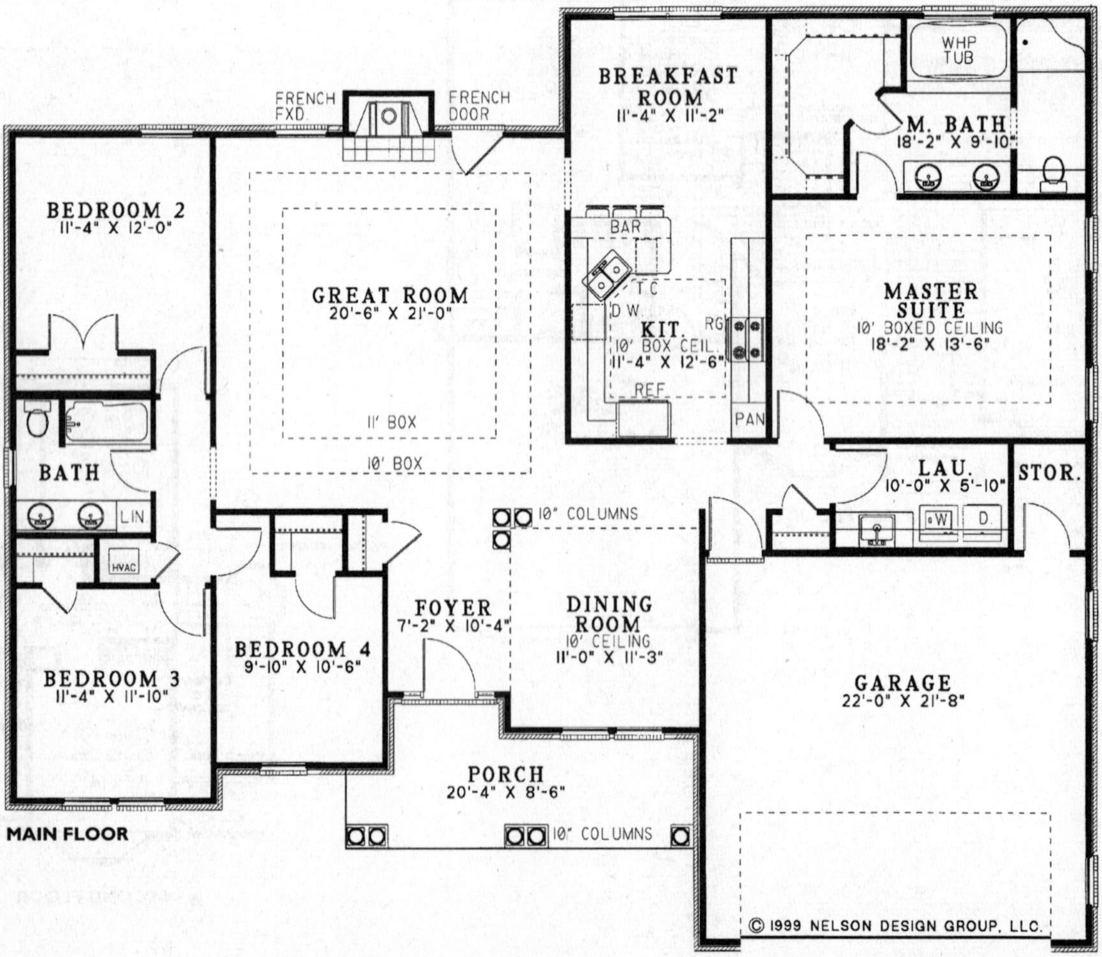
FRENCH FXD.
FRENCH DOOR
BREAKFAST ROOM
11'-4" X 11'-2"
WHP TUB
M. BATH
18'-2" X 9'-10"
BEDROOM 2
11'-4" X 12'-0"
GREAT ROOM
20'-6" X 21'-0"
11' BOX
10' BOX
BAR
T C
D W.
KIT.
10' BOX CEIL.
11'-4" X 12'-6"
RG
REF.
PAN
MASTER SUITE
10' BOXED CEILING
18'-2" X 13'-6"
BATH
LIN
HVAC
10" COLUMNS
LAU.
10'-0" X 5'-10"
STOR.
W
D
FOYER
7'-2" X 10'-4"
DINING ROOM
10' CEILING
11'-0" X 11'-3"
BEDROOM 4
9'-10" X 10'-6"
BEDROOM 3
11'-4" X 11'-10"
GARAGE
22'-0" X 21'-8"
PORCH
20'-4" X 8'-6"
10" COLUMNS
© 1999 NELSON DESIGN GROUP, LLC.

MAIN FLOOR

Design 60112

See Order Pages and Index for Info

Units	Single
Price Code	A
Total Finished	1,149 sq. ft.
Main Finished	1,149 sq. ft.
Basement Unfinished	1,166 sq. ft.
Garage Unfinished	422 sq. ft.
Dimensions	47'6"x42'4"
Foundation	Basement
Bedrooms	3
Full Baths	2
Main Ceiling	9'
Max Ridge Height	21'10"
Roof Framing	Stick
Exterior Walls	2x4

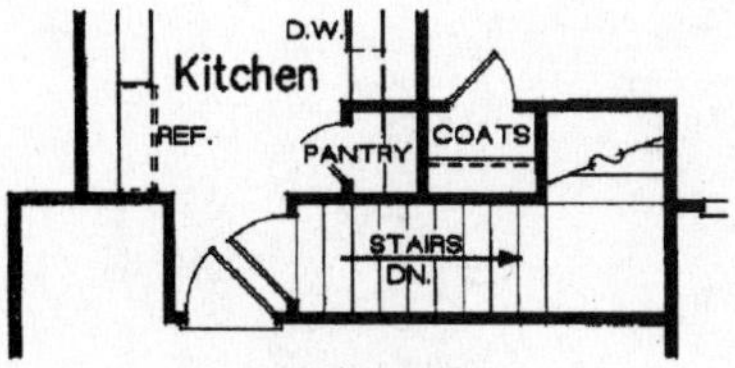
D.W.
Kitchen
REF.
PANTRY
COATS
STAIRS DN.

OPTIONAL

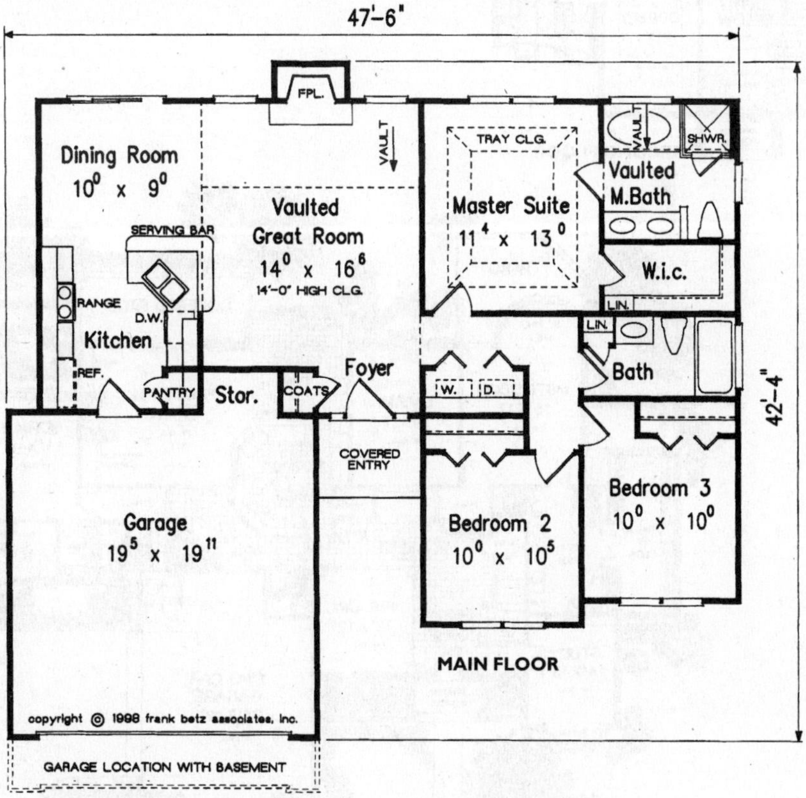
47'-6"
42'-4"
FPL.
VAULT
Dining Room 10^0 x 9^0
SERVING BAR
Vaulted Great Room 14^0 x 16^6
14'-0" HIGH CLG.
RANGE
D.W.
Kitchen
REF.
PANTRY
Stor.
COATS
Foyer
TRAY CLG.
Master Suite 11^4 x 13^0
VAULT
SHWR.
Vaulted M.Bath
W.i.c.
LIN.
LIN.
Bath
W.
D.
COVERED ENTRY
Bedroom 2 10^0 x 10^5
Bedroom 3 10^0 x 10^0
Garage 19^5 x 19^11
copyright © 1998 frank betz associates, inc.
GARAGE LOCATION WITH BASEMENT

MAIN FLOOR

Design 96327

See Order Pages and Index for Info

Units	Single
Price Code	L
Total Finished	4,047 sq. ft.
First Finished	2,994 sq. ft.
Second Finished	1,053 sq. ft.
Garage Unfinished	818 sq. ft.
Porch Unfinished	48 sq. ft.
Dimensions	127'9.5"x61'1"
Foundation	Basement Crawlspace Slab
Bedrooms	4
Full Baths	4
Half Baths	1
First Ceiling	10'
Second Ceiling	8'
Roof Framing	Stick
Exterior Walls	2x4

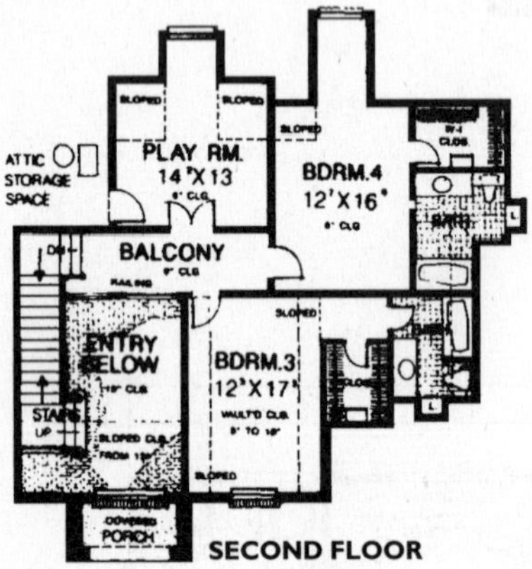
ATTIC STORAGE SPACE
PLAY RM. 14'X13
BDRM.4 12'X16'
BALCONY
ENTRY BELOW
BDRM.3 12'X17'
STAIRS UP
COVERED PORCH

SECOND FLOOR

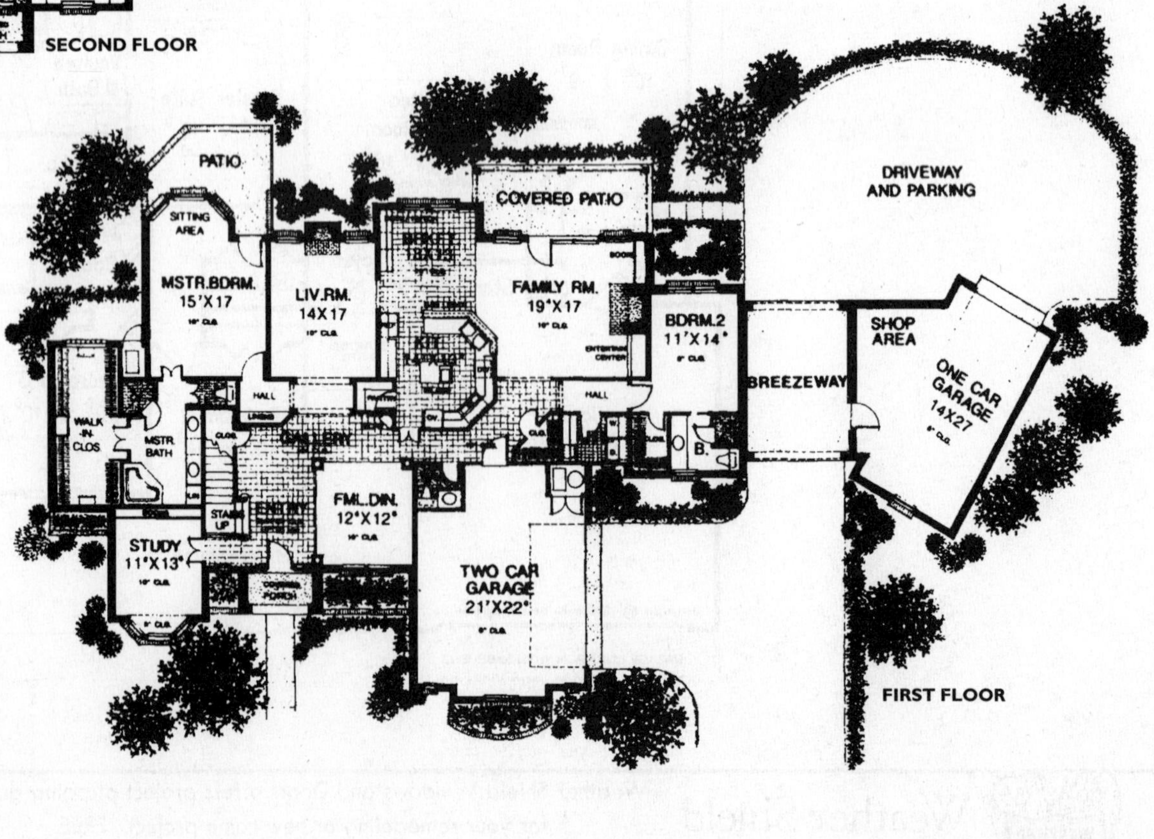
PATIO
SITTING AREA
MSTR.BDRM. 15'X17
LIV.RM. 14X17
COVERED PATIO
FAMILY RM. 19'X17
BDRM.2 11'X14'
DRIVEWAY AND PARKING
SHOP AREA
ONE CAR GARAGE 14X27
BREEZEWAY
HALL
WALK-IN-CLOS.
MSTR. BATH
GALLERY
ENTRY
FML.DIN. 12'X12'
STUDY 11'X13'
COVERED PORCH
TWO CAR GARAGE 21'X22'

FIRST FLOOR

Design 93254

See Order Pages and Index for Info

Units	Single
Price Code	F
Total Finished	2,509 sq. ft.
First Finished	1,282 sq. ft.
Second Finished	1,227 sq. ft.
Bonus Unfinished	314 sq. ft.
Basement Unfinished	1,154 sq. ft.
Garage Unfinished	528 sq. ft.
Dimensions	62'x36'
Foundation	Basement Crawlspace Slab
Bedrooms	3
Full Baths	3
Half Baths	1
First Ceiling	9'
Max Ridge Height	38'
Roof Framing	Stick
Exterior Walls	2x4

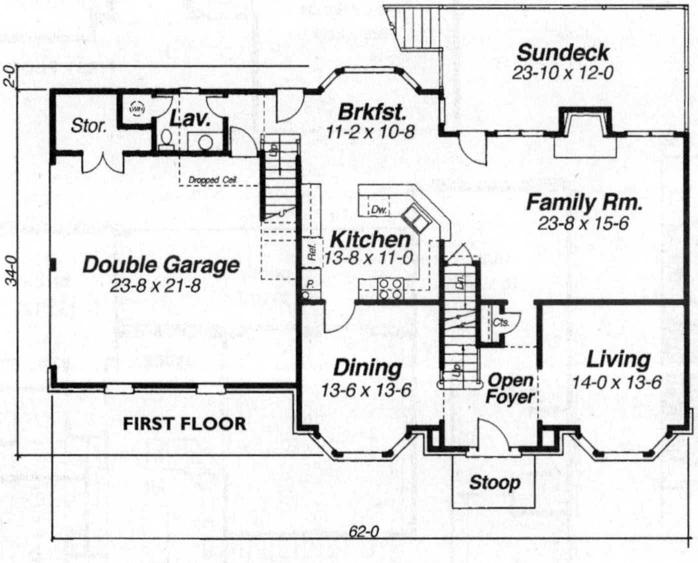
Sundeck
23-10 x 12-0
Brkfst.
11-2 x 10-8
Stor.
Lav.
Dropped Ceil
Family Rm.
23-8 x 15-6
Kitchen
13-8 x 11-0
Double Garage
23-8 x 21-8
Dining
13-6 x 13-6
Open
Foyer
Living
14-0 x 13-6
Stoop
FIRST FLOOR
2-0
34-0
62-0

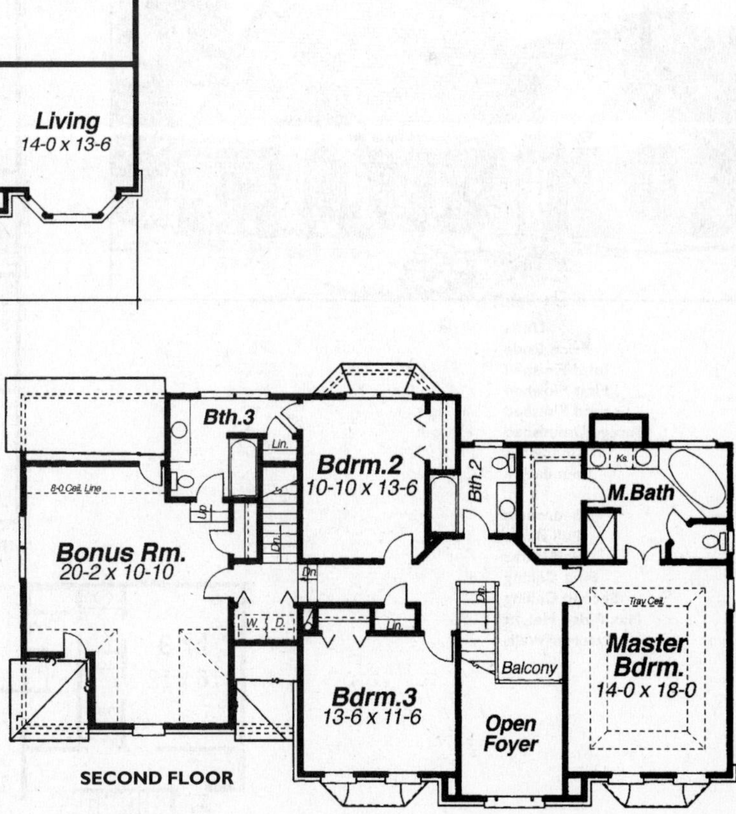
Bth.3
Lin.
Bdrm.2
10-10 x 13-6
Bth.2
M.Bath
8-0 Ceil. Line
Bonus Rm.
20-2 x 10-10
W.
D.
Lin.
Tray Ceil.
Master
Bdrm.
14-0 x 18-0
Balcony
Bdrm.3
13-6 x 11-6
Open
Foyer
SECOND FLOOR

Design 92642

See Order Pages and Index for Info

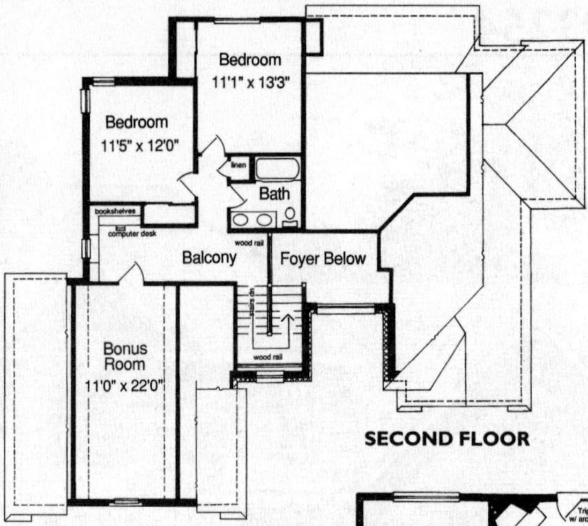
Bedroom
11'1" x 13'3"
Bedroom
11'5" x 12'0"
linen
Bath
bookshelves
computer desk
wood rail
Balcony
Foyer Below
Bonus Room
11'0" x 22'0"
wood rail

SECOND FLOOR

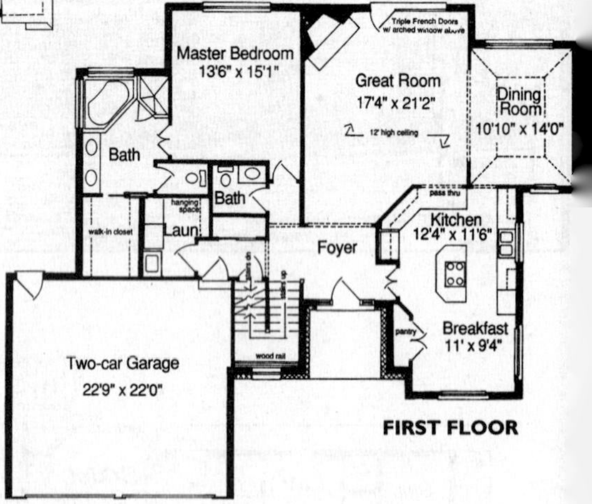
Triple French Doors w/ arched window above
Master Bedroom
13'6" x 15'1"
Great Room
17'4" x 21'2"
12' high ceiling
Dining Room
10'10" x 14'0"
Bath
hanging space
Bath
pass thru
Kitchen
12'4" x 11'6"
walk-in closet
Laun
Foyer
pantry
Breakfast
11' x 9'4"
Two-car Garage
22'9" x 22'0"
wood rail

FIRST FLOOR

Units	Single
Price Code	D
Total Finished	2,082 sq. ft.
First Finished	1,524 sq. ft.
Second Finished	558 sq. ft.
Bonus Unfinished	267 sq. ft.
Basement Unfinished	1,460 sq. ft.
Dimensions	60'x50'4"
Foundation	Basement
Bedrooms	3
Full Baths	2
Half Baths	1
First Ceiling	8'
Second Ceiling	8'
Max Ridge Height	26'
Roof Framing	Truss
Exterior Walls	2x4

Design 92582

See Order Pages and Index for Info.

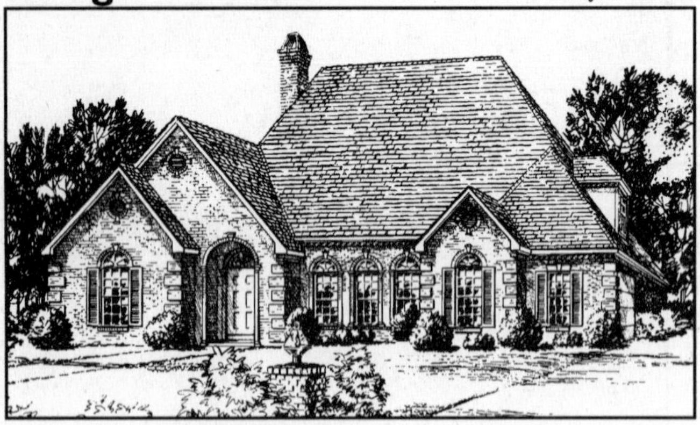

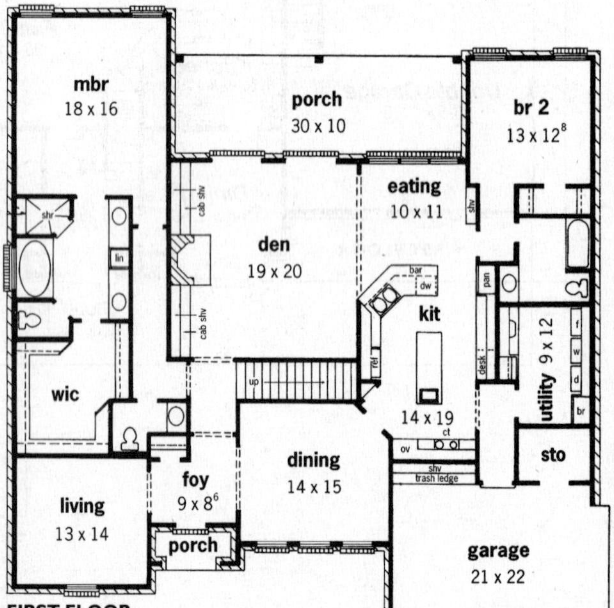
mbr
18 x 16
porch
30 x 10
br 2
13 x 12[8]
eating
10 x 11
den
19 x 20
cab shv
shr
lin
bar
dw
kit
14 x 19
pan
utility 9 x 12
wic
up
ref
desk
ct
living
13 x 14
foy
9 x 8[6]
dining
14 x 15
ov
shv
trash ledge
sto
porch
garage
21 x 22
sto

FIRST FLOOR

Units	Single
Price Code	I
Total Finished	3,256 sq. ft.
First Finished	2,545 sq. ft.
Second Finished	711 sq. ft.
Garage Unfinished	484 sq. ft.
Dimensions	59'10"x72'10"
Foundation	Crawlspace Slab
Bedrooms	4
Full Baths	3
Half Baths	1
First Ceiling	9'
Second Ceiling	8'
Max Ridge Height	29'6"
Exterior Walls	2x4

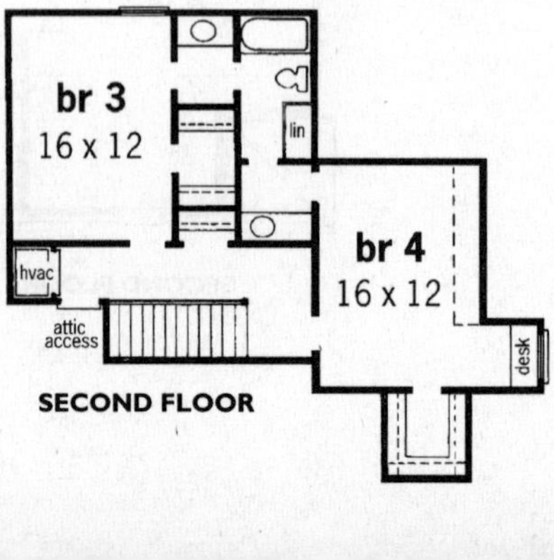
br 3
16 x 12
lin
br 4
16 x 12
hvac
attic access
desk

SECOND FLOOR

Design 93333

See Order Pages and Index for Info

Units	Single
Price Code	H
Total Finished	3,198 sq. ft.
First Finished	1,743 sq. ft.
Second Finished	1,455 sq. ft.
Dimensions	94'6"x60'2"
Foundation	Basement
Bedrooms	4
Full Baths	2
Half Baths	1
First Ceiling	8'4.5"
Second Ceiling	8'4.5"
Max Ridge Height	29'
Roof Framing	Stick
Exterior Walls	2x6

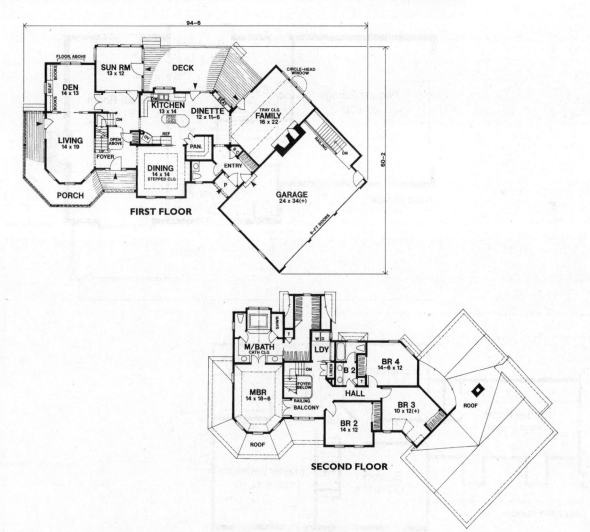

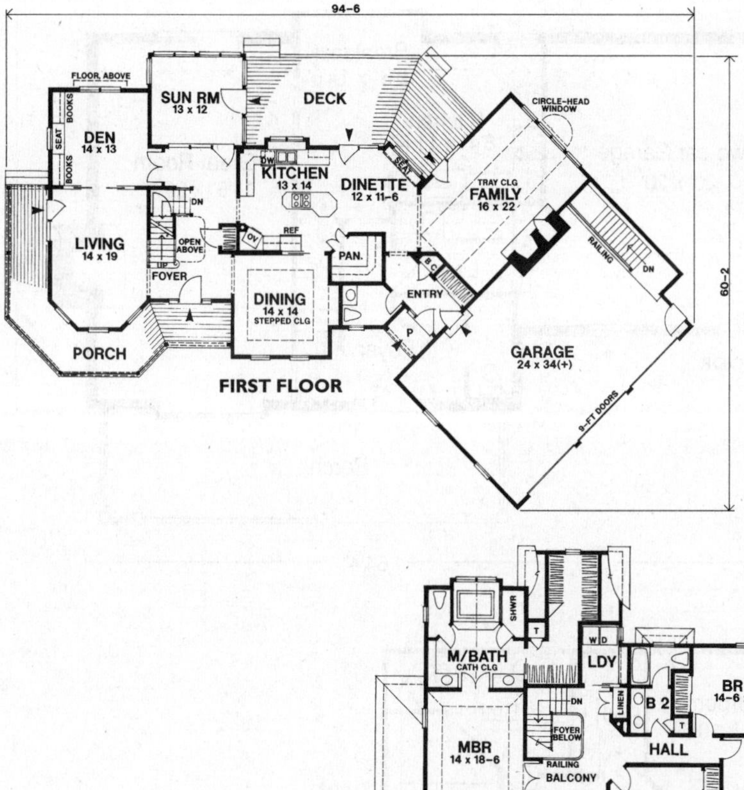
94-6
60-2
FLOOR ABOVE
SUN RM 13 x 12
DECK
DEN 14 x 13
BOOKS
SEAT
KITCHEN 13 x 14
DW
DINETTE 12 x 11-6
SEAT
CIRCLE-HEAD WINDOW
TRAY CLG FAMILY 16 x 22
LIVING 14 x 19
DN
OPEN ABOVE
OV
REF
PAN.
RAILING
DN
UP
FOYER
DINING 14 x 14 STEPPED CLG
ENTRY
P
GARAGE 24 x 34(+)
9-FT DOORS
PORCH
FIRST FLOOR

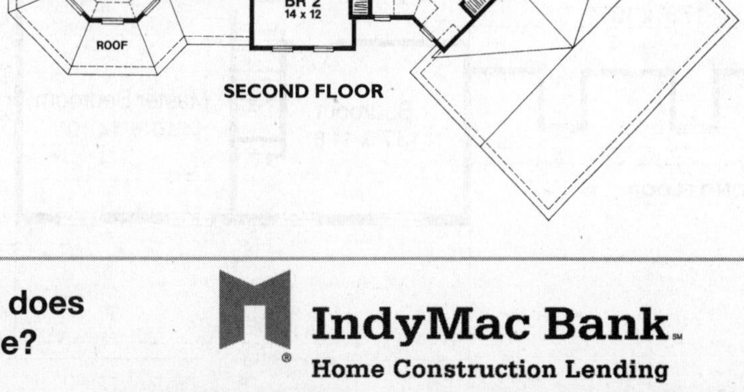
SHWR
T
W D
M/BATH CATH CLG
LDY
LINEN
B 2
T
BR 4 14-6 x 12
DN
FOYER BELOW
MBR 14 x 18-6
HALL
RAILING
BALCONY
BR 3 10 x 12(+)
ROOF
BR 2 14 x 12
ROOF
SECOND FLOOR

Design 92690

See Order Pages and Index for Info

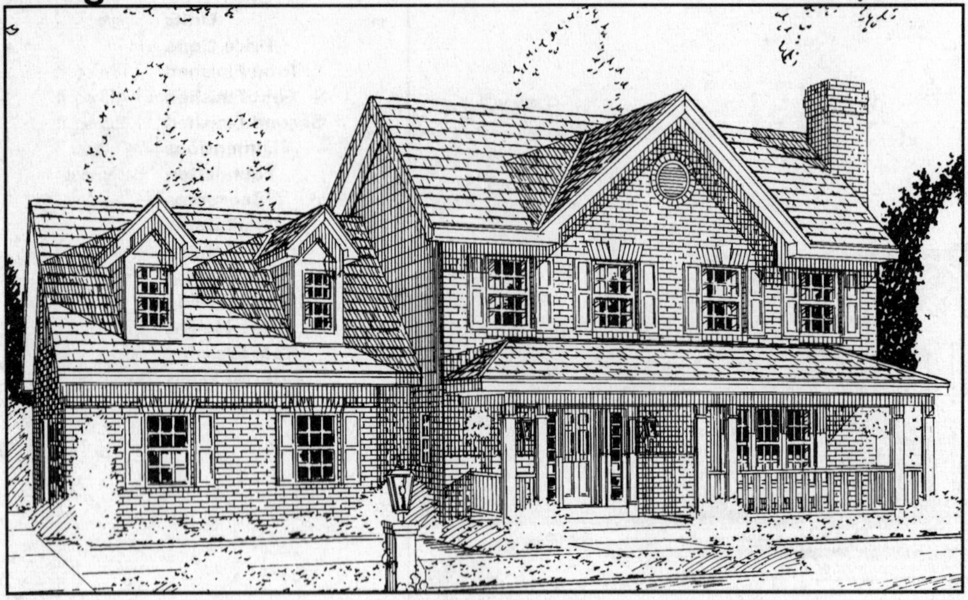

Units	Single
Price Code	B
Total Finished	1,698 sq. ft.
First Finished	868 sq. ft.
Second Finished	830 sq. ft.
Bonus Unfinished	269 sq. ft.
Basement Unfinished	850 sq. ft.
Garage Unfinished	417 sq. ft.
Porch Unfinished	239 sq. ft.
Dimensions	54'4"x28'4"
Foundation	Basement
Bedrooms	3
Full Baths	2
Half Baths	1
Max Ridge Height	28'
Roof Framing	Truss
Exterior Walls	2x4

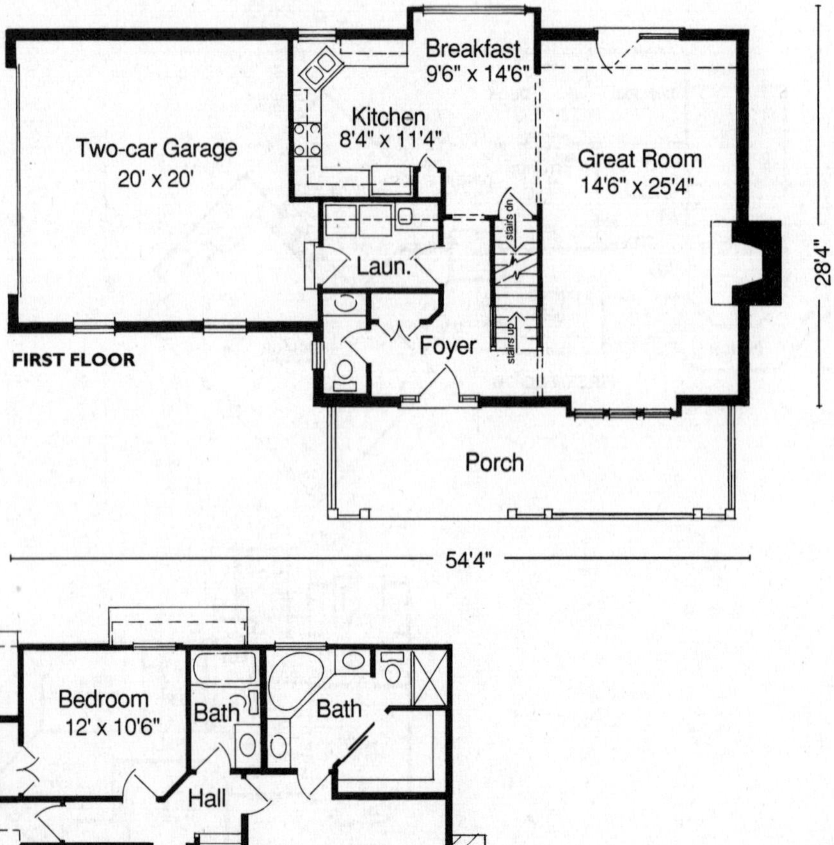
Breakfast
9'6" x 14'6"
Kitchen
8'4" x 11'4"
Two-car Garage
20' x 20'
Great Room
14'6" x 25'4"
stairs dn
Laun.
Foyer
stairs up
28'4"
Porch
54'4"

FIRST FLOOR

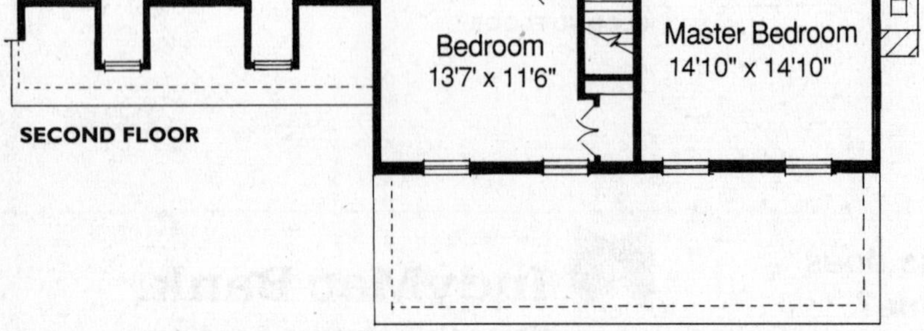
Bedroom
12' x 10'6"
Bath
Bath
Bonus Room
17'5" x 10'7"
Hall
Bedroom
13'7" x 11'6"
Master Bedroom
14'10" x 14'10"

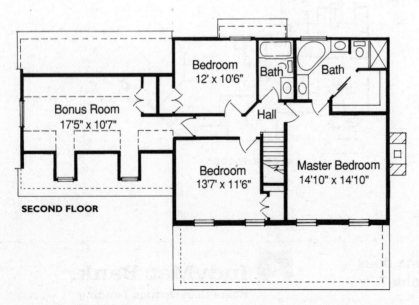

SECOND FLOOR

Design 67005

See Order Pages and Index for Info

Units	Single
Price Code	D
Total Finished	2,084 sq. ft.
First Finished	1,203 sq. ft.
Second Finished	881 sq. ft.
Garage Unfinished	462 sq. ft.
Porch Unfinished	323 sq. ft.
Dimensions	56'x44'5"
Foundation	Slab
Bedrooms	3
Full Baths	2
Half Baths	1
First Ceiling	9'
Second Ceiling	8'
Roof Framing	Stick
Exterior Walls	2x4

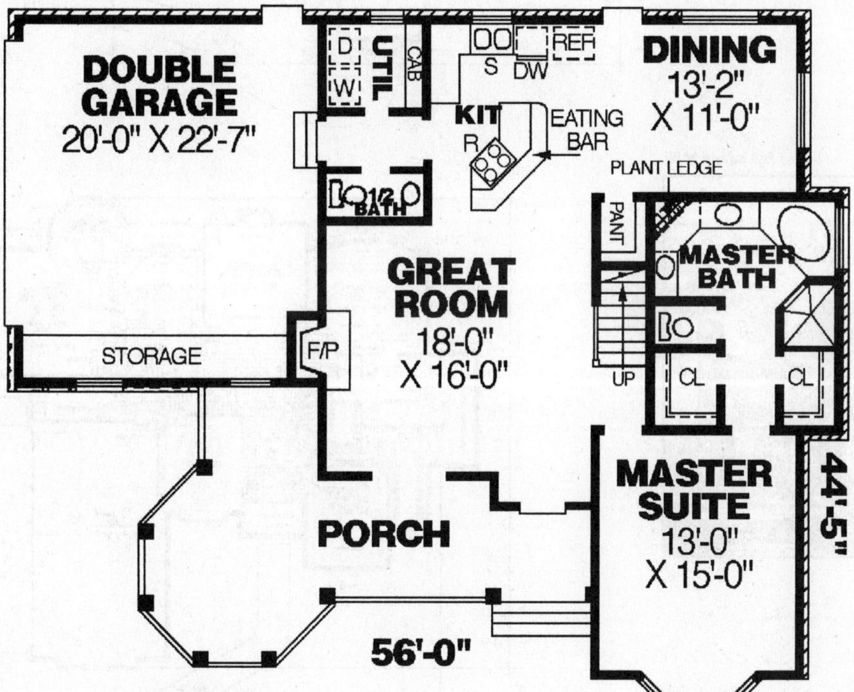
DOUBLE GARAGE
20'-0" X 22'-7"
STORAGE
D
W
UTIL
CAB
S
DW
REF
KIT
R
EATING BAR
DINING
13'-2" X 11'-0"
PLANT LEDGE
1/2 BATH
PANT
MASTER BATH
GREAT ROOM
18'-0" X 16'-0"
F/P
UP
CL
CL
MASTER SUITE
13'-0" X 15'-0"
PORCH
56'-0"
44'-5"

FIRST FLOOR

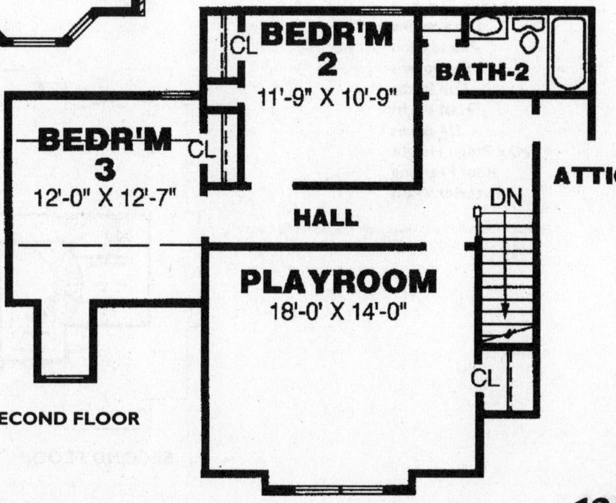
BEDR'M 2
11'-9" X 10'-9"
CL
BATH-2
BEDR'M 3
12'-0" X 12'-7"
CL
ATTIC
DN
HALL
PLAYROOM
18'-0' X 14'-0"
CL

SECOND FLOOR

Design 99437

See Order Pages and Index for Info

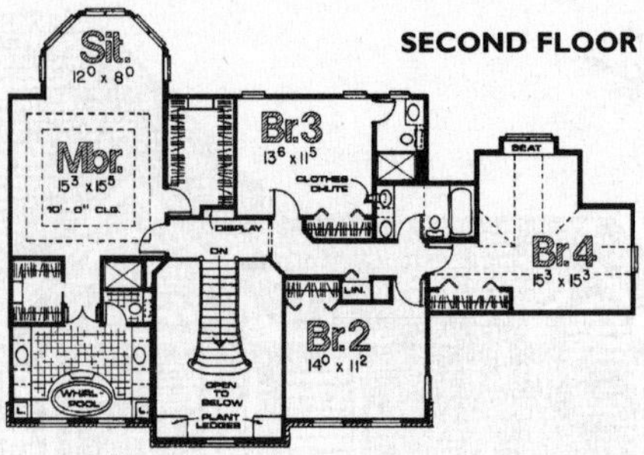
Sit.
12⁰ x 8⁰
Mbr.
15³ x 15⁶
Br.3
13⁶ x 11⁵
Br.4
15³ x 15³
Br.2
14⁰ x 11²
OPEN TO BELOW
PLANT LEDGE
WHIRL POOL
DISPLAY
CLOTHES CHUTE

SECOND FLOOR

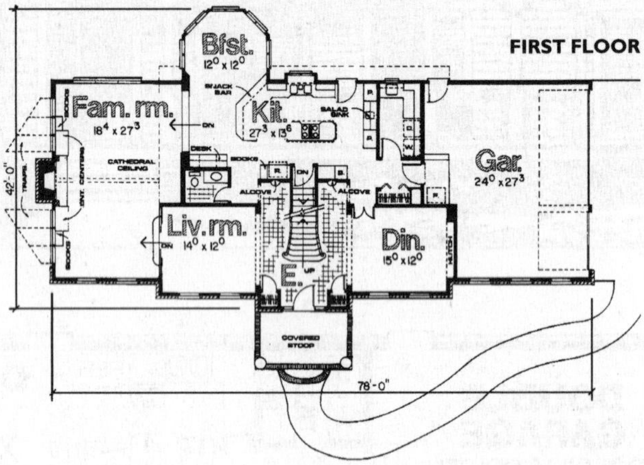
Bfst.
12⁰ x 12⁰
Fam. rm.
18⁴ x 27³
Kit.
27³ x 13⁶
Gar.
24⁰ x 27³
Liv.rm.
14⁰ x 12⁰
Din.
15⁰ x 12⁰
E.
COVERED STOOP
ALCOVE
CATHEDRAL CEILING
78'-0"
42'-0"

FIRST FLOOR

Units	Single
Price Code	H
Total Finished	3,235 sq. ft.
First Finished	1,717 sq. ft.
Second Finished	1,518 sq. ft.
Basement Unfinished	1,717 sq. ft.
Garage Unfinished	633 sq. ft.
Dimensions	78'x42'
Foundation	Basement
Bedrooms	4
Full Baths	2
Half Baths	1
3/4 Baths	1
Max Ridge Height	30'5"
Roof Framing	Stick
Exterior Walls	2x4

* Alternate foundation options available at an additional charge.
Please call 1-800-235-5700 for more information.

Design 99466

See Order Pages and Index for Info

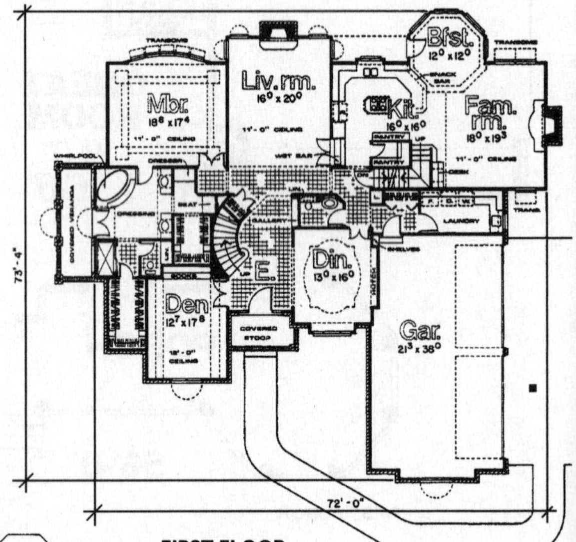
Bfst.
12⁰ x 12⁰
Mbr.
18⁶ x 17⁴
Liv.rm.
16⁰ x 20⁰
Kit.
16⁰ x 16⁰
Fam. rm.
18⁰ x 19³
Din.
13⁰ x 16⁰
Den
12⁷ x 17⁸
Gar.
21³ x 38⁰
E.
COVERED STOOP
LAUNDRY
72'-0"
73'-4"

FIRST FLOOR

Units	Single
Price Code	K
Total Finished	3,827 sq. ft.
First Finished	2,789 sq. ft.
Second Finished	1,038 sq. ft.
Dimensions	72'x73'4"
Foundation	Basement
Bedrooms	4
Full Baths	2
Half Baths	1
3/4 Baths	1
Max Ridge Height	29'6"
Roof Framing	Stick
Exterior Walls	2x4

* Alternate foundation options available at an additional charge.
Please call 1-800-235-5700 for more information.

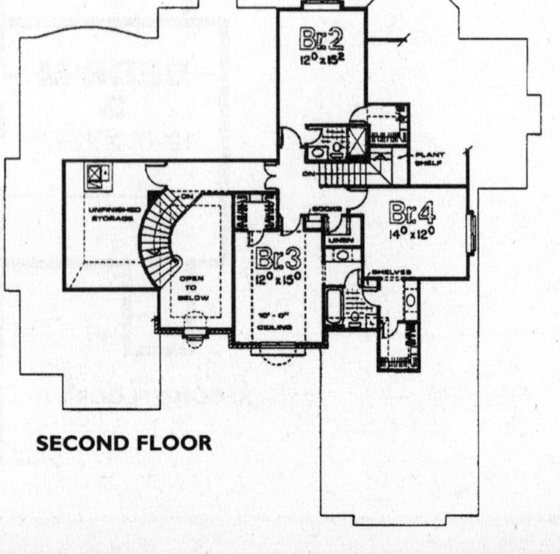
Br.2
12⁰ x 15²
Br.4
14⁰ x 12⁰
Br.3
12⁰ x 15⁰
UNFINISHED STORAGE
OPEN TO BELOW
PLANT SHELF

SECOND FLOOR

Design 63049

See Order Pages and Index for Info

Units	Single
Price Code	C
Total Finished	1,997 sq. ft.
Main Finished	1,997 sq. ft.
Bonus Unfinished	310 sq. ft.
Garage Unfinished	502 sq. ft.
Dimensions	64'x57'
Foundation	Basement
Bedrooms	3
Full Baths	2
Half Baths	1
Main Ceiling	10'
Max Ridge Height	23'
Roof Framing	Truss
Exterior Walls	2x4

MAIN FLOOR

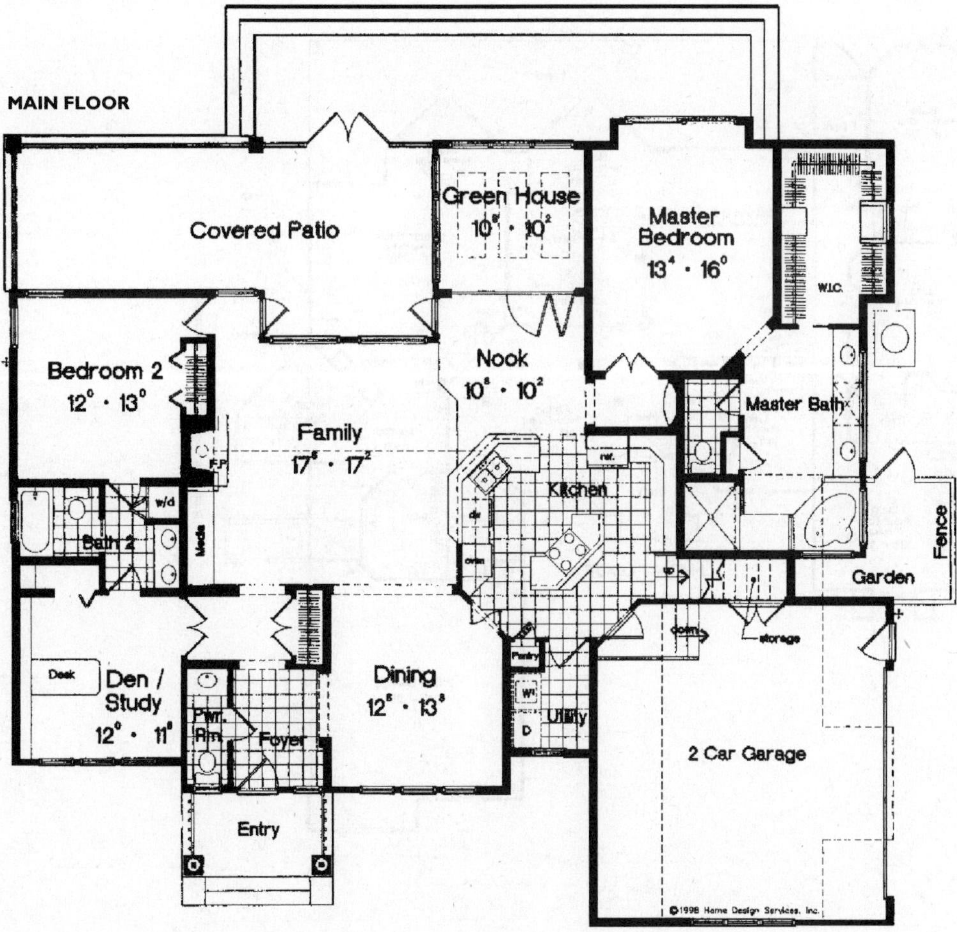
Covered Patio
Green House
$10^{6} \cdot 10^{2}$
Master Bedroom
$13^{4} \cdot 16^{0}$
W.I.C.
Bedroom 2
$12^{0} \cdot 13^{0}$
Nook
$10^{8} \cdot 10^{2}$
Master Bath
Family
$17^{6} \cdot 17^{2}$
F.P.
w/d
Bath 2
Media
Kitchen
Fence
Garden
storage
Desk
Den / Study
$12^{0} \cdot 11^{8}$
Dining
$12^{6} \cdot 13^{8}$
Pantry
Utility
Pwr. Rm.
Foyer
2 Car Garage
Entry
©1998 Home Design Services, Inc.

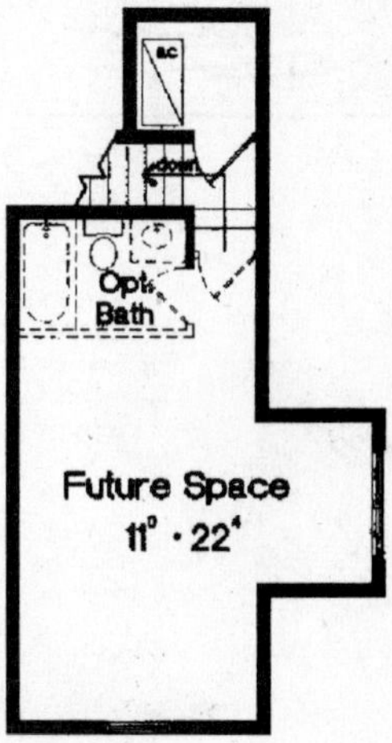
Opt. Bath
Future Space
$11^{0} \cdot 22^{4}$

BONUS

Design 63038

See Order Pages and Index for Info

Units	Single
Price Code	G
Total Finished	3,280 sq. ft.
Main Finished	3,280 sq. ft.
Garage Unfinished	596 sq. ft.
Dimensions	72'4"x82'10"
Foundation	Slab
Bedrooms	4
Full Baths	3
Main Ceiling	10'
Max Ridge Height	24'8"
Roof Framing	Truss
Exterior Walls	2x4

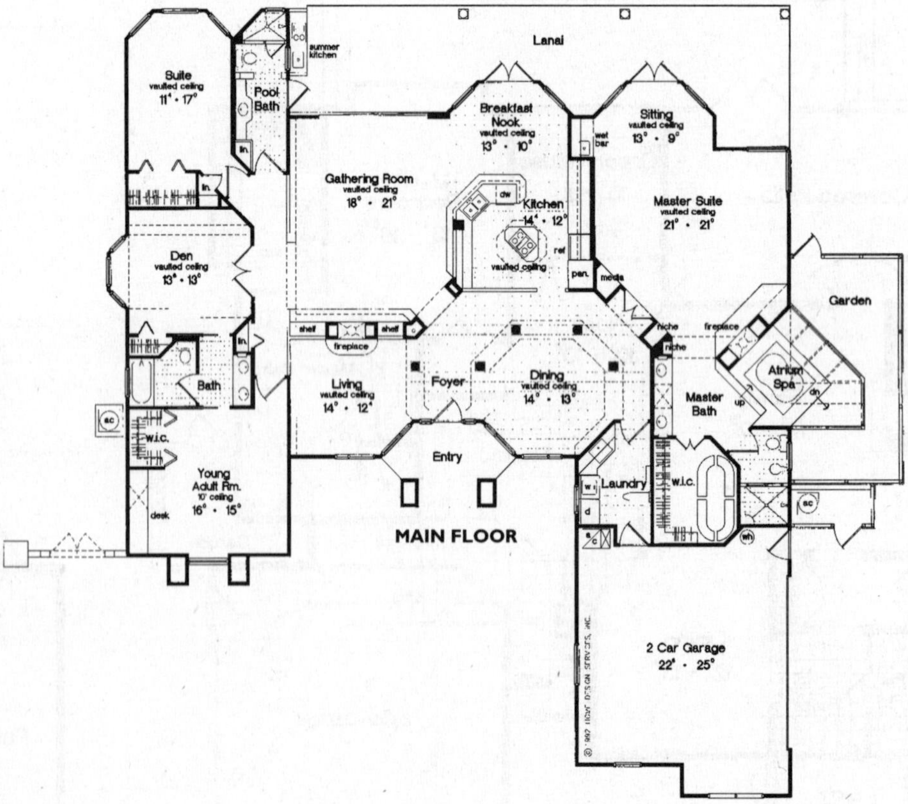
Lanai
summer kitchen
Suite
vaulted ceiling
11⁴ · 17⁰
Pool Bath
Breakfast Nook
vaulted ceiling
13⁰ · 10⁰
Sitting
vaulted ceiling
13⁰ · 9⁰
wet bar
Gathering Room
vaulted ceiling
18⁰ · 21⁰
Kitchen
14⁴ · 12⁰
Master Suite
vaulted ceiling
21⁰ · 21⁰
Den
vaulted ceiling
13⁸ · 13⁰
pan.
media
Garden
fireplace
niche
Atrium
Spa
Living
vaulted ceiling
14⁰ · 12⁴
Foyer
Dining
vaulted ceiling
14⁰ · 13⁰
Bath
Master Bath
Entry
Laundry
w.i.c.
Young
Adult Rm.
10' ceiling
16⁰ · 15⁰
desk
2 Car Garage
22⁸ · 25⁰

MAIN FLOOR

Design 92630

See Order Pages and Index for Info

Units	Single
Price Code	C
Total Finished	1,782 sq. ft.
Main Finished	1,782 sq. ft.
Basement Unfinished	1,735 sq. ft.
Garage Unfinished	407 sq. ft.
Dimensions	67'2"x47'
Foundation	Basement
Bedrooms	3
Full Baths	2
Max Ridge Height	20'
Roof Framing	Truss
Exterior Walls	2x4

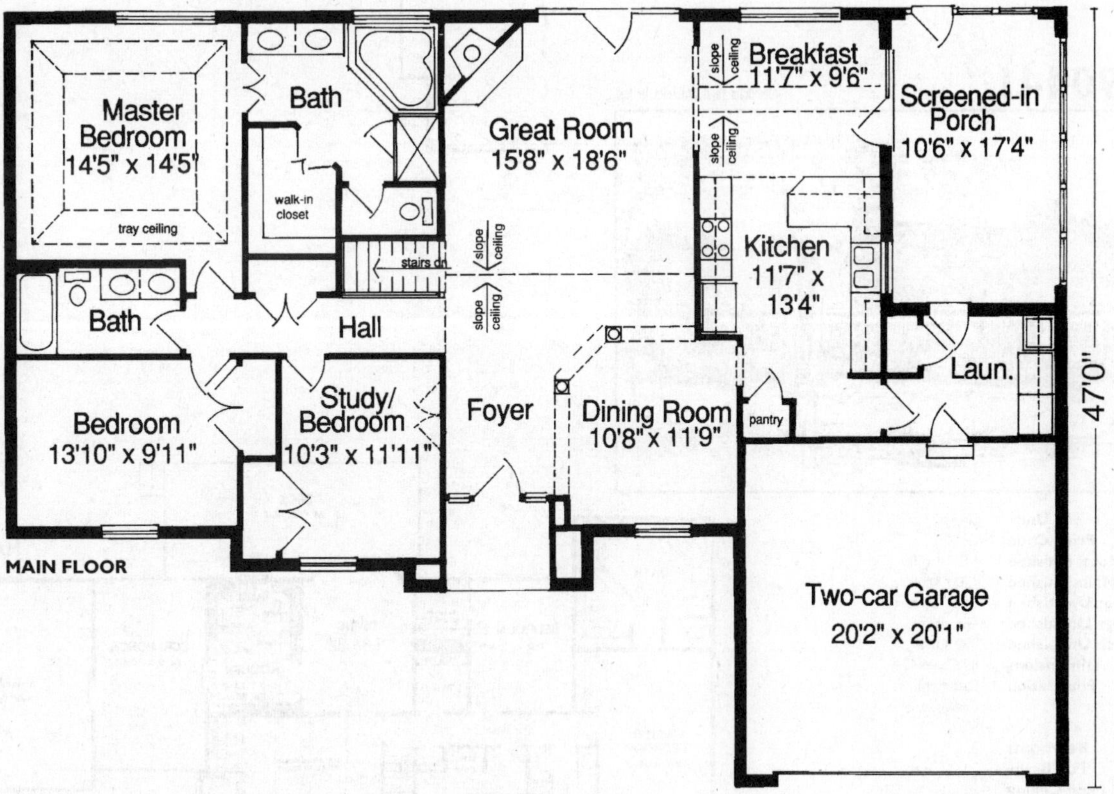
Master Bedroom
14'5" x 14'5"
tray ceiling
Bath
walk-in closet
stairs dn
Great Room
15'8" x 18'6"
slope ceiling
Breakfast
11'7" x 9'6"
Screened-in Porch
10'6" x 17'4"
Kitchen
11'7" x 13'4"
Bath
Hall
Laun.
Study/ Bedroom
10'3" x 11'11"
Foyer
Dining Room
10'8" x 11'9"
pantry
Bedroom
13'10" x 9'11"
MAIN FLOOR
Two-car Garage
20'2" x 20'1"
67'-2"
47'0"

Design 63075

See Order Pages and Index for Info

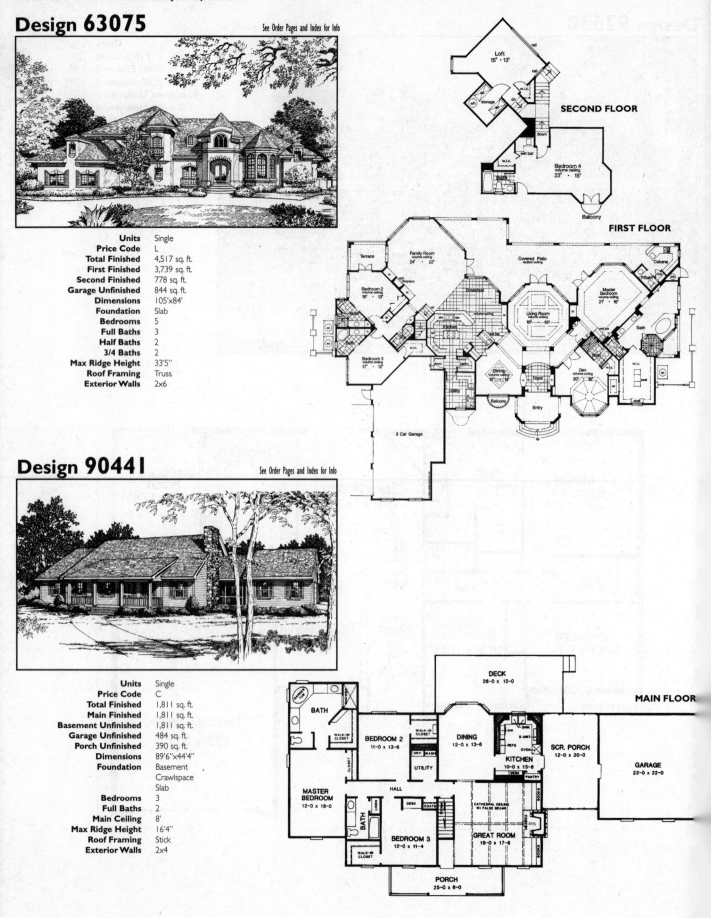

Units	Single
Price Code	L
Total Finished	4,517 sq. ft.
First Finished	3,739 sq. ft.
Second Finished	778 sq. ft.
Garage Unfinished	844 sq. ft.
Dimensions	105'x84'
Foundation	Slab
Bedrooms	5
Full Baths	3
Half Baths	2
3/4 Baths	2
Max Ridge Height	33'5"
Roof Framing	Truss
Exterior Walls	2x6

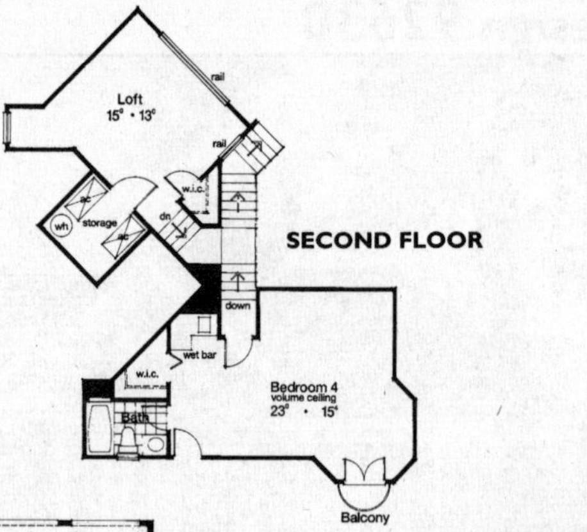
SECOND FLOOR
Loft
storage
wet bar
Bedroom 4
Bath
Balcony

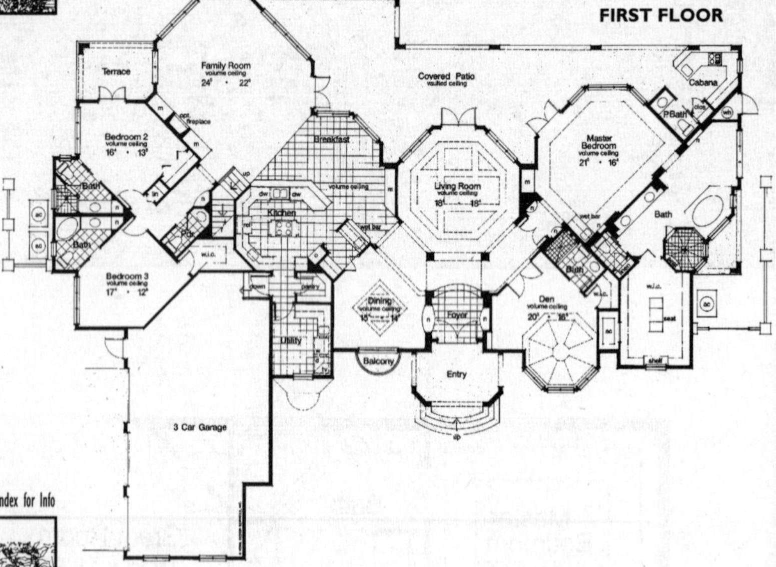
FIRST FLOOR
Terrace
Family Room
Covered Patio
Cabana
Bedroom 2
Breakfast
Living Room
Master Bedroom
Kitchen
Bath
Bedroom 3
Dining
Foyer
Den
Utility
Balcony
Entry
3 Car Garage

Design 90441

See Order Pages and Index for Info

Units	Single
Price Code	C
Total Finished	1,811 sq. ft.
Main Finished	1,811 sq. ft.
Basement Unfinished	1,811 sq. ft.
Garage Unfinished	484 sq. ft.
Porch Unfinished	390 sq. ft.
Dimensions	89'6"x44'4"
Foundation	Basement Crawlspace Slab
Bedrooms	3
Full Baths	2
Main Ceiling	8'
Max Ridge Height	16'4"
Roof Framing	Stick
Exterior Walls	2x4

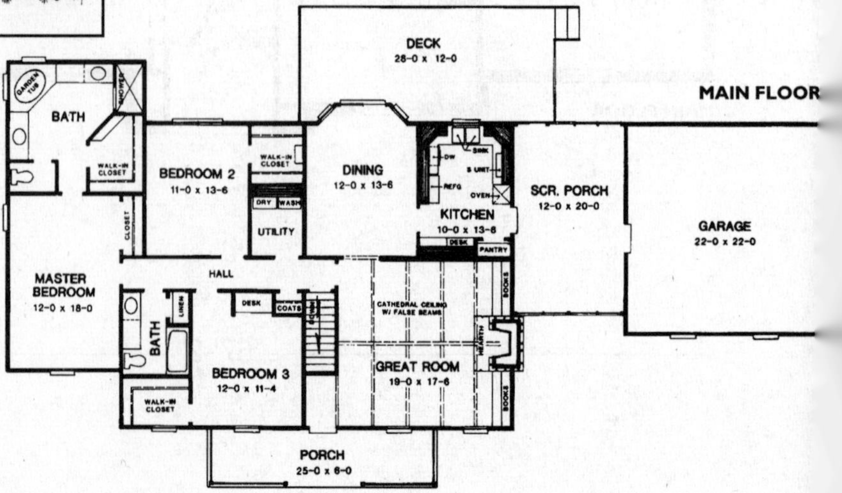
DECK
28-0 x 12-0
MAIN FLOOR
BATH
WALK-IN CLOSET
BEDROOM 2
11-0 x 13-6
DINING
12-0 x 13-6
KITCHEN
10-0 x 13-8
SCR. PORCH
12-0 x 20-0
GARAGE
22-0 x 22-0
UTILITY
HALL
MASTER BEDROOM
12-0 x 18-0
CATHEDRAL CEILING W/ FALSE BEAMS
GREAT ROOM
19-0 x 17-6
BEDROOM 3
12-0 x 11-4
BATH
PORCH
25-0 x 8-0

Design 92259

See Order Pages and Index for Info

Units	Single
Price Code	A
Total Finished	1,432 sq. ft.
Main Finished	1,432 sq. ft.
Garage Unfinished	409 sq. ft.
Porch Unfinished	42 sq. ft.
Dimensions	50'x49'2"
Foundation	Slab
Bedrooms	3
Full Baths	2
Max Ridge Height	21'
Roof Framing	Stick
Exterior Walls	2x4

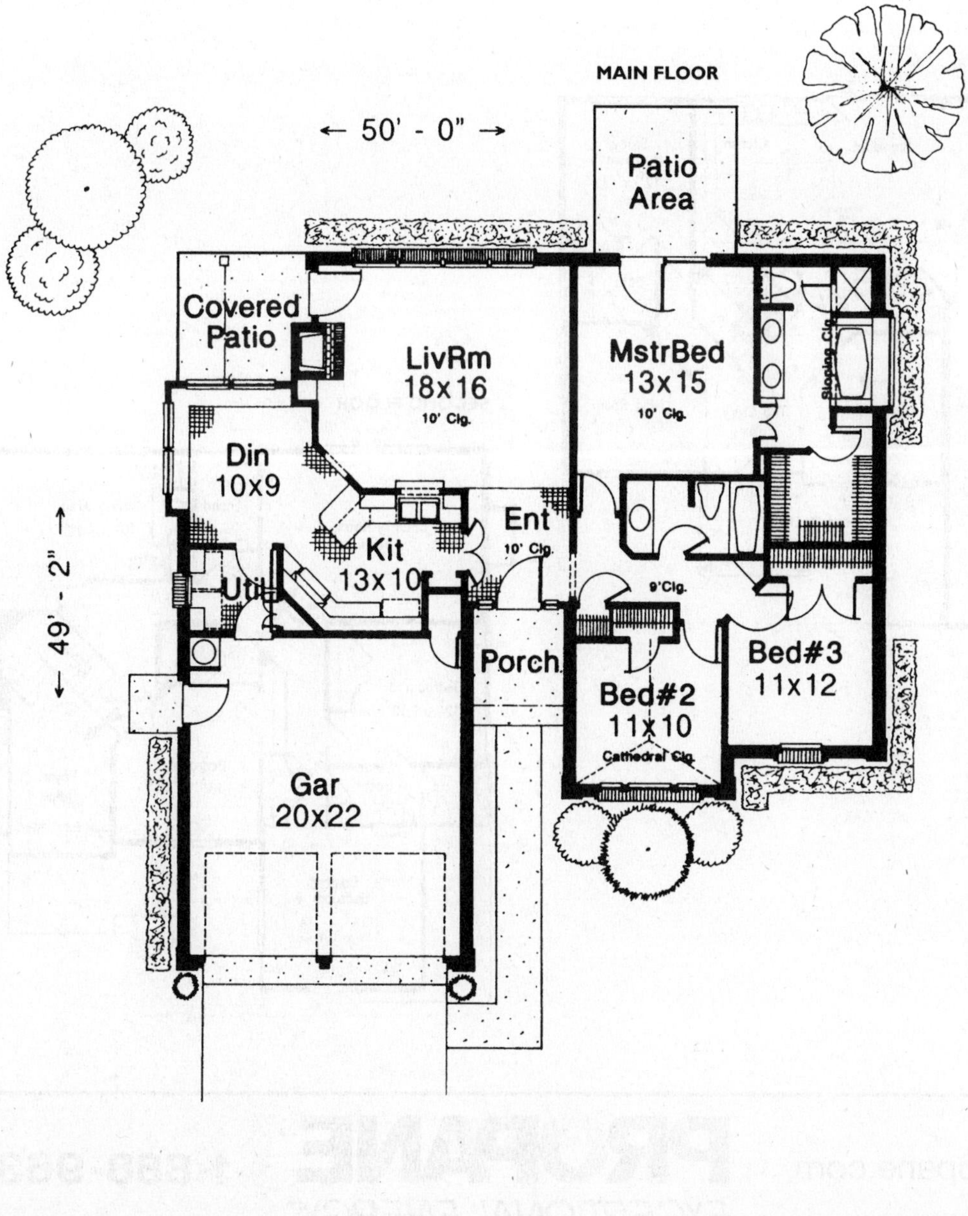
MAIN FLOOR
← 50' - 0" →
Patio Area
Covered Patio
LivRm 18x16 10' Clg.
MstrBed 13x15 10' Clg.
Sloping Clg.
Din 10x9
Kit 13x10
Ent 10' Clg.
9'Clg.
Util
← 49' - 2" →
Porch
Bed#2 11x10 Cathedral Clg.
Bed#3 11x12
Gar 20x22

Design 97633

See Order Pages and Index for Info

Units	Single
Price Code	I
Total Finished	3,266 sq. ft.
First Finished	1,577 sq. ft.
Second Finished	1,689 sq. ft.
Basement Unfinished	1,577 sq. ft.
Garage Unfinished	694 sq. ft.
Dimensions	59'4"x49'
Foundation	Basement Crawlspace
Bedrooms	5
Full Baths	4
Half Baths	1
First Ceiling	9'
Second Ceiling	8'
Max Ridge Height	32'6"
Roof Framing	Stick
Exterior Walls	2x4

FIRST FLOOR

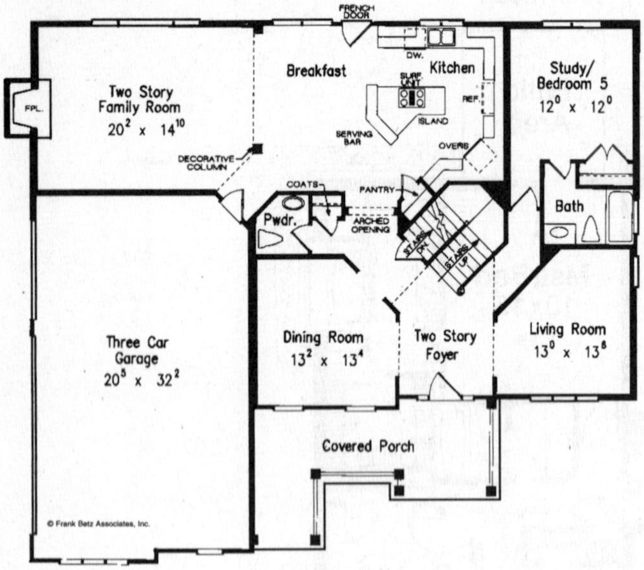
FRENCH DOOR
Two Story Family Room
20² x 14¹⁰
FPL.
Breakfast
Kitchen
DW.
SURF UNIT
ISLAND
REF.
SERVING BAR
OVENS
DECORATIVE COLUMN
Study/ Bedroom 5
12⁰ x 12⁰
COATS
PANTRY
Pwdr.
ARCHED OPENING
STAIRS DN
STAIRS UP
Bath
Three Car Garage
20⁵ x 32²
Dining Room
13² x 13⁴
Two Story Foyer
Living Room
13⁰ x 13⁸
Covered Porch
© Frank Betz Associates, Inc.

SECOND FLOOR

RADIUS WINDOW
Family Room Below
Laund.
SINK
LINEN
BUILT-IN SHELVES
FPL.
Sitting Area
10⁰ x 11³
BUILT-IN SHELVES
TRAY CLG.
Master Suite
18⁰ x 14⁰
OPEN RAIL
OVERLOOK
Bath
STAIRS DN
FRENCH DOORS
Vaulted M.Bath
KS.
SHWR.
Bedroom 3
12⁰ x 12³
OVERLOOK
OPEN RAIL
Bedroom 2
13² x 13⁹
Foyer Below
PLANT SHELF
PLANT SHELF ABOVE
W.i.c.
LINEN
Bath
LINEN
Vaulted Bedroom 4
14⁵ x 14³
10'-0" HIGH CLG.
VLT.
VLT.

Design 93080

See Order Pages and Index for Info

Units	Single
Price Code	C
Total Finished	1,890 sq. ft.
Main Finished	1,890 sq. ft.
Garage Unfinished	565 sq. ft.
Porch Unfinished	241 sq. ft.
Dimensions	65'10"x53'5"
Foundation	Crawlspace Slab
Bedrooms	3
Full Baths	2
Main Ceiling	10'
Max Ridge Height	21'6"
Roof Framing	Stick
Exterior Walls	2x4

MAIN FLOOR

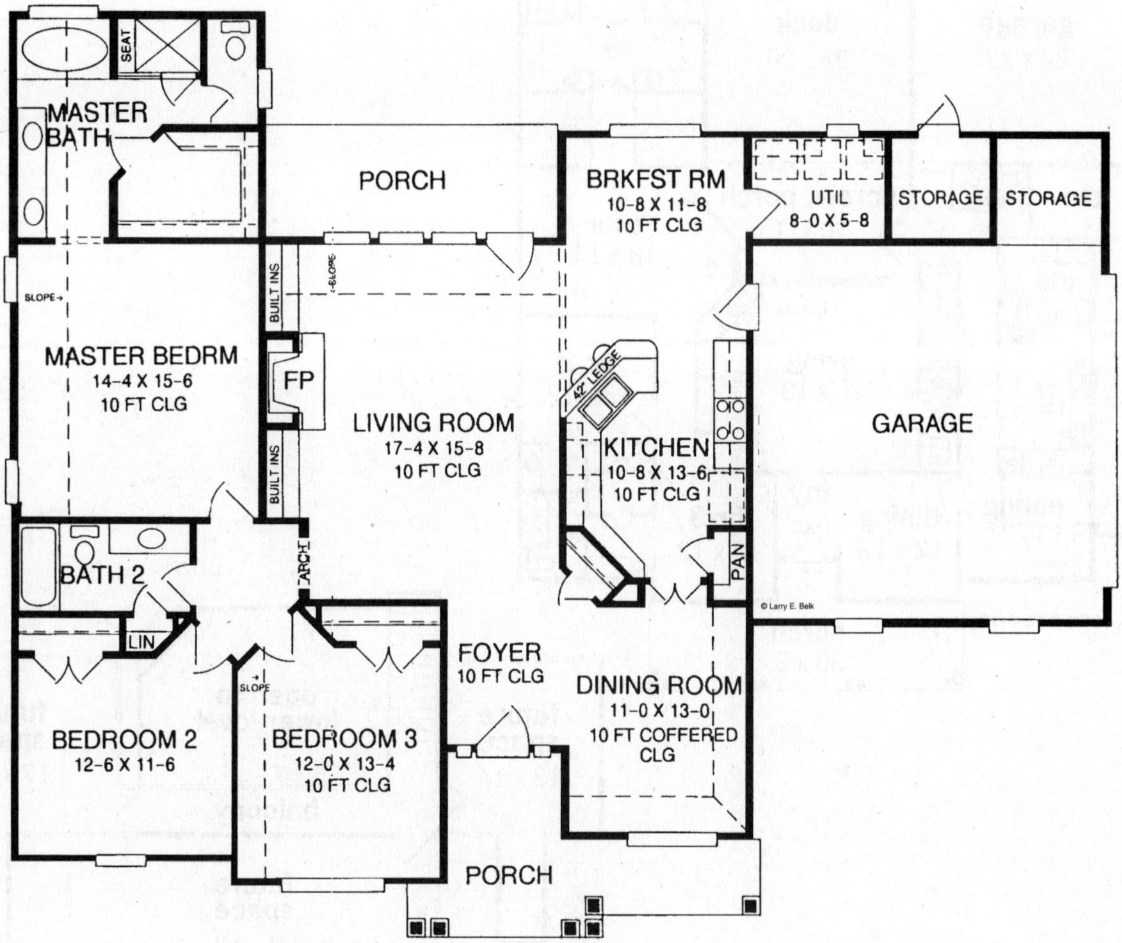
SEAT
MASTER BATH
PORCH
BRKFST RM
10-8 X 11-8
10 FT CLG
UTIL
8-0 X 5-8
STORAGE
STORAGE
SLOPE
BUILT INS
MASTER BEDRM
14-4 X 15-6
10 FT CLG
FP
LIVING ROOM
17-4 X 15-8
10 FT CLG
42" LEDGE
KITCHEN
10-8 X 13-6
10 FT CLG
GARAGE
BUILT INS
PAN
BATH 2
ARCH
© Larry E. Belk
LIN
FOYER
10 FT CLG
DINING ROOM
11-0 X 13-0
10 FT COFFERED CLG
SLOPE
BEDROOM 2
12-6 X 11-6
BEDROOM 3
12-0 X 13-4
10 FT CLG
PORCH

Design 65633

See Order Pages and Index for Info

Units	Single
Price Code	L
Total Finished	2,393 sq. ft.
First Finished	2,281 sq. ft.
Second Finished	112 sq. ft.
Bonus Unfinished	912 sq. ft.
Dimensions	60'x71'
Bedrooms	3
Full Baths	2
Half Baths	1
First Ceiling	9'

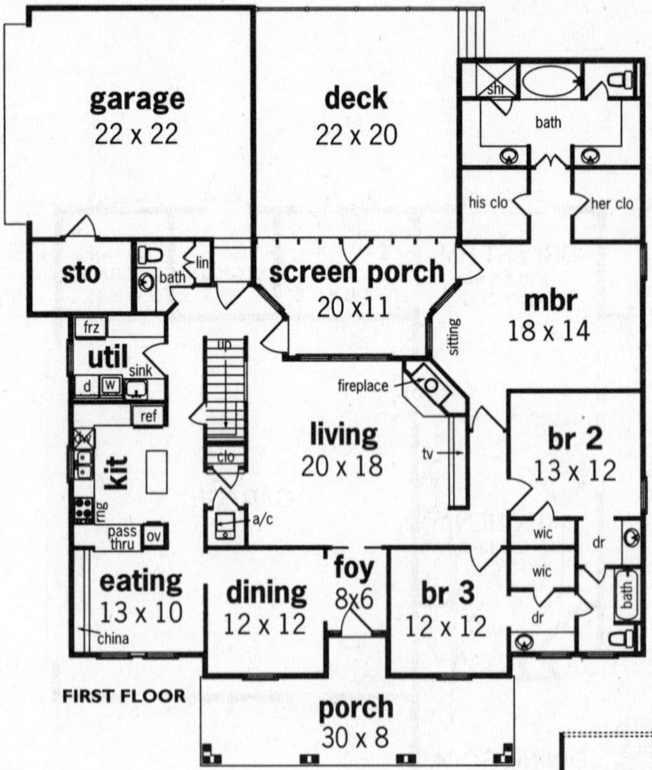
garage
22 x 22
deck
22 x 20
shr
bath
his clo
her clo
sto
bath
lin
screen porch
20 x11
mbr
18 x 14
sitting
frz
util
sink
d
w
ref
up
fireplace
living
20 x 18
tv
br 2
13 x 12
kit
clo
a/c
rng
pass thru
ov
wic
dr
wic
eating
13 x 10
china
dining
12 x 12
foy
8x6
br 3
12 x 12
dr
bath
porch
30 x 8

FIRST FLOOR

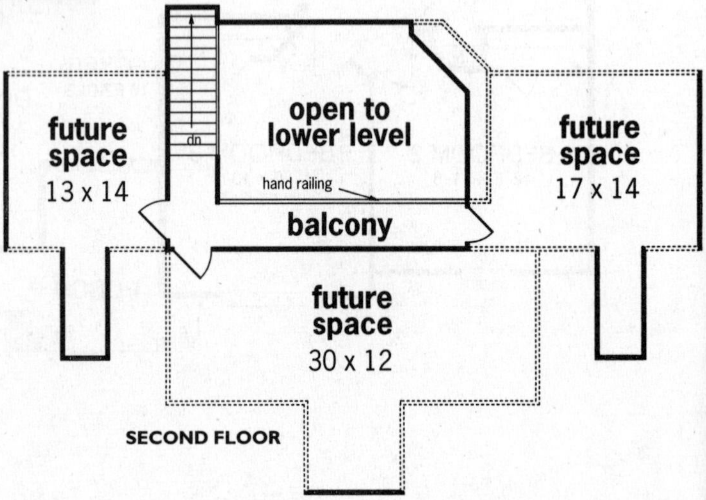
future
space
13 x 14
dn
open to
lower level
hand railing
balcony
future
space
17 x 14
future
space
30 x 12

SECOND FLOOR

Design 94230

See Order Pages and Index for Info

Units	Single
Price Code	L
Total Finished	4,759 sq. ft.
First Finished	3,546 sq. ft.
Second Finished	1,213 sq. ft.
Garage Unfinished	822 sq. ft.
Porch Unfinished	719 sq. ft.
Dimensions	95'4"x83'
Foundation	Slab
Bedrooms	4
Full Baths	2
Half Baths	1
3/4 Baths	1
First Ceiling	10'
Second Ceiling	9'
Max Ridge Height	37'8"
Roof Framing	Truss
Exterior Walls	2x6

* Alternate foundation options available at an additional charge. Please call 1-800-235-5700 for more information.

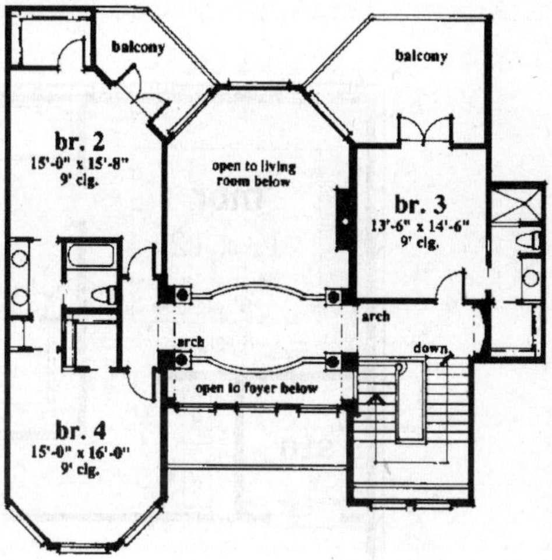
balcony
balcony
br. 2
15'-0" x 15'-8"
9' clg.
open to living room below
br. 3
13'-6" x 14'-6"
9' clg.
arch
arch
down
open to foyer below
br. 4
15'-0" x 16'-0"
9' clg.

SECOND FLOOR

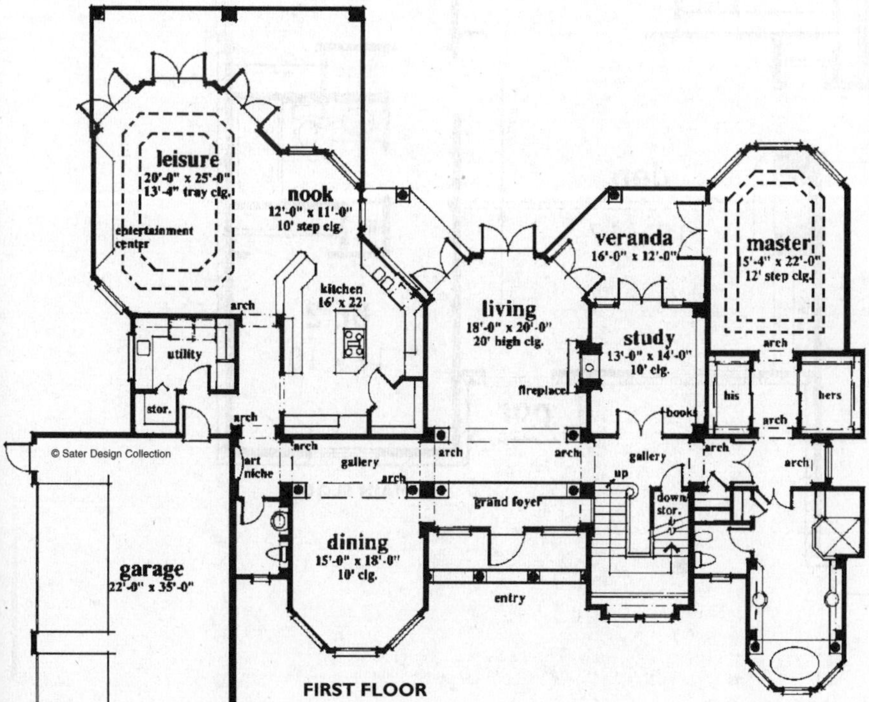
leisure
20'-0" x 25'-0"
13'-4" tray clg.
entertainment center
nook
12'-0" x 11'-0"
10' step clg.
kitchen
16' x 22'
veranda
16'-0" x 12'-0"
master
15'-4" x 22'-0"
12' step clg.
living
18'-0" x 20'-0"
20' high clg.
study
13'-0" x 14'-0"
10' clg.
fireplace
books
utility
stor.
arch
his
hers
© Sater Design Collection
art niche
gallery
gallery
up
down
stor.
grand foyer
dining
15'-0" x 18'-0"
10' clg.
garage
22'-0" x 35'-0"
entry

FIRST FLOOR

Design 92502

See Order Pages and Index for Info

Units	Single
Price Code	A
Total Finished	1,237 sq. ft.
Main Finished	1,237 sq. ft.
Garage Unfinished	436 sq. ft.
Dimensions	50'x38'
Foundation	Crawlspace Slab
Bedrooms	3
Full Baths	2
Main Ceiling	8'
Max Ridge Height	18'6"
Roof Framing	Stick
Exterior Walls	2x4

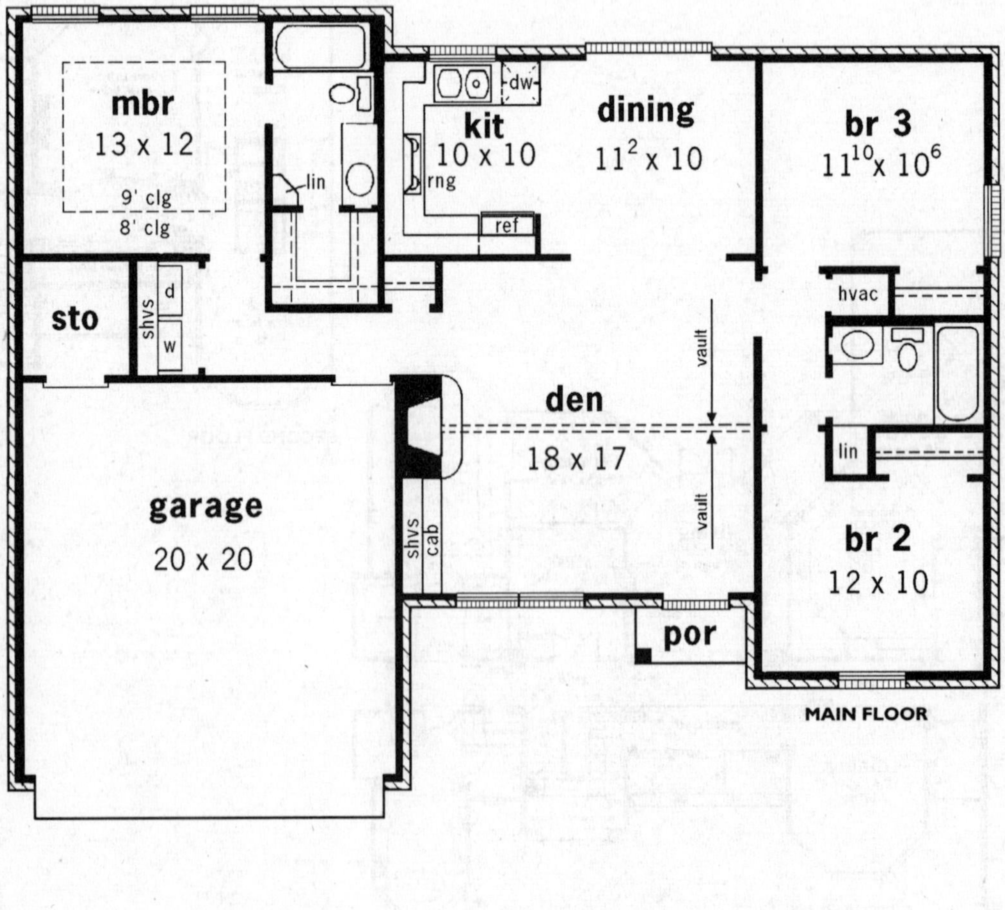
mbr
13 x 12
9' clg
8' clg
lin
kit
10 x 10
dw
rng
ref
dining
11² x 10
br 3
11¹⁰ x 10⁶
hvac
sto
shvs
d
w
vault
den
18 x 17
vault
lin
garage
20 x 20
shvs
cab
br 2
12 x 10
por

MAIN FLOOR

Design 92419

See Order Pages and Index for Info

Units	Single
Price Code	F
Total Finished	2,546 sq. ft.
First Finished	1,818 sq. ft.
Second Finished	728 sq. ft.
Bonus Unfinished	579 sq. ft.
Basement Unfinished	1,818 sq. ft.
Dimensions	56'x67'
Foundation	Basement
Bedrooms	4
Full Baths	2
Half Baths	1
3/4 Baths	1
First Ceiling	9'
Second Ceiling	8'
Vaulted Ceiling	18'
Max Ridge Height	29'8"
Roof Framing	Stick
Exterior Walls	2x4

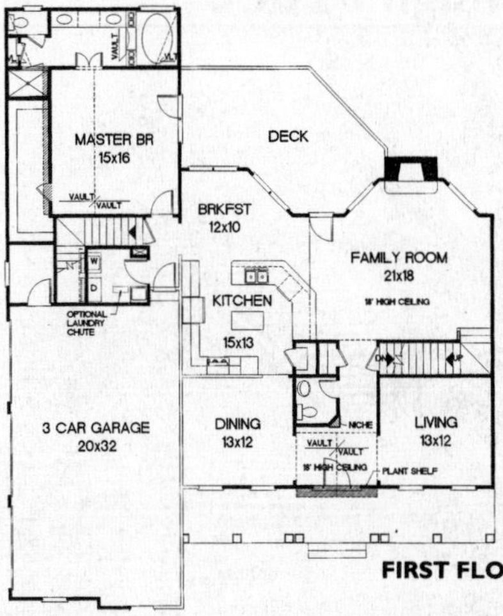
MASTER BR
15x16
DECK
BRKFST
12x10
FAMILY ROOM
21x18
KITCHEN
15x13
3 CAR GARAGE
20x32
DINING
13x12
LIVING
13x12

FIRST FLOOR

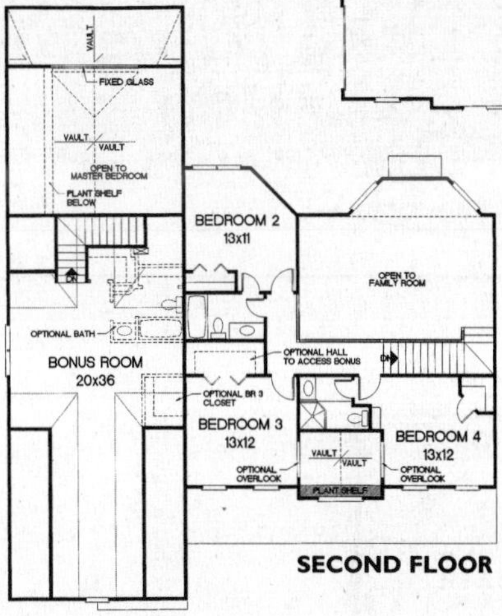
BEDROOM 2
13x11
BONUS ROOM
20x36
BEDROOM 3
13x12
BEDROOM 4
13x12

SECOND FLOOR

Design 92423

See Order Pages and Index for Info

Units	Single
Price Code	B
Total Finished	1,643 sq. ft.
First Finished	1,064 sq. ft.
Second Finished	579 sq. ft.
Dimensions	38'x34'
Foundation	Basement
Bedrooms	3
Full Baths	2
Half Baths	1
First Ceiling	8'
Second Ceiling	8'
Vaulted Ceiling	14'
Max Ridge Height	21'6"
Exterior Walls	2x4

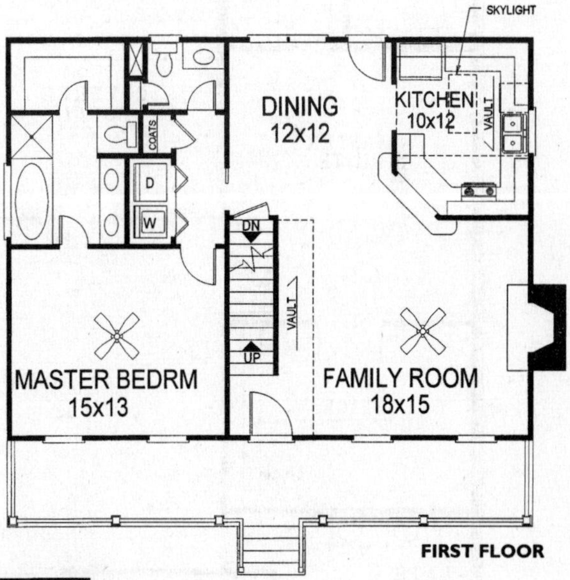
SKYLIGHT
DINING
12x12
KITCHEN
10x12
VAULT
COATS
D
W
DN
UP
VAULT
MASTER BEDRM
15x13
FAMILY ROOM
18x15

FIRST FLOOR

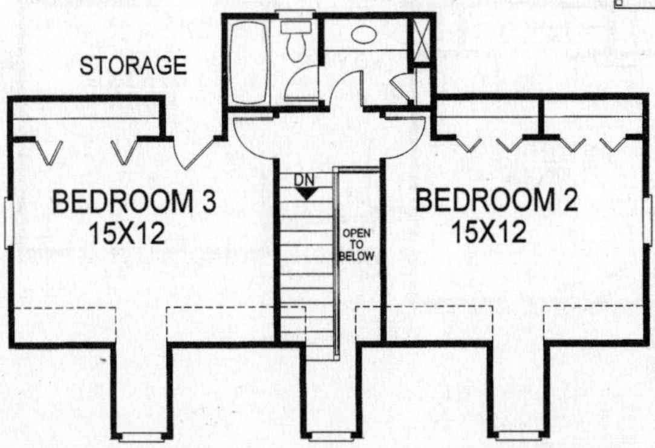
STORAGE
BEDROOM 3
15X12
DN
OPEN TO BELOW
BEDROOM 2
15X12

SECOND FLOOR

Design 82080

See Order Pages and Index for Info

Units	Single
Price Code	C
Total Finished	1,994 sq. ft.
Main Finished	1,994 sq. ft.
Garage Unfinished	417 sq. ft.
Porch Unfinished	118 sq. ft.
Dimensions	65'2"x63'
Foundation	Basement Crawlspace Slab
Bedrooms	3
Full Baths	2
Roof Framing	Stick
Exterior Walls	2x4

MAIN FLOOR

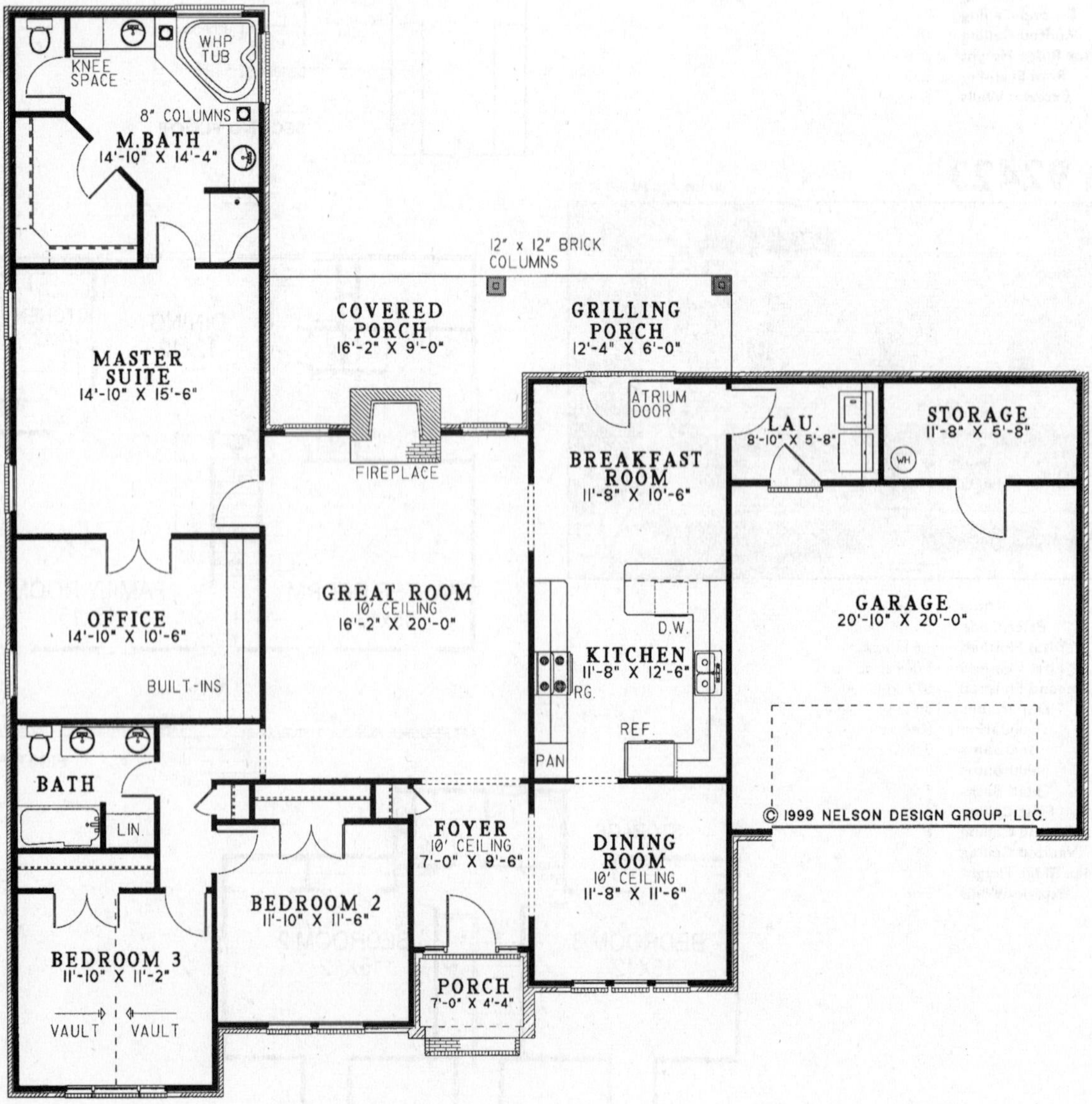
WHP TUB
KNEE SPACE
8" COLUMNS
M.BATH 14'-10" X 14'-4"
12" x 12" BRICK COLUMNS
COVERED PORCH 16'-2" X 9'-0"
GRILLING PORCH 12'-4" X 6'-0"
MASTER SUITE 14'-10" X 15'-6"
ATRIUM DOOR
LAU. 8'-10" X 5'-8"
STORAGE 11'-8" X 5'-8"
WH
FIREPLACE
BREAKFAST ROOM 11'-8" X 10'-6"
GREAT ROOM 10' CEILING 16'-2" X 20'-0"
OFFICE 14'-10" X 10'-6"
BUILT-INS
D.W.
KITCHEN 11'-8" X 12'-6"
RG.
REF.
PAN
GARAGE 20'-10" X 20'-0"
BATH
LIN.
FOYER 10' CEILING 7'-0" X 9'-6"
DINING ROOM 10' CEILING 11'-8" X 11'-6"
© 1999 NELSON DESIGN GROUP, LLC.
BEDROOM 2 11'-10" X 11'-6"
BEDROOM 3 11'-10" X 11'-2"
VAULT
VAULT
PORCH 7'-0" X 4'-4"

Design 97762

See Order Pages and Index for Info

Units	Single
Price Code	B
Total Finished	1,594 sq. ft.
Main Finished	1,594 sq. ft.
Basement Unfinished	1,594 sq. ft.
Garage Unfinished	512 sq. ft.
Porch Unfinished	125 sq. ft.
Dimensions	52'8"x55'5"
Foundation	Basement
Bedrooms	3
Full Baths	2
Main Ceiling	8'
Vaulted Ceiling	10'
Max Ridge Height	23'6"
Roof Framing	Truss
Exterior Walls	2x4

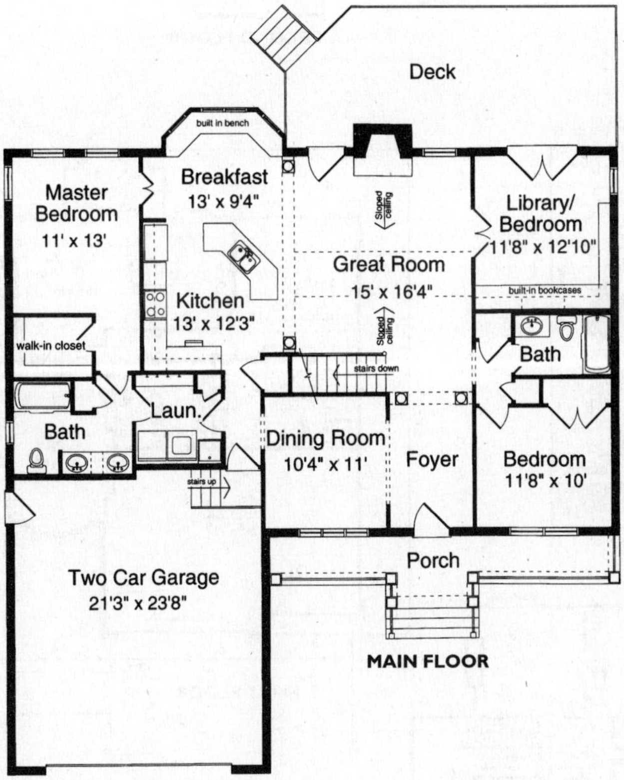
Deck
built in bench
Breakfast
13' x 9'4"
Master Bedroom
11' x 13'
Sloped ceiling
Library/ Bedroom
11'8" x 12'10"
Great Room
15' x 16'4"
Kitchen
13' x 12'3"
built-in bookcases
walk-in closet
Bath
stairs down
Laun.
Bath
Dining Room
10'4" x 11'
Foyer
Bedroom
11'8" x 10'
stairs up
Porch
Two Car Garage
21'3" x 23'8"

MAIN FLOOR

Bedroom
11'8" x 10'5"

OPTIONAL 3RD BEDROOM

Design 97436

See Order Pages and Index for Info

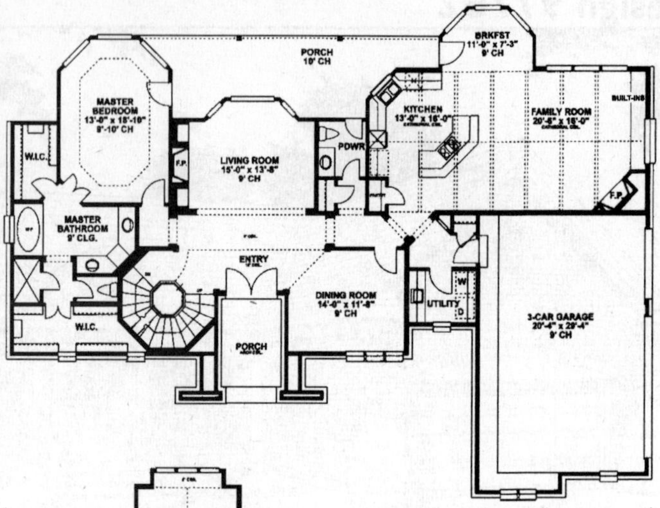
PORCH
BRKFST
KITCHEN
FAMILY ROOM
BUILT-INS
MASTER BEDROOM
W.I.C.
F.P.
LIVING ROOM
PDWR
MASTER BATHROOM
ENTRY
DINING ROOM
UTILITY
3-CAR GARAGE
W.I.C.
PORCH

FIRST FLOOR

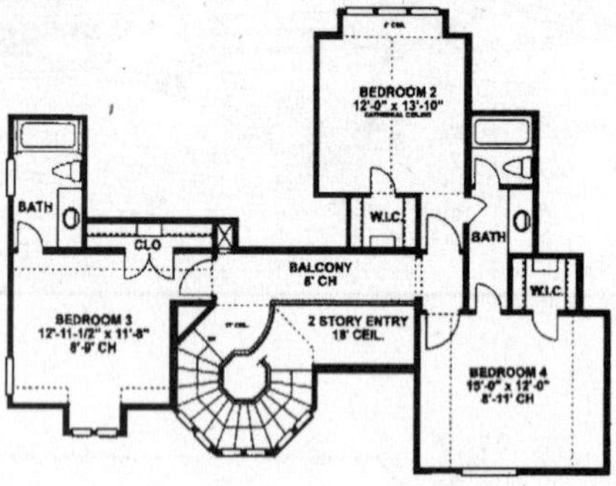
BEDROOM 2
BATH
W.I.C.
CLO
BATH
BALCONY
W.I.C.
BEDROOM 3
2 STORY ENTRY
BEDROOM 4

SECOND FLOOR

Units	Single
Price Code	G
Total Finished	2,961 sq. ft.
First Finished	2,044 sq. ft.
Second Finished	917 sq. ft.
Garage Unfinished	640 sq. ft.
Dimensions	77'3"x56'5"
Foundation	Slab
Bedrooms	4
Full Baths	3
Half Baths	1
First Ceiling	9'
Max Ridge Height	29'9"
Roof Framing	Stick
Exterior Walls	2x4

* Alternate foundation options available at an additional charge. Please call 1-800-235-5700 for more information.

Design 97437

See Order Pages and Index for Info

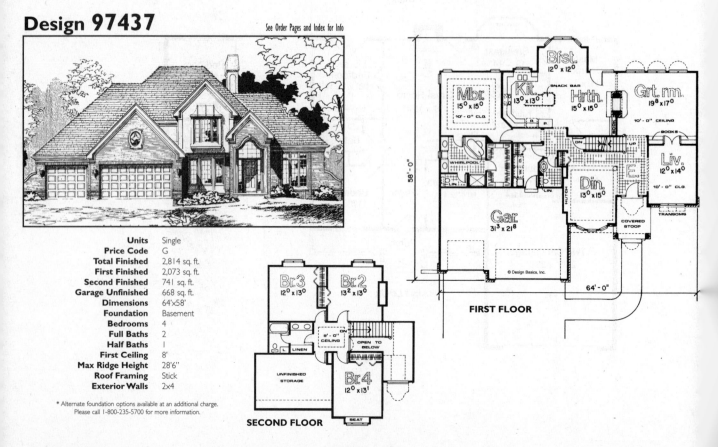

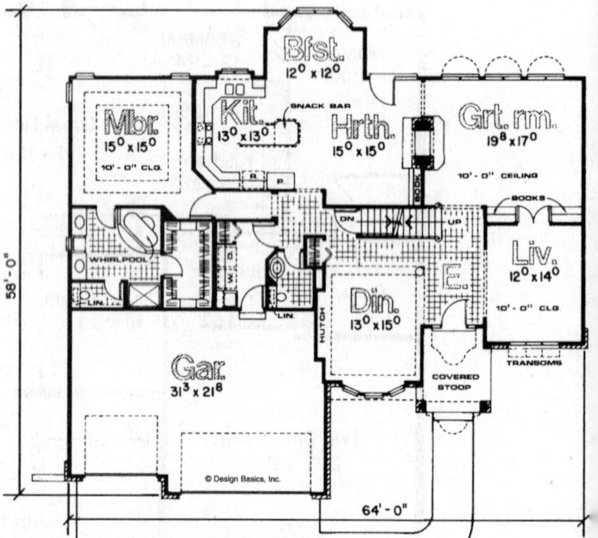
Bfst.
12⁰ x 12⁰
Mbr.
15⁰ x 15⁰
10'-0" CLG.
Kit.
13⁰ x 13⁰
SNACK BAR
Hrth.
15⁰ x 15⁰
Grt. rm.
19⁸ x 17⁰
10'-0" CEILING
BOOKS
WHIRLPOOL
Liv.
12⁰ x 14⁰
10'-0" CLG.
E.
Din.
13⁰ x 15⁰
HUTCH
TRANSOMS
COVERED STOOP
Gar.
31³ x 21⁸
58'-0"
64'-0"
© Design Basics, Inc.

FIRST FLOOR

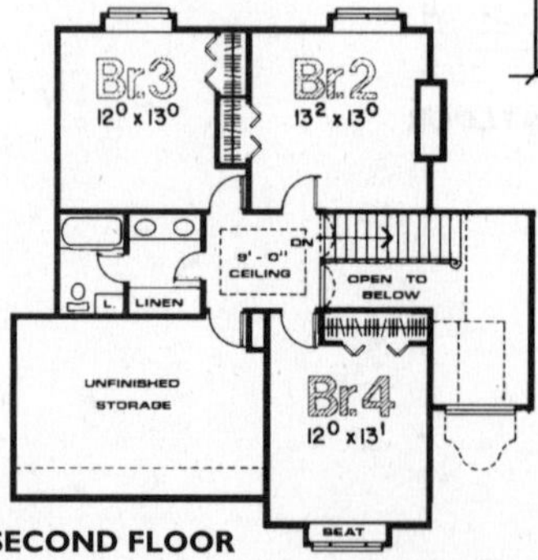
Br.3
12⁰ x 13⁰
Br.2
13² x 13⁰
9'-0" CEILING
DN
OPEN TO BELOW
LINEN
UNFINISHED STORAGE
Br.4
12⁰ x 13¹
SEAT

SECOND FLOOR

Units	Single
Price Code	G
Total Finished	2,814 sq. ft.
First Finished	2,073 sq. ft.
Second Finished	741 sq. ft.
Garage Unfinished	668 sq. ft.
Dimensions	64'x58'
Foundation	Basement
Bedrooms	4
Full Baths	2
Half Baths	1
First Ceiling	8'
Max Ridge Height	28'6"
Roof Framing	Stick
Exterior Walls	2x4

* Alternate foundation options available at an additional charge. Please call 1-800-235-5700 for more information.

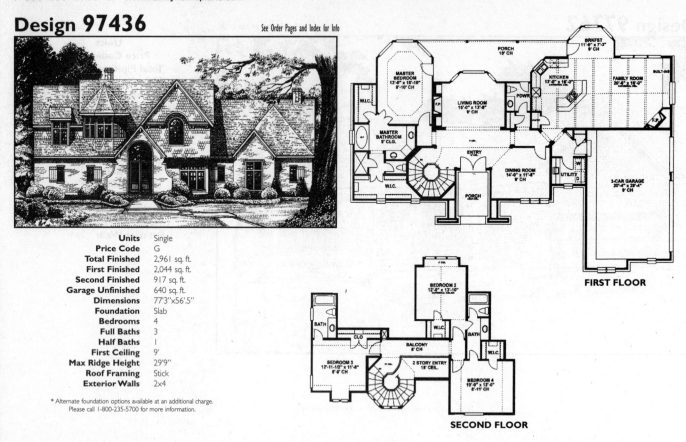

Design 97227

See Order Pages and Index for Info

Units	Single
Price Code	C
Total Finished	1,960 sq. ft.
Main Finished	1,960 sq. ft.
Basement Unfinished	1,993 sq. ft.
Garage Unfinished	476 sq. ft.
Dimensions	59'x62'
Foundation	Basement Crawlspace
Bedrooms	4
Full Baths	3
Main Ceiling	9'1 1/8"
Max Ridge Height	24'
Roof Framing	Stick
Exterior Walls	2x4

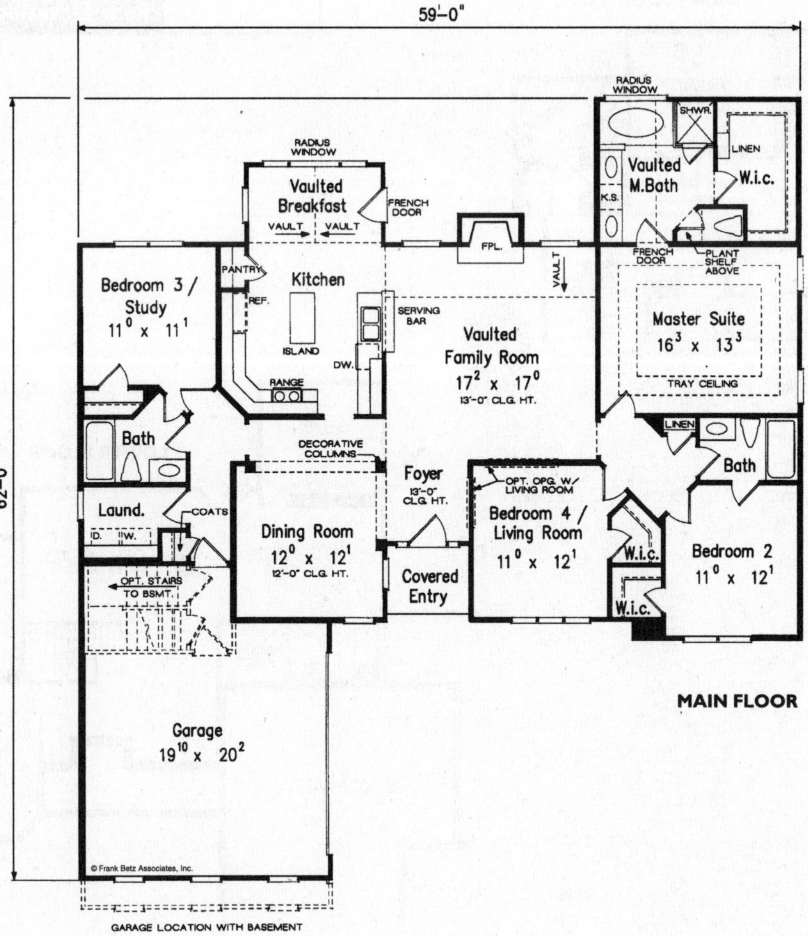
59'-0"
62'-0"
RADIUS WINDOW
Vaulted Breakfast
VAULT VAULT
FRENCH DOOR
FPL.
VAULT
RADIUS WINDOW
SHWR.
LINEN
W.i.c.
Vaulted M.Bath
K.S.
FRENCH DOOR
PLANT SHELF ABOVE
Bedroom 3 / Study
11⁰ x 11¹
PANTRY
Kitchen
REF.
ISLAND
RANGE
DW.
SERVING BAR
Vaulted Family Room
17² x 17⁰
13'-0" CLG. HT.
Master Suite
16³ x 13³
TRAY CEILING
Bath
DECORATIVE COLUMNS
Foyer
13'-0" CLG. HT.
LINEN
Bath
Laund.
COATS
D. W.
OPT. STAIRS TO BSMT.
Dining Room
12⁰ x 12¹
12'-0" CLG. HT.
Covered Entry
OPT. OPG. W/ LIVING ROOM
Bedroom 4 / Living Room
11⁰ x 12¹
W.i.c.
W.i.c.
Bedroom 2
11⁰ x 12¹
Garage
19¹⁰ x 20²
© Frank Betz Associates, Inc.
GARAGE LOCATION WITH BASEMENT

MAIN FLOOR

Design 97319

See Order Pages and Index for Info

Units	Single
Price Code	J
Total Finished	2,047 sq. ft.
Main Finished	2,047 sq. ft.
Lower Finished	1,668 sq. ft.
Basement Unfinished	379 sq. ft.
Dimensions	73'x71'
Foundation	Basement
Bedrooms	3
Full Baths	2
Half Baths	1
Roof Framing	Truss

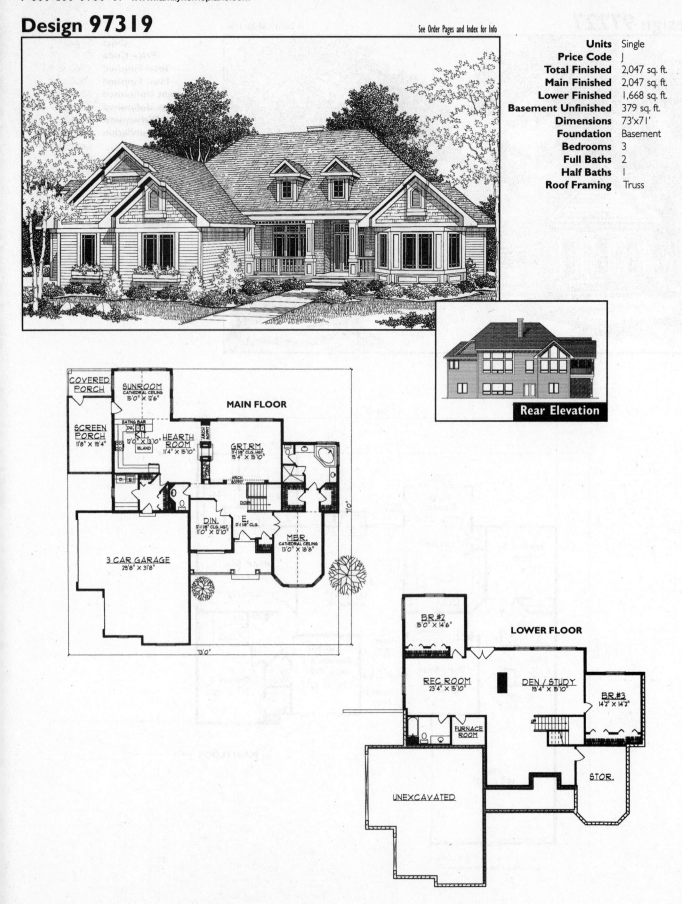

Rear Elevation

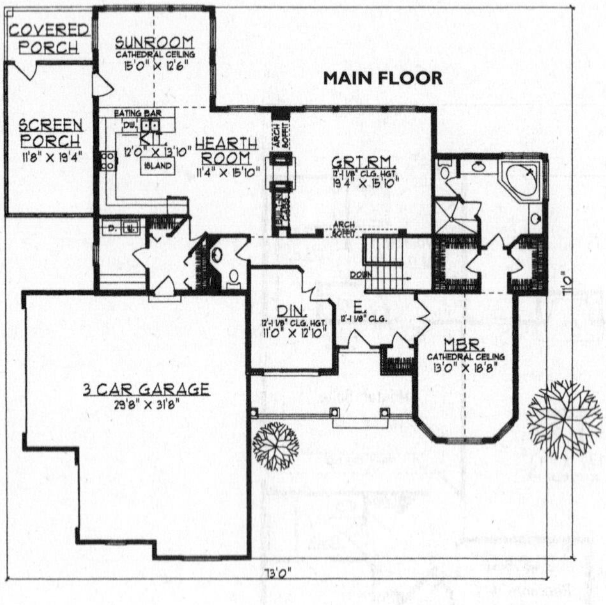
MAIN FLOOR
COVERED PORCH
SUNROOM CATHEDRAL CEILING 15'0" X 12'6"
SCREEN PORCH 11'8" X 19'4"
EATING BAR
KIT 12'0" X 13'10"
ISLAND
HEARTH ROOM 11'4" X 15'10"
ARCH SOFFIT
GRT.RM. 17'-1 1/8" CLG. HGT. 19'4" X 15'10"
DOWN
DIN. 12'-1 1/8" CLG. HGT. 11'0" X 12'10"
E. 12'-1 1/8" CLG.
MBR. CATHEDRAL CEILING 13'0" X 18'8"
3 CAR GARAGE 29'8" X 31'8"
73'0"
71'0"

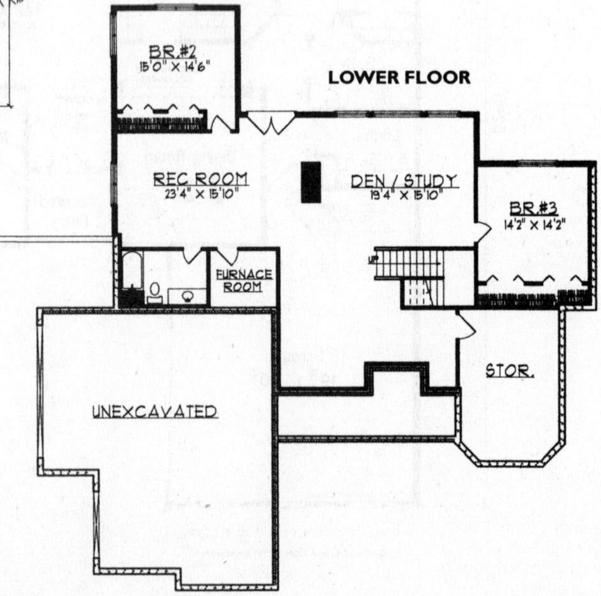
LOWER FLOOR
BR.#2 15'0" X 14'6"
REC ROOM 23'4" X 15'10"
DEN / STUDY 19'4" X 15'10"
BR.#3 14'2" X 14'2"
FURNACE ROOM
UP
STOR.
UNEXCAVATED

Design 98455

See Order Pages and Index for Info

Units	Single
Price Code	E
Total Finished	2,349 sq. ft.
First Finished	1,761 sq. ft.
Second Finished	588 sq. ft.
Bonus Unfinished	267 sq. ft.
Basement Unfinished	1,761 sq. ft.
Garage Unfinished	435 sq. ft.
Dimensions	56'x47'6"
Foundation	Basement Crawlspace
Bedrooms	4
Full Baths	3
First Ceiling	9'
Second Ceiling	8'
Max Ridge Height	31'6"
Roof Framing	Stick
Exterior Walls	2x4

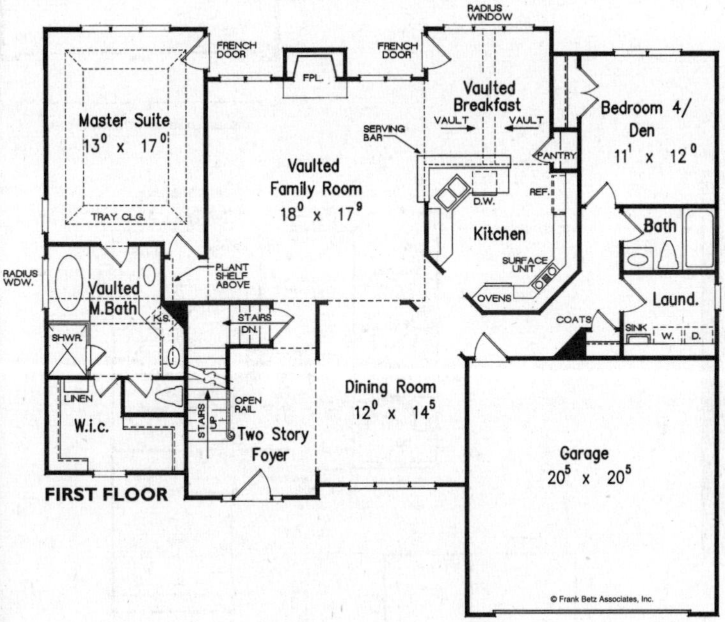
RADIUS WINDOW
FRENCH DOOR
FPL.
FRENCH DOOR
Vaulted Breakfast
VAULT
VAULT
Master Suite
13⁰ x 17⁰
TRAY CLG.
SERVING BAR
Vaulted Family Room
18⁰ x 17⁹
PANTRY
Bedroom 4/ Den
11¹ x 12⁰
D.W.
REF.
Kitchen
Bath
SURFACE UNIT
OVENS
Laund.
RADIUS WDW.
Vaulted M.Bath
PLANT SHELF ABOVE
STAIRS DN.
COATS
SINK
W.
D.
SHWR.
LINEN
W.i.c.
OPEN RAIL
STAIRS UP
Two Story Foyer
Dining Room
12⁰ x 14⁵
Garage
20⁵ x 20⁵
© Frank Betz Associates, Inc.

FIRST FLOOR

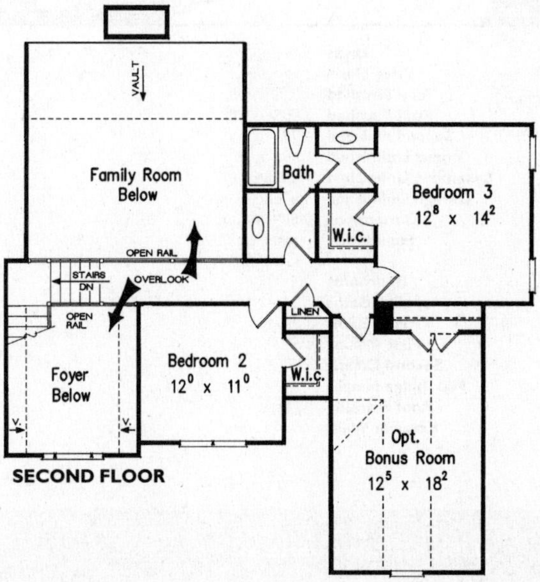
VAULT
Family Room Below
Bath
Bedroom 3
12⁸ x 14²
W.i.c.
OPEN RAIL
STAIRS DN
OVERLOOK
OPEN RAIL
LINEN
Foyer Below
Bedroom 2
12⁰ x 11⁰
W.i.c.
Opt. Bonus Room
12⁵ x 18²

SECOND FLOOR

Design 98411

See Order Pages and Index for Info

Units	Single
Price Code	A
Total Finished	1,373 sq. ft.
Main Finished	1,373 sq. ft.
Basement Unfinished	1,386 sq. ft.
Dimensions	50'4"x45'
Foundation	Basement Crawlspace
Bedrooms	3
Full Baths	2
Main Ceiling	9'
Max Ridge Height	23'6"
Roof Framing	Stick
Exterior Walls	2x4,2x6

MAIN FLOOR

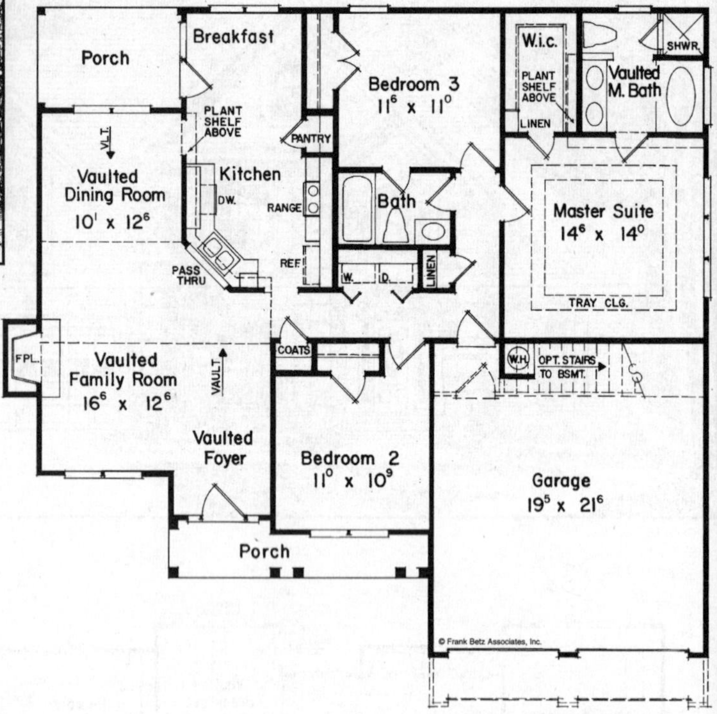

Porch
Breakfast
Bedroom 3
11⁶ x 11⁰
W.i.c.
PLANT SHELF ABOVE
LINEN
Vaulted M. Bath
SHWR.
PLANT SHELF ABOVE
PANTRY
Vaulted Dining Room
10¹ x 12⁶
Kitchen
DW.
RANGE
Bath
Master Suite
14⁶ x 14⁰
TRAY CLG.
REF
W.
D.
LINEN
PASS THRU
FPL.
Vaulted Family Room
16⁶ x 12⁶
VAULT
COATS
W.H.
OPT. STAIRS TO BSMT.
Vaulted Foyer
Bedroom 2
11⁰ x 10⁹
Garage
19⁵ x 21⁶
Porch
© Frank Betz Associates, Inc.

GARAGE LOCATION WITH BASEMENT

Design 97662

See Order Pages and Index for Info

Units	Single
Price Code	H
Total Finished	3,025 sq. ft.
First Finished	2,238 sq. ft.
Second Finished	787 sq. ft.
Bonus Unfinished	408 sq. ft.
Basement Unfinished	2,238 sq. ft.
Garage Unfinished	506 sq. ft.
Dimensions	58'4"x67'
Foundation	Basement Crawlspace
Bedrooms	4
Full Baths	3
Half Baths	1
First Ceiling	9'
Second Ceiling	8'
Max Ridge Height	30'
Roof Framing	Stick
Exterior Walls	2x4

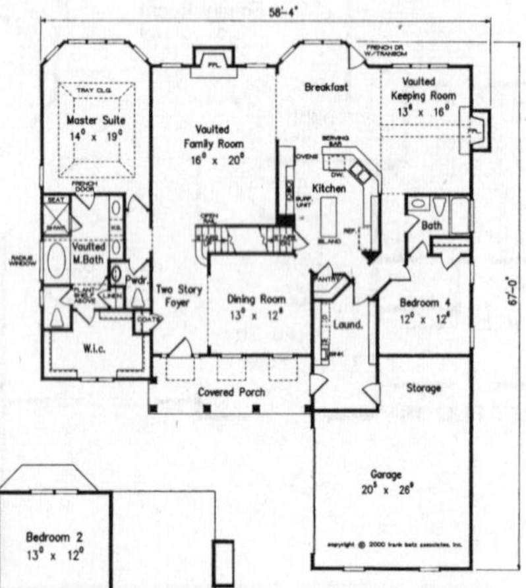

58'-4"
Master Suite
Vaulted Family Room
Breakfast
Vaulted Keeping Room
Kitchen
Bath
Two Story Foyer
Dining Room
Bedroom 4
Laund.
W.i.c.
Covered Porch
Storage
Garage
67'-0"

FIRST FLOOR

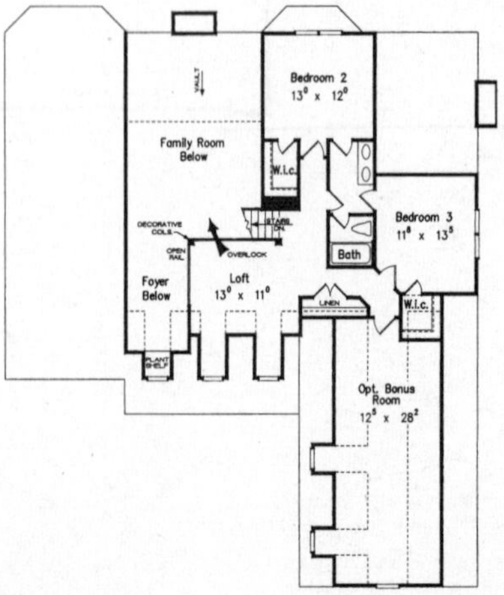

Bedroom 2
13⁰ x 12⁰
Family Room Below
Bedroom 3
11⁶ x 13⁵
Bath
Foyer Below
Loft
13⁰ x 11⁰
OVERLOOK
LINEN
W.i.c.
Opt. Bonus Room
12⁵ x 28²

SECOND FLOOR

Design 98403

See Order Pages and Index for Info

Units	Single
Price Code	I
Total Finished	3,395 sq. ft.
First Finished	2,467 sq. ft.
Second Finished	928 sq. ft.
Bonus Unfinished	296 sq. ft.
Basement Unfinished	2,467 sq. ft.
Garage Unfinished	566 sq. ft.
Dimensions	64'6"x62'10"
Foundation	Basement Crawlspace Slab
Bedrooms	4
Full Baths	3
Half Baths	1
First Ceiling	9'
Second Ceiling	8'
Max Ridge Height	32'8"
Roof Framing	Stick
Exterior Walls	2x4

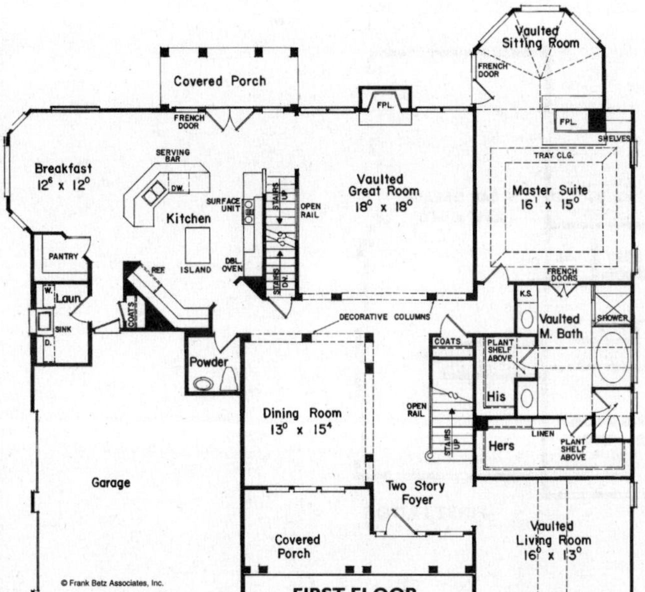
Vaulted Sitting Room
Covered Porch
FRENCH DOOR
FPL.
FPL.
SHELVES
TRAY CLG.
Breakfast 12⁶ x 12⁰
SERVING BAR
DW.
SURFACE UNIT
Kitchen
REF.
ISLAND
DBL OVEN
OPEN RAIL
Vaulted Great Room 18⁰ x 18⁰
Master Suite 16' x 15⁰
FRENCH DOORS
PANTRY
Laun.
SINK
COATS
DECORATIVE COLUMNS
K.S.
Vaulted M. Bath
SHOWER
Powder
COATS
PLANT SHELF ABOVE
His
Dining Room 13⁰ x 15⁴
OPEN RAIL
LINEN
Hers
PLANT SHELF ABOVE
Garage
Two Story Foyer
Covered Porch
Vaulted Living Room 16⁰ x 13⁰
© Frank Betz Associates, Inc.
FPL.

FIRST FLOOR

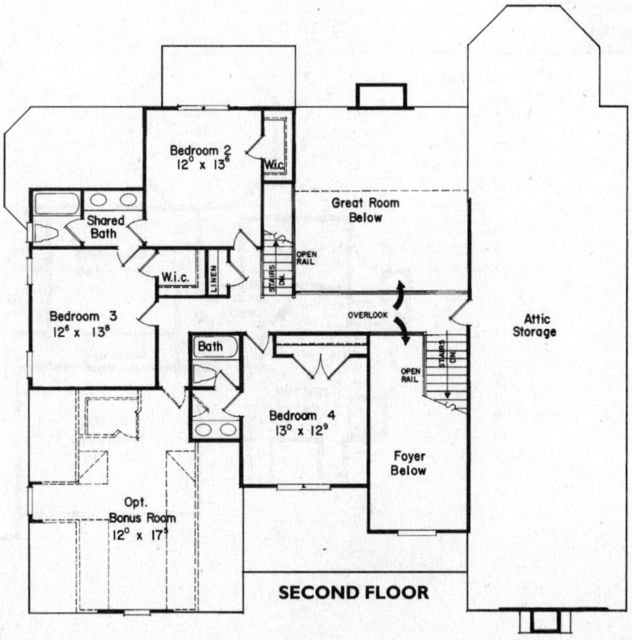
Bedroom 2 12⁰ x 13⁶
W.i.c.
Shared Bath
Great Room Below
OPEN RAIL
W.i.c.
LINEN
OVERLOOK
Bedroom 3 12⁶ x 13⁸
Bath
Attic Storage
OPEN RAIL
Bedroom 4 13⁰ x 12⁹
Foyer Below
Opt. Bonus Room 12⁰ x 17⁵

SECOND FLOOR

Design 99093

See Order Pages and Index for Info

Units	Single
Price Code	L
Total Finished	5,825 sq. ft.
First Finished	3,180 sq. ft.
Second Finished	2,645 sq. ft.
Basement Unfinished	3,175 sq. ft.
Garage Unfinished	1,260 sq. ft.
Porch Unfinished	230 sq. ft.
Dimensions	109'6"x54'3"
Foundation	Basement
Bedrooms	4
Full Baths	3
Half Baths	2
First Ceiling	9'
Second Ceiling	9'
Max Ridge Height	36'
Roof Framing	Stick
Exterior Walls	2x6

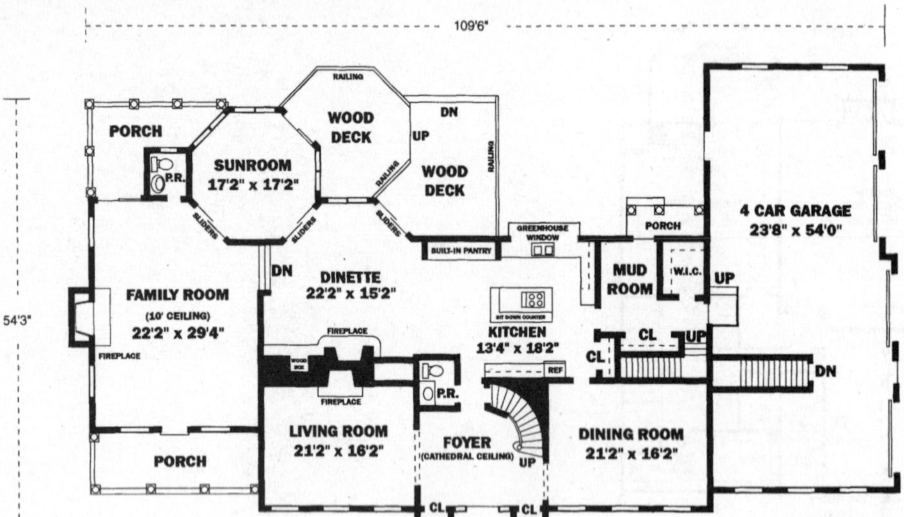
109'6"
54'3"
PORCH
P.R.
SUNROOM
17'2" x 17'2"
RAILING
WOOD
DECK
UP
DN
WOOD
DECK
RAILING
SLIDERS
SLIDERS
SLIDERS
GREENHOUSE
WINDOW
BUILT-IN PANTRY
PORCH
4 CAR GARAGE
23'8" x 54'0"
DN
DINETTE
22'2" x 15'2"
MUD
ROOM
W.I.C.
UP
FAMILY ROOM
(10' CEILING)
22'2" x 29'4"
FIREPLACE
FIREPLACE
KITCHEN
13'4" x 18'2"
CL
CL
UP
REF
DN
FIREPLACE
P.R.
LIVING ROOM
21'2" x 16'2"
FOYER
(CATHEDRAL CEILING)
UP
DINING ROOM
21'2" x 16'2"
PORCH
CL
CL

FIRST FLOOR

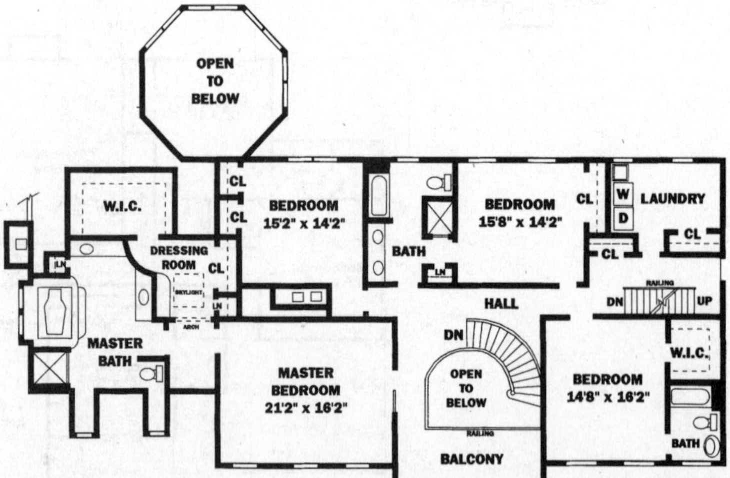
OPEN
TO
BELOW
W.I.C.
CL
CL
BEDROOM
15'2" x 14'2"
BEDROOM
15'8" x 14'2"
CL
W
D
LAUNDRY
CL
CL
DRESSING
ROOM
CL
SKYLIGHT
ARCH
BATH
LN
HALL
RAILING
DN
UP
LN
DN
W.I.C.
MASTER
BATH
MASTER
BEDROOM
21'2" x 16'2"
OPEN
TO
BELOW
RAILING
BEDROOM
14'8" x 16'2"
BATH
BALCONY

SECOND FLOOR

Design 98524

See Order Pages and Index for Info

Units	Single
Price Code	G
Total Finished	2,902 sq. ft.
First Finished	2,036 sq. ft.
Second Finished	866 sq. ft.
Garage Unfinished	720 sq. ft.
Porch Unfinished	46 sq. ft.
Dimensions	65'x53'4"
Foundation	Basement Slab
Bedrooms	4
Full Baths	3
Half Baths	1
Max Ridge Height	23'6"
Roof Framing	Stick
Exterior Walls	2x4

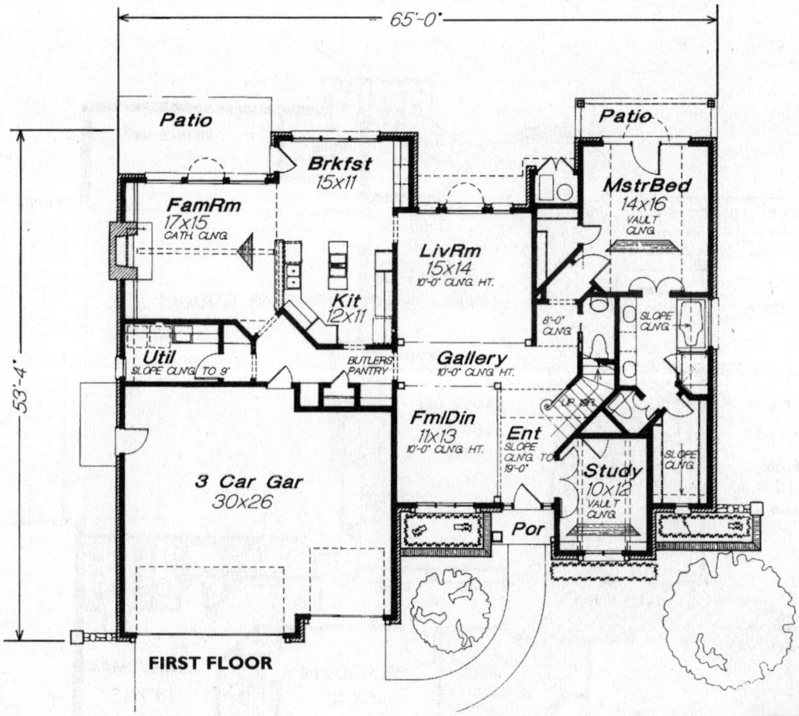
65'-0"
53'-4"
Patio
Brkfst 15x11
Patio
MstrBed 14x16 VAULT CLNG.
FamRm 17x15 CATH. CLNG.
LivRm 15x14 10'-0" CLNG. HT.
Kit 12x11
8'-0" CLNG.
SLOPE CLNG.
Util SLOPE CLNG. TO 9'
BUTLERS PANTRY
Gallery 10'-0" CLNG. HT.
UP 19R.
FmlDin 11x13 10'-0" CLNG. HT.
Ent SLOPE CLNG. TO 19'-0"
Study 10x12 VAULT CLNG.
SLOPE CLNG.
3 Car Gar 30x26
Por

FIRST FLOOR

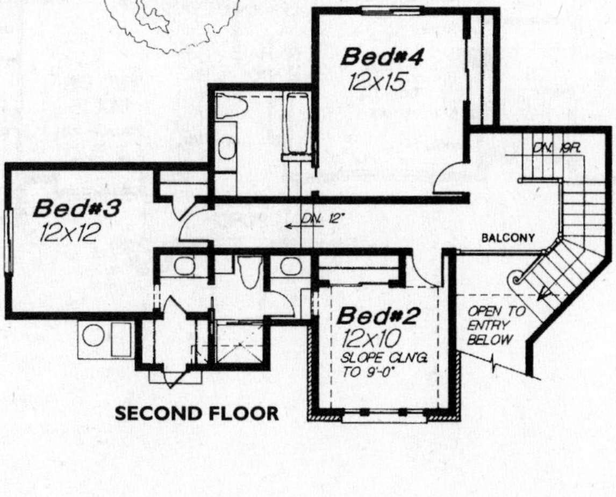
Bed#4 12x15
DN. 19R.
Bed#3 12x12
DN. 12"
BALCONY
Bed#2 12x10 SLOPE CLNG. TO 9'-0"
OPEN TO ENTRY BELOW

SECOND FLOOR

Design 97877

See Order Pages and Index for Info

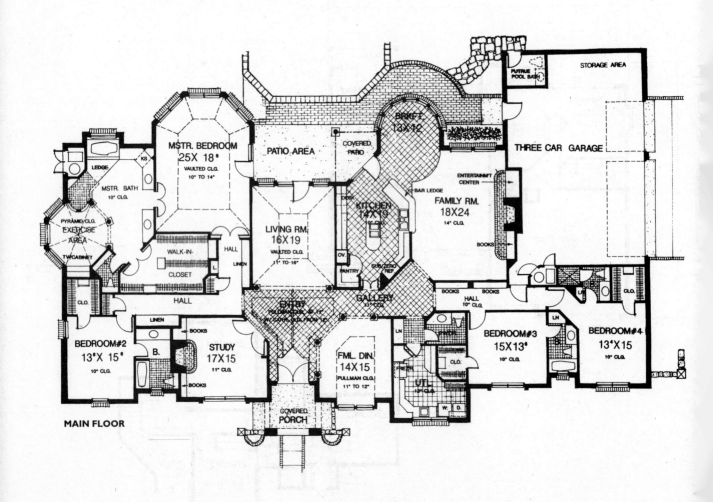

Units	Single
Price Code	L
Total Finished	4,615 sq. ft.
Main Finished	4,615 sq. ft.
Garage Unfinished	748 sq. ft.
Dimensions	113'4"x69'4"
Foundation	Slab
Bedrooms	4
Full Baths	3
Half Baths	1
3/4 Baths	1
Max Ridge Height	34'
Roof Framing	Stick
Exterior Walls	2x4

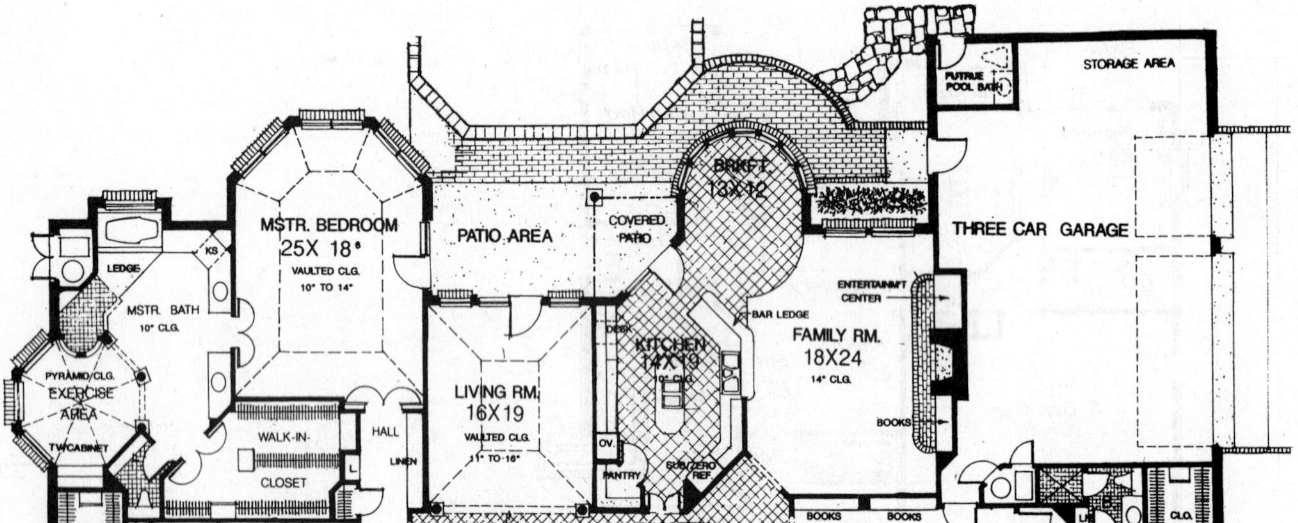
STORAGE AREA
BRKFT. 13X12
THREE CAR GARAGE
MSTR. BEDROOM 25X 18⁶ VAULTED CLG. 10" TO 14"
PATIO AREA
COVERED PATIO
ENTERTAINMT CENTER
BAR LEDGE
FAMILY RM. 18X24 14" CLG.
LEDGE
MSTR. BATH 10" CLG.
KITCHEN 14X19
LIVING RM. 16X19 VAULTED CLG. 11" TO 16"
PYRAMID CLG. EXERCISE AREA
WALK-IN-CLOSET
HALL
LINEN
BOOKS
PANTRY
SUB/ZERO REF.
CLO.
HALL
ENTRY
GALLERY
BOOKS
HALL 10" CLG.
BEDROOM#2 13⁶X 15⁶ 10" CLG.
STUDY 17X15 11" CLG.
FML. DIN. 14X15 PULLMAN CLG. 11" TO 12"
PWDR
BEDROOM#3 15X13⁶ 10" CLG.
BEDROOM#4 13⁶X15 10" CLG.
UTL.
W. D.
COVERED PORCH

MAIN FLOOR

Design 98912

See Order Pages and Index for Info

MAIN FLOOR

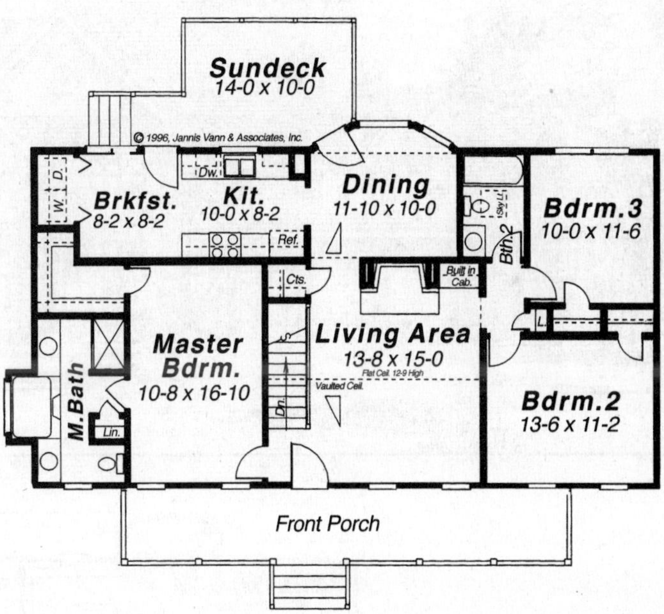

Sundeck
14-0 x 10-0
© 1996, Jannis Vann & Associates, Inc.
Brkfst.
8-2 x 8-2
Kit.
10-0 x 8-2
Dining
11-10 x 10-0
Bdrm.3
10-0 x 11-6
Master
Bdrm.
10-8 x 16-10
Living Area
13-8 x 15-0
Bdrm.2
13-6 x 11-2
M.Bath
Front Porch

Units	Single
Price Code	A
Total Finished	1,345 sq. ft.
Main Finished	1,325 sq. ft.
Lower Finished	20 sq. ft.
Basement Unfinished	556 sq. ft.
Garage Unfinished	724 sq. ft.
Porch Unfinished	216 sq. ft.
Dimensions	52'x42'
Foundation	Basement
Bedrooms	3
Full Baths	2
Main Ceiling	8'
Max Ridge Height	19'
Roof Framing	Stick
Exterior Walls	2x4

Design 97462

See Order Pages and Index for Info

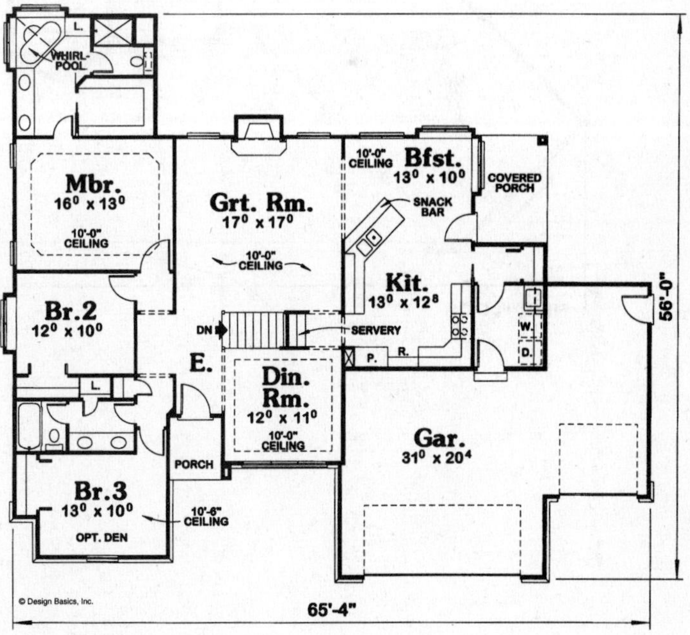

WHIRL-POOL
Mbr.
16⁰ x 13⁰
10'-0" CEILING
Grt. Rm.
17⁰ x 17⁰
10'-0" CEILING
10'-0" CEILING
Bfst.
13⁰ x 10⁰
SNACK BAR
COVERED PORCH
Kit.
13⁰ x 12⁸
SERVERY
Br.2
12⁰ x 10⁰
DN
E.
Din. Rm.
12⁰ x 11⁰
10'-0" CEILING
Gar.
31⁰ x 20⁴
PORCH
Br.3
13⁰ x 10⁰
OPT. DEN
10'-6" CEILING
56'-0"
65'-4"
© Design Basics, Inc.

MAIN FLOOR

Units	Single
Price Code	B
Total Finished	1,806 sq. ft.
Main Finished	1,806 sq. ft.
Garage Unfinished	655 sq. ft.
Dimensions	65'4"x56'
Foundation	Basement
Bedrooms	3
Full Baths	2
Main Ceiling	9'
Max Ridge Height	21'
Roof Framing	Stick
Exterior Walls	2x4

* Alternate foundation options available at an additional charge. Please call 1-800-235-5700 for more information.

Design 97401

See Order Pages and Index for Info

Units	Single
Price Code	I
Total Finished	3,404 sq. ft.
First Finished	1,824 sq. ft.
Second Finished	1,580 sq. ft.
Bonus Unfinished	479 sq. ft.
Dimensions	83'4"x65'10"
Foundation	Basement
Bedrooms	4
Full Baths	3
Half Baths	1
First Ceiling	8'
Max Ridge Height	30'8"
Roof Framing	Stick
Exterior Walls	2x4

* Alternate foundation options available at an additional charge
Please call 1-800-235-5700 for more information.

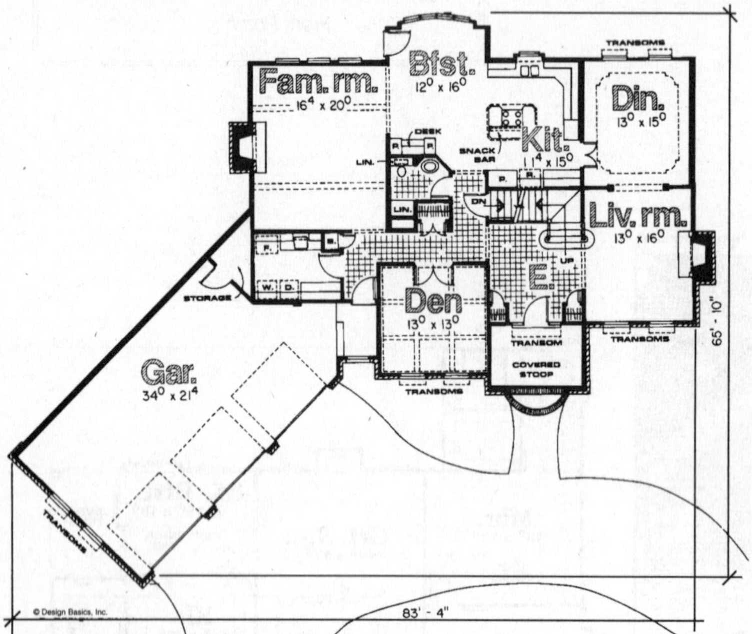

TRANSOMS
Bfst.
12⁰ x 16⁰
Fam. rm.
16⁴ x 20⁰
Din.
13⁰ x 15⁰
DESK
SNACK BAR
Kit.
11⁴ x 15⁰
LIN.
Liv. rm.
13⁰ x 16⁰
E.
STORAGE
Den
13⁰ x 13⁰
TRANSOM
COVERED STOOP
TRANSOMS
Gar.
34⁰ x 21⁴
65' - 10"
83' - 4"
© Design Basics, Inc.

FIRST FLOOR

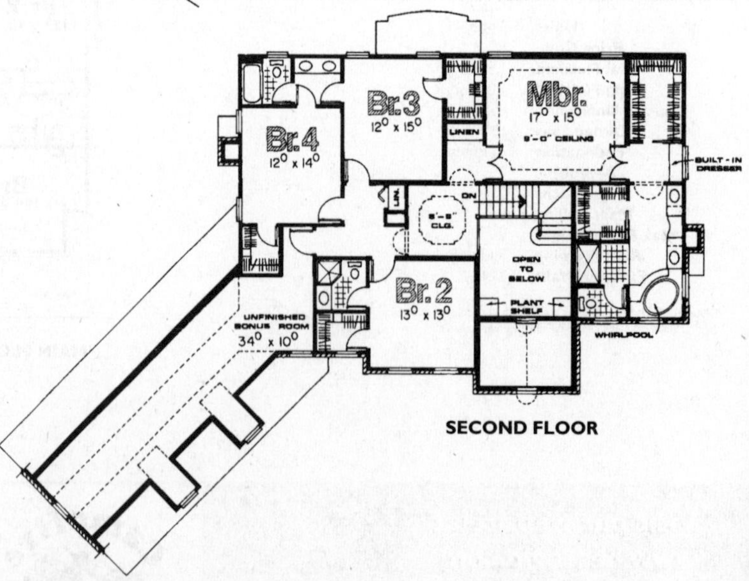

Br. 3
12⁰ x 15⁰
Mbr.
17⁰ x 15⁰
9'-0" CEILING
LINEN
Br. 4
12⁰ x 14⁰
BUILT-IN DRESSER
LIN.
CLO.
OPEN TO BELOW
Br. 2
13⁰ x 13⁰
PLANT SHELF
WHIRLPOOL
UNFINISHED BONUS ROOM
34⁰ x 10⁰

SECOND FLOOR

Design 92067

See Order Pages and Index for Info

Units	Single
Price Code	F
Total Finished	2,647 sq. ft.
Main Finished	1,431 sq. ft.
Lower Finished	1,216 sq. ft.
Basement Unfinished	215 sq. ft.
Dimensions	52'x49'
Foundation	Basement
Bedrooms	4
Full Baths	3
Max Ridge Height	23'
Roof Framing	Truss

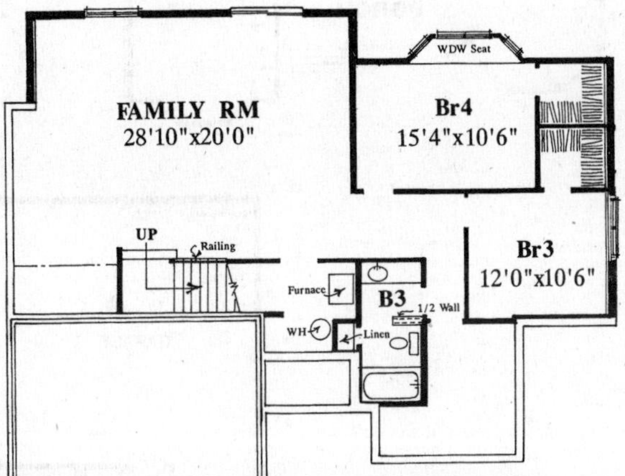
FAMILY RM
28'10"x20'0"
WDW Seat
Br4
15'4"x10'6"
Br3
12'0"x10'6"
UP
Railing
Furnace
B3
1/2 Wall
WH
Linen

LOWER FLOOR

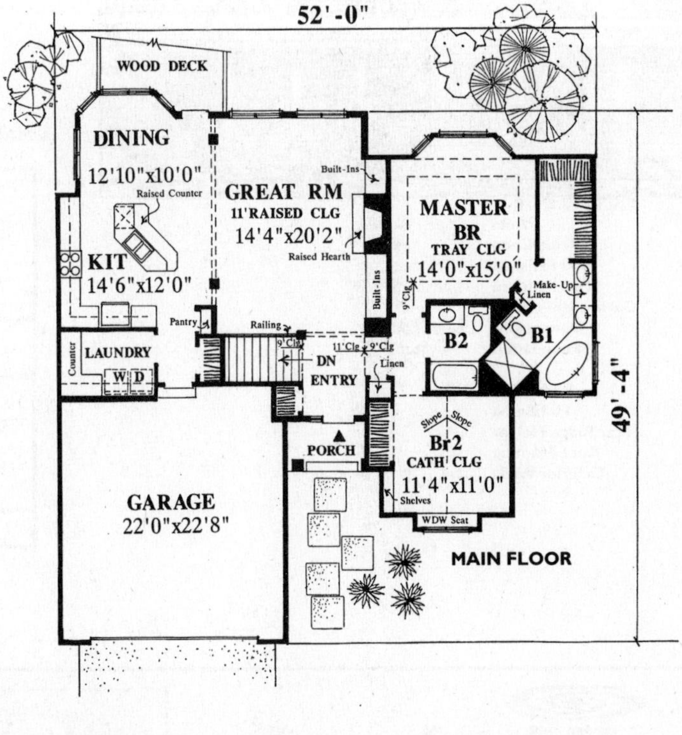
52'-0"
WOOD DECK
DINING
12'10"x10'0"
Raised Counter
KIT
14'6"x12'0"
GREAT RM
11'RAISED CLG
14'4"x20'2"
Built-Ins
Raised Hearth
MASTER
BR
TRAY CLG
14'0"x15'0"
Make-Up
Linen
B1
B2
Pantry
Railing
LAUNDRY
Counter
DN
ENTRY
Linen
PORCH
Br2
CATH CLG
11'4"x11'0"
Shelves
WDW Seat
GARAGE
22'0"x22'8"
49'-4"

MAIN FLOOR

Design 67003

See Order Pages and Index for Info

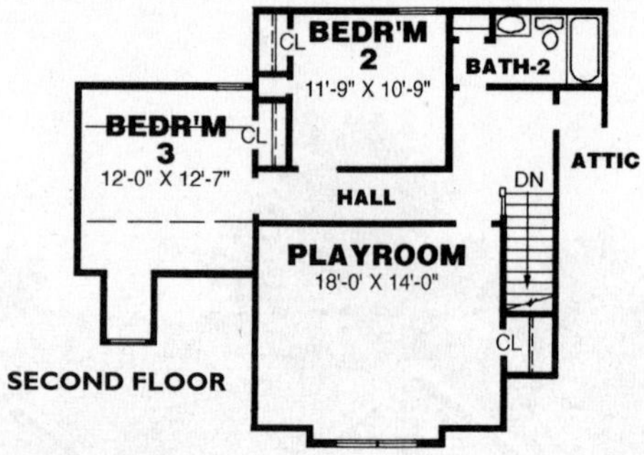
BEDR'M 2
11'-9" X 10'-9"
CL
BATH-2
BEDR'M 3
12'-0" X 12'-7"
CL
ATTIC
DN
HALL
PLAYROOM
18'-0' X 14'-0"
CL
SECOND FLOOR

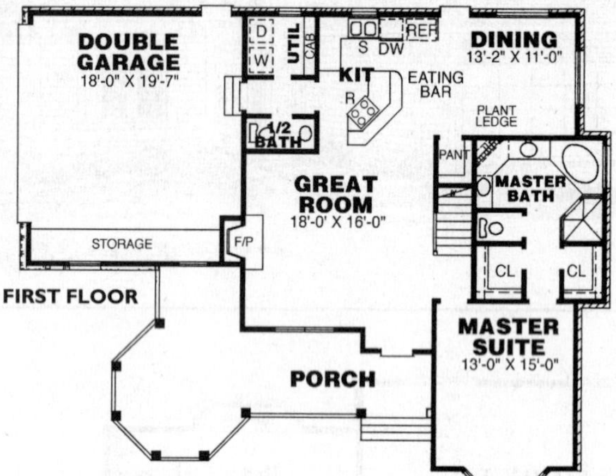
DOUBLE GARAGE
18'-0" X 19'-7"
D
W
UTIL
CAB
S
DW
REF
KIT
R
EATING BAR
DINING
13'-2" X 11'-0"
PLANT LEDGE
1/2 BATH
PANT
MASTER BATH
GREAT ROOM
18'-0' X 16'-0"
STORAGE
F/P
CL
CL
FIRST FLOOR
MASTER SUITE
13'-0" X 15'-0"
PORCH

Units	Single
Price Code	D
Total Finished	2,044 sq. ft.
First Finished	1,203 sq. ft.
Second Finished	841 sq. ft.
Garage Unfinished	462 sq. ft.
Porch Unfinished	323 sq. ft.
Dimensions	56'x44'5"
Foundation	Slab
Bedrooms	3
Full Baths	2
Half Baths	1
First Ceiling	8'
Second Ceiling	8'
Vaulted Ceiling	16'
Max Ridge Height	28'9"
Roof Framing	Stick
Exterior Walls	2x4

Design 93079

See Order Pages and Index for Info

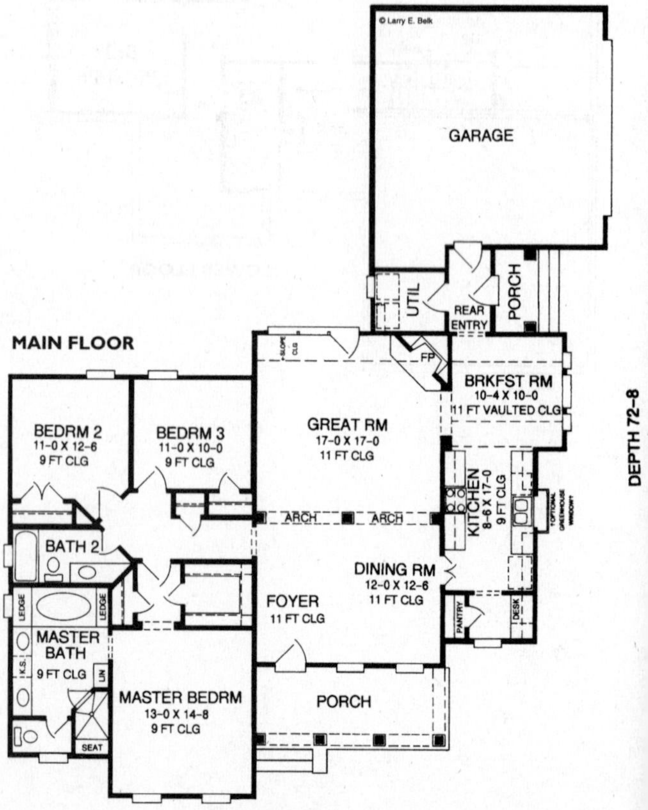
© Larry E. Belk
GARAGE
UTIL
REAR ENTRY
PORCH
MAIN FLOOR
FP
BRKFST RM
10-4 X 10-0
11 FT VAULTED CLG
DEPTH 72-8
BEDRM 2
11-0 X 12-6
9 FT CLG
BEDRM 3
11-0 X 10-0
9 FT CLG
GREAT RM
17-0 X 17-0
11 FT CLG
ARCH
ARCH
KITCHEN
8-6 X 17-0
9 FT CLG
BATH 2
DINING RM
12-0 X 12-6
11 FT CLG
LEDGE
LEDGE
FOYER
11 FT CLG
PANTRY
DESK
MASTER BATH
9 FT CLG
K.S.
LIN
MASTER BEDRM
13-0 X 14-8
9 FT CLG
PORCH
SEAT
WIDTH 56-4

Units	Single
Price Code	B
Total Finished	1,725 sq. ft.
Main Finished	1,725 sq. ft.
Garage Unfinished	496 sq. ft.
Dimensions	56'4"x72'8"
Foundation	Crawlspace Slab
Bedrooms	3
Full Baths	2
Max Ridge Height	23'
Roof Framing	Stick
Exterior Walls	2x4

Design 92651

See Order Pages and Index for Info

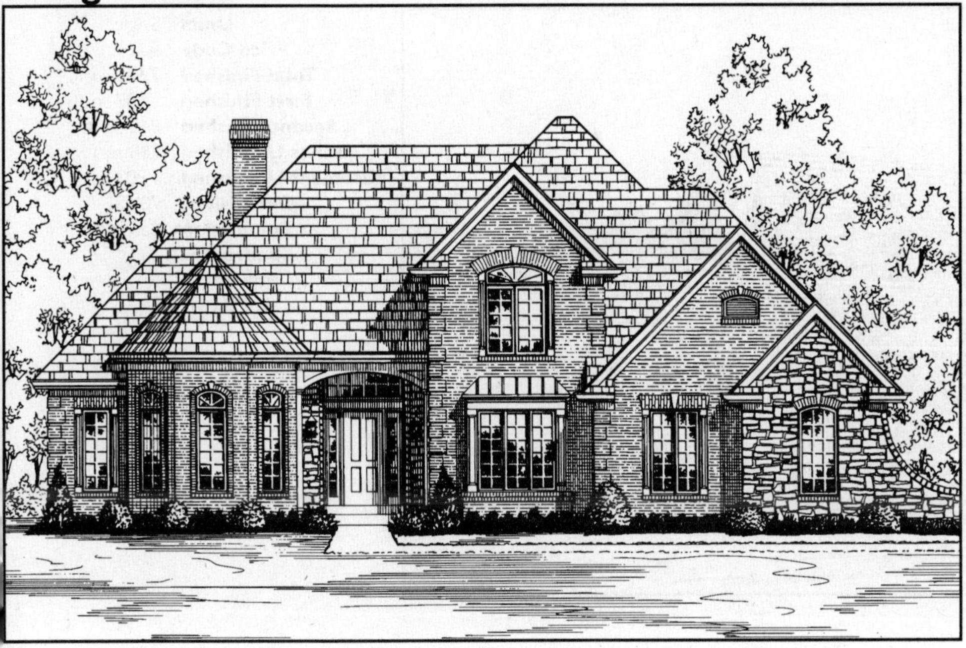

Units	Single
Price Code	E
Total Finished	2,403 sq. ft.
First Finished	1,710 sq. ft.
Second Finished	693 sq. ft.
Basement Unfinished	1,620 sq. ft.
Garage Unfinished	467 sq. ft.
Porch Unfinished	43 sq. ft.
Dimensions	63'4"x48'
Foundation	Basement Slab
Bedrooms	4
Full Baths	3
Half Baths	1
First Ceiling	8'
Second Ceiling	8'
Vaulted Ceiling	11'
Tray Ceiling	17'
Max Ridge Height	20'
Roof Framing	Truss
Exterior Walls	2x4

FIRST FLOOR

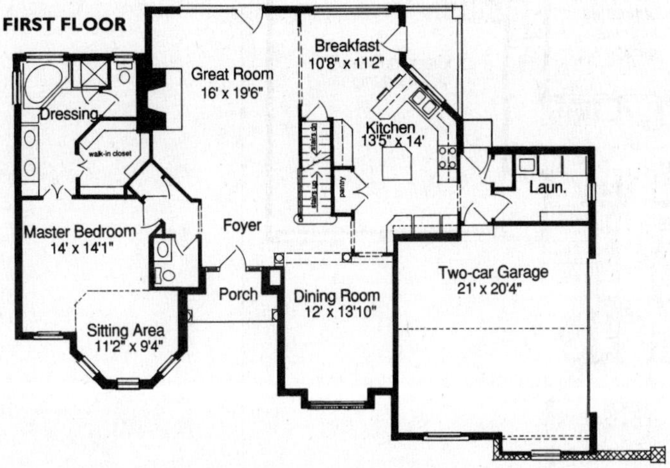
Great Room
16' x 19'6"
Breakfast
10'8" x 11'2"
Dressing
walk-in closet
Kitchen
13'5" x 14'
Laun.
Master Bedroom
14' x 14'1"
Foyer
Porch
Dining Room
12' x 13'10"
Two-car Garage
21' x 20'4"
Sitting Area
11'2" x 9'4"

SECOND FLOOR

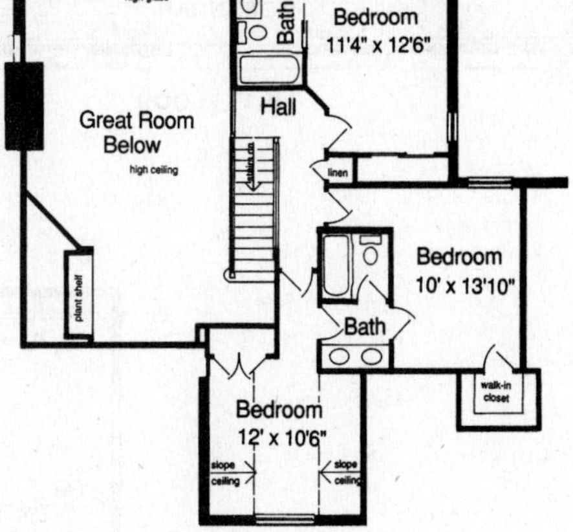
high glass
Bath
Bedroom
11'4" x 12'6"
Hall
Great Room
Below
high ceiling
linen
Bedroom
10' x 13'10"
plant shelf
Bath
walk-in
closet
Bedroom
12' x 10'6"
slope
ceiling
slope
ceiling

Design 90838

See Order Pages and Index for Info

Units	Single
Price Code	F
Total Finished	2,685 sq. ft.
First Finished	1,837 sq. ft.
Second Finished	848 sq. ft.
Bonus Unfinished	288 sq. ft.
Basement Unfinished	1,803 sq. ft.
Dimensions	78'x51'
Foundation	Basement
Bedrooms	3
Full Baths	1
3/4 Baths	2

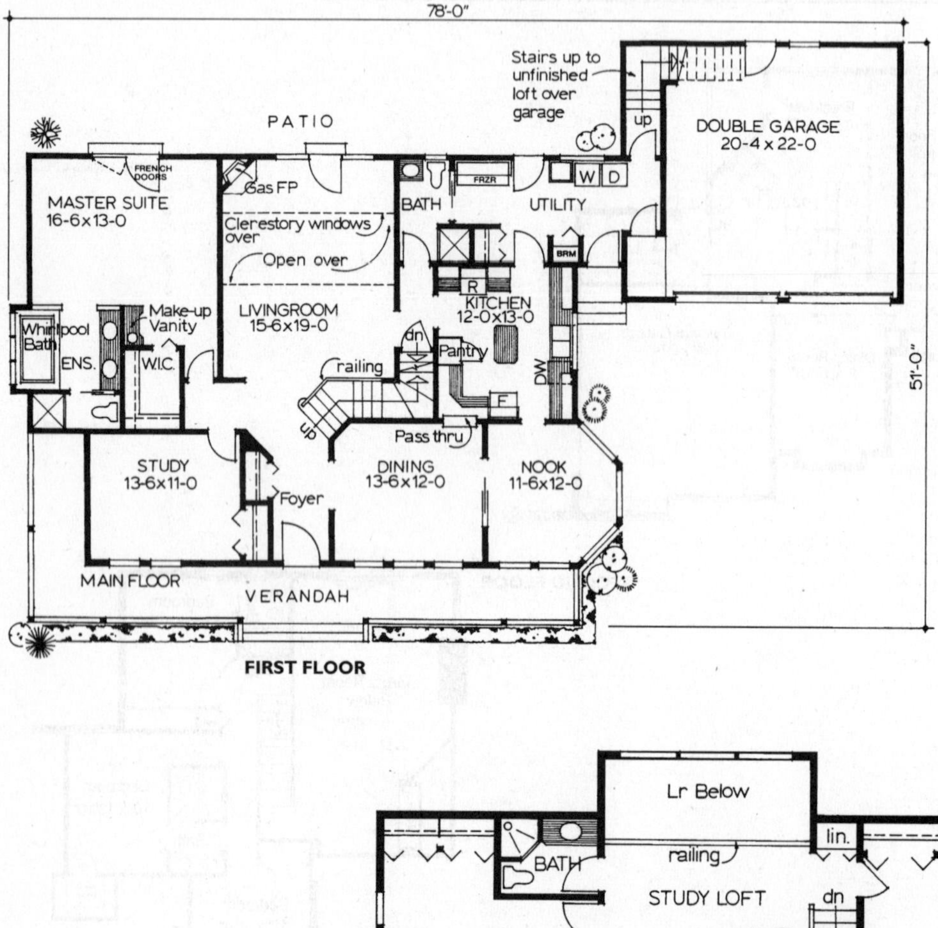
78'-0"
51'-0"
Stairs up to unfinished loft over garage
PATIO
up
DOUBLE GARAGE 20-4 x 22-0
FRENCH DOORS
MASTER SUITE 16-6x13-0
Gas FP
Clerestory windows over
Open over
BATH
FRZR
UTILITY
W
D
BRM
KITCHEN 12-0x13-0
LIVINGROOM 15-6x19-0
Make-up Vanity
Whirlpool Bath
ENS.
W.I.C.
railing
dn
Pantry
DW
F
up
Pass thru
STUDY 13-6x11-0
Foyer
DINING 13-6x12-0
NOOK 11-6x12-0
MAIN FLOOR
VERANDAH

FIRST FLOOR

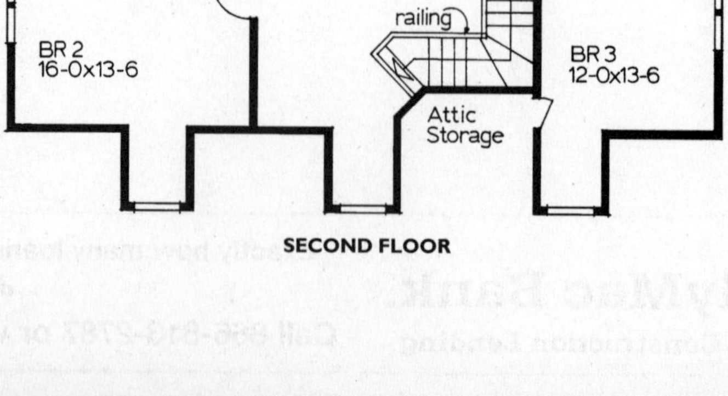
Lr Below
lin.
BATH
railing
STUDY LOFT
dn
railing
BR 2 16-0x13-6
BR 3 12-0x13-6
Attic Storage

SECOND FLOOR

Design 93133

See Order Pages and Index for Info

Units	Single
Price Code	C
Total Finished	1,761 sq. ft.
Main Finished	1,761 sq. ft.
Basement Unfinished	1,761 sq. ft.
Garage Unfinished	658 sq. ft.
Dimensions	67'8"x42'8"
Foundation	Basement
Bedrooms	3
Full Baths	2
Main Ceiling	8'
Vaulted Ceiling	14'
Max Ridge Height	22'
Roof Framing	Truss
Exterior Walls	2x6

MAIN FLOOR

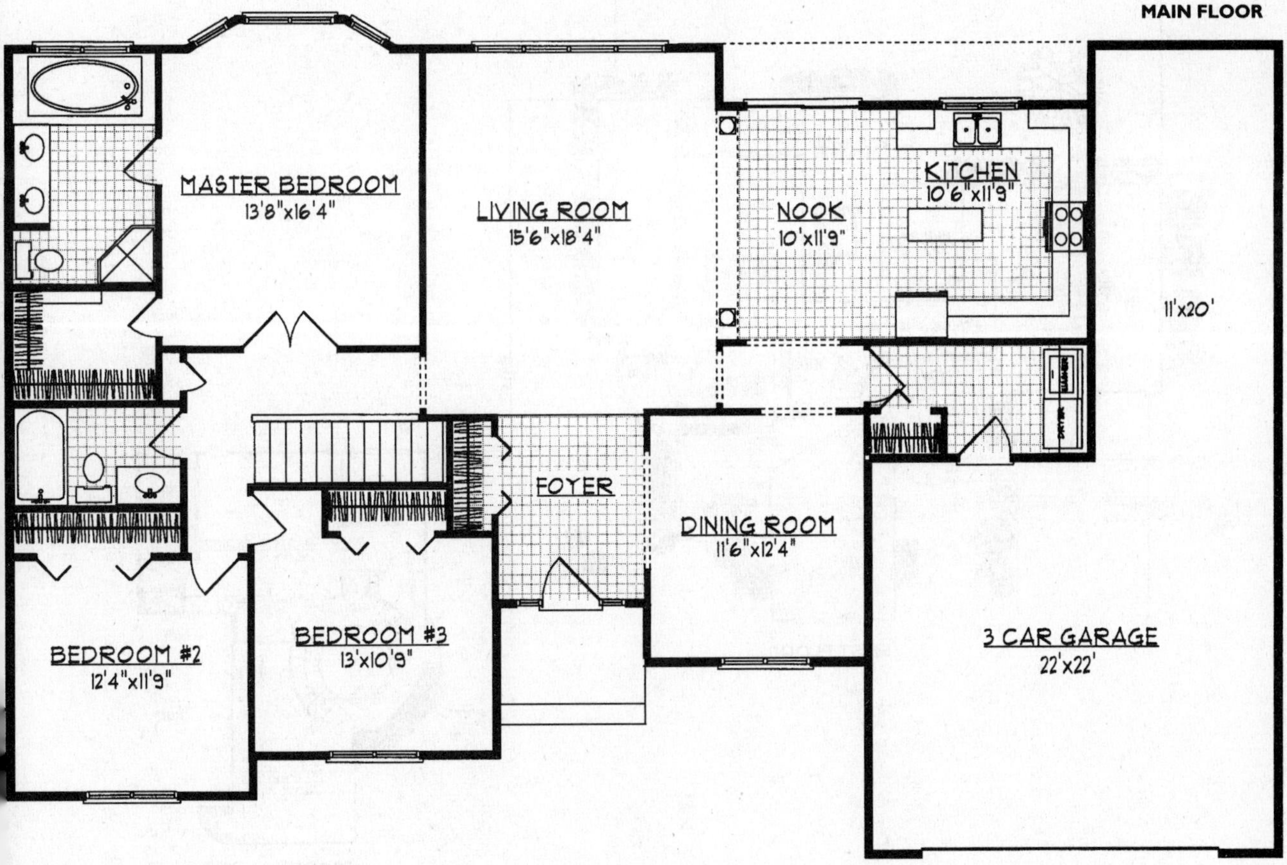
MASTER BEDROOM
13'8"x16'4"
LIVING ROOM
15'6"x18'4"
NOOK
10'x11'9"
KITCHEN
10'6"x11'9"
11'x20'
FOYER
DINING ROOM
11'6"x12'4"
BEDROOM #2
12'4"x11'9"
BEDROOM #3
13'x10'9"
3 CAR GARAGE
22'x22'

Design 91022

See Order Pages and Index for Info

Units	Single
Price Code	F
Total Finished	2,700 sq. ft.
First Finished	1,985 sq. ft.
Second Finished	715 sq. ft.
Basement Unfinished	1,985 sq. ft.
Garage Unfinished	608 sq. ft.
Dimensions	70'3"x64'
Foundation	Basement Crawlspace Slab
Bedrooms	3
Full Baths	2
Half Baths	1
Max Ridge Height	26'
Roof Framing	Stick
Exterior Walls	2x6

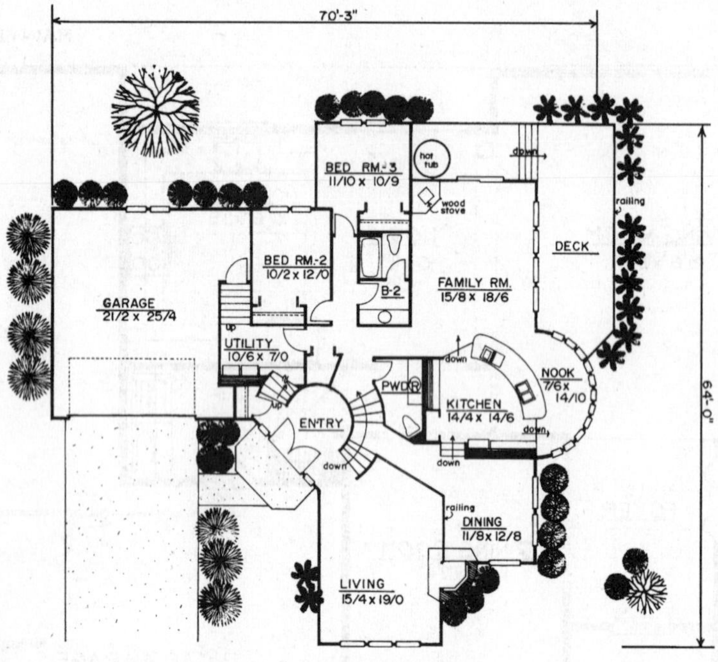
70'-3"
64'-0"
BED RM-3
11/10 x 10/9
hot tub
wood stove
down
railing
DECK
BED RM-2
10/2 x 12/0
B-2
FAMILY RM.
15/8 x 18/6
GARAGE
21/2 x 25/4
UTILITY
10/6 x 7/0
up
NOOK
7/6 x 14/10
PWDR
KITCHEN
14/4 x 14/6
ENTRY
down
DINING
11/8 x 12/8
LIVING
15/4 x 19/0

FIRST FLOOR

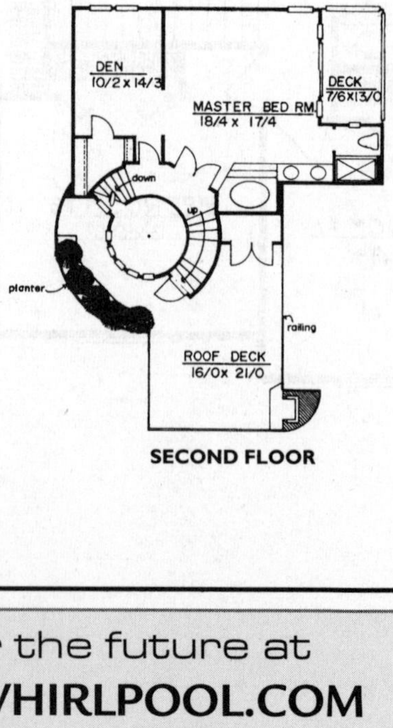
DEN
10/2 x 14/3
DECK
7/6 x 13/0
MASTER BED RM
18/4 x 17/4
down
up
planter
railing
ROOF DECK
16/0 x 21/0

SECOND FLOOR

Design 98518

See Order Pages and Index for Info

Units	Single
Price Code	E
Total Finished	2,455 sq. ft.
First Finished	1,447 sq. ft.
Second Finished	1,008 sq. ft.
Garage Unfinished	756 sq. ft.
Bonus Unfinished	352 sq. ft
Porch Unfinished	210 sq. ft.
Dimensions	65'x37'11"
Foundation	Basement Slab
Bedrooms	3
Full Baths	2
Half Baths	1
First Ceiling	9'
Second Ceiling	8'
Max Ridge Height	30'
Roof Framing	Stick
Exterior Walls	2x4

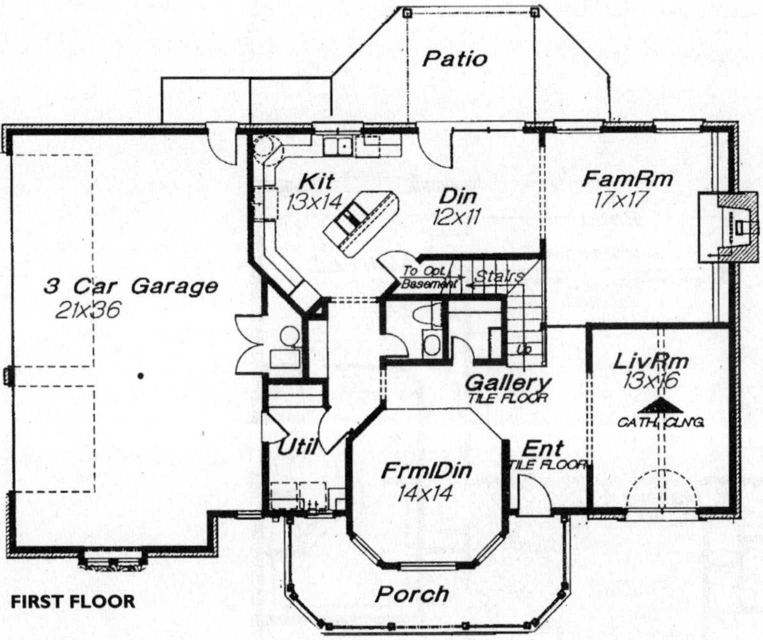
Patio
Kit
13x14
Din
12x11
FamRm
17x17
3 Car Garage
21x36
To Opt. Basement
Stairs
Up
Gallery
TILE FLOOR
LivRm
13x16
CATH. CLNG.
Util
FrmlDin
14x14
Ent
TILE FLOOR
Porch

FIRST FLOOR

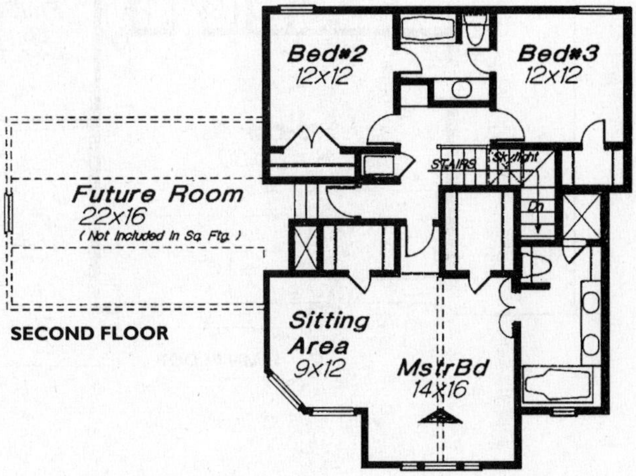
Bed#2
12x12
Bed#3
12x12
STAIRS
Skylight
Dn
Future Room
22x16
(Not Included In Sq. Ftg.)
Sitting
Area
9x12
MstrBd
14x16

SECOND FLOOR

Design 92275

See Order Pages and Index for Info

Units	Single
Price Code	F
Total Finished	2,675 sq. ft.
Main Finished	2,675 sq. ft.
Garage Unfinished	638 sq. ft.
Dimensions	69'x59'10"
Foundation	Slab
Bedrooms	4
Full Baths	3
Max Ridge Height	28'
Roof Framing	Stick
Exterior Walls	2x4

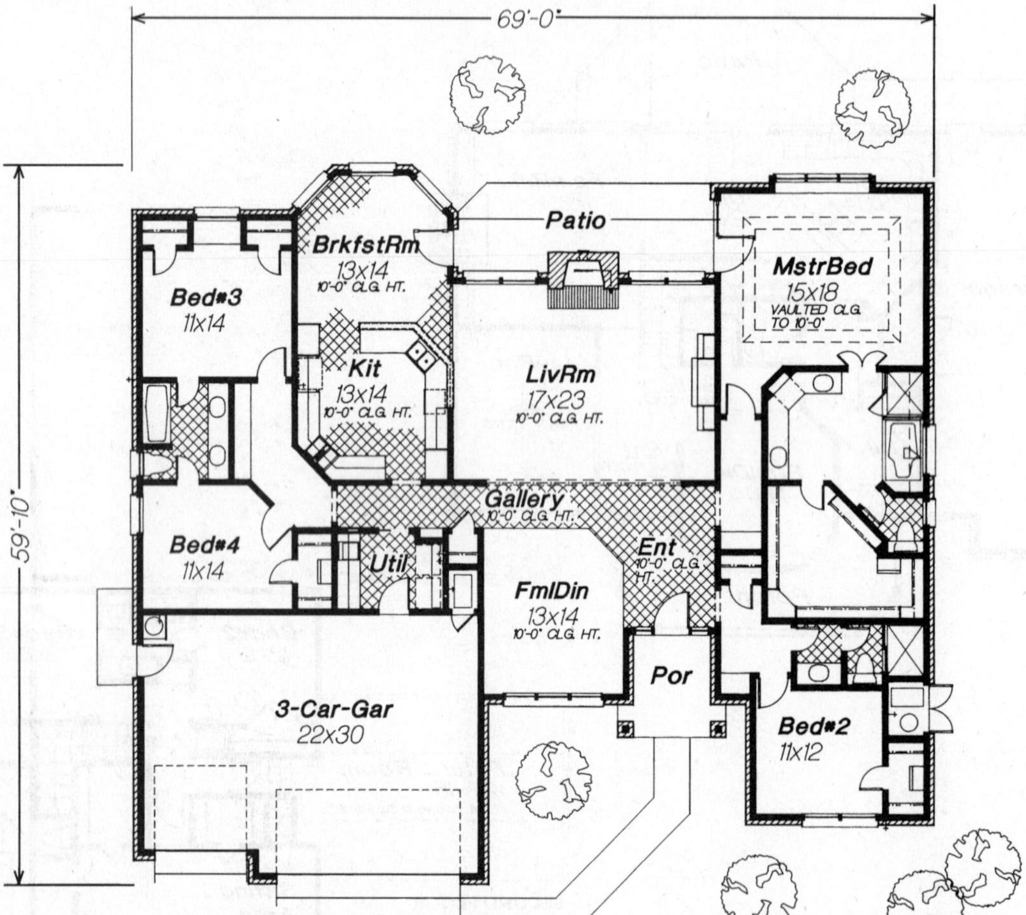
69'-0"
59'-10"
Patio
BrkfstRm 13x14 10'-0" CLG. HT.
MstrBed 15x18 VAULTED CLG. TO 10'-0"
Bed#3 11x14
Kit 13x14 10'-0" CLG. HT.
LivRm 17x23 10'-0" CLG. HT.
Gallery 10'-0" CLG. HT.
Bed#4 11x14
Util
Ent 10'-0" CLG. HT.
FmlDin 13x14 10'-0" CLG. HT.
Por
3-Car-Gar 22x30
Bed#2 11x12

MAIN FLOOR

Design 91840

See Order Pages and Index for Info

Units	Single
Price Code	B
Total Finished	1,588 sq. ft.
Main Finished	1,588 sq. ft.
Basement Unfinished	1,576 sq. ft.
Garage Unfinished	528 sq. ft.
Porch Unfinished	80 sq. ft.
Dimensions	66'x50'
Foundation	Basement
Bedrooms	3
Full Baths	2
Main Ceiling	8'
Max Ridge Height	20'
Roof Framing	Truss
Exterior Walls	2x6

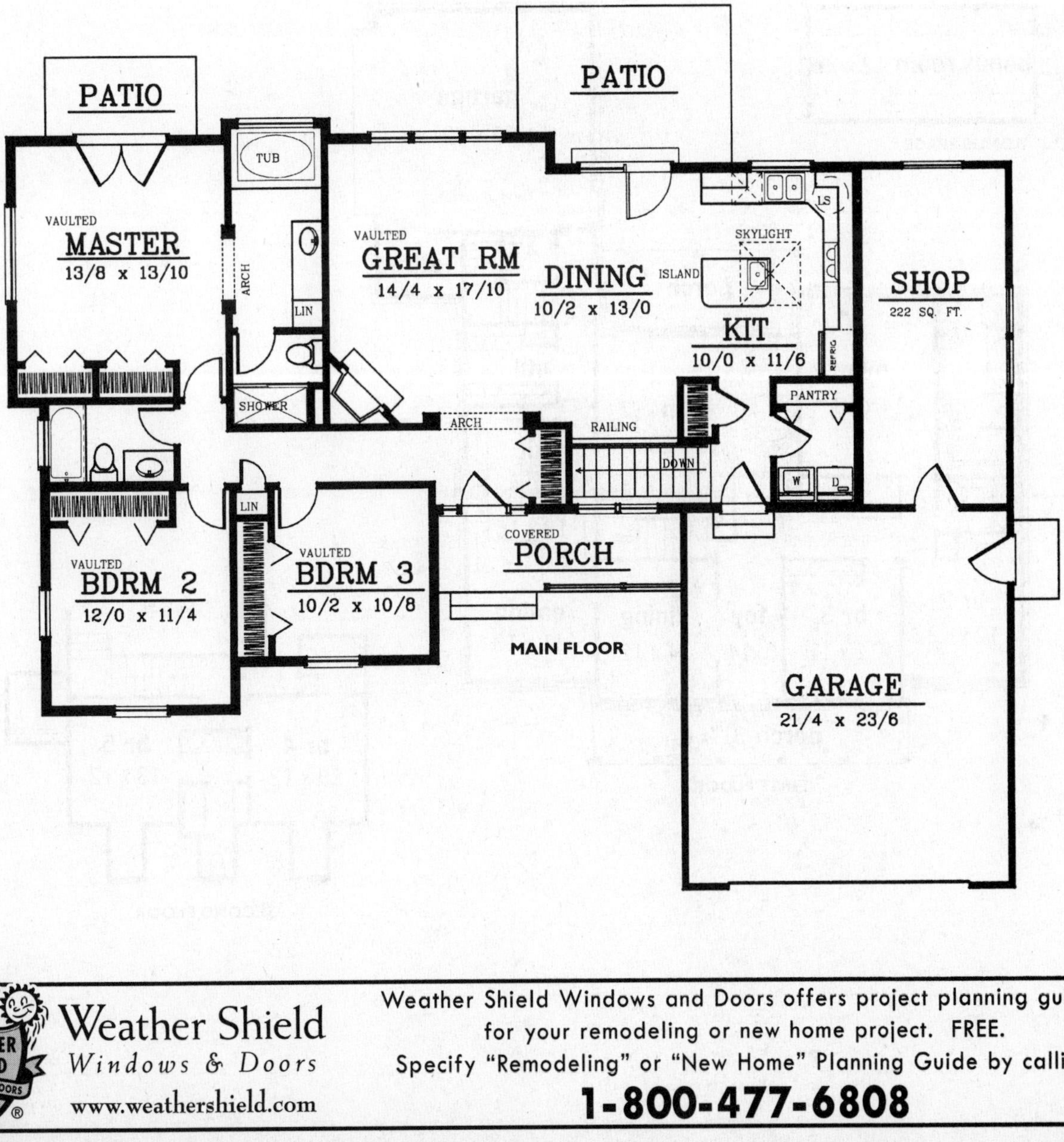
PATIO
PATIO
TUB
VAULTED
MASTER
13/8 x 13/10
ARCH
LIN
SHOWER
VAULTED
GREAT RM
14/4 x 17/10
DINING
10/2 x 13/0
SKYLIGHT
ISLAND
LS
KIT
10/0 x 11/6
REFRIG
SHOP
222 SQ. FT.
PANTRY
W
D
ARCH
RAILING
DOWN
LIN
VAULTED
BDRM 2
12/0 x 11/4
VAULTED
BDRM 3
10/2 x 10/8
COVERED
PORCH
MAIN FLOOR
GARAGE
21/4 x 23/6

Design 92576

See Order Pages and Index for Info

Units	Single
Price Code	G
Total Finished	2,858 sq. ft.
First Finished	2,256 sq. ft.
Second Finished	602 sq. ft.
Bonus Unfinished	264 sq. ft.
Garage Unfinished	484 sq. ft.
Dimensions	65'6"x74'5"
Foundation	Crawlspace Slab
Bedrooms	5
Full Baths	3
Half Baths	1
First Ceiling	9'
Second Ceiling	8'

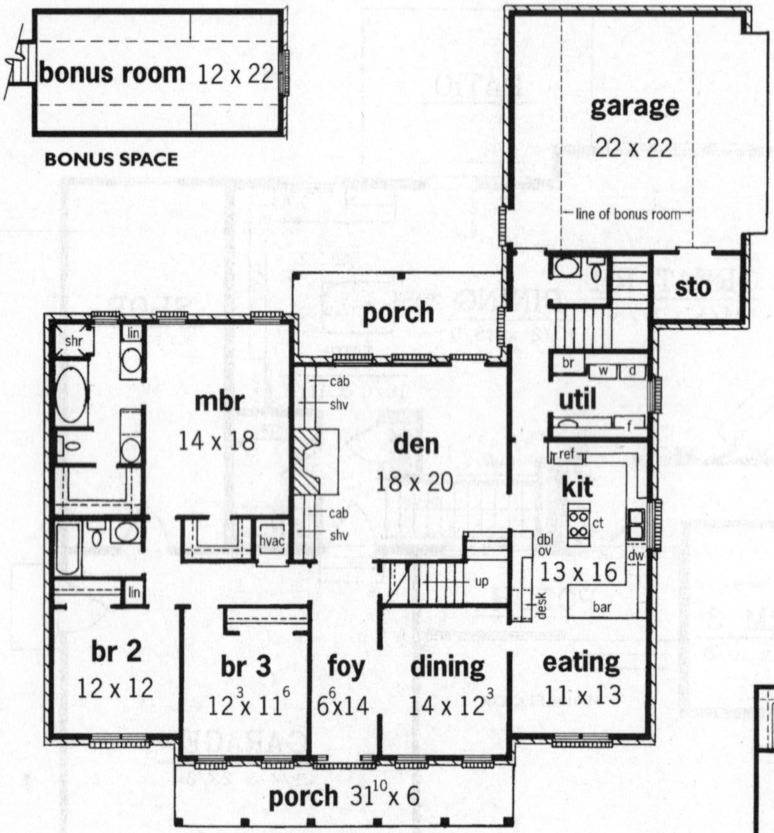
bonus room 12 x 22
garage
22 x 22
line of bonus room
sto
porch
shr
lin
mbr
14 x 18
cab
shv
den
18 x 20
br
w
d
util
f
ref
kit
ct
hvac
dbl ov
13 x 16
dw
up
desk
bar
lin
br 2
12 x 12
br 3
12³ x 11⁶
foy
6⁶x14
dining
14 x 12³
eating
11 x 13
porch 31¹⁰ x 6

BONUS SPACE

FIRST FLOOR

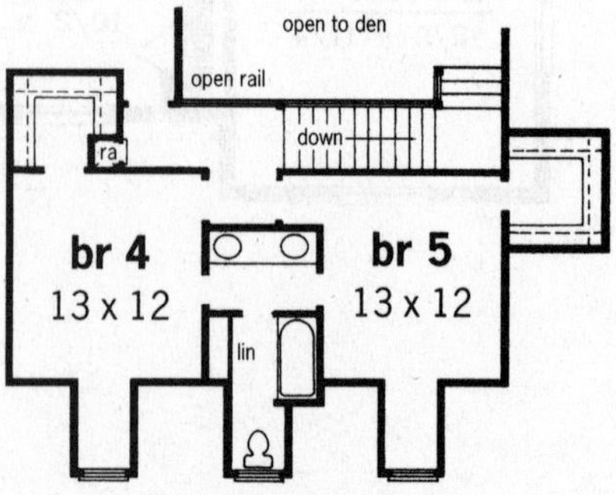
open to den
open rail
ra
down
br 4
13 x 12
br 5
13 x 12
lin

SECOND FLOOR

Design 97731

See Order Pages and Index for Info

Units	Single
Price Code	A
Total Finished	1,315 sq. ft.
Main Finished	1,315 sq. ft.
Basement Unfinished	1,315 sq. ft.
Garage Unfinished	488 sq. ft.
Porch Unfinished	75 sq. ft.
Dimensions	50'x54'8"
Foundation	Basement
Bedrooms	3
Full Baths	2
Main Ceiling	8'
Max Ridge Height	18'
Roof Framing	Truss
Exterior Walls	2x4

Deck
Master Bedroom
12'-4" x 13'-0"
Great Room
18'-8" x 17'-4"
SLOPE CEIL
Bedroom
11'-4" x 10'-8"
DN 13 RISERS
Bath
Dining
Bath
Kitchen
13'-4" x 9'-11"
SLOPE CEIL
Foyer
Bedroom
12'-4" x 10'-10"
Laun.
Porch
MAIN FLOOR
Garage
20'-0" x 26'-2"

Design 34901

See Order Pages and Index for Info

Rear Elevation

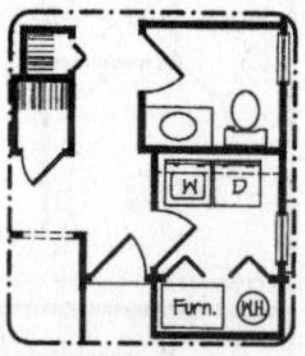
W
D
Furn.
W.H.

CRAWLSPACE/SLAB OPTION

Units	Single
Price Code	C
Total Finished	1,763 sq. ft.
First Finished	909 sq. ft.
Second Finished	854 sq. ft.
Basement Unfinished	899 sq. ft.
Garage Unfinished	491 sq. ft.
Dimensions	48'x44'
Foundation	Basement Crawlspace Slab
Bedrooms	3
Full Baths	2
Half Baths	1
First Ceiling	8'
Second Ceiling	8'
Tray Ceiling	9'
Max Ridge Height	29'
Roof Framing	Stick
Exterior Walls	2x4,2x6

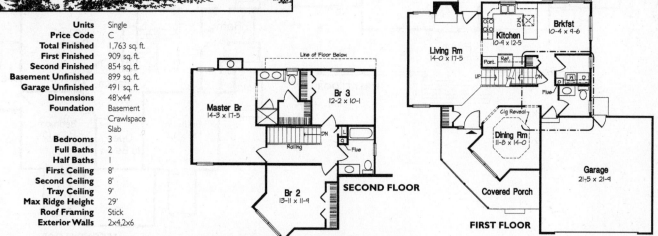

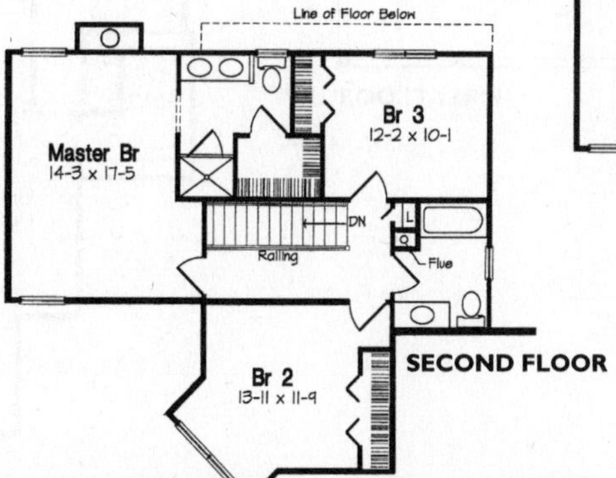
Line of Floor Below
Master Br
14-3 x 17-5
Br 3
12-2 x 10-1
DN
Railing
Flue
Br 2
13-11 x 11-9
SECOND FLOOR

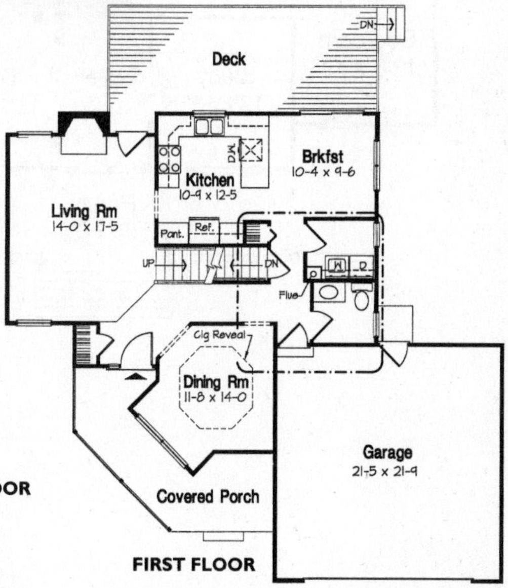
DN
Deck
DW
Kitchen
10-9 x 12-5
Brkfst
10-4 x 9-6
Living Rm
14-0 x 17-5
Pant.
Ref.
UP
DN
Flue
Clg Reveal
Dining Rm
11-8 x 14-0
Garage
21-5 x 21-9
Covered Porch
FIRST FLOOR

Design 94686

See Order Pages and Index for Info

Units	Single
Price Code	J
Total Finished	3,590 sq. ft.
First Finished	2,390 sq. ft.
Second Finished	1,200 sq. ft.
Porch Unfinished	271 sq. ft.
Dimensions	61'x64'4"
Foundation	Pier/Post
Bedrooms	4
Full Baths	3
First Ceiling	9'
Second Ceiling	9'
Max Ridge Height	40'
Roof Framing	Stick
Exterior Walls	2x4

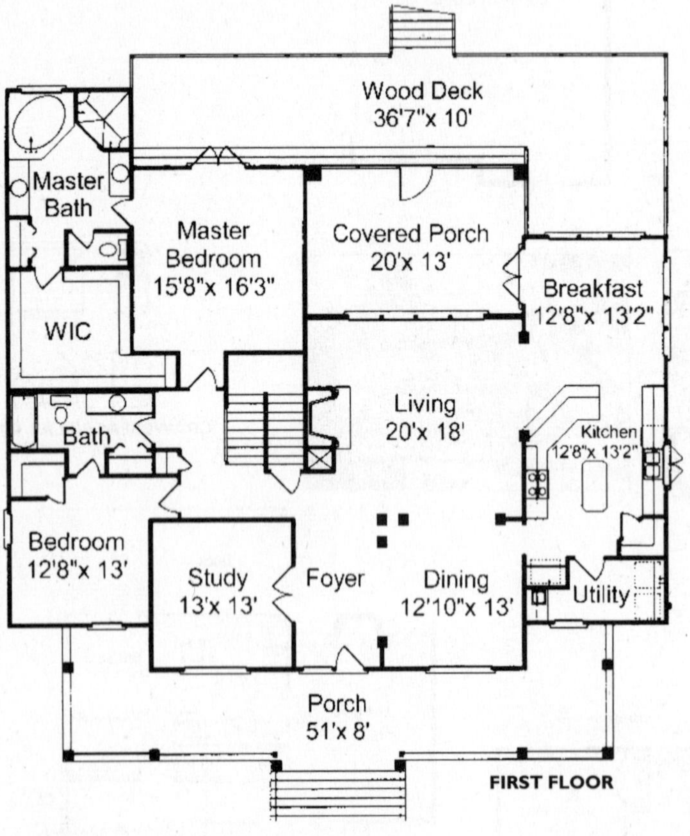
Wood Deck
36'7"x 10'
Master
Bath
Master
Bedroom
15'8"x 16'3"
Covered Porch
20'x 13'
Breakfast
12'8"x 13'2"
WIC
Living
20'x 18'
Kitchen
12'8"x 13'2"
Bath
Bedroom
12'8"x 13'
Study
13'x 13'
Foyer
Dining
12'10"x 13'
Utility
Porch
51'x 8'

FIRST FLOOR

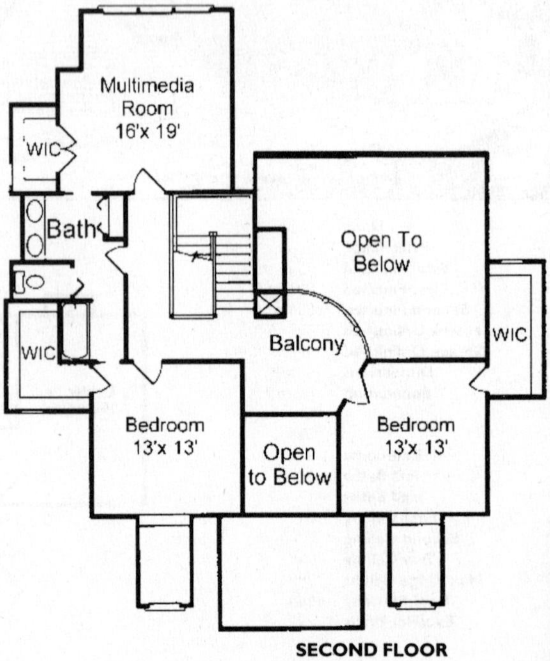
Multimedia
Room
16'x 19'
WIC
Bath
Open To
Below
WIC
Balcony
WIC
Bedroom
13'x 13'
Open
to Below
Bedroom
13'x 13'

SECOND FLOOR

Design 97448

See Order Pages and Index for Info

Units	Single
Price Code	B
Total Finished	1,660 sq. ft.
First Finished	1,265 sq. ft.
Second Finished	395 sq. ft.
Garage Unfinished	475 sq. ft.
Dimensions	46'x48'
Foundation	Basement Slab
Bedrooms	3
Full Baths	2
Half Baths	1
First Ceiling	8'
Max Ridge Height	25'
Exterior Walls	2x4

* Alternate foundation options available at an additional charge. Please call 1-800-235-5700 for more information.

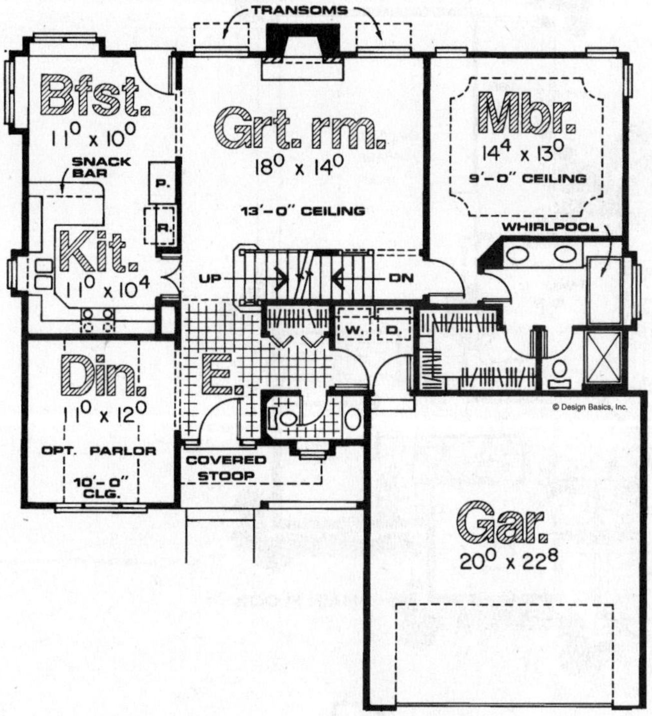
TRANSOMS
Bfst.
11^{0} x 10^{0}
Grt. rm.
18^{0} x 14^{0}
Mbr.
14^{4} x 13^{0}
9'-0" CEILING
SNACK BAR
P.
R.
13'-0" CEILING
WHIRLPOOL
Kit.
11^{0} x 10^{4}
UP
DN
W.
D.
Din.
11^{0} x 12^{0}
E.
OPT. PARLOR
10'-0" CLG.
COVERED STOOP
© Design Basics, Inc.
Gar.
20^{0} x 22^{8}

FIRST FLOOR

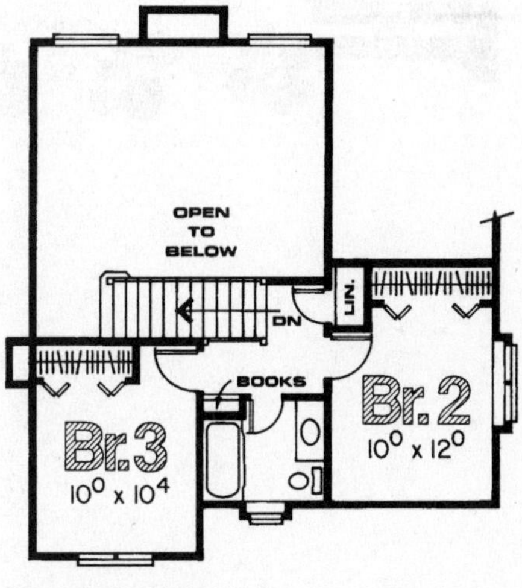
OPEN TO BELOW
LIN.
DN
BOOKS
Br. 2
10^{0} x 12^{0}
Br. 3
10^{0} x 10^{4}

SECOND FLOOR

Design 96325

See Order Pages and Index for Info

Units	Single
Price Code	J
Total Finished	3,578 sq. ft.
Main Finished	3,578 sq. ft.
Bonus Unfinished	522 sq. ft.
Garage Unfinished	864 sq. ft.
Porch Unfinished	264 sq. ft.
Dimensions	100'x72'8"
Foundation	Basement Crawlspace Slab
Bedrooms	4
Full Baths	3
Half Baths	1
Main Ceiling	10'
Max Ridge Height	31'
Roof Framing	Stick
Exterior Walls	2x4

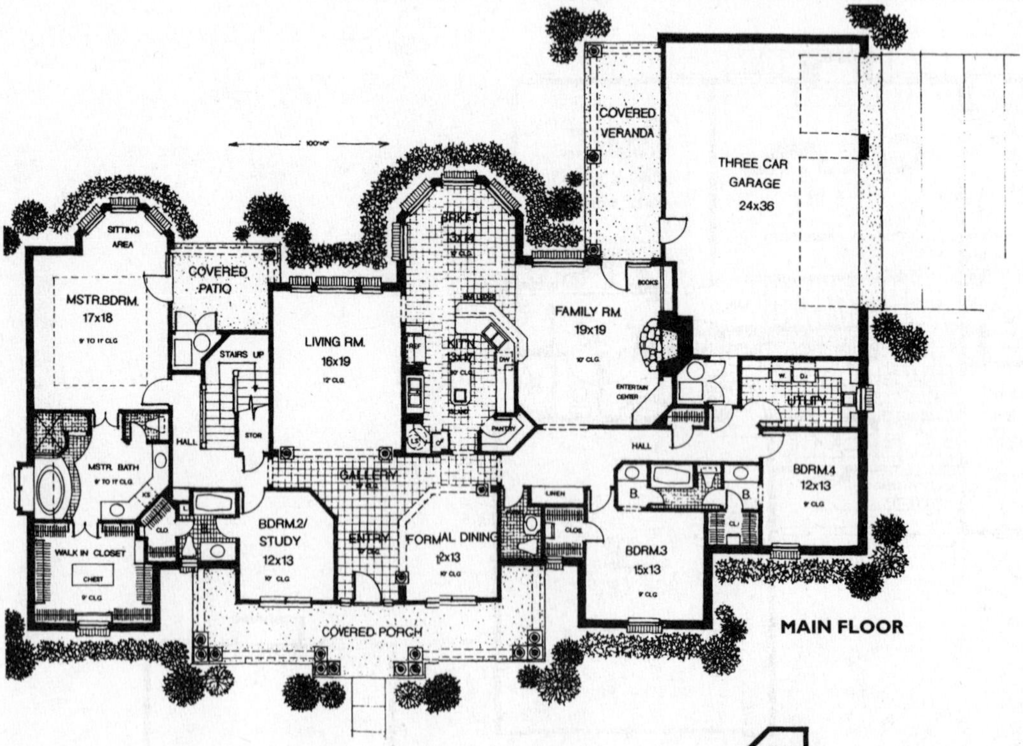
COVERED VERANDA
THREE CAR GARAGE 24x36
SITTING AREA
COVERED PATIO
MSTR. BDRM. 17x18
STAIRS UP
LIVING RM. 16x19
FAMILY RM. 19x19
MSTR. BATH
HALL
STOR
PANTRY
UTILITY
HALL
GALLERY
BDRM.4 12x13
WALK IN CLOSET
BDRM.2/ STUDY 12x13
ENTRY
FORMAL DINING 12x13
BDRM.3 15x13
COVERED PORCH

MAIN FLOOR

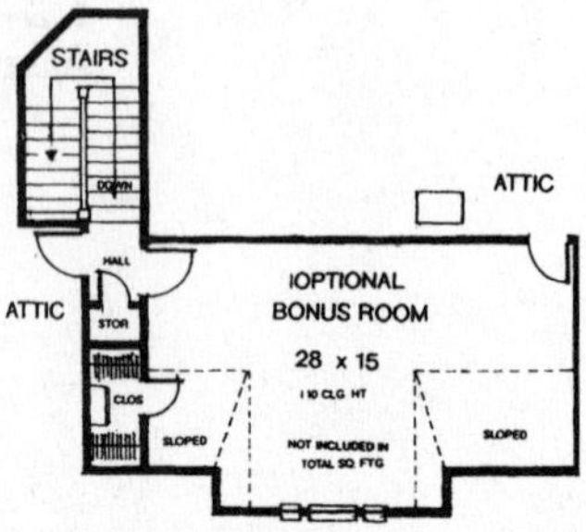
STAIRS
ATTIC
ATTIC
OPTIONAL BONUS ROOM
28 x 15
SLOPED
SLOPED

BONUS

Design 96326

See Order Pages and Index for Info

Units	Single
Price Code	J
Total Finished	3,510 sq. ft.
Main Finished	3,510 sq. ft.
Garage Unfinished	704 sq. ft.
Porch Unfinished	62 sq. ft.
Dimensions	91'x72'10"
Foundation	Slab
Bedrooms	4
Full Baths	3
Half Baths	1
Main Ceiling	10'
Max Ridge Height	33'
Roof Framing	Stick
Exterior Walls	2x4

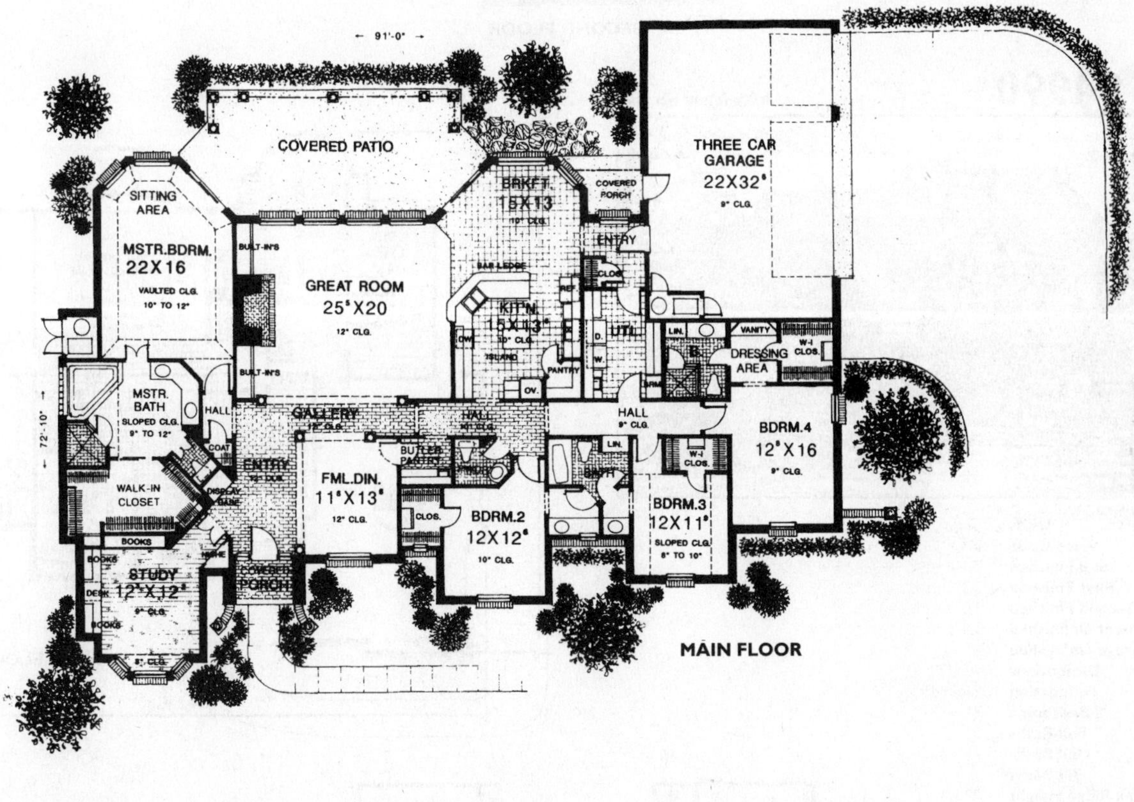

91'-0"
72'-10"
COVERED PATIO
SITTING AREA
MSTR.BDRM.
22X16
VAULTED CLG. 10" TO 12"
BUILT-IN'S
GREAT ROOM
25⁵X20
12" CLG.
BRKFT.
15X13
COVERED PORCH
ENTRY
THREE CAR GARAGE
22X32⁶
9" CLG.
KIT'N
UTL
DRESSING AREA
MSTR. BATH
SLOPED CLG. 9" TO 12"
HALL
COAT
GALLERY
ENTRY
WALK-IN CLOSET
FML.DIN.
11⁶X13⁶
12" CLG.
BUTLER PANTRY
PANTRY
BDRM.2
12X12⁶
10" CLG.
BDRM.3
12X11⁶
SLOPED CLG. 8" TO 10"
BDRM.4
12⁶X16
9" CLG.
STUDY
12⁸X12⁸
COVERED PORCH
BOOKS
DESK

MAIN FLOOR

Design 94994

See Order Pages and Index for Info

Units	Single
Price Code	G
Total Finished	2,957 sq. ft.
First Finished	2,063 sq. ft.
Second Finished	894 sq. ft.
Basement Unfinished	2,063 sq. ft.
Garage Unfinished	666 sq. ft.
Dimensions	72'8"x51'4"
Foundation	Basement
Bedrooms	4
Full Baths	2
Half Baths	1
3/4 Baths	2
First Ceiling	8'
Max Ridge Height	27'
Roof Framing	Stick
Exterior Walls	2x4

* Alternate foundation options available at an additional charge. Please call 1-800-235-5700 for more information.

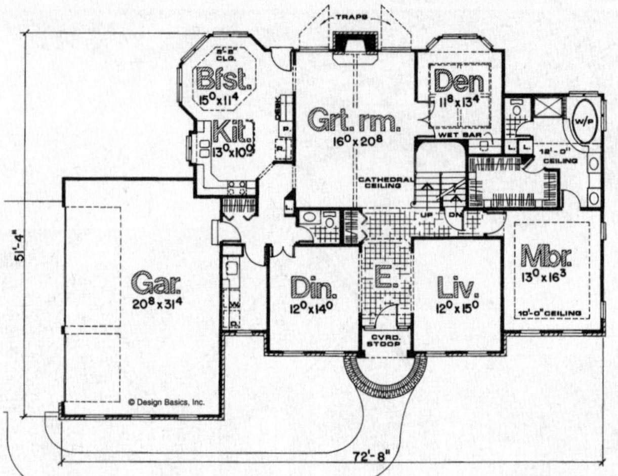
TRAPS
Bfst.
15⁰x11⁴
Kit.
13⁰x10⁹
Grt. rm.
16⁰x20⁸
CATHEDRAL CEILING
Den
11⁸x13⁴
WET BAR
Gar.
20⁸x31⁴
Din.
12⁰x14⁰
E.
Liv.
12⁰x15⁰
Mbr.
13⁰x16³
10'-0" CEILING
CVRD. STOOP
51'-4"
72'-8"
© Design Basics, Inc.

FIRST FLOOR

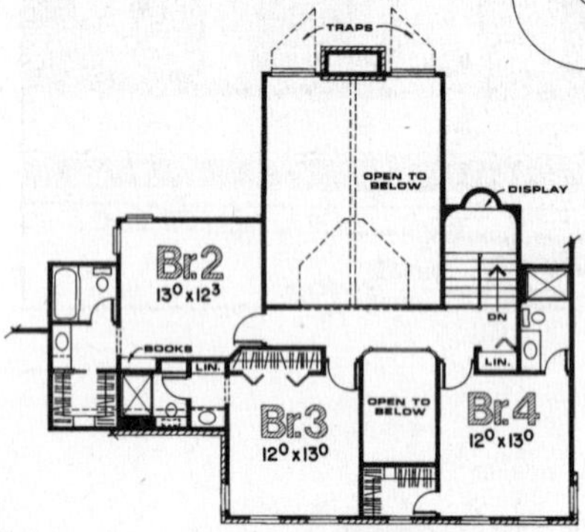
TRAPS
OPEN TO BELOW
DISPLAY
Br.2
13⁰x12³
BOOKS
LIN.
Br.3
12⁰x13⁰
OPEN TO BELOW
Br.4
12⁰x13⁰
LIN.
DN

SECOND FLOOR

Design 94990

See Order Pages and Index for Info

Units	Single
Price Code	I
Total Finished	3,448 sq. ft.
First Finished	2,375 sq. ft.
Second Finished	1,073 sq. ft.
Basement Unfinished	2,375 sq. ft.
Garage Unfinished	672 sq. ft.
Dimensions	70'x62'
Foundation	Basement
Bedrooms	4
Full Baths	2
Half Baths	1
3/4 Baths	1
Max Ridge Height	29'
Roof Framing	Stick
Exterior Walls	2x4

* Alternate foundation options available at an additional charge. Please call 1-800-235-5700 for more information.

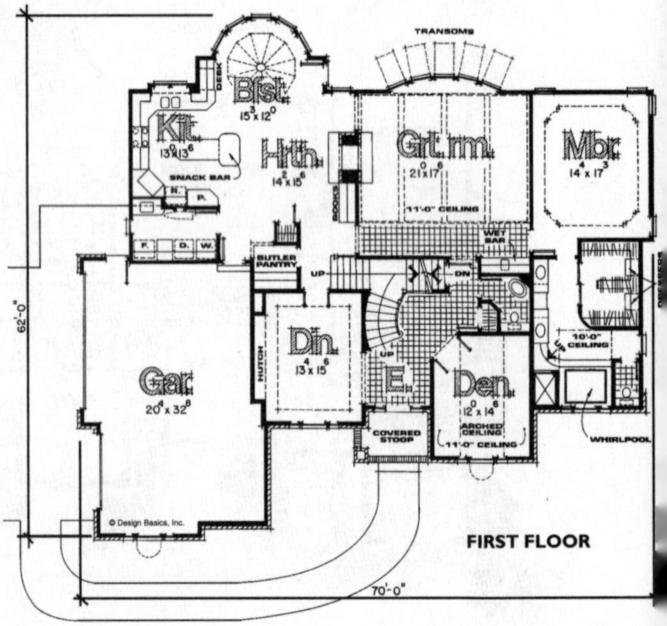
TRANSOMS
Bfst.
15³x12⁰
Kit.
13⁰x13⁶
SNACK BAR
Hrth.
14⁰x15⁶
Grt. rm.
21⁰x17⁶
11'-0" CEILING
Mbr.
14⁴x17³
WET BAR
BUTLER PANTRY
Din.
13⁴x15⁶
HUTCH
Gar.
20⁴x32⁸
E.
Den.
12⁰x14⁶
ARCHED CEILING
11'-0" CEILING
COVERED STOOP
10'-0" CEILING
WHIRLPOOL
62'-0"
70'-0"
© Design Basics, Inc.

FIRST FLOOR

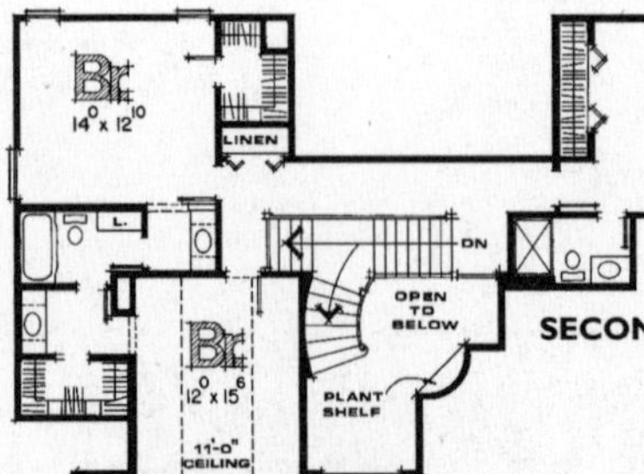
Br.
14⁰x12¹⁰
LINEN
Br.
14⁴x13⁴
DN
OPEN TO BELOW
Br.
12⁰x15⁶
11'-0" CEILING
PLANT SHELF
TRANS.

SECOND FLOOR

Design 96813

See Order Pages and Index for Info

Units	Single
Price Code	E
Total Finished	2,437 sq. ft.
Main Finished	2,437 sq. ft.
Bonus Unfinished	90 sq. ft.
Garage Unfinished	646 sq. ft.
Porch Unfinished	213 sq. ft.
Dimensions	64'9"x59'
Foundation	Basement Crawlspace Slab
Bedrooms	3
Full Baths	2
Main Ceiling	9'
Max Ridge Height	26'
Roof Framing	Stick
Exterior Walls	2x4

MAIN FLOOR

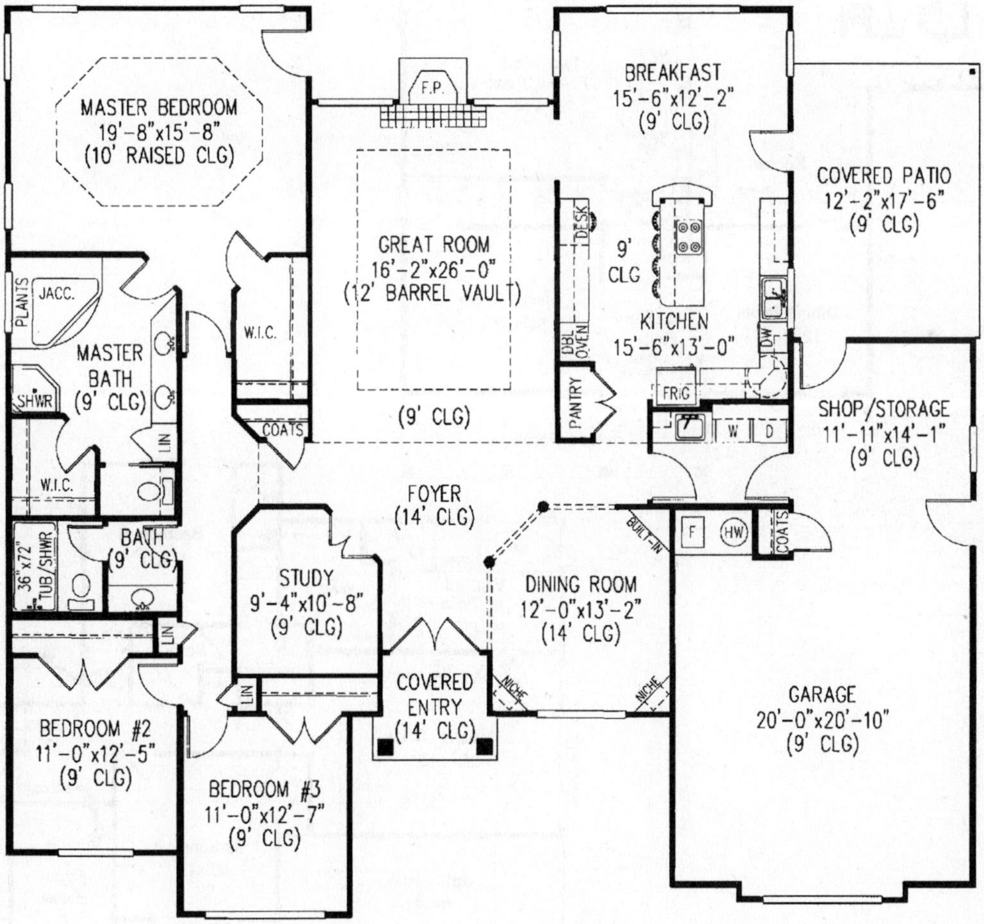
MASTER BEDROOM
19'-8"x15'-8"
(10' RAISED CLG)
F.P.
BREAKFAST
15'-6"x12'-2"
(9' CLG)
COVERED PATIO
12'-2"x17'-6"
(9' CLG)
GREAT ROOM
16'-2"x26'-0"
(12' BARREL VAULT)
DESK
9' CLG
KITCHEN
15'-6"x13'-0"
JACC.
PLANTS
MASTER BATH
(9' CLG)
W.I.C.
SHWR
DBL OVEN
PANTRY
FRIG
DW
W
D
SHOP/STORAGE
11'-11"x14'-1"
(9' CLG)
COATS
(9' CLG)
LIN
W.I.C.
FOYER
(14' CLG)
BUILT-IN
F
HW
COATS
36"x72" TUB/SHWR
BATH
(9' CLG)
STUDY
9'-4"x10'-8"
(9' CLG)
DINING ROOM
12'-0"x13'-2"
(14' CLG)
LIN
COVERED ENTRY
(14' CLG)
NICHE
NICHE
GARAGE
20'-0"x20'-10"
(9' CLG)
LIN
BEDROOM #2
11'-0"x12'-5"
(9' CLG)
BEDROOM #3
11'-0"x12'-7"
(9' CLG)

Design 98409

See Order Pages and Index for Info

Units	Single
Price Code	E
Total Finished	2,368 sq. ft.
First Finished	1,200 sq. ft.
Second Finished	1,168 sq. ft.
Basement Unfinished	1,200 sq. ft.
Garage Unfinished	527 sq. ft.
Dimensions	56'x39'
Foundation	Basement Crawlspace Slab
Bedrooms	4
Full Baths	2
Half Baths	1
First Ceiling	9'
Second Ceiling	8'
Max Ridge Height	31'6"
Roof Framing	Stick
Exterior Walls	2x4

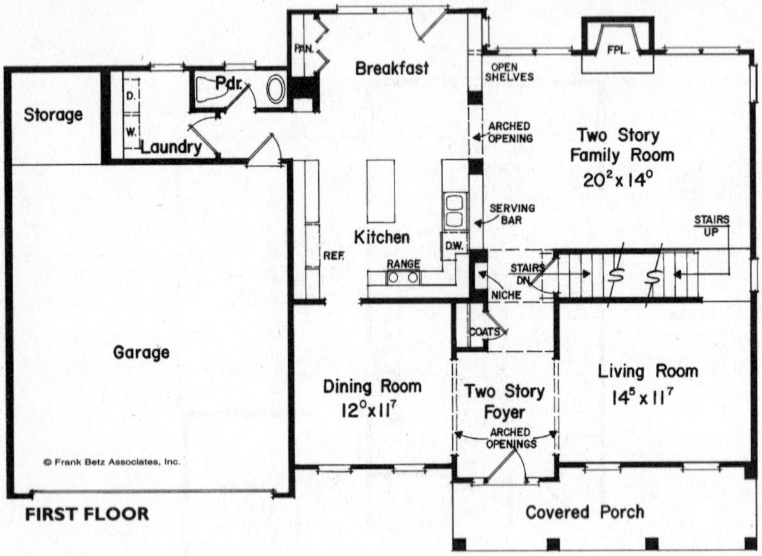
Breakfast
P.N.
FPL.
OPEN SHELVES
Pdr.
Storage
D.
W.
Laundry
ARCHED OPENING
Two Story Family Room 20^2x14^0
SERVING BAR
Kitchen
STAIRS UP
REF.
RANGE
DW.
STAIRS DN.
NICHE
COATS
Garage
Dining Room 12^0x11^7
Two Story Foyer
Living Room 14^5x11^7
ARCHED OPENINGS
© Frank Betz Associates, Inc.
Covered Porch

FIRST FLOOR

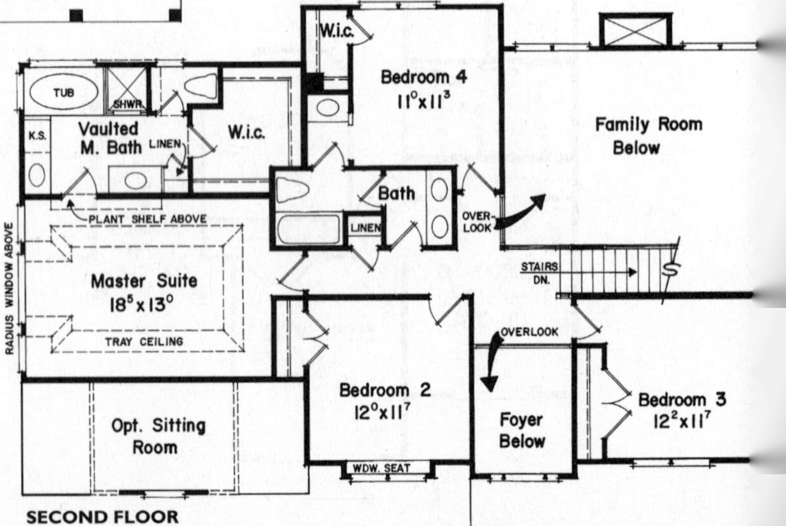
W.i.c.
Bedroom 4 11^0x11^3
TUB
SHWR.
K.S.
Vaulted M. Bath
LINEN
W.i.c.
Family Room Below
Bath
LINEN
OVER-LOOK
PLANT SHELF ABOVE
RADIUS WINDOW ABOVE
Master Suite 18^5x13^0
TRAY CEILING
STAIRS DN.
OVERLOOK
Bedroom 2 12^0x11^7
Foyer Below
Bedroom 3 12^2x11^7
Opt. Sitting Room
WDW. SEAT

SECOND FLOOR

Design 64125

See Order Pages and Index for Info

Units	Single
Price Code	H
Total Finished	2,487 sq. ft.
Main Finished	2,487 sq. ft.
Basement Finished	1,742 sq. ft.
Dimensions	70'x72'
Foundation	Basement Slab
Bedrooms	3
Full Baths	2
Max Ridge Height	27'4"
Exterior Walls	2x6

* Alternate foundation options available at an additional charge. Please call 1-800-235-5700 for more information.

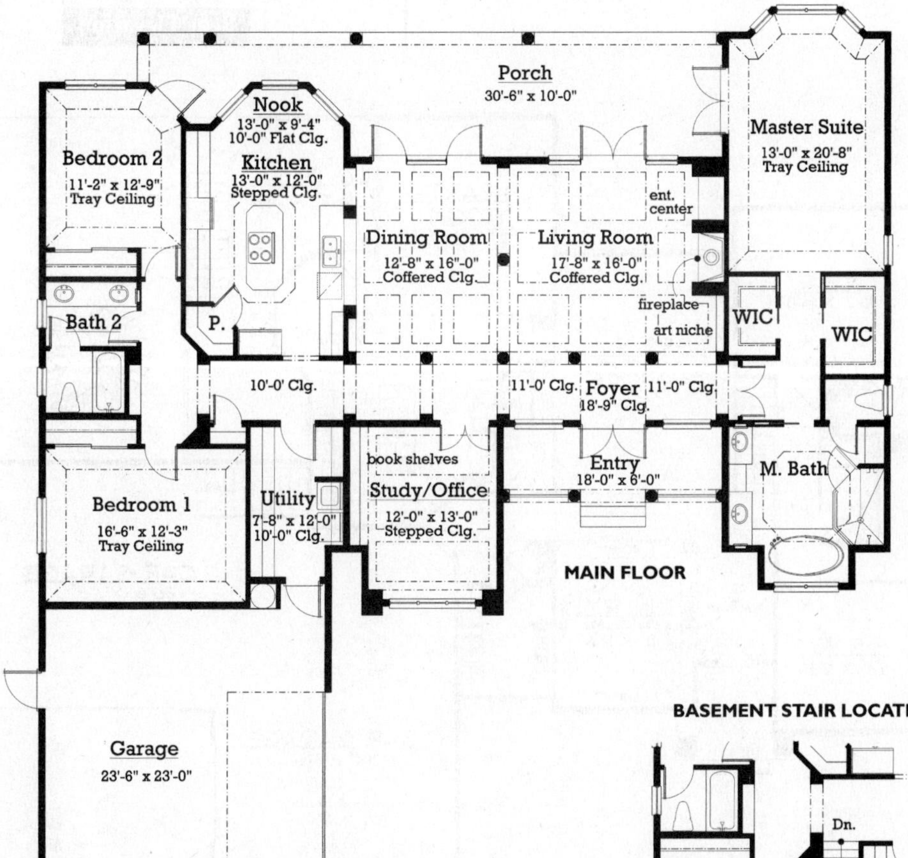
Porch
30'-6" x 10'-0"
Nook
13'-0" x 9'-4"
10'-0" Flat Clg.
Kitchen
13'-0" x 12'-0"
Stepped Clg.
Bedroom 2
11'-2" x 12'-9"
Tray Ceiling
Master Suite
13'-0" x 20'-8"
Tray Ceiling
ent. center
Dining Room
12'-8" x 16'-0"
Coffered Clg.
Living Room
17'-8" x 16'-0"
Coffered Clg.
fireplace
art niche
WIC
WIC
Bath 2
P.
10'-0' Clg.
11'-0' Clg.
Foyer
18'-9" Clg.
11'-0" Clg.
book shelves
Study/Office
12'-0" x 13'-0"
Stepped Clg.
Entry
18'-0" x 6'-0"
M. Bath
Bedroom 1
16'-6" x 12'-3"
Tray Ceiling
Utility
7'-8" x 12'-0"
10'-0" Clg.
MAIN FLOOR
Garage
23'-6" x 23'-0"
© Sater Design Collection

BASEMENT STAIR LOCATION

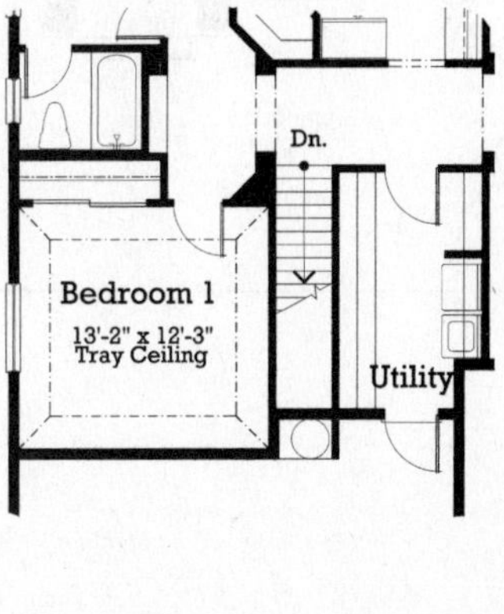
Dn.
Bedroom 1
13'-2" x 12'-3"
Tray Ceiling
Utility

Design 97312

See Order Pages and Index for Info

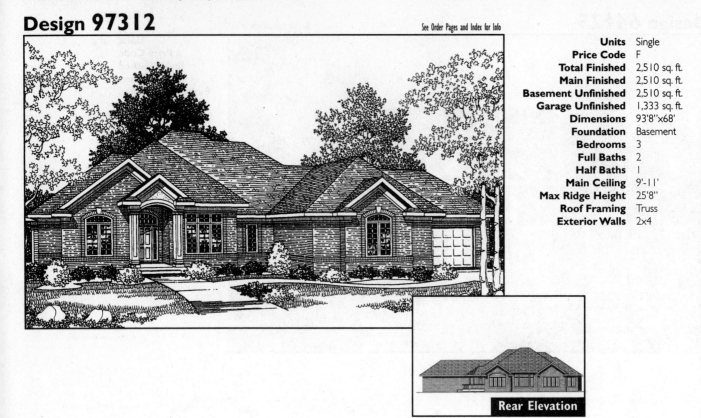

Units	Single
Price Code	F
Total Finished	2,510 sq. ft.
Main Finished	2,510 sq. ft.
Basement Unfinished	2,510 sq. ft.
Garage Unfinished	1,333 sq. ft.
Dimensions	93'8"x68'
Foundation	Basement
Bedrooms	3
Full Baths	2
Half Baths	1
Main Ceiling	9'-11'
Max Ridge Height	25'8"
Roof Framing	Truss
Exterior Walls	2x4

Rear Elevation

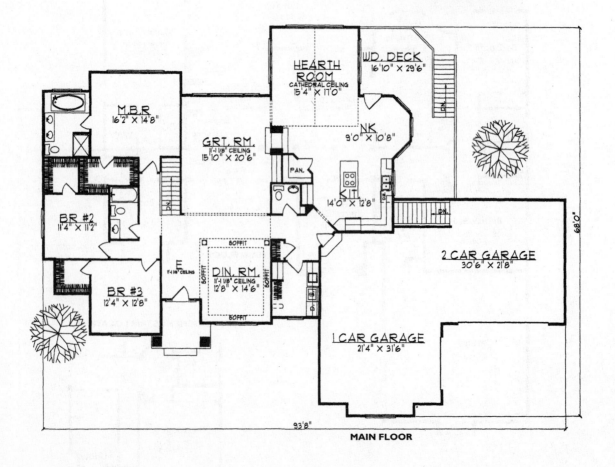

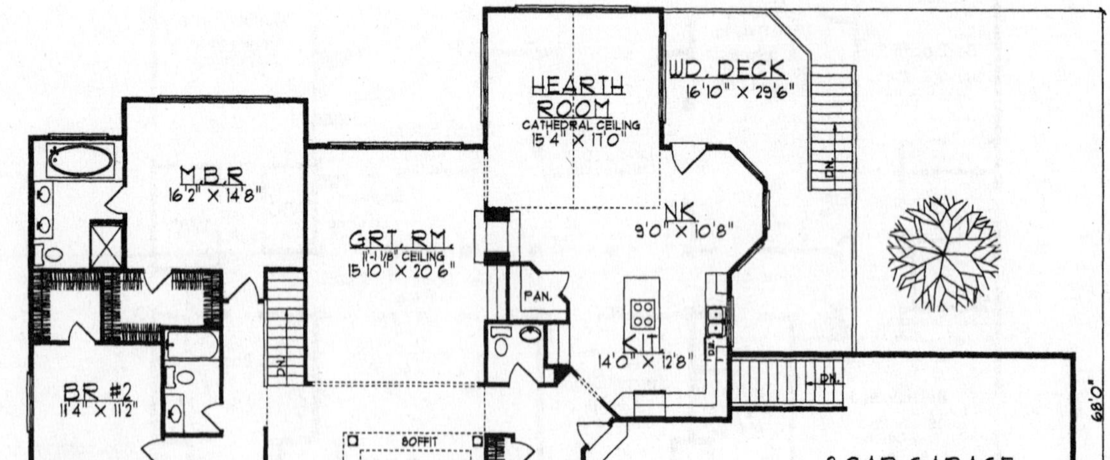
HEARTH ROOM
CATHEDRAL CEILING
15'4" X 17'0"
WD. DECK
16'10" X 29'6"
M.B.R.
16'2" X 14'8"
GRT. RM.
11'-1 1/8" CEILING
15'10" X 20'6"
NK
9'0" X 10'8"
PAN.
KIT
14'0" X 12'8"
BR #2
11'4" X 11'2"
SOFFIT
E
11'-1 1/8" CEILING
DIN. RM.
11'-1 1/8" CEILING
12'8" X 14'6"
BR #3
12'4" X 12'8"
2 CAR GARAGE
30'6" X 21'8"
1 CAR GARAGE
21'4" X 31'6"
68'0"
93'8"

MAIN FLOOR

Design 96511

See Order Pages and Index for Info

Units	Single
Price Code	A
Total Finished	1,247 sq. ft.
Main Finished	1,247 sq. ft.
Garage Unfinished	512 sq. ft.
Dimensions	43'x60'
Foundation	Crawlspace Slab
Bedrooms	3
Full Baths	2
Main Ceiling	8'
Max Ridge Height	19'
Roof Framing	Stick
Exterior Walls	2x4

MAIN FLOOR

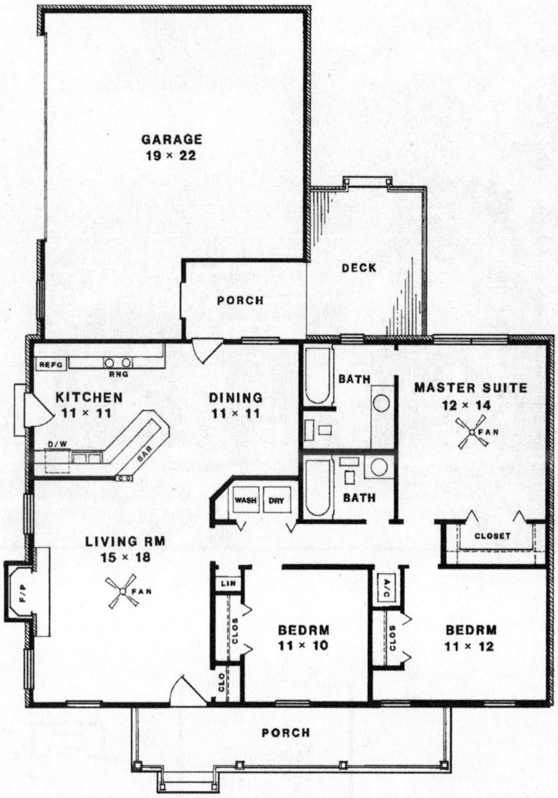
GARAGE
19 × 22
DECK
PORCH
REFG
RNG
KITCHEN
11 × 11
D/W
BAR
DINING
11 × 11
BATH
MASTER SUITE
12 × 14
FAN
WASH
DRY
BATH
CLOSET
LIVING RM
15 × 18
FAN
F/P
LIN
CLOS
A/C
CLOS
BEDRM
11 × 10
BEDRM
11 × 12
CLO
PORCH

Design 98497

See Order Pages and Index for Info

Units	Single
Price Code	A
Total Finished	1,169 sq. ft.
Main Finished	1,169 sq. ft.
Basement Unfinished	1,194 sq. ft.
Garage Unfinished	400 sq. ft.
Dimensions	40'x49'6"
Foundation	Basement Crawlspace Slab
Bedrooms	3
Full Baths	2
Main Ceiling	9'
Max Ridge Height	21'
Roof Framing	Stick
Exterior Walls	2x4

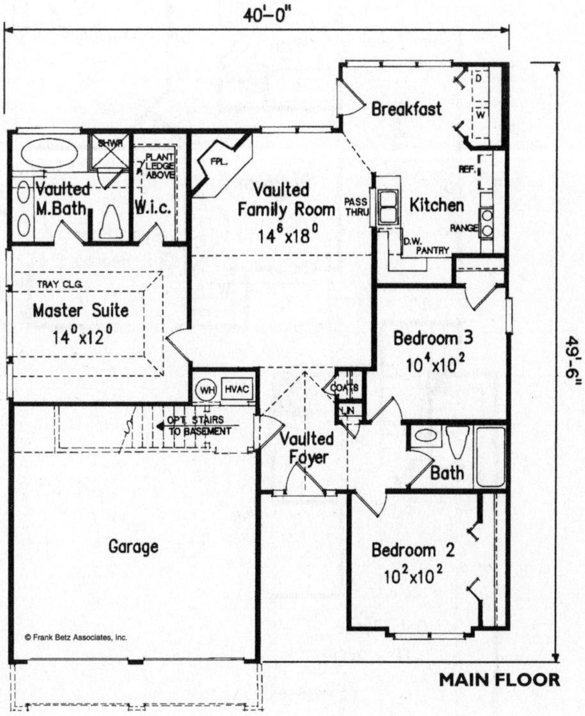
40'-0"
49'-6"
Breakfast
D
W
SHWR
PLANT LEDGE ABOVE
FPL.
Vaulted
Family Room
14^6x18^0
PASS THRU
Kitchen
REF.
RANGE
D.W.
PANTRY
Vaulted
M.Bath
W.i.c.
TRAY CLG.
Master Suite
14^0x12^0
Bedroom 3
10^4x10^2
WH
HVAC
COATS
LIN
OPT. STAIRS TO BASEMENT
Vaulted
Foyer
Bath
Garage
Bedroom 2
10^2x10^2
© Frank Betz Associates, Inc.

MAIN FLOOR

Design 98466

See Order Pages and Index for Info

Units	Single
Price Code	D
Total Finished	2,193 sq. ft.
Main Finished	2,193 sq. ft.
Bonus Unfinished	400 sq. ft.
Basement Unfinished	2,193 sq. ft.
Garage Unfinished	522 sq. ft.
Dimensions	64'6"x59'
Foundation	Basement Crawlspace Slab
Bedrooms	4
Full Baths	2
Main Ceiling	9'
Bonus Ceiling	8'
Max Ridge Height	27'
Roof Framing	Stick
Exterior Walls	2x4

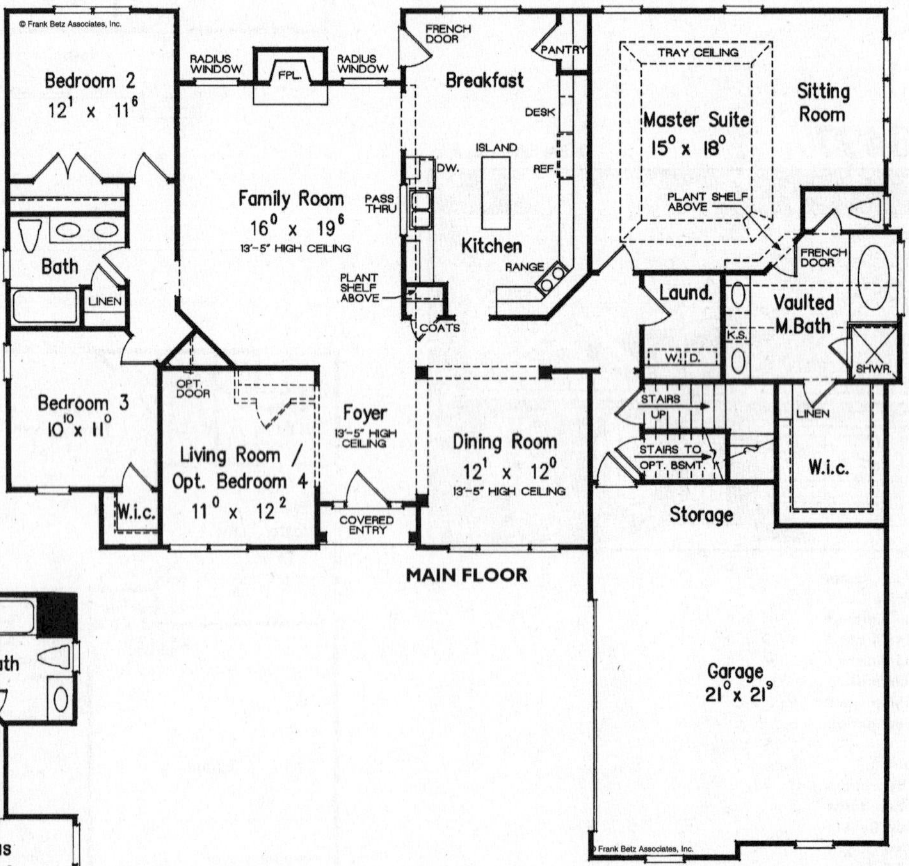
© Frank Betz Associates, Inc.
Bedroom 2
12¹ x 11⁶
RADIUS WINDOW
FPL.
RADIUS WINDOW
FRENCH DOOR
PANTRY
Breakfast
DESK
ISLAND
REF.
DW.
PASS THRU
Family Room
16⁰ x 19⁶
13'-5" HIGH CEILING
Kitchen
RANGE
PLANT SHELF ABOVE
COATS
TRAY CEILING
Master Suite
15⁰ x 18⁰
Sitting Room
PLANT SHELF ABOVE
FRENCH DOOR
Laund.
Vaulted M.Bath
K.S.
W. D.
SHWR.
Bath
LINEN
Bedroom 3
10¹⁰ x 11⁰
OPT. DOOR
Living Room / Opt. Bedroom 4
11⁰ x 12²
Foyer
13'-5" HIGH CEILING
Dining Room
12¹ x 12⁰
13'-5" HIGH CEILING
STAIRS UP
STAIRS TO OPT. BSMT.
LINEN
W.i.c.
W.i.c.
COVERED ENTRY
Storage
Garage
21⁰ x 21⁹
© Frank Betz Associates, Inc.

MAIN FLOOR

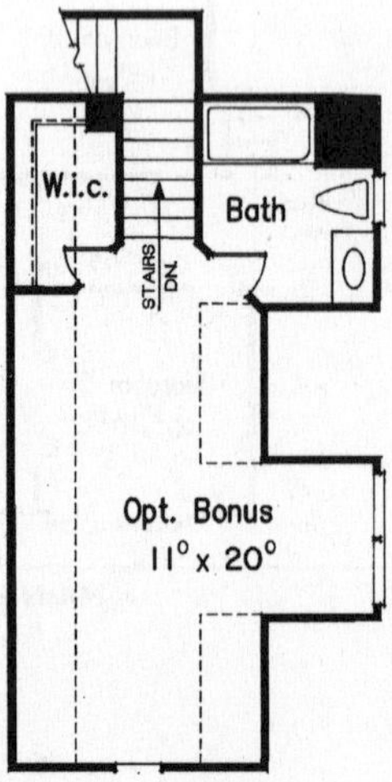
W.i.c.
Bath
STAIRS DN.
Opt. Bonus
11⁰ x 20⁰

BONUS

Design 97404

See Order Pages and Index for Info

Units	Single
Price Code	E
Total Finished	2,311 sq. ft.
Main Finished	2,311 sq. ft.
Garage Unfinished	657 sq. ft.
Dimensions	64'x57'2"
Foundation	Basement
Bedrooms	3
Full Baths	2
Half Baths	1
Main Ceiling	8'
Max Ridge Height	21'4"
Roof Framing	Stick
Exterior Walls	2x4

* Alternate foundation options available at an additional charge. Please call 1-800-235-5700 for more information.

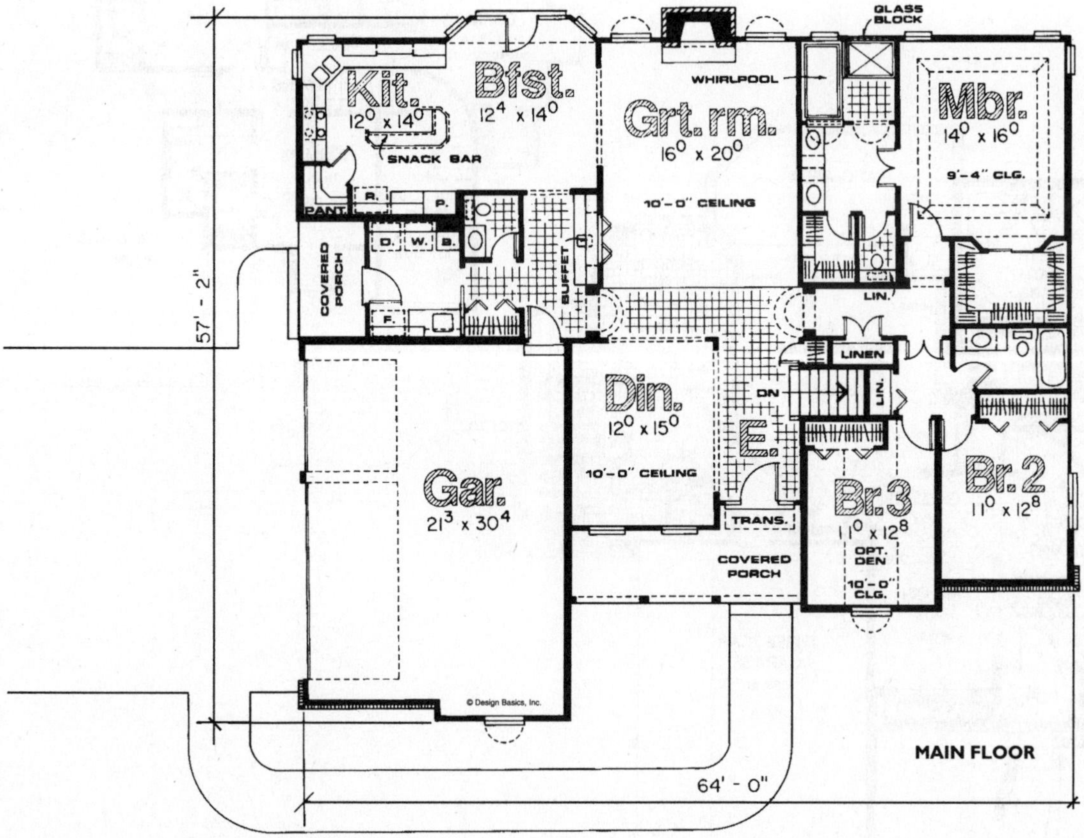
GLASS BLOCK
WHIRLPOOL
Kit.
12^{0} x 14^{0}
SNACK BAR
Bfst.
12^{4} x 14^{0}
Grt. rm.
16^{0} x 20^{0}
10'-0" CEILING
Mbr.
14^{0} x 16^{0}
9'-4" CLG.
PANT.
R.
P.
D. W. B.
COVERED PORCH
F.
BUFFET
LIN.
LINEN
DN
LIN.
Din.
12^{0} x 15^{0}
10'-0" CEILING
E.
Gar.
21^{3} x 30^{4}
Br. 3
11^{0} x 12^{8}
OPT. DEN
10'-0" CLG.
Br. 2
11^{0} x 12^{8}
TRANS.
COVERED PORCH
57' - 2"
64' - 0"
© Design Basics, Inc.

MAIN FLOOR

Design 98588

See Order Pages and Index for Info

Units	Single
Price Code	H
Total Finished	3,219 sq. ft.
First Finished	2,337 sq. ft.
Second Finished	882 sq. ft.
Garage Unfinished	640 sq. ft.
Bonus Unfinished	357 sq. ft.
Porch Unfinished	120 sq. ft.
Dimensions	70'x63'2"
Foundation	Basement Slab
Bedrooms	4
Full Baths	2
3/4 Baths	2
Half Baths	1
Max Ridge Height	32'6"
Roof Framing	Stick
Exterior Walls	2x4

SECOND FLOOR

B.
B.
BDRM.#2
12X12
8" CLG.
CLO.
BDRM.#3
12X14
SLOPED CLG. TO 8"
HALL
LIN.
STAIRS
DN.
CL.
BDRM.#4
12X12
8" CLG.
B.
CLO.
OPEN ABOVE
ENTRY
SLOPED CLG.
TO 2 STORY
FUTURE BONUS
ROOM

FIRST FLOOR

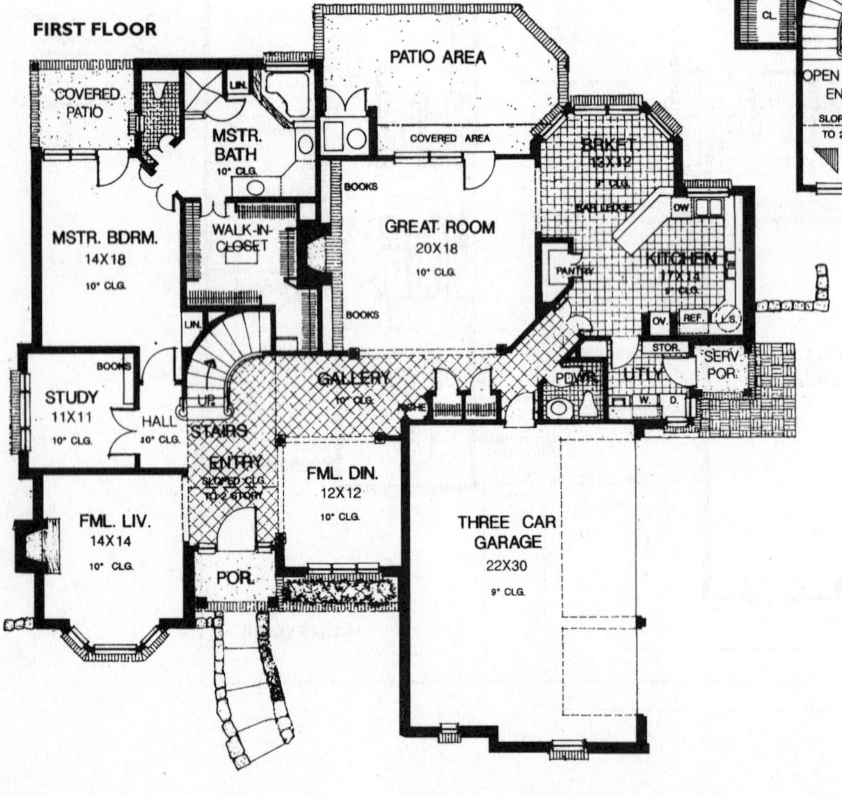
PATIO AREA
COVERED
PATIO
LIN.
MSTR.
BATH
10" CLG.
COVERED AREA
BRKFT
12X12
9" CLG.
BAR LEDGE
DW
BOOKS
GREAT ROOM
20X18
10" CLG.
BOOKS
MSTR. BDRM.
14X18
10" CLG.
WALK-IN-
CLOSET
PANTRY
KITCHEN
17X14
9" CLG.
OV.
REF.
L.S.
LIN.
STOR.
SERV.
POR.
BOOKS
STUDY
11X11
10" CLG.
HALL
10" CLG.
UP
STAIRS
GALLERY
10" CLG.
NICHE
PDR.
UTLY.
W.
D.
ENTRY
SLOPED CLG.
TO 2 STORY
FML. DIN.
12X12
10" CLG.
FML. LIV.
14X14
10" CLG.
THREE CAR
GARAGE
22X30
9" CLG.
POR.

Design 98408

See Order Pages and Index for Info

Units	Single
Price Code	C
Total Finished	1,856 sq. ft.
Main Finished	1,856 sq. ft.
Basement Unfinished	1,856 sq. ft.
Garage Unfinished	429 sq. ft.
Dimensions	59'x54'6"
Foundation	Basement Crawlspace Slab
Bedrooms	3
Full Baths	2
Main Ceiling	9'
Max Ridge Height	25'6"
Roof Framing	Stick
Exterior Walls	2x4

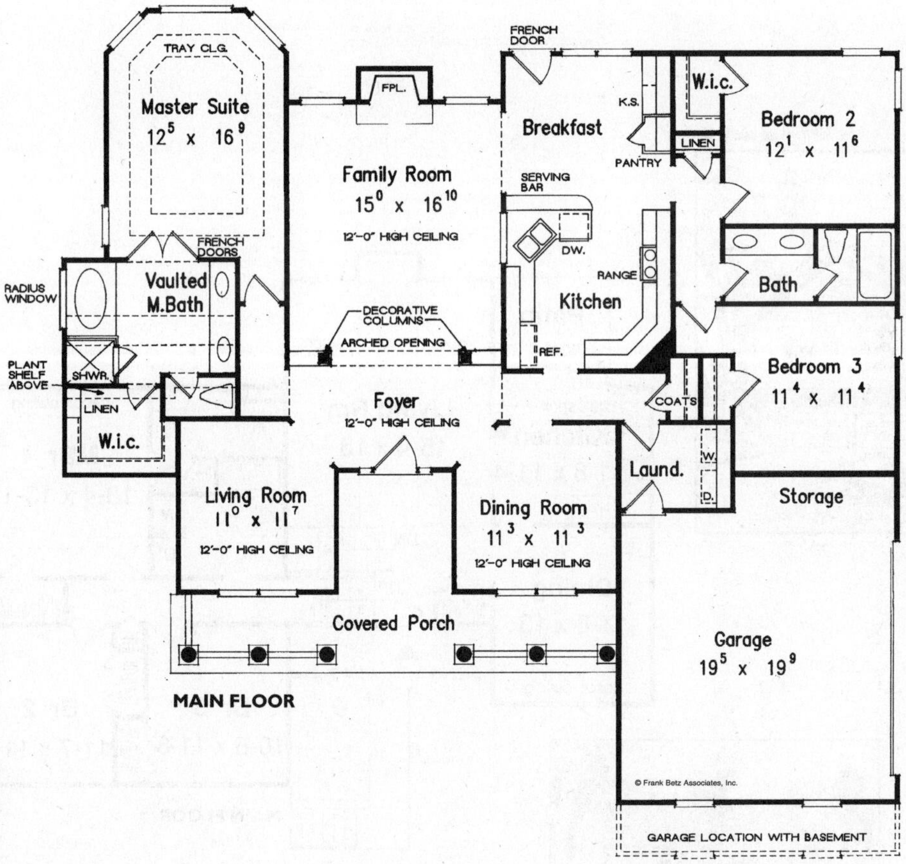

TRAY CLG.
Master Suite
12⁵ x 16⁹
FPL.
FRENCH DOOR
Family Room
15⁰ x 16¹⁰
12'-0" HIGH CEILING
Breakfast
K.S.
PANTRY
W.i.c.
LINEN
Bedroom 2
12¹ x 11⁶
SERVING BAR
DW.
RANGE
Kitchen
REF.
FRENCH DOORS
RADIUS WINDOW
Vaulted M.Bath
PLANT SHELF ABOVE
SHWR.
LINEN
W.i.c.
DECORATIVE COLUMNS
ARCHED OPENING
Foyer
12'-0" HIGH CEILING
Bath
COATS
Bedroom 3
11⁴ x 11⁴
W.
D.
Laund.
Storage
Living Room
11⁰ x 11⁷
12'-0" HIGH CEILING
Dining Room
11³ x 11³
12'-0" HIGH CEILING
Covered Porch
Garage
19⁵ x 19⁹
© Frank Betz Associates, Inc.
GARAGE LOCATION WITH BASEMENT

MAIN FLOOR

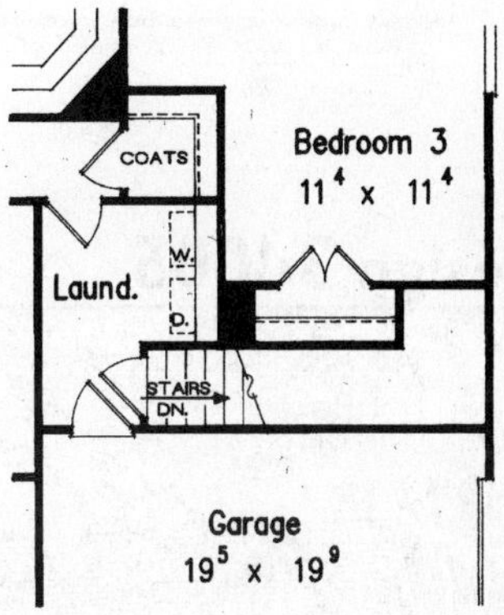

COATS
Bedroom 3
11⁴ x 11⁴
Laund.
W.
D.
STAIRS DN.
Garage
19⁵ x 19⁹

OPTIONAL BASEMENT STAIR LOCATION

Design 94985

See Order Pages and Index for Info

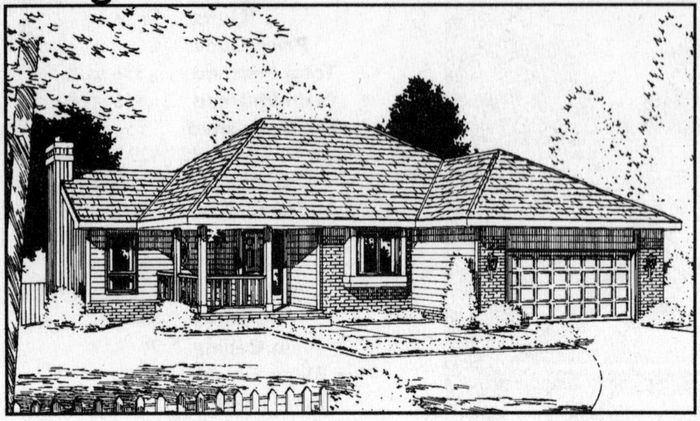

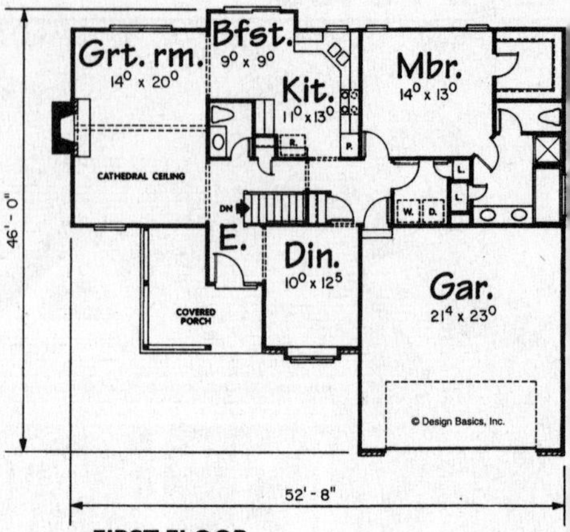
Grt. rm.
14^0 x 20^0
Bfst.
9^0 x 9^0
Kit.
11^0 x 13^0
Mbr.
14^0 x 13^0
CATHEDRAL CEILING
DN
E.
Din.
10^0 x 12^5
Gar.
21^4 x 23^0
COVERED PORCH
46' - 0"
52' - 8"
© Design Basics, Inc.

FIRST FLOOR

Units	Single
Price Code	A
Total Finished	1,279 sq. ft.
First Finished	1,279 sq. ft.
Bonus Unfinished	984 sq. ft.
Garage Unfinished	509 sq. ft.
Dimensions	52'8"x46'
Foundation	Basement
Bedrooms	3
Full Baths	2
Half Baths	1
Max Ridge Height	17'3"
Roof Framing	Stick
Exterior Walls	2x4

* Alternate foundation options available at an additional charge. Please call 1-800-235-5700 for more information.

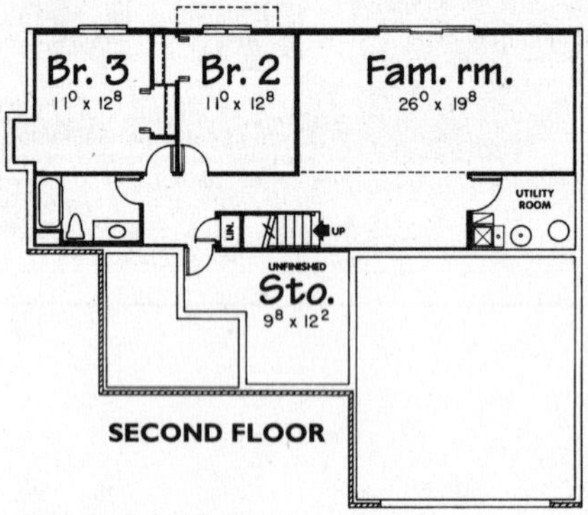
Br. 3
11^0 x 12^8
Br. 2
11^0 x 12^8
Fam. rm.
26^0 x 19^8
UTILITY ROOM
UP
UNFINISHED
Sto.
9^8 x 12^2

SECOND FLOOR

Design 34005

See Order Pages and Index for Info

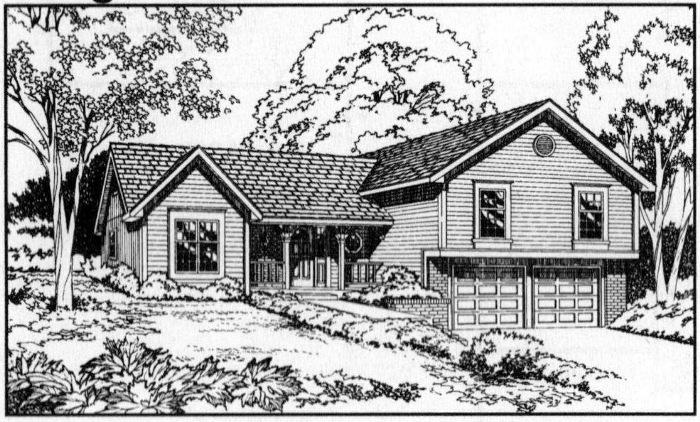

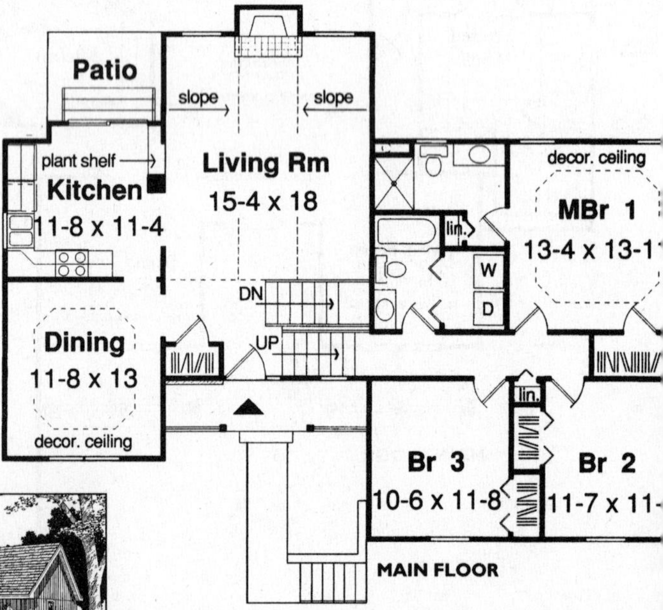
Patio
slope
slope
plant shelf
Kitchen
11-8 x 11-4
Living Rm
15-4 x 18
decor. ceiling
MBr 1
13-4 x 13-1
lin.
W
D
DN
UP
Dining
11-8 x 13
decor. ceiling
lin.
Br 3
10-6 x 11-8
Br 2
11-7 x 11-

MAIN FLOOR

Units	Single
Price Code	A
Total Finished	1,441 sq. ft.
Main Finished	1,441 sq. ft.
Basement Unfinished	769 sq. ft.
Garage Unfinished	672 sq. ft.
Dimensions	52'x38'
Foundation	Basement Crawlspace
Bedrooms	3
Full Baths	1
3/4 Baths	1
Max Ridge Height	26'
Roof Framing	Stick
Exterior Walls	2x4,2x6

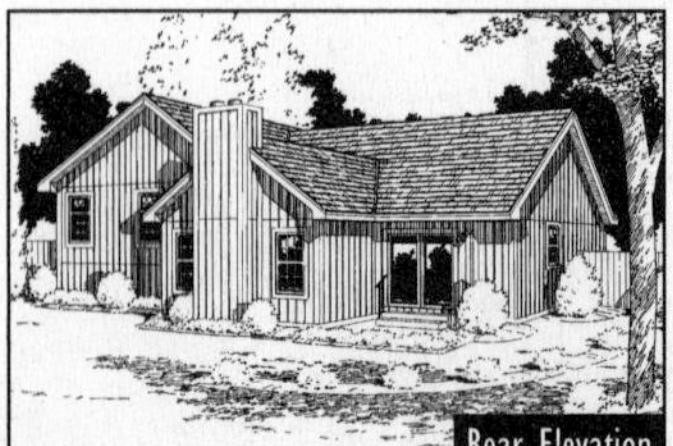

Rear Elevation

Design 98590

See Order Pages and Index for Info

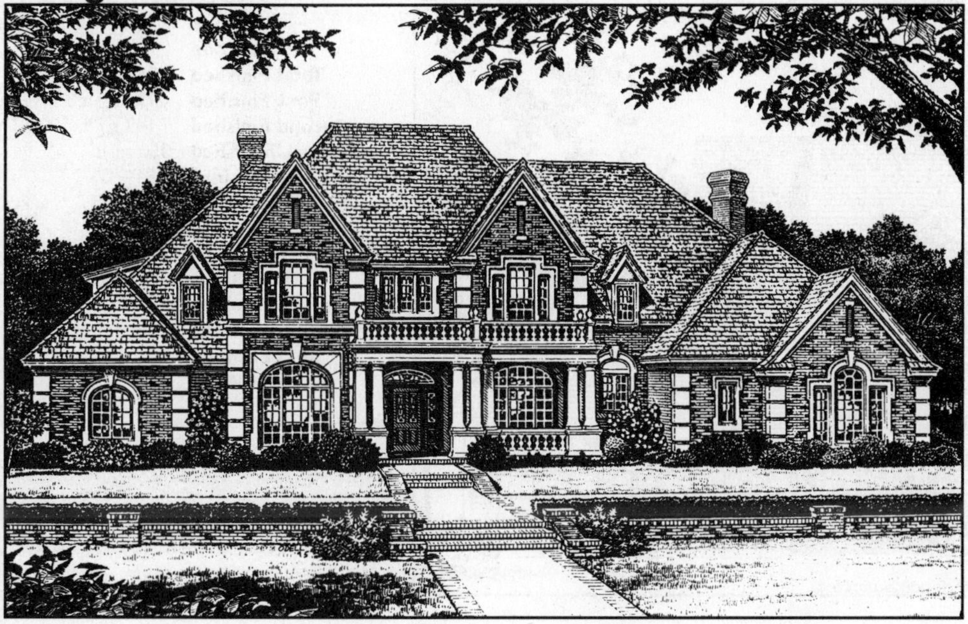

Units	Single
Price Code	L
Total Finished	4,166 sq. ft.
First Finished	3,168 sq. ft.
Second Finished	998 sq. ft.
Bonus Unfinished	320 sq. ft.
Garage Unfinished	810 sq. ft.
Porch Unfinished	180 sq. ft.
Dimensions	90'x63'5"
Foundation	Basement Crawlspace Slab
Bedrooms	4
Full Baths	3
Half Baths	1
First Ceiling	10'
Second Ceiling	9'
Max Ridge Height	36'
Roof Framing	Stick
Exterior Walls	2x4

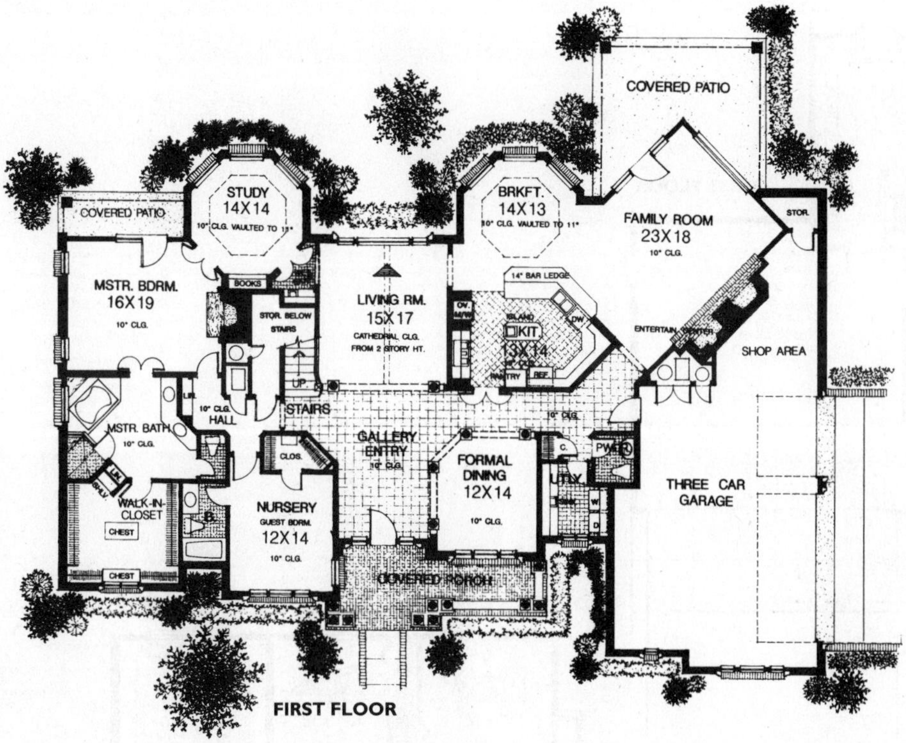
COVERED PATIO
STUDY
14X14
10" CLG. VAULTED TO 13"
BRKFT.
14X13
10" CLG. VAULTED TO 11"
FAMILY ROOM
23X18
10" CLG.
COVERED PATIO
STOR.
MSTR. BDRM.
16X19
10" CLG.
BOOKS
LIVING RM.
15X17
CATHEDRAL CLG. FROM 2 STORY HT.
14" BAR LEDGE
ISLAND
KIT.
13X14
PANTRY
REF.
ENTERTAIN. CENTER
SHOP AREA
STOR. BELOW STAIRS
UP
STAIRS
10" CLG. HALL
MSTR. BATH
10" CLG.
GALLERY ENTRY
10" CLG.
FORMAL DINING
12X14
10" CLG.
PWDR.
UTLY.
THREE CAR GARAGE
WALK-IN-CLOSET
CHEST
CLOS.
NURSERY
GUEST BDRM.
12X14
10" CLG.
CHEST
COVERED PORCH

FIRST FLOOR

SECOND FLOOR

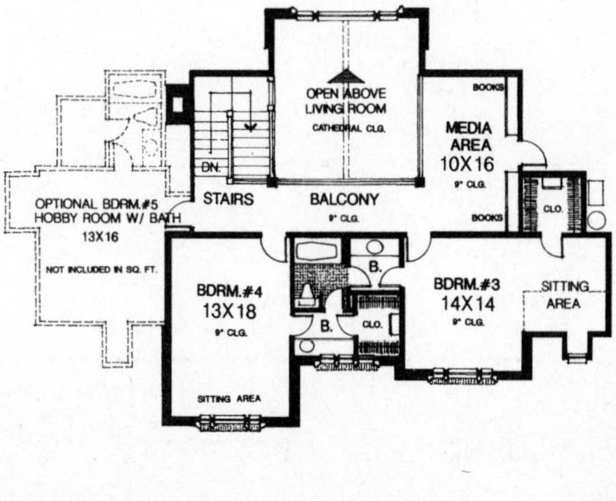
OPEN ABOVE LIVING ROOM
CATHEDRAL CLG.
BOOKS
MEDIA AREA
10X16
9" CLG.
DN.
STAIRS
BALCONY
9" CLG.
BOOKS
CLO.
OPTIONAL BDRM.#5 HOBBY ROOM W/ BATH
13X16
NOT INCLUDED IN SQ. FT.
BDRM.#4
13X18
9" CLG.
B.
B.
CLO.
BDRM.#3
14X14
9" CLG.
SITTING AREA
SITTING AREA

Design 97428

See Order Pages and Index for Info

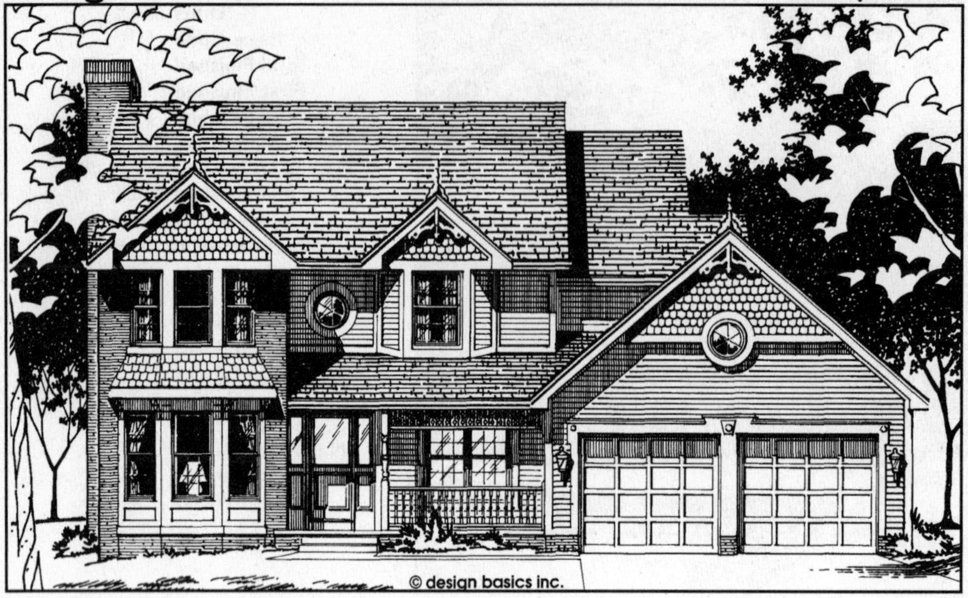
© design basics inc.

Units	Single
Price Code	E
Total Finished	2,283 sq. ft.
First Finished	1,134 sq. ft.
Second Finished	1,149 sq. ft.
Garage Unfinished	560 sq. ft.
Dimensions	53'4"x42'
Foundation	Basement
Bedrooms	4
Full Baths	2
Half Baths	1
First Ceiling	8'
Max Ridge Height	27'9"
Roof Framing	Stick
Exterior Walls	2x4

* Alternate foundation options available at an additional charge. Please call 1-800-235-5700 for more information.

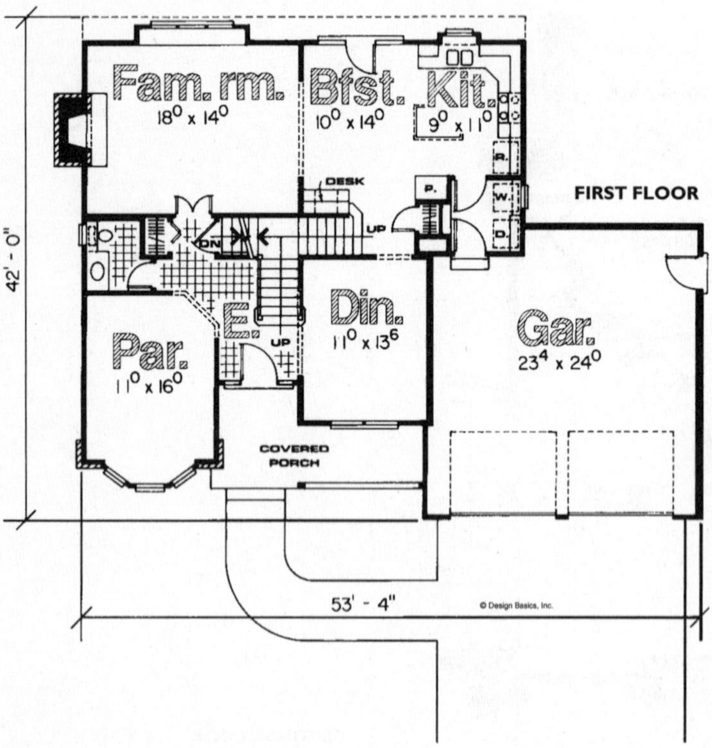
FIRST FLOOR
Fam. rm.
18⁰ x 14⁰
Bfst.
10⁰ x 14⁰
Kit.
9⁰ x 11⁰
DESK
P.
R.
W.
D.
UP
DN
E.
UP
Din.
11⁰ x 13⁶
Par.
11⁰ x 16⁰
Gar.
23⁴ x 24⁰
COVERED PORCH
42' - 0"
53' - 4"
© Design Basics, Inc.

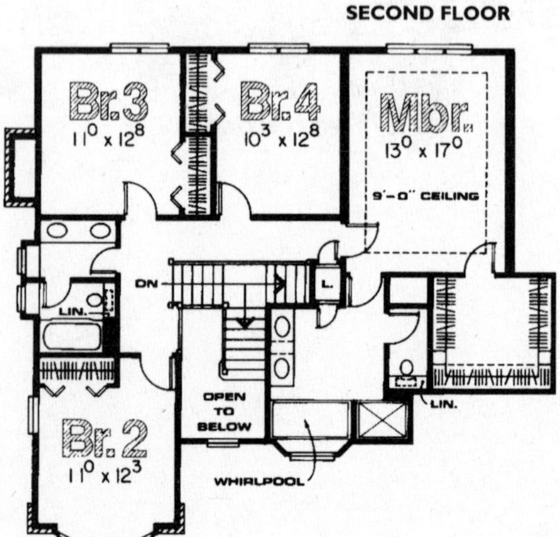
SECOND FLOOR
Br.3
11⁰ x 12⁸
Br.4
10³ x 12⁸
Mbr.
13⁰ x 17⁰
9'-0" CEILING
DN
L.
LIN.
OPEN TO BELOW
Br. 2
11⁰ x 12³
WHIRLPOOL
LIN.

Design 97618

See Order Pages and Index for Info

Units	Single
Price Code	C
Total Finished	1,915 sq. ft.
Main Finished	1,915 sq. ft.
Basement Unfinished	1,932 sq. ft.
Garage Unfinished	489 sq. ft.
Dimensions	56'6"x57'6"
Foundation	Basement Crawlspace
Bedrooms	4
Full Baths	3
Max Ridge Height	22'6"
Roof Framing	Stick
Exterior Walls	2x4

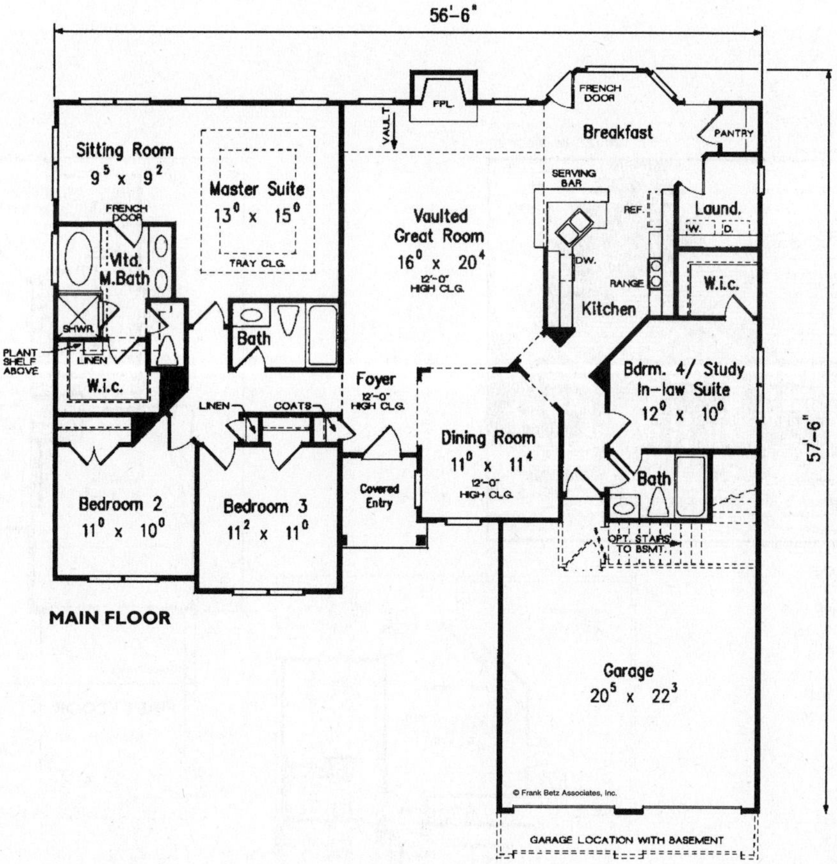
56'-6"
57'-6"
Sitting Room 9⁵ x 9²
Master Suite 13⁰ x 15⁰
TRAY CLG.
FRENCH DOOR
Vltd. M.Bath
SHWR.
LINEN
W.i.c.
PLANT SHELF ABOVE
Bath
VAULT
FPL.
Vaulted Great Room 16⁰ x 20⁴ 12'-0" HIGH CLG.
FRENCH DOOR
Breakfast
PANTRY
SERVING BAR
REF.
DW.
RANGE
Kitchen
Laund.
W. D.
W.i.c.
Bdrm. 4/ Study In-law Suite 12⁰ x 10⁰
Bath
OPT. STAIRS TO BSMT.
Foyer 12'-0" HIGH CLG.
LINEN
COATS
Dining Room 11⁰ x 11⁴ 12'-0" HIGH CLG.
Covered Entry
Bedroom 2 11⁰ x 10⁰
Bedroom 3 11² x 11⁰
Garage 20⁵ x 22³
© Frank Betz Associates, Inc.
GARAGE LOCATION WITH BASEMENT

MAIN FLOOR

Design 92530

See Order Pages and Index for Info

Units	Single
Price Code	A
Total Finished	1,128 sq. ft.
Main Finished	1,128 sq. ft.
Dimensions	61'10"x30'10"
Foundation	Crawlspace Slab
Bedrooms	3
Full Baths	2
Max Ridge Height	21'
Roof Framing	Stick
Exterior Walls	2x4

MAIN FLOOR

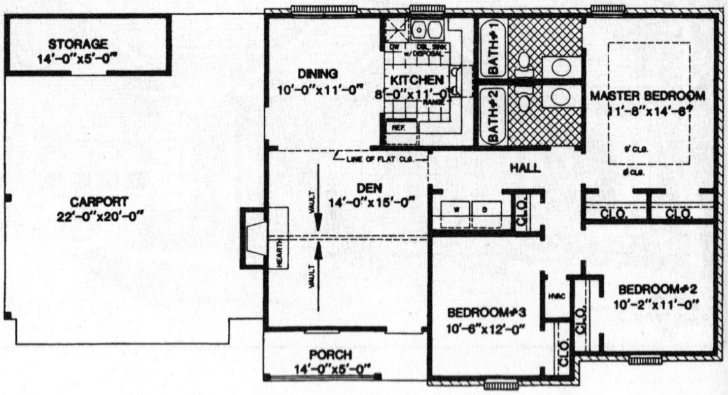
STORAGE
14'-0"x5'-0"
DINING
10'-0"x11'-0"
KITCHEN
8'-0"x11'-0"
BATH#1
BATH#2
MASTER BEDROOM
11'-8"x14'-6"
LINE OF FLAT CLG.
HALL
CARPORT
22'-0"x20'-0"
DEN
14'-0"x15'-0"
VAULT
HEARTH
CLO.
BEDROOM#3
10'-6"x12'-0"
HVAC
BEDROOM#2
10'-2"x11'-0"
PORCH
14'-0"x5'-0"

Design 97489

See Order Pages and Index for Info

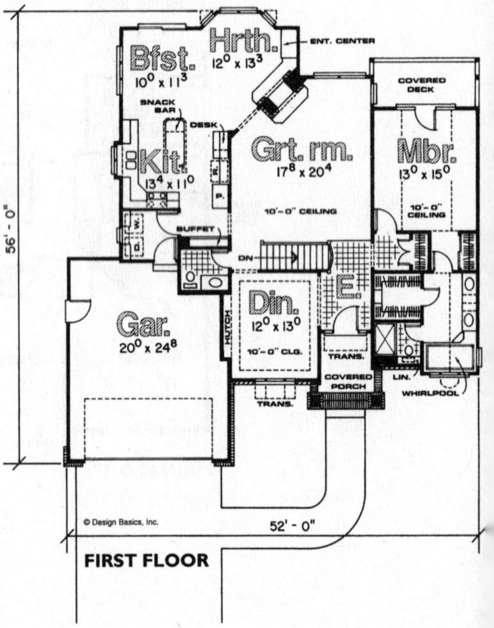
Bfst.
10⁰ x 11³
Hrth.
12⁰ x 13³
ENT. CENTER
COVERED DECK
SNACK BAR
DESK
Kit.
13⁴ x 11⁰
Grt. rm.
17⁸ x 20⁴
10'-0" CEILING
Mbr.
13⁰ x 15⁰
10'-0" CEILING
BUFFET
DN
E.
56' - 0"
Gar.
20⁰ x 24⁸
HUTCH
Din.
12⁰ x 13⁰
10'-0" CLG.
TRANS.
COVERED PORCH
LIN.
WHIRLPOOL
© Design Basics, Inc.
52' - 0"

FIRST FLOOR

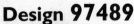

Units	Single
Price Code	B
Total Finished	1,595 sq. ft.
First Finished	1,595 sq. ft.
Basement Unfinished	790 sq. ft.
Garage Unfinished	476 sq. ft.
Dimensions	52'x56'
Foundation	Basement
Bedrooms	3
Full Baths	2
Half Baths	1
First Ceiling	8'
Max Ridge Height	20'9"
Roof Framing	Stick
Exterior Walls	2x4

* Alternate foundation options available at an additional charge.
Please call 1-800-235-5700 for more information.

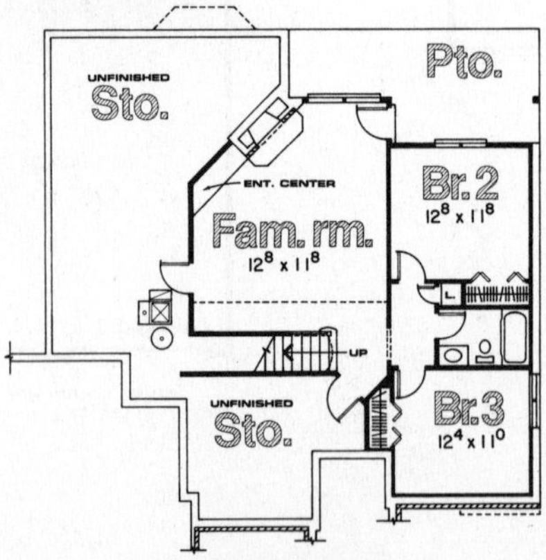
UNFINISHED
Sto.
Pto.
ENT. CENTER
Br. 2
12⁸ x 11⁸
Fam. rm.
12⁸ x 11⁸
UP
UNFINISHED
Sto.
Br. 3
12⁴ x 11⁰

SECOND FLOOR

Design 93407

See Order Pages and Index for Info

Units	Single
Price Code	F
Total Finished	2,613 sq. ft.
First Finished	1,625 sq. ft.
Second Finished	988 sq. ft.
Basement Unfinished	1,625 sq. ft.
Garage Unfinished	491 sq. ft.
Dimensions	59'x50'
Foundation	Basement
Bedrooms	4
Full Baths	2
Half Baths	1
Max Ridge Height	32'
Roof Framing	Stick
Exterior Walls	2x4

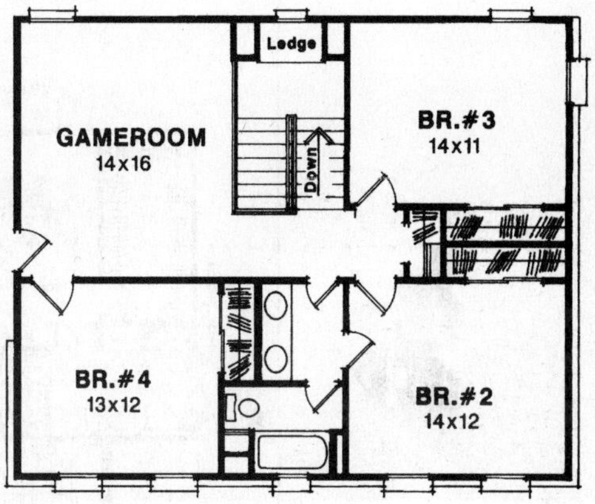
Ledge
GAMEROOM
14x16
Down
BR.#3
14x11
BR.#4
13x12
BR.#2
14x12

SECOND FLOOR

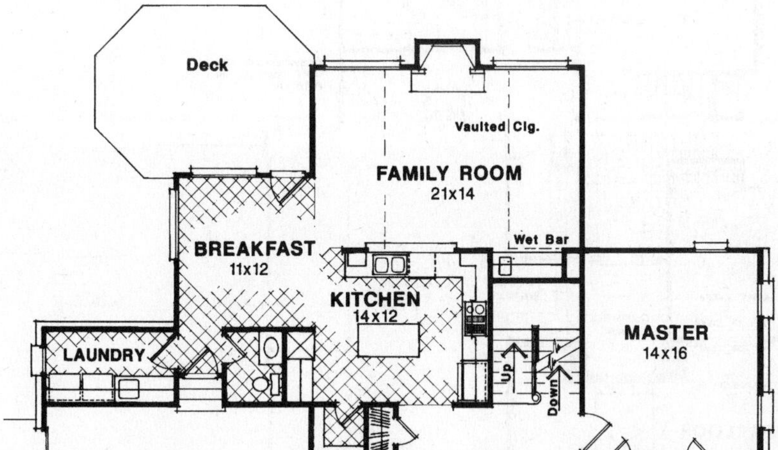
Deck
Vaulted Clg.
FAMILY ROOM
21x14
Wet Bar
BREAKFAST
11x12
KITCHEN
14x12
MASTER
14x16
LAUNDRY
Up
Down
Drive
GARAGE
21x22
DINING
14x12
FOYER

FIRST FLOOR

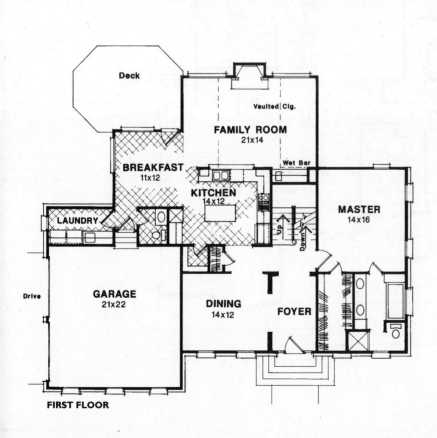

Design 97494

See Order Pages and Index for Info

Units	Single
Price Code	D
Total Finished	2,186 sq. ft.
Main Finished	2,186 sq. ft.
Garage Unfinished	720 sq. ft.
Dimensions	64'x66'
Foundation	Basement
Bedrooms	3
Full Baths	2
Half Baths	1
Main Ceiling	8'
Max Ridge Height	25'
Roof Framing	Stick
Exterior Walls	2x4

* Alternate foundation options available at an additional charge. Please call 1-800-235-5700 for more information.

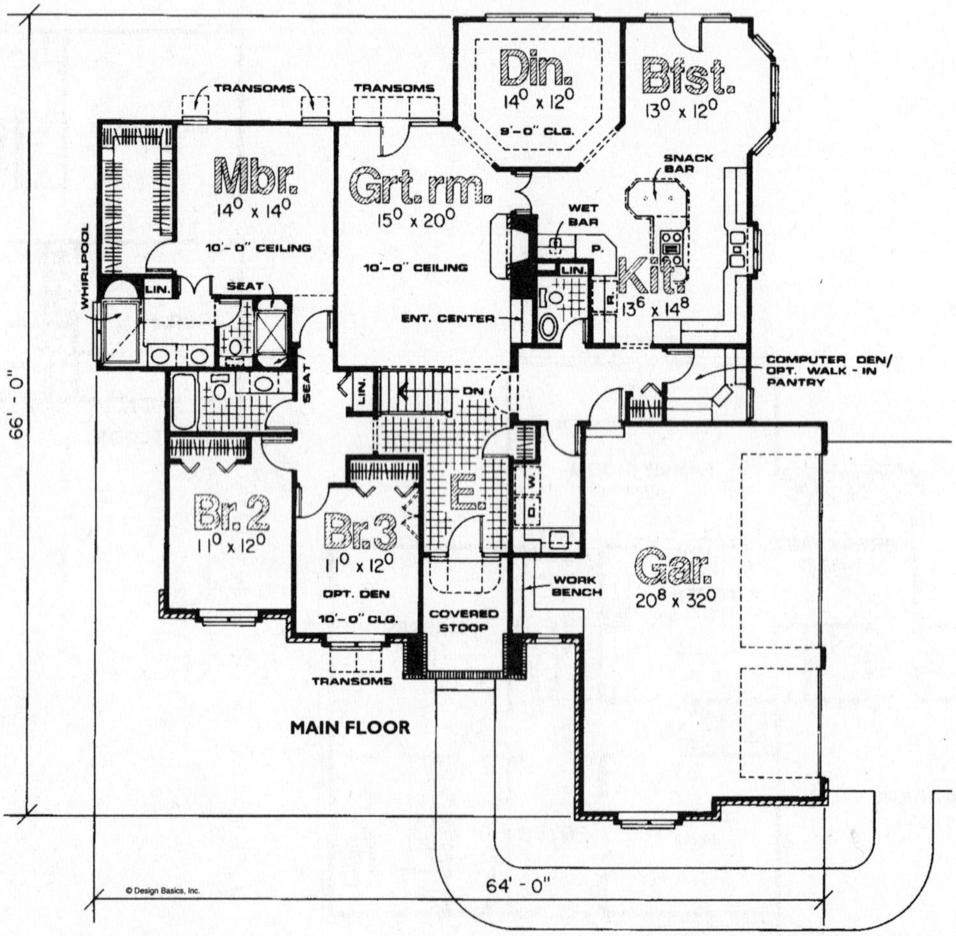
TRANSOMS
TRANSOMS
Din.
14⁰ x 12⁰
9'-0" CLG.
Bfst.
13⁰ x 12⁰
SNACK BAR
Mbr.
14⁰ x 14⁰
10'-0" CEILING
Grt. rm.
15⁰ x 20⁰
10'-0" CEILING
WET BAR
P.
LIN.
Kit.
13⁶ x 14⁸
WHIRLPOOL
LIN.
SEAT
ENT. CENTER
R.
COMPUTER DEN/ OPT. WALK - IN PANTRY
SEAT
LIN.
DN
66' - 0"
W.
D.
E.
Br. 2
11⁰ x 12⁰
Br. 3
11⁰ x 12⁰
OPT. DEN
10'-0" CLG.
COVERED STOOP
WORK BENCH
Gar.
20⁸ x 32⁰
TRANSOMS
MAIN FLOOR
© Design Basics, Inc.
64' - 0"

Design 99194

See Order Pages and Index for Info

Units	Single
Price Code	F
Total Finished	2,570 sq. ft.
Main Finished	2,570 sq. ft.
Garage Unfinished	808 sq. ft.
Dimensions	79'x63'
Foundation	Basement
Bedrooms	4
Full Baths	2
3/4 Baths	1
Main Ceiling	9'
Max Ridge Height	28'
Roof Framing	Truss
Exterior Walls	2x6

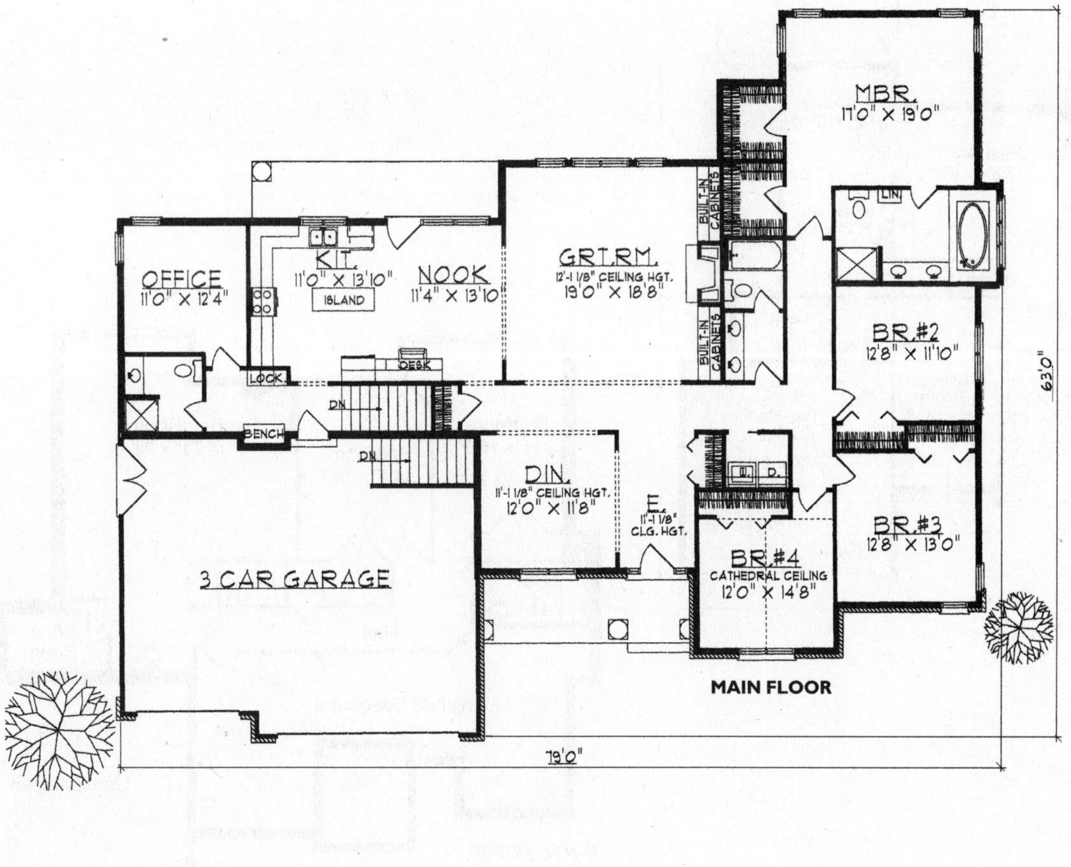
MBR.
11'0" X 19'0"
LIN
BUILT-IN CABINETS
GRT.RM.
12'-1 1/8" CEILING HGT.
19'0" X 18'8"
BUILT-IN CABINETS
BR.#2
12'8" X 11'10"
OFFICE
11'0" X 12'4"
KIT.
11'0" X 13'10"
ISLAND
NOOK
11'4" X 13'10"
DESK
LOCK.
DN
BENCH
DN
DIN.
11'-1 1/8" CEILING HGT.
12'0" X 11'8"
E.
11'-1 1/8"
CLG. HGT.
BR.#3
12'8" X 13'0"
BR.#4
CATHEDRAL CEILING
12'0" X 14'8"
3 CAR GARAGE
63'0"
79'0"

MAIN FLOOR

Design 97776

See Order Pages and Index for Info

Units	Single
Price Code	G
Total Finished	2,769 sq. ft.
Main Finished	1,681 sq. ft.
Lower Finished	1,088 sq. ft.
Basement Unfinished	382 sq. ft.
Garage Unfinished	426 sq. ft.
Porch Unfinished	137 sq. ft.
Dimensions	57'6"x63'11"
Foundation	Basement
Bedrooms	3
Full Baths	2
Half Baths	1
Main Ceiling	9'
Vaulted Ceiling	10'
Max Ridge Height	24'10"
Roof Framing	Truss
Exterior Walls	2x4

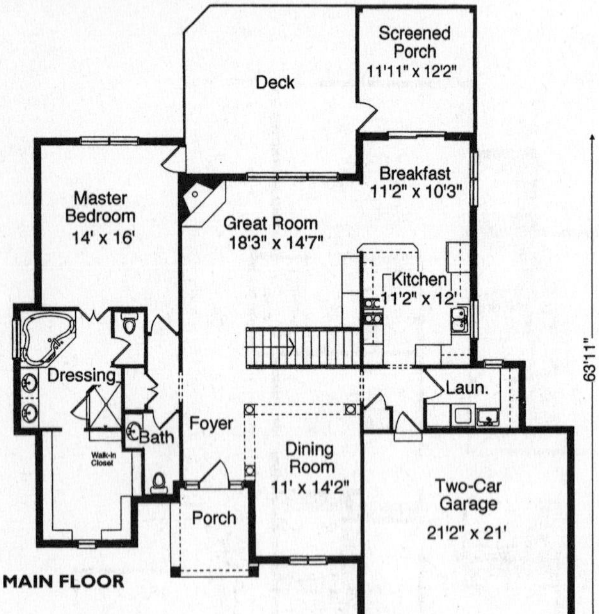
Screened Porch
11'11" x 12'2"
Deck
Master Bedroom
14' x 16'
Great Room
18'3" x 14'7"
Breakfast
11'2" x 10'3"
Kitchen
11'2" x 12'
Dressing
Walk-in Closet
Bath
Foyer
Laun.
Dining Room
11' x 14'2"
Porch
Two-Car Garage
21'2" x 21'
63'11"
57'6"

MAIN FLOOR

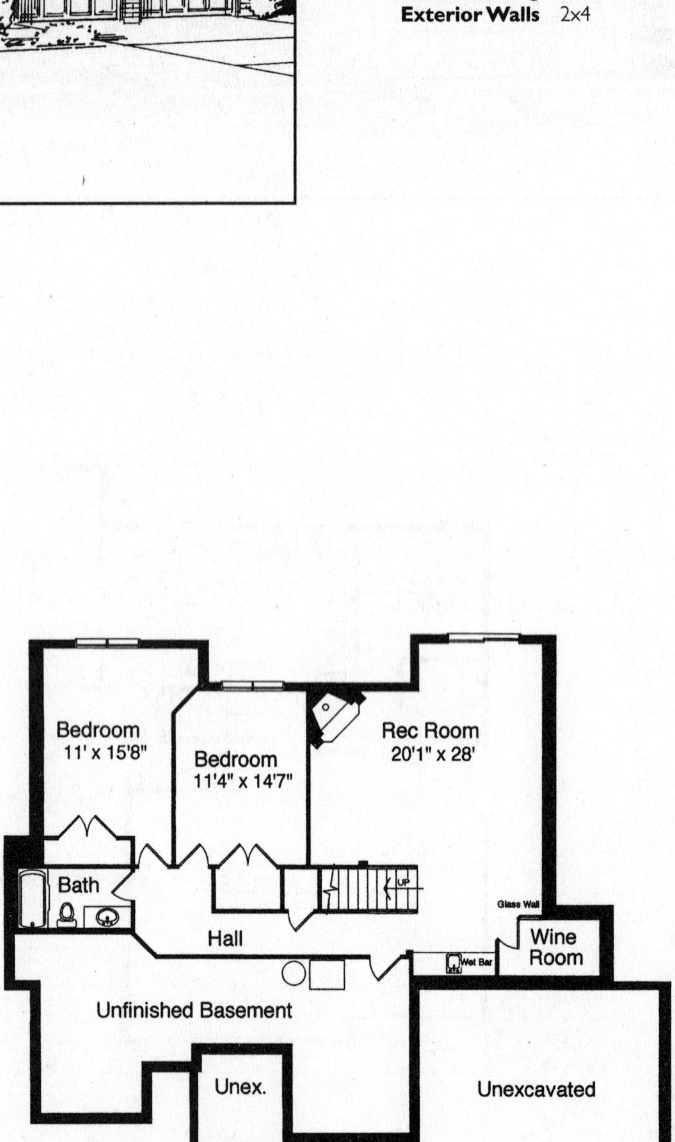
Bedroom
11' x 15'8"
Bedroom
11'4" x 14'7"
Rec Room
20'1" x 28'
Bath
UP
Glass Wall
Hall
Wet Bar
Wine Room
Unfinished Basement
Unex.
Unexcavated

LOWER FLOOR

Design 99451

See Order Pages and Index for Info

Units	Single
Price Code	G
Total Finished	2,764 sq. ft.
First Finished	2,000 sq. ft.
Second Finished	764 sq. ft.
Basement Unfinished	2,000 sq. ft.
Garage Unfinished	696 sq. ft.
Dimensions	59'4"x60'8"
Foundation	Basement
Bedrooms	4
Full Baths	2
Half Baths	1
3/4 Baths	1
Max Ridge Height	29'9"
Roof Framing	Stick
Exterior Walls	2x4

* Alternate foundation options available at an additional charge. Please call 1-800-235-5700 for more information.

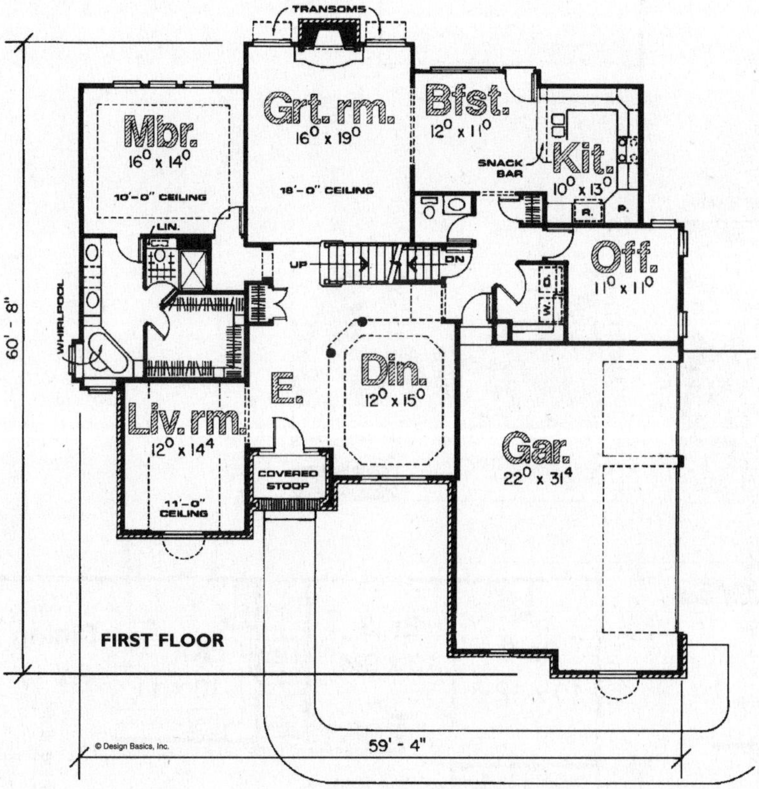
TRANSOMS
Grt. rm.
16^{0} x 19^{0}
18'-0" CEILING
Bfst.
12^{0} x 11^{0}
Mbr.
16^{0} x 14^{0}
10'-0" CEILING
SNACK BAR
Kit.
10^{0} x 13^{0}
R.
P.
LIN.
UP
DN
Off.
11^{0} x 11^{0}
W.
D.
WHIRLPOOL
60' - 8"
E.
Din.
12^{0} x 15^{0}
Liv. rm.
12^{0} x 14^{4}
11'-0" CEILING
COVERED STOOP
Gar.
22^{0} x 31^{4}
59' - 4"
© Design Basics, Inc.

FIRST FLOOR

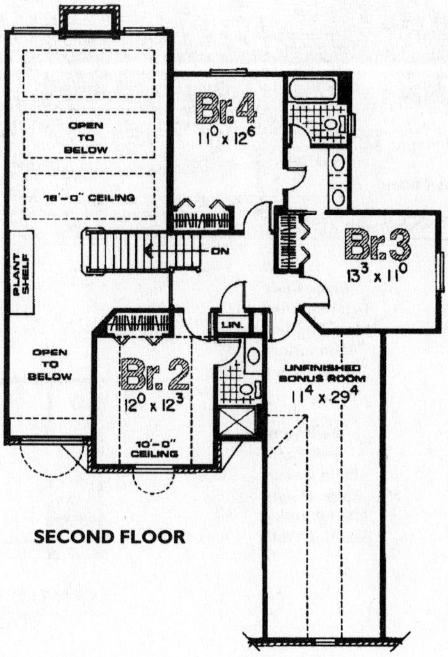
OPEN TO BELOW
18'-0" CEILING
PLANT SHELF
Br. 4
11^{0} x 12^{6}
Br. 3
13^{3} x 11^{0}
DN
LIN.
OPEN TO BELOW
Br. 2
12^{0} x 12^{3}
10'-0" CEILING
UNFINISHED BONUS ROOM
11^{4} x 29^{4}

SECOND FLOOR

Design 97274

See Order Pages and Index for Info

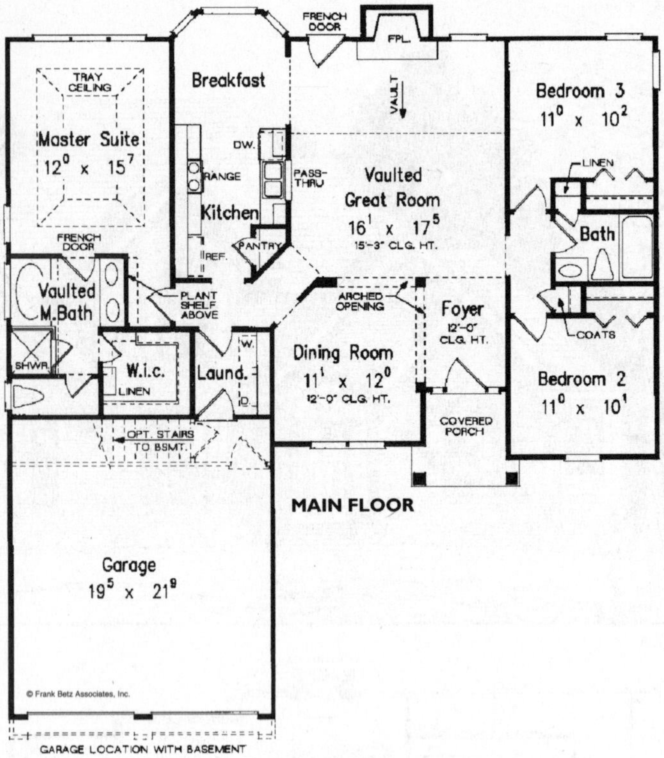
Master Suite
12⁰ x 15⁷
TRAY CEILING
FRENCH DOOR
Vaulted M.Bath
SHWR.
W.i.c.
LINEN
Breakfast
Kitchen
DW.
RANGE
PASS-THRU
PANTRY
REF.
PLANT SHELF ABOVE
Laund.
W.
D.
OPT. STAIRS TO BSMT.
FRENCH DOOR
FPL.
VAULT
Vaulted Great Room
16¹ x 17⁵
15'-3" CLG. HT.
ARCHED OPENING
Dining Room
11¹ x 12⁰
12'-0" CLG. HT.
Foyer
12'-0" CLG. HT.
COVERED PORCH
Bedroom 3
11⁰ x 10²
LINEN
Bath
COATS
Bedroom 2
11⁰ x 10¹
MAIN FLOOR
Garage
19⁵ x 21⁹
© Frank Betz Associates, Inc.
GARAGE LOCATION WITH BASEMENT

Units	Single
Price Code	A
Total Finished	1,432 sq. ft.
Main Finished	1,432 sq. ft.
Basement Unfinished	1,454 sq. ft.
Garage Unfinished	440 sq. ft.
Dimensions	49'x52'4"
Foundation	Basement Crawlspace
Bedrooms	3
Full Baths	2
Max Ridge Height	24'2"
Roof Framing	Stick
Exterior Walls	2x4

Design 34003

See Order Pages and Index for Info

Rear Elevation

Units	Single
Price Code	A
Total Finished	1,146 sq. ft.
Main Finished	1,146 sq. ft.
Dimensions	44'x28'
Foundation	Basement Crawlspace Slab
Bedrooms	3
Full Baths	2
Main Ceiling	8'
Max Ridge Height	16'
Roof Framing	Stick
Exterior Walls	2x4,2x6

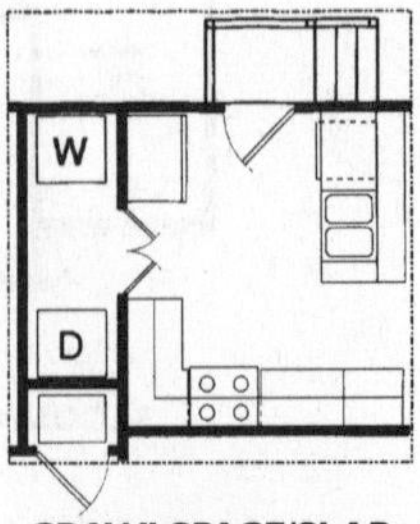
W
D

CRAWLSPACE/SLAB OPTION

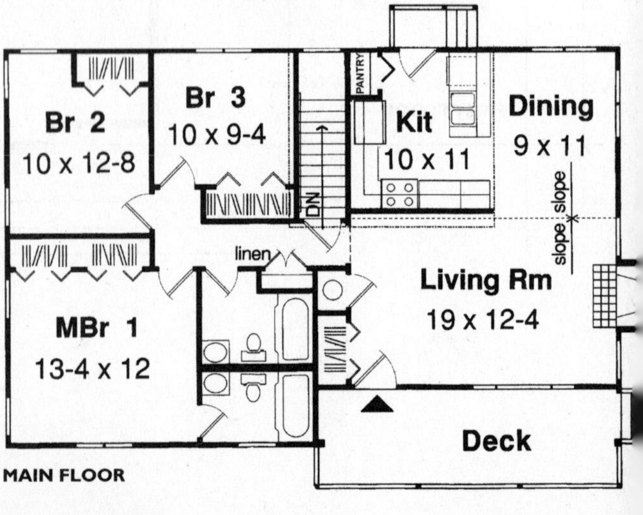
Br 2
10 x 12-8
Br 3
10 x 9-4
PANTRY
Kit
10 x 11
Dining
9 x 11
DN
slope
slope
linen
Living Rm
19 x 12-4
MBr 1
13-4 x 12
Deck

MAIN FLOOR

Design 99143

See Order Pages and Index for Info

Units Single
Price Code F
Total Finished 2,702 sq. ft.
First Finished 2,032 sq. ft.
Second Finished 670 sq. ft.
Basement Unfinished 2,032 sq. ft.
Porch Unfinished 224 sq. ft.
Dimensions 81'x53'
Foundation Basement
Bedrooms 3
Full Baths 2
Half Baths 1
Max Ridge Height 29'
Roof Framing Truss
Exterior Walls 2x6

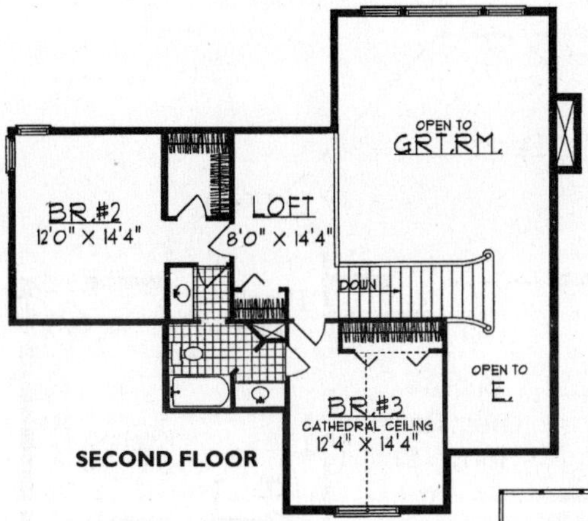
OPEN TO
GRT.RM.
BR.#2
12'0" X 14'4"
LOFT
8'0" X 14'4"
DOWN
OPEN TO
E.
BR.#3
CATHEDRAL CEILING
12'4" X 14'4"

SECOND FLOOR

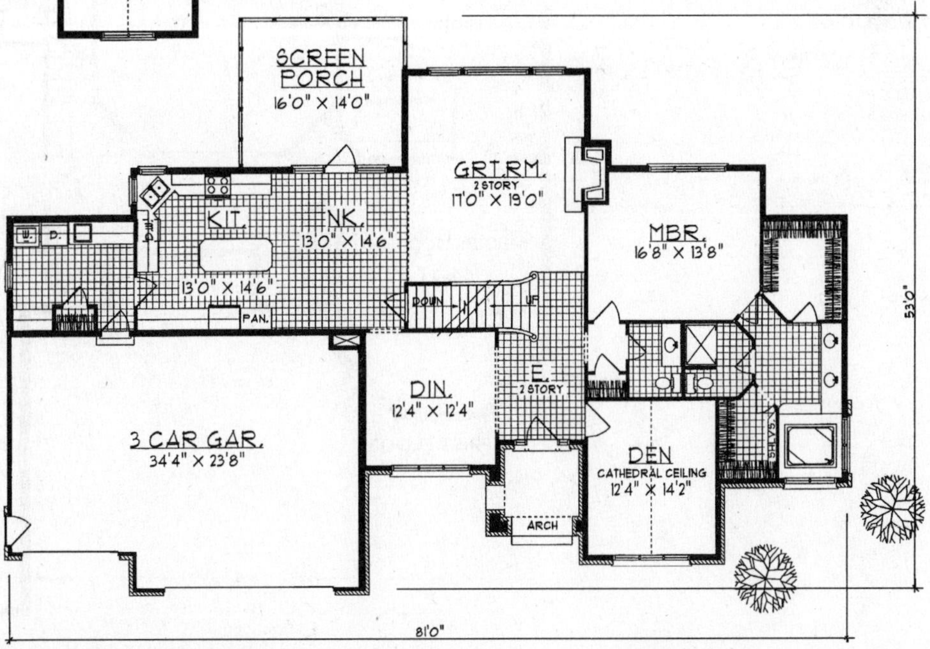
SCREEN
PORCH
16'0" X 14'0"
GRT.RM.
2 STORY
17'0" X 19'0"
KIT.
NK.
13'0" X 14'6"
13'0" X 14'6"
PAN.
MBR.
16'8" X 13'8"
DOWN
UP
DIN.
12'4" X 12'4"
E.
2 STORY
3 CAR GAR.
34'4" X 23'8"
DEN
CATHEDRAL CEILING
12'4" X 14'2"
ARCH
53'0"
81'0"

FIRST FLOOR

Design 92610

See Order Pages and Index for Info

Photography by Donna & Ron Kolb, Exposures Unlimited

Units	Single
Price Code	D
Total Finished	2,101 sq. ft.
First Finished	1,626 sq. ft.
Second Finished	475 sq. ft.
Basement Unfinished	1,512 sq. ft.
Garage Unfinished	438 sq. ft.
Dimensions	59'x60'8"
Foundation	Basement
Bedrooms	3
Full Baths	2
Half Baths	1
First Ceiling	8'
Second Ceiling	8'
Max Ridge Height	31'
Roof Framing	Truss
Exterior Walls	2x4

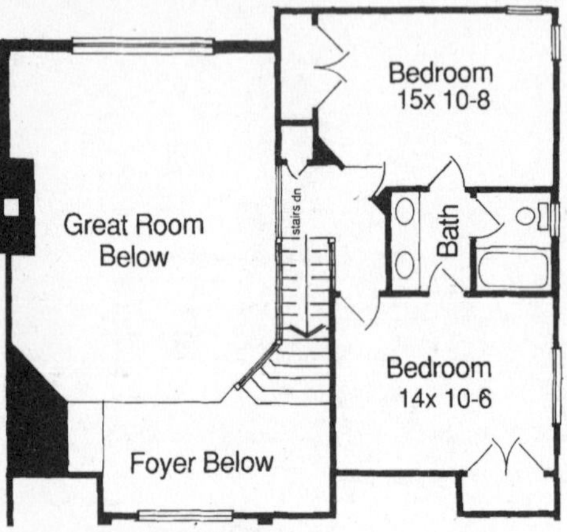
Bedroom
15x 10-8
Great Room
Below
stairs dn
Bath
Bedroom
14x 10-6
Foyer Below

SECOND FLOOR

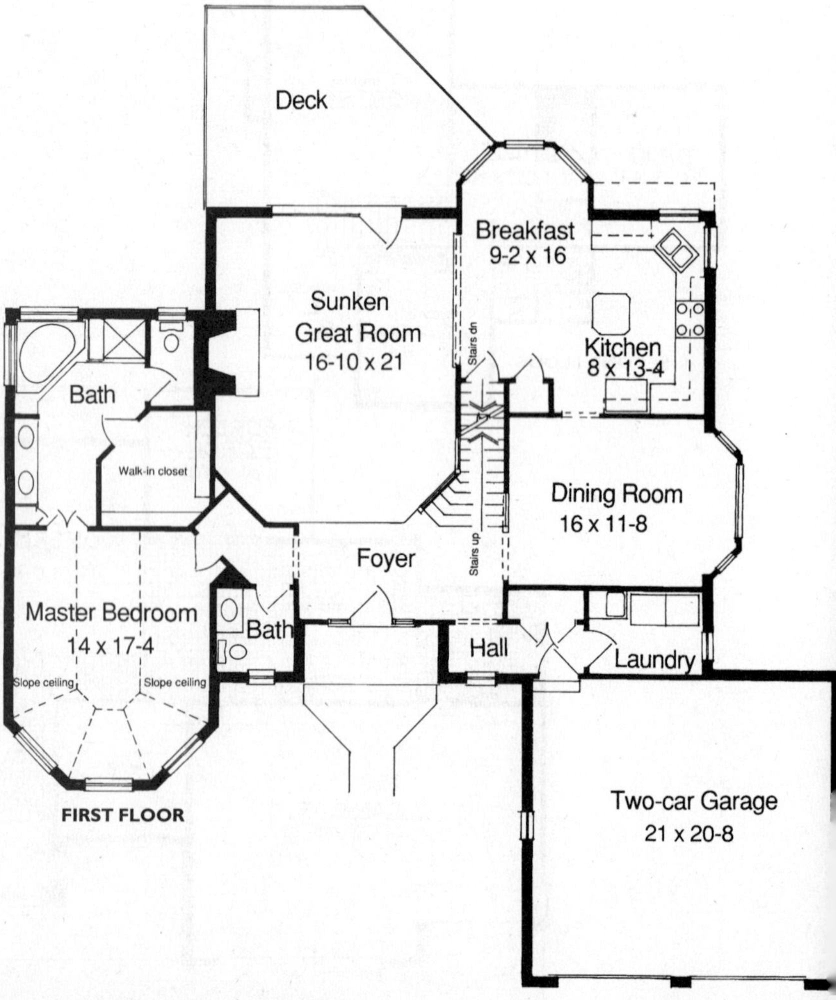
Deck
Breakfast
9-2 x 16
Sunken
Great Room
16-10 x 21
Stairs dn
Kitchen
8 x 13-4
Bath
Walk-in closet
Dining Room
16 x 11-8
Foyer
Stairs up
Master Bedroom
14 x 17-4
Bath
Hall
Laundry
Slope ceiling
Slope ceiling
Two-car Garage
21 x 20-8

FIRST FLOOR

Design 99486

See Order Pages and Index for Info

Units	Single
Price Code	I
Total Finished	3,422 sq. ft.
First Finished	2,367 sq. ft.
Second Finished	1,055 sq. ft.
Dimensions	74'8"x62'
Foundation	Basement
Bedrooms	4
Full Baths	3
Half Baths	1
Max Ridge Height	31'4"

* Alternate foundation options available at an additional charge. Please call 1-800-235-5700 for more information.

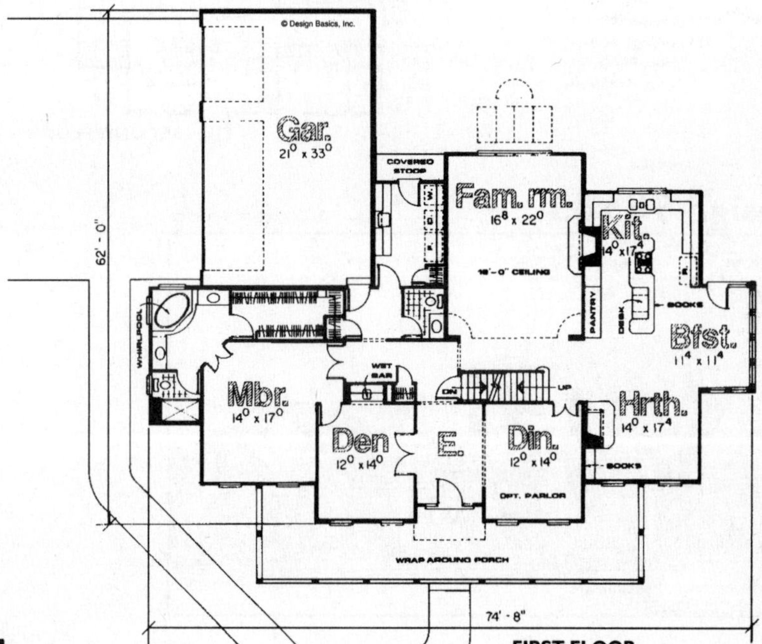

© Design Basics, Inc.
Gar.
21⁰ x 33⁰
COVERED STOOP
Fam. rm.
16⁸ x 22⁰
18'-0" CEILING
Kit.
14⁰ x 17⁴
PANTRY
DESK
BOOKS
Bfst.
11⁴ x 11⁴
WHIRLPOOL
WET BAR
DN
UP
Mbr.
14⁰ x 17⁰
Hrth.
14⁰ x 17⁴
Den
12⁰ x 14⁰
E.
Din.
12⁰ x 14⁰
OPT. PARLOR
BOOKS
WRAP AROUND PORCH
62' - 0"
74' - 8"

FIRST FLOOR

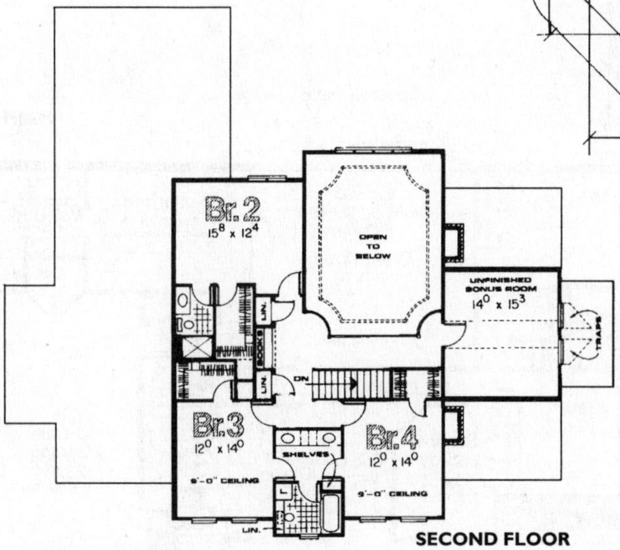

Br. 2
15⁸ x 12⁴
OPEN TO BELOW
UNFINISHED BONUS ROOM
14⁰ x 15³
LIN.
DN
Br. 3
12⁰ x 14⁰
9'-0" CEILING
SHELVES
Br. 4
12⁰ x 14⁰
9'-0" CEILING
LIN.

SECOND FLOOR

Design 98520

See Order Pages and Index for Info

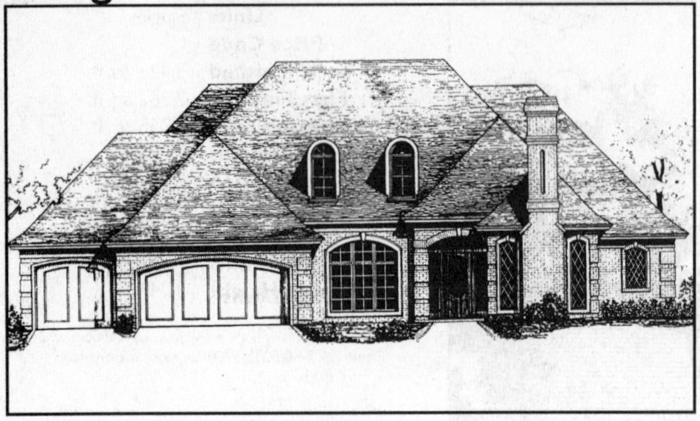

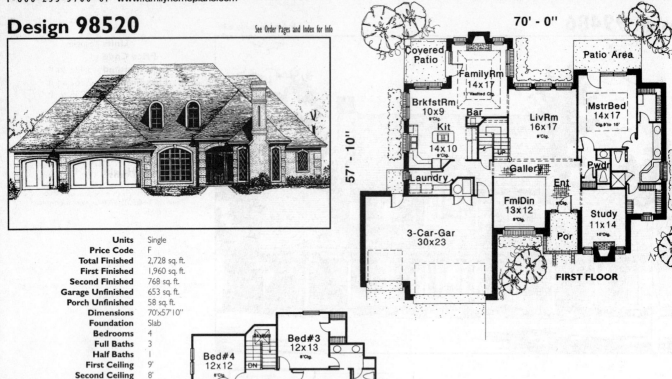

Units	Single
Price Code	F
Total Finished	2,728 sq. ft.
First Finished	1,960 sq. ft.
Second Finished	768 sq. ft.
Garage Unfinished	653 sq. ft.
Porch Unfinished	58 sq. ft.
Dimensions	70'x57'10"
Foundation	Slab
Bedrooms	4
Full Baths	3
Half Baths	1
First Ceiling	9'
Second Ceiling	8'
Max Ridge Height	27'
Roof Framing	Stick
Exterior Walls	2x4

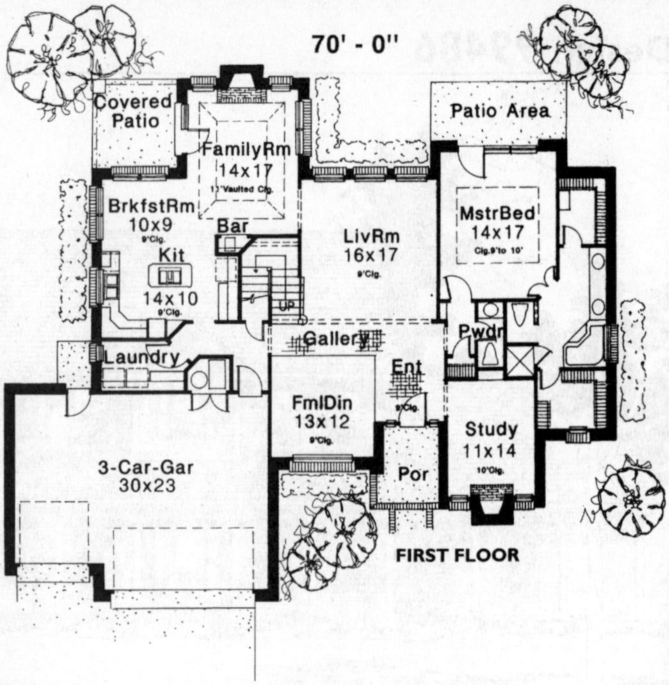
70' - 0"
57' - 10"
Covered Patio
FamilyRm
14x17
BrkfstRm
10x9
Bar
LivRm
16x17
Patio Area
MstrBed
14x17
Kit
14x10
Gallery
Pwdr
Laundry
Ent
FmlDin
13x12
Study
11x14
3-Car-Gar
30x23
Por
FIRST FLOOR

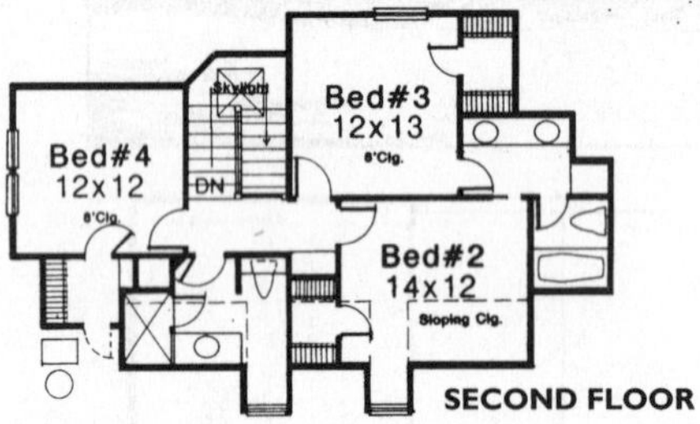
Bed#3
12x13
Bed#4
12x12
DN
Bed#2
14x12
Sloping Clg.
SECOND FLOOR

Design 98583

See Order Pages and Index for Info

Units	Single
Price Code	D
Total Finished	2,078 sq. ft.
Main Finished	2,078 sq. ft.
Garage Unfinished	734 sq. ft.
Porch Unfinished	240 sq. ft.
Dimensions	75'x47'10"
Foundation	Crawlspace Slab
Bedrooms	4
Full Baths	2
Max Ridge Height	27'
Roof Framing	Stick
Exterior Walls	2x4

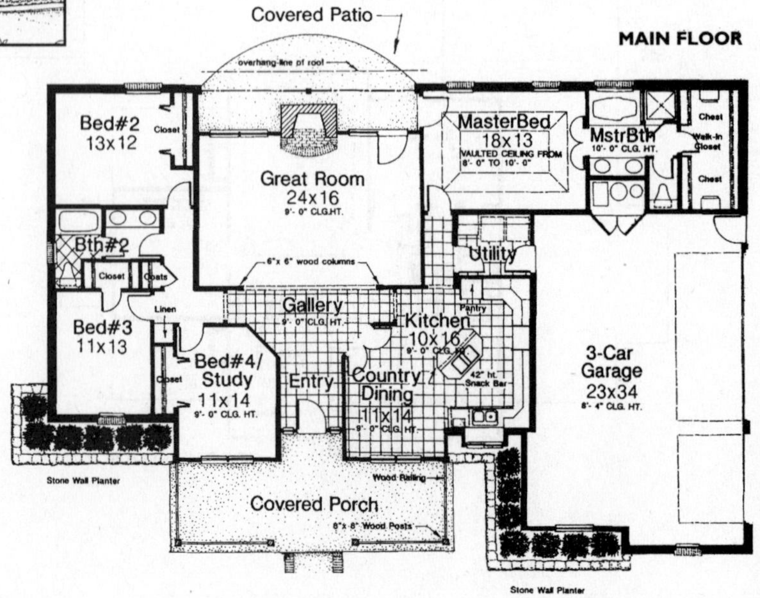
Covered Patio
MAIN FLOOR
Bed#2
13x12
Closet
Great Room
24x16
9'- 0" CLG.HT.
MasterBed
18x13
MstrBth
Chest
Bth#2
Closet
Coats
Utility
Gallery
Kitchen
10x16
Bed#3
11x13
Linen
Bed#4/
Study
11x14
Entry
Country
Dining
11x14
3-Car
Garage
23x34
Stone Wall Planter
Wood Railing
Covered Porch
Stone Wall Planter

Design 99473

See Order Pages and Index for Info

Units	Single
Price Code	F
Total Finished	2,639 sq. ft.
First Finished	2,087 sq. ft.
Second Finished	552 sq. ft.
Basement Unfinished	2,087 sq. ft.
Garage Unfinished	673 sq. ft.
Dimensions	68'7"x57'4"
Foundation	Basement Slab
Bedrooms	4
Full Baths	3
Half Baths	1
First Ceiling	9'
Second Ceiling	8'
Max Ridge Height	30'9"
Roof Framing	Stick
Exterior Walls	2x4

* Alternate foundation options available at an additional charge.
Please call 1-800-235-5700 for more information.

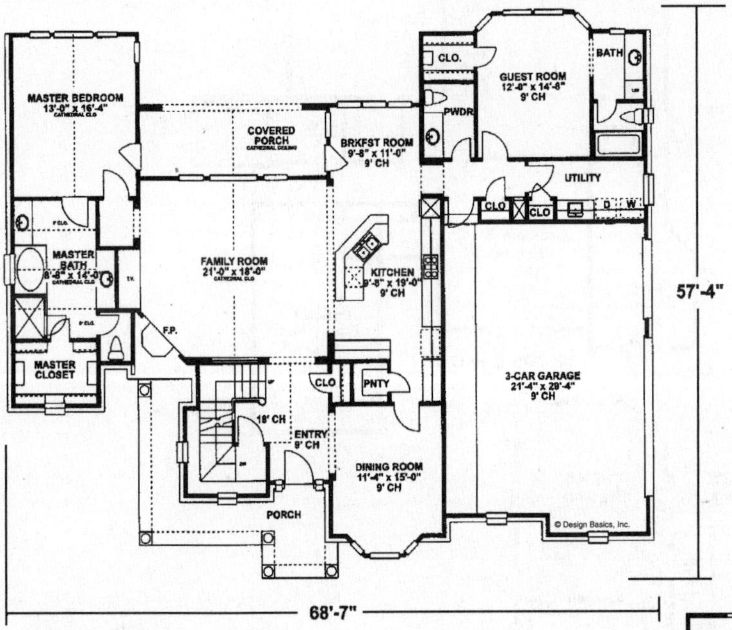

MASTER BEDROOM
13'-0" x 16'-4"
COVERED PORCH
BRKFST ROOM
9'-8" x 11'-0"
9' CH
CLO.
GUEST ROOM
12'-8" x 14'-8"
9' CH
BATH
PWDR
UTILITY
CLO
CLO
MASTER BATH
FAMILY ROOM
21'-0" x 18'-0"
KITCHEN
9'-8" x 19'-0"
9' CH
57'-4"
F.P.
MASTER CLOSET
CLO
PNTY
3-CAR GARAGE
21'-4" x 29'-4"
9' CH
18' CH
ENTRY
9' CH
DINING ROOM
11'-4" x 15'-0"
9' CH
PORCH
© Design Basics, Inc.
68'-7"

FIRST FLOOR

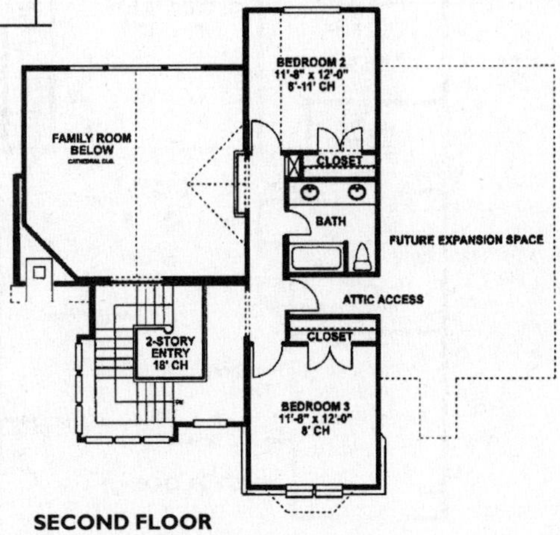

BEDROOM 2
11'-8" x 12'-0"
8'-11' CH
FAMILY ROOM BELOW
CLOSET
BATH
FUTURE EXPANSION SPACE
ATTIC ACCESS
2-STORY ENTRY
18' CH
CLOSET
BEDROOM 3
11'-8" x 12'-0"
8' CH

SECOND FLOOR

Design 98419

See Order Pages and Index for Info

Units	Single
Price Code	E
Total Finished	2,425 sq. ft.
First Finished	1,796 sq. ft.
Second Finished	629 sq. ft.
Bonus Unfinished	208 sq. ft.
Basement Unfinished	1,796 sq. ft.
Garage Unfinished	588 sq. ft.
Dimensions	54'x53'10"
Foundation	Basement Crawlspace Slab
Bedrooms	3
Full Baths	2
Half Baths	1
First Ceiling	9'
Second Ceiling	8'
Max Ridge Height	32'
Roof Framing	Stick
Exterior Walls	2x4

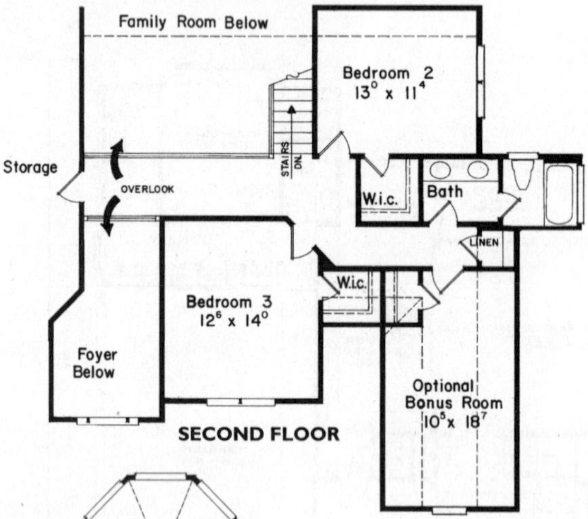
Family Room Below
Bedroom 2
13⁰ x 11⁴
Storage
OVERLOOK
STAIRS DN.
W.i.c.
Bath
LINEN
W.i.c.
Bedroom 3
12⁶ x 14⁰
Foyer
Below
Optional
Bonus Room
10⁵ x 18⁷

SECOND FLOOR

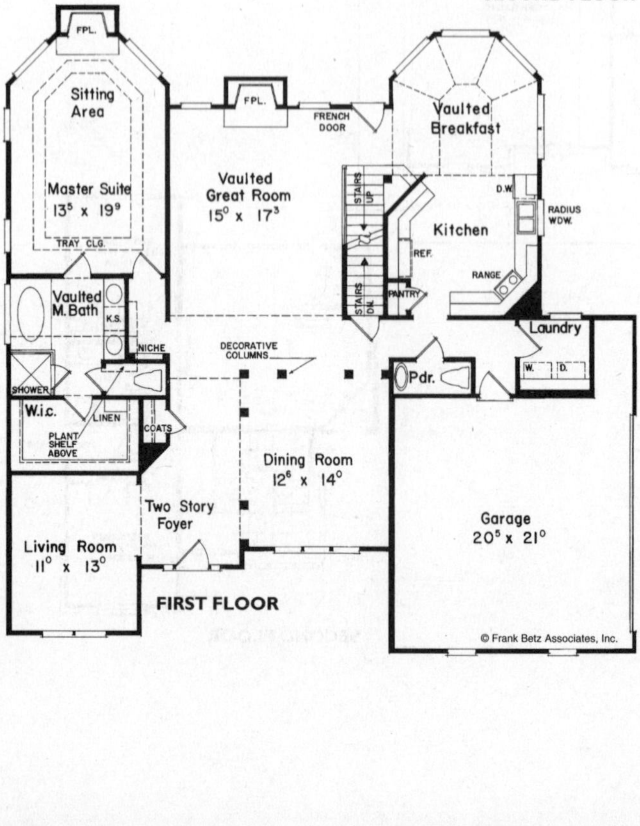
FPL.
Sitting
Area
Master Suite
13⁵ x 19⁹
TRAY CLG.
FPL.
FRENCH
DOOR
Vaulted
Great Room
15⁰ x 17³
Vaulted
Breakfast
STAIRS UP
STAIRS DN.
D.W.
RADIUS
WDW.
Kitchen
REF.
PANTRY
RANGE
Vaulted
M.Bath
K.S.
NICHE
DECORATIVE
COLUMNS
Laundry
W.
D.
SHOWER
Pdr.
W.i.c.
LINEN
PLANT
SHELF
ABOVE
COATS
Dining Room
12⁶ x 14⁰
Two Story
Foyer
Garage
20⁵ x 21⁰
Living Room
11⁰ x 13⁰

FIRST FLOOR

Design 98536

See Order Pages and Index for Info

Units	Single
Price Code	I
Total Finished	3,423 sq. ft.
First Finished	2,787 sq. ft.
Second Finished	636 sq. ft.
Garage Unfinished	832 sq. ft.
Porch Unfinished	212 sq. ft.
Dimensions	101'x58'8"
Foundation	Crawlspace Slab
Bedrooms	4
Full Baths	2
Half Baths	1
First Ceiling	9'
Second Ceiling	7'-9'
Max Ridge Height	28'6"
Roof Framing	Stick
Exterior Walls	2x4

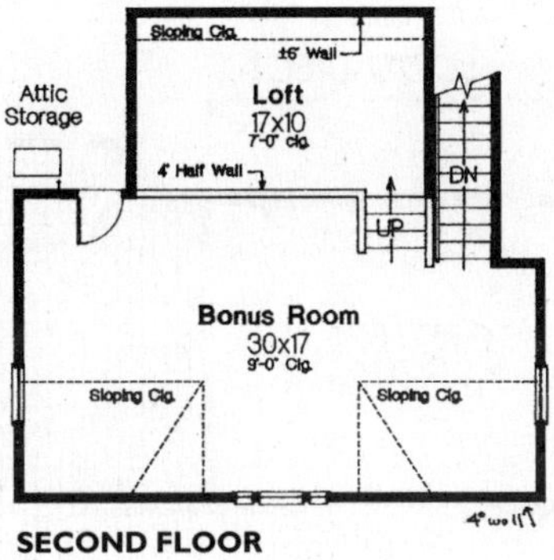
Sloping Clg.
Loft
17x10
7'-0" clg.
4' Half Wall
Attic Storage
UP
DN
Bonus Room
30x17
9'-0" Clg.
Sloping Clg.
Sloping Clg.

SECOND FLOOR

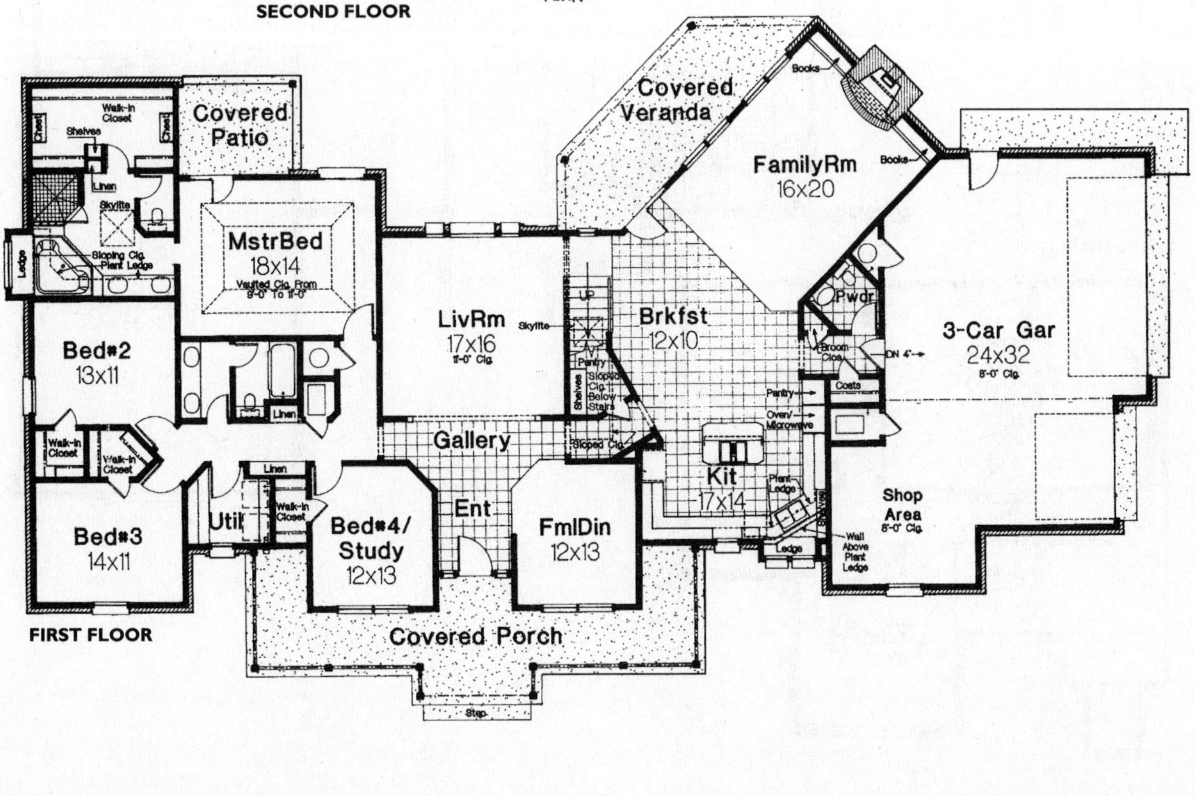
Covered Patio
Walk-in Closet
Shelves
Linen
Skylite
Sloping Clg. Plant Ledge
Ledge
MstrBed
18x14
Vaulted Clg. From 9'-0" To 11'-0"
Covered Veranda
Books
FamilyRm
16x20
Bed#2
13x11
LivRm
17x16
11'-0" Clg.
Skylite
Brkfst
12x10
Pwdr
3-Car Gar
24x32
8'-0" Clg.
Pantry
Shelves
Broom Clos.
DN
Coats
Linen
Walk-in Closet
Gallery
Over/Microwave
Plant Ledge
Kit
17x14
Shop Area
8'-0" Clg.
Bed#3
14x11
Util
Bed#4/ Study
12x13
Ent
FmlDin
12x13
Ledge
Wall Above Plant Ledge
Covered Porch
Step

FIRST FLOOR

Design 99149

See Order Pages and Index for Info

Units	Single
Price Code	H
Total Finished	3,009 sq. ft.
First Finished	2,039 sq. ft.
Second Finished	970 sq. ft.
Dimensions	69'8"x72'
Foundation	Basement
Bedrooms	4
Full Baths	2
Half Baths	1
First Ceiling	9'
Second Ceiling	8'
Max Ridge Height	32'4"
Roof Framing	Truss
Exterior Walls	2x6

FIRST FLOOR

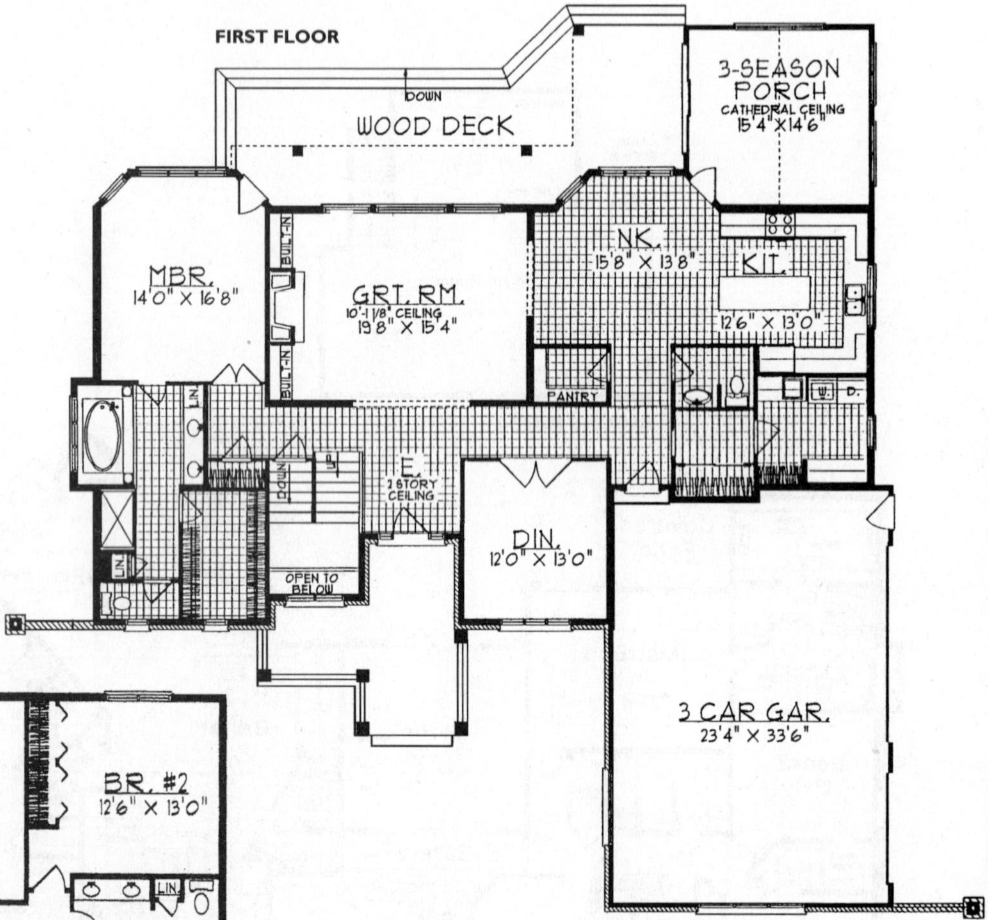
DOWN
WOOD DECK
3-SEASON PORCH
CATHEDRAL CEILING
15'4" X 14'6"
MBR.
14'0" X 16'8"
BUILT-IN
GRT. RM.
10'-1 1/8" CEILING
19'8" X 15'4"
NK.
15'8" X 13'8"
KIT.
12'6" X 13'0"
PANTRY
W.
D.
LIN.
UP
E.
2 STORY CEILING
OPEN TO BELOW
DIN.
12'0" X 13'0"
3 CAR GAR.
23'4" X 33'6"

SECOND FLOOR

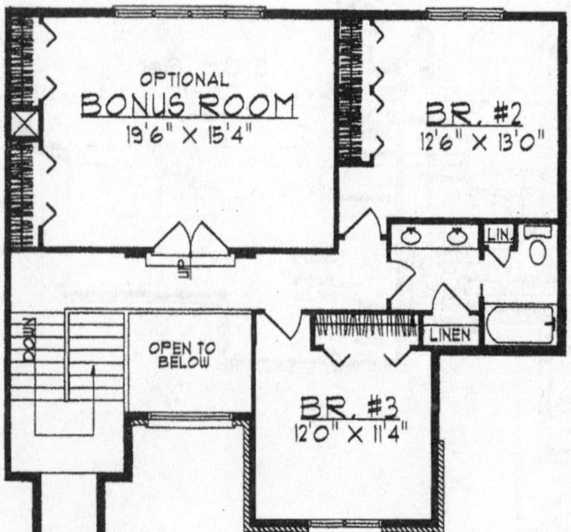
OPTIONAL
BONUS ROOM
19'6" X 15'4"
BR. #2
12'6" X 13'0"
LIN.
UP
DOWN
OPEN TO BELOW
LINEN
BR. #3
12'0" X 11'4"

Design 97439

See Order Pages and Index for Info

© design basics inc. 1986

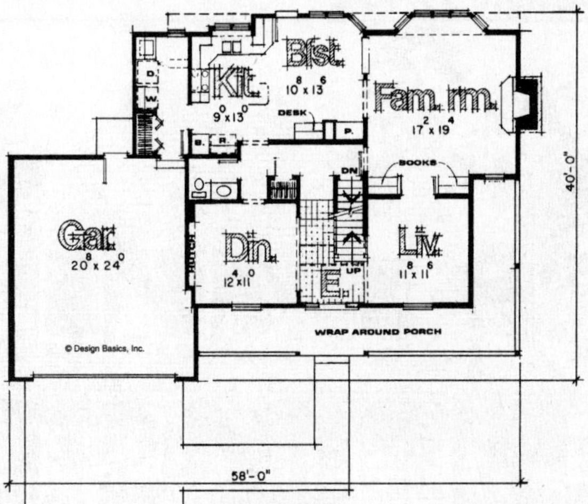
Bfst. 10⁸ x 13⁶
Kit. 9⁰ x 13⁰
Fam. rm. 17² x 19⁴
DESK
BOOKS
Gar. 20⁸ x 24⁰
Din. 12⁴ x 11⁰
Liv. 11⁸ x 11⁶
WRAP AROUND PORCH
© Design Basics, Inc.
40'-0"
58'-0"

FIRST FLOOR

Units	Single
Price Code	E
Total Finished	2,360 sq. ft.
First Finished	1,188 sq. ft.
Second Finished	1,172 sq. ft.
Garage Unfinished	504 sq. ft.
Dimensions	58'x40'
Foundation	Basement
Bedrooms	4
Full Baths	2
Half Baths	1
First Ceiling	8'
Max Ridge Height	25'6"
Roof Framing	Stick
Exterior Walls	2x4

* Alternate foundation options available at an additional charge. Please call 1-800-235-5700 for more information.

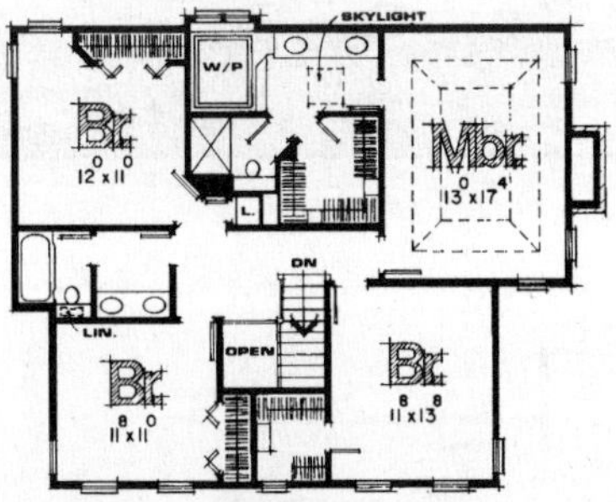
SKYLIGHT
W/P
Br. 12⁰ x 11⁰
Mbr. 13⁰ x 17⁴
DN
LIN.
OPEN
Br. 11⁰ x 11⁸
Br. 11⁸ x 13⁸

SECOND FLOOR

Design 97440

See Order Pages and Index for Info

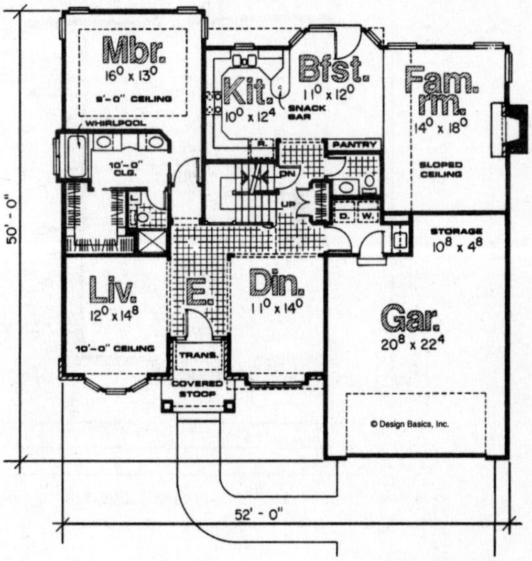
Mbr. 16⁰ x 13⁰
9'-0" CEILING
WHIRLPOOL
10'-0" CLG.
Kit. 10⁰ x 12⁴
SNACK BAR
Bfst. 11⁰ x 12⁰
Fam. rm. 14⁰ x 18⁰
SLOPED CEILING
PANTRY
STORAGE 10⁸ x 4⁸
Liv. 12⁰ x 14⁸
10'-0" CEILING
E.
Din. 11⁰ x 14⁰
TRANS.
COVERED STOOP
Gar. 20⁸ x 22⁴
© Design Basics, Inc.
50'-0"
52'-0"

FIRST FLOOR

Units	Single
Price Code	E
Total Finished	2,285 sq. ft.
First Finished	1,651 sq. ft.
Second Finished	634 sq. ft.
Garage Unfinished	530 sq. ft.
Dimensions	52'x50'
Foundation	Basement
Bedrooms	4
Full Baths	2
Half Baths	1
First Ceiling	8'
Second Ceiling	8'
Max Ridge Height	27'6"
Roof Framing	Stick
Exterior Walls	2x4

* Alternate foundation options available at an additional charge. Please call 1-800-235-5700 for more information.

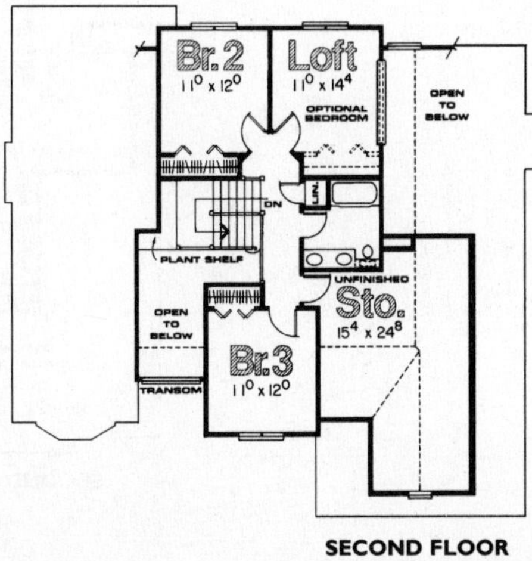
Br. 2 11⁰ x 12⁰
Loft 11⁰ x 14⁴
OPTIONAL BEDROOM
OPEN TO BELOW
DN
PLANT SHELF
OPEN TO BELOW
UNFINISHED
Sto. 15⁴ x 24⁸
Br. 3 11⁰ x 12⁰
TRANSOM

SECOND FLOOR

Design 97432

See Order Pages and Index for Info

Units	Single
Price Code	F
Total Finished	2,543 sq. ft.
First Finished	1,406 sq. ft.
Second Finished	1,137 sq. ft.
Bonus Unfinished	96 sq. ft.
Garage Unfinished	792 sq. ft.
Dimensions	62'x51'4"
Foundation	Basement
Bedrooms	4
Full Baths	2
Half Baths	1
First Ceiling	9'
Max Ridge Height	30'
Roof Framing	Stick
Exterior Walls	2x4

* Alternate foundation options available at an additional charge. Please call 1-800-235-5700 for more information.

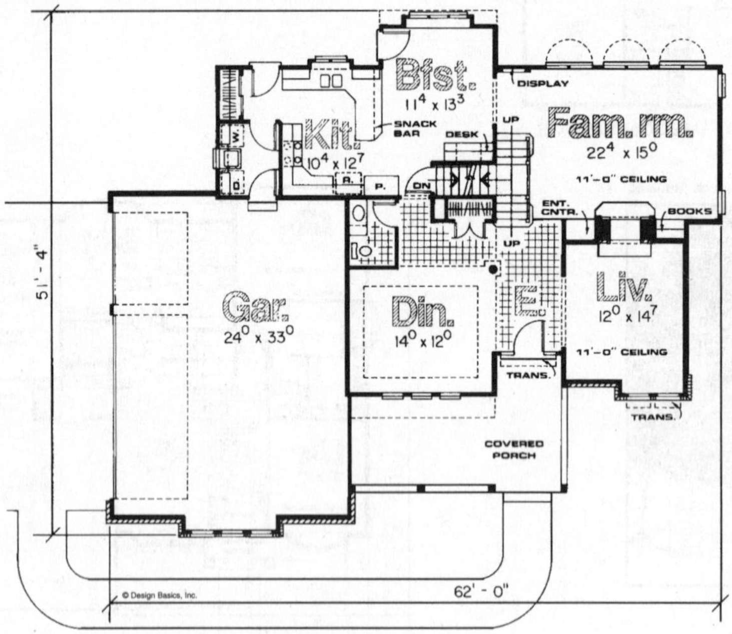

Bfst.
11⁴ x 13³
DISPLAY
Kit.
10⁴ x 12⁷
SNACK BAR
DESK
UP
Fam. rm.
22⁴ x 15⁰
11'-0" CEILING
ENT. CNTR.
BOOKS
DN
UP
Gar.
24⁰ x 33⁰
Din.
14⁰ x 12⁰
E
Liv.
12⁰ x 14⁷
11'-0" CEILING
TRANS.
TRANS.
COVERED PORCH
51'-4"
62'-0"
© Design Basics, Inc.

FIRST FLOOR

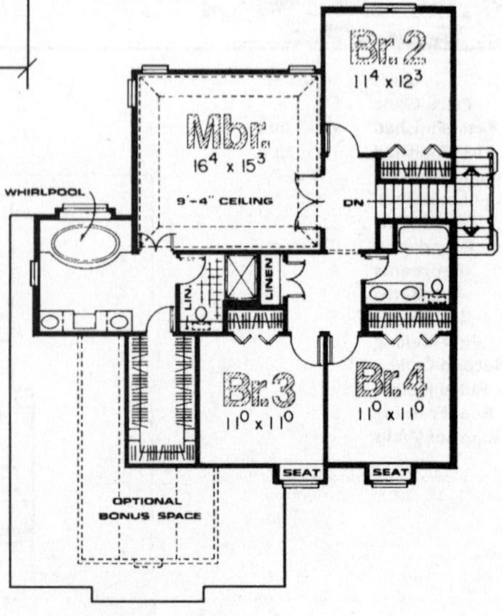

Br. 2
11⁴ x 12³
Mbr.
16⁴ x 15³
9'-4" CEILING
WHIRLPOOL
DN
LIN.
LINEN
Br. 3
11⁰ x 11⁰
Br. 4
11⁰ x 11⁰
SEAT
SEAT
OPTIONAL BONUS SPACE

SECOND FLOOR

Design 98430

See Order Pages and Index for Info

Units	Single
Price Code	C
Total Finished	1,884 sq. ft.
Main Finished	1,884 sq. ft.
Basement Unfinished	1,908 sq. ft.
Garage Unfinished	495 sq. ft.
Dimensions	50'x55'4"
Foundation	Basement Crawlspace Slab
Bedrooms	3
Full Baths	2
Half Baths	1
Main Ceiling	9'
Max Ridge Height	25'
Roof Framing	Stick
Exterior Walls	2x4

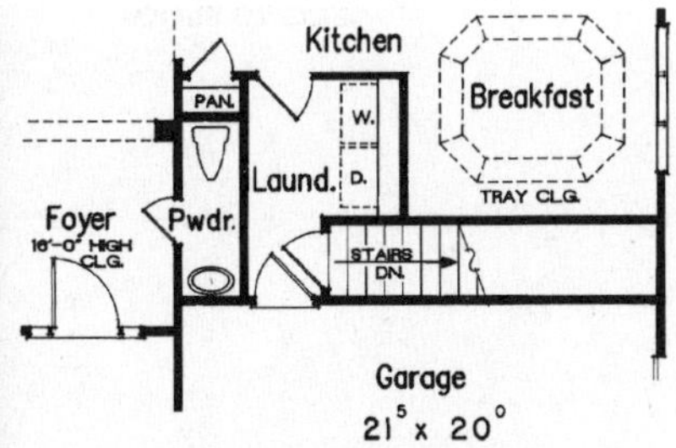
Kitchen
PAN.
W.
D.
Breakfast
Laund.
TRAY CLG.
Foyer
16'-0" HIGH CLG.
Pwdr.
STAIRS DN.
Garage
21^5 x 20^0

OPTIONAL BASEMENT STAIRS LOCATION

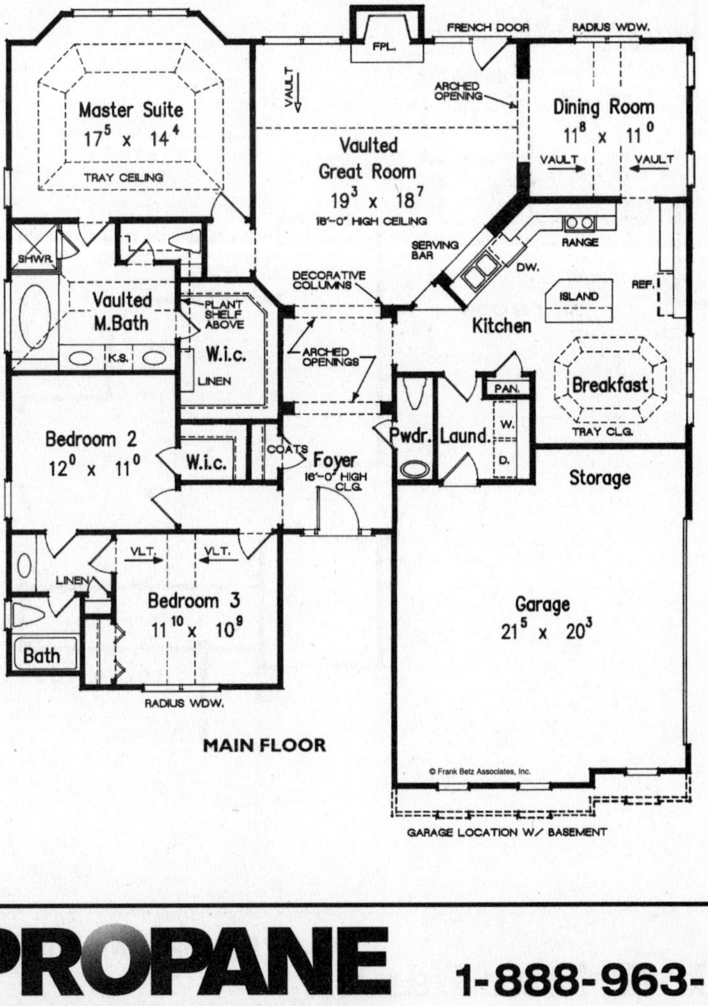
FRENCH DOOR
RADIUS WDW.
FPL.
VAULT
ARCHED OPENING
Master Suite
17^5 x 14^4
TRAY CEILING
Vaulted
Great Room
19^3 x 18^7
18'-0" HIGH CEILING
Dining Room
11^8 x 11^0
VAULT
VAULT
RANGE
SERVING BAR
DW.
ISLAND
REF.
SHWR.
Vaulted
M.Bath
PLANT SHELF ABOVE
K.S.
W.i.c.
LINEN
DECORATIVE COLUMNS
ARCHED OPENINGS
Kitchen
PAN.
Breakfast
TRAY CLG.
Bedroom 2
12^0 x 11^0
W.i.c.
COATS
Foyer
16'-0" HIGH CLG.
Pwdr.
Laund.
W.
D.
Storage
VLT.
VLT.
LINEN
Bedroom 3
11^{10} x 10^9
Bath
RADIUS WDW.
Garage
21^5 x 20^3
© Frank Betz Associates, Inc.
GARAGE LOCATION W/ BASEMENT

MAIN FLOOR

Design 94294

See Order Pages and Index for Info

Units	Single
Price Code	F
Total Finished	2,513 sq. ft.
First Finished	1,542 sq. ft.
Second Finished	971 sq. ft.
Bonus Unfinished	747 sq. ft.
Garage Unfinished	663 sq. ft.
Porch Unfinished	330 sq. ft.
Dimensions	46'x51'
Foundation	Basement
Bedrooms	4
Full Baths	3
Max Ridge Height	39'4"
Roof Framing	Truss
Exterior Walls	2x6

* Alternate foundation options available at an additional charge. Please call 1-800-235-5700 for more information.

br. 2
11'-4" x 13'-0"
10'-0"h. clg.
covered porch
built ins
great room
19'-0" x 18'-0"
2-story clg.
fireplace
built ins
dining
12'-0" x 14'-0"
10'-0" h. clg.
up
up
foyer
kitchen
10'-8" x 13'-6"
butler pantry
util.
built ins
study
13'-4" x 12'-0"
vaulted clg.
entry porch

FIRST FLOOR

br. 3
11'-4" x 13'-0"
vaulted clg.
deck
sitting
open to below
master suite
16'-0" x 14'-0"
vaulted clg.
dn
overlook
dn
open
master bath
w.i.c.

SECOND FLOOR

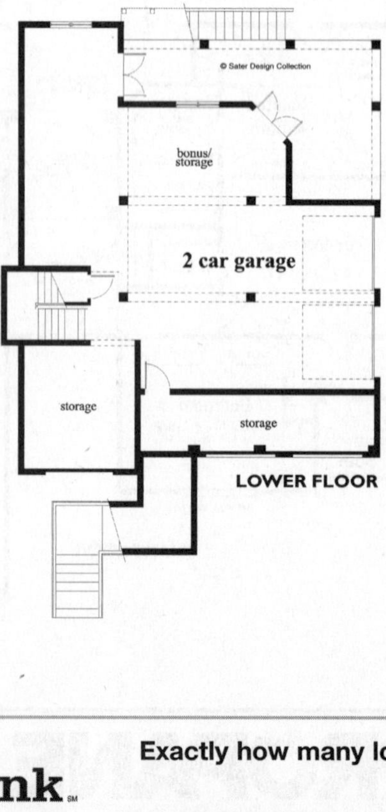
© Sater Design Collection
bonus/ storage
2 car garage
storage
storage

LOWER FLOOR

Design 98246

See Order Pages and Index for Info

Units	Single
Price Code	G
Total Finished	2,588 sq. ft.
Main Finished	2,588 sq. ft.
Basement Unfinished	2,588 sq. ft.
Garage Unfinished	469 sq. ft.
Porch Unfinished	150 sq. ft.
Dimensions	77'x52'6"
Foundation	Basement
Bedrooms	4
Full Baths	3
Main Ceiling	8'
Vaulted Ceiling	12'
Max Ridge Height	22'
Roof Framing	Stick
Exterior Walls	2x4

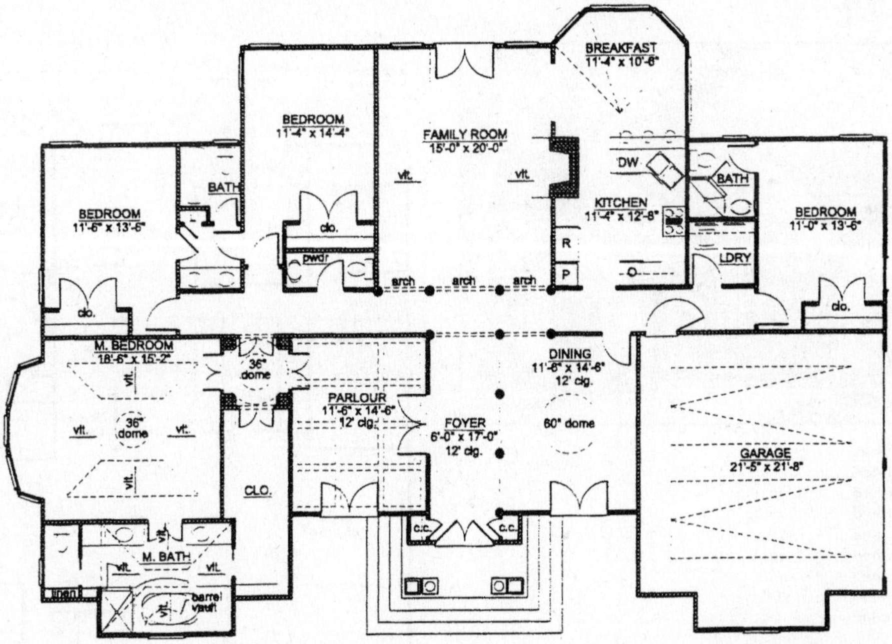
BREAKFAST
11'-4" x 10'-6"
BEDROOM
11'-4" x 14'-4"
FAMILY ROOM
15'-0" x 20'-0"
vlt.
vlt.
DW
KITCHEN
11'-4" x 12'-8"
BATH
BEDROOM
11'-0" x 13'-6"
LDRY
clo.
BEDROOM
11'-6" x 13'-6"
BATH
clo.
clo.
pwdr
R
P
arch
arch
arch
M. BEDROOM
18'-6" x 15'-2"
36" dome
36" dome
PARLOUR
11'-6" x 14'-6"
12' clg.
FOYER
6'-0" x 17'-0"
12' clg.
DINING
11'-6" x 14'-6"
12' clg.
60" dome
GARAGE
21'-5" x 21'-8"
CLO.
c.c.
c.c.
M. BATH
linen
barrel vault

MAIN FLOOR

Design 97248

See Order Pages and Index for Info

Units	Single
Price Code	C
Total Finished	1,901 sq. ft.
First Finished	996 sq. ft.
Second Finished	905 sq. ft.
Basement Unfinished	996 sq. ft.
Garage Unfinished	476 sq. ft.
Dimensions	40'x39'4"
Foundation	Basement Crawlspace
Bedrooms	3
Full Baths	2
Half Baths	1
Max Ridge Height	32'9"
Roof Framing	Stick
Exterior Walls	2x4

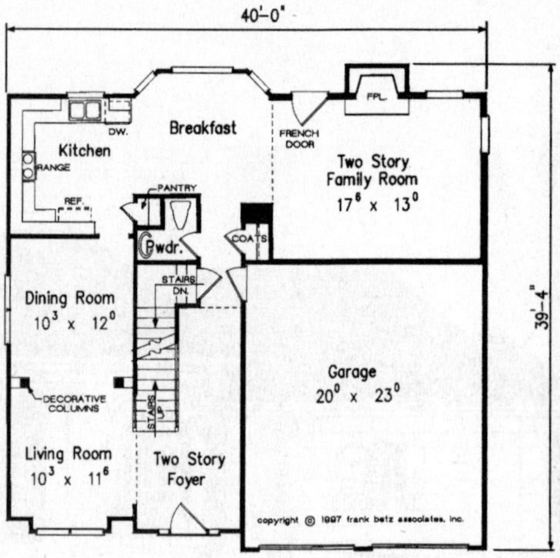
40'-0"
Breakfast
Kitchen
DW.
RANGE
REF.
PANTRY
FRENCH DOOR
FPL.
Two Story Family Room 17⁶ x 13⁰
Pwdr.
COATS
STAIRS DN.
Dining Room 10³ x 12⁰
DECORATIVE COLUMNS
Garage 20⁰ x 23⁰
39'-4"
Living Room 10³ x 11⁶
Two Story Foyer
copyright © 1997 frank betz associates, inc.

FIRST FLOOR

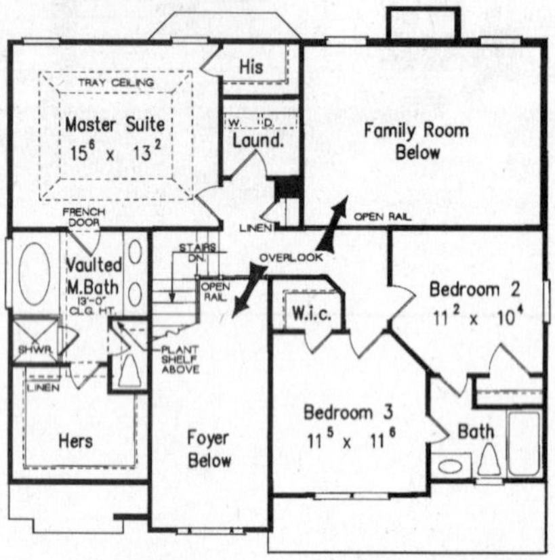
TRAY CEILING
Master Suite 15⁶ x 13²
His
Laund.
Family Room Below
FRENCH DOOR
LINEN
OPEN RAIL
OVERLOOK
Vaulted M.Bath
STAIRS DN.
OPEN RAIL
W.i.c.
Bedroom 2 11² x 10⁴
SHWR.
PLANT SHELF ABOVE
LINEN
Hers
Foyer Below
Bedroom 3 11⁵ x 11⁶
Bath

SECOND FLOOR

Design 97277

See Order Pages and Index for Info

Units	Single
Price Code	C
Total Finished	1,927 sq. ft.
Main Finished	1,927 sq. ft.
Bonus Unfinished	424 sq. ft.
Basement Unfinished	1,927 sq. ft.
Garage Unfinished	494 sq. ft.
Dimensions	55'6"x64'
Foundation	Basement Crawlspace
Bedrooms	3
Full Baths	2
Main Ceiling	9'
Max Ridge Height	28'2"
Roof Framing	Stick
Exterior Walls	2x4

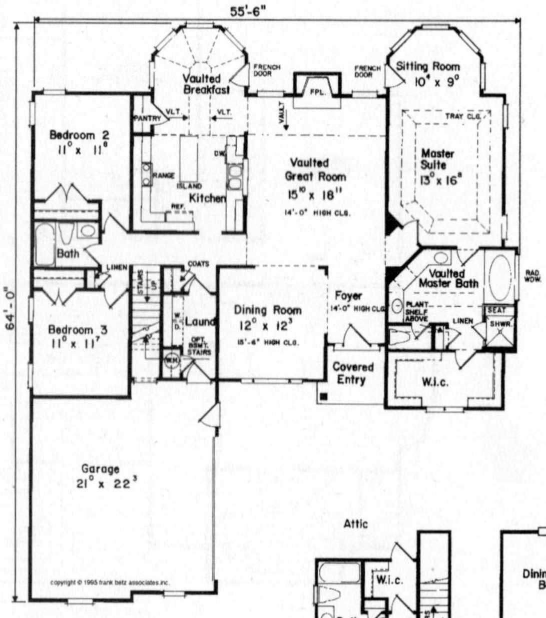
55'-6"
Vaulted Breakfast
FRENCH DOOR
FPL.
FRENCH DOOR
Sitting Room 10⁴ x 9⁰
PANTRY
TRAY CLG.
Bedroom 2 11⁰ x 11⁸
Vaulted Great Room 15¹⁰ x 18¹¹
14'-0" HIGH CLG.
Master Suite 13⁰ x 16⁸
RANGE
ISLAND
Kitchen
REF.
Bath
LINEN
COATS
Vaulted Master Bath
Foyer
Laund.
Dining Room 12⁰ x 12³
Bedroom 3 11⁰ x 11⁷
W.i.c.
Covered Entry
64'-0"
Garage 21⁰ x 22³
copyright © 1995 frank betz associates inc.

MAIN FLOOR

Attic

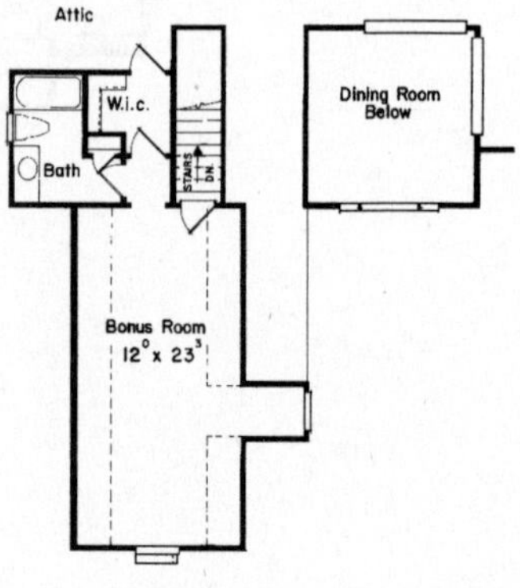
W.i.c.
Bath
Dining Room Below
Bonus Room 12⁰ x 23³

BONUS

Design 97450

See Order Pages and Index for Info

Units	Single
Price Code	D
Total Finished	2,118 sq. ft.
First Finished	1,453 sq. ft.
Second Finished	665 sq. ft.
Garage Unfinished	566 sq. ft.
Dimensions	55'x49'
Foundation	Basement
Bedrooms	4
Full Baths	2
Half Baths	1
Max Ridge Height	27'6"
Roof Framing	Stick
Exterior Walls	2x4

* Alternate foundation options available at an additional charge. Please call 1-800-235-5700 for more information.

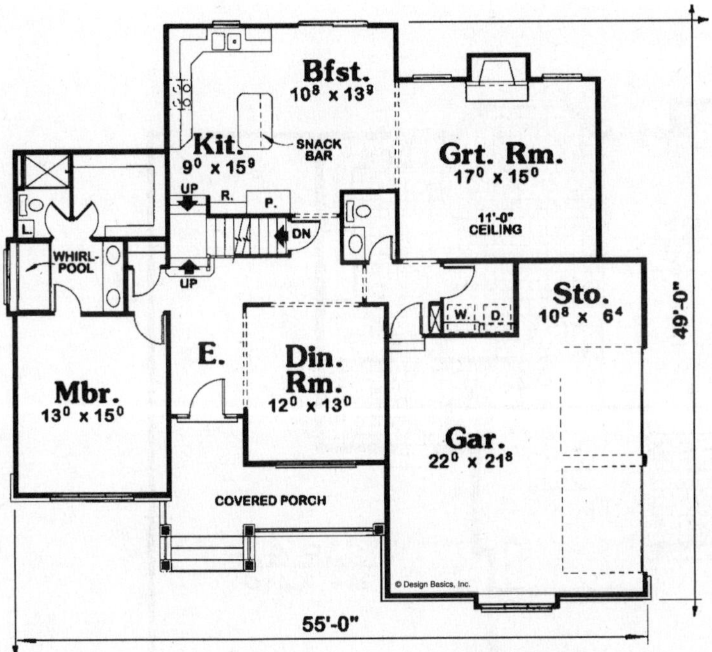
Bfst.
10⁸ x 13⁹
Kit.
9⁰ x 15⁹
SNACK BAR
Grt. Rm.
17⁰ x 15⁰
11'-0" CEILING
UP
R.
P.
DN
L
WHIRL-POOL
UP
Sto.
10⁸ x 6⁴
W.
D.
E.
Din. Rm.
12⁰ x 13⁰
Mbr.
13⁰ x 15⁰
Gar.
22⁰ x 21⁸
COVERED PORCH
49'-0"
55'-0"
© Design Basics, Inc.

FIRST FLOOR

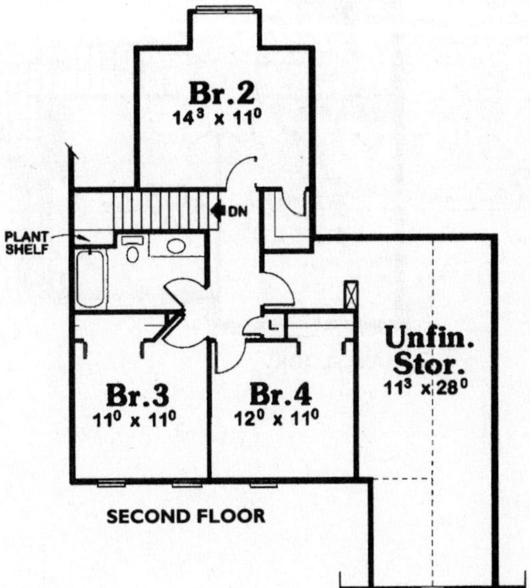
Br.2
14³ x 11⁰
DN
PLANT SHELF
L
Unfin. Stor.
11³ x 28⁰
Br.3
11⁰ x 11⁰
Br.4
12⁰ x 11⁰

SECOND FLOOR

Design 99115

See Order Pages and Index for Info

Units	Single
Price Code	C
Total Finished	1,947 sq. ft.
Main Finished	1,947 sq. ft.
Basement Unfinished	1,947 sq. ft.
Dimensions	69'8"x46'
Foundation	Basement
Bedrooms	3
Full Baths	2
Half Baths	1
Main Ceiling	8'
Max Ridge Height	22'4"
Roof Framing	Truss
Exterior Walls	2x6

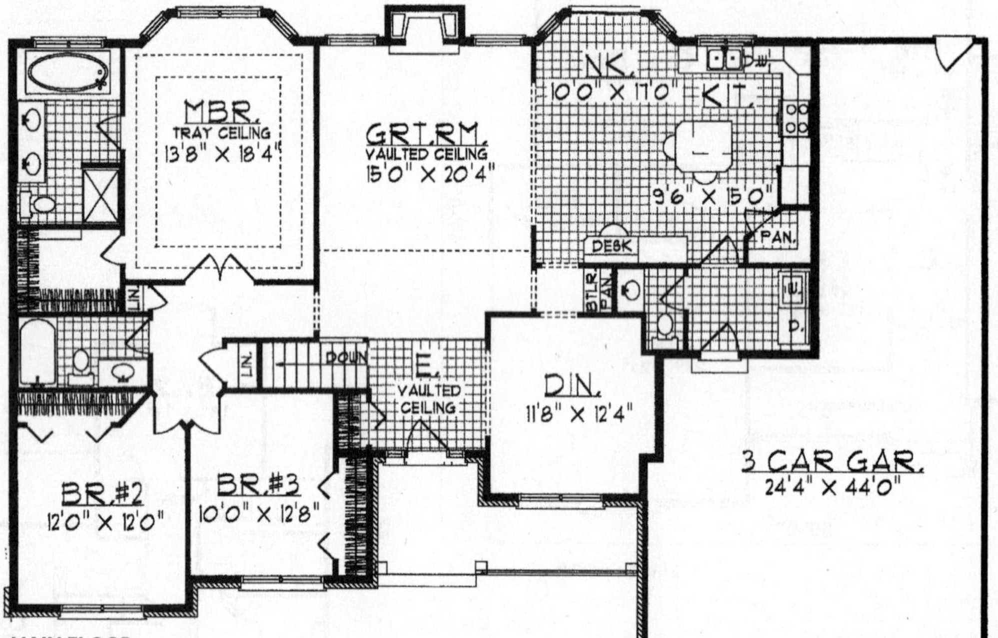
MBR.
TRAY CEILING
13'8" X 18'4"
GRT.RM.
VAULTED CEILING
15'0" X 20'4"
NK.
10'0" X 17'0"
KIT.
9'6" X 15'0"
PAN.
DESK
BTR. PAN.
W.
D.
LIN.
LIN.
DOWN
E.
VAULTED CEILING
DIN.
11'8" X 12'4"
3 CAR GAR.
24'4" X 44'0"
BR.#2
12'0" X 12'0"
BR.#3
10'0" X 12'8"

MAIN FLOOR

Design 97283

See Order Pages and Index for Info

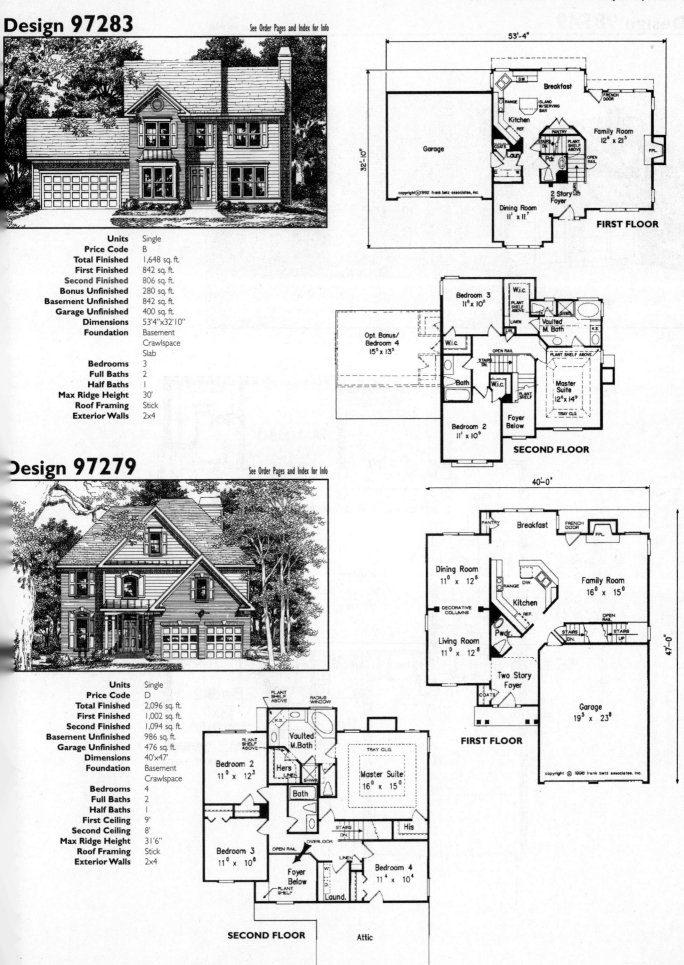

Units	Single
Price Code	B
Total Finished	1,648 sq. ft.
First Finished	842 sq. ft.
Second Finished	806 sq. ft.
Bonus Unfinished	280 sq. ft.
Basement Unfinished	842 sq. ft.
Garage Unfinished	400 sq. ft.
Dimensions	53'4"x32'10"
Foundation	Basement Crawlspace Slab
Bedrooms	3
Full Baths	2
Half Baths	1
Max Ridge Height	30'
Roof Framing	Stick
Exterior Walls	2x4

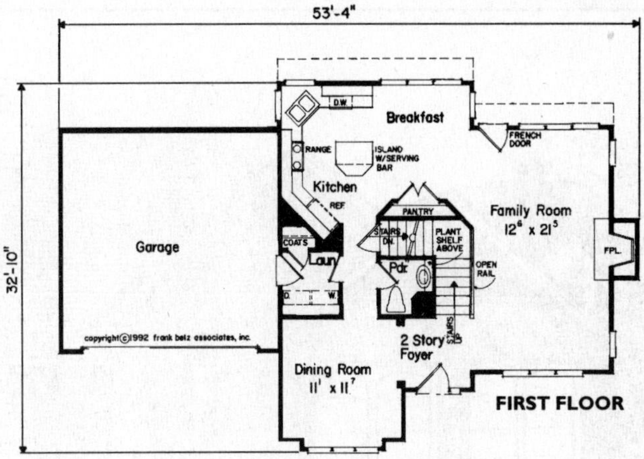
53'-4"
32'-10"
Breakfast
D.W.
RANGE
ISLAND W/SERVING BAR
FRENCH DOOR
Kitchen
REF.
Family Room
12^6 x 21^5
FPL.
Garage
COATS
Laun.
PANTRY
STAIRS DN.
PLANT SHELF ABOVE
Pdr.
OPEN RAIL
copyright © 1992 frank betz associates, inc.
2 Story Foyer
Dining Room
11' x 11^7
FIRST FLOOR

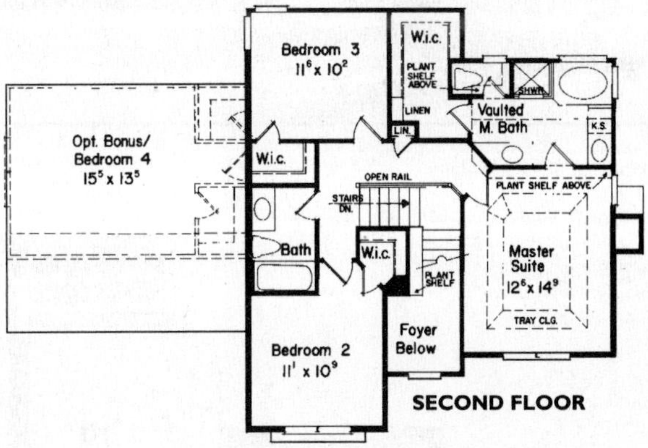
Bedroom 3
11^6 x 10^2
W.i.c.
PLANT SHELF ABOVE
LINEN
LIN.
SHWR.
Vaulted M. Bath
K.S.
Opt. Bonus/ Bedroom 4
15^5 x 13^5
W.i.c.
OPEN RAIL
STAIRS DN.
PLANT SHELF ABOVE
Bath
W.i.c.
PLANT SHELF
Master Suite
12^6 x 14^9
TRAY CLG.
Foyer Below
Bedroom 2
11' x 10^9
SECOND FLOOR

Design 97279

See Order Pages and Index for Info

Units	Single
Price Code	D
Total Finished	2,096 sq. ft.
First Finished	1,002 sq. ft.
Second Finished	1,094 sq. ft.
Basement Unfinished	986 sq. ft.
Garage Unfinished	476 sq. ft.
Dimensions	40'x47'
Foundation	Basement Crawlspace
Bedrooms	4
Full Baths	2
Half Baths	1
First Ceiling	9'
Second Ceiling	8'
Max Ridge Height	31'6"
Roof Framing	Stick
Exterior Walls	2x4

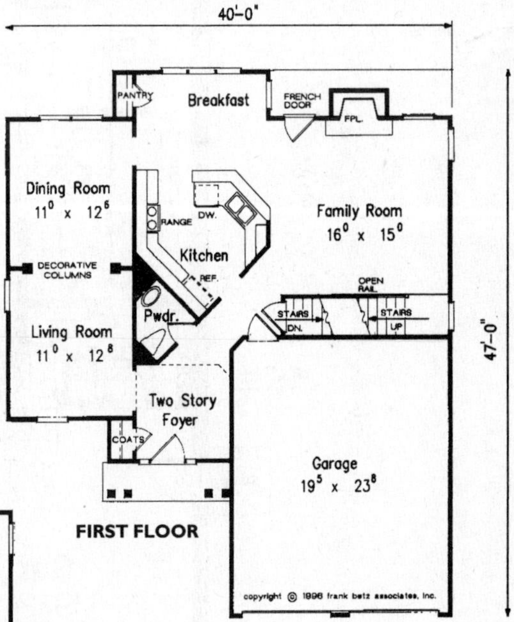
40'-0"
47'-0"
PANTRY
Breakfast
FRENCH DOOR
FPL.
Dining Room
11^0 x 12^6
RANGE
DW.
Kitchen
REF.
Family Room
16^0 x 15^0
DECORATIVE COLUMNS
OPEN RAIL
STAIRS DN.
STAIRS UP
Pwdr.
Living Room
11^0 x 12^8
Two Story Foyer
COATS
Garage
19^5 x 23^8
copyright © 1996 frank betz associates, inc.
FIRST FLOOR

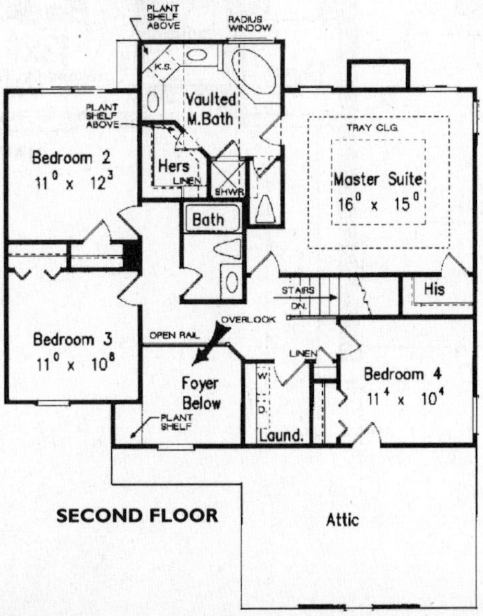
PLANT SHELF ABOVE
RADIUS WINDOW
K.S.
Vaulted M.Bath
PLANT SHELF ABOVE
Bedroom 2
11^0 x 12^3
Hers
LINEN
SHWR.
TRAY CLG.
Master Suite
16^0 x 15^0
Bath
His
STAIRS DN.
OPEN RAIL
OVERLOOK
Bedroom 3
11^0 x 10^8
Foyer Below
LINEN
Bedroom 4
11^4 x 10^4
PLANT SHELF
Laund.
SECOND FLOOR
Attic

Design 98549

See Order Pages and Index for Info

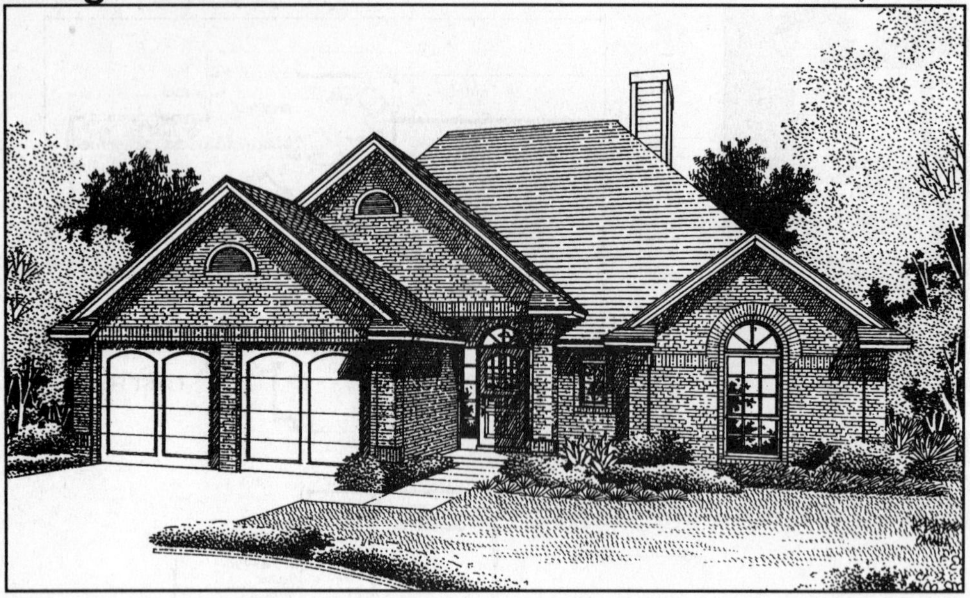

Units	Single
Price Code	A
Total Finished	1,431 sq. ft.
Main Finished	1,431 sq. ft.
Garage Unfinished	410 sq. ft.
Dimensions	44'x57'1"
Foundation	Slab
Bedrooms	3
Full Baths	2
Max Ridge Height	23'2"
Roof Framing	Stick
Exterior Walls	2x4

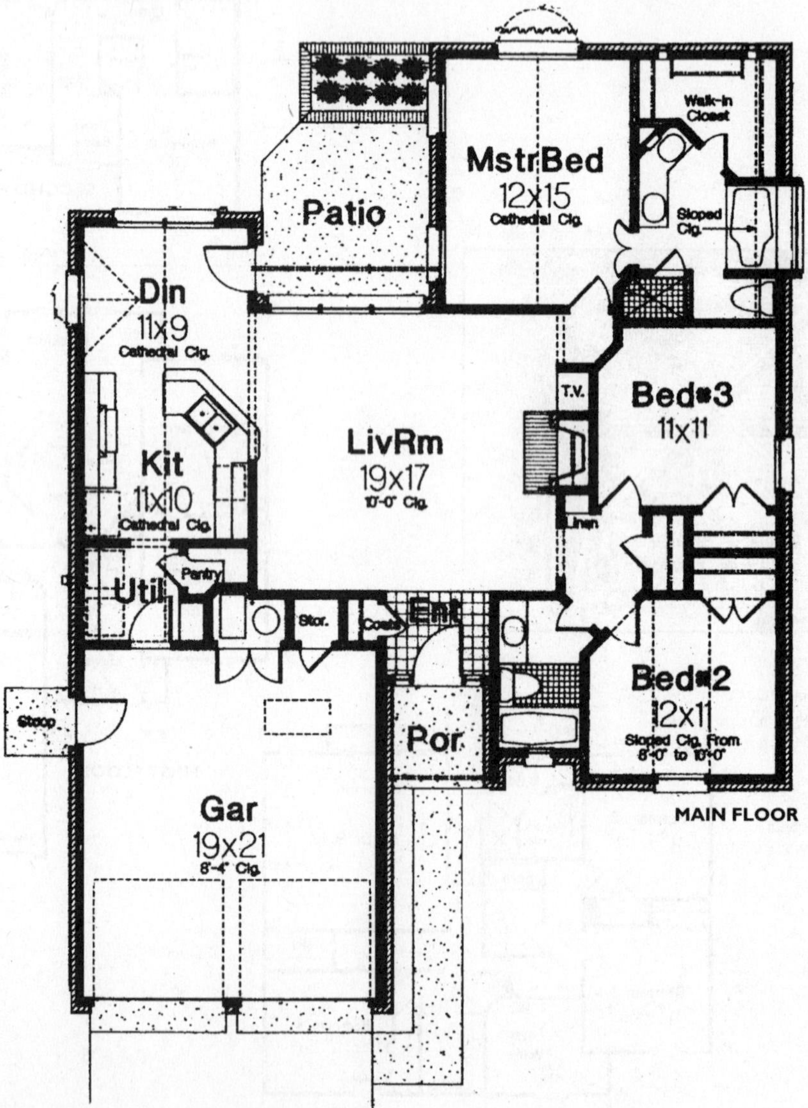
Walk-in Closet
MstrBed
12x15
Cathedral Clg.
Patio
Sloped Clg.
Din
11x9
Cathedral Clg.
T.V.
Bed#3
11x11
LivRm
19x17
10'-0" Clg.
Kit
11x10
Cathedral Clg.
Linen
Pantry
Util
Stor.
Coats
Ent
Bed#2
12x11
Sloped Clg. From 8'-0" to 10'-0"
Stoop
Por
Gar
19x21
8'-4" Clg.

MAIN FLOOR

Design 98435

See Order Pages and Index for Info

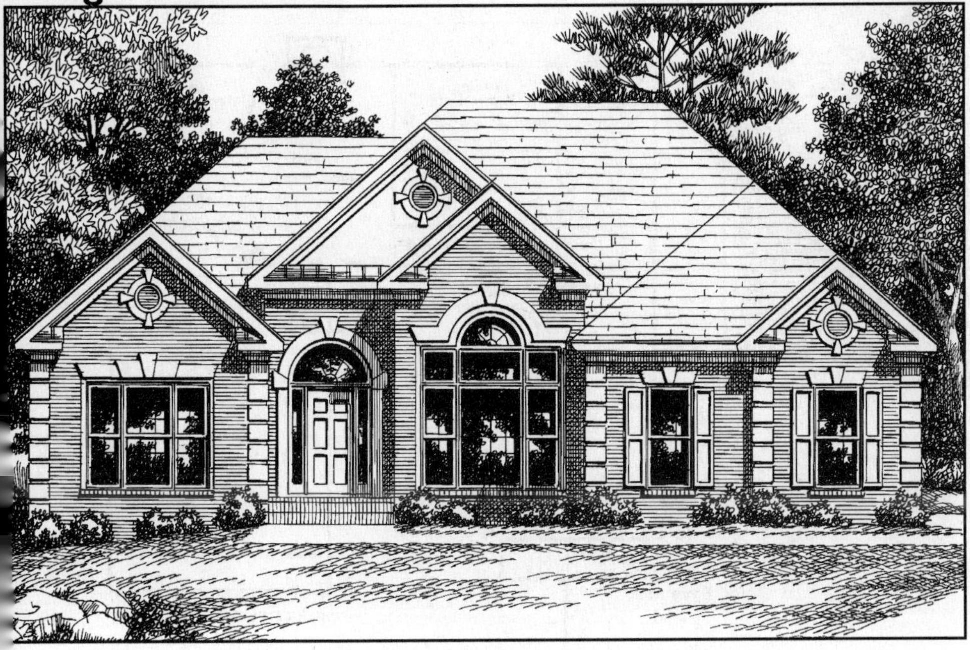

Units	Single
Price Code	C
Total Finished	1,945 sq. ft.
Main Finished	1,945 sq. ft.
Dimensions	56'6"x52'6"
Foundation	Basement Crawlspace
Bedrooms	4
Full Baths	2
Main Ceiling	9'
Max Ridge Height	26'4"
Roof Framing	Stick
Exterior Walls	2x4

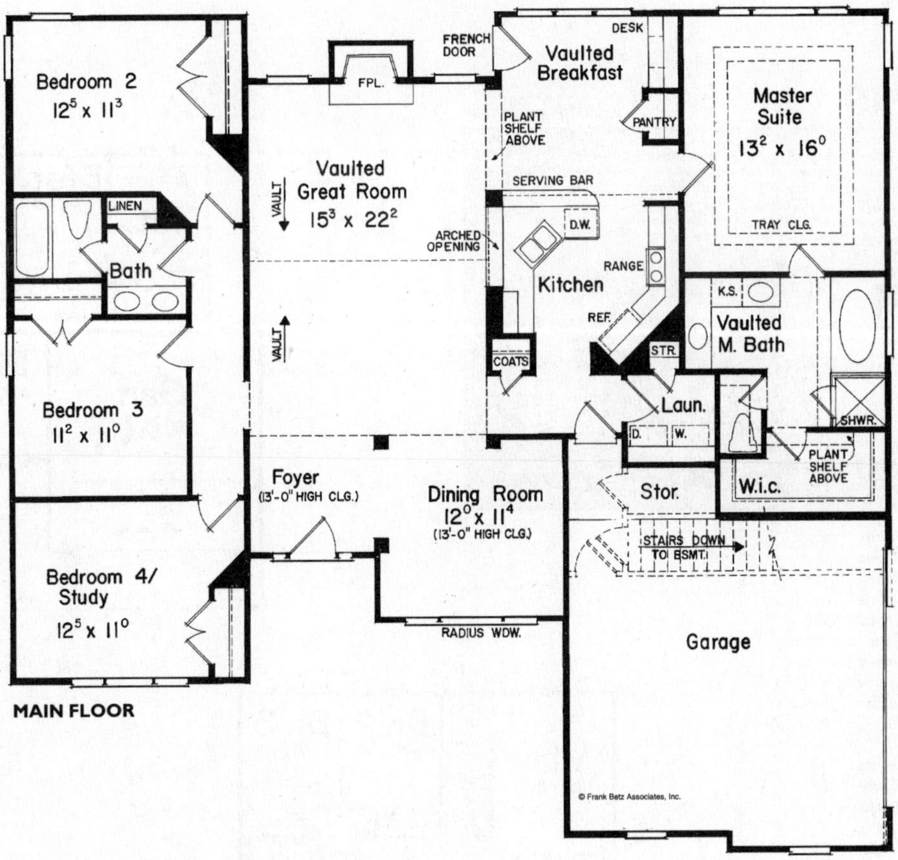
Bedroom 2
12⁵ x 11³
FPL.
FRENCH DOOR
Vaulted Breakfast
DESK
PANTRY
Master Suite
13² x 16⁰
TRAY CLG.
PLANT SHELF ABOVE
VAULT
Vaulted Great Room
15³ x 22²
SERVING BAR
LINEN
Bath
D.W.
ARCHED OPENING
RANGE
Kitchen
REF.
K.S.
Vaulted M. Bath
STR
COATS
VAULT
Bedroom 3
11² x 11⁰
Laun.
D.
W.
SHWR.
PLANT SHELF ABOVE
Foyer
(13'-0" HIGH CLG.)
Dining Room
12⁰ x 11⁴
(13'-0" HIGH CLG.)
Stor.
W.i.c.
STAIRS DOWN TO BSMT.
Bedroom 4/ Study
12⁵ x 11⁰
RADIUS WDW.
Garage
MAIN FLOOR
© Frank Betz Associates, Inc.

Design 97678

See Order Pages and Index for Info

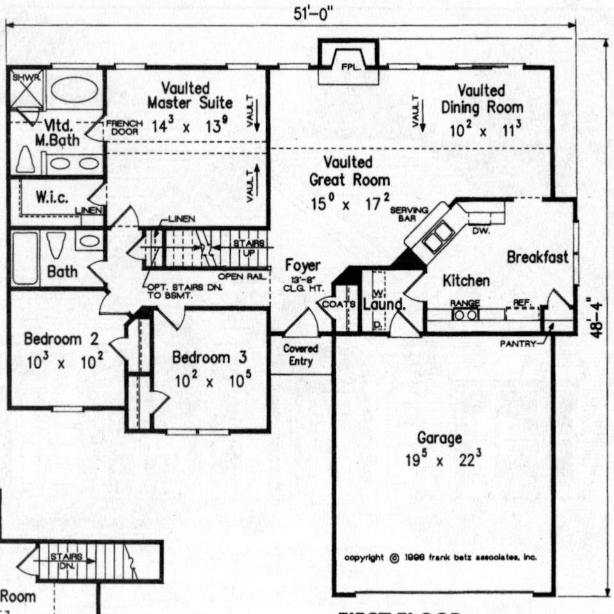
51'-0"
48'-4"
SHWR.
Vltd. M.Bath
FRENCH DOOR
Vaulted Master Suite
14^3 x 13^9
VAULT
FPL.
Vaulted Great Room
15^0 x 17^2
Vaulted Dining Room
10^2 x 11^3
W.i.c.
LINEN
Bath
STAIRS UP
OPEN RAIL
OPT. STAIRS DN. TO BSMT.
SERVING BAR
DW.
Breakfast
Foyer
13'-8" CLG. HT.
COATS
Laund.
Kitchen
RANGE
REF.
PANTRY
Bedroom 2
10^3 x 10^2
Bedroom 3
10^2 x 10^5
Covered Entry
Garage
19^5 x 22^3
copyright © 1998 frank betz associates, inc.

FIRST FLOOR

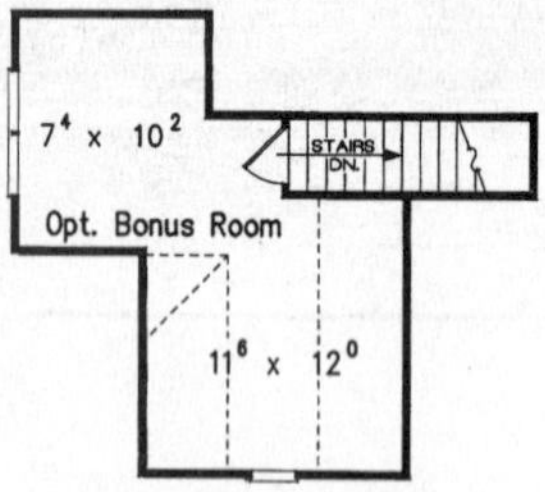
7^4 x 10^2
STAIRS DN.
Opt. Bonus Room
11^6 x 12^0

SECOND FLOOR

Units	Single
Price Code	A
Total Finished	1,354 sq. ft.
First Finished	1,354 sq. ft.
Bonus Unfinished	246 sq. ft.
Basement Unfinished	1,354 sq. ft.
Garage Unfinished	450 sq. ft.
Dimensions	51'x48'4"
Foundation	Basement Crawlspace
Bedrooms	3
Full Baths	2
First Ceiling	8'
Second Ceiling	8'
Max Ridge Height	22'
Roof Framing	Stick
Exterior Walls	2x4

Design 97930

See Order Pages and Index for Info

Photography supplied by Design Basics, Inc.

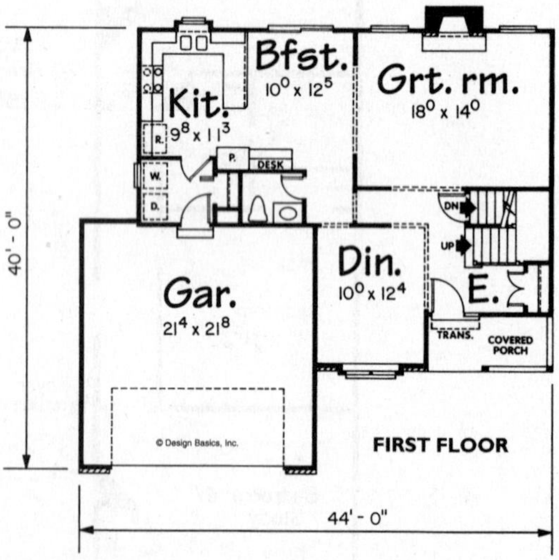
Bfst.
10^0 x 12^5
Grt. rm.
18^0 x 14^0
Kit.
9^8 x 11^3
R.
P.
DESK
W.
D.
DN
UP
Din.
10^0 x 12^4
E.
Gar.
21^4 x 21^8
TRANS.
COVERED PORCH
40' - 0"
44' - 0"
© Design Basics, Inc.

FIRST FLOOR

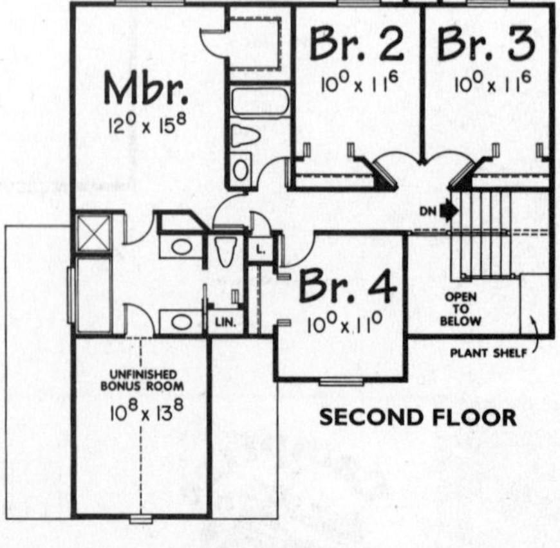
Mbr.
12^0 x 15^8
Br. 2
10^0 x 11^6
Br. 3
10^0 x 11^6
DN
L.
Br. 4
10^0 x 11^0
LIN.
OPEN TO BELOW
PLANT SHELF
UNFINISHED BONUS ROOM
10^8 x 13^8

SECOND FLOOR

Units	Single
Price Code	C
Total Finished	1,844 sq. ft.
First Finished	924 sq. ft.
Second Finished	920 sq. ft.
Bonus Unfinished	159 sq. ft.
Garage Unfinished	483 sq. ft.
Dimensions	44'x40'
Foundation	Basement Crawlspace Slab
Bedrooms	4
Full Baths	2
Half Baths	1
First Ceiling	8'
Max Ridge Height	26'2"
Roof Framing	Stick
Exterior Walls	2x4

* Alternate foundation options available at an additional charge.
Please call 1-800-235-5700 for more information.

Design 97433

See Order Pages and Index for Info

Units	Single
Price Code	D
Total Finished	2,119 sq. ft.
First Finished	1,086 sq. ft.
Second Finished	1,033 sq. ft.
Bonus Unfinished	215 sq. ft.
Garage Unfinished	547 sq. ft.
Dimensions	56'x38'
Foundation	Basement
Bedrooms	4
Full Baths	2
Half Baths	1
First Ceiling	8'
Max Ridge Height	24'8"
Roof Framing	Stick
Exterior Walls	2x4

* Alternate foundation options available at an additional charge.
Please call 1-800-235-5700 for more information.

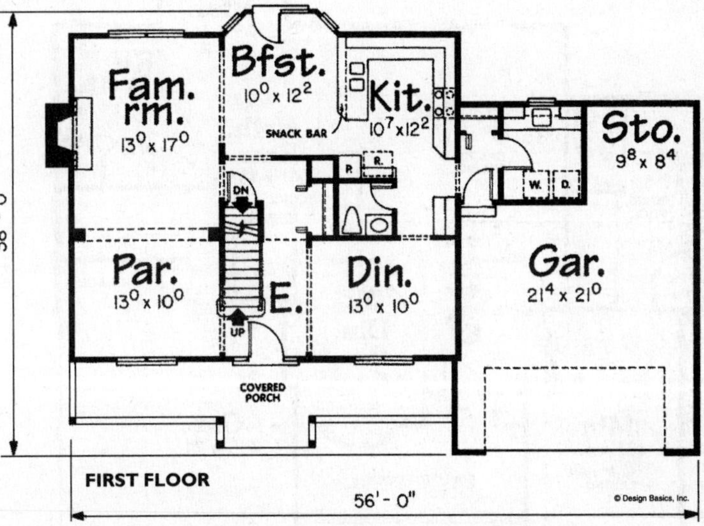
Fam. rm.
13⁰ x 17⁰
Bfst.
10⁰ x 12²
Kit.
10⁷x12²
SNACK BAR
Sto.
9⁸ x 8⁴
W.
D.
P.
R.
DN
UP
Par.
13⁰ x 10⁰
E.
Din.
13⁰ x 10⁰
Gar.
21⁴ x 21⁰
COVERED PORCH
38' - 0"
56' - 0"
© Design Basics, Inc.

FIRST FLOOR

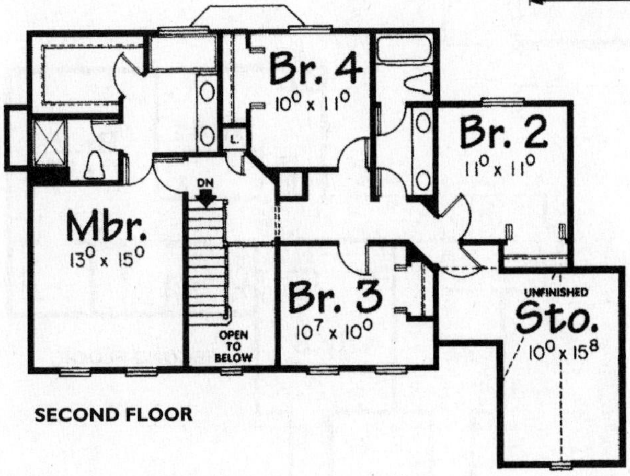
Br. 4
10⁰ x 11⁰
L.
Br. 2
11⁰ x 11⁰
DN
Mbr.
13⁰ x 15⁰
Br. 3
10⁷ x 10⁰
OPEN TO BELOW
UNFINISHED
Sto.
10⁰ x 15⁸

SECOND FLOOR

Design 97438

See Order Pages and Index for Info

Units	Single
Price Code	F
Total Finished	2,512 sq. ft.
First Finished	1,795 sq. ft.
Second Finished	717 sq. ft.
Garage Unfinished	472 sq. ft.
Dimensions	57'x51'
Foundation	Basement
Bedrooms	4
Full Baths	2
Half Baths	1
Max Ridge Height	30'
Roof Framing	Stick
Exterior Walls	2x4

* Alternate foundation options available at an additional charge. Please call 1-800-235-5700 for more information.

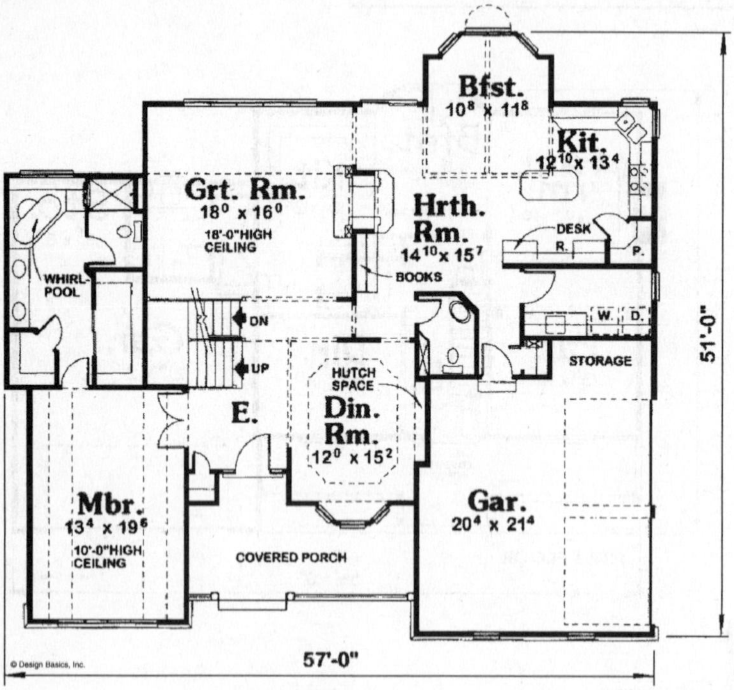

Bfst.
10⁸ x 11⁸
Kit.
12¹⁰ x 13⁴
Grt. Rm.
18⁰ x 16⁰
18'-0"HIGH CEILING
Hrth. Rm.
14¹⁰ x 15⁷
DESK
R.
P.
BOOKS
WHIRL-POOL
DN
UP
W.
D.
STORAGE
HUTCH SPACE
Din. Rm.
12⁰ x 15²
E.
Mbr.
13⁴ x 19⁶
10'-0"HIGH CEILING
COVERED PORCH
Gar.
20⁴ x 21⁴
51'-0"
57'-0"
© Design Basics, Inc.

FIRST FLOOR

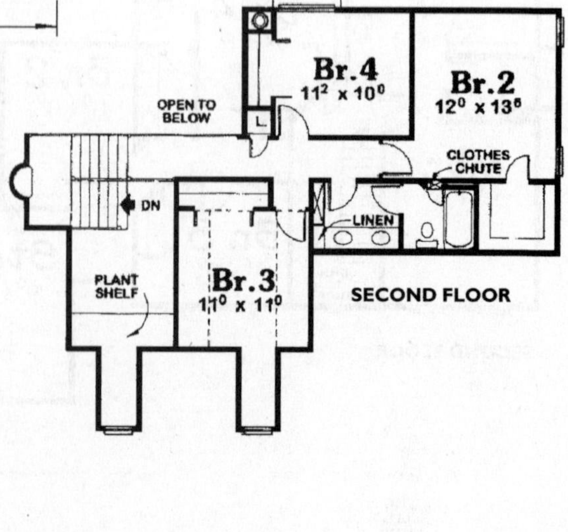

Br.4
11² x 10⁰
Br.2
12⁰ x 13⁶
OPEN TO BELOW
L
CLOTHES CHUTE
DN
LINEN
PLANT SHELF
Br.3
11⁰ x 11⁰

SECOND FLOOR

Design 97269

See Order Pages and Index for Info

Units	Single
Price Code	E
Total Finished	2,398 sq. ft.
First Finished	1,290 sq. ft.
Second Finished	1,108 sq. ft.
Bonus Unfinished	399 sq. ft.
Basement Unfinished	1,290 sq. ft.
Garage Unfinished	504 sq. ft.
Dimensions	67'4"x38'6"
Foundation	Basement Crawlspace
Bedrooms	4
Full Baths	2
Half Baths	1
First Ceiling	9'
Second Ceiling	8'
Max Ridge Height	33'
Roof Framing	Stick
Exterior Walls	2x4

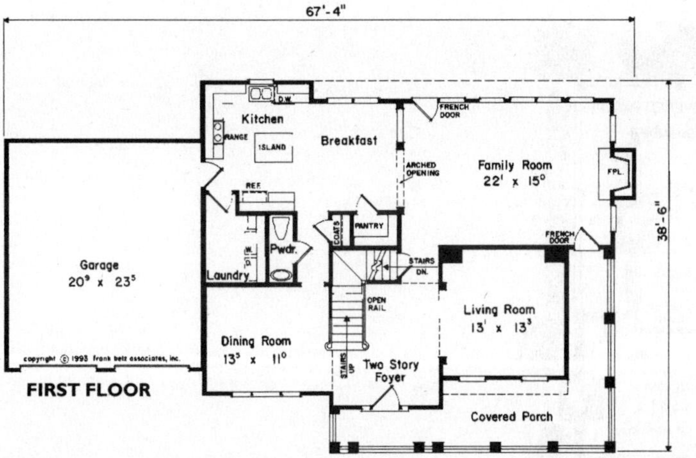

67'-4"
38'-6"
Kitchen
D.W.
RANGE
ISLAND
Breakfast
FRENCH DOOR
ARCHED OPENING
Family Room
22' x 15°
FPL.
REF.
PANTRY
COATS
FRENCH DOOR
Garage
20⁹ x 23⁵
W.
D.
Pwdr.
Laundry
STAIRS DN.
OPEN RAIL
Living Room
13' x 13³
Dining Room
13⁵ x 11°
STAIRS UP
Two Story Foyer
Covered Porch
copyright © 1993 frank betz associates, inc.

FIRST FLOOR

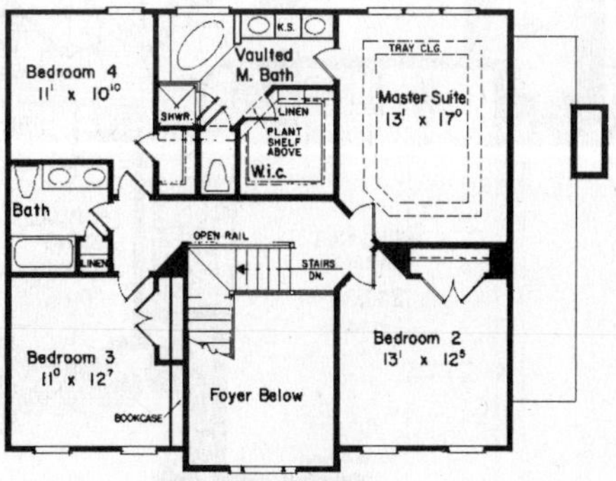

Bedroom 4
11' x 10¹⁰
K.S.
Vaulted M. Bath
TRAY CLG.
Master Suite
13' x 17°
SHWR.
LINEN
PLANT SHELF ABOVE
W.i.c.
Bath
LINEN
OPEN RAIL
STAIRS DN.
Bedroom 3
11° x 12⁷
BOOKCASE
Foyer Below
Bedroom 2
13' x 12⁵

SECOND FLOOR

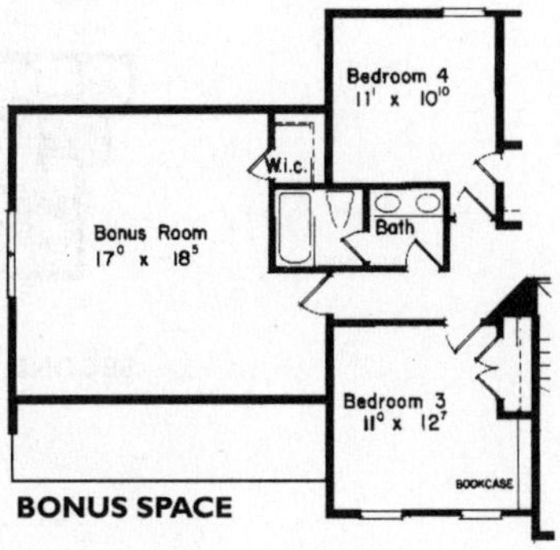

Bedroom 4
11' x 10¹⁰
W.i.c.
Bath
Bonus Room
17° x 18⁵
Bedroom 3
11° x 12⁷
BOOKCASE

BONUS SPACE

Design 98596

See Order Pages and Index for Info

Units	Single
Price Code	H
Total Finished	3,062 sq. ft.
First Finished	2,115 sq. ft.
Second Finished	947 sq. ft.
Bonus Unfinished	195 sq. ft.
Garage Unfinished	635 sq. ft.
Porch Unfinished	32 sq. ft.
Dimensions	68'10"x58'1"
Foundation	Basement Crawlspace Slab
Bedrooms	4
Full Baths	3
Half Baths	1
First Ceiling	10'
Second Ceiling	8'
Max Ridge Height	32'6"
Roof Framing	Stick
Exterior Walls	2x4

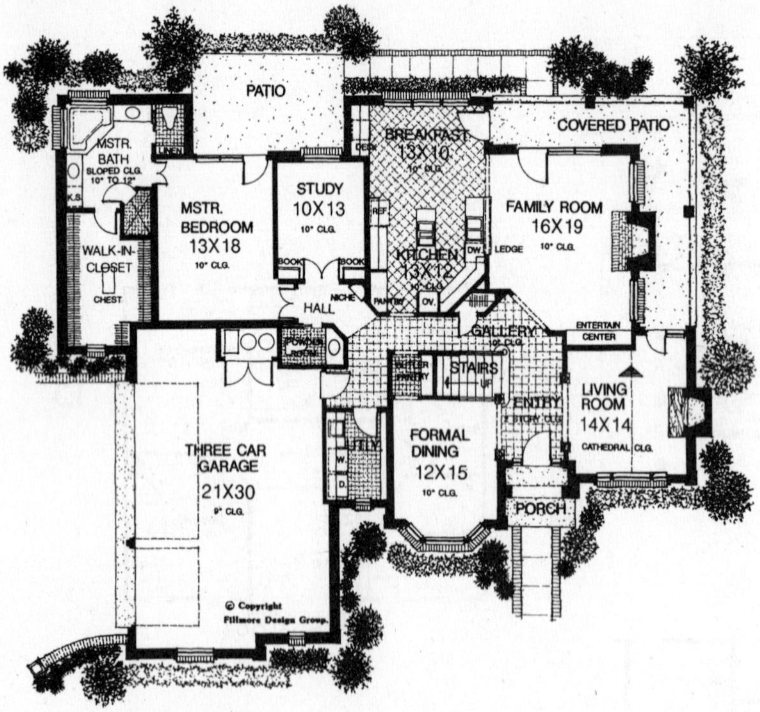
PATIO
BREAKFAST 13X10
COVERED PATIO
MSTR. BATH SLOPED CLG. 10" TO 12"
MSTR. BEDROOM 13X18 10" CLG.
STUDY 10X13 10" CLG.
FAMILY ROOM 16X19 10" CLG.
WALK-IN-CLOSET
CHEST
BOOK
BOOK
KITCHEN 13X12
LEDGE
HALL
NICHE
PANTRY
OV.
GALLERY
ENTERTAIN CENTER
STAIRS
ENTRY
LIVING ROOM 14X14 CATHEDRAL CLG.
THREE CAR GARAGE 21X30 9" CLG.
UTILITY
FORMAL DINING 12X15 10" CLG.
PORCH
© Copyright Fillmore Design Group.

FIRST FLOOR

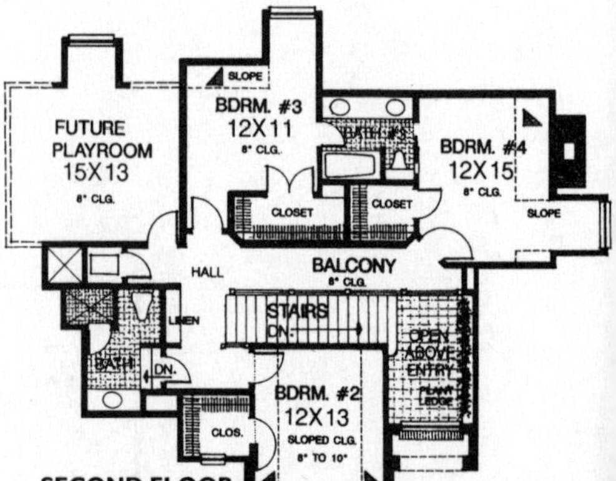
SLOPE
FUTURE PLAYROOM 15X13 8" CLG.
BDRM. #3 12X11 8" CLG.
BATH #3
BDRM. #4 12X15 8" CLG.
CLOSET
CLOSET
SLOPE
HALL
BALCONY 8" CLG.
STAIRS
DN.
LINEN
BATH
DN.
OPEN ABOVE ENTRY
PLANT LEDGE
CLOS.
BDRM. #2 12X13 SLOPED CLG. 8" TO 10"

SECOND FLOOR

Design 63067

See Order Pages and Index for Info

Units	Single
Price Code	I
Total Finished	3,064 sq. ft.
Main Finished	3,064 sq. ft.
Bonus Unfinished	366 sq. ft.
Garage Unfinished	716 sq. ft.
Dimensions	79'6"x91'
Foundation	Slab
Bedrooms	4
Full Baths	4
Main Ceiling	10'-12'
Second Ceiling	8'
Max Ridge Height	24'4"
Roof Framing	Truss

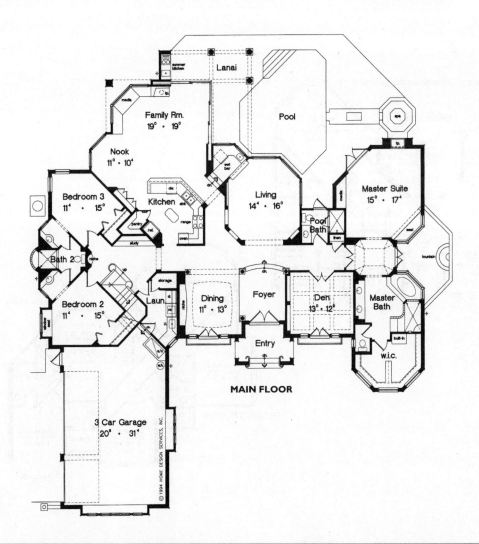

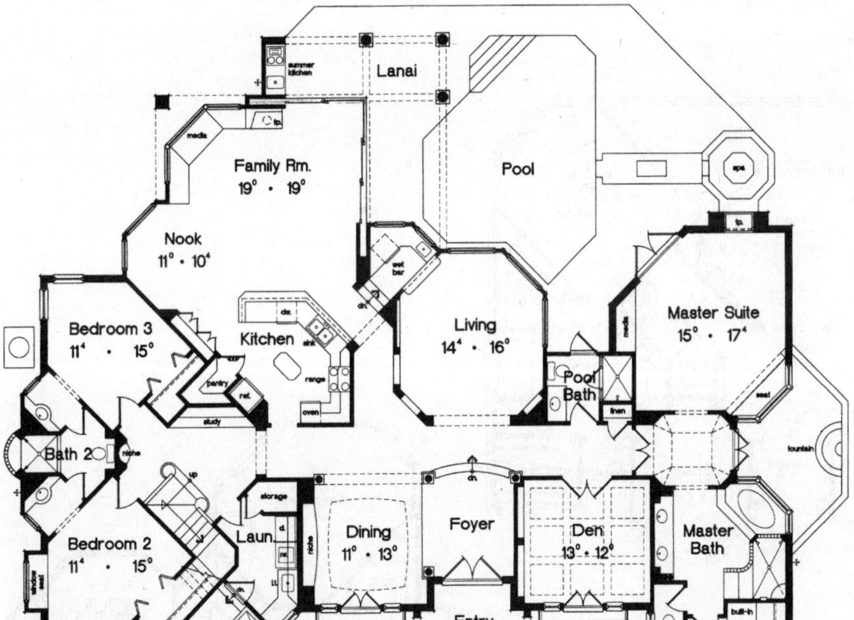
Lanai
Pool
Family Rm.
19^0 · 19^0
Nook
11^0 · 10^4
Bedroom 3
11^4 · 15^0
Kitchen
Living
14^4 · 16^0
Master Suite
15^0 · 17^4
Pool Bath
Bath 2
Bedroom 2
11^4 · 15^0
Laun.
Dining
11^0 · 13^0
Foyer
Den
13^0 · 12^6
Master Bath
Entry
W.I.C.
3 Car Garage
20^8 · 31^4
© 1994 HOME DESIGN SERVICES, INC.

MAIN FLOOR

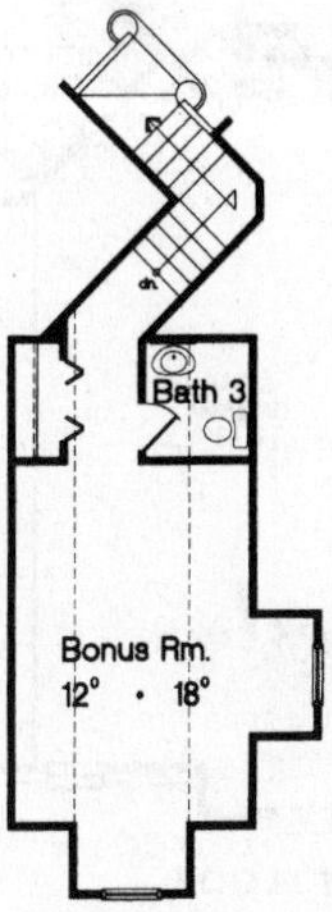
Bath 3
Bonus Rm.
12^0 · 18^0

BONUS

Design 97400

See Order Pages and Index for Info

Units	Single
Price Code	H
Total Finished	3,094 sq. ft.
First Finished	2,112 sq. ft.
Second Finished	982 sq. ft.
Basement Unfinished	2,112 sq. ft.
Garage Unfinished	650 sq. ft.
Dimensions	67'1"x65'10.1"
Foundation	Basement Slab
Bedrooms	4
Full Baths	3
Half Baths	1
First Ceiling	9'
Max Ridge Height	30'4"
Roof Framing	Stick
Exterior Walls	2x4

* Alternate foundation options available at an additional charge. Please call 1-800-235-5700 for more information.

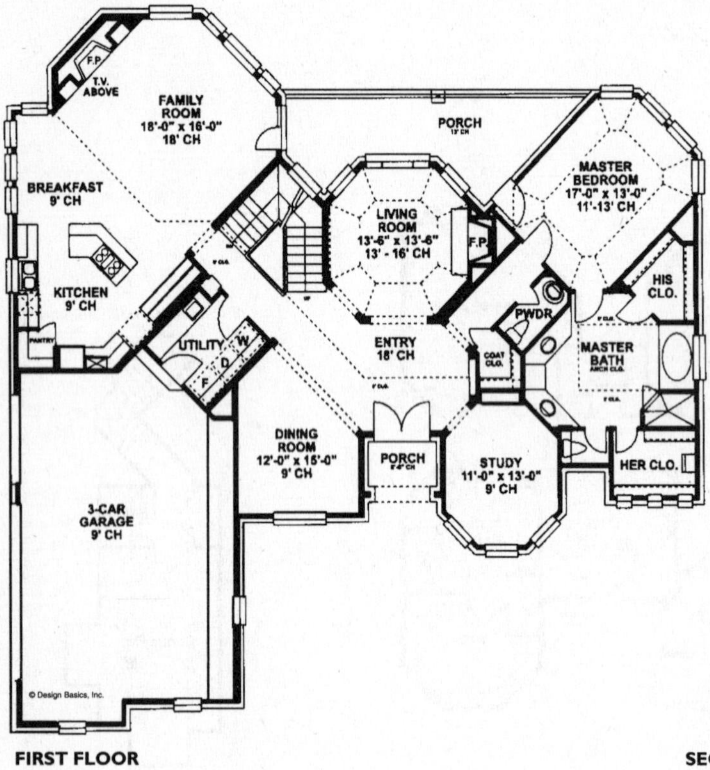
F.P.
T.V. ABOVE
FAMILY ROOM 18'-0" x 16'-0" 18' CH
BREAKFAST 9' CH
KITCHEN 9' CH
PANTRY
UTILITY
W
D
F
PORCH
LIVING ROOM 13'-6" x 13'-6" 13' - 16' CH
F.P.
MASTER BEDROOM 17'-0" x 13'-0" 11'-13' CH
HIS CLO.
PWDR
ENTRY 18' CH
COAT CLO.
MASTER BATH
DINING ROOM 12'-0" x 15'-0" 9' CH
PORCH
STUDY 11'-0" x 13'-0" 9' CH
HER CLO.
3-CAR GARAGE 9' CH
© Design Basics, Inc.

FIRST FLOOR

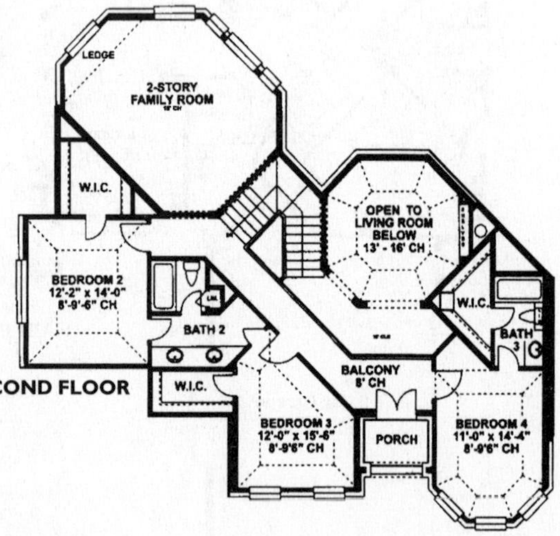
LEDGE
2-STORY FAMILY ROOM
W.I.C.
BEDROOM 2 12'-2" x 14'-0" 8'-9'-6" CH
BATH 2
W.I.C.
OPEN TO LIVING ROOM BELOW 13' - 16' CH
W.I.C.
BATH 3
BALCONY 8' CH
BEDROOM 3 12'-0" x 15'-6" 8'-9'6" CH
PORCH
BEDROOM 4 11'-0" x 14'-4" 8'-9'6" CH

SECOND FLOOR

Design 97449

See Order Pages and Index for Info

Units	Single
Price Code	C
Total Finished	1,996 sq. ft.
First Finished	1,398 sq. ft.
Second Finished	598 sq. ft.
Garage Unfinished	460 sq. ft.
Dimensions	54'x50'8"
Foundation	Basement
Bedrooms	4
Full Baths	2
Half Baths	1
First Ceiling	8'
Max Ridge Height	24'10"
Roof Framing	Stick
Exterior Walls	2x4

* Alternate foundation options available at an additional charge. Please call 1-800-235-5700 for more information.

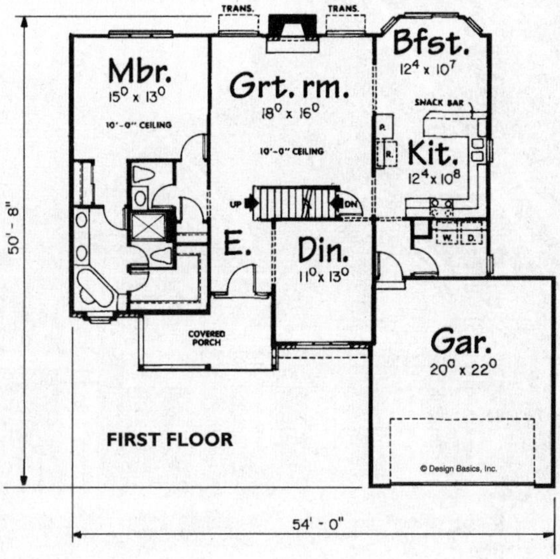
TRANS.
TRANS.
Mbr.
15⁰ x 13⁰
10'-0" CEILING
Grt. rm.
18⁰ x 16⁰
10'-0" CEILING
Bfst.
12⁴ x 10⁷
SNACK BAR
Kit.
12⁴ x 10⁸
UP
DN
E.
Din.
11⁰ x 13⁰
COVERED PORCH
Gar.
20⁰ x 22⁰
50' - 8"
54' - 0"
© Design Basics, Inc.

FIRST FLOOR

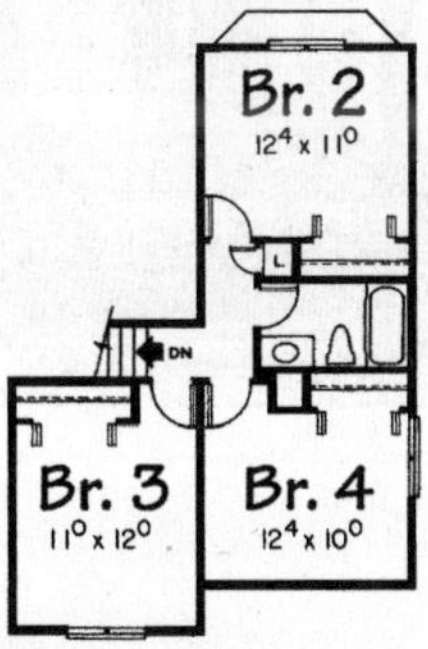
Br. 2
12⁴ x 11⁰
DN
Br. 3
11⁰ x 12⁰
Br. 4
12⁴ x 10⁰

SECOND FLOOR

Design 97777

See Order Pages and Index for Info

Units	Single
Price Code	C
Total Finished	1,861 sq. ft.
Main Finished	1,861 sq. ft.
Basement Unfinished	1,861 sq. ft.
Garage Unfinished	433 sq. ft.
Porch Unfinished	21 sq. ft.
Dimensions	50'8"x59'10"
Foundation	Basement
Bedrooms	3
Full Baths	2
Main Ceiling	9'
Tray Ceiling	10'
Max Ridge Height	23'
Roof Framing	Truss
Exterior Walls	2x4

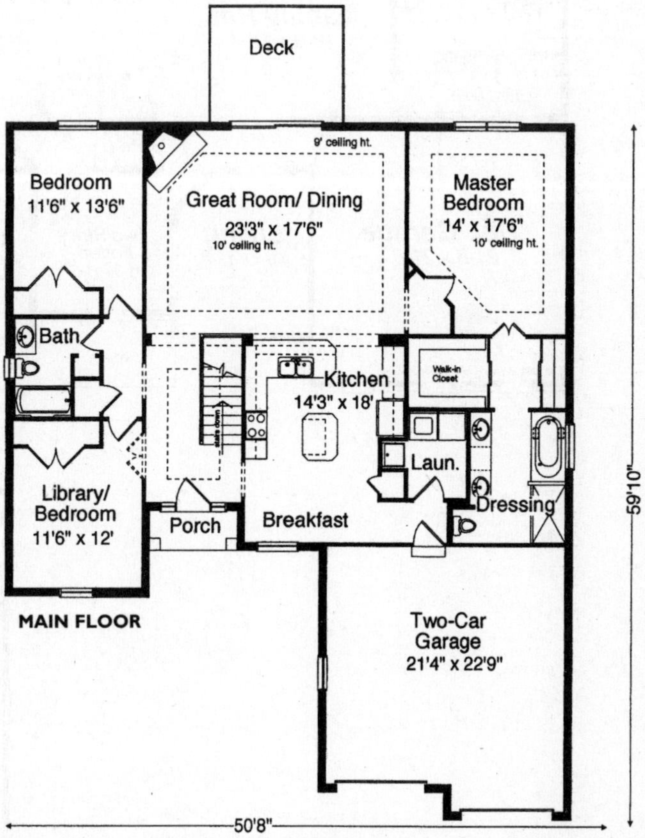
Deck
9' ceiling ht.
Bedroom
11'6" x 13'6"
Great Room/ Dining
23'3" x 17'6"
10' ceiling ht.
Master
Bedroom
14' x 17'6"
10' ceiling ht.
Bath
Kitchen
14'3" x 18'
Walk-in Closet
Laun.
Library/
Bedroom
11'6" x 12'
Porch
Breakfast
Dressing
Two-Car
Garage
21'4" x 22'9"
59'10"
50'8"

MAIN FLOOR

Design 98929

See Order Pages and Index for Info

Units	Single
Price Code	H
Total Finished	3,140 sq. ft.
First Finished	1,553 sq. ft.
Second Finished	1,587 sq. ft.
Basement Unfinished	1,553 sq. ft.
Garage Unfinished	485 sq. ft.
Porch Unfinished	73 sq. ft.
Dimensions	58'x40'4"
Foundation	Basement
Bedrooms	5
Full Baths	4
First Ceiling	9'
Second Ceiling	8'
Max Ridge Height	34'
Roof Framing	Stick
Exterior Walls	2x4

FIRST FLOOR

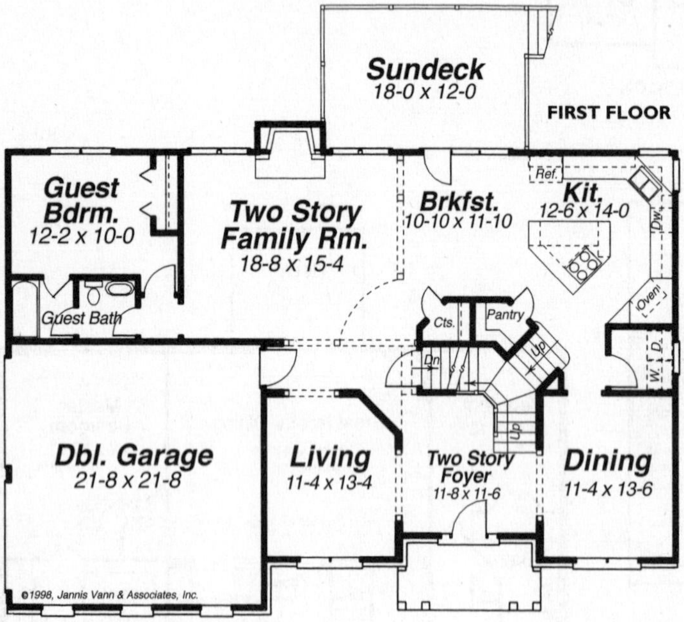
Sundeck
18-0 x 12-0
Guest Bdrm.
12-2 x 10-0
Two Story Family Rm.
18-8 x 15-4
Brkfst.
10-10 x 11-10
Kit.
12-6 x 14-0
Ref.
Dw.
Oven
Cts.
Pantry
Dn
Up
W. D.
Guest Bath
Dbl. Garage
21-8 x 21-8
Living
11-4 x 13-4
Two Story Foyer
11-8 x 11-6
Dining
11-4 x 13-6
©1998, Jannis Vann & Associates, Inc.

SECOND FLOOR

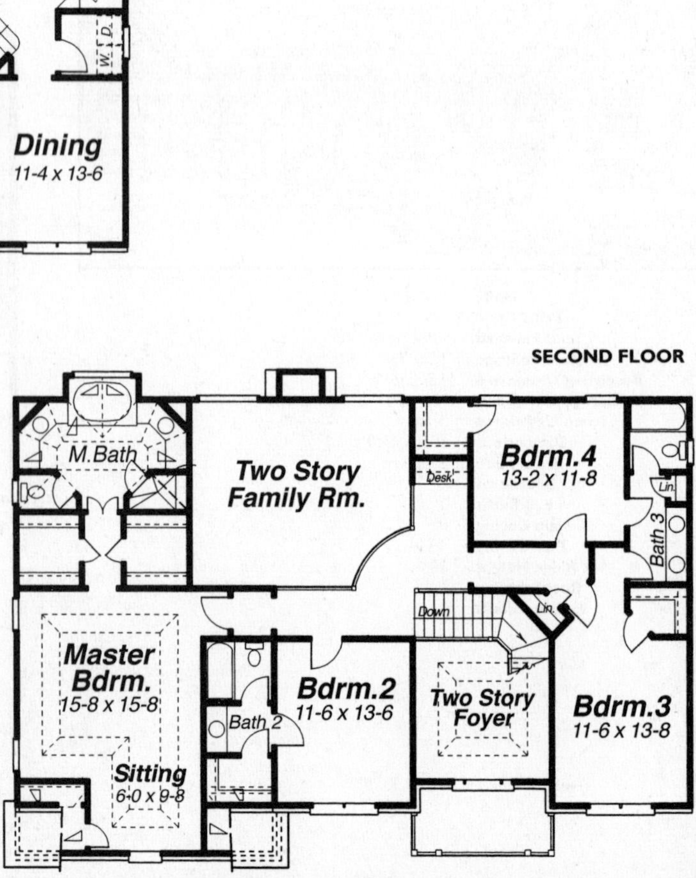
M.Bath
Two Story Family Rm.
Desk
Bdrm.4
13-2 x 11-8
Lin.
Bath 3
Down
Lin.
Master Bdrm.
15-8 x 15-8
Bath 2
Bdrm.2
11-6 x 13-6
Two Story Foyer
Bdrm.3
11-6 x 13-8
Sitting
6-0 x 9-8

Design 97748

See Order Pages and Index for Info

Units	Single
Price Code	E
Total Finished	2,286 sq. ft.
First Finished	1,625 sq. ft.
Second Finished	661 sq. ft.
Basement Unfinished	1,625 sq. ft.
Garage Unfinished	469 sq. ft.
Porch Unfinished	26 sq. ft.
Dimensions	56'8"x46'8"
Foundation	Basement
Bedrooms	3
Full Baths	2
Half Baths	1
First Ceiling	8'
Second Ceiling	8'
Max Ridge Height	30'
Roof Framing	Truss
Exterior Walls	2x4

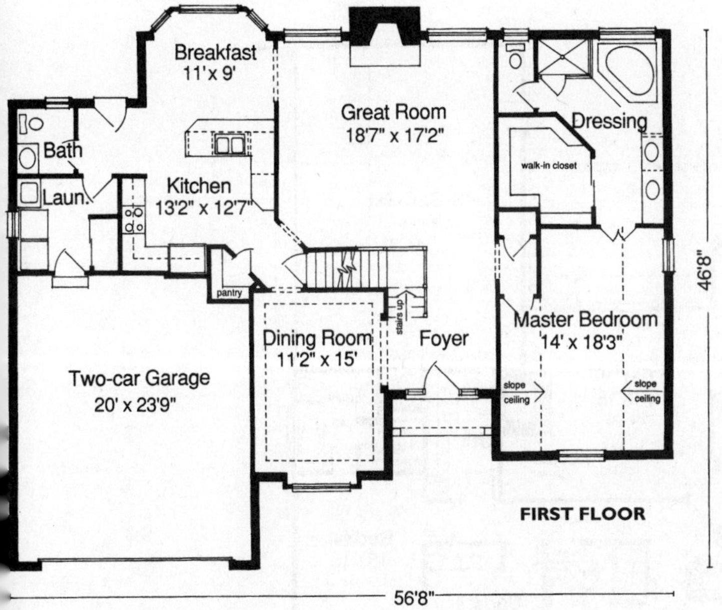
Breakfast
11'x 9'
Great Room
18'7" x 17'2"
Dressing
walk-in closet
Bath
Laun.
Kitchen
13'2" x 12'7"
pantry
stairs up
Dining Room
11'2" x 15'
Foyer
Master Bedroom
14' x 18'3"
slope ceiling
slope ceiling
Two-car Garage
20' x 23'9"
46'8"
56'8"

FIRST FLOOR

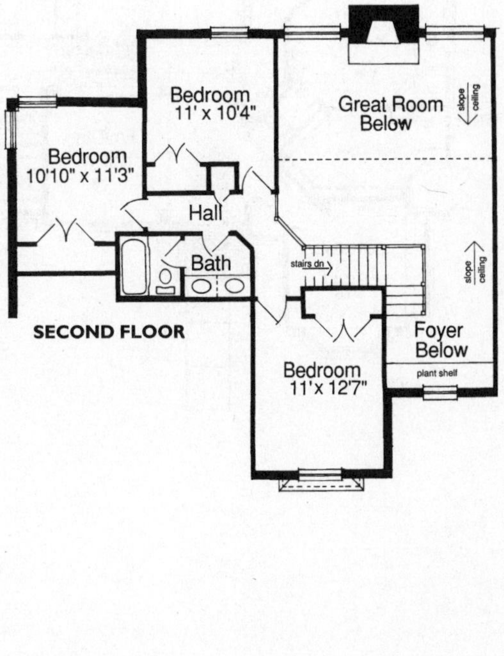
Bedroom
11' x 10'4"
Great Room
Below
slope ceiling
Bedroom
10'10" x 11'3"
Hall
Bath
stairs dn
slope ceiling
Foyer
Below
plant shelf
Bedroom
11'x 12'7"

SECOND FLOOR

Design 98513

See Order Pages and Index for Info

Units	Single
Price Code	I
Total Finished	3,352 sq. ft.
Main Finished	3,352 sq. ft.
Garage Unfinished	672 sq. ft.
Porch Unfinished	60 sq. ft.
Dimensions	91'x71'9"
Foundation	Slab
Bedrooms	4
Full Baths	3
Half Baths	1
Main Ceiling	9'-11'
Max Ridge Height	28'2"
Roof Framing	Stick
Exterior Walls	2x4

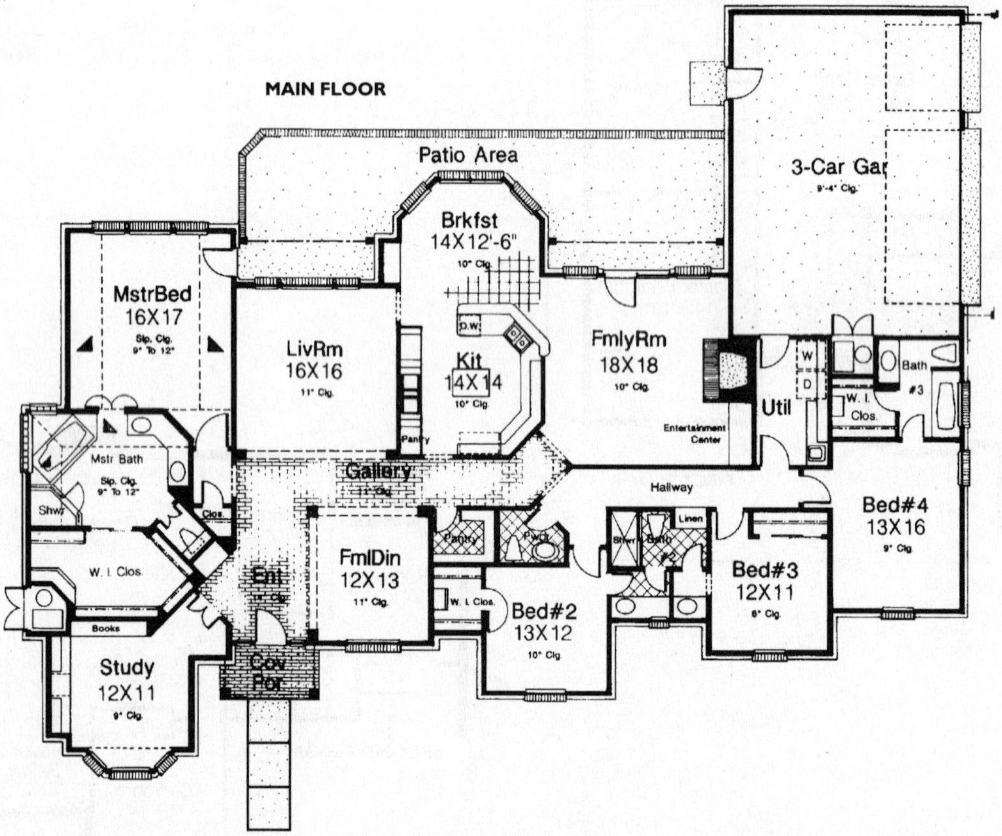
MAIN FLOOR
Patio Area
3-Car Gar
Brkfst
14X12'-6"
MstrBed
16X17
LivRm
16X16
Kit
14X14
FmlyRm
18X18
Entertainment Center
Util
W
D
Bath
#3
W. I. Clos.
Mstr Bath
Shwr
Clos
Gallery
Hallway
Bed#4
13X16
W. I. Clos.
Books
Study
12X11
Ent
FmlDin
12X13
Pantry
Linen
Bed#3
12X11
W. I. Clos.
Bed#2
13X12
Cov Por

Design 98499

See Order Pages and Index for Info

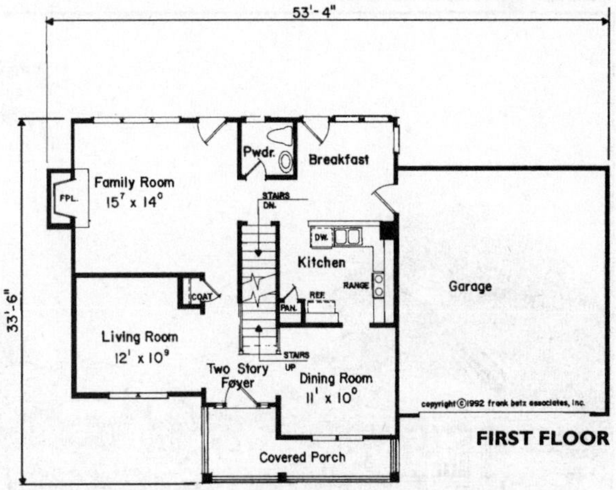

53'-4"
33'-6"
FPL.
Family Room
15' x 14'
Pwdr.
Breakfast
STAIRS DN.
DW.
Kitchen
RANGE
COAT
PAN.
REF.
Garage
Living Room
12' x 10'
Two Story Foyer
STAIRS UP
Dining Room
11' x 10'
Covered Porch
copyright © 1992 frank betz associates, inc.

FIRST FLOOR

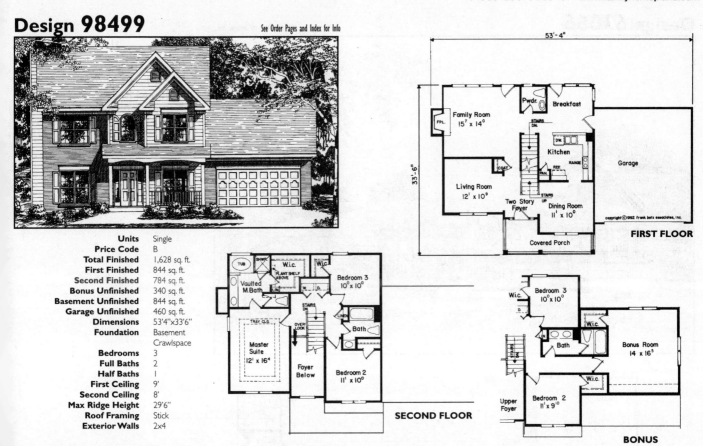

Units	Single
Price Code	B
Total Finished	1,628 sq. ft.
First Finished	844 sq. ft.
Second Finished	784 sq. ft.
Bonus Unfinished	340 sq. ft.
Basement Unfinished	844 sq. ft.
Garage Unfinished	460 sq. ft.
Dimensions	53'4"x33'6"
Foundation	Basement Crawlspace
Bedrooms	3
Full Baths	2
Half Baths	1
First Ceiling	9'
Second Ceiling	8'
Max Ridge Height	29'6"
Roof Framing	Stick
Exterior Walls	2x4

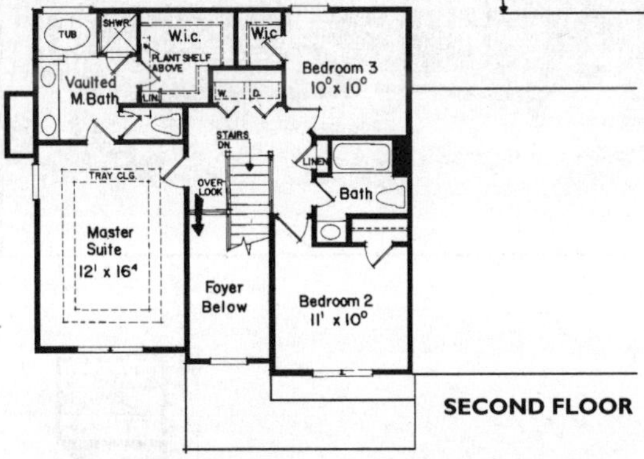

TUB
SHWR.
W.i.c.
W.i.c.
PLANT SHELF ABOVE
Vaulted M.Bath
LIN.
W.
D.
Bedroom 3
10' x 10'
STAIRS DN.
TRAY CLG.
OVER LOOK
LINEN
Bath
Master Suite
12' x 16'
Foyer Below
Bedroom 2
11' x 10'

SECOND FLOOR

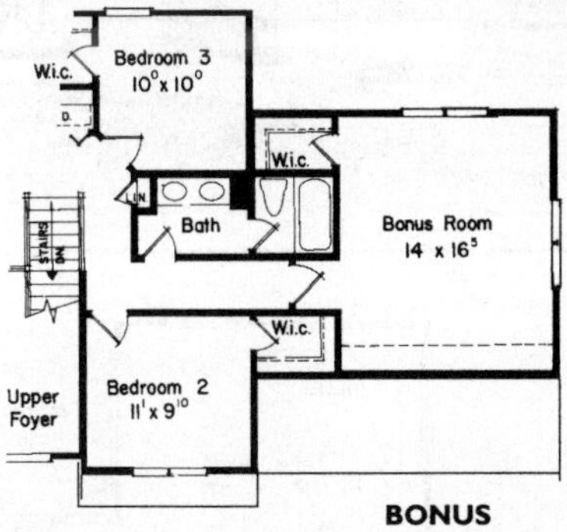

W.i.c.
Bedroom 3
10' x 10'
D.
W.i.c.
LIN.
Bath
Bonus Room
14 x 16
STAIRS DN.
W.i.c.
Upper Foyer
Bedroom 2
11' x 9'

BONUS

Design 99164

See Order Pages and Index for Info

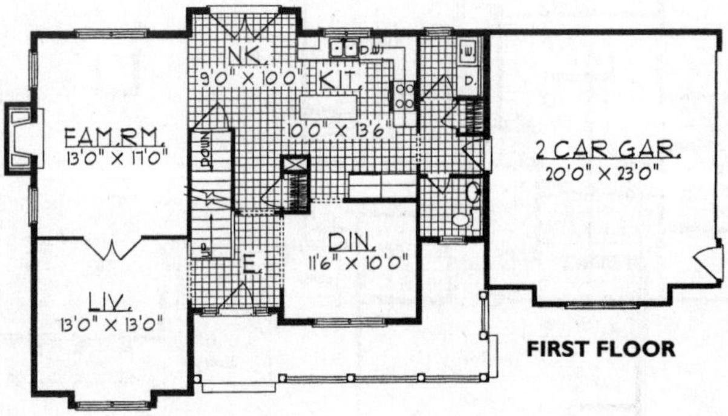

NK.
9'0" X 10'0"
KIT.
10'0" X 13'6"
FAM.RM.
13'0" X 17'0"
DOWN
UP
E.
2 CAR GAR.
20'0" X 23'0"
DIN.
11'6" X 10'0"
LIV.
13'0" X 13'0"

FIRST FLOOR

Units	Single
Price Code	C
Total Finished	1,986 sq. ft.
First Finished	1,065 sq. ft.
Second Finished	921 sq. ft.
Basement Unfinished	1,065 sq. ft.
Dimensions	60'x34'
Foundation	Basement
Bedrooms	3
Full Baths	2
Half Baths	1
Max Ridge Height	27'8"
Roof Framing	Truss
Exterior Walls	2x6

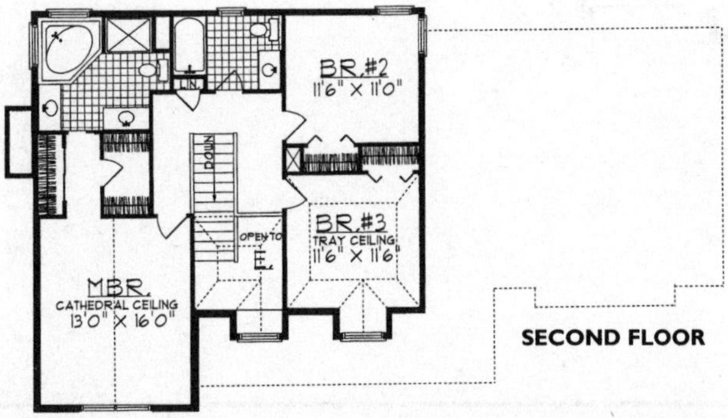

LIN.
BR.#2
11'6" X 11'0"
DOWN
OPEN TO
E.
BR.#3
TRAY CEILING
11'6" X 11'6"
MBR.
CATHEDRAL CEILING
13'0" X 16'0"

SECOND FLOOR

Design 63066

See Order Pages and Index for Info

Units	Single
Price Code	H
Total Finished	3,200 sq. ft.
First Finished	2,531 sq. ft.
Second Finished	669 sq. ft.
Garage Unfinished	656 sq. ft.
Dimensions	70'x82'4"
Foundation	Slab
Bedrooms	4
Full Baths	3
Half Baths	2
Max Ridge Height	26'10"

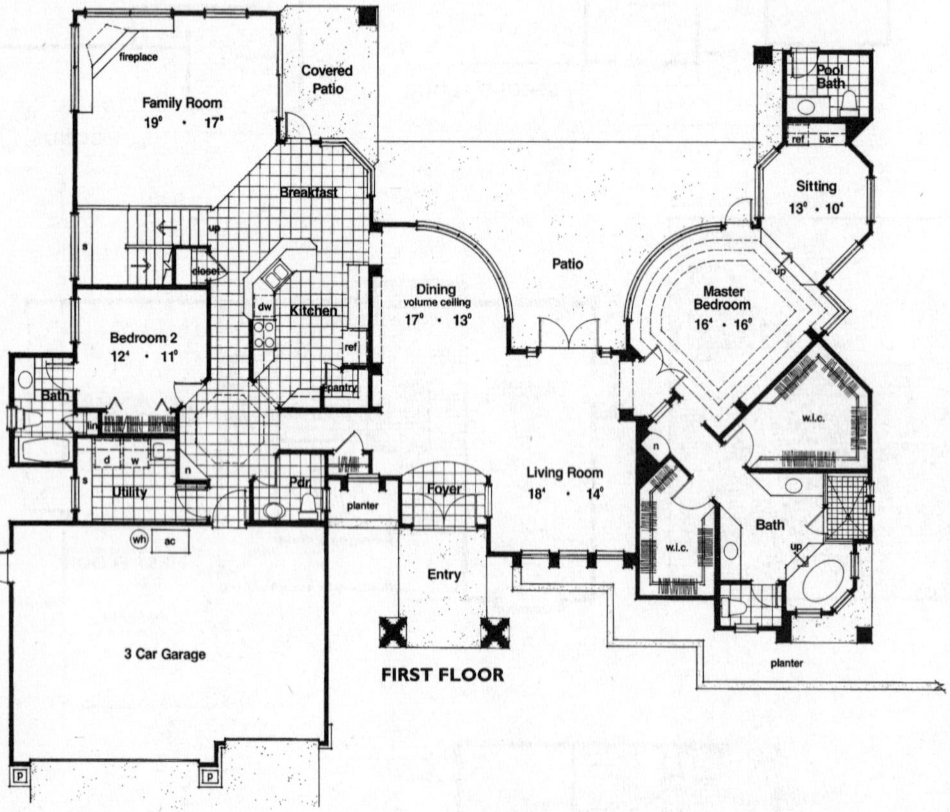
fireplace
Family Room
$19^0 \cdot 17^8$
Covered Patio
Breakfast
up
closet
dw
Kitchen
ref
pantry
Dining
volume ceiling
$17^0 \cdot 13^0$
Patio
Pool Bath
ref bar
Sitting
$13^0 \cdot 10^4$
up
Master Bedroom
$16^4 \cdot 16^0$
w.i.c.
Bedroom 2
$12^4 \cdot 11^0$
Bath
lin
d w
n
Utility
Pdr.
planter
Foyer
Living Room
$18^4 \cdot 14^0$
n
w.i.c.
Bath
up
wh ac
Entry
3 Car Garage
planter

FIRST FLOOR

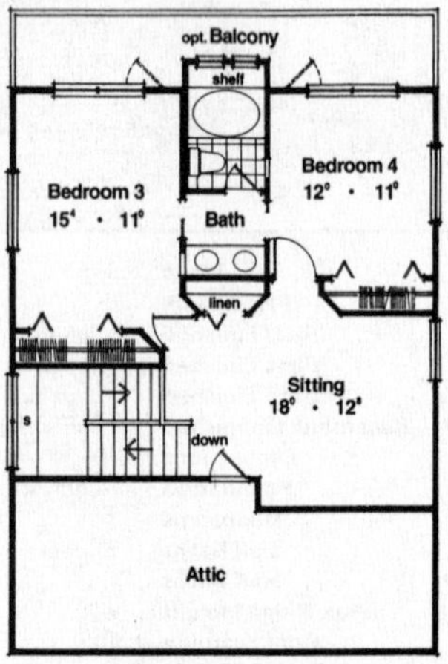
opt. Balcony
shelf
Bedroom 3
$15^4 \cdot 11^0$
Bath
Bedroom 4
$12^0 \cdot 11^0$
linen
Sitting
$18^0 \cdot 12^8$
down
Attic

SECOND FLOOR

Design 63064

See Order Pages and Index for Info

© HOME DESIGN SERVICES, INC.
J.H. HANSEN

Units	Single
Price Code	H
Total Finished	3,164 sq. ft.
First Finished	2,624 sq. ft.
Second Finished	540 sq. ft.
Garage Unfinished	802 sq. ft.
Dimensions	66'x83'
Foundation	Slab
Bedrooms	4
Full Baths	3
3/4 Baths	1
Max Ridge Height	27'
Roof Framing	Truss
Exterior Walls	2x4

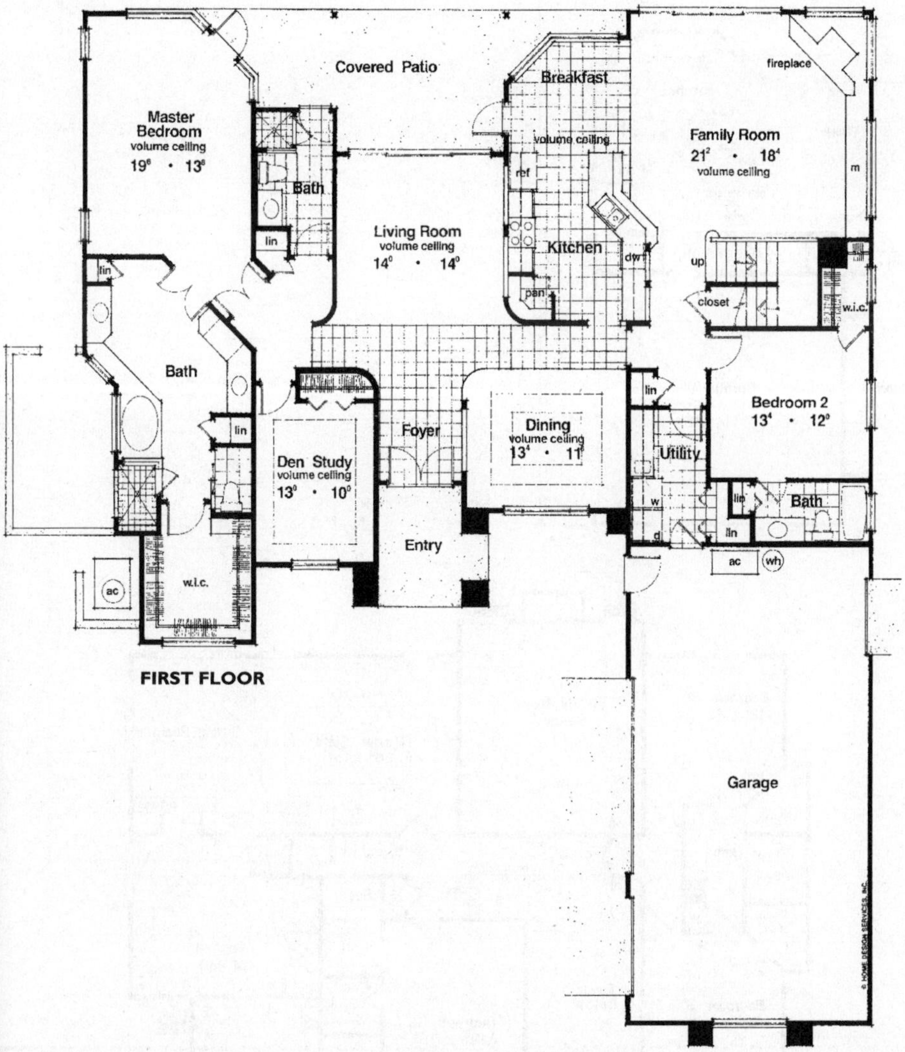
Covered Patio
Breakfast
volume ceiling
fireplace
Master Bedroom
volume ceiling
19^{6} · 13^{6}
Bath
lin
Living Room
volume ceiling
14^{0} · 14^{0}
ref
Kitchen
dw
pan
Family Room
21^{2} · 18^{4}
volume ceiling
up
closet
w.i.c.
Bath
lin
Den Study
volume ceiling
13^{0} · 10^{0}
Foyer
Dining
volume ceiling
13^{4} · 11^{0}
lin
Utility
Bedroom 2
13^{4} · 12^{0}
Bath
lin
w
d
ac
wh
Entry
w.i.c.
ac
Garage

FIRST FLOOR

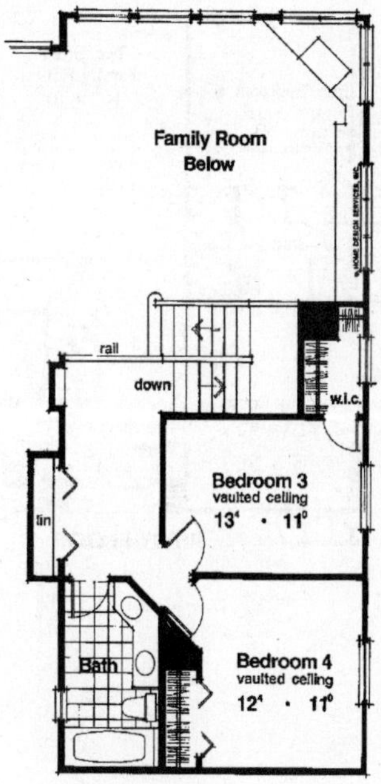
Family Room
Below
rail
down
w.i.c.
Bedroom 3
vaulted ceiling
13^{4} · 11^{0}
lin
Bath
Bedroom 4
vaulted ceiling
12^{4} · 11^{0}

SECOND FLOOR

Design 98401

See Order Pages and Index for Info

Units	Single
Price Code	H
Total Finished	3,219 sq. ft.
First Finished	1,665 sq. ft.
Second Finished	1,554 sq. ft.
Basement Unfinished	1,665 sq. ft.
Garage Unfinished	462 sq. ft.
Dimensions	58'6"x44'10"
Foundation	Basement Crawlspace
Bedrooms	5
Full Baths	4
First Ceiling	9'
Second Ceiling	8'
Max Ridge Height	33'
Roof Framing	Stick
Exterior Walls	2x4

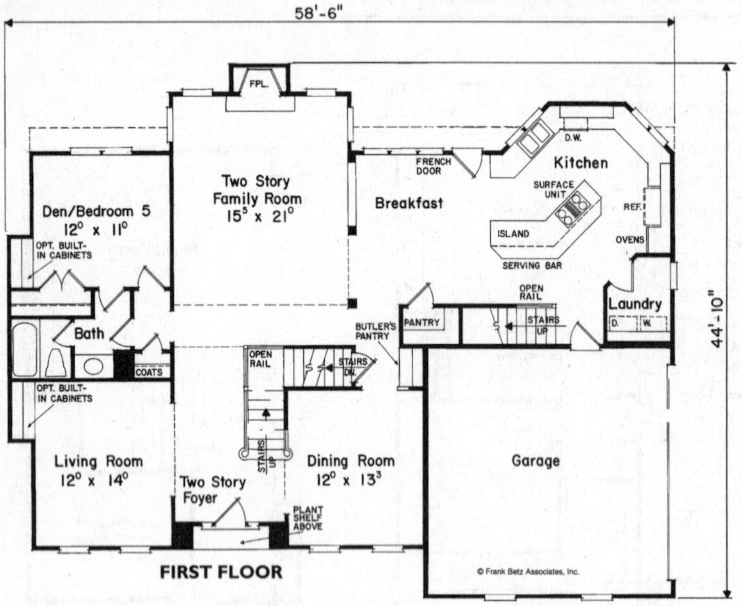
58'-6"
FPL.
Two Story Family Room 15^{5} x 21^{0}
Den/Bedroom 5 12^{0} x 11^{0}
OPT. BUILT-IN CABINETS
FRENCH DOOR
Breakfast
Kitchen
D.W.
SURFACE UNIT
REF.
ISLAND
OVENS
SERVING BAR
OPEN RAIL
PANTRY
STAIRS UP
Laundry
D. W.
BUTLER'S PANTRY
Bath
COATS
OPEN RAIL
STAIRS DN.
OPT. BUILT-IN CABINETS
Living Room 12^{0} x 14^{0}
STAIRS UP
Two Story Foyer
Dining Room 12^{0} x 13^{3}
PLANT SHELF ABOVE
Garage
44'-10"
© Frank Betz Associates, Inc.

FIRST FLOOR

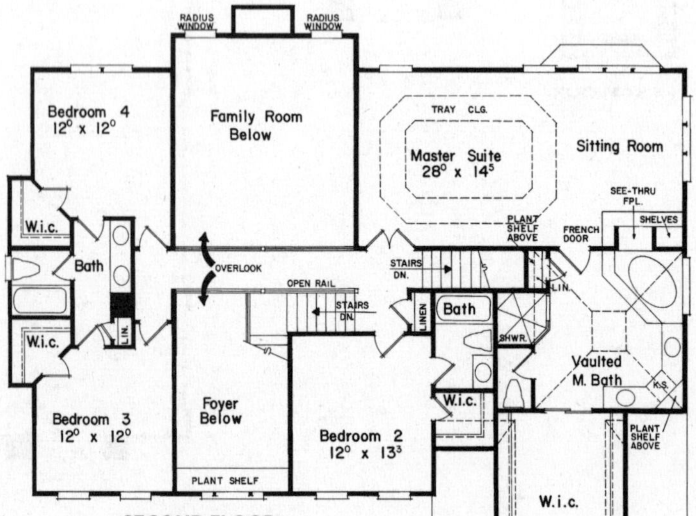
RADIUS WINDOW
RADIUS WINDOW
Bedroom 4 12^{0} x 12^{0}
Family Room Below
TRAY CLG.
Master Suite 28^{0} x 14^{5}
Sitting Room
SEE-THRU FPL.
SHELVES
PLANT SHELF ABOVE
FRENCH DOOR
W.i.c.
Bath
OVERLOOK
STAIRS DN.
OPEN RAIL
STAIRS DN.
LIN.
LINEN
Bath
SHWR.
W.i.c.
LIN.
Vaulted M. Bath
K.S.
Bedroom 3 12^{0} x 12^{0}
Foyer Below
Bedroom 2 12^{0} x 13^{3}
W.i.c.
PLANT SHELF ABOVE
PLANT SHELF
W.i.c.

SECOND FLOOR

Design 99475

See Order Pages and Index for Info

Units	Single
Price Code	C
Total Finished	1,999 sq. ft.
First Finished	1,421 sq. ft.
Second Finished	578 sq. ft.
Dimensions	52'x47'4"
Foundation	Basement
Bedrooms	4
Full Baths	2
Half Baths	1
First Ceiling	8'
Second Ceiling	8'
Max Ridge Height	25'5"
Roof Framing	Stick
Exterior Walls	2x4

* Alternate foundation options available at an additional charge. Please call 1-800-235-5700 for more information.

SECOND FLOOR

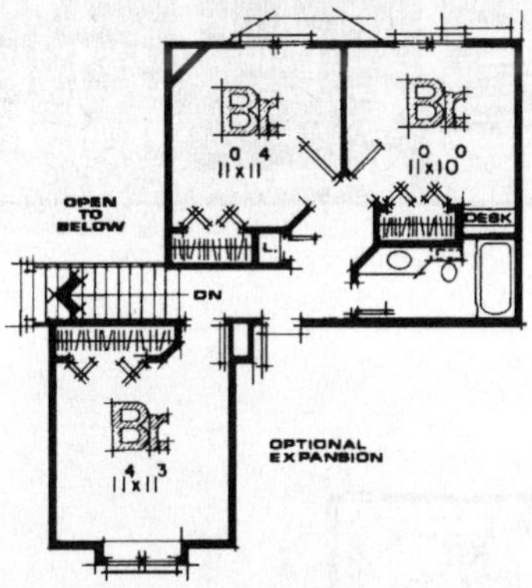
Br. 11⁰x11⁴
Br. 11⁰x10⁰
OPEN TO BELOW
DESK
DN
Br. 11⁴x11³
OPTIONAL EXPANSION

FIRST FLOOR

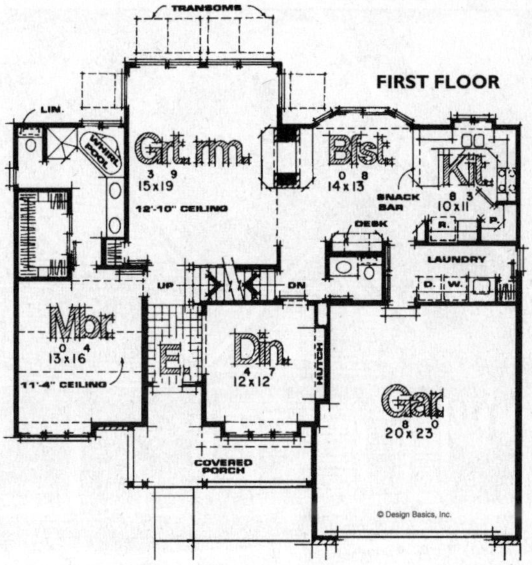
TRANSOMS
LIN.
Grt. rm. 15x19
12'-10" CEILING
Bfst. 14x13
Kit. 10x11
SNACK BAR
DESK
LAUNDRY
D.W.
UP
DN
Mbr. 13x16
11'-4" CEILING
E.
Din. 12x12
HUTCH
Gar. 20x23
COVERED PORCH
© Design Basics, Inc.

Design 97993

See Order Pages and Index for Info

Rear Elevation

Units	Single
Price Code	C
Total Finished	1,948 sq. ft.
Main Finished	1,948 sq. ft.
Basement Unfinished	1,948 sq. ft.
Garage Unfinished	517 sq. ft.
Dimensions	64'x52'
Foundation	Basement Crawlspace Slab
Bedrooms	3
Full Baths	2
Half Baths	1
Main Ceiling	8'
Max Ridge Height	20'
Roof Framing	Stick
Exterior Walls	2x4

* Alternate foundation options available at an additional charge. Please call 1-800-235-5700 for more information.

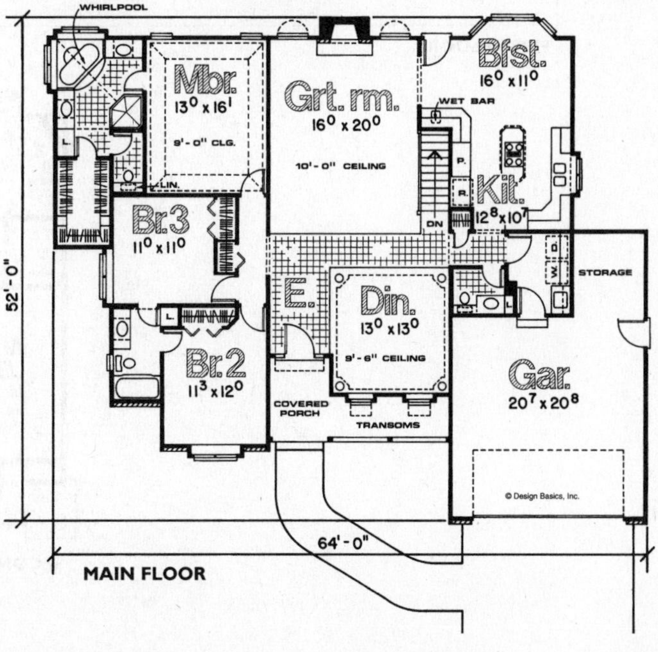
WHIRLPOOL
Mbr. 13⁰ x 16¹
9'-0" CLG.
LIN.
Grt. rm. 16⁰ x 20⁰
10'-0" CEILING
Bfst. 16⁰ x 11⁰
WET BAR
Kit. 12⁸ x 10⁷
DN
Br. 3 11⁰ x 11⁰
STORAGE
E.
Din. 13⁰ x 13⁰
9'-6" CEILING
Br. 2 11³ x 12⁰
COVERED PORCH
TRANSOMS
Gar. 20⁷ x 20⁸
52'-0"
64'-0"
© Design Basics, Inc.

MAIN FLOOR

Design 98975

See Order Pages and Index for Info

Units	Single
Price Code	H
Total Finished	3,140 sq. ft.
First Finished	1,553 sq. ft.
Second Finished	1,587 sq. ft.
Garage Unfinished	485 sq. ft.
Dimensions	58'x40'4"
Foundation	Basement
Bedrooms	4
Full Baths	3
Half Baths	1
First Ceiling	9'

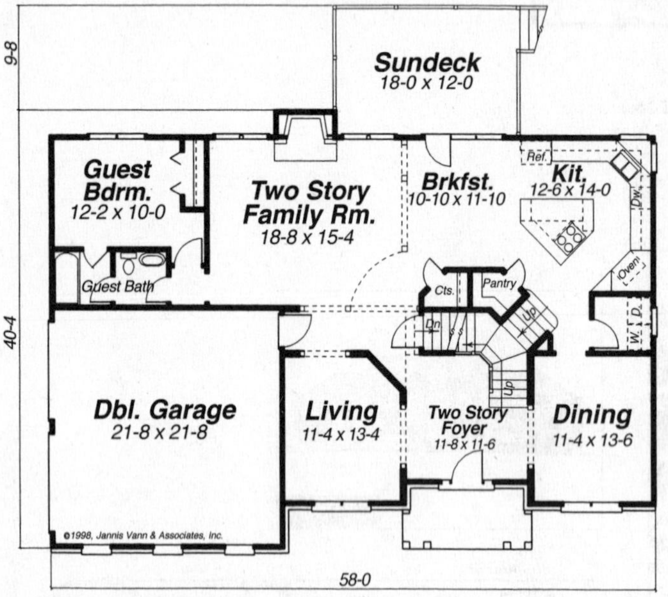
9-8
Sundeck
18-0 x 12-0
Guest Bdrm.
12-2 x 10-0
Two Story Family Rm.
18-8 x 15-4
Brkfst.
10-10 x 11-10
Ref.
Kit.
12-6 x 14-0
Dw.
Guest Bath
Cts.
Pantry
Oven
Dn
Up
W. D.
40-4
Dbl. Garage
21-8 x 21-8
Living
11-4 x 13-4
Two Story Foyer
11-8 x 11-6
Dining
11-4 x 13-6
©1998, Jannis Vann & Associates, Inc.
58-0

FIRST FLOOR

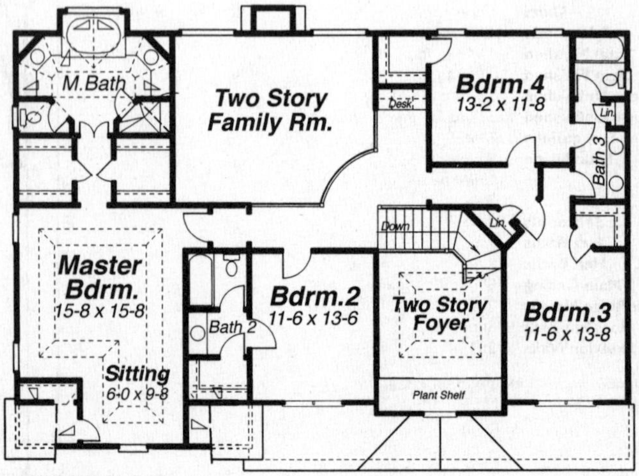
M.Bath
Two Story Family Rm.
Desk
Bdrm.4
13-2 x 11-8
Lin.
Bath 3
Down
Lin.
Master Bdrm.
15-8 x 15-8
Bath 2
Bdrm.2
11-6 x 13-6
Two Story Foyer
Bdrm.3
11-6 x 13-8
Sitting
6-0 x 9-8
Plant Shelf

SECOND FLOOR

Design 98581

See Order Pages and Index for Info

Units	Single
Price Code	G
Total Finished	2,772 sq. ft.
First Finished	2,023 sq. ft.
Second Finished	749 sq. ft.
Bonus Unfinished	256 sq. ft.
Garage Unfinished	546 sq. ft.
Dimensions	77'2"x57'11"
Foundation	Basement Slab
Bedrooms	4
Full Baths	3
Half Baths	1
First Ceiling	9'
Second Ceiling	9'
Max Ridge Height	33'
Roof Framing	Stick
Exterior Walls	2x4

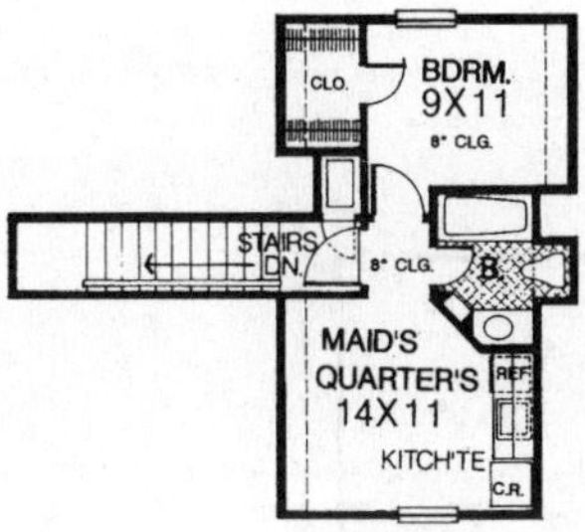
CLO.
BDRM.
9X11
8" CLG.
STAIRS
DN.
8" CLG.
B.
MAID'S
QUARTER'S
14X11
REF.
KITCH'TE
C.R.

BONUS

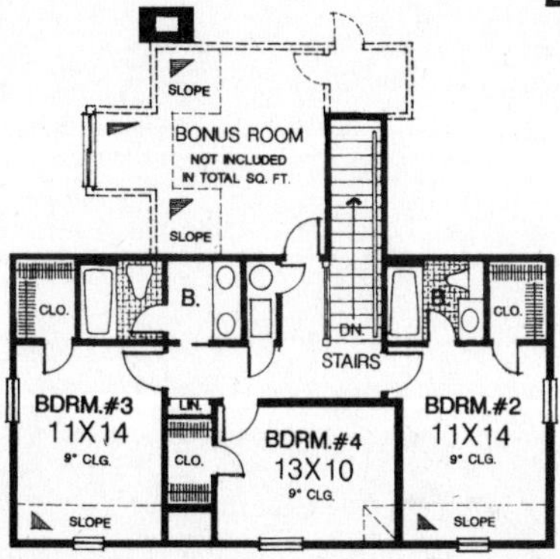
SLOPE
BONUS ROOM
NOT INCLUDED
IN TOTAL SQ. FT.
SLOPE
CLO.
B.
B.
CLO.
DN.
STAIRS
BDRM.#3
11X14
9" CLG.
LIN.
CLO.
BDRM.#4
13X10
9" CLG.
BDRM.#2
11X14
9" CLG.
SLOPE
SLOPE

SECOND FLOOR

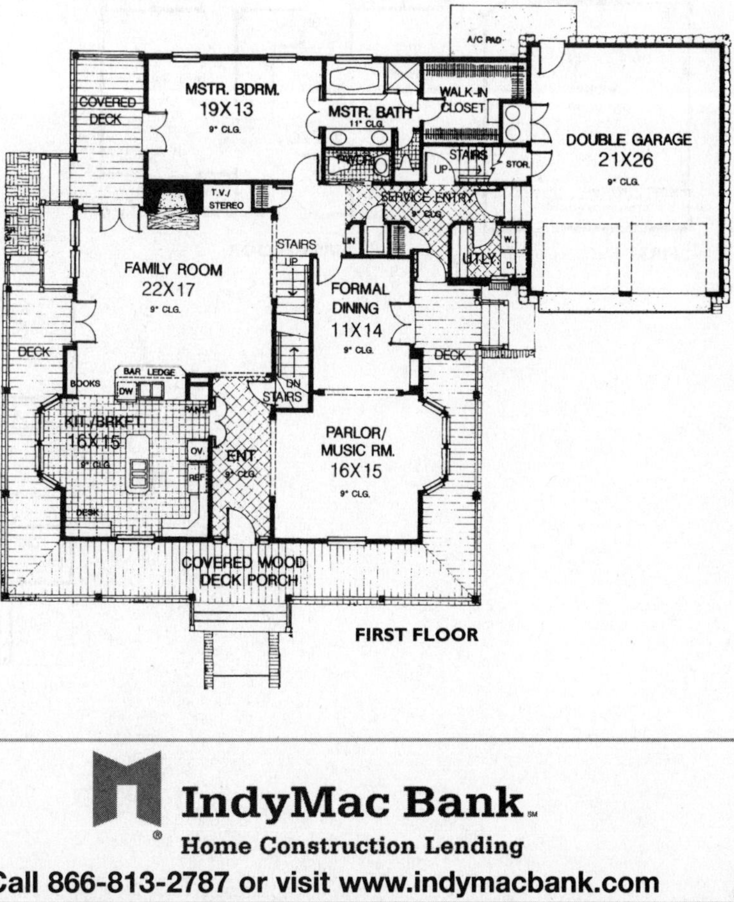
A/C PAD
COVERED
DECK
MSTR. BDRM.
19X13
9" CLG.
MSTR. BATH
11" CLG.
WALK-IN
CLOSET
STAIRS
UP
STOR.
PWDR.
DOUBLE GARAGE
21X26
9" CLG.
T.V./
STEREO
SERVICE ENTRY
9" CLG.
LIN.
W.
D.
UTLY.
STAIRS
UP
FAMILY ROOM
22X17
9" CLG.
FORMAL
DINING
11X14
9" CLG.
DECK
DECK
BAR LEDGE
BOOKS
DW
DN
STAIRS
KIT./BRKFT.
16X15
9" CLG.
PAN.
OV.
REF.
ENT
9" CLG.
PARLOR/
MUSIC RM.
16X15
9" CLG.
DESK
COVERED WOOD
DECK PORCH

FIRST FLOOR

Design 98490

See Order Pages and Index for Info

Units	Single
Price Code	J
Total Finished	3,559 sq. ft.
First Finished	1,865 sq. ft.
Second Finished	1,694 sq. ft.
Basement Unfinished	1,865 sq. ft.
Garage Unfinished	481 sq. ft.
Dimensions	59'x50'
Foundation	Basement Crawlspace
Bedrooms	5
Full Baths	3
First Ceiling	9'
Second Ceiling	8'
Max Ridge Height	34'
Roof Framing	Stick
Exterior Walls	2x4

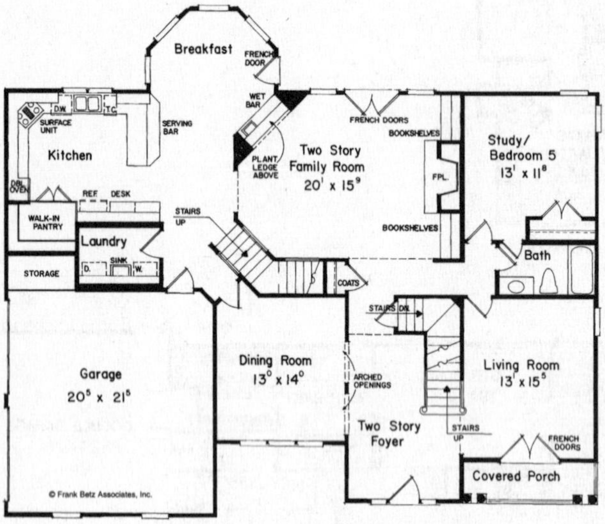

Breakfast
FRENCH DOOR
WET BAR
SURFACE UNIT
D.W.
SERVING BAR
Kitchen
PLANT LEDGE ABOVE
FRENCH DOORS
BOOKSHELVES
Two Story Family Room
20' x 15⁹
FPL.
Study/ Bedroom 5
13' x 11⁸
DBL OVEN
REF.
DESK
WALK-IN PANTRY
STAIRS UP
Laundry
SINK
BOOKSHELVES
Bath
STORAGE
COATS
STAIRS DN.
Garage
20⁵ x 21⁵
Dining Room
13⁰ x 14⁰
ARCHED OPENINGS
Living Room
13' x 15⁵
Two Story Foyer
STAIRS UP
FRENCH DOORS
Covered Porch
© Frank Betz Associates, Inc.

FIRST FLOOR

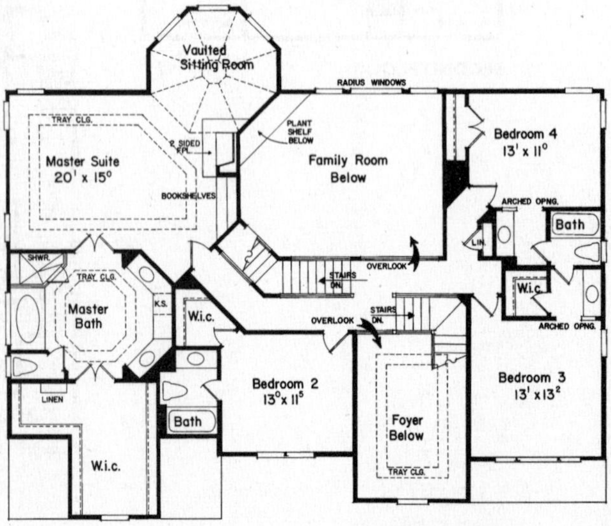

Vaulted Sitting Room
RADIUS WINDOWS
TRAY CLG.
PLANT SHELF BELOW
2 SIDED FPL
Master Suite
20' x 15⁰
Family Room Below
Bedroom 4
13' x 11⁰
BOOKSHELVES
ARCHED OPNG.
Bath
SHWR.
TRAY CLG.
Master Bath
K.S.
STAIRS DN.
OVERLOOK
W.i.c.
OVERLOOK
STAIRS DN.
ARCHED OPNG.
Bedroom 2
13⁰ x 11⁵
Bedroom 3
13' x 13²
LINEN
Bath
Foyer Below
TRAY CLG.
W.i.c.

SECOND FLOOR

Design 98974

See Order Pages and Index for Info

Units	Single
Price Code	G
Total Finished	2,814 sq. ft.
First Finished	1,465 sq. ft.
Second Finished	1,349 sq. ft.
Dimensions	72'4"x38'4"
Foundation	Basement Crawlspace Slab
Bedrooms	4
Full Baths	3
Half Baths	1
First Ceiling	10'
Second Ceiling	8'
Max Ridge Height	33'
Roof Framing	Stick
Exterior Walls	2x4

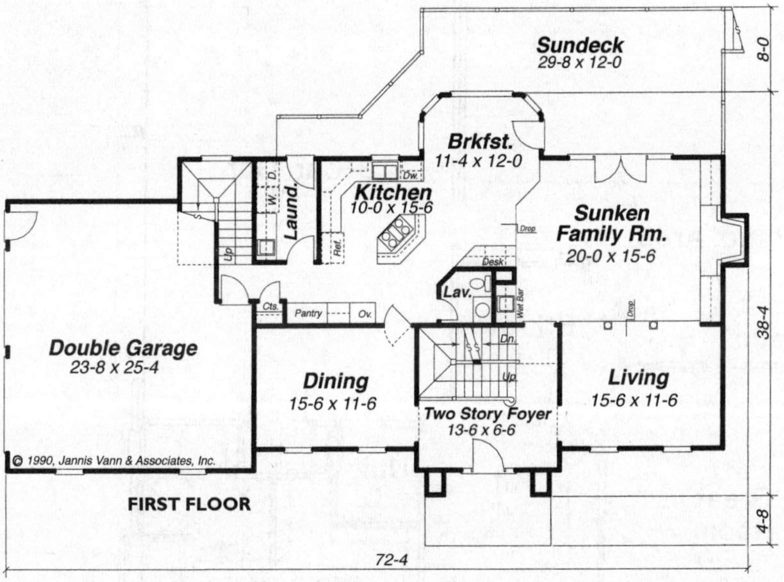
Sundeck
29-8 x 12-0
Brkfst.
11-4 x 12-0
Kitchen
10-0 x 15-6
Laund.
Sunken
Family Rm.
20-0 x 15-6
Lav.
Pantry
Double Garage
23-8 x 25-4
Dining
15-6 x 11-6
Living
15-6 x 11-6
Two Story Foyer
13-6 x 6-6
© 1990, Jannis Vann & Associates, Inc.
8-0
38-4
4-8
72-4

FIRST FLOOR

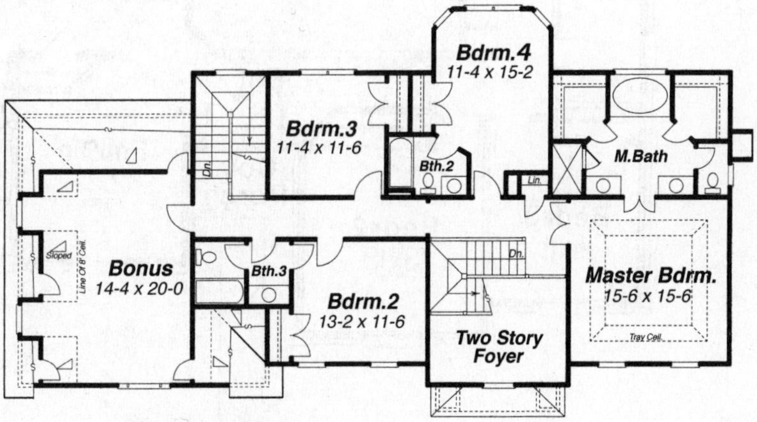
Bdrm.4
11-4 x 15-2
Bdrm.3
11-4 x 11-6
Bth.2
M.Bath
Bonus
14-4 x 20-0
Bth.3
Bdrm.2
13-2 x 11-6
Two Story
Foyer
Master Bdrm.
15-6 x 15-6
Tray Ceil.

SECOND FLOOR

Design 98548

See Order Pages and Index for Info

Units	Single
Price Code	E
Total Finished	2,257 sq. ft.
Main Finished	2,257 sq. ft.
Garage Unfinished	601 sq. ft.
Porch Unfinished	325 sq. ft.
Dimensions	65'x65'10'
Foundation	Crawlspace Slab
Bedrooms	4
Full Baths	2
Half Baths	1
Main Ceiling	9'-11'
Max Ridge Height	25'
Roof Framing	Stick
Exterior Walls	2x4

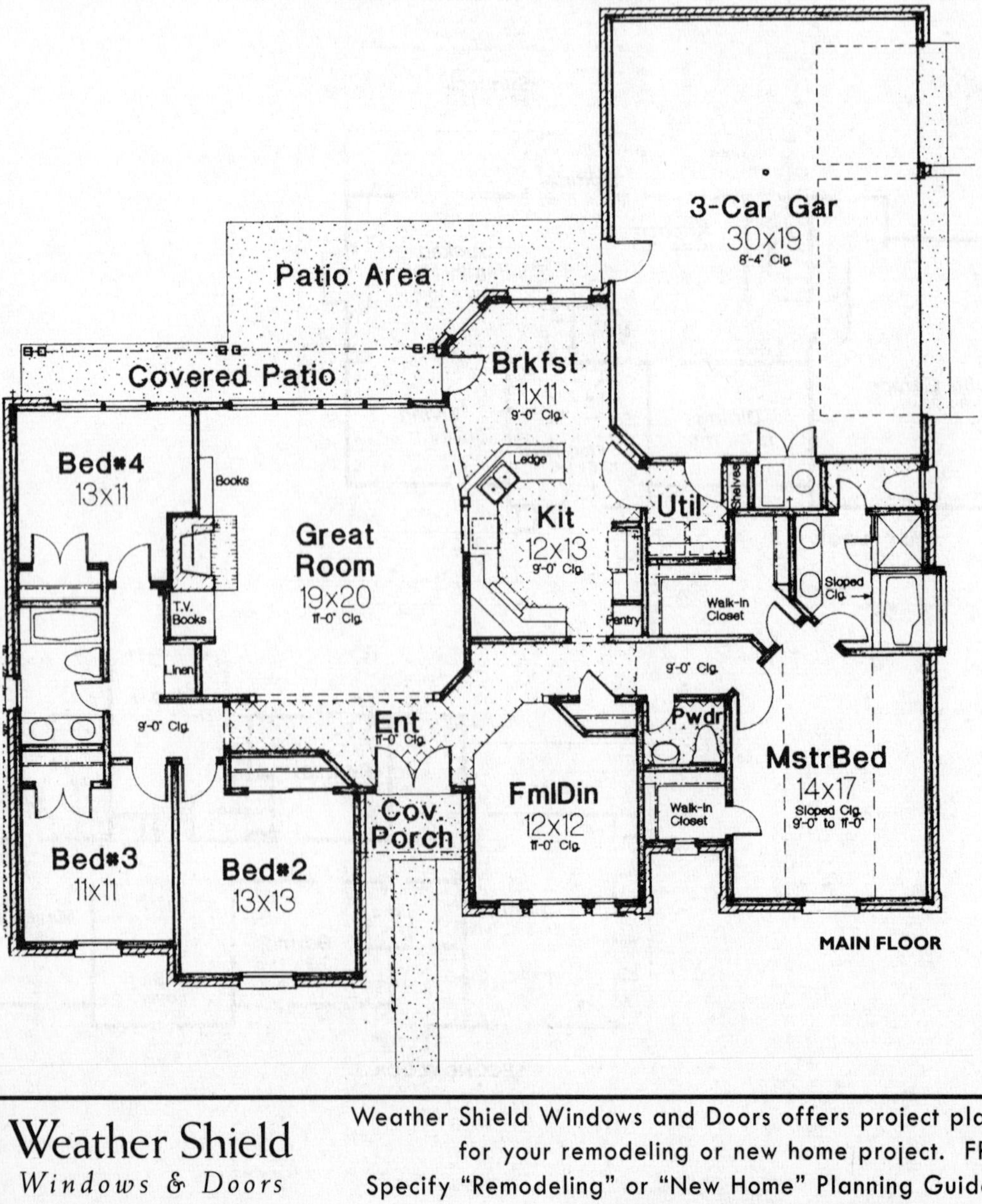
3-Car Gar
30x19
8'-4" Clg.
Patio Area
Covered Patio
Brkfst
11x11
9'-0" Clg.
Bed#4
13x11
Books
Great
Room
19x20
11'-0" Clg.
T.V.
Books
Linen
Ledge
Kit
12x13
9'-0" Clg.
Pantry
Util
Shelves
Walk-in
Closet
Sloped
Clg.
9'-0" Clg.
9'-0" Clg.
Ent
11'-0" Clg.
Pwdr
MstrBed
14x17
Sloped Clg.
9'-0" to 11'-0"
FmlDin
12x12
11'-0" Clg.
Walk-in
Closet
Cov.
Porch
Bed#3
11x11
Bed#2
13x13

MAIN FLOOR

Design 93285

See Order Pages and Index for Info

Units	Single
Price Code	F
Total Finished	2,574 sq. ft.
First Finished	1,135 sq. ft.
Second Finished	1,439 sq. ft.
Bonus Unfinished	193 sq. ft.
Basement Unfinished	1,112 sq. ft.
Dimensions	49'x38'
Foundation	Basement Crawlspace Slab
Bedrooms	4
Full Baths	2
Half Baths	1
Max Ridge Height	30'4"
Roof Framing	Truss
Exterior Walls	2x4

FIRST FLOOR

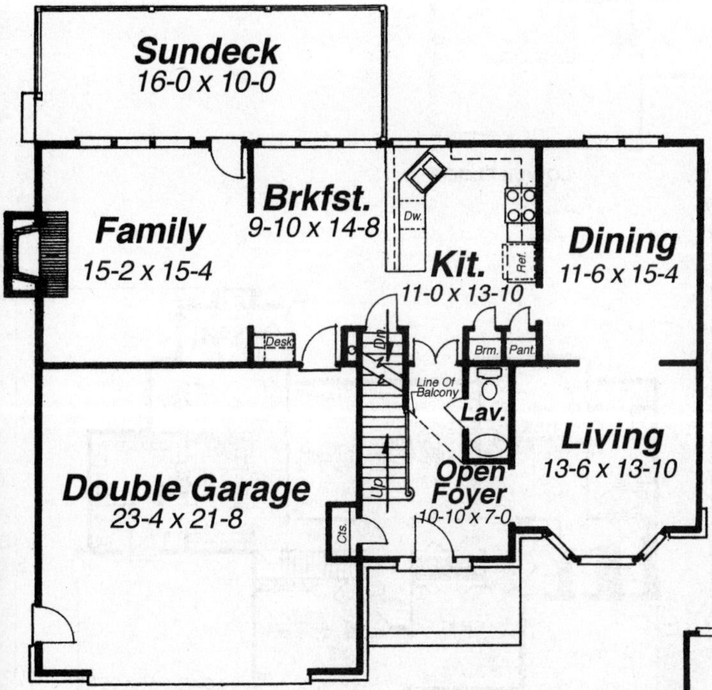
Sundeck
16-0 x 10-0
Brkfst.
9-10 x 14-8
Family
15-2 x 15-4
Dw.
Kit.
11-0 x 13-10
Ref.
Dining
11-6 x 15-4
Desk
Dn.
Brm.
Pant.
Line Of Balcony
Lav.
Living
13-6 x 13-10
Double Garage
23-4 x 21-8
Up
Open Foyer
10-10 x 7-0
Cts.

SECOND FLOOR

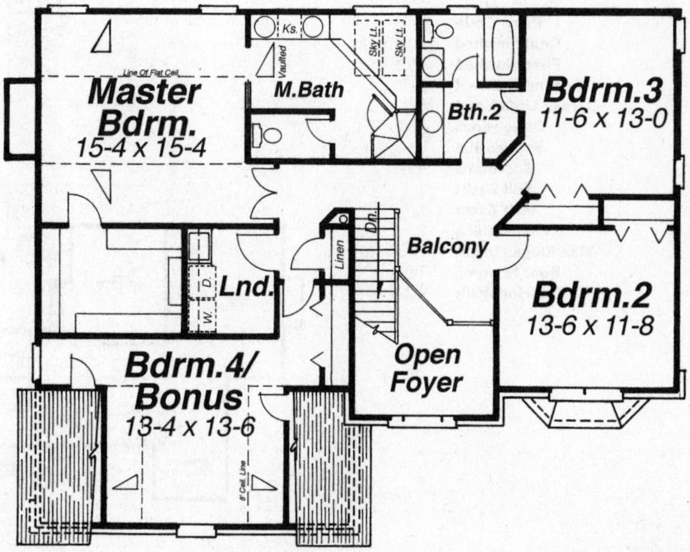
Ks.
Sky Lt.
Sky Lt.
Line Of Flat Ceil.
Master Bdrm.
15-4 x 15-4
Vaulted
M.Bath
Bth.2
Bdrm.3
11-6 x 13-0
Dn.
Balcony
Lnd.
D.
W.
Linen
Bdrm.2
13-6 x 11-8
Bdrm.4/ Bonus
13-4 x 13-6
8' Ceil. Line
Open Foyer

Design 99195

See Order Pages and Index for Info

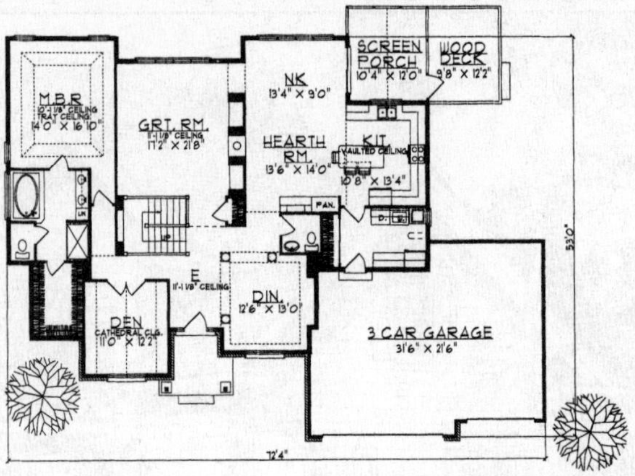
SCREEN PORCH 10'4" X 12'0"
WOOD DECK 9'8" X 12'2"
M.B.R. 14'0" X 16'10"
GRT. RM. 17'2" X 21'8"
NK 13'4" X 9'0"
HEARTH RM. 13'6" X 14'0"
KIT 10'8" X 13'4"
DEN CATHEDRAL CLG. 11'0" X 12'2"
E
DIN. 12'6" X 13'0"
3 CAR GARAGE 31'6" X 21'6"
72'4"
53'0"

MAIN FLOOR

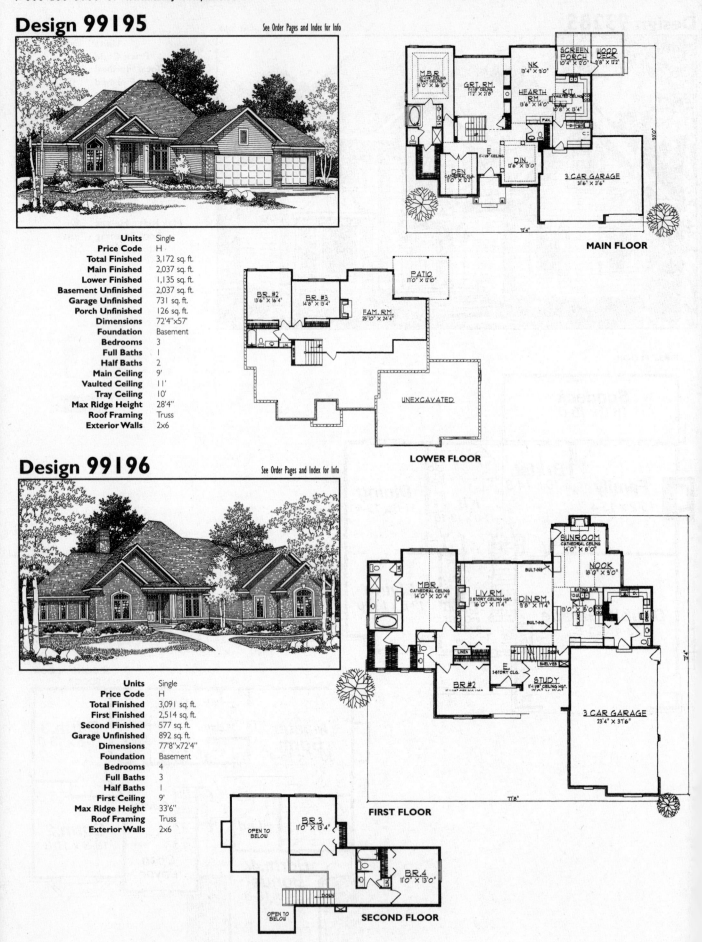

Units	Single
Price Code	H
Total Finished	3,172 sq. ft.
Main Finished	2,037 sq. ft.
Lower Finished	1,135 sq. ft.
Basement Unfinished	2,037 sq. ft.
Garage Unfinished	731 sq. ft.
Porch Unfinished	126 sq. ft.
Dimensions	72'4"x57'
Foundation	Basement
Bedrooms	3
Full Baths	1
Half Baths	2
Main Ceiling	9'
Vaulted Ceiling	11'
Tray Ceiling	10'
Max Ridge Height	28'4"
Roof Framing	Truss
Exterior Walls	2x6

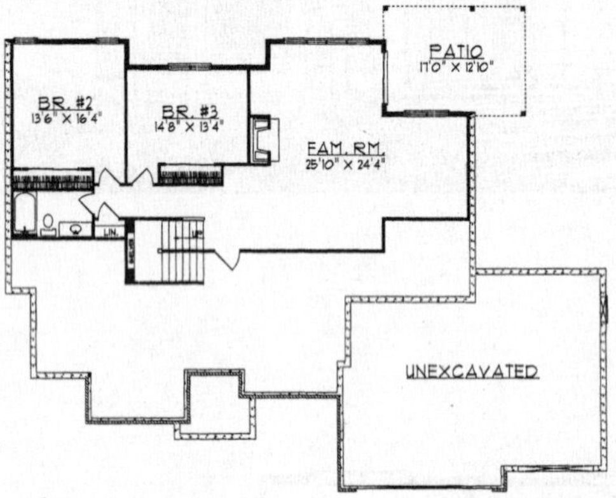
PATIO 17'0" X 12'10"
BR. #2 13'6" X 16'4"
BR. #3 14'8" X 13'4"
FAM. RM. 25'10" X 24'4"
UNEXCAVATED

LOWER FLOOR

Design 99196

See Order Pages and Index for Info

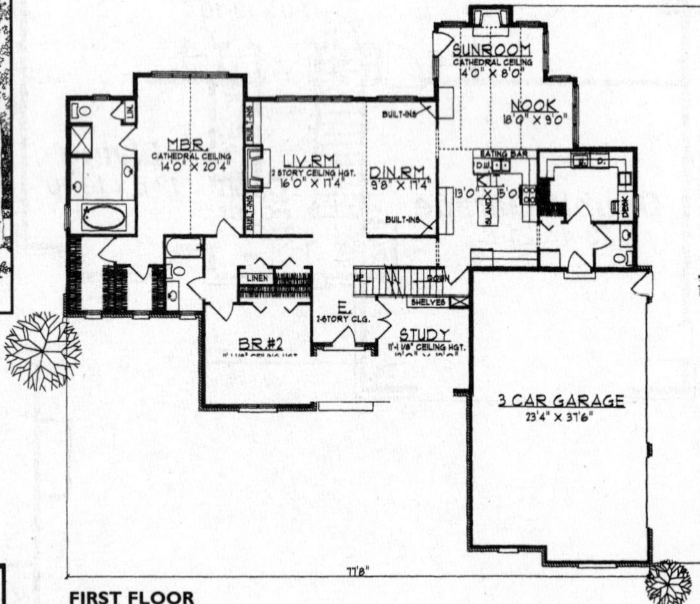
SUNROOM CATHEDRAL CEILING 14'0" X 8'0"
NOOK 18'0" X 9'0"
MBR. CATHEDRAL CEILING 14'0" X 20'4"
LIV. RM. 2 STORY CEILING HGT. 16'0" X 17'4"
DIN. RM. 9'8" X 11'4"
BUILT-INS
EATING BAR
BR #2
E 2-STORY CLG.
STUDY
3 CAR GARAGE 23'4" X 37'6"
77'8"
72'4"

FIRST FLOOR

Units	Single
Price Code	H
Total Finished	3,091 sq. ft.
First Finished	2,514 sq. ft.
Second Finished	577 sq. ft.
Garage Unfinished	892 sq. ft.
Dimensions	77'8"x72'4"
Foundation	Basement
Bedrooms	4
Full Baths	3
Half Baths	1
First Ceiling	9'
Max Ridge Height	33'6"
Roof Framing	Truss
Exterior Walls	2x6

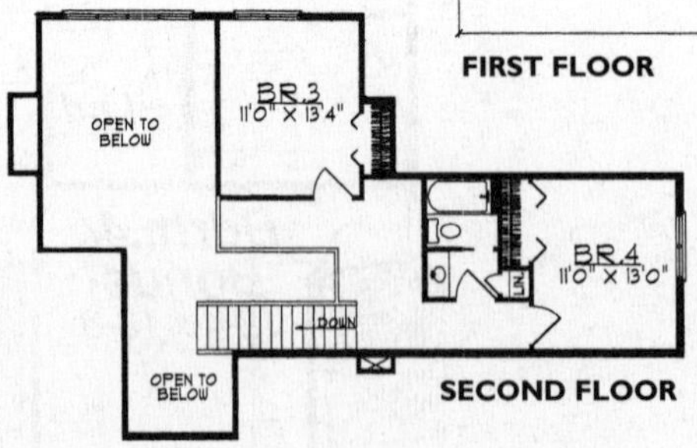
OPEN TO BELOW
BR.3 11'0" X 13'4"
BR.4 11'0" X 13'0"
DOWN
OPEN TO BELOW

SECOND FLOOR

Design 99197

See Order Pages and Index for Info

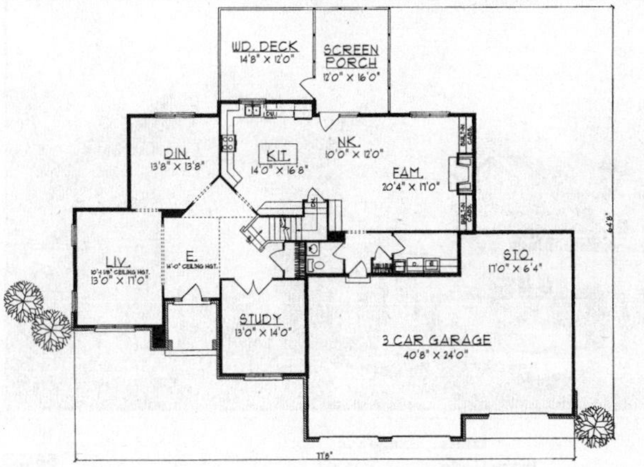
WD. DECK
14'8" X 12'0"
SCREEN PORCH
12'0" X 16'0"
DIN.
13'8" X 13'8"
KIT.
14'0" X 16'8"
NK.
10'0" X 12'0"
FAM.
20'4" X 17'0"
LIV.
13'0" X 17'0"
E.
STUDY
13'0" X 14'0"
STO.
17'0" X 6'4"
3 CAR GARAGE
40'8" X 24'0"

FIRST FLOOR

Units	Single
Price Code	H
Total Finished	3,204 sq. ft.
First Finished	1,768 sq. ft.
Second Finished	1,436 sq. ft.
Basement Unfinished	1,768 sq. ft.
Garage Unfinished	1,065 sq. ft.
Dimensions	77'8"x64'8'
Foundation	Basement
Bedrooms	4
Full Baths	2
Half Baths	1
First Ceiling	9'
Second Ceiling	8'
Max Ridge Height	33'
Roof Framing	Truss
Exterior Walls	2x6

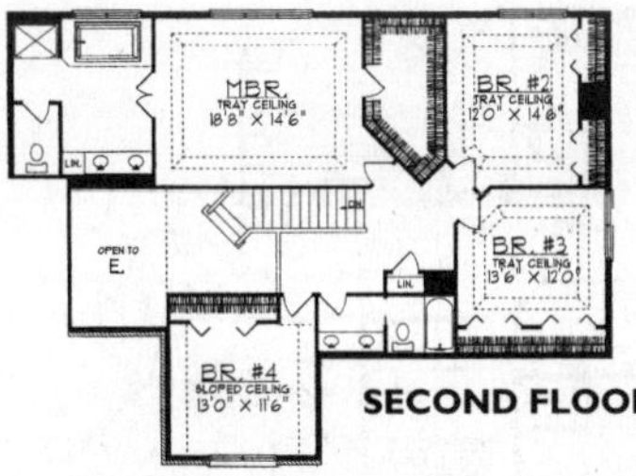
MBR.
TRAY CEILING
18'8" X 14'6"
BR. #2
TRAY CEILING
12'0" X 14'8"
BR. #3
TRAY CEILING
13'6" X 12'0"
BR. #4
SLOPED CEILING
13'0" X 11'6"
OPEN TO E.

SECOND FLOOR

Rear Elevation

Design 99199

See Order Pages and Index for Info

Units	Single
Price Code	H
Total Finished	3,125 sq. ft.
Main Finished	1,800 sq. ft.
Lower Finished	1,325 sq. ft.
Garage Unfinished	948 sq. ft.
Porch Unfinished	136 sq. ft.
Dimensions	74'8"x65'8"
Foundation	Basement
Bedrooms	4
Full Baths	2
3/4 Baths	1
Main Ceiling	10'
Max Ridge Height	25'
Roof Framing	Truss
Exterior Walls	2x6

Rear Elevation

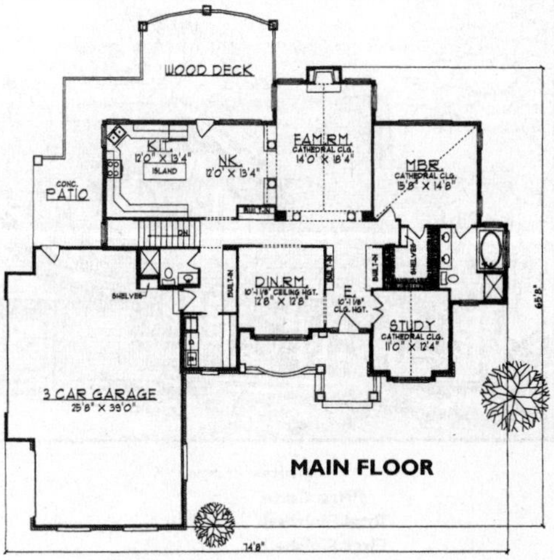
WOOD DECK
KIT.
12'0" X 13'4"
ISLAND
NK.
12'0" X 13'4"
FAM.RM.
CATHEDRAL CLG.
14'0" X 18'4"
MBR
CATHEDRAL CLG.
15'8" X 14'8"
PATIO
DIN.RM.
12'8" X 12'8"
E.
STUDY
CATHEDRAL CLG.
11'0" X 12'4"
3 CAR GARAGE
25'8" X 35'0"

MAIN FLOOR

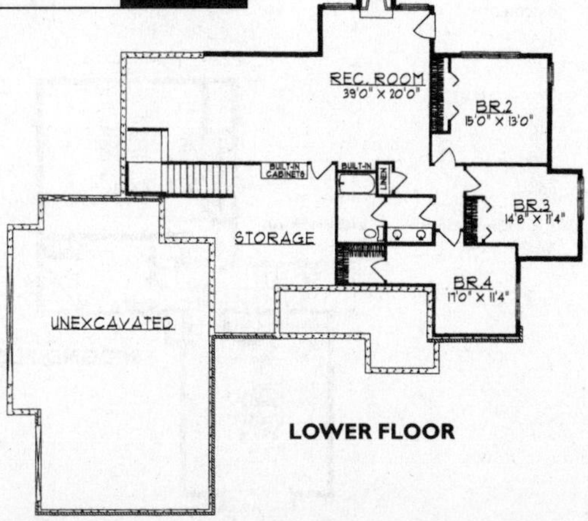
REC. ROOM
39'0" X 20'0"
BR.2
15'0" X 13'0"
BR.3
14'8" X 11'4"
BR.4
17'0" X 11'4"
STORAGE
UNEXCAVATED

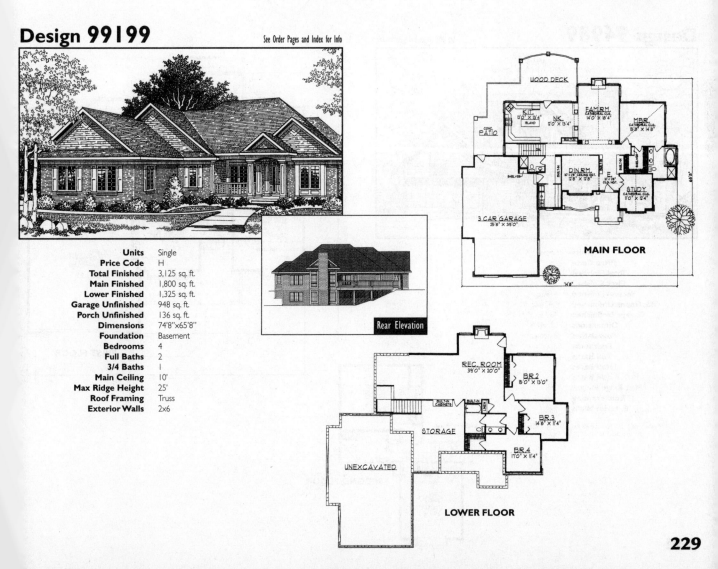

LOWER FLOOR

Design 99441

See Order Pages and Index for Info

FIRST FLOOR

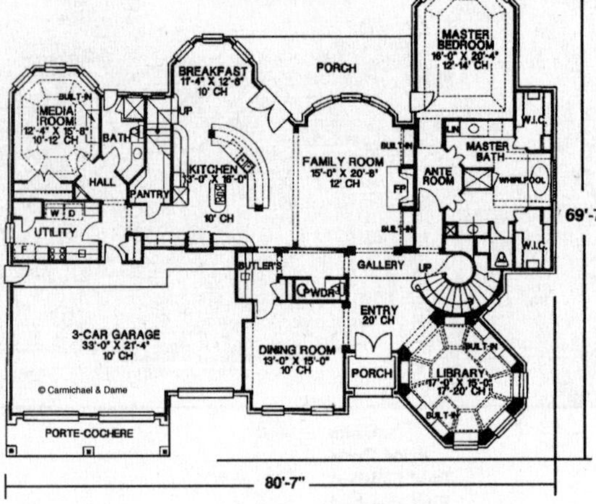

MASTER BEDROOM 16'-0" X 20'-4" 12'-14' CH
BREAKFAST 11'-4" X 12'-8" 10' CH
PORCH
MEDIA ROOM 12'-4" X 15'-8" 10'-12' CH
BATH
HALL
KITCHEN 13'-0" X 18'-0"
PANTRY
FAMILY ROOM 15'-0" X 20'-8" 12' CH
ANTE ROOM
MASTER BATH
WHIRLPOOL
UTILITY
BUTLER'S
PWDR
GALLERY
3-CAR GARAGE 33'-0" X 21'-4" 10' CH
ENTRY 20' CH
DINING ROOM 13'-0" X 15'-0" 10' CH
PORCH
LIBRARY 17'-0" X 15'-0" 17'-20' CH
PORTE-COCHERE
© Carmichael & Dame
69'-7"
80'-7"

SECOND FLOOR

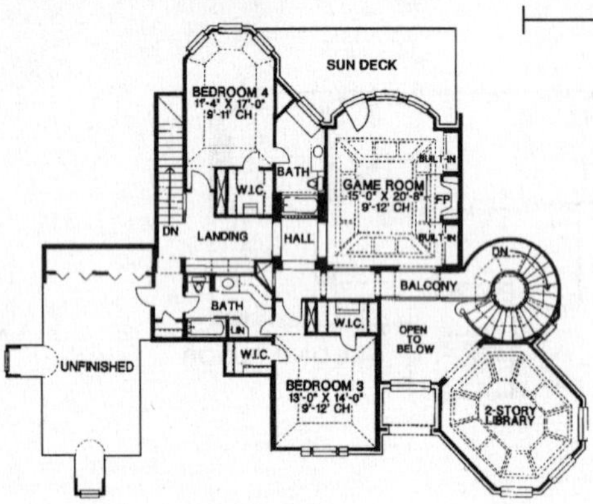

SUN DECK
BEDROOM 4 11'-4" X 17'-0" 9'-11' CH
GAME ROOM 15'-0" X 20'-8" 9'-12' CH
LANDING
HALL
BATH
W.I.C.
BALCONY
OPEN TO BELOW
UNFINISHED
BEDROOM 3 13'-0" X 14'-0" 9'-12' CH
2-STORY LIBRARY

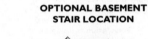

OPTIONAL BASEMENT STAIR LOCATION

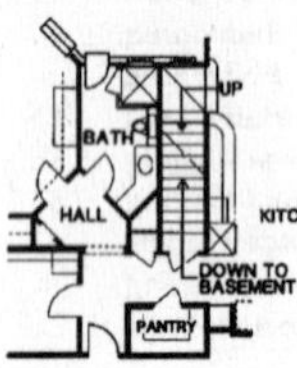

BATH
HALL
KITCHEN
DOWN TO BASEMENT
PANTRY

Units	Single
Price Code	L
Total Finished	4,339 sq. ft.
First Finished	2,932 sq. ft.
Second Finished	1,407 sq. ft.
Basement Unfinished	2,932 sq. ft.
Garage Unfinished	739 sq. ft.
Dimensions	80'7"x69'7"
Foundation	Basement Slab
Bedrooms	3
Full Baths	3
3/4 Baths	1
Max Ridge Height	37'
Roof Framing	Stick
Exterior Walls	2x4

* Alternate foundation options available at an additional charge. Please call 1-800-235-5700 for more information.

Design 94989

See Order Pages and Index for Info

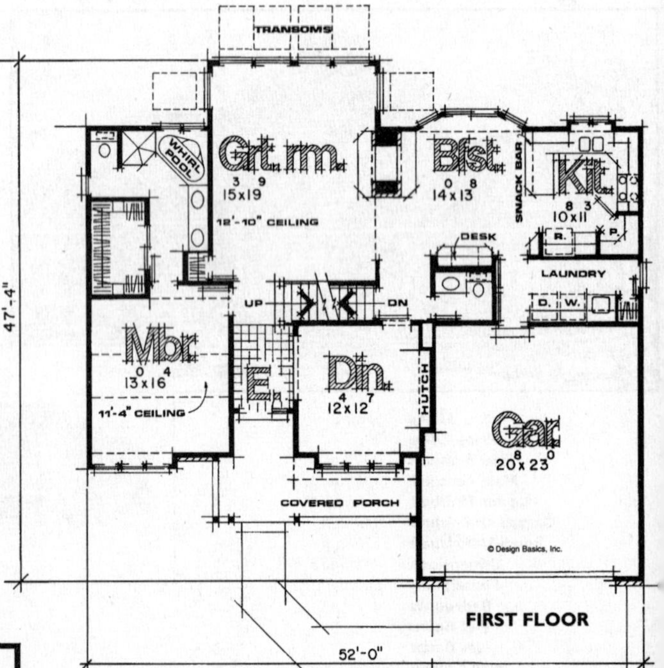

TRANSOMS
WHIRLPOOL
Grt. rm. 15x19
12'-10" CEILING
Bkst 14x13
SNACK BAR
Kit 10x11
DESK
LAUNDRY
UP
DN
Mbr 13x16
11'-4" CEILING
E
Din 12x12
HUTCH
Gar 20x23
COVERED PORCH
© Design Basics, Inc.
47'-4"
52'-0"

FIRST FLOOR

Units	Single
Price Code	C
Total Finished	1,869 sq. ft.
First Finished	1,421 sq. ft.
Second Finished	448 sq. ft.
Basement Unfinished	1,421 sq. ft.
Garage Unfinished	480 sq. ft.
Dimensions	52'x47'4"
Foundation	Basement
Bedrooms	3
Full Baths	1
Half Baths	1
3/4 Baths	1
Max Ridge Height	25'
Roof Framing	Stick
Exterior Walls	2x4

* Alternate foundation options available at an additional charge. Please call 1-800-235-5700 for more information.

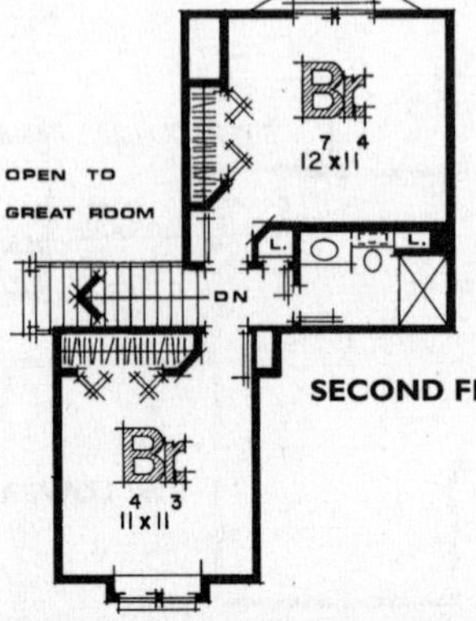

Br 12x11
OPEN TO GREAT ROOM
DN
Br 11x11

SECOND FLOOR

Design 99448

See Order Pages and Index for Info

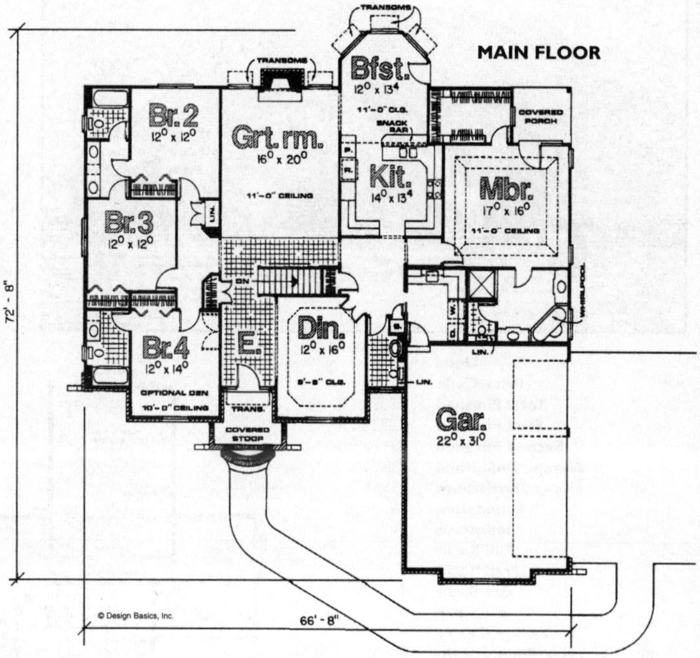
TRANSOMS
TRANSOMS
Bfst.
12⁰ x 13⁴
11'-0" CLG.
SNACK BAR
COVERED PORCH
Br. 2
12⁰ x 12⁰
Grt. rm.
16⁰ x 20⁰
11'-0" CEILING
Kit.
14⁰ x 13⁴
Mbr.
17⁰ x 16⁰
11'-0" CEILING
Br. 3
12⁰ x 12⁰
LIN.
DN
WHIRLPOOL
Br. 4
12⁰ x 14⁰
E.
Din.
12⁰ x 16⁰
9'-0" CLG.
LIN.
LIN.
OPTIONAL DEN
10'-0" CEILING
TRANS.
COVERED STOOP
Gar.
22⁰ x 31⁰
72' - 8"
© Design Basics, Inc.
66' - 8"

MAIN FLOOR

Units	Single
Price Code	F
Total Finished	2,655 sq. ft.
Main Finished	2,655 sq. ft.
Basement Unfinished	2,655 sq. ft.
Garage Unfinished	695 sq. ft.
Dimensions	66'8"x72'8"
Foundation	Basement
Bedrooms	4
Full Baths	3
Half Baths	1
Max Ridge Height	23'
Roof Framing	Stick
Exterior Walls	2x4

* Alternate foundation options available at an additional charge. Please call 1-800-235-5700 for more information.

Design 99465

See Order Pages and Index for Info

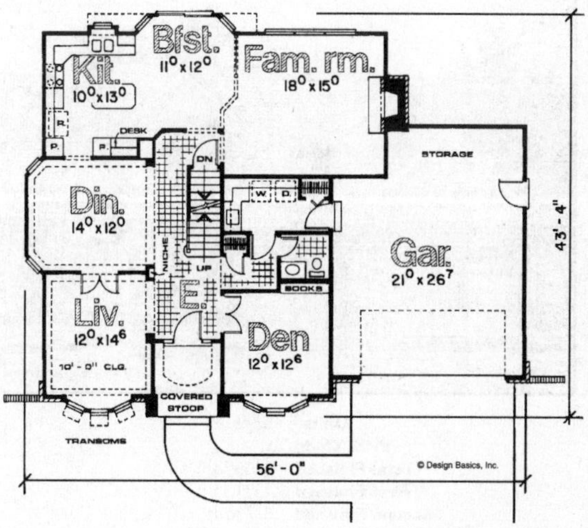
Bfst.
11⁰ x 12⁰
Kit.
10⁰ x 13⁰
Fam. rm.
18⁰ x 15⁰
DESK
STORAGE
DN
Din.
14⁰ x 12⁰
W. D.
Gar.
21⁰ x 26⁷
NICHE
UP
BOOKS
Liv.
12⁰ x 14⁶
10'-0" CLG.
E.
Den
12⁰ x 12⁶
COVERED STOOP
TRANSOMS
43' - 4"
56' - 0"
© Design Basics, Inc.

FIRST FLOOR

Units	Single
Price Code	F
Total Finished	2,545 sq. ft.
First Finished	1,392 sq. ft.
Second Finished	1,153 sq. ft.
Garage Unfinished	549 sq. ft.
Dimensions	56'x43'4"
Foundation	Basement
Bedrooms	4
Full Baths	2
Half Baths	1
3/4 Baths	1
Max Ridge Height	27'
Roof Framing	Stick
Exterior Walls	2x4

* Alternate foundation options available at an additional charge. Please call 1-800-235-5700 for more information.

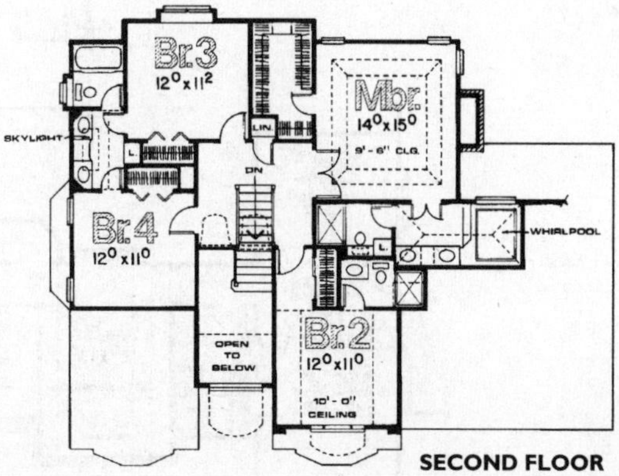
Br. 3
12⁰ x 11²
Mbr.
14⁰ x 15⁰
9'-6" CLG.
SKYLIGHT
LIN.
DN
Br. 4
12⁰ x 11⁰
WHIRLPOOL
OPEN TO BELOW
Br. 2
12⁰ x 11⁰
10'-0" CEILING

SECOND FLOOR

Design 99461

See Order Pages and Index for Info

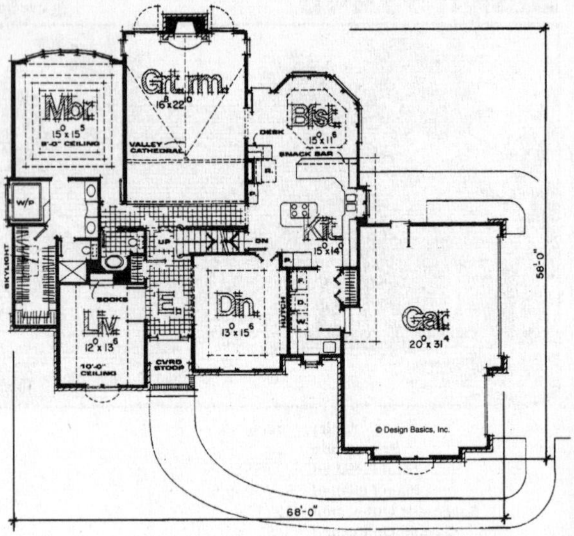
Mbr.
15⁰ x 15⁵
9'-0" CEILING
Grt. rm.
16⁸ x 22¹⁰
VALLEY CATHEDRAL
Bfst.
15⁰ x 11⁶
DESK
SNACK BAR
W/D
SKYLIGHT
Kit.
15⁰ x 14⁰
BOOKS
Liv.
12⁰ x 13⁶
10'-0" CEILING
E.
Din.
13⁰ x 15⁶
HUTCH
CVRD STOOP
Gar.
20⁰ x 31⁴
58'-0"
68'-0"
© Design Basics, Inc.

FIRST FLOOR

Units	Single
Price Code	G
Total Finished	2,865 sq. ft.
First Finished	1,972 sq. ft.
Second Finished	893 sq. ft.
Garage Unfinished	658 sq. ft.
Dimensions	68'x58'
Foundation	Basement
Bedrooms	4
Full Baths	2
Half Baths	1
3/4 Baths	1
First Ceiling	8'
Second Ceiling	8'
Max Ridge Height	25'7"
Roof Framing	Stick
Exterior Walls	2x4

* Alternate foundation options available at an additional charge. Please call 1-800-235-5700 for more information.

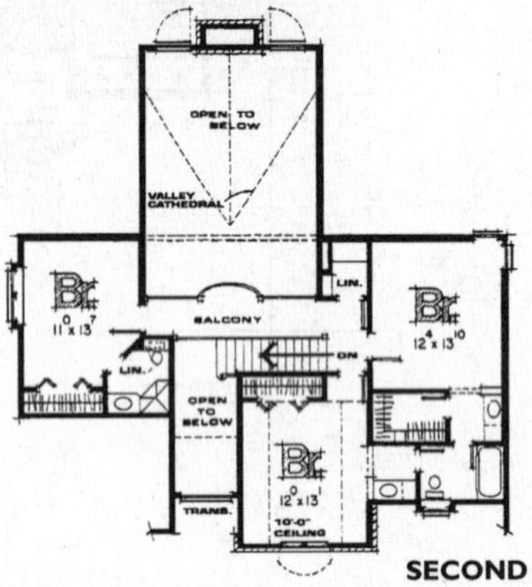
OPEN TO BELOW
VALLEY CATHEDRAL
Br.
11⁰ x 13⁷
BALCONY
LIN.
Br.
12⁴ x 13¹⁰
OPEN TO BELOW
Br.
12⁰ x 13⁰
10'-0" CEILING
TRANS.

SECOND FLOOR

Design 99468

See Order Pages and Index for Info

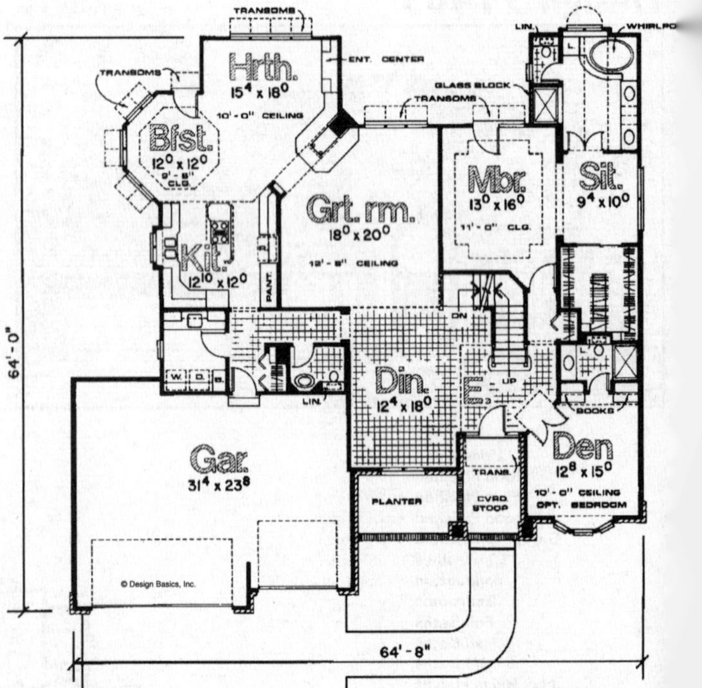
TRANSOMS
Hrth.
15⁴ x 18⁰
10'-0" CEILING
ENT. CENTER
Bfst.
12⁰ x 12⁰
9'-8" CLG.
GLASS BLOCK
TRANSOMS
WHIRLPOOL
Mbr.
13⁰ x 16⁰
11'-0" CLG.
Sit.
9⁴ x 10⁰
Grt. rm.
18⁰ x 20⁰
12'-8" CEILING
Kit.
12¹⁰ x 12⁰
PANT.
Din.
12⁴ x 18⁰
E.
Den
12⁸ x 15⁰
10'-0" CEILING
OPT. BEDROOM
BOOKS
TRANS.
CVRD. STOOP
PLANTER
Gar.
31⁴ x 23⁸
64'-0"
64'-8"
© Design Basics, Inc.

FIRST FLOOR

Units	Single
Price Code	H
Total Finished	3,138 sq. ft.
First Finished	2,321 sq. ft.
Second Finished	817 sq. ft.
Basement Unfinished	2,321 sq. ft.
Garage Unfinished	758 sq. ft.
Dimensions	64'8"x64'
Foundation	Basement
Bedrooms	3
Full Baths	2
Half Baths	1
3/4 Baths	2
Max Ridge Height	28'
Roof Framing	Stick
Exterior Walls	2x4

* Alternate foundation options available at an additional charge. Please call 1-800-235-5700 for more information.

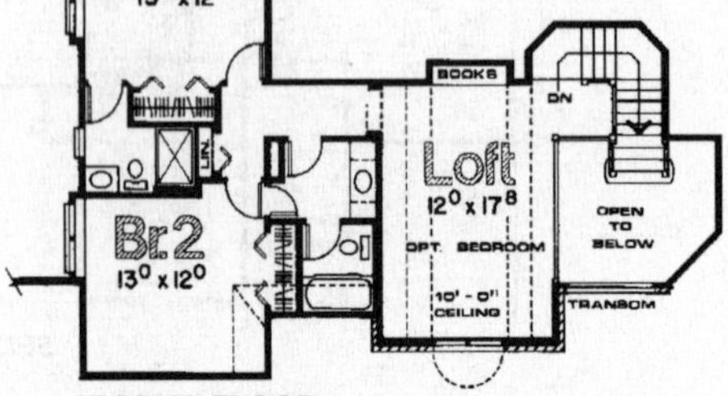
Br.3
13⁰ x 12⁰
Br.2
13⁰ x 12⁰
BOOKS
Loft
12⁰ x 17⁸
OPT. BEDROOM
10'-0" CEILING
OPEN TO BELOW
TRANSOM

SECOND FLOOR

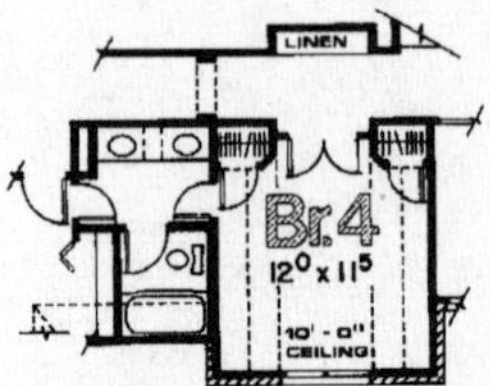
LINEN
Br.4
12⁰ x 11⁵
10'-0" CEILING

OPTIONAL BEDROOM

Design 99278

See Order Pages and Index for Info

Units	Single
Price Code	L
Total Finished	4,116 sq. ft.
First Finished	3,166 sq. ft.
Second Finished	950 sq. ft.
Dimensions	154'x94'8"
Foundation	Slab
Bedrooms	6
Full Baths	5
Max Ridge Height	28'
Roof Framing	Truss
Exterior Walls	2x6

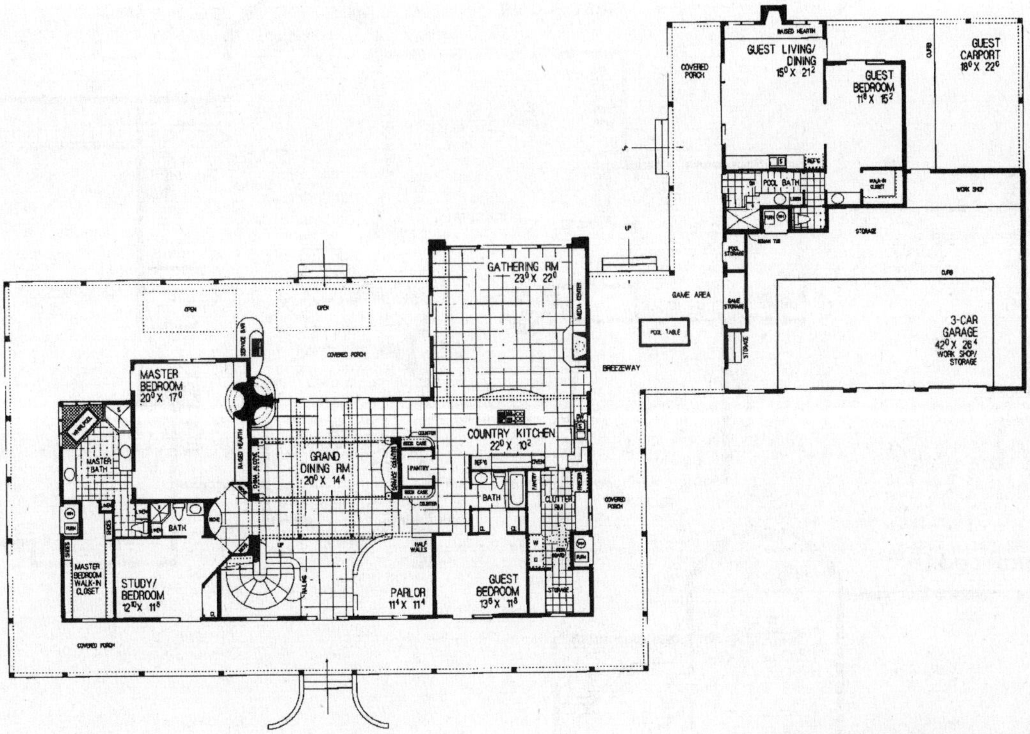
GUEST LIVING/ DINING 15⁰ X 21²
GUEST BEDROOM 11⁶ X 15²
GUEST CARPORT 18⁰ X 22⁰
COVERED PORCH
POOL BATH
WORK SHOP
STORAGE
GATHERING RM 23⁰ X 22⁸
GAME AREA
POOL TABLE
3-CAR GARAGE 42⁰ X 26⁴ WORK SHOP/ STORAGE
BREEZEWAY
COVERED PORCH
MASTER BEDROOM 20⁰ X 17⁰
COUNTRY KITCHEN 22⁰ X 10²
GRAND DINING RM 20⁰ X 14⁴
MASTER BATH
BATH
PANTRY
MASTER BEDROOM WALK-IN CLOSET
STUDY/ BEDROOM 12¹⁰ X 11⁸
PARLOR 11⁴ X 11⁴
GUEST BEDROOM 13⁶ X 11⁸
CLUTTER RM
COVERED PORCH

FIRST FLOOR

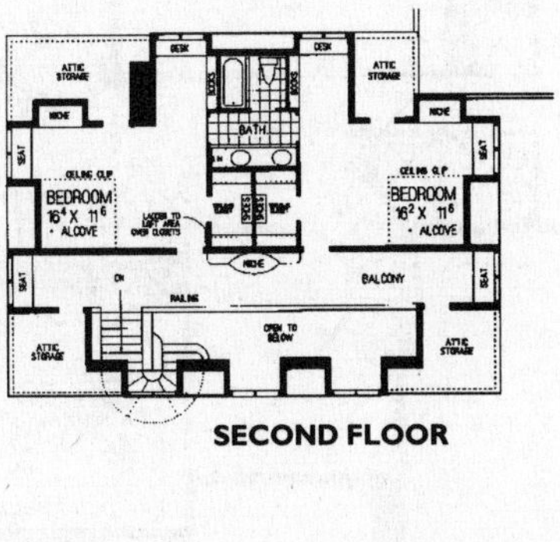
ATTIC STORAGE
BATH
BEDROOM 16⁴ X 11⁶ + ALCOVE
BEDROOM 16² X 11⁶ + ALCOVE
BALCONY
OPEN TO BELOW
RAILING

SECOND FLOOR

Design 97199

See Order Pages and Index for Info

Units	Single
Price Code	J
Total Finished	3,688 sq. ft.
First Finished	2,065 sq. ft.
Second Finished	1,623 sq. ft.
Garage Unfinished	869 sq. ft.
Porch Unfinished	214 sq. ft.
Dimensions	82'x50'4"
Foundation	Basement
Bedrooms	4
Full Baths	2
Half Baths	2
3/4 Baths	1
First Ceiling	9'1 1/8"
Second Ceiling	9' 1 1/8"
Max Ridge Height	27'
Roof Framing	Truss
Exterior Walls	2x6

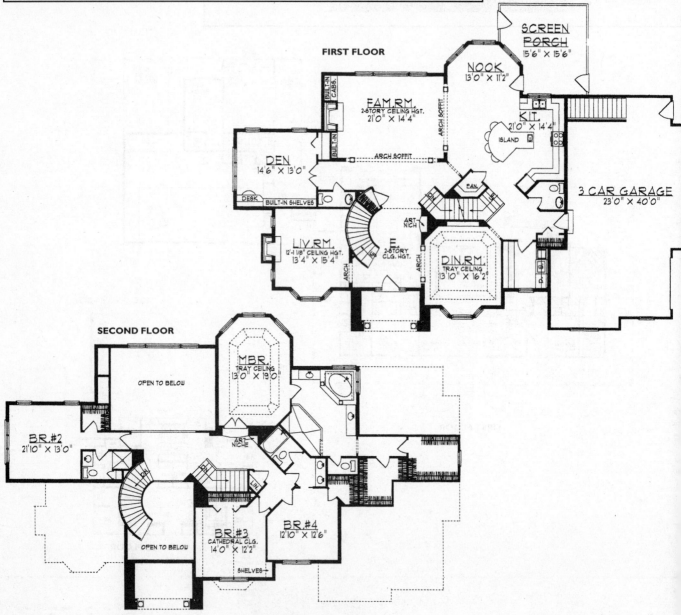

FIRST FLOOR

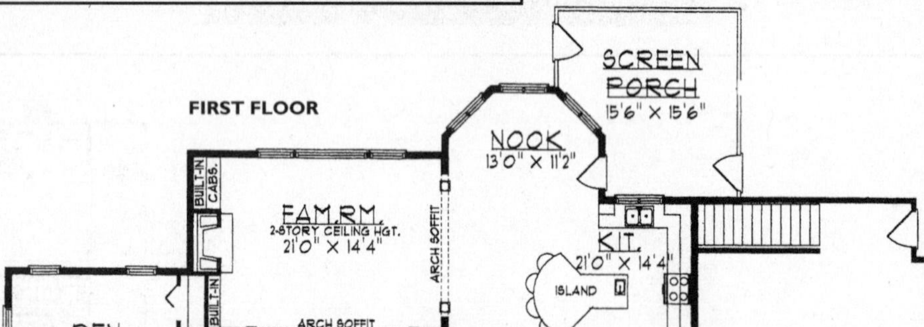
SCREEN PORCH
15'6" X 15'6"
NOOK
13'0" X 11'2"
FAM.RM.
2-STORY CEILING HGT.
21'0" X 14'4"
BUILT-IN CABS.
BUILT-IN
ARCH SOFFIT
ARCH SOFFIT
KIT.
21'0" X 14'4"
ISLAND
DEN
14'6" X 13'0"
DESK
BUILT-IN SHELVES
PAN.
ART NICH
3 CAR GARAGE
23'0" X 40'0"
LIV.RM.
12'-1 1/8" CEILING HGT.
13'4" X 15'4"
E.
2-STORY CLG. HGT.
ARCH
ARCH
DIN.RM.
TRAY CEILING
13'10" X 16'2"

SECOND FLOOR

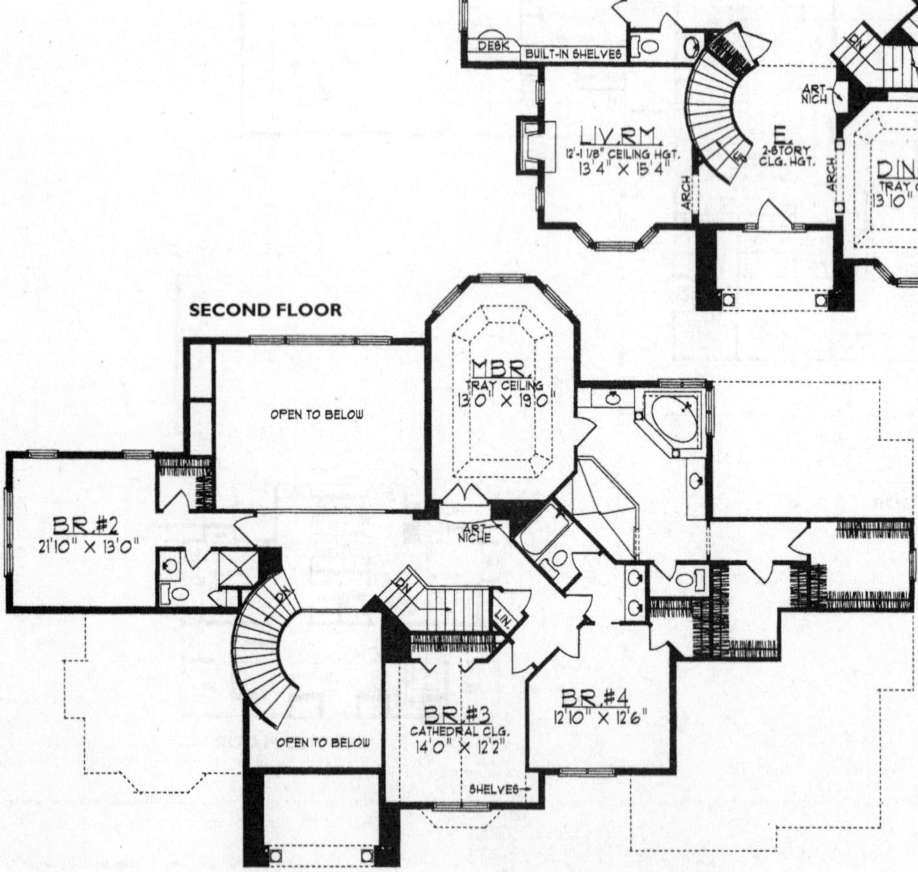
OPEN TO BELOW
MBR.
TRAY CEILING
13'0" X 19'0"
BR.#2
21'10" X 13'0"
ART NICHE
LIN.
BR.#3
CATHEDRAL CLG.
14'0" X 12'2"
BR.#4
12'10" X 12'6"
OPEN TO BELOW
SHELVES

Design 32146

See Order Pages and Index for Info

Photography supplied by the Meredith Corporation

Units	Single
Price Code	K
Total Finished	3,895 sq. ft.
First Finished	2,727 sq. ft.
Second Finished	1,168 sq. ft.
Bonus Unfinished	213 sq. ft.
Basement Unfinished	2,250 sq. ft.
Garage Unfinished	984 sq. ft.
Dimensions	73'8"x72'2"
Foundation	Basement
Bedrooms	4
Full Baths	4
Half Baths	1
First Ceiling	9'
Second Ceiling	8'
Vaulted Ceiling	22'
Max Ridge Height	43'
Roof Framing	Stick
Exterior Walls	2x6

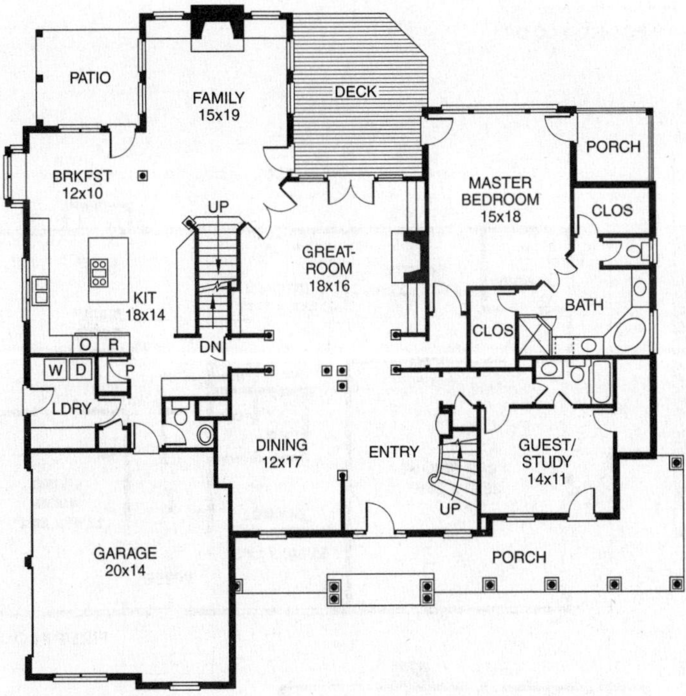
PATIO
FAMILY 15x19
DECK
PORCH
BRKFST 12x10
MASTER BEDROOM 15x18
CLOS
UP
GREAT-ROOM 18x16
KIT 18x14
BATH
CLOS
O R
DN
W D
P
LDRY
DINING 12x17
ENTRY
GUEST/ STUDY 14x11
UP
GARAGE 20x14
PORCH

FIRST FLOOR

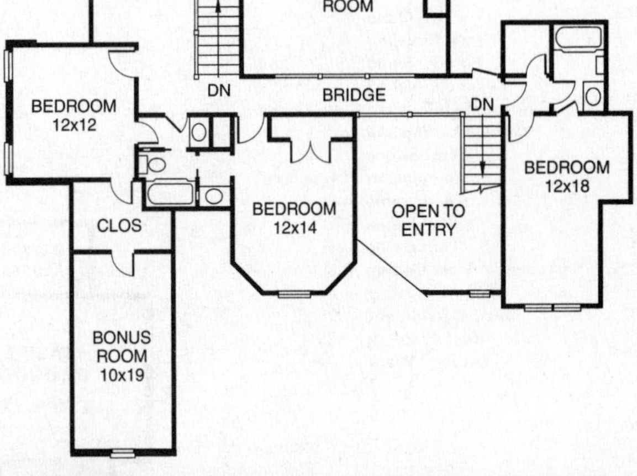
OPEN TO FAMILY
OFFICE 10x13
OPEN TO GREAT-ROOM
BEDROOM 12x12
DN
BRIDGE
DN
BEDROOM 12x18
BEDROOM 12x14
OPEN TO ENTRY
CLOS
BONUS ROOM 10x19

SECOND FLOOR

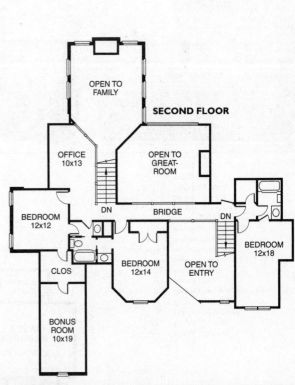

Design 99471

See Order Pages and Index for Info

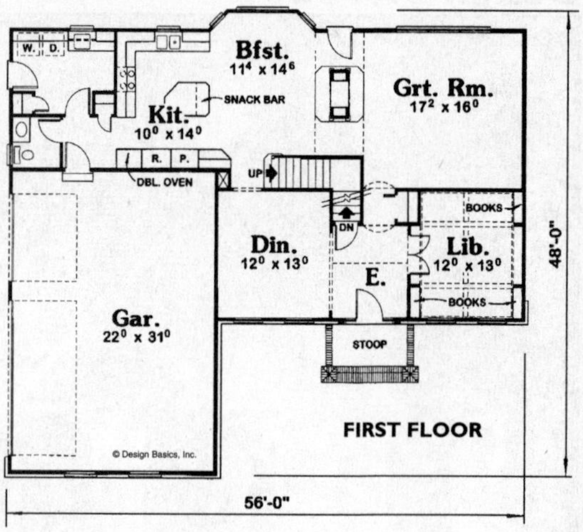
W.
D.
Bfst.
11⁴ x 14⁶
SNACK BAR
Kit.
10⁰ x 14⁰
Grt. Rm.
17² x 16⁰
R.
P.
DBL. OVEN
UP
DN
BOOKS
Din.
12⁰ x 13⁰
Lib.
12⁰ x 13⁰
E.
BOOKS
Gar.
22⁰ x 31⁰
STOOP
© Design Basics, Inc.
48'-0"
56'-0"

FIRST FLOOR

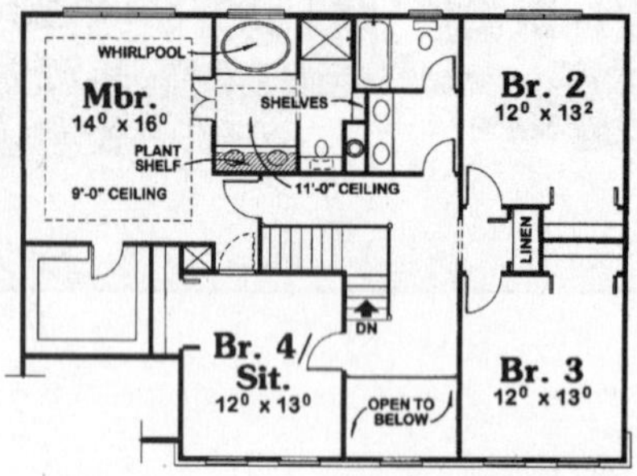
WHIRLPOOL
Mbr.
14⁰ x 16⁰
SHELVES
PLANT SHELF
9'-0" CEILING
11'-0" CEILING
Br. 2
12⁰ x 13²
LINEN
DN
Br. 4/ Sit.
12⁰ x 13⁰
OPEN TO BELOW
Br. 3
12⁰ x 13⁰

SECOND FLOOR

Units	Single
Price Code	F
Total Finished	2,642 sq. ft.
First Finished	1,357 sq. ft.
Second Finished	1,285 sq. ft.
Basement Unfinished	1,357 sq. ft.
Garage Unfinished	705 sq. ft.
Dimensions	56'x48'
Foundation	Basement
Bedrooms	4
Full Baths	2
Half Baths	1
Max Ridge Height	29'9"
Roof Framing	Stick
Exterior Walls	2x4

* Alternate foundation options available at an additional charge. Please call 1-800-235-5700 for more information.

Design 99092

See Order Pages and Index for Info

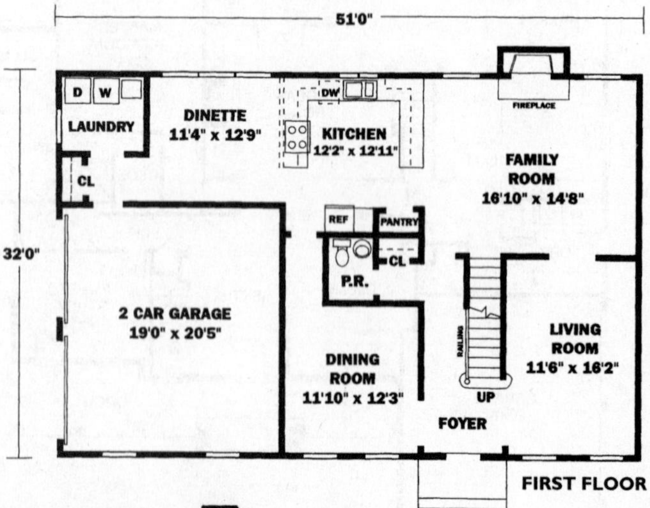
51'0"
D
W
LAUNDRY
DINETTE
11'4" x 12'9"
DW
KITCHEN
12'2" x 12'11"
FIREPLACE
FAMILY ROOM
16'10" x 14'8"
CL
REF
PANTRY
CL
P.R.
32'0"
2 CAR GARAGE
19'0" x 20'5"
RAILING
DINING ROOM
11'10" x 12'3"
LIVING ROOM
11'6" x 16'2"
UP
FOYER

FIRST FLOOR

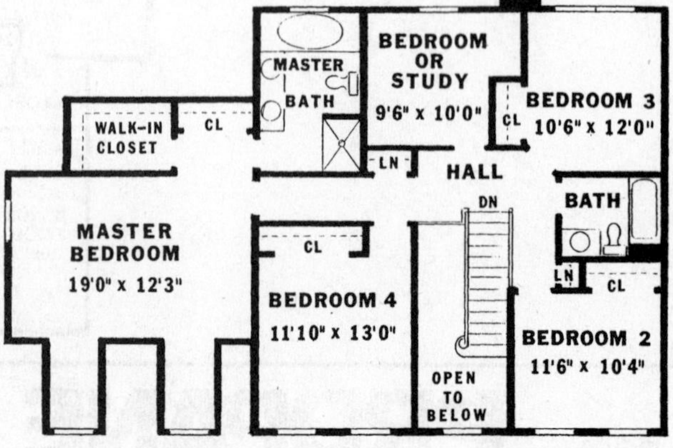
MASTER BATH
BEDROOM OR STUDY
9'6" x 10'0"
CL
BEDROOM 3
10'6" x 12'0"
WALK-IN CLOSET
CL
LN
HALL
DN
BATH
MASTER BEDROOM
19'0" x 12'3"
CL
BEDROOM 4
11'10" x 13'0"
LN
CL
BEDROOM 2
11'6" x 10'4"
OPEN TO BELOW

SECOND FLOOR

Units	Single
Price Code	F
Total Finished	2,549 sq. ft.
First Finished	1,246 sq. ft.
Second Finished	1,303 sq. ft.
Basement Unfinished	1,230 sq. ft.
Garage Unfinished	383 sq. ft.
Dimensions	51'x32'
Foundation	Basement
Bedrooms	5
Full Baths	2
Half Baths	1
First Ceiling	8'
Second Ceiling	8'
Max Ridge Height	29'
Roof Framing	Stick
Exterior Walls	2x4

Design 99456

See Order Pages and Index for Info

Units	Single
Price Code	H
Total Finished	3,057 sq. ft.
First Finished	1,631 sq. ft.
Second Finished	1,426 sq. ft.
Basement Unfinished	1,631 sq. ft.
Garage Unfinished	681 sq. ft.
Dimensions	60'x58'
Foundation	Basement
Bedrooms	4
Full Baths	2
Half Baths	1
3/4 Baths	1
Max Ridge Height	26'
Roof Framing	Stick
Exterior Walls	2x4

* Alternate foundation options available at an additional charge. Please call 1-800-235-5700 for more information.

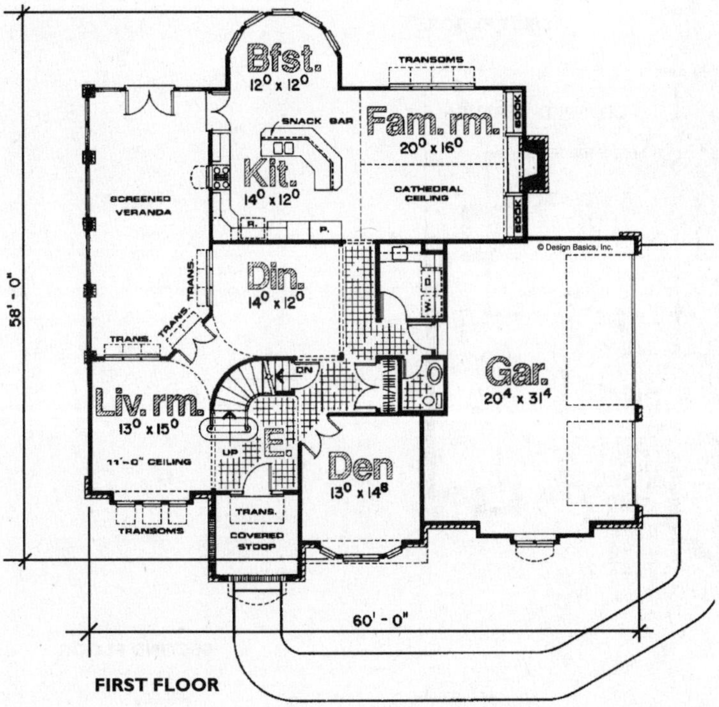
Bfst.
12⁰ x 12⁰
TRANSOMS
SNACK BAR
Fam. rm.
20⁰ x 16⁰
Kit.
14⁰ x 12⁰
CATHEDRAL CEILING
SCREENED VERANDA
© Design Basics, Inc.
Din.
14⁰ x 12⁰
TRANS.
Gar.
20⁴ x 31⁴
Liv. rm.
13⁰ x 15⁰
11'-0" CEILING
Den
13⁰ x 14⁸
TRANSOMS
COVERED STOOP
58' - 0"
60' - 0"

FIRST FLOOR

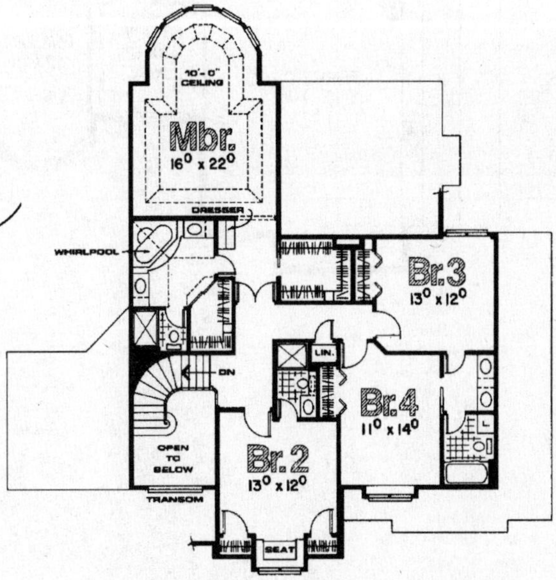
10'-0" CEILING
Mbr.
16⁰ x 22⁰
DRESSER
WHIRLPOOL
Br. 3
13⁰ x 12⁰
LIN.
DN
Br. 4
11⁰ x 14⁰
OPEN TO BELOW
Br. 2
13⁰ x 12⁰
TRANSOM
SEAT

SECOND FLOOR

Design 98539

See Order Pages and Index for Info

Units	Single
Price Code	K
Total Finished	3,936 sq. ft.
First Finished	2,751 sq. ft.
Second Finished	1,185 sq. ft.
Bonus Unfinished	343 sq. ft.
Garage Unfinished	790 sq. ft.
Porch Unfinished	36 sq. ft.
Dimensions	79'x66'4"
Foundation	Basement Slab
Bedrooms	4
Full Baths	3
Half Baths	1
First Ceiling	10'
Max Ridge Height	35'
Roof Framing	Stick
Exterior Walls	2x4

FIRST FLOOR

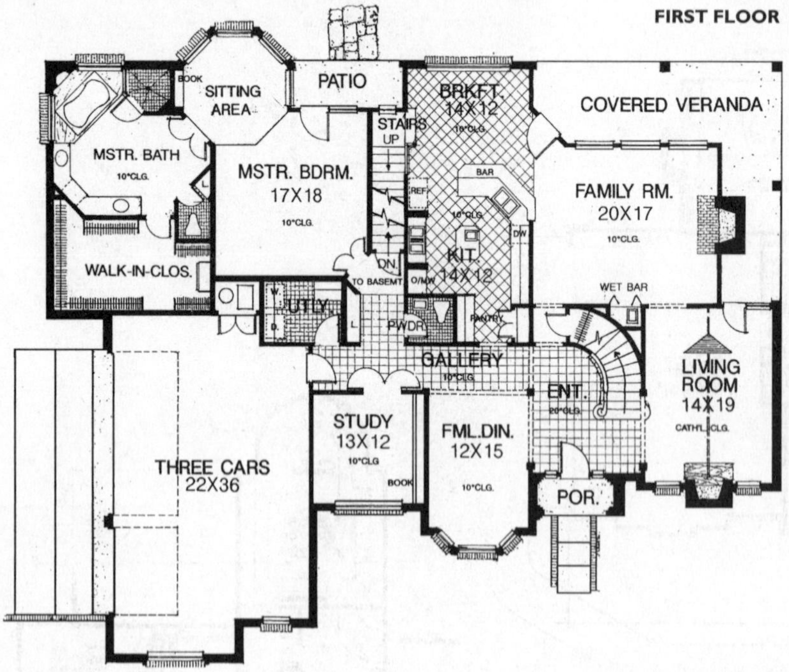
BOOK
SITTING AREA
PATIO
BRKFT. 14X12
COVERED VERANDA
MSTR. BATH
MSTR. BDRM. 17X18
STAIRS UP
BAR
REF
FAMILY RM. 20X17
KIT. 14X12
DW
DN.
TO BASEMT
O/MW
WALK-IN-CLOS.
UTLY
WET BAR
PWDR
PANTRY
GALLERY
ENT.
LIVING ROOM 14X19
CATH'L CLG.
STUDY 13X12
FML.DIN. 12X15
BOOK
THREE CARS 22X36
POR.

SECOND FLOOR

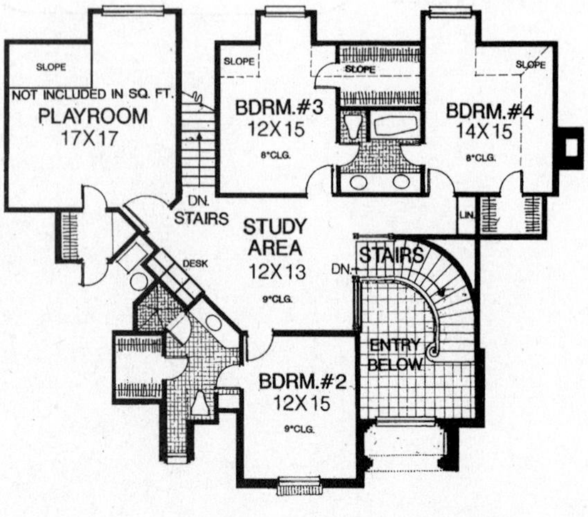
SLOPE
NOT INCLUDED IN SQ. FT.
PLAYROOM 17X17
SLOPE
BDRM.#3 12X15
SLOPE
BDRM.#4 14X15
DN.
STAIRS
STUDY AREA 12X13
LIN.
STAIRS
DN.
DESK
ENTRY BELOW
BDRM.#2 12X15

Design 92551

See Order Pages and Index for Info

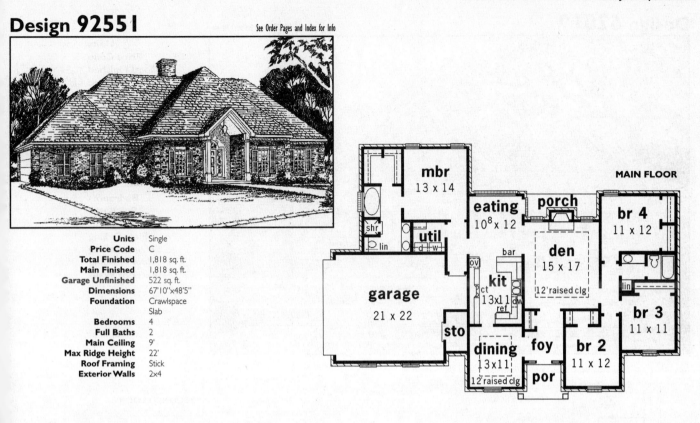

Units	Single
Price Code	C
Total Finished	1,818 sq. ft.
Main Finished	1,818 sq. ft.
Garage Unfinished	522 sq. ft.
Dimensions	67'10"x48'5"
Foundation	Crawlspace Slab
Bedrooms	4
Full Baths	2
Main Ceiling	9'
Max Ridge Height	22'
Roof Framing	Stick
Exterior Walls	2x4

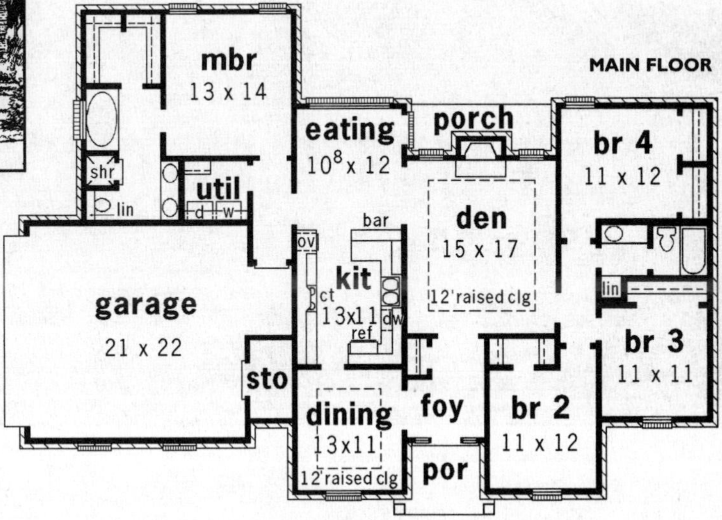
mbr
13 x 14
eating
10^8 x 12
porch
br 4
11 x 12
shr
lin
util
d w
bar
den
15 x 17
12'raised clg
ov
kit
13x11
ct
ref
dw
lin
br 3
11 x 11
garage
21 x 22
sto
dining
13x11
12'raised clg
foy
por
br 2
11 x 12

MAIN FLOOR

Design 93063

See Order Pages and Index for Info

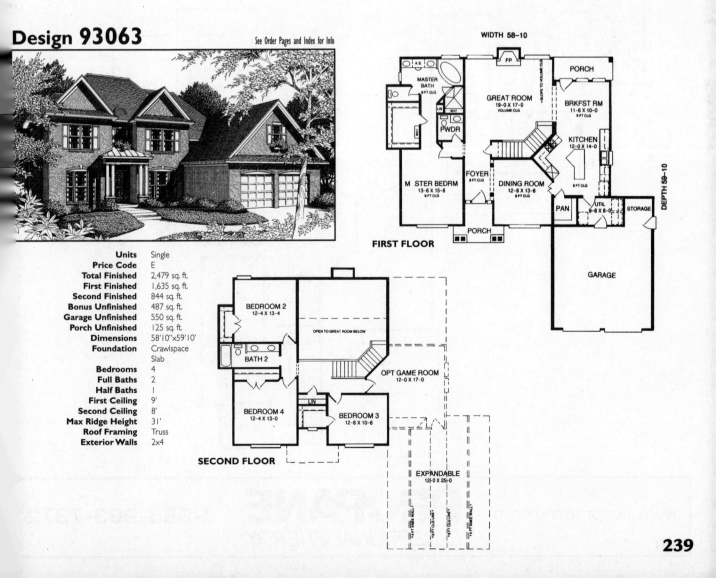

Units	Single
Price Code	E
Total Finished	2,479 sq. ft.
First Finished	1,635 sq. ft.
Second Finished	844 sq. ft.
Bonus Unfinished	487 sq. ft.
Garage Unfinished	550 sq. ft.
Porch Unfinished	125 sq. ft.
Dimensions	58'10"x59'10'
Foundation	Crawlspace Slab
Bedrooms	4
Full Baths	2
Half Baths	1
First Ceiling	9'
Second Ceiling	8'
Max Ridge Height	31'
Roof Framing	Truss
Exterior Walls	2x4

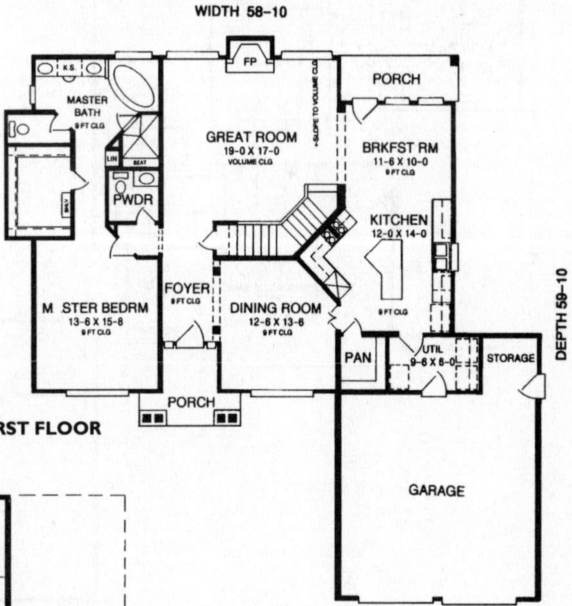
WIDTH 58-10
FP
MASTER BATH
9 FT CLG
GREAT ROOM
19-0 X 17-0
VOLUME CLG
PORCH
BRKFST RM
11-6 X 10-0
9 FT CLG
PWDR
KITCHEN
12-0 X 14-0
M STER BEDRM
13-6 X 15-8
9 FT CLG
FOYER
9 FT CLG
DINING ROOM
12-6 X 13-6
9 FT CLG
PAN
UTIL
9-6 X 6-0
STORAGE
PORCH
GARAGE
DEPTH 59-10

FIRST FLOOR

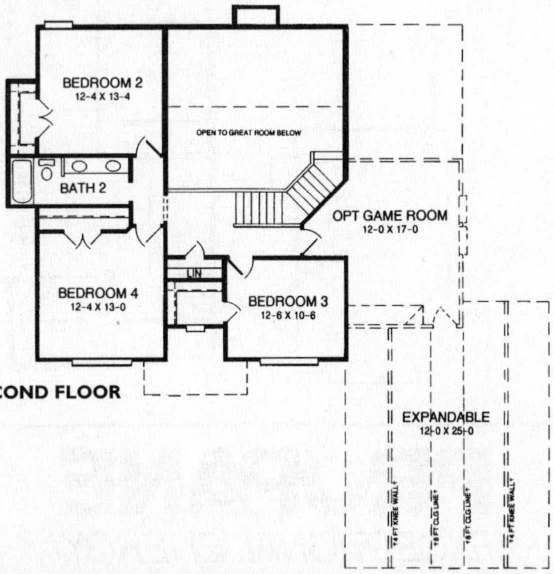
BEDROOM 2
12-4 X 13-4
OPEN TO GREAT ROOM BELOW
BATH 2
OPT GAME ROOM
12-0 X 17-0
LIN
BEDROOM 4
12-4 X 13-0
BEDROOM 3
12-6 X 10-6
EXPANDABLE
12-0 X 25-0

SECOND FLOOR

Design 62019

See Order Pages and Index for Info

Units	Single
Price Code	K
Total Finished	3,947 sq. ft.
First Finished	2,777 sq. ft.
Second Finished	1,170 sq. ft.
Lower Unfinished	1,616 sq. ft.
Garage Unfinished	794 sq. ft.
Porch Unfinished	704 sq. ft.
Dimensions	70'x75'10"
Foundation	Basement Crawlspace Slab
Bedrooms	3
Full Baths	3
Half Baths	2
First Ceiling	10'
Second Ceiling	9'
Roof Framing	Stick
Exterior Walls	2x4

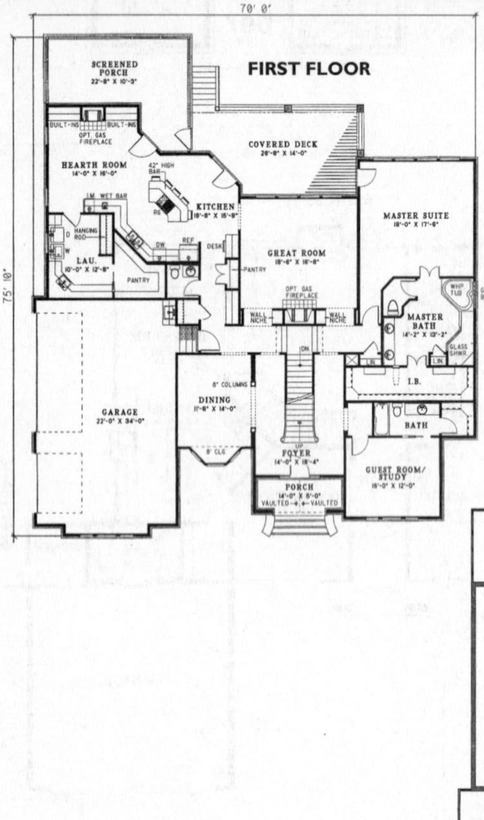

70' 0"
75' 10"
FIRST FLOOR
SCREENED PORCH
COVERED DECK
HEARTH ROOM
KITCHEN
MASTER SUITE
GREAT ROOM
LAU.
PANTRY
MASTER BATH
GARAGE
DINING
FOYER
PORCH
BATH
GUEST ROOM/ STUDY

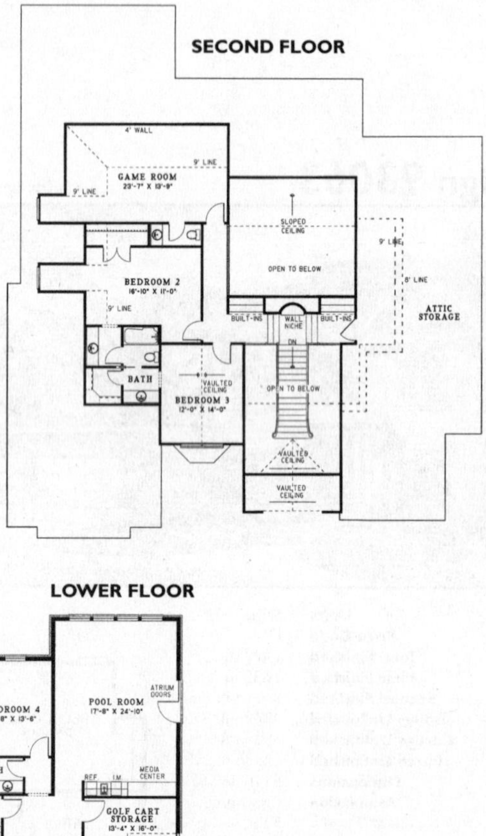

SECOND FLOOR
GAME ROOM
BEDROOM 2
OPEN TO BELOW
ATTIC STORAGE
BATH
BEDROOM 3

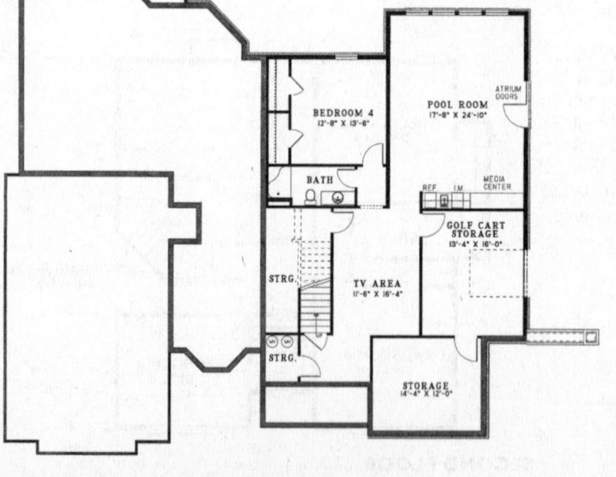

LOWER FLOOR
BEDROOM 4
POOL ROOM
BATH
GOLF CART STORAGE
STRG.
TV AREA
STORAGE

Design 93094

See Order Pages and Index for Info

Units	Single
Price Code	F
Total Finished	2,586 sq. ft.
First Finished	2,028 sq. ft.
Second Finished	558 sq. ft.
Bonus Unfinished	272 sq. ft.
Garage Unfinished	551 sq. ft.
Porch Unfinished	223 sq. ft.
Dimensions	64'10"x61'
Foundation	Basement Crawlspace Slab
Bedrooms	4
Full Baths	3
Max Ridge Height	29'
Roof Framing	Stick
Exterior Walls	2x4

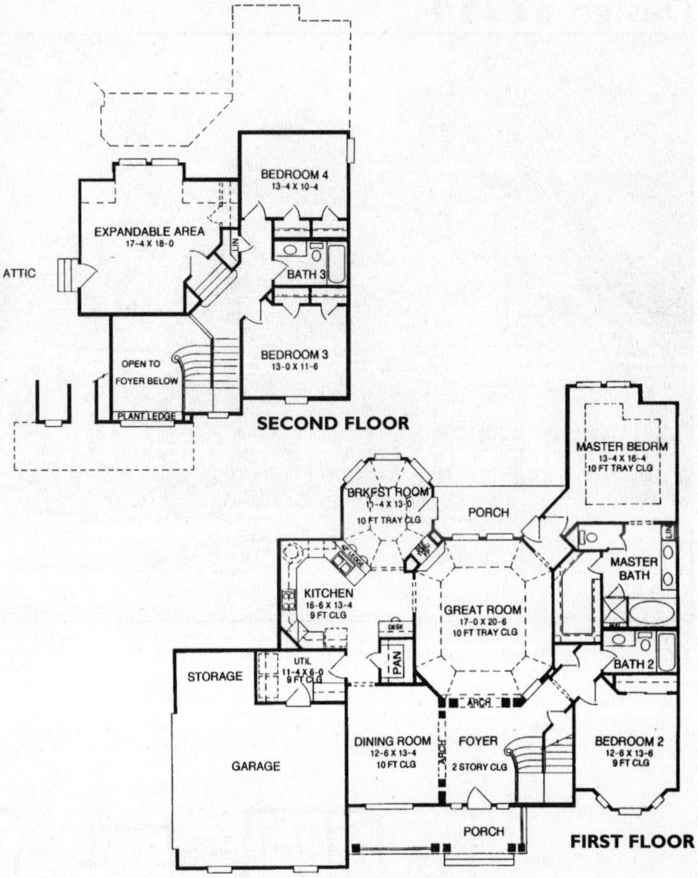
BEDROOM 4
13-4 X 10-4
EXPANDABLE AREA
17-4 X 18-0
ATTIC
LIN
BATH 3
OPEN TO
FOYER BELOW
PLANT LEDGE
BEDROOM 3
13-0 X 11-6
SECOND FLOOR
MASTER BEDRM
13-4 X 16-4
10 FT TRAY CLG
BRKFST ROOM
11-4 X 13-0
10 FT TRAY CLG
PORCH
KITCHEN
16-6 X 13-4
9 FT CLG
GREAT ROOM
17-0 X 20-6
10 FT TRAY CLG
MASTER
BATH
STORAGE
UTIL
11-4 X 6-0
9 FT CLG
PAN
BATH 2
ARCH
GARAGE
DINING ROOM
12-6 X 13-4
10 FT CLG
FOYER
2 STORY CLG
BEDROOM 2
12-6 X 13-6
9 FT CLG
PORCH
FIRST FLOOR

Design 93098

See Order Pages and Index for Info

Units	Single
Price Code	C
Total Finished	1,932 sq. ft.
Main Finished	1,932 sq. ft.
Garage Unfinished	552 sq. ft.
Dimensions	65'10"x53'5"
Foundation	Crawlspace Slab
Bedrooms	3
Full Baths	2
Max Ridge Height	22'4"
Roof Framing	Stick
Exterior Walls	2x4

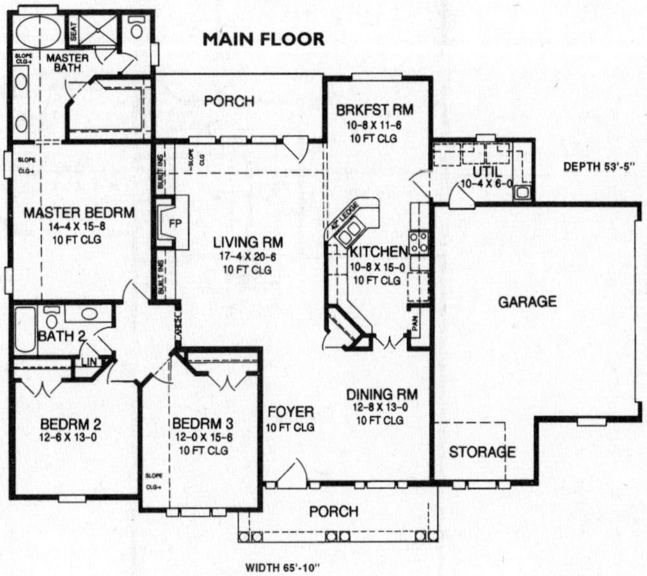
MAIN FLOOR
MASTER
BATH
SEAT
PORCH
BRKFST RM
10-8 X 11-6
10 FT CLG
UTIL
10-4 X 6-0
DEPTH 53'-5"
MASTER BEDRM
14-4 X 15-8
10 FT CLG
FP
LIVING RM
17-4 X 20-8
10 FT CLG
KITCHEN
10-8 X 15-0
10 FT CLG
GARAGE
BATH 2
LIN
PAN
BEDRM 2
12-6 X 13-0
BEDRM 3
12-0 X 15-6
10 FT CLG
FOYER
10 FT CLG
DINING RM
12-8 X 13-0
10 FT CLG
STORAGE
PORCH
WIDTH 65'-10"

Design 97254

See Order Pages and Index for Info

Units	Single
Price Code	B
Total Finished	1,692 sq. ft.
Main Finished	1,692 sq. ft.
Bonus Unfinished	358 sq. ft.
Basement Unfinished	1,705 sq. ft.
Garage Unfinished	472 sq. ft.
Dimensions	54'x56'6"
Foundation	Basement Crawlspace
Bedrooms	3
Full Baths	2
Max Ridge Height	27'
Roof Framing	Stick
Exterior Walls	2x4

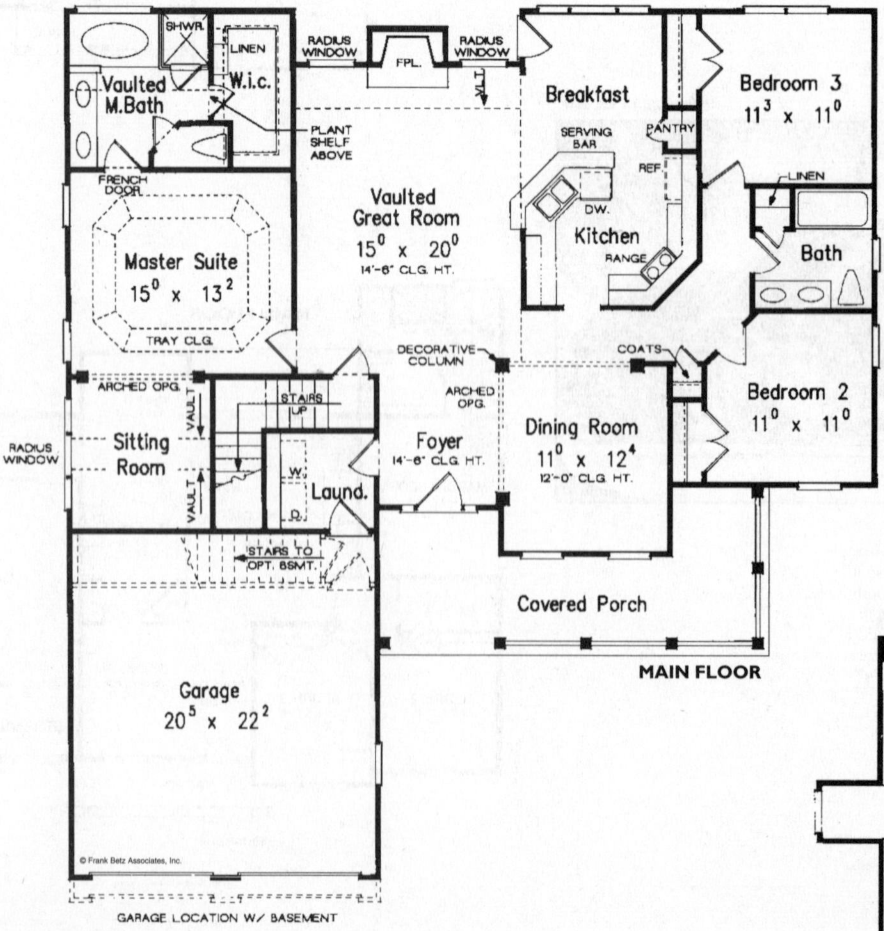
SHWR.
LINEN
Vaulted M.Bath
W.i.c.
RADIUS WINDOW
FPL.
RADIUS WINDOW
VLT.
PLANT SHELF ABOVE
FRENCH DOOR
Breakfast
SERVING BAR
PANTRY
REF.
DW.
Kitchen
RANGE
Bedroom 3
11^3 x 11^0
LINEN
Bath
Vaulted Great Room
15^0 x 20^0
14'-6" CLG. HT.
Master Suite
15^0 x 13^2
TRAY CLG.
DECORATIVE COLUMN
COATS
Bedroom 2
11^0 x 11^0
ARCHED OPG.
ARCHED OPG.
STAIRS UP
VAULT
VAULT
RADIUS WINDOW
Sitting Room
Foyer
14'-6" CLG. HT.
Dining Room
11^0 x 12^4
12'-0" CLG. HT.
W.
D.
Laund.
STAIRS TO OPT. BSMT.
Covered Porch
Garage
20^5 x 22^2
© Frank Betz Associates, Inc.
GARAGE LOCATION W/ BASEMENT

MAIN FLOOR

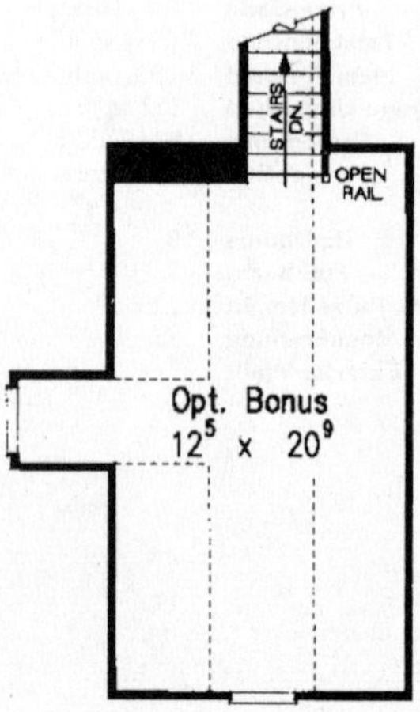
STAIRS DN.
OPEN RAIL
Opt. Bonus
12^5 x 20^9

BONUS

Design 32063

See Order Pages and Index for Info

Photography supplied by the Meredith Corporation

Units	Single
Price Code	L
Total Finished	4,283 sq. ft.
First Finished	1,642 sq. ft.
Second Finished	1,411 sq. ft.
Lower Finished	1,230 sq. ft.
Basement Unfinished	412 sq. ft.
Porch Unfinished	1,000 sq. ft.
Dimensions	92'x61'
Foundation	Basement
Bedrooms	4
Full Baths	4
Half Baths	1
First Ceiling	9'
Second Ceiling	8'
Max Ridge Height	35'
Roof Framing	Stick
Exterior Walls	2x6

Rear Elevation

SECOND FLOOR
BEDROOM 11x14
BATH
CLOS
CLOS
DN
BATH
BEDROOM 11x14
CLOS
MASTER BEDROOM 16x16
CLOS
UP
DECK
LIBRARY/ DEN 11x13
W D
LDRY
UP
GARAGE 23x37
BRZWY 9x11
DINING 14x13
ENTRY
FIRST FLOOR
DN
UP
R
P
SCREEN PORCH 11x11
GREAT-RM 20x16
KITCHEN 16x18
BRKFST 9x11
DN
DECK
LOWER FLOOR
MEDIA ROOM 22x18
MECH
GUEST 16x14
UP
CLOS
DRESS
BATH
STORAGE 32x6
PLAYRM/ EXERCISE 12x17

Design 93089

See Order Pages and Index for Info

Units	Single
Price Code	I
Total Finished	3,494 sq. ft.
First Finished	2,469 sq. ft.
Second Finished	1,025 sq. ft.
Bonus Unfinished	320 sq. ft.
Garage Unfinished	795 sq. ft.
Porch Unfinished	249 sq. ft.
Dimensions	67'8"x74'2"
Foundation	Basement Crawlspace Slab
Bedrooms	4
Full Baths	3
Half Baths	1
Max Ridge Height	31'
Roof Framing	Stick
Exterior Walls	2x4

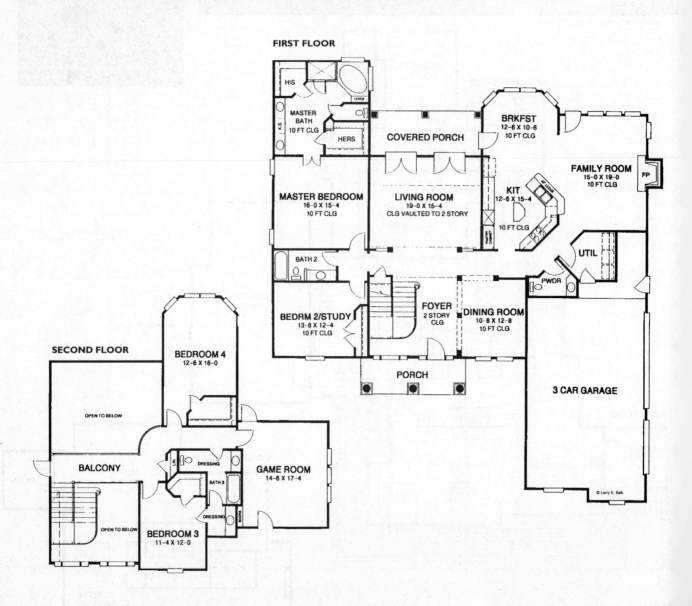

FIRST FLOOR

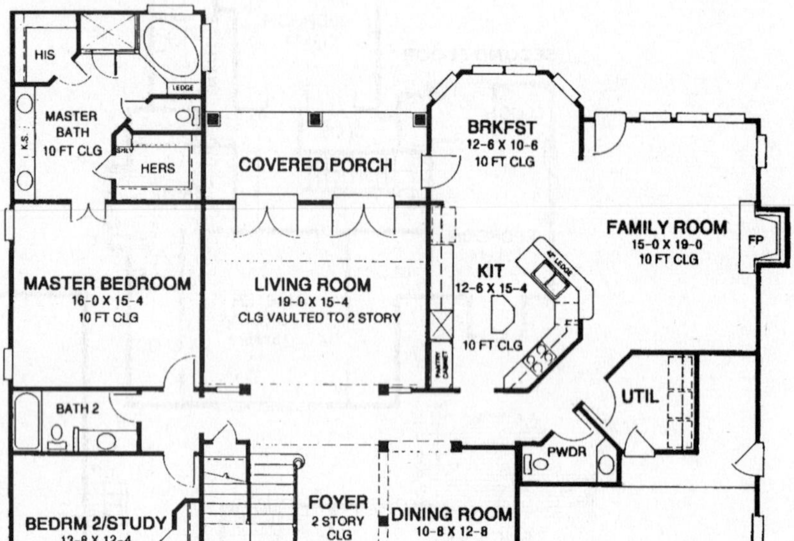
HIS
LEDGE
MASTER BATH 10 FT CLG
HERS
COVERED PORCH
BRKFST 12-6 X 10-6 10 FT CLG
FAMILY ROOM 15-0 X 19-0 10 FT CLG
FP
KIT 12-6 X 15-4
10 FT CLG
MASTER BEDROOM 16-0 X 15-4 10 FT CLG
LIVING ROOM 19-0 X 15-4 CLG VAULTED TO 2 STORY
BATH 2
UTIL
PWDR
FOYER 2 STORY CLG
BEDRM 2/STUDY 13-8 X 12-4 10 FT CLG
DINING ROOM 10-8 X 12-8 10 FT CLG
PORCH
3 CAR GARAGE
© Larry E. Belk

SECOND FLOOR

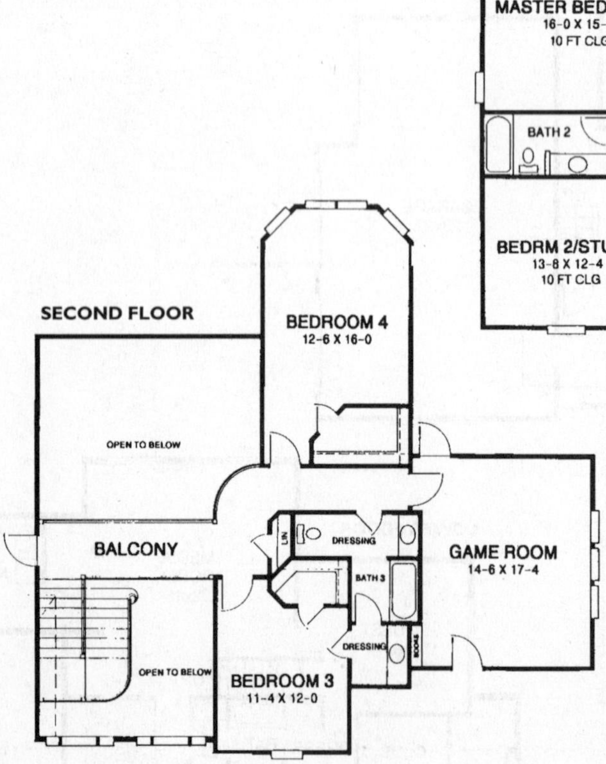
BEDROOM 4 12-6 X 16-0
OPEN TO BELOW
BALCONY
DRESSING
BATH 3
GAME ROOM 14-6 X 17-4
DRESSING
BOOKS
OPEN TO BELOW
BEDROOM 3 11-4 X 12-0

Design 98427

See Order Pages and Index for Info

Units	Single
Price Code	D
Total Finished	2,051 sq. ft.
Main Finished	2,051 sq. ft.
Basement Unfinished	2,051 sq. ft.
Garage Unfinished	441 sq. ft.
Dimensions	56'x60'6"
Foundation	Basement Crawlspace Slab
Bedrooms	3
Full Baths	2
Main Ceiling	9'
Max Ridge Height	27'5"
Roof Framing	Stick
Exterior Walls	2x4

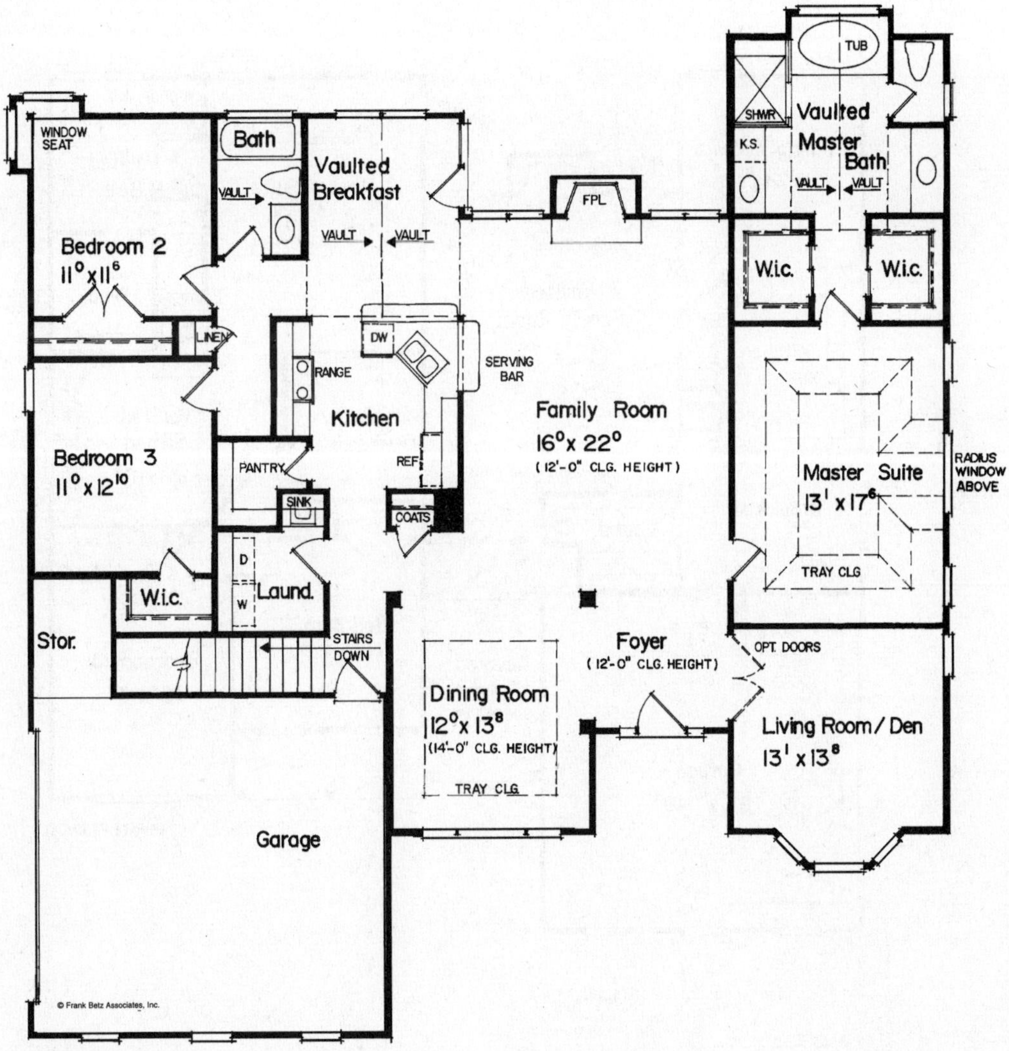

Window Seat
Bath
Vault
Vaulted Breakfast
Vault
Vault
Bedroom 2
11⁰x11⁶
Linen
DW
Range
Serving Bar
Kitchen
Pantry
Ref
Sink
Coats
Bedroom 3
11⁰x12¹⁰
D
W
Laund.
W.i.c.
Stor.
Stairs Down
FPL
Family Room
16⁰x 22⁰
(12'-0" CLG. HEIGHT)
TUB
SHWR
K.S.
Vaulted Master Bath
Vault
Vault
W.i.c.
W.i.c.
Master Suite
13¹ x 17⁶
Radius Window Above
Tray CLG
Foyer
(12'-0" CLG. HEIGHT)
OPT. DOORS
Dining Room
12⁰x 13⁸
(14'-0" CLG. HEIGHT)
Tray CLG
Living Room / Den
13¹ x 13⁸
Garage
© Frank Betz Associates, Inc.

MAIN FLOOR

Design 98423

See Order Pages and Index for Info

Units	Single
Price Code	B
Total Finished	1,671 sq. ft.
Main Finished	1,671 sq. ft.
Basement Unfinished	1,685 sq. ft.
Garage Unfinished	400 sq. ft.
Dimensions	50'x51'
Foundation	Basement Crawlspace Slab
Bedrooms	3
Full Baths	2
Main Ceiling	9'
Max Ridge Height	22'6"
Roof Framing	Stick
Exterior Walls	2x4

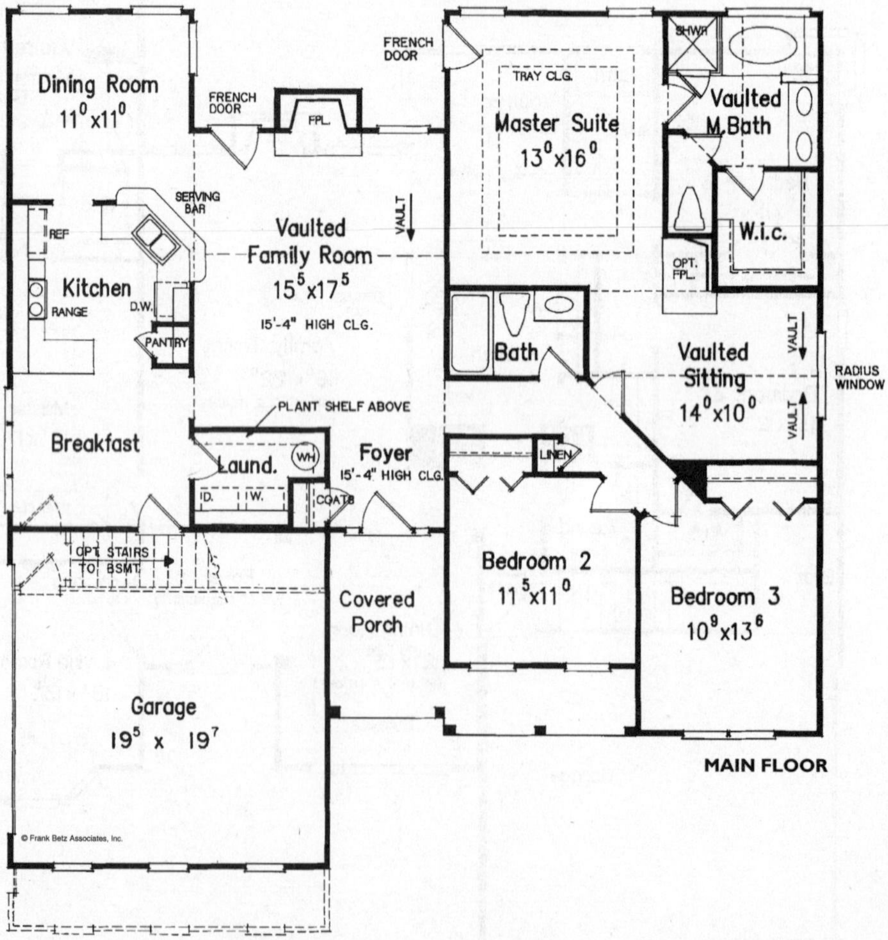
Dining Room
11^0x11^0
FRENCH DOOR
FPL.
FRENCH DOOR
SERVING BAR
REF
Kitchen
RANGE
D.W.
PANTRY
Vaulted Family Room
15^5x17^5
15'-4" HIGH CLG.
VAULT
PLANT SHELF ABOVE
Breakfast
Laund.
WH
D. W.
COATS
Foyer
15'-4" HIGH CLG.
OPT. STAIRS TO BSMT.
Covered Porch
Garage
19^5 x 19^7
© Frank Betz Associates, Inc.
TRAY CLG.
Master Suite
13^0x16^0
SHWR
Vaulted M.Bath
W.i.c.
OPT. FPL.
Bath
LINEN
Vaulted Sitting
14^0x10^0
VAULT
RADIUS WINDOW
Bedroom 2
11^5x11^0
Bedroom 3
10^9x13^6

MAIN FLOOR

Design 93209

See Order Pages and Index for Info

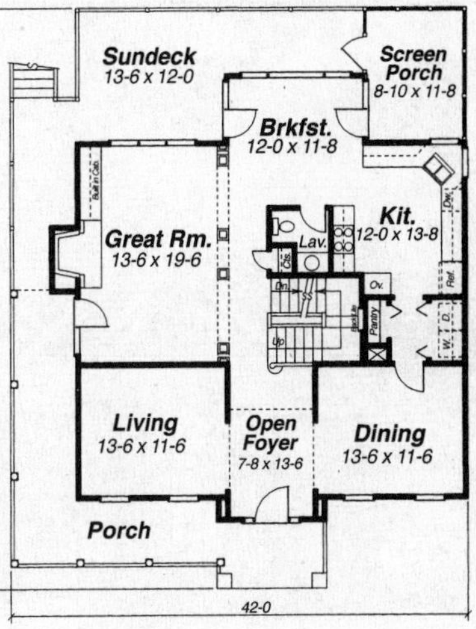
Sundeck
13-6 x 12-0
Screen Porch
8-10 x 11-8
Brkfst.
12-0 x 11-8
Great Rm.
13-6 x 19-6
Lav.
Kit.
12-0 x 13-8
Living
13-6 x 11-6
Open Foyer
7-8 x 13-6
Dining
13-6 x 11-6
Porch
50-0
42-0

FIRST FLOOR

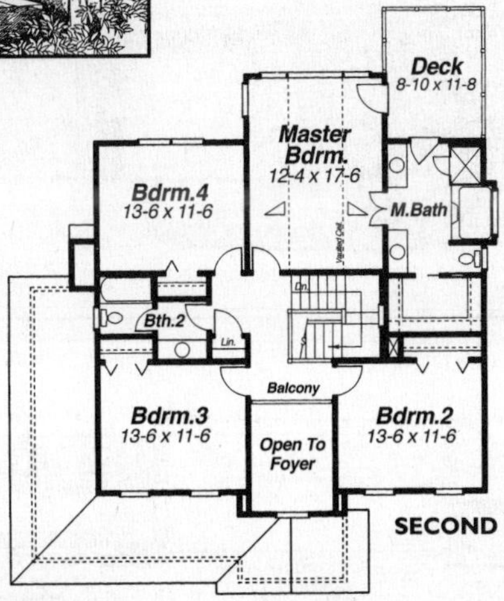
Deck
8-10 x 11-8
Master Bdrm.
12-4 x 17-6
Bdrm.4
13-6 x 11-6
M.Bath
Bth.2
Lin.
Balcony
Bdrm.3
13-6 x 11-6
Open To Foyer
Bdrm.2
13-6 x 11-6

SECOND FLOOR

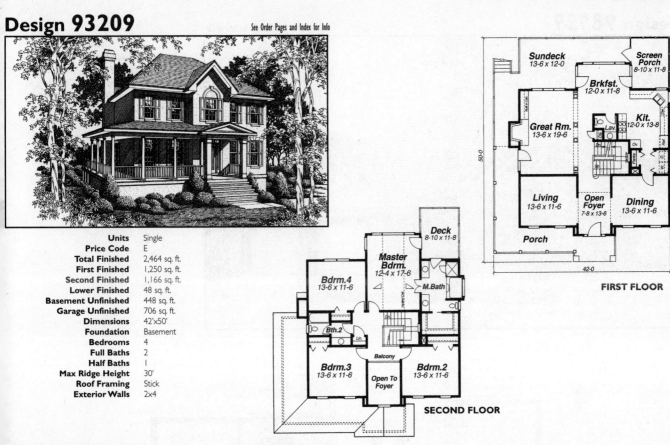

Units	Single
Price Code	E
Total Finished	2,464 sq. ft.
First Finished	1,250 sq. ft.
Second Finished	1,166 sq. ft.
Lower Finished	48 sq. ft.
Basement Unfinished	448 sq. ft.
Garage Unfinished	706 sq. ft.
Dimensions	42'x50'
Foundation	Basement
Bedrooms	4
Full Baths	2
Half Baths	1
Max Ridge Height	30'
Roof Framing	Stick
Exterior Walls	2x4

Design 94112

See Order Pages and Index for Info

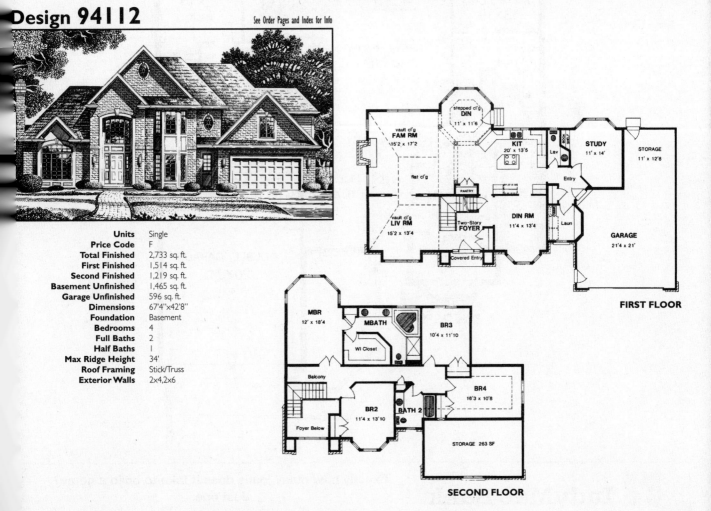

Units	Single
Price Code	F
Total Finished	2,733 sq. ft.
First Finished	1,514 sq. ft.
Second Finished	1,219 sq. ft.
Basement Unfinished	1,465 sq. ft.
Garage Unfinished	596 sq. ft.
Dimensions	67'4"x42'8"
Foundation	Basement
Bedrooms	4
Full Baths	2
Half Baths	1
Max Ridge Height	34'
Roof Framing	Stick/Truss
Exterior Walls	2x4,2x6

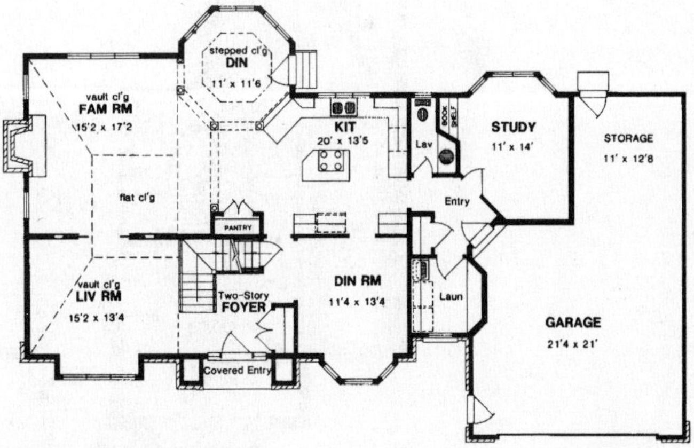
stepped cl'g
DIN
11' x 11'6
vault cl'g
FAM RM
15'2 x 17'2
KIT
20' x 13'5
STUDY
11' x 14'
STORAGE
11' x 12'8
Lav
flat cl'g
Entry
PANTRY
vault cl'g
LIV RM
15'2 x 13'4
Two-Story
FOYER
DIN RM
11'4 x 13'4
Laun
GARAGE
21'4 x 21'
Covered Entry

FIRST FLOOR

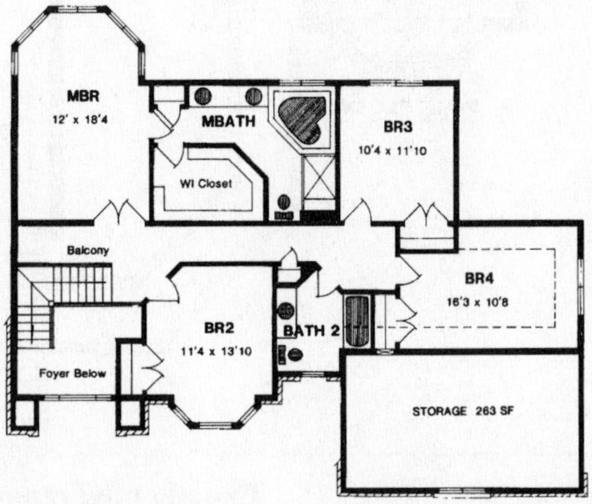
MBR
12' x 18'4
MBATH
BR3
10'4 x 11'10
WI Closet
Balcony
BR4
16'3 x 10'8
BR2
11'4 x 13'10
BATH 2
Foyer Below
STORAGE 263 SF

SECOND FLOOR

Design 98559

See Order Pages and Index for Info

Units	Single
Price Code	D
Total Finished	2,081 sq. ft.
Main Finished	2,081 sq. ft.
Garage Unfinished	422 sq. ft.
Porch Unfinished	240 sq. ft.
Dimensions	55'x57'10"
Foundation	Slab
Bedrooms	3
Full Baths	2
3/4 Baths	1
Max Ridge Height	24'6"
Roof Framing	Stick
Exterior Walls	2x4

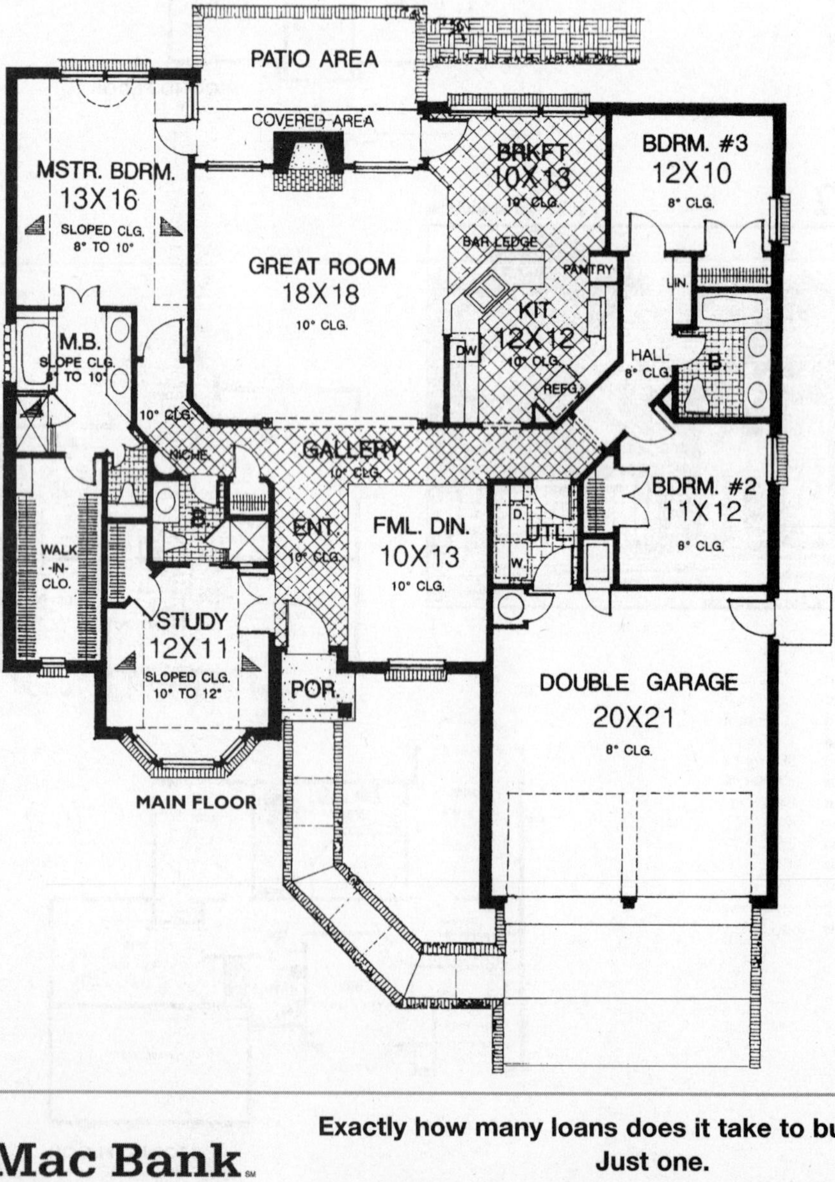
PATIO AREA
COVERED AREA
MSTR. BDRM.
13X16
SLOPED CLG.
8° TO 10°
BRKFT
10X13
10° CLG.
BDRM. #3
12X10
8° CLG.
GREAT ROOM
18X18
10° CLG.
BAR LEDGE
PANTRY
LIN.
KIT.
12X12
10° CLG.
DW
REFG.
HALL
8° CLG.
B.
M.B.
SLOPE CLG.
8° TO 10°
10° CLG.
NICHE
GALLERY
10° CLG.
BDRM. #2
11X12
8° CLG.
B.
ENT.
10° CLG.
FML. DIN.
10X13
10° CLG.
D.
W.
UTL.
WALK-IN-CLO.
STUDY
12X11
SLOPED CLG.
10° TO 12°
POR.
DOUBLE GARAGE
20X21
8° CLG.

MAIN FLOOR

Design 94810

See Order Pages and Index for Info

WHEELCHAIR BATH

MAIN FLOOR

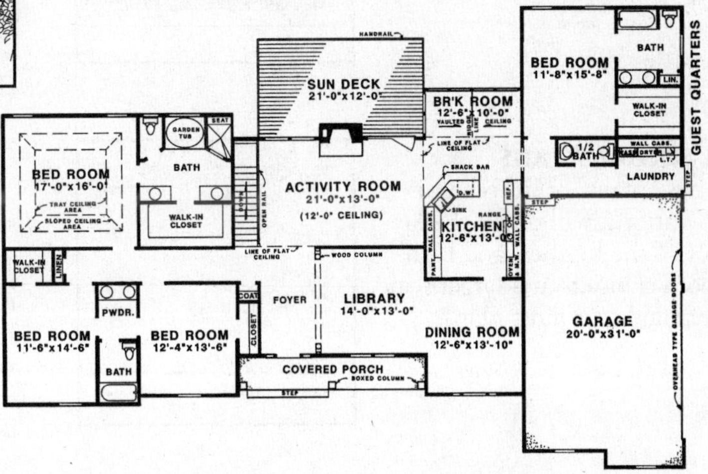

SUN DECK 21'-0"x12'-0"
BR'K ROOM 12'-6"x10'-0"
BED ROOM 11'-8"x15'-8"
BATH
GUEST QUARTERS
BED ROOM 17'-0"x16'-0"
BATH
WALK-IN CLOSET
ACTIVITY ROOM 21'-0"x13'-0" (12'-0" CEILING)
KITCHEN 12'-6"x13'-0"
1/2 BATH
LAUNDRY
PWDR.
FOYER
LIBRARY 14'-0"x13'-0"
BED ROOM 11'-6"x14'-6"
BED ROOM 12'-4"x13'-6"
BATH
COVERED PORCH
DINING ROOM 12'-6"x13'-10"
GARAGE 20'-0"x31'-0"

Units	Single
Price Code	F
Total Finished	2,690 sq. ft.
Main Finished	2,690 sq. ft.
Basement Unfinished	2,690 sq. ft.
Garage Unfinished	660 sq. ft.
Porch Unfinished	95 sq. ft.
Dimensions	87'6"x56'10"
Foundation	Basement
Bedrooms	4
Full Baths	3
Half Baths	1
Main Ceiling	9'
Vaulted Ceiling	14'
Tray Ceiling	11'
Max Ridge Height	25'4"
Roof Framing	Stick
Exterior Walls	2x4

Design 94917

See Order Pages and Index for Info

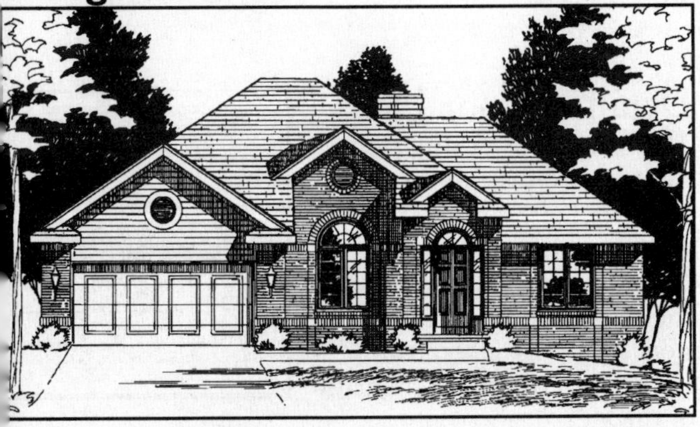

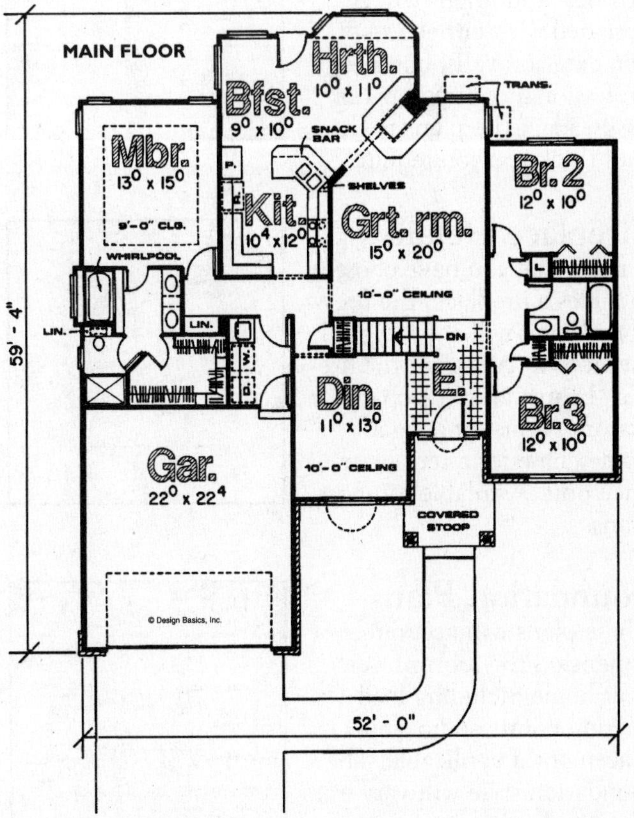

MAIN FLOOR
Hrth. 10⁰ x 11⁰
Bfst. 9⁰ x 10⁰
Mbr. 13⁰ x 15⁰
9'-0" CLG.
SNACK BAR
Kit. 10⁴ x 12⁰
Grt. rm. 15⁰ x 20⁰
10'-0" CEILING
Br. 2 12⁰ x 10⁰
WHIRLPOOL
Din. 11⁰ x 13⁰
10'-0" CEILING
E.
Br. 3 12⁰ x 10⁰
Gar. 22⁰ x 22⁴
COVERED STOOP
59' - 4"
52' - 0"
© Design Basics, Inc.

Units	Single
Price Code	C
Total Finished	1,782 sq. ft.
Main Finished	1,782 sq. ft.
Basement Unfinished	1,782 sq. ft.
Garage Unfinished	466 sq. ft.
Dimensions	52'x59'4"
Foundation	Basement Slab
Bedrooms	3
Full Baths	2
Max Ridge Height	21'
Roof Framing	Stick
Exterior Walls	2x4

* Alternate foundation options available at an additional charge. Please call 1-800-235-5700 for more information.

Everything you need...to Make Your Dream Come True!

Exterior Elevations
Scaled drawings of the front, rear, sides of the home. Information pertaining to the exterior finish materials, roof pitches and exterior height dimensions.

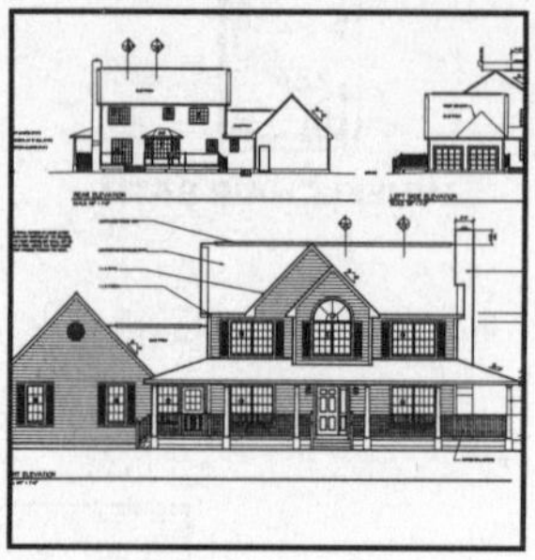

Cabinet Plans
These plans, or in some cases elevations, will detail the layout of the kitchen and bathroom cabinets at a larger scale. Available for most plans.

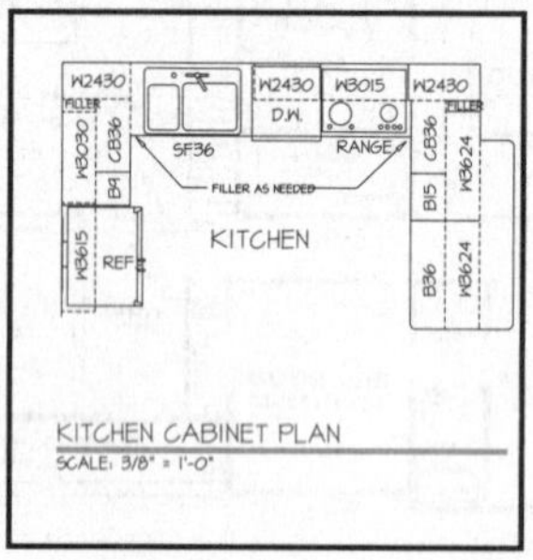
W2430
W2430
W3015
W2430
D.W.
RANGE
SF36
FILLER AS NEEDED
KITCHEN
REF.
KITCHEN CABINET PLAN
SCALE: 3/8" = 1'-0"

Typical Wall Section
This section will address insulation, roof components, and interior and exterior wall finishes. Your plans will be designed with either 2x4 or 2x6 exterior walls, but most professional contractors can easily adapt the plans to the wall thickness you require.

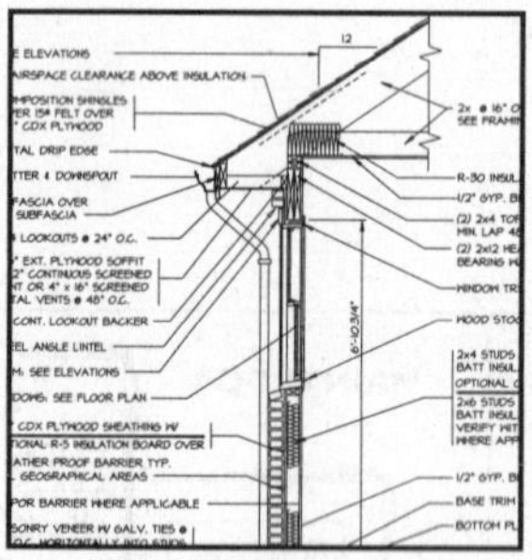

Fireplace Details
If the home you have chosen includes a fireplace, the fireplace detail will show typical methods to construct the firebox, hearth and flue chase for masonry units, or a wood frame chase for a zero-clearance unit. Available for most plans.

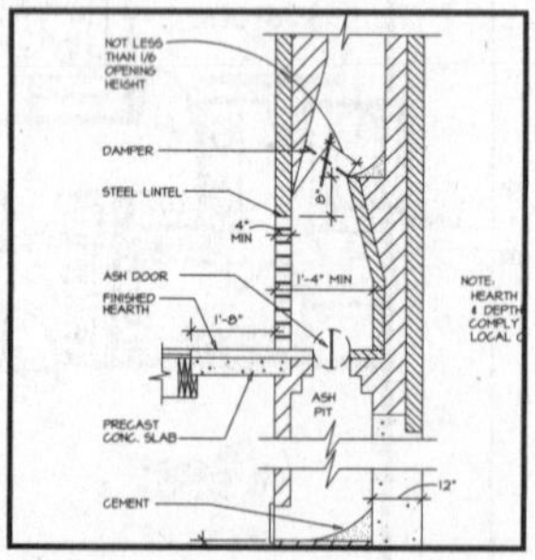
DAMPER
STEEL LINTEL
ASH DOOR
PRECAST CONC. SLAB
CEMENT

Foundation Plan
These plans will accurately dimension the footprint of your home including load bearing points and beam placement if applicable. The foundation style will vary from plan to plan.

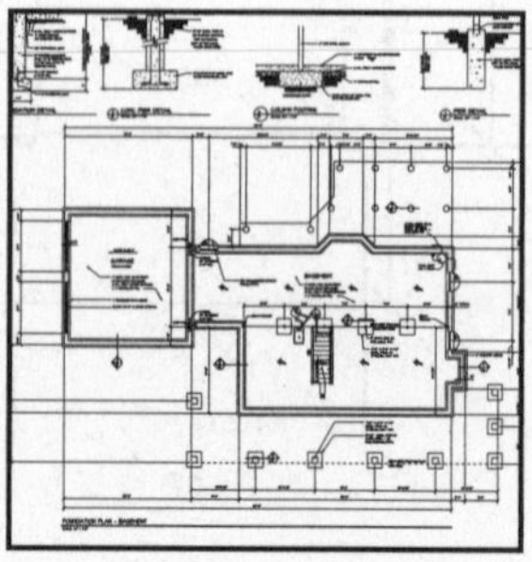

Roof Plan
The information necessary to construct the roof will be included with your home plans. Some plans will reference roof trusses, while many others contain schematic framing plans. These framing plans will indicate the lumber sizes necessary for the rafters and ridgeboards based on the designated roof loads.

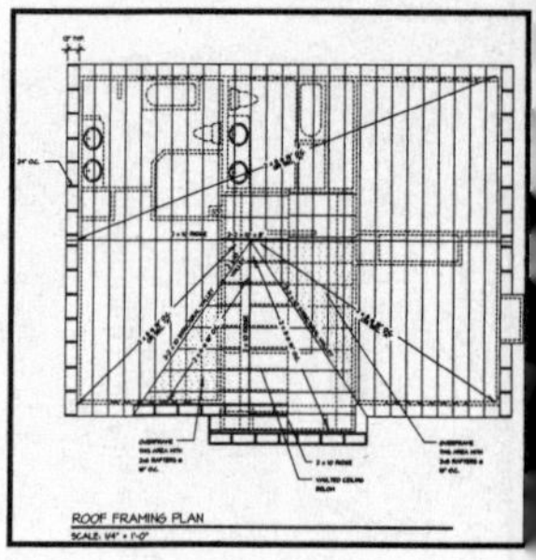
ROOF FRAMING PLAN

Typical Cross Section
A cut-away cross-section through the entire home shows your building contractor the exact correlation of construction components at all levels of the house. It will help to clarify the load bearing points from the roof all the way down to the basement. Available for most plans.

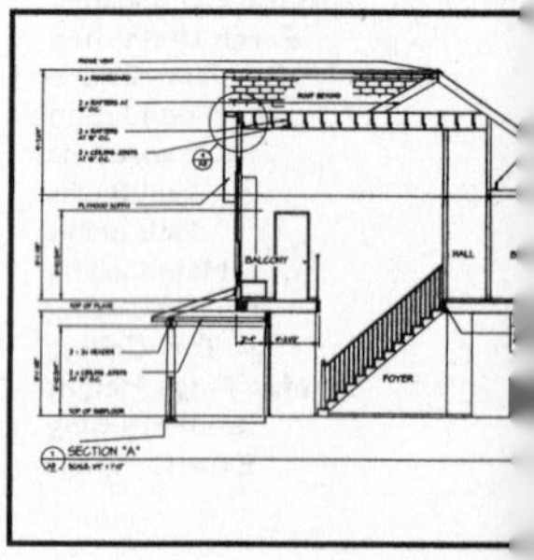
SECTION "A"

Detailed Floor Plans
The floor plans of your home accurately dimension the positioning of all walls, doors, windows, stairs and permanent fixtures. They will show you the relationship and dimensions of rooms, closets and traffic patterns. The schematic of the electrical layout may be included in the plan.

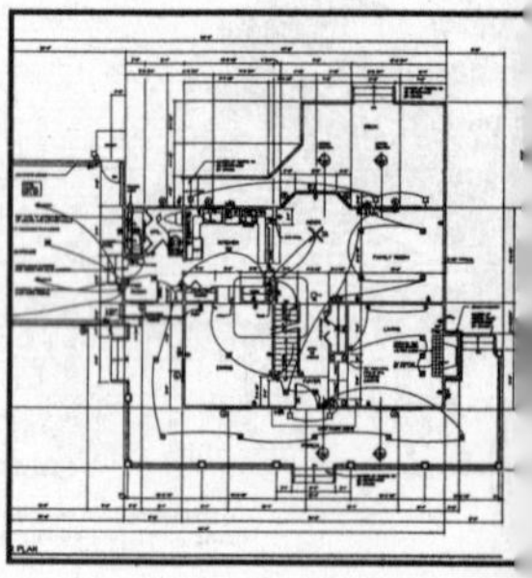

Stair Details
If stairs are an element of the design you have chosen, the plans will show the necessary information to build these, either through a stair cross section, or on the floor plans.

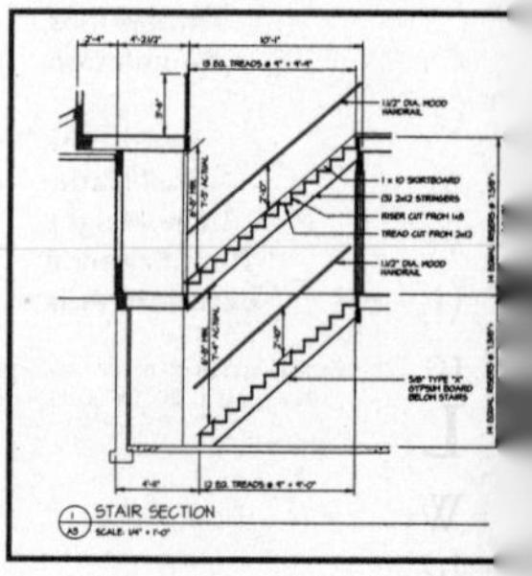
STAIR SECTION

Reversed Plans Can Make Your Dream Home Just Right!

You could have exactly the home you want by flipping it end-for-end. Simply order your plans "reversed." We'll send you one full set of mirror-image plans (with the writing backwards) as a master guide for you and your builder.

The remaining sets of your order will come as shown in this book so the dimensions and specifications are easily read on the job site...but most plans in our collection come stamped "reversed" so there is no confusion.

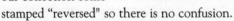

As Shown
Reversed

We can only send reversed plans with multiple-set orders. There is a $50 charge for this service.

Some plans in our collection are available in Right Reading Reverse. Right Reading Reverse plans will show your home in reverse, with the writing on the plan being readable. This easy-to-read format will save you valuable time and money. Please contact our Customer Service Department to check for Right Reading Reverse availability. There is a $135 charge for Right Reading Reverse. RRR

Remember To Order Your Materials List

Available at a modest additional charge, the Materials List gives the quantity, dimensions, and specifications for the major materials needed to build your home. You will get faster, more accurate bids from your contractors and building suppliers — and avoid paying for unused materials and waste. Materials Lists are available for all home plans except as otherwise indicated, but can only be ordered with a set of home plans. Due to differences in regional requirements and homeowner or builder preferences... electrical, plumbing and heating/air conditioning equipment specifications are not designed specifically for each plan. ML

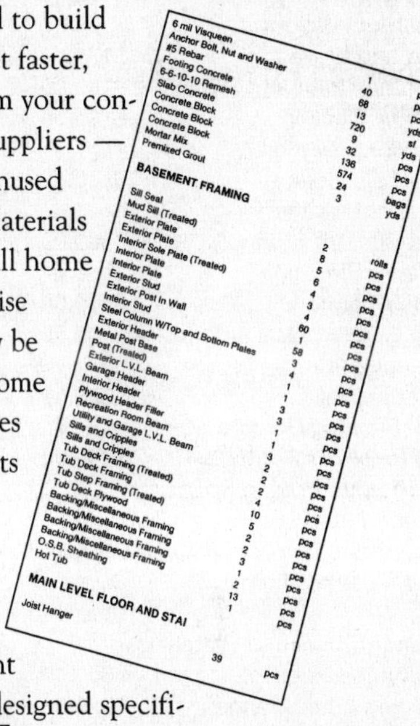
6 mil Visqueen
Anchor Bolt, Nut and Washer
#5 Rebar
Footing Concrete
6-6-10-10 Remesh
Slab Concrete
Concrete Block
Concrete Block
Concrete Block
Mortar Mix
Premixed Grout
BASEMENT FRAMING
Sill Seal
Mud Sill (Treated)
Exterior Plate
Exterior Plate
Interior Sole Plate (Treated)
Interior Plate
Interior Plate
Exterior Stud
Exterior Post In Wall
Interior Stud
Steel Column W/Top and Bottom Plates
Exterior Header
Metal Post Base
Post (Treated)
Exterior L.V.L. Beam
Garage Header
Interior Header
Plywood Header Filler
Recreation Room Beam
Utility and Garage L.V.L. Beam
Sills and Cripples
Sills and Cripples
Tub Deck Framing (Treated)
Tub Deck Framing
Tub Step Framing (Treated)
Tub Deck Plywood
Backing/Miscellaneous Framing
Backing/Miscellaneous Framing
Backing/Miscellaneous Framing
Backing/Miscellaneous Framing
O.S.B. Sheathing
Hot Tub
MAIN LEVEL FLOOR AND STAI
Joist Hanger
1 40 68 13 720 9 32 136 574 24 3
2 8 5 6 4 3 4 60 1 58 3 4 1 1 3 3 1 1 3 2 2 2 4 10 5 2 2 3 1 2 13 1
39
pcs pcs pcs yds sf yds pcs pcs pcs bags yds
rolls pcs pcs pcs pcs pcs pcs pcs pcs pcs pcs pcs pcs pcs pcs pcs pcs pcs pcs pcs pcs pcs pcs pcs pcs pcs pcs pcs pcs pcs pcs pcs
pcs

What Garlinghouse Offers

Home Plan Blueprint Package

By purchasing a multiple set package of blueprints or a vellum from Garlinghouse, you not only receive the physical blueprint documents necessary for construction, but you are also granted a license to build one, and only one, home. You can also make simple modifications, including minor non-structural changes and material substitutions, to our design, as long as these changes are made directly on the blueprints purchased from Garlinghouse and no additional copies are made.

Home Plan Vellums

By purchasing vellums for one of our home plans, you receive the same construction drawings found in the blueprints, but printed on vellum paper. Vellums can be erased and are perfect for making design changes. They are also semi-transparent making them easy to duplicate. But most importantly, the purchase of home plan vellums comes with a broader license that allows you to make changes to the design (ie, create a hand drawn or CAD derivative work), to make copies of the plan, and to build one home from the plan.

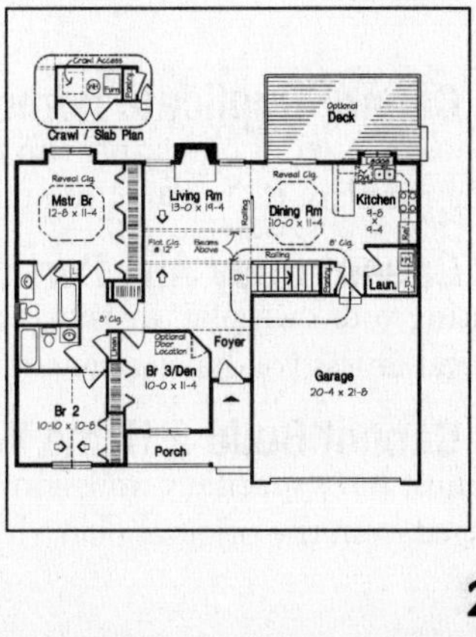
Crawl / Slab Plan
Deck
Mstr Br
Living Rm
Dining Rm
Kitchen
Laun.
Foyer
Br 3/Den
Br 2
Garage
Porch

License To Build Additional Homes

With the purchase of a blueprint package or vellums you automatically receive a license to build one home and only one home, respectively. If you want to build more homes than you are licensed to build through your purchase of a plan, then additional licenses may be purchased at reasonable costs from Garlinghouse. Inquire for more information.

Modify Your Favorite Design, Made Easy

MODIFICATION PRICING GUIDE

CATEGORIES	ESTIMATED COST
Kitchen Layout Plan and Elevation	$175.00
Bathroom Layout Plan and Elevation	$175.00
Fireplace Plan and Details	$200.00
Interior Elevation	$125.00
Exterior Elevation Material Change	$140.00
Exterior Elevation Add Brick or Stone	$400.00
Exterior Elevation Style Change	$450.00
Non Bearing Walls(interior)	$200.00
Bearing and/or Exterior Walls	$325.00
Wall Framing Change 2x4 to 2x6 or 2x6 to 2x4	$240.00
Add/Reduce Living Space Square Footage	Quote Required
New Materials List	Quote Required
Change Trusses to Rafters or Change Roof Pitch	$300.00
Framing Plan Changes	$325.00
Garage Changes	$325.00
Add a Foundation Option	$300.00
Foundation Changes	$250.00
Right Reading Plan Reverse	$575.00
Architects Seal (available for most states)	$300.00
Energy Certificate	$150.00
Light and Ventilation Schedule	$150.00

Questions?

Call our customer service department at 1.860.659.5667

#1 Modifying Your Garlinghouse Home Plan

Simple modifications to your dream home, including minor non-structural changes and material substitutions, can be made between you and your builder by marking the changes directly on your blueprints. However, if you are considering making significant changes to your chosen design, we recommend that you use the services of The Garlinghouse Design Staff. We will help take your ideas and turn them into a reality, just the way you want. Here's our procedure:

When you place your Vellum order, you may also request a free Garlinghouse Modification Kit. In this kit, you will receive a red marking pencil, furniture cut-out sheet, ruler, a self-addressed mailing label and a form for specifying any additional notes or drawings that will help us understand your design ideas. Mark your desired changes directly on the Vellum drawings. NOTE: Please use only a ***red pencil*** to mark your desired changes on the Vellum. Then, return the red-lined Vellum set in the original box to us.

Important: Please roll the Vellums for shipping, ***do not fold.***

We also offer modification estimates. We will provide you with an estimate to draft your changes based on your specific modifications before you purchase the vellums, for a $50 fee. After you receive your estimate, if you decide to have us do the changes, the $50 estimate fee will be deducted from the cost of your modifications. If, however, you choose to use a different service, the $50 estimate fee is non-refundable. (Note: Personal checks cannot be accepted for the estimate.)

Within 5 days of receipt of your plans, you will be contacted by a member of the design staff with an estimate for the design services to draw those changes. A 50% deposit is required before we begin making the actual modifications to your plans.

Once the design changes have been completed to your vellum plan, a representative will call to inform you that your modified Vellum plan is complete and will be shipped as soon as the final payment has been made. For additional information call us at 1-860-659-5667. Please refer to the Modification Pricing Guide for estimated modification costs.

#2 Reproducible Vellums for Local Modification Ease

If you decide not to use Garlinghouse for your modifications, we recommend that you follow our same procedure of purchasing Vellums. You then have the option of using the services of the original designer of the plan, a local professional designer, or architect to make the modifications.

With a Vellum copy of our plans, a design professional can alter the drawings just the way you want, then you can print as many copies of the modified plans as you need to build your house. And, since you have already started with our complete detailed plans, the cost of those expensive professional services will be significantly less than starting from scratch. Refer to the price schedule for Vellum costs.

Ignoring Copyright Laws Can Be A $100,000 Mistake

Recent changes in the US copyright laws allow for statutory penalties of up to $100,000 per incident for copyright infringement involving any of the copyrighted plans found in this publication. The law can be confusing. So, for your own protection, take time to understand what you can and cannot do when it comes to home plans.

What You Can't Do!

You Cannot Duplicate Home Plans

Purchasing a set of blueprints and making additional sets by reproducing the original is illegal. If you need multiple sets of a particular home plan, then you must purchase them.

You Cannot Copy Any Part of a Home Plan to Create Another

Creating your own plan by copying even part of a home design found in this publication is called "creating a derivative work" and is illegal unless you have permission to do so.

You Cannot Build a Home Without a License

You must have specific permission or license to build a home from a copyrighted design, even if the finished home has been changed from the original plan. It is illegal to build one of the homes found in this publication without a license.

How to obtain a construction cost calculation based on labor rates and building material costs in your Zip code area!

Why? Do you wish you could quickly find out the building cost for your new home without waiting for a contractor to compile hundreds of bids? Would you like to have a benchmark to compare your contractor(s) bids against? Well, Now You Can!!, with Zip-Quote Home Cost Calculator. Zip-Quote is only available for zip code areas within the United States.

How? Our Zip-Quote Home Cost Calculator will enable you to obtain the calculated building cost to construct your new home, based on labor rates and building material costs within your zip code area, without the normal delays or has-sles usually associated with the bidding process. Zip-Quote :an be purchased in two separate formats, an itemized or a oottom line format.

How does Zip-Quote actually work? When you call to order, you must choose from the options available, for your pecific home, in order for us to process your order. Once we eceive your Zip-Quote order, we process your specific home plan building materials list through our Home Cost Calculator which contains up-to-date rates for all residential abor trades and building material costs in your zip code area. The result? A calculated cost to build your dream home in our Zip code area. This calculation will help you (as a con-umer or a builder) evaluate your building budget.

All database information for our calculations is furnished y Marshall & Swift, L.P. For over 60 years, Marshall & wift L.P. has been a leading provider of cost data to profes-ionals in all aspects of the construction and remodeling ndustries.

ption 1 The **Itemized Zip-Quote** is a detailed building aterial list. Each building material list line item will sepa-tely state the labor cost, material cost and equipment cost f applicable) for the use of that building material in the onstruction process. This building materials list will be mmarized by the individual building categories and will ave additional columns where you can enter data from your ontractor's estimates for a cost comparison between the dif-rent suppliers and contractors who will actually quote you eir products and services.

ption 2 The **Bottom Line Zip-Quote** is a one line sum-arized total cost for the home plan of your choice. This st calculation is also based on the labor cost, material cost d equipment cost (if applicable) within your Zip code area. ottom Line Zip-Quote is available for most plans. Please ll for availability.

ost The price of your Itemized Zip-Quote is based upon e pricing schedule of the plan you have selected, in addition to the price of the materials list. Please refer to the pricing schedule on our order form. The price of your initial Bottom Line Zip-Quote is $29.95. Each additional Bottom Line Zip-Quote ordered in conjunction with the initial order is only $14.95. Bottom Line Zip-Quote may be purchased separately and does NOT have to be purchased in conjunc-tion with a home plan order.

FYI An Itemized Zip-Quote Home Cost Calculation can ONLY be purchased in conjunction with a Home Plan order. The Itemized Zip-Quote can not be purchased separately. If you find within 60 days of your order date that you will be unable to build this home, then you may exchange the plans and the materials list towards the price of a new set of plans (see order info pages for plan exchange policy). The Itemized Zip-Quote and the Bottom Line Zip-Quote are NOT returnable. The price of the initial Bottom Line Zip-Quote order can be credited toward the purchase of an Itemized Zip-Quote order, only if available. Additional Bottom Line Zip-Quote orders, within the same order can not be credited. Please call our Customer Service Department for more information.

An Itemized Zip-Quote is available for plans where you see this symbol. ZIP

A Bottom-line Zip-Quote is available for all plans under 4,000 sq. ft. or where you see this symbol. BL

Please call for current availability.

Some More Information The Itemized and Bottom Line Zip-Quotes give you approximated costs for constructing the particular house in your area. These costs are not exact and are only intended to be used as a preliminary estimate to help determine the affordability of a new home and/or as a guide to evaluate the general competitiveness of actual price quotes obtained through local suppliers and contractors. However, Zip-Quote cost figures should never be relied upon as the only source of information in either case. **Land, land-scaping, sewer systems, site work, contractor overhead and profit, and other expenses are not included in our building cost figures. Excluding land and landscaping, you may incur an additional 20% to 40% in costs from the original estimate.** Garlinghouse and Marshall & Swift L.P. cannot guarantee any level of data accuracy or correctness in a Zip-Quote and disclaim all liability for loss with respect to the same, in excess of the original purchase price of the Zip-Quote product. All Zip-Quote calculations are based upon the actual blueprints and do not reflect any differences or options that may be shown on the published house render-ings, floor plans, or photographs.

the Garlinghouse company

BEST PLAN VALUE IN THE INDUSTRY!

Order Code No. **H2NH1**

Order Form

Plan prices guaranteed until 5/21/03 After this date call for updated pricing

_______ foundation

___ set(s) of blueprints for plan #_______ $_____

___ Vellum & Modification kit for plan #_______ $_____

___ Additional set(s) @ $50 each for plan #_______ $_____

___ Mirror Image Reverse @ $50 each $_____

___ Right Reading Reverse @ $135 each $_____

___ Materials list for plan #_______ $_____

___ Detail Plans @ $19.95 each

❑ Construction ❑ Plumbing ❑ Electrical $_____

___ Bottom Line Zip-Quote@$29.95 for plan #_______ $_____

___ Additional Bottom Line Zip-Quote

@ $14.95 for plan(s) #_______ $_____

Zip code where building _______

___ Itemized Zip-Quote for plan(s) #_______ $_____

Shipping $_____

Subtotal $_____

Sales Tax (CT residents add 6% sales tax) (Not required for other states) $_____

TOTAL AMOUNT ENCLOSED $_____

Send your check, money order or credit card information to:
(No C.O.D.'s Please)

Please submit all United States & Other Nations orders to:
Garlinghouse Company
174 Oakwood Drive
Glastonbury, CT. 06033
CALL: (800) 235-5700 FAX: (860) 659-5692

Please Submit all Canadian plan orders to:
Garlinghouse Company
102 Ellis Street
Penticton, BC V2A 4L5
CALL: (800) 361-7526 FAX: (250) 493-7526

ADDRESS INFORMATION:

NAME: _______________

STREET: _______________

CITY: _______________

STATE: _______ ***ZIP:*** _______

DAYTIME PHONE: _______________

EMAIL ADDRESS: _______________

Credit Card Information		
Charge To:	❑ Visa	❑ Mastercard
Card #	|_|_|_|_|_|_|_|_|_|_|_|_|_|_|_|_|	
Signature _______________		Exp. ___/___

Payment must be made in U.S. funds. Foreign Mail Orders: Certified bank checks in U.S. funds only

Privacy Statement (please read)

Dear Valued Garlinghouse Customer,

Your privacy is extremely important to us. We'd like to take a little of your time to explain our privacy policy.

As a service to you, we would like to provide your name to companies such as the following:

- Building material manufacturers that we are affiliated with. In these cases, our affiliates would like to keep you current with their product line and specials.
- Building material retailers that would like to offer you competitive prices to help you save money.
- Financing companies that would like to offer you competitive mortgage rates.

In addition, as our valued customer, we would like to send you newsletters to assist your building experience. *We* would appreciate your feedback with a customer service survey to improve our operations.

You have total control over the use of your contact information. You can let us know exactly how you want to be contacted. Please check all boxes that apply. Thank you.

☐ Don't mail
☐ Don't call
☐ Don't email
☐ Only send Garlinghouse newsletters and customer service surveys

In closing, we hope this shows Garlinghouse's commitment to providing superior customer service and protection of your privacy. We thank you for your time and consideration.

Sincerely,

James D. McNair III
CEO

BEFORE ORDERING PLEASE READ ALL ORDERING INFORMATION

For Our **USA** Customers:
Order Toll Free — 1-800-235-5700
Monday-Friday 8:00 a.m. to 8:00 p.m. Eastern Time
or FAX your Credit Card order to 1-860-659-5692
All foreign residents call 1-860-659-5667

For Our **Canadian** Customers:
Order Toll Free — 1-800-361-7526
Monday-Friday 8:00 a.m. to 5:00 p.m. Pacific Time
or FAX your Credit Card order to 1-250-493-7526
Customer Service: 1-250-493-0942

Please have ready: 1. Your credit card number 2. The plan number 3. The order code number ⇨ ***H2NH1***

Garlinghouse 2002 Blueprint Price Code Schedule

	1 Set	4 Sets	8 Sets	Vellums	ML	Itemized ZIP Quote
A	$345	$385	$435	$525	$60	$50
B	$375	$415	$465	$555	$60	$50
C	$410	$450	$500	$590	$60	$50
D	$450	$490	$540	$630	$60	$50
E	$495	$535	$585	$675	$70	$60
F	$545	$585	$635	$725	$70	$60
G	$595	$635	$685	$775	$70	$60
H	$640	$680	$730	$820	$70	$60
I	$685	$725	$775	$865	$80	$70
J	$725	$765	$815	$905	$80	$70
K	$765	$805	$855	$945	$80	$70
L	$800	$840	$890	$980	$80	$70

Shipping — (Plans 1-59999)	1-3 Sets	4-6 Sets	7+ & Vellums
Standard Delivery (UPS 2-Day)	$25.00	$30.00	$35.00
Overnight Delivery	$35.00	$40.00	$45.00

Shipping — (Plans 60000-99999)	1-3 Sets	4-6 Sets	7+ & Vellums
Ground Delivery (7-10 Days)	$15.00	$20.00	$25.00
Express Delivery (3-5 Days)	$20.00	$25.00	$30.00

International Shipping & Handling	1-3 Sets	4-6 Sets	7+ & Vellums
Regular Delivery Canada (10-14 Days)	$25.00	$30.00	$35.00
Express Delivery Canada (7-10 Days)	$40.00	$45.00	$50.00
Overseas Delivery Airmail (3-4 Weeks)	$50.00	$60.00	$65.00

Additional sets with original order $50

IMPORTANT INFORMATION TO READ BEFORE YOU PLACE YOUR ORDER

ow Many Sets Of Plans Will You Need?

he Standard 8-Set Construction Package

*Our experience shows that you'll speed every step of construction and avoid costly building errors by ordering enough sets to go around. Each radesperson wants a set — the general contractor and all subcontractors: foundation, electrical, plumbing, heating/air conditioning and framers. Don't forget our lending institution, building department and, of course, a set for yourself. * Recommended For Construction **

he Minimum 4-Set Construction Package

*If you're comfortable with arduous follow-up, this package can save you a few dollars by giving you the option of passing down plan sets as work rogresses. You might have enough copies to go around if work goes exactly as scheduled and no plans are lost or damaged by subcontrators. But for only $60 nore, the 8-set package eliminates these worries. *Recommended For Bidding **

he Single Study Set

We offer this set so you can study the blueprints to plan your dream home in detail. They are stamped "study set only-not for construction" and you cannot uild a home from them. In pursuant to copyright laws, it is illegal to reproduce any blueprint.

ur Reorder and Exchange Policies

If you find after your initial purchase that you require additional sets of plans you may purchase them from us at special reorder prices (please call for pricing details) rovided that you reorder within six months of your original order date. There is a $28 reorder processing fee that is charged on all reorders. For more information on eordering plans, please contact our Customer Service Department. Your plans are custom printed especially for you once you place your order. For that reason we cannot ccept any returns. If for some reason you find that the plan you have purchased from us does not meet your needs, then you may exchange that plan for any other plan our collection. We allow you sixty days from your original invoice date to make an exchange. At the time of the exchange you will be charged a processing fee of 20% of e total amount of your original order plus the difference in price between the plans (if applicable) plus the cost to ship the new plans to you. Call our Customer Service epartment for more information. Please Note: Reproducible vellums can only be exchanged if they are unopened.

mportant Shipping Information

ease refer to the shipping charts on the order form for service availability for your specific plan number. Our delivery service must have a street address or Rural oute Box number — never a post office box. (PLEASE NOTE: Supplying a P.O. Box number only will delay the shipping of your order.) Use a work address if no one home during the day. Orders being shipped to APO or FPO must go via First Class Mail. Please include the proper postage.

For our International Customers, only Certified bank checks and money orders are accepted and must be payable in U.S. currency. For speed, we ship interna-nal orders Air Parcel Post. Please refer to the chart for the correct shipping cost.

mportant Canadian Shipping Information

To our friends in Canada, we have a plan design affiliate in Penticton, BC. This relationship will help you avoid the delays and charges associated with ship-ents from the United States. Moreover, our affiliate is familiar with the building requirements in your community and country. We prefer payments in U.S. Currency. you, however, are sending Canadian funds please add 45% to the prices of the plans and shipping fees.

n Important Note About uilding Code Requirements

All plans are drawn to conform to one or more of the industry's major national building standards. However, due to the variety of local building regulations, your an may need to be modified to comply with local requirements — snow loads, energy loads, seismic zones, etc. Do check them fully and consult your local ilding officials.

A few states require that all building plans used be drawn by an architect registered in that state. While having your plans reviewed and stamped by such an chitect may be prudent, laws requiring non-conforming plans like ours to be completely redrawn forces you to unnecessarily pay very large fees. If your state has ch a law, we strongly recommend you contact your state representative to protest.

The rendering, floor plans, and technical information contained within this publication are not guaranteed to be totally accurate. Consequently, no information m this publication should be used either as a guide to constructing a home or for estimating the cost of building a home. Complete blueprints must be purchased such purposes.

Option Key

BL Bottom-line Zip Quote **ML** Materials List Available **ZIP** Itemized Zip Quote **RRR** Right Reading Reverse **DUP** Duplex Plan